T0163268

ARCHAEOLOGICAL FORMATION PROCESSES

The representativity of archaeological remains from Danish Prehistory

ARCHAEOLOGICAL FORMATION PROCESSES

The representativity of archaeological remains
from Danish Prehistory

Editor
Kristian Kristiansen

Nationalmuseet 1985

© 1985 The individual authors
Nationalmuseets forlag
Ny Vestergade 10
DK-1471 København K

Cover and lay-out: Catharina Oksen

Printed by: Special-Trykkeriet Viborg a-s

ISBN 87-480-0571-1

Sale and distribution:
Arnold Busck, International Booksellers
49 Købmagergade
DK-1150 Copenhagen K

This book is published with grants from

Dronning Margrethe II's Arkæologiske Fond
The Danish Research Counsil for the Humanities
Prehistoric Museum, Moesgård
The National Agency for the Protection of Nature,
Monuments and Sites

Contents

Preface

This book was planned in 1976. Manuscripts were finished in 1978, translations and drawings in late 1979. It remains a regrettable fact that publication was delayed for four years according to the original plan, due to a change in the publication policy of the National Museum. Consequently, this volume terminates the proposed series: Studies in Scandinavian Prehistory and Early History. Volumes 3 and 5 will appear elsewhere and volume 4 has been cancelled.

The present selection of articles represents the first complete national survey of the effect of historical post-depositional factors for archaeological representativity to appear in print. Hopefully, it retains and transmits some of the inspiration and enthusiasm which originally made the book possible.

I wish to thank the authors both for their willingness to invest a large amount of work in this joint project, based on common methodological standards, and for their patience. Each article is founded upon a complete survey of original finds in museums. I also wish to thank the Prehistoric Museum of Moesgård for making all drawings without cost for the project. Most drawings were made by Svend Kaae, supplemented by Catharina Oksen. Financial support for translation and publication was granted by the Research Council of the Humanities. Additional support for publication was given by Queen Margrethe II Archaeological Foundation. All translations were carried out by Ole Bay-Petersen, except the articles about Bronze Age burials and hoards which were translated by Jean Olsen and Peter Crabb.

To facilitate the practical usefulness of the book and to help foreign archaeologists in dealing with Danish prehistory, appendixes 1-4 were added.

Copenhagen, April 1984
Kristian Kristiansen

Post-Depositional Formation Processes and the Archaeological Record

A Danish Perspective

by KRISTIAN KRISTANSEN

Denmark's history of systematic archaeological research is probably one of the longest in the world, going back to the foundation of the "Royal Commission for the Preservation of Northern Antiquities" in 1807. Consequently, a major part of the archaeological data available to researchers has been accumulated over a period of nearly 200 years. This implies that any systematic study of the major find groups will have to deal with the question of the effect of the influence of post-depositional factors in the period 1807 up to the present date. This book represents an attempt to establish a systematic methodological framework for this kind of historical-archaeological research in order to establish a general evaluation of the representativity of the data. Quite obviously, this only represents a starting point which will have to be followed by the formulation of more specific research programs to test the representativity with respect to more specific hypotheses and the effect of predepositional factors. Thus, the articles in this book represent an attempt to systematize but one aspect within an overall theory of the formation processes of the archaeological record (Schiffer 1976). It should further be added that even within this historical-archaeological field of research of post-depositional formation processes the methodological framework was deliberately designed to elucidate representativity on a national and regional scale. In local areas this should be supported by field surveying and a closer study of local historical archives. It should also be stressed that such specialized historical-archaeological studies may be successfully extended back to before 1800 as demonstrated in some recent works (Knudsen 1982).

The approach presented will probably be foreign to most New World archaeologists, who have been mainly concerned with the effect of post-depositional factors on the individual site (Schiffer 1983) and regional sampling techniques (Mueller 1975, Schiffer and Gummerman

1977). The approach presented here, however, is based on a European research tradition of source criticism, as presented in the works of H. J. Eggers (1950 and 1957), Clark (1968), Geislinger (1967) and Torbrügge (1959). It was developed by systematizing and operationalizing the various source critical concepts and attitudes which had been employed in European archaeology throughout the last 30-40 years into a more coherent methodological framework (Kristiansen 1976 and 1978) (note 1). For heuristic and practical reasons I found it necessary to distinguish between a *general* and *specific* level of representativity – the general level being basic to the specific insofar as problems relating to the latter are so numerous that even before asking them it is a great advantage to first have the general aspects analyzed and brought under some scientific control. When this is done, one can more profitably proceed to relate various hypotheses and problems at hand to the more specific aspects of representativity. Thus, general representativity as presented in this book may be said to establish a foundation unrelated to any specific archaeological hypothesis, but with implications for an indefinite number of hypotheses. This does not imply any static or a priori inductive approach. Source criticism is to be regarded as an integrated part of the research process within a wider theoretical inductive/deductive framework of scientific inference. The major goal of this book is to facilitate the exploitation of the rich archaeological data base from Denmark by determining its general representativity in terms of its history of recovery. This is determined by 3 major factors:

Physical and environmental factors. The influence of physical and environmental factors is in general constant within a given geographical and climatic region. When examining the representativity of a certain group of finds within a research area, it is therefore of great importance to draw systematic distinctions between the various sta-

.tes of preservation of identical materials which are due to variations in the physical surroundings and the various states of preservation under uniform physical conditions which are due to differing properties of the material (Clark 1968, chapter III).

In Denmark it is necessary to distinguish between the area inside and outside the last glacial, since the soil in the area outside is acid, owing to a washing out of chalk (Iversen 1973). This determines the preservation of organic material in bogs. The iso- and eustatic processes responsible for drastic changes of the land/sea relationship since the last glacial has also influenced representativity. This implies that a major part of the mesolithic and early neolithic coastal sites are today under water. To this should be added the effects of soil erosion, which, however, in Denmark only has occurred sporadically since the last glacial which eroded and covered all previous palaeolithic sites with moraine.

Cultural and economic factors. The influence of cultural and economic factors depends on the relationship between the formation of the present cultural landscape and the state of the prehistoric material. These factors are variable and can be divided into *active* and *passive*. The active factors include such activities as the cultivation of new areas, ploughing, peat cutting, industrialization and war. By passive factors are meant the presence of wastelands like heaths and moors. These may often cause gaps in our knowledge of the hidden sources lying buried in the ground, but offer great potential in terms of completeness and state of preservation when systematically recorded and excavated.

Economic factors have been examined most systematically to determine the representativity of graves and hoards (Geislinger 1967, chapter 3, Torbrügge 1959, p. 20-48, Torbrügge 1971, Sprockhoff 1938, abb 62-63). In Denmark the Celtic fields of the Iron Age are among the best known examples of how uncultivated areas of heath preserve traces of farming, in the rest of the country such traces only occur, sporadically, in forests (Nielsen 1983, Müller-Wille 1965, chapter 1).

Research factors and archaeological factors of registration are variable and may either be of *quantitative* or *qualitative* nature. A quantitative factor is the intensity of registration, which is defined by the relationship between the size of an area and its archaeological coverage (Binford 1964 is optimistic for theoretical reasons, Struever 1968 is pessimistic for practical reasons). Qualitative factors refer to indirect information, which is dependent on the

scope of documentation. As pointed out by Jensen (1966, p. 14) archaeologists must often subject the recorded evidence to historical source criticism, if it is based on assumptions other than his own.

In Denmark the regional settlement analyses of Mathiassen (1948 and 1959) have provided a very good measure of the potential of archaeological remains, compared with the general level of registration (Thrane 1973).

Archaeological representativity is strongly affected by the dynamic interaction between the above factors and the various properties of archaeological data. However, the agricultural transformation of the Danish landscape throughout the past 200 years has been one of the major factors responsible for the destruction of monuments and the accumulation of archaeological finds. Therefore the first article provides a general background for the understanding of this development, followed by a survey of the history of research and of legislation. Together these articles establish a historical framework for the following articles, all dealing with the interaction between historical formation processes and the archaeological record.

The major categories of finds dealt with are:
1. Monuments (megaliths and Bronze Age barrows)
2. Settlement sites
3. Burials
4. Hoards
5. Particular groups of finds (wooden implements).

Two articles deal with monuments. Bronze Age barrows are analysed by Baudou and megalithic monuments by Ebbesen. These studies provide a background for understanding regional variation in rates of destruction/preservation of monuments. Especially Baudou's article has implications for the subsequent analyses of Bronze and Iron Age grave finds.

With respect to the articles dealing with settlement sites, burials and hoards I shall try to extract some of the general trends in representativity rather than present each article separately. Thus, it is quite obvious when comparing the various figures that certain recurrent trends are observable. With respect to settlements the find accumulation curves all display a similar pattern. Most of them do not begin until the later part of the 19th century, and they maintain a low level until the last 3-4 decades, when the curve rises exponentially. This pattern is a direct reversion of the curve of grave finds and hoards. Most of them reach a climax in the decades around the turn of the century and then decline steeply during the last 3-4 decades.

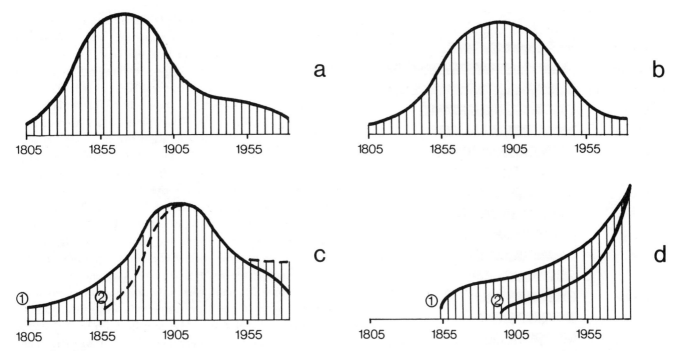

Fig. 1. Generalized find curves at national (and regional) levels for various types of finds.
a) Hoards with precious metals (bronze, silver, gold), unprofessionally excavated burials from Eastern Denmark
b) less precious hoards (only bronze, mainly single objects), unprofessionally excavated burials from Western Denmark (in level ground = c),
c) Neolithic hoards of stone and flint axes/daggers (1), professionally excavated burials (2),
d) Neolithic (1) and Bronze Age (2) settlement sites both unprofessionally and professionally excavated or registrated.

These two general trends naturally reflect the history of research. Burials and hoards were the first find groups to achieve archaeological attention, especially if they contained objects made of copper, bronze or other precious metals that were remunerated when handed in to the museum. In contrast to these find groups settlements achieved archaeological attention rather late, and it was not until the last few decades that settlement research developed beyond excavations of a few randomly selected, well preserved settlements. These trends in the development of archaeological research are also clearly demonstrated by the analysis of agricultural tools of wood (spades, wagons) mainly found in bogs. They must have been destroyed by the thousands throughout the previous 150 years, and the same is true of settlements. A second destruction phase began in the 1940's with the rapid spread of tractors and subsequent deeper ploughing bringing up fresh new cultural layers. Thus it is the interplay between mechanization, deeper ploughing, and a rapidly growing interest in settlement research which

explains the steeply rising curves for this group of finds. From the previous phase of settlement destruction only artefacts that cannot be decomposed remain as indicators, whereas all pottery, bones, charcoal etc. vanished long ago.

If we now take a closer look at the various curves for hoards and burials, certain interesting variations can be observed. With respect to hoards, several curves conform rather closely to a normal distribution, showing the discovery, exploitation, and exhaustion of an archaeological source. It is interesting to note, however, that whereas hoards from the Germanic Iron Age show a skewed distribution with a climax in the middle of the 19th century and then a rather prolonged decline, Neolithic hoards show a later climax around the turn of the century. The time lag between the 2 curves reflects the different values attached to such finds. Whereas Germanic hoards rather often contain finds of precious metals (bronze and gold), Neolithic hoards were not as highly rewarded and their archaeological value not recognized as early as that of the

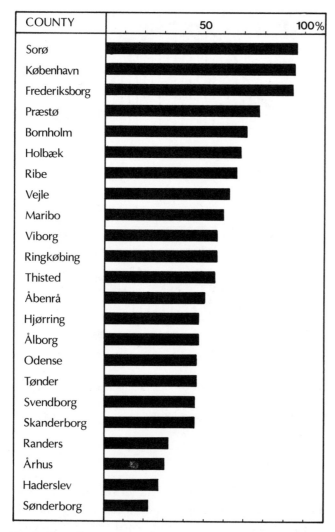

COUNTY	50	100%
Sorø		
København		
Frederiksborg		
Præstø		
Bornholm		
Holbæk		
Ribe		
Vejle		
Maribo		
Viborg		
Ringkøbing		
Thisted		
Åbenrå		
Hjørring		
Ålborg		
Odense		
Tønder		
Svendborg		
Skanderborg		
Randers		
Århus		
Haderslev		
Sønderborg		

Fig. 2. The relative share of Early Bronze Age finds in the National Museum in 1970. Counties are used as geographical units and arranged in rank order. Each county is 100 %. (Based on the catalogues of Aner and Kersten).

metal hoards. From this we can infer that quite a large number of Neolithic hoards must have been lost in the early and middle part of the century. The same type of variation is seen on a regional level with respect to early Bronze Age hoards.

We now turn to grave finds. Here we find basically the same patterns, but with regional variations that can be related to regional trends in agricultural expansion, as revealed in the statistics of article 1 and in Baudou's article. Although professional excavations have played a dominant role since the late 19th century, it is interesting to note that burials also show a declining trend through-

out the last 3 decades. However, future analysis will most probably show that throughout the late 1970's and 1980's this declining trend was reversed due to the expansion of rescue archaeology and the work of the Ancient Monument Administration (Kristiansen 1983).

These general trends can naturally be further specified by analyzing the data according to other parameters. With respect to hoards a division can be made between finds from moors and dry fields respectively; similarly, the depth of deposition is an important parameter showing regularities throughout the Neolithic, Bronze Age, and Iron Age. With respect to grave finds a fundamental distinction is naturally that between professionally versus unprofessionally excavated finds, which also shows general trends cross-cutting the various periods and types of finds (barrows/flat ground). Also, the activities of the National Museum versus the regional museums show general trends for the various periods, just as the number of finds in the National Museum declines with distance (fig. 2). Even so, however, the National Museum contains the majority of finds, thereby creating a unique basis for research. Here the regional analysis of the single grave culture shows the impact of the extensive excavation campaigns directed by the National Museum around the turn of the century in Jutland, just as it confirms the general trends noted in Baudou's article, regarding the relationship between cultivation and destruction of monuments.

In conclusion the articles in this book represent a systematic analysis of the recovery of archaeological finds in Denmark throughout the last 200 years. By applying a common methodological framework, it has been possible to demonstrate a number of general trends linked to a systematic interaction between the dominant post-depositional factors at work, the various properties of archaeological data and the history of research, indicating various levels of representativity. It may be further suggested that these findings are valid not only in Denmark but also in most of Northern and Central Europe, due to common historical traditions of archaeological research and common economic and political developmental processes throughout the last 200 years.

Kristian Kristiansen,
The National Agency for the Protection of Nature,
Monuments and Sites,
Amaliegade 13,
DK – 1256 Copenhagen K.

NOTES

1. In recent years problems of field surveying and sampling techniques have been increasingly discussed in European archaeology, in pace with the development of regional settlement studies and large scale rescue projects. However, most of this discussion is hidden away in various research reports etc. and only few articles deal primarily with such problems (e.g. articles in Cherry, Gamble and Shennan 1978, Fowler 1972).

REFERENCES

BINFORD, L.R. 1964: A Consideration of Archaeological Research Design. *American Antiquity 29.*

CHERRY, J.F., GAMBLE, C., AND SHENNAN, St. (eds.) 1978: *Sampling in Contemporary British Archaeology.* B.A.R. British Series 50. Oxford.

CLARK, J.G.D. 1968: *Archaeology and Society.* University Paperback 3, ed. 1968.

EGGERS, H.J. 1951: *Der römische Import im freien Germanien.* Atlas der Urgeschichte 1. Hamburg.

– 1959: *Einführung in die Vorgeschichte.* R. Piber & Co., München.

FOWLER, P. (ed.) 1972: *Field Survey in British Archaeology.* London, Council of British Archaeology.

GEISSLINGER, H. 1967: *Horte als Geschichtsquelle.* Offa-Bücher, Band 19. Neumünster.

IVERSEN, J. 1973: The Development of Denmark's Nature since the last Glacial. *Geol. Survey of Denmark V, Series No. 7-c.* Copenhagen.

JENSEN, J. 1966: Arkæologi og kulturforskning. *Historisk Tidsskrift 12,11.*

KNUDSEN, S.Aa. 1982: *Landskab og oldtid.* Atlas over Søllerød og Lyngby-Taarbæk Kommuner. København 1982.

KRISTIANSEN, K. 1976: En kildekritisk analyse af depotfund fra Danmarks yngre bronzealder (periode IV-V). Et bidrag til den arkæologiske kildekritik. *Årbøger for nordisk oldkyndighed* 1974.

– 1978: The Application of Source Criticism to Archaeology. *Norwegian Arch. Review.* Vol. 11, No. 7, Oslo.

– 1983: Rescue Archaeology in Denmark 1970-82. *Journal of Danish Archaeology Vol. 2.* Odense University Press.

MATHIASSEN, T. 1948: *Studier over Vestjyllands oldtidsbebyggelse.* (Studies of the Prehistoric Settlement of West Jutland). Nationalmuseets skrifter. Arkæol.-Hist. Rk. II. København.

– 1959: *Nordvestsjællands oldtidsbebyggelse.* (The Prehistoric Settlement of Northwestern Zealand). Nationalmuseets skrifter. Arkæol.-Hist. Rk. VII. København.

MUELLER, J.W. (ed.) 1975: *Sampling in Archaeology.* The University of Arizona Press, Tuscon.

MÜLLER-WILLE, M. 1965: *Eisenzeitliche Fluren in den festländischen Nordseegebieten.* Siedlung und Handschaft in Westfalen 5.

NIELSEN, V. 1983: Prehistoric Field Boundaries in Eastern Denmark. To appear in *Journal of Danish Archaeology, Vol. 3.*

SCHIFFER, M. 1976: *Behavioral Archaeology.* New York. Academic Press.

SCHIFFER, M. AND GUMMERMAN, G.J. (eds.) 1977: *Conservation Archaeology.* A Guide for Cultural Resource Management Studies. Academic Press.

SCHIFFER, M. 1983: Towards the Identification of Formation Processes. *American Antiquity* vol. 48, No. 4.

SPROCKHOFF, E. 1938: *Die nordische Megalithkultur.* Handbuch der Urgeschichte Deutschlands 3. Berlin und Leipzig.

STRUEVER, S. 1968: Problems, Methods and Organization. A Disparity in the Growth of Archaeology. In Meggers, B.J. (ed.). *Anthropological Archaeology in the Americas.* Washington.

THRANE, H. 1973: Bebyggelsesarkæologi – en arkæologisk arbejdsopgave. *Fortid og Nutid XXV, 3/4.*

TORBRÜGGE, W. 1959: Die Bronzezeit in der Oberpfalz. *Materialhefte zur Bayrischen Vorgeschichte 13. Heft.*

– 1971: Vor- und Frühgeschichtliche Flussfunde. *Ber.röm.-germ. Kommission 51-52,* p. 3-138.

A Short History of Danish Archaeology

An Analytical Perspective

by KRISTIAN KRISTIANSEN

INTRODUCTION

Traditional accounts of the history of Danish archaeology are centred on the description of the leading scholars – C.J. Thomsen, J.J.A. Worsaae, Sophus Müller and Johannes Brøndsted (Brøndsted 1962; Klindt-Jensen 1975). The development of archaeology is seen in the light of these scholars' contribution to museums and to knowledge. This is because their names, not only in Denmark but also abroad, are associated with a number of fundamental scientific advances. Thomsen and the Three Ages: the Stone, Bronze and Iron Ages, a turning-point for the role of museums in archaeology. Worsaae and the first excavations, the first registrations of monuments and the first interdisciplinary collaboration (the interpretation of shell middens), a turningpoint for archaeology in terms of culture history and protection. Müller and the classification and publication of material, the scientific consolidation of archaeological knowledge. And finally Brøndsted, who maintained and advanced this tradition. From 1837 for app. a century Danish and Scandinavian archaeology helped to set scientific standards for the whole discipline. This was partly due to these eminent scholars, but a number of other factors were no less important. The following paper is an attempt to describe this interplay of factors by tracing some of the major trends in the development of Danish archaeology.

DISCOVERIES AND SCHOLARS

Though archaeology is a young science, it has a tradition of centuries behind it as part of the aristocratic passion for collecting. The princely collections of curios fashionable during the Renaissance also contained prehistoric artefacts. They were a fairly small number since excavations had not yet begun; besides, treasure hunting was only practised on a small scale in Northern Europe (Werlauff 1807, 15 ff.; Hermansen 1954). Objects recognized as archaeological were primarily the monuments: grave mounds, dolmens and runic stones. Some of these had already been described in 1643 by Ole Worm in the "*Danicorum Monumentorum Libri Sex*", a book which attracted international attention. Prehistoric remains were, however, rare in this period. Both in Ole Worm's famous collection of curios and in later antiquarian collections they were simply random elements in a varied repertoire of objects (Neergaard 1916). This rarity was also because up till the end of the reign of King Christian IV, treasure trove was regarded as a source of state income, and was melted down (Hindenburg 1859, 24). Not until King Frederik III established his "Kunstkammer" (: Chamber of Arts) in 1663, was treasure trove awarded antiquarian status and placed on exhibition (Bering Liisberg 1897, 18).

This situation changed abruptly after the agrarian reforms of the 1780's (Vibæk 1964). These were followed by the increased destruction of burial mounds, and treasure and hoard finds turned up in newly cultivated areas. While archaeological finds were becoming common, thousands of prehistoric remains were being destroyed. This alarming situation led to the establishment in 1807 of a Royal Commission for Antiquities and a "national museum", which was housed in the loft of the Trinitatis Church in Copenhagen, where the Educational Library was also to be found (Hermansen 1931 and 1953; Hildebrand 1938, 175 ff.). There followed a time of great activity. Questionnaires were sent to all clergymen and other interested private citizens to obtain a comprehensive survey of the nation's antiquities. The results were published at once by B. Thorlacius in 1809 in his "Bemærkninger over de i Danmark endnu tilværende hedenolds

Fig. 1. Demolition of large barrow in the late 19th century (photograph: the National Museum).

Høie og Steensætninger" – the earliest systematic survey known. Voluntary conservation schemes were carried out and a periodical, *Antiquariske Annaler,* was founded. *The outer framework had now been created for archaeological activity.* But museum accessions were still few in number, c. 100 p.a.

The next step was taken when, contrary to the usual practice, a merchant with no academic qualifications, C.J. Thomsen, was appointed Secretary of the Commission for Antiquities. Now things were put in order;[1] the collection was systematically arranged, accessions were registered, and in 1819 it was opened to the public in the form of a free, weekly guided tour conducted by Thomsen himself, as he continued to do for the rest of his life. In a short time the museum became an object of great interest throughout Scandinavia: "The most interesting and instructive sight in Copenhagen," wrote the Swedish poet and professor of history Erik Gustaf Geijer in 1825 (Hildebrand 1938, 511). During the almost fifty years (up to 1865) Thomsen was in charge – ending up as the director of five museums – the foundations of the collections were laid. The number of accessions now rose steadily (in Thomsen's time there were 540 each year). This was due to two factors: firstly the expansion of agricultu-

re, and secondly the reputation Thomsen had created for the museum as a unique national institution. This led to the acquisition in 1832 of 4 to 5 rooms in Christiansborg Palace, and still more in 1838[2]. This was occasioned by the visit of the Russian Czarprince. Finally in 1854 the museum was housed in Prinsens Palæ, where it is still to be found after extensive alterations and additions in the 1930's (Müller 1907; Mackeprang 1938 and 1939; Brøndsted 1957). A major factor in the progress of archaeology was Thomsen's principle that the collections should be open to everyone so that the guided tours could instruct people about the past and create an interest in antiquities among all classes of society. Thomsen thus established a practice fundamental to all museums today.

In this period only a few random excavations were carried out, such as the discovery of the famous Bronze Age "Hvidegård" find, described by Magnus Petersen (Petersen 1909, 11-20). Finds were acquired primarily from the many destroyed burial mounds, and were catalogued and exhibited. The public transport of the time did not permit frequent field trips, while museum work was carried out part-time and unpaid until Worsaae received the first royal appointment to the position of "Inspector for Ancient Monuments"[3]. Great importance was at-

Fig. 2. The parish survey in 1892 (photograph: the National Museum).

tached to developing contacts with interested collectors, and in 1836 Thomsen gave advice in his "Guide" on how best to carry out excavations and how to treat artefacts (Thomsen 1836, 87 ff.)[4]. However, there was still a considerable gap between the finders of artefacts, usually peasants and farm labourers, and the museum in Copenhagen. That a successful contact was nevertheless established at an early stage was due to two factors: the increasing popularity of archaeology at a time of national economic depression, and not least the payment of rewards to the finders. *The foundations of archaeological activity had now been laid,* and after 1850 this activity began to expand. This expansion took place on several fronts.

From 1855 onwards a growing number of provincial collections were established. These were all the result of private initiative originating from a museum society of interested collectors. Museums were first established in the large cathedral cities of Ribe (1855), Odense (1860),

Viborg and Århus (1861), and Ålborg (1863). The other provincial towns of Jutland followed suit from the 1880's, and after the turn of the century the founding of museums continued in the islands (Jensen and Møller 1939). With the collecting activity of King Frederik VII as a model, a large number of aristocratic private collections were established in the decades after 1850, while a corresponding number of private citizens' collections were begun in the towns. An expanding market for artefacts developed, and dealers flourished as never before, not only Danes but also dealers from Hamburg and England[5]. In these decades the destruction of burial mounds reached a climax (fig. 1) as a result of the new prosperity and the many subsequent advances in agriculture: drainage, marling, heath cultivation etc. (cf. Kristiansen 1974b)[6].

Worsaae became Museum Curator in the midst of this sudden expansion (1866). Now one fresh initiative followed another. The collections were re-arranged, and the

Fig. 3. Excavation at the shell midden Ertebølle in 18. The Scandinavian Kitchen-Midden Commission (photograph: the National Museum).

National Museum, having created new positions and received special grants, began a more systematic excavation programme. Thomsen's students, Herbst and Engelhardt, and the draughtsmen Kornerup, Magnus Pedersen and others, were often out on field work. The great Iron Age bog finds of Thorsbjerg, Nydam, Kragehul and Vimose were excavated and published by Engelhardt. The first rich grave finds from the Roman Iron Age from Varpelev and Valløby were published by Herbst and Engelhardt; Worsaae excavated at the Jellinge burial mounds and at Dannevirke; and as early as the 1850's he collaborated with the zoologist Steenstrup and the geologist Forchhammer in excavating oyster shell middens which he interpreted as the remains of Stone Age hunting people. From 1873 a system of regular local parish visits was carried out, in which participated some of Worsaae's new staff, Henry Petersen and Sophus Müller[7] (fig. 2). New finds and excavations often resulted from these vi-

sits. They were made possible by the many new railway lines – which also destroyed a fair number of burial mounds, as did the new roads. In short, this was a season of growth, not only for Denmark as a whole but also for archaeology, in which Worsaae's talent for organization was brought into full play (Müller 1886). Accessions rose in this period to an average number of 810 p.a.

After Worsaae's sudden death in 1885, Herbst became Museum Curator, but the dominant figure was Sophus Müller, who became Curator in 1892[8]. The projects begun by Worsaae were carried on. These included the interdisciplinary study of "kitchen middens" (fig. 3), the results of which were published in 1900, as well as the joint publication with Neergaard on Dannevirke in 1902. Moreover, a great many new finds were published, including the sun-chariot from Trundholm and the silver cauldron from Gundestrup, and most large find groups were re-assessed. Among the new activities carried out

Fig. 4. Group of single barrows near Viborg in Central Jutland, photographed around the turn of the century, when the landscape still retained some

was the major single-grave project in Jutland, designed to save some of the thousands of grave mounds destroyed in those years (fig. 4). A regional study of settlements was begun, and the first Maglemosean habitation site was excavated by Sarauw. The large Iron Age grave yards in Jutland were also systematically studied by Neergaard. In fact, a large part of the National Museum's work now focused on Jutland. Systematic excavation techniques were developed (Müller 1897), and Müller gradually created his own staff of assistants, including Raklev, Blom, Neergaard, Kjær, Th. Thomsen, Rosenberg, Sarauw, Blinkenberg, and later Friis Johansen, Broholm, Nordman, Hatt and Brøndsted. Finally, under both Worsaae and Müller there were several colleagues associated on a kind of freelance basis, e.g. Daniel Bruun and A.P. Madsen.

During this period, until Müller's retirement in 1921, find accessions reached their peak and stabilized, coinciding with the consolidation of agriculture. The most important development in this period, however, was scientific; we shall return to this later.

In one crucial respect Sophus Müller did not follow

Worsaae's tradition, viz. with regard to the growing number of provincial museums. Where Worsaae embraced decentralization and recommended that each county should have its own curator, Müller sought to concentrate all scientific and administrative ability in the National Museum. Confrontation arose when the "old" provincial museums wanted state support. In 1887 this led to a situation where in return for a state contribution of 1,000 kroner a year they had to sign an agreement which, in effect, terminated all possibility of independent activity. They were placed under the administration of the National Museum. All excavations were to be directed by the National Museum, which was entitled to all important finds – not that the latter was anything new. The function of the provincial museums was confined to exhibitions of a popular and instructive kind. As a result these institutions ceased to be actively engaged in excavation, while private digging continued. In Funen, for instance, most of the work formerly done by the local museum was carried out by the apothecary C. Mikkelsen, and later by his son P. Helveg Mikkelsen, who conducted far more excavations than the museum, particularly of Iron Age graves

of its original open treeless character (photograph: The National Museum).

(Larsen 1935, 56 ff.). In Langeland the merchant Winther established his own museum and excavated some of the most significant settlement sites of that time, which he published himself. Private collectors and private excavations had of course always played an important role and from the beginning they had formed the basis of all museum development. Naturally, these private initiatives were supported by the National Museum under Worsaae (Worsaae 1877), because the collections were known and usually acquired later. The collectors were part of the archaeological world, were sometimes represented in archaeological journals, and in economic and social terms were members of the upper class and the more affluent middle class, who could afford to build up a collection. In contrast to these were the itinerant dealers, who belonged to the opposite end of the social scale and lived by selling antiquities. With improved outlets, especially after the banning of museum excavations in 1887, their enterprise increased and led to the systematic looting of thousands of burial mounds in Jutland. Most famous of these dealers were the so-called Vorbasse boys (Quist 1975). Sophus Müller began a ruthless, systematic fight against the looting by means of proclamations, newsbills and popular meetings conducted by the poet Johan Skjoldborg (Thorsen 1983). Müller's admirably steadfast commitment was reflected in the chapter entitled "Devoted Friends and Dangerous Enemies" in the book of the National Museum's centenary (Müller 1907, 44 ff.). But this black and white view distorted the real situation, which after all was a reflection of the great class divisions of the time (Thorsen 1979); besides, Müller himself had helped to create a market for antiquities. With the spread of education and the gradual improvement of social conditions among the rural proletariat this type of itinerant dealer slowly vanished from the scene.

The development of provincial museums in these years took a new direction in many places. Interest in peasant culture rose significantly over the whole of Scandinavia, coinciding with the growth of industrialization. A large number of folk museums were now established. From 1855 to 1887 eight (county) museums were founded; from 1880 to 1900 another eight; from 1901 to 1914 twenty-seven; and from 1915 to 1929 there were thirty-two (fig. 5). The work of many of these museums had an

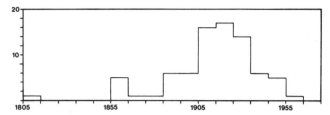

Fig. 5a. The frequency of culture-historical museums with an archaeological collection plotted against the date of their foundation (after Kristiansen 1981, p. 32).

	1965	1970	1976	1982
Universities	4	8	10	9
National Museum	8	9	9	11
Ancient Mon. Adm.	3	3	4	8
Regional Museums	6(3)	11(5)	23(5)	41(6)
Total	21	31	46	69

Fig. 6b. Diagram showing prehistoric archaeologists with a major university degree in permanent jobs (full- or parttime) in Denmark in respectively 1965, 1970, 1976 and in 1982. In brackets Prehistoric Museum Moesgaard. To this should in 1982/83 be added 7 prehistoric archaeologists employed in other institutions, plus 2 in Greenland and 1 in the Faroe Islands.

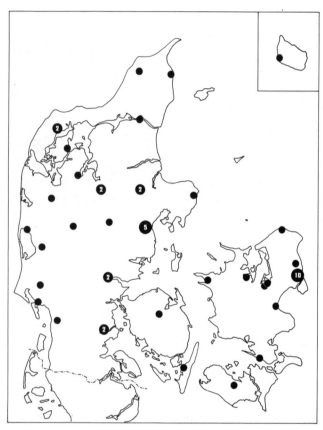

Fig. 6a. Museums with prehistoric archaeologists in permanent jobs in Denmark in 1982 (Medieval archaeologists are excluded).

orientation towards local history (Knudsen 1939). The number of museums receiving state support increased in 1915, and again in 1941. Some museums, such as Haderslev, Kolding, Odense and Ålborg, were given a professional curator during this period. Only in 1958 and 1976 were the legislative changes introduced which redefined the administrative and professional status of local museums and which radically improved their situation (Govt. Report No. 152; Nielsen 1964 and Govt. Report

No. 727). This led to considerable activity as a result of the appointment of professionally trained staff (fig. 6).

From 1930 up to the present day further important changes have occurred: new nature conservation legislation was passed in 1937 which protected all prehistoric remains *in situ*. Between 1937 and 1957 all parishes in Denmark were inspected by staff from the National Museum. Undisturbed and particularly significant burial mounds and monuments were placed under complete protection, a total of 24,000, while all the 78,000 burial mounds which had been ploughed were protected against excavation and destruction (Mathiassen 1938 and 1957) (fig. 7-9). All previous conservation had been voluntary, and in this way 7,500 prehistoric sites had already been protected when the new legislation was passed. Preservation initiatives had been started by the Commission for Antiquities in 1807, and between 1927 and 1934 nearly 100 sites a year were placed under protection. The new legislation, however, ensured a uniform legislative and administrative framework within which antiquities could be protected as part of the natural and cultural landscape. Both for archaeology and the environment, therefore, this was a major advance[9]. Of equal importance was the fact that in 1929 a lectureship in prehistoric archaeology was created at the University of Copenhagen with Brøndsted as lecturer, and from 1941 as professor. Worsaae had taught at the University from 1855-66, with little noticeable effect. Now a new generation of young archaeologists were trained who were to influence the development of Danish archaeology up to the present day (Becker 1979). In 1949 a chair of archae-

Region	in 1000						Protected mon. in %
	5	10	15	20	25	30	
Jutland						61095	28
Funen							34
Lolland–Falster							59
Zealand							36
Bornholm							42

Fig. 7. Diagram showing the relationship between the total number af recorded monuments and protected monuments in the major Danish provinces (after Mathiassen 1957).

ology was established in Århus. This guaranteed scientific continuity. Furthermore, in 1932-33 Brøndsted had become Curator of the 1st department of the National Museum, which had been settling into an attitude of learned intolerance[10]. Now things changed. The collections were re-arranged, while as early as 1928 the journal "Fra Nationalmuseets Arbejdsmark" had been established to provide popular information on archaeology. Several new members of staff were appointed, the first and most important of whom was Therkel Mathiassen, who laid the basis for a new tradition in the regional surveying of settlements and their environment. Around this time there was a change in the archaeological material received. There was a gradual but significant decline in the number of new grave and hoard finds brought to the museums. This was partly because certain find groups were nearly exhausted, partly because of the conservation legislation. The growing interest in settlement finds may also have been relevant. A new type of active archaeologist arose as a result of the attention paid by Therkel Mathiassen to this group of sites. The popularity of archaeology drew people into the fields. This was also reflected in the composition of private collections which now consisted predominantly of settlement finds. It was during the same period that Gudmund Hatt carried out his classic pioneer work, the registration of Iron Age field systems and the excavation of their house sites. For the third time a research programme on an interdisciplinary basis was begun, which studied the Ertebølle culture and the development of early agriculture. Here, for the first time, interpretations were aided significantly by pollen analyses. The "Mose" (: bog) Laboratory was set up during the war, and in 1956 the 8th dept. of the National Museum was established to deal with pollen analysis and C14 dating etc. Among new sites should be mentioned the large-scale excavation of Trelleborg and later of Fyrkat.

Fig. 8. Map showing the distribution of protected monuments in Denmark.

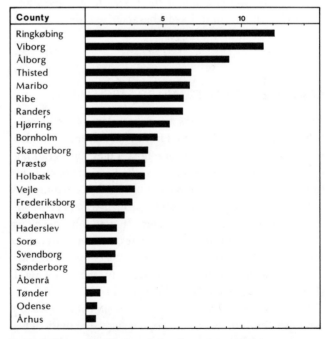

Fig. 9. Diagram showing the relative share of protected monuments in the Danish counties. All counties = 100%. (after Mathiassen 1957).

2*

All these trends have been followed and further developed in recent decades by a growing staff of archaeologists (Becker 1977, 38 ff. & 518 ff.). The period has been characterized by steadily improving methods of recording and excavation, and this has resulted in the accumulation of essential new knowledge on both a detailed and a comprehensive level. The composition of settlement layers is now recorded in terms of its archaeology, geology and botany. Crumbling skeletal remains are exposed in graves with a brush, or recorded by means of phosphate analysis. The use of machinery to uncover large surface areas has also added to our knowledge of the nature of settlements, since it has become possible to expose whole villages[11]. The work of the Settlement Committee (established by the Research Council) has been very important in this respect and has initiated development the main results of which will appear in the years to come. Excavation activity has also increased with the setting up of the "Fortidsmindeforvaltning" (: Administration of Ancient Monuments), which also conducts the excavation of endangered sites (as laid down in Act No. 314 of 1969, revising the Act of Conservation).

The preceding pages have described some principal features and characters involved in the development of archaeology, as reflected in the growth of museums, their accessions, and their excavation activity. In the following, I shall discuss some of the research objectives and research milieus that have characterized the scientific development of archaeology.

RESEARCH OBJECTIVES AND RESEARCH MILIEUS

Every field of science has its own system of well-established assumptions inherited from past research. Handed down through generations of scholars they have gradually turned into self-evident truths, the basis of which is no longer questioned or doubted. This basis is communicated, developed and established through teaching, publications, journals and congresses. It gradually develops into a research tradition and creates a strong protective sense of solidarity between the researchers involved. This is also true of Danish archaeology. In the following I shall attempt to show how this came about.

In the period before Thomsen the main concern was to establish the framework for archaeological activity. This was done with great skill and consistency, which has been somewhat obscured by Thomsen's achievements.

The early work of the Committee for Antiquities – during the first enthusiastic years – should be emphasized, since the actual creation of the Committee is a well known and frequently described achievement (Hermansen 1931 and 1954). In 1808 Werlauff published and commented on the general policy guiding the Committee's work. The objects of investigation were:

a. "Which prehistoric monuments found scattered over the fields, which presumably cannot be removed because of their size, deserve to be reserved for posterity by Royal Charter; and which, on the other hand, being less important, every farmer may be entitled to use in whichever way he wishes".

b. "What steps can be taken to rescue from destruction such remains from Antiquity and the Middle Ages as are to be found in churches and other public buildings."

c. "How common people can best be taught the value of the antiquities frequently dug up from the ground, and which are usually destroyed because nobody knows that they might be useful".

d. "How, at a minimum cost to the state, a State Museum can be founded to house all existing antiquities, whether they are already in the Royal Collections or might eventually be incorporated in them".

e. "How such a museum can be useful to the public".

In the context of the time, the formulation of these aims in 1807 must be regarded as epoch-making. For the first time archaeology was defined as an independent subject, studying the silent evidence of monuments and artefacts. As a next step a plan was proposed for their protection and exhibition[12]. The awareness of the importance of archaeology as an independent discipline did not arise by chance. Both the 1808 publication and a book published in 1807, "*Udkast til den nordiske Archæologies Historie i vort Fædreland, indtil Ole Worm*" (: A Survey of the History of Nordic Archaeology in Our Country, up to the Time of Ole Worm), by the same Werlauff, described the "new archaeology" in sharp contrast to earlier diffuse archaeological efforts, and stressed the need for scientific survey and excavation. The Commission made its first attempt by sending out questionnaires to all clergymen, which were hoped to provide information on 12 different types of archaeological material, from dolmens to runic stones. Thorlacius immediately analysed this information, as mentioned above. Werlauff, however, expressed some scepticism on the suitability of the clergy for such a task, and suggested archaeological field trips throughout the country and the founding of an archaeological journal. The latter proposal was carried out in 1812 with the publication of *Antiquariske Annaler,* whereas the archaeological field trips were not begun until two generations later. Werlauff finished by saying: "As long as these two *pia desideria* remain unrealized, we shall doubtless lack much of the possible information about our past. So, then, out into the field! must be the first and last cry of the antiquarian, eager for knowledge, to those who honour and speak on behalf of our past. This would crown the work of our Commission with laurels. When all this has come to pass, when all our antiquities have been collected and placed in our museums, then will be the time for the archaeologist to arrange and set in order all this material, and if possible organise it into a system; only then can he decide what we know with some degree of certainty, and where gaps exist which cannot be filled. The historian then will assist by comparing the data the archaeologist gives him with the insights gleaned from nature and myth, and from all that he can *perhaps* shed new light on the early mythical past of the Nordic countries"[13].

These promising beginnings of the Commission for Antiquities did not, however, continue with equal success, mainly because all its members were engaged full-time in other disciplines.

Without antiquities and arrangements for their display no further progress could be made. C.J. Thomsen was the first to realize this, and do something about it. Thomsen saw that a large, systematically arranged comparative collection was a necessary basis for the most elementary scientific progress. At that time the most pressing elementary problem was the rough chronological ordering of the many artefacts, the function of which as primitive tools, ornaments etc. was generally known. Thomsen was also aware that this knowledge should be based on observations from "closed finds", i.e. objects found in association. This appears from Thomsen's many letters. In 1822 he wrote to Schröder: "No less important is that the antiquarian should observe which objects are found together – we have been neglectful in this respect. I hope that the careful inventory we keep on everything that comes into our Museum will be of some help. By exercising some caution, one can be fairly sure of what belongs to pagan times, but with most artefacts we know no more than that. Future antiquarians may determine whether they are from the year zero, 100 A.D. or 900 A.D., or even before the worship of Odin began in Scandinavia, but this will only become possible if we observe which

finds occur together, and our collections are made as perfect as possible" (quoted in Hildebrand 1938, 353).

Not until 1836 did Thomsen publish his *results,* which turned out to be of fundamental importance; their underlying *assumptions,* however, were equally significant for the scientific development of archaeology (Gräslund 1974, 101 ff.). The importance of this advance must be seen in relation to the "general archaeological situation" in Europe at the time, which was chaotic, to put it mildly. Thomsen's aim was to make archaeology into an empirical science, and this is part of the reason for his reluctance to publish. It was quite simply too early to achieve any major scientific progress, given the existing conditions of museums and archaeological data. In this respect Thomsen can be said to have laid the foundations for archaeological activity. Others, including the young Worsaae, were to reap the first scientific harvest of this work. Finally, Thomsen's well-known prejudice against the academic world should be seen in relation to the historical background of his contribution (Hildebrand 1938, 13-146; Petersen 1938, 1-85)[14]. In Thomsen's day there was a fight for supremacy between the literary and the empirical concept of prehistory. Finn Magnussen's book of 1820, *"Bidrag til nordisk Archæologie meddelt i Forelæsninger"* (: Lectures on Nordic Archaeology), was on the whole a philological and historical study concentrating on Tacitus, the sagas etc., to which monuments and artefacts were seen merely as a supplement. This situation lasted well into the nineteenth century. It was this sort of speculative work to which Thomsen was opposed, since it might compromise the fragile beginnings of archaeology as a scientific discipline. If the historians more or less neglected archaeology, it was also because it was still not possible to relate Thomsen's Three-Age System to patterns in culture history or any chronological framework. The historian P.A. Munch stated in 1838 that "southern Sweden and Denmark were inhabited by primitive men, who lived by hunting and fishing, and used weapons and household equipment of stone or copper, later also of bronze... We know nothing more about these early inhabitants of Scandinavia" (quoted in Petersen 1938, 77). N.M. Petersen gave a fuller explanation in 1837: "Today new paths to knowledge are being cleared, and the time will probably come when we can illuminate the past by the light of the present: interpret written records by material remains from the past. Much material for this purpose has been collected and arranged, particularly as a result of the tireless efforts of one man, but definite results have not yet emerged; more must be collected, and must be analysed" (quoted in Petersen 1938, 73).

Thomsen began a scientific tradition which was as important as his museum work in the development of archaeology, in that he created a milieu for archaeological research – a precondition for the development and continuity of every field of study. This is reflected in his comprehensive correspondance, the immense bulk of which stands in sharp contrast to his limited scientific writings. These letters show the real Thomsen, the archaeologist to whom the subject was more important than scholarly renown, and who shared out all his knowledge and experience in private and thereby decisively influenced the development of museums and archaeology in Scandinavia (Hildebrand 1938). A scholar cannot work in isolation. Thomsen realized this. Similarly, scientific continuity had to be ensured, and Thomsen did this by gathering round him young voluntary assistants, who all were to achieve distinction as archaeologists. This patriarchal tradition of instruction has continued right up to our time[15].

An important figure in the field of scholarship at that time was Thomsen's contemporary C.C. Rafn, who in 1825 was a founding member of the Society of Northern Antiquaries: (in 1828 it became a Royal society). Rafn was the prime mover in the Society, which was to become the foremost scientific medium for Danish archaeology. Its growing membership, at home and abroad, helped to give Danish archaeology a prominent place during the middle and later part of the 19th century. This was also the time when a special French edition of the Society's annual publication was issued – French being then, together with Danish, the main language of archaeology (Worsaae 1866 and 1875; Grøndal 1869). The Society aimed at the publication of Icelandic manuscripts, partly for scholars and partly for the general reader. This soon ensured a sound economic position, which was further consolidated by the international best-seller of 1837, "Antiquitates Americanæ". Its scholarly reputation as well as its capital increased steadily during the 19th century, partly because a growing proportion of its core membership consisted of scientists, heads of state, princes etc. from all over the world. From 1832 archaeology was represented in the periodical "*Nordisk Tidsskrift for Oldkyndighed*" – from 1836 called "*Antiquarisk Tidsskrift*". These journals were succeeded in 1866 by "*Aarbøger for nordisk Oldkyndighed*". During the first few decades, however, they served primarily the study of history and philo-

logy. To change this required an improvement in the status of archaeology, reflected partly in greater activity, partly in an archaeological objective defined in terms of social and cultural history. This was brought about by the followers of Thomsen in the years after 1850, with Worsaae as the guiding spirit.

The ground had already been prepared in the 1840's when the young Worsaae elegantly refuted some of the period's more imaginative manifestations of archaelogical enterprise: a body found in a bog at Haraldskjær was alleged to be that of Queen Gunhild, known as the wife of Erik Bloodaxe; and the dramatic runic inscriptions "Runamo", which – subjected to Worsaae's critical scrutiny – dissolved into natural cracks and crevices (Worsaae 1934, 94-126; Petersen 1938, 84-116). This caused a sensation because on this occasion a young student floored academically some of the most eminent scholars of the time, as was confirmed later during a debate in the Academy of Sciences and Letters. But Worsaae's main point, as revealed in his conclusion to the Runamo affair, should be noted: "There is no doubt," Worsaae stated, "that many will take a humorous view of the Runamo affair and become sceptical, even contemptuous, of the study of Antiquity. However, such a point of view is completely unjustified." Worsaae substantiated this and concluded: "Admittedly, in this case *the imagination, which has hitherto played far too great a role in the study of the past*, seems to have reached its peak, and *fearing similar mistakes science will now undoubtedly learn to adopt a more critical attitude* so that the attempted reading of Runamo rather than harming science may exercise a highly beneficial influence over its future development" (quoted in Petersen 1938, 111) (my italics).

By his effective and tactically well-chosen criticism of a few grave examples of the erroneous and uncritical use of archaeological sources, Worsaae had achieved an important victory for the independence of the new science. But this success had to be followed up in such a way as to demonstrate how archaeological sources might contribute to the knowledge of prehistoric cultures. With this in mind Worsaae published, as early as 1843, a popular booklet aimed at educating the general reader, "*Danmarks Oldtid oplyst ved Oldsager og Gravhøie*" (: Denmark's prehistory as revealed in antiquities and burial mounds). It was translated into German in 1844 and into English in 1849. It was built around Thomsen's Three-Age System, and moreover contained a clear emphasis on the inadequacy of written sources. It argued against legendary traditions and also proposed a process of culture historical evolution, and gave the three ages an approximate dating (Worsaae 1843, 98-143). In the following decades, as mentioned above, the excavations and registration work were carried out which were to justify Worsaae's bold and, in the context of the time, extremely polemical statements. In these years Thomsen's students did their pioneer work in Danish archaeology "on constant journeys of exploration into the Danish landscape and through persistent studies of the collected material they sketched the first rough outline of Nordic prehistory, which was then more of a *terra incognita* than are the planets of the universe today", as Mogens Ørsnes has so vividly expressed it (Ørsnes 1969, V). The Stone Age, the Bronze Age and the Iron Age were each divided into an early and a late period (Gräslund 1974, 113 ff.). Methodological analysis was still rough and ready, and it was the many new finds that were mainly conducive to progress in chronology. Worsaae himself worked out the main outline, and formulated it in several publications for popular readership, the last in 1882. It was a period when broad outlines were being produced for science in general, since developments during these years in natural history, geology, zoology, archaeology and ethnography constituted nothing less than a conceptual revolution. And the basic results were achieved by interdisciplinary collaboration. Worsaae himself had helped to demonstrate the existence of primitive hunting people in Denmark, and around this time man-made flint tools were being found in France in geological association with bones of a glacial fauna, e.g. the woolly rhinoceros, mammoth, reindeer etc. (Eggers 1959, 54-73). Simultaneously, Darwin was formulating his theory of evolution, while ethnographic theories of evolution were also in the melting-pot. It was thus a time of interdisciplinary growth, when new grand perspectives were being opened up, perspectives which revolutionized the world view of the time and at one stroke took the history of mankind thousands of years back beyond the date of 4004 B.C. allotted it by the church. It was in this context that Worsaae wrote in his introduction to the book "*Danish Arts*": "As long as there was nothing to refer to but historical documents, the immeasurable pre-historic periods of the existence of the human race lay in the deepest obscurity" (Worsaae 1882, 2).

Let us attempt to summarize the most important results achieved in the period 1850-75. In general it was a turning-point for the natural and historical sciences throughout Europe. In archaeology Thomsen's Three-Age System was seen to be valid in a large part of the world. In Denmark itself archaeology was established as an independent discipline. The cultural and historical framework which later research has sought to develop was formulated in Worsaae's published work. It was based on the hypothesis of a cultural development from south to north, and aimed at identifying new stimuli in the form of migrations. "It would be of the greatest significance to show – as Rask was trying to do with languages – the migrations of peoples from their first origins by means of the evidence from finds" (quoted in Petersen 1938, 139). Thomsen's system was also developed chronologically, and dates were provided. The archaeological world in these decades was dynamic and open to new ideas, with no sharp divisions between professional and "amateur" archaeologists, or between the various disciplines of social and cultural history. There was as yet no formal archaeological training in existence. Important scientific contributions were made by "non-professionals", such as the County Prefect Vedel and the Court Chamberlain Sehested. Major results had already been achieved. Nevertheless Worsaae realized, in 1882, that "it was self-evident that such a newly established and singularly comprehensive study of prehistory could not yet have achieved many general, and in every respect irrefutable, scientific results which in a manner convincing to everybody could replace the old prevailing prejudices" (Worsaae 1882, 1 f.). This statement contains the key for an understanding of the research of the subsequent 50 years, which was a time of consolidation and stabilization during which the many problems formulated by Worsaae were tackled, while a few new problems arose.

Under Sophus Müller archaeology followed a narrower path. A well-defined scientific methodology was worked out, both in resolving chronologies and in excavation, and at the same time there were stricter demands placed on archaeological work. This is one of the reasons for his conflict with provincial museums. On one point Müller's policy of centralisation was well-founded, and did not depart from previous practice[16], viz. where the statutory obligation to deliver important finds to the National Museum was concerned. This, combined with the National Museum's function as a central museum, was an essential prerequisite for the scientific progress made during these years in the field of chronological research. It is clearly illustrated by a comparison of Müller's article of

1876 on Bronze Age chronology with that of 1909. The former opposes any kind of chronological division; the latter subdivides the Late Bronze Age alone into six periods. The greatest accession of Bronze Age finds by the National Museum took place in the intervening years. Müller could, so to speak, develop his chronological system year by year on the basis of new important finds.

Another equally essential prerequisite was the working out of a well-defined scientific method to build a chronology. Former research had been based on a comparison of associated and non-associated finds (e.g. stone axes and iron artefacts). This was the principle underlying the Three-Age System. Intermediate stages – finds combining e.g. stone axes and bronze artefacts, or bronze and iron – indicated the direction of development. With the growing interest in a finer chronological division, attention was increasingly focused on the gradual changes that could be observed in individual objects belonging to the same period. It was soon realized that such changes occurred fairly regularly, so that it was possible to establish whole "developmental series" of artefacts, which could be divided according to type. When these type series were compared with each other, in the context of closed finds, the main periods could now be subdivided with great accuracy. Formerly, divisions had primarily been based on differences. Now they were based on graduated similarity. This method had been developed in Sweden in the 1870's by H. Hildebrand and Oscar Montelius, who gave it its methodologically most precise version under the name of "typology" (e.g. Montelius 1903). In fact, typology reflected a general methodological tendency in contemporary archaeological research. That is probably one reason why Müller argued so vehemently against it – in his opinion it was nothing new (Müller 1884; also Gräslund 1974, 167-216).

The decades around the turn of the century thus saw two major achievements: a representative collection was acquired as a result of substantial accessions and this, combined with improved typological methods, made possible the final working out of the chronological systems. Broadly speaking, later research has only added minor chronological adjustments. Bronze Age chronology was the first to find its final version in 1885, followed by the Iron Age and after the turn of the century Stone Age chronology. Only the Old Stone Age was still inadequately studied, while settlements from the other periods also began to attract scholarly attention. It was now possible to show the distribution over large geographical areas of specific artefact types, and typological studies – not of chronological changes, but of the geographical ones – could demonstrate the spread of cultural influences, often from south to north. The distribution areas of specific artefact types were termed "culture groups", and these groups were identified with different peoples. One such culture group, the single-grave culture, had been discovered in systematic excavations in Jutland, and it was thought to represent a new immigration from the south-east. Worsaae's desiderata had now been fulfilled. – It was a time when similar theories of culture were also being worked out in philology, anthropology (the study of races) and ethnography (the culture group theory in Europe, the Boas school in the U.S.). There was widespread interest in cultural diffusion, which was linked with theories on migration etc. Race, language and culture were the basic elements (Kristiansen 1974, with references). Archaeologists managed to date the Bronze and Iron Age periods by linking finds from the north with those from the south until the sanctuary of safe dates was reached in Greece and Egypt (Eggers 1959, 34 ff.). This fundamental progress enabled Sophus Müller to give the first really comprehensive account, in 1897, of cultural developments in Danish prehistory (Müller 1897).

Under Sophus Müller and his successor C. Neergaard (1921-33) the research milieu was restrictive, and rigid lines of demarcation were drawn up in many directions. Müller laid down the objectives which all had to pursue, and he controlled publication rights. Consequently, able assistants with an independent outlook, such as Georg Sarauw – and later on Blinkenberg, Friis Johansen and Hatt – eventually left the Museum. Yet considerable results were obtained and archaeological material was not allowed to remain unpublished. At the end of the 19th century there were several major publications of material by A.P. Madsen, Boye and Sehested *et al.*, and the monograph series "*Nordiske Fortidsminder*" was begun in 1889 to present new important finds.

When Johannes Brøndsted began lecturing at the University of Copenhagen in 1929 and then – almost by a palace revolution – replaced Neergaard as head of the 1st dept. of the National Museum in 1932-33, an open and dynamic research environment was restored, and there was an impressive increase in activity in all areas. Contacts were re-established with natural science, with the University and with amateur archaeologists. Efforts were directed towards two goals: elucidating Old Stone Age cultures and the problem of settlements in general, and renewed chronological studies in order to improve the older systems. The following couple of decades are among the most productive in the history of Danish archaeology – one major publication followed another –, and to present many of the new results to an international public "*Acta Archaeologica*" was begun in 1930. In 1938-40 Brøndsted summarized the results in his impressive outline "*Danmarks Oldtid*". The book covered no new theoretical ground, but the picture of Danish prehistory was presented with more detail and subtlety than ever before, and the book was followed by a steadily increasing flow of popular books and pamphlets.

It can reasonably be claimed that Brøndsted's students have left their mark on developments up to the present day – in positions at the National Museum, in institutes of archaeology, and in a few provincial museums. Yet a kind of dividing line appears towards the year 1950. In 1949 P.V. Glob became professor in Århus, as did C. J. Becker in Copenhagen in 1952. Glob devoted himself to great practical tasks – at first in the newly founded "Jydsk Arkæologisk Selskab" (: Archaeological Society of Jutland), as founder of the Prehistoric Museum of Moesgård, and on expeditions to the Persian Gulf, later as Keeper of National Antiquities, in which capacity he has no doubt succeeded better than anybody else in giving archaeology a popular image. By contrast, Becker carried on the scientific traditions of the discipline in Copenhagen with special emphasis on chronological research and later settlement excavations. In subsequent decades Becker trained most of the younger generation of archaeologists. In this way, and as editor of the chief publications, Becker has helped to influence scientific developments during this period more than anyone else. There is, however, a kind of interaction between Århus and Copenhagen. In Århus an enterprising, outgoing archaeological environment was created around the "Jydsk Arkæologisk Selskab" and the new journal "*Kuml*", from 1961 intensified by Ole Klindt-Jensen as professor, while a more restrictive research community developed in Copenhagen, based on research within the framework laid down by Becker. This was furthered by the publication from 1973 of the new monograph series "*Arkæologiske Studier*". The period has not been characterized by fundamental methodological progress, although there has been more precise methodological formulation, by e.g. Mogens Ørsnes and Olfert Voss, and increasing use of statistical methods. In terms of social and cultural history it

has been a period of stagnation; Brøndsted and Glob have had their work reprinted, and new publications in the field add nothing new.

Let us summarize briefly. The first and chief aim of archaeology after the Committee for Antiquities was founded in 1807 was to provide a systematically arranged collection of artefacts and a rough chronology (Thomsen). The next step was a concentrated effort to establish archaeology as an independent branch of social and cultural history (Worsaae). Its scientific status was consolidated under Müller, above all by the working out of a chronological method and by systematic publication of material. All later archaeological research has taken place within this framework – with chronology as the scientific basis and cultural history as the national superstructure. In these years the research milieu has changed its character several times. The archaeological community in Denmark shows two main currents. One is represented by J.J.A. Worsaae and J. Brøndsted, P.V. Glob and O. Klindt-Jensen: expansive personalities who gathered a group of widely differing researchers around them and allowed them to work and develop in their own chosen field. They initiated periods in Danish archaeology characterized by innovation and diverse patterns of activity. The other main current is represented by C.J. Thomsen, Sophus Müller and C.J. Becker: all archaeologists with a capital "A", who were more inclined to shape Danish archaeology in accordance with their own views. They inaugurated periods characterized by preoccupation with and consolidation of achieved results. Both scientific communities have produced significant research, but of a different kind and on a different basis.

We shall now examine the position of archaeology in the development of society during the same period.

ARCHAEOLOGY IN SOCIETY

In highly developed and expanding societies like those of Western Europe the historical changes take place, as it were, before our very eyes. A historical consciousness is therefore "inevitably part of our mental equipment – and the historical outlook is part of ourselves. Thus the historical view is not something we can form an opinion about – it simply happens to be there" (Witt 1977, 18 ff.). But it is a far cry from this to initiating archaeological activity. Why did it happen and why was such activity maintained and developed? Only an examination of the function of archaeology in society can answer these questions.

Such an examination will necessarily be short and tentative, since we are dealing with a problem which has not received much attention. Yet it is undoubtedly of considerable importance for an understanding of the expansion of archaeology in Denmark – and in other West European countries. Besides, an understanding of this relationship is a *sine qua non* if a cultural policy for archaeology is to be formulated for the future.

A general and well-known feature of archaeology is the fact that throughout its development it has been part of the national moral rearmament. This hardly requires documentation. The "fateful years" of 1807, 1848, 1864, 1920 and 1940-45 are all reflected in the archaeological activity of the time, and prehistory in these years of crisis was frequently used as a symbol of national identity. After all, it was not only through museums and archaeological books that knowledge of archaeology spread. Most of the population got to know of it at second or third hand – primarily through the literary tradition extending from Oehlenschläger, Ingemann and Grundtvig to Johannes V. Jensen and Martin A. Hansen, but also in an attenuated form through school text books, children's books, folk high schools etc. In this way knowledge of prehistory, and of the past in general, reached a large section of society in a complex process of dissemination during which it underwent several changes and was used in many disguises. The question is whether it is possible to discern behind these general tendencies any important changes in the social position of archaeology and its ideological affiliations. Was archaeology used? For what? And by whom? We can approach the answer to this problem in several ways. The records of the National Museum, for instance, show us the route from finder to museum, and the fact that it changed. The other route, from archaeologists out to different segments of society via literature, popular outlines etc. is also informative. Finally, the founding of museums and the active interest shown by people outside the circle of professional archaeologists provide us with more tangible information. I shall now attempt a brief sketch of the development of archaeology in Danish society, with examples from each of these three categories.

There seems to be no doubt that the Commission for Antiquities was set up as the indirect result of the Romantic movement and the national defeats of the time (e.g. Hildebrand 1938, 175 ff.; Klindt-Jensen 1975, 58 ff.). Thorlacius' conclusion is significant: "They remind us of the heroic deeds of the Nordic peoples, they speak aloud of their vigour and fighting strength, they offer abundant cause for comparing the past and the present" (Thorlacius 1809, 68).[17]. There is also no doubt that during its first fifty years archaeology was a leisure pursuit of the educated upper class. So-called popular backing was found only on a small scale. The clergy and local government officials (magistrates and county prefects) played a crucial role by maintaining contact with the Museum of Antiquities during this early period, as is apparent from the old records[18]. It was the payment of rewards which counted among those people who actually made the finds, since their standard of living was miserably low throughout most of the 19th century (Riismøller 1971; Engberg 1973). The educational ideas which were part of the archaeological effort were expressed by archaeologists and the educated upper class of government officials and landowners. One of the latter was the Royal Councillor Bülow from Funen, who as early as 1816 was active in setting up an archaeological collection in Odense and was supported by Prince Christian Frederik (later King Christian VIII), who wrote to the Commission for Antiquities in 1817 with a request for contributions of duplicates. The relics of the past being an important means of kindling love of the native country, "thus I believe the effects of these means will be even stronger and more comprehensive if ... in all major provincial towns there were small collections of antiquities, the suitable use of which would undoubtedly disseminate at large the appreciation of a sense of the past already created by the *Zeitgeist* and the measures of the Government" (quoted in Hermansen 1960, 21). Inculcating a knowledge of the past thus had a clear purpose. Worsaae introduced his book of 1843 with the words: "A people with respect for themselves and their independence cannot possibly rest content with a consideration of their present circumstances only. They must also of necessity look to the past ... to learn how they became what they are. Only when this is clear in their minds, can a people fully understand their heritage, only then can they defend their independence with all their might and work with zeal for future progress, and thereby safeguard the prosperity and honour of their mother country" (Worsaae 1843, 1)[19].

But those who were to become enlightened by the past were not themselves actively involved in this process. The initiatives came from the people at the top. Several attempts were made at this time to set up public archaeological collections in the provinces, often attached to a county library, i.e. as part of the educational effort. This happened first in Odense in 1818, then in Århus in 1837, then in Odense again in 1840 and in Ålborg in 1844 (Kjær 1974, 116 ff., fig. 3). But they were only attempts. Both administratively and ideologically, archaeology remained an integral part of the period's autocracy.

In the inter-war years 1850-64 five provincial museums were suddenly established in rapid succession: Ribe, Odense, Århus, Viborg and Ålborg. These five museums had a number of characteristics in common: in each case the initiative had been taken by people who shared the same social background, the educated "upper middle class"; their administration was also dominated by academics from the upper middle class of Copenhagen, and the leading personality in each of the five museums was an academic with a background in natural history. This is an interesting point, since natural history and archaeology made great joint progress at this particular time, as already mentioned. Their statement of aims stressed the need for preservation of ancient monuments by educating the population about their historical and national significance: "The aim is to provide a collection of antiquities and exhibit them, so that the people will be in spiritual possession of the relics of the past, and learn to understand them so that a general interest is aroused for the history of the native country". The widespread destruction of monuments during that time played a contributory role, but the chief purpose was to establish *provincial* collections in order to educate *local* people. J. Forchhammer associated this with the post-autocratic decentralization because he saw provincial museums as a part of the new democracy and its popular education policy (Forchhammer 1866). In these and other views Forchhammer was amazingly far-sighted, and his opinions were supported by Worsaae, as mentioned above. The initiative in founding the first provincial museums thus came from people in the towns. The social group they were most concerned with – the peasants – did not yet themselves take the initiative. It is also remarkable that in every case the founding occurred at a time when the towns were experiencing rapid population increase and economic expansion. The museums were a product of the growing provincial middle class, and it is also during this time that the many large private collections were set up by aristocrats and wealthy middle class people (Kjær 1974).

By this time archaeology had won general recognition as an important branch of national history, which was further emphasized by the active interest taken by King Frederik VII in archaeology. Moreover, investigations were begun during these years at a number of national monuments, such as Jelling and Danevirke, and in the relationship with Germany archaeology was used as a political weapon, by means of which Worsaae denied German claims of ethnic and cultural affinities between South Jutland and Germany in his 1865 publication of Schleswig's prehistoric monuments. Sophus Müller repeated the same thing when he wrote about South Jutland's prehistory in 1913-14. On the whole, the discussion of such nationalist themes has always thrived in times of national crisis or consolidation.

The great period of museum foundations was at the end of the 19th century and the first decades of the 20th century (up to and including the 1930's). This was also the time of expansion for the folk high schools. The farmers and peasantry were the new dominant class (Skovmand 1964; Dybdahl 1965; Falk and Hansen 1974). While they organized themselves politically and economically – the "Venstre (: Left) party, co-operative societies, banks etc. – the folk high schools provided their cultural education. The farmers and peasantry received from these schools a sense of cultural and historical identity, of spreading and renewing fundamental national values, as reflected, for instance, in the high school song books. And as a result of this the farmers and school teachers began to establish their own museums, the folk and regional museums. These museums expressed the cultural self-assurance of farming people, e.g. as keepers and intermediaries of the old vanishing peasant culture[20]. They also reflected the desire for a more tangible historical identity based on the district where they lived and which they knew well. As a further sign of this a large number of county historical journals were published from the turn of the century (Hvidtfeldt 1949-52). In the museums prehistory was usually only part of an exhibition of more local interest, whereas the first provincial museums had been primarily archaeological. The archaeological collections mainly derived from the local private collections which appeared in their hundreds in the decades around the turn of the century. Such collections were offered to the National Museum in increasing numbers after the turn of the century, but were usually referred to the local museum. They reflect a keen interest in the past among the farmers themselves, who had previously simply handed over or sold artefacts to local land-owners or dealers. New social groups had become exponents of archaeological activity, and of historical activity taken as a whole. For these people both history and prehistory had a definite function, which gave perspective and meaning to their own role of transmitting historical traditions. At the same time it should be remembered that below the new class of independent farmers there still existed a large uneducated rural proletariat, many of whom emigrated to the U.S. in the 1880's and 1890's. They did not receive their share of the progress until the small-holders' legislation and social reforms of the 20th century. As mentioned above, these social contrasts were also expressed archaeologically in the relationship between burial mound looters/dealers: the "dangerous enemies", on the one hand, and the more affluent collectors: the "devoted friends", on the other.

If we look at the records of the National Museum again, we can see that teachers have replaced the clergy as museum middlemen. In fact, school teachers played a major role in the archaeological and historical work of this period (Olrik 1913). "A growing people" was the title of one of the chapters about this period in the History of Denmark published by the national newspaper "Politiken" (Skovmand 1964, 355 ff.). The desire of professional archaeologists to be associated with this development is clearly expressed in a statement by Sophus Müller in 1896 and 1907. After stressing the skill of the prehistoric Scandinavian peoples, he wrote: "Southern Scandinavia at all times had a culture with a character of its own, markedly different from that found in northern Germany. From South Jutland to Scania there lived a uniform people; on our soil the Nordic Tribe grew strong and plentiful until much later, around the middle of the millennium after Christ, it separated into Danes, Norwegians and Swedes. Prehistoric Denmark was a good country, its soil and seas, its climate and situation, half separated and half united as it was with other countries. It was a country where an able population could evolve, independent and progressive. The great value of antiquities for all Danes is that they teach us this; it is also useful knowledge for the man who prefers to think of the present and the future. The great record of our country's prehistoric past gives us confidence that the work to protect her future independence, to uphold our national identity, and to develop our prosperity and culture will not be in vain" (Müller 1907, 26). In keeping with this view Müller saw archaeology as a product of the new era: "Rather than tracing its ancestry to the Middle Ages, in the manner of aristocrats, the study of prehistory prefers to re-

gard itself as a child of the new era, born as an ordinary citizen in the dawn of the Century of Liberty" (Müller 1896, 702).

The period between 1930 and 1950 was a time of consolidation, during which the cultural activities in the countryside were continued, e.g. in youth and gymnastic clubs and in regional historical societies. A growing number of interested individuals, with affiliations to the tradition of regional history, became actively involved as amateur archaeologists and made their own collections, many of which became the nucleus of small regional museums. These private collectors had a different background from their predecessors, being often gardeners or workmen. Amateur archaeologists, the active collectors, became a new concept. This tendency towards a proliferation of archaeological interest has been accentuated in the last two decades. In the towns a new and large circle of educated middle-class readers are reached, primarily through the periodical "Skalk" but also through an increasing number of popular archaeological books, for which there is now a ready market. These readers are not actively involved in archaeology, they see it as exciting – and interesting – entertainment. This is underlined by the way prehistory is presented: in "Skalk" as "newspaper items", prehistoric news in the form of sensational and exciting new finds; the slightly piquant and macabre appeal of Glob's book "The Bog People" etc. Archaeology has long ago abandoned its nationalistic commitment and has become entertainment for the rising middle classes. New types of exhibitions and museums also seek to attract this public. The national commitment, the attempt to use archaeology, has continued mainly among non-archaeologists, most explicitly in the writings of Martin A. Hansen, who regretted the fact that continuity in historiography had been replaced by isolated details and fragments: "The subject is reduced to bits and pieces. Cross sections, excerpts, isolated extracts are preferred to continuity" (1957, 9). And he continued: "We are not only members of society, citizens of the state, we are members, we discover, of a more potent, more profound community, the Danish people, whose foundations are the mother tongue, the history of Denmark, its literature. But history is also something else; it is a weapon. What is needed is a history that has been forged and tempered. And it becomes that the moment we recount it as it deserves to be recounted. "Skræp"* must be dug up, not to be recorded, analysed for pollen and placed in a museum, but to be used".

Generally speaking, the spread of archaeology has thus been brought about by three different groups of society: the aristocracy, the middle classes, and the peasantry, in that historical order but with considerable overlap. The historical and archaeological commitment coincides with periods either of decline or progress for these groups, which is hardly accidental. Admittedly, it may be argued that an interest in archaeology, especially the urge to collect, is a common human trait, and this does lend variety to the picture. But the purpose for which archaeology could be used – and was used – is specifically historical. It is hardly a matter of chance that national archaeology was to arise during the decline of absolutism, and the fact that archaeology – and history – was used first by the rising middle classes and then by the peasantry is hardly accidental either; nor the fact that the working classes never used it. It would seem that archaeology fulfilled important functions, e.g. by publicising and legitimatizing the interests and aims of these social groups, and by identifying them with the cultural heritage of the nation and the "people". The ultimate effect was to change the focus from internal to external contradictions, stressing national identity and solidarity as a precondition for progress and sovereignty. Seen in this light, it is not surprising that archaeology is hardly used for anything today, in a time characterized by supra-national organizations, and this despite the fact that archaeology has never had a larger public. But then it has hardly ever had so little to offer. The same old wine in new bottles.

SUMMARY AND CONCLUSION

After this discussion of some of the main trends in the development of Danish archaeology, I shall attempt to give a brief summary of my conclusions, according to period (see also fig. 10):

I. 1807-16. A slight growth in archaeological material (grave and hoard finds). Broad outlines, the framework for *archaeological* activity, are formulated by the Commission for Antiquities.

II. 1817-50. Increasing accessions (grave and hoard finds). First principles are laid down by Thomsen. A systematically arranged collection is established, on the basis of which the Three-Age System (chronology) is formulated. Archaeological interest is stimulated by guided Museum tours. Archaeological activity begins.

III. 1850-75. Explosive increase in accessions (grave and hoard finds). The main outlines are formulated by Worsaae during the period 1843-82. New activities resulting from this include systematic excavations and the registration of all prehistoric monuments. The principles governing archaeology as a scientific discipline are laid down. The museums of the provincial middle class are set up (county museums).

IV. 1875-1930. The accessions reach their peak and stabilize (grave and hoard finds). Settlements are found. Archaeology is consolidated scientifically under Müller, and expands by means of museums and popular support. Chronological systems are given their final shape. Archaeological material and outlines of prehistory are published. An increasing number of regional museums are set up by farmers and teachers.

V. 1930-50. Accessions from grave and hoard finds decline, but those from settlements increase. The broad outlines are re-formulated by Brøndsted and lead to new activities: new preservation legislation is followed by inspections for conservation purposes, and by regional surveys. The University training of archaeologists begins, new outlines are published. Archaeology is consolidated through museums and popular support, and scientific continuity is ensured.

VI. 1950-. There is a sudden decrease in archaeological material from graves and hoard finds, but a sharp increase in that from settlements. The period after 1950 can be seen as a consolidation of the progress achieved under Brøndsted. A new archaeological institute it established in Århus, legislation concerning museums and preservation is revised several times, and more and more professional staff are appointed to provincial museums, the activities of which rise dramatically as those of the National Museum decline. The Administration of Ancient Monuments is established to excavate endangered sites. Archaeological outlines are reprinted. Archaeology increasingly becomes a leisure pursuit of the middle classes.

The preceding pages have sketched the historical research framework for the representativity analyses which follow. In conclusion we shall summarize the historical significance of Danish archaeology. Danish – and later Scandinavian – archaeology achieved its international reputation in the 19th century because the fundamental methods were developed and representative material was collected earlier here than in other countries. In this way

30

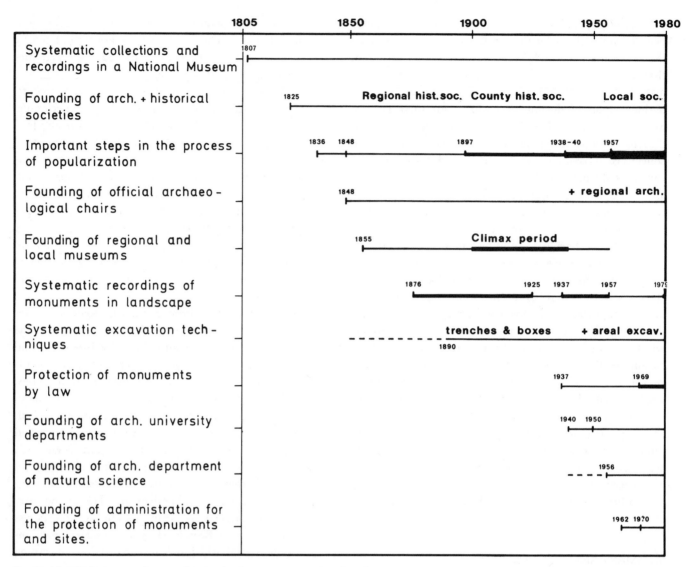

Fig. 10. Historical summary diagram of major developments in Danish archaeology.

Scandinavian archaeological activity became a yardstick for archaeology elsewhere. Subsequently, as comparable material was acquired and classified in Europe, Scandinavia gradually lost its initial advantage, a change that only began after the turn of this century. European archaeology at this time was still orientated towards the Scandinavian methodology and chronological systems. But now the situation has changed. In the last 20-25 years, European archaeology has evolved its own systems of chronology, and has achieved a high level of documentation by the publication of material. In the same period the new archaeology has been developed in England and

the U.S., which has also changed the scientific world picture considerably. It must be admitted that Danish archaeology – with a few exceptions – is today internationally famous mainly in Denmark. A renewal is needed in the cultural sciences, not only in Danish but in Continental archaeology as a whole. This is necessary if one wishes to keep abreast of scientific development, but also if one wishes to supplement and adjust the former function of archaeology as a form of national history in favour of a global scientific perspective. This requires the application of new theoretical perspectives, and not least the development of new methods which can convincingly relate archaeological material to theoretical aims, a process which is already under way. This involves, however, a number of fundamental problems concerning sampling and representativity, and although the centuries old tradition of European research has resulted in a very comprehensive collection of data, systematic representativity analysis is a necessary part of the new theoretical and methodological orientation of the future. This book is the first step in this direction.

Acknowledgements

The author wishes to express his gratitude to Jens Henrik Bech, Lotte Hedeager, Jørgen Street-Jensen, Birgitte Kjær, Viggo Nielsen and Olfert Voss for their critical comments and supplementary information during the final preparation of the manuscript, which was finished in 1977, with a few additions in 1979.

Kristian Kristiansen,
National Agency for The Protection of Nature,
Monuments and Sites,
Amaliegade 13,
1256 Copenhagen K.

NOTES

1. When Thomsen became Secretary, the collection was a shambles and he spent his first three years bringing it in order: "It was *intolerable* for me to display.....
 – Covered in dust, in complete disorder, hidden away in drawers, corners, kerchiefs, paper – everything was chaotic" (extract from a letter to Vedel Simonsen, quoted in Hermansen 1934, 112 f.).
2. In 1832 the governing body of the University, who wanted the premises for their own use, urged strongly that the Museum be moved. The letter contains a vivid description of museum activities and the inconvenience caused to the University Library. The premises, it says, were "a suitable place to deposit things as long as the Museum collected little and had few visitors". "But", it continued, "an entirely new situation has now arisen: the Museum has acquired a considerable collection, including a dozen sizeable heaps of stone etc., which weigh heavily on the floor; whole parties visit it from the city, the country, and from abroad, including scores of journeymen and school children, for whom the Library itself serves as a passageway or entrance hall; when all cannot be admitted, they assemble in the entrance to the Library where they cause much inconvenience by their noisy behaviour and by taking up room intended for the regular visitors to the University Library. Further, the Museum is governed, and the exhibition tours conducted, by persons who are complete strangers to the Library, indeed, most of them, to the University" (quoted in Mackeprang 1929, 6).
3. But first there was a temporary break with Thomsen because he refused to help Worsaae become permanently employed, whereas two of Thomsen's other assistants had joined the permanent staff. To make matters worse, Worsaae was in economic difficulties following the death of his father. This "break", with all its psychological and emotional overtones, appears vividly in their letters. Thomsen wrote: "although you are a stiff-necked person, I do like you. This is said to you by your Thomsen" (Worsaae 1934, 247). Worsaae sought advice and consolation from Hildebrand, who wrote to him: "You must step aside, but do not disappear from the scene. However, do not regard as a misfortune the fact that you are *forced* into an independent position. Among all the pleasures in the world that is the one I myself cherish the most" (Worsaae 1934).
4. As early as 1831 The Royal Society of Northern Antiquaries had issued a pamphlet to school teachers throughout the country containing instructions on excavation of burial mounds, the search for antiquities, and their proper conservation. The pamphlet was written by Thomsen, assisted by Finn Magnussen and Rafn, but was published anonymously, as were several of the Society's publications. Worsaae's book in 1843 also contained an appendix on excavation of burial mounds and the preservation of antiquities.
5. Vedel Simonsen, who had been a collector since 1807 and a member of the Commission since 1810, complained loudly about this in letters to his friend Werlauff. Vedel Simonsen employed four assistants to roam round Funen searching for antiquities, and yet the yield decreased "because collecting antiquities is becoming a mania, since not only does the White Doctor drive from house to house but also the King has his officers purchase everything for his private collection; in addition English emissaries and Jews from Hamburg buy up indiscriminately, and finally Count Ahlefeld, the Court Chamberlains Holsteen, Blixen, Wind, and War Councillor Theil etc. etc. are setting up private collections, and thus one outbids the other" (Wad 1916, 298 f.). Nevertheless, from 1851 till his death in 1858 Vedel Simonsen delivered c. 500 items to the Museum a year. By comparison, from 1807-23 he collected 363 items, and during the period 1824-51 873 items.
6. In 1852 Vedel Simonsen wrote to Werlauff: "You should not be surprised at all that more antiquities are found today than in olden times, for there is no question that people are now more on the lookout for them. Besides, they litterally *grow out of the earth:* the more the soil is worked and cultivated the more easily they are brought to the surface by the frost; furthermore, marl is now dug at a depth of several fathoms, which was not done before. Similarly, peat is now dug at a much greater depth than before" (Wad 1916, 267).
7. Worsaae was the first archaeologist who had the possibility to travel and excavate widely, and this is vividly illustrated in his letters to Thomsen back at the Museum, and later to his wife (Worsaae 1938). The regular parish visits have also been described, both by Magnus Petersen (1909) and by Løffler (1905).
8. Considerations of space rule out a discussion of the many complicated structural changes that have taken place at the National Museum over the years, including the splitting up of the present departments. The historical sections were made separate only in 1892, and the department of ethnography did not become independent until 1920. It is therefore difficult to categorize many of the old archaeologists. Most of them at various times dealt with archaeology, mediaeval history, and ethnology. Even under Müller they were ethnographers during the winter and archaeologists during the summer.

9. After Worsaae was appointed Inspector of Ancient Monuments, preservation efforts resumed. In 1848 all burial mounds on royal territory and in state forests were protected, and in 1849 government circulars on preservation were forwarded to all landowners. New preservation initiatives were inaugurated in the 1880's and 1890's: all glebes were protected (1885), the Heath Society was drawn into a joint conservation programme (1899), while Railway and Highway Authorities were prohibited by an injunction from removing any more stones from burial mounds (1887, 1890), which had been authorized by a provision of 1793 – a request in 1829 had had little effect. In 1911 the setting up of state small-holdings was accompanied by preservation regulations, and the obligation to observe existing provisions was stressed several times in Government circulars. In other words, a very active policy of preservation had been carried out. Moreover, all acts of preservation were published in the newspapers. (Cf. preservation reports 1873-90 by Worsaae, 1897-1902 by Müller and 1927-34 by Brøndsted in the National Museum Library).

10. It was during this period that the disgraceful rejection took place of Erik Westerby's basic investigation of "Stone Age Settlements around Klampenborg", just as Therkel Mathiassen was kept out of the 1st dept. of the National Museum.

11. This progress in documentary methods has also had its drawbacks, since it is time-consuming. The number of unfinished excavations reports has therefore risen markedly during the 50's and 60's, but has subsided again after the Administration of Ancient Monuments was set up – first under the Keeper of National Antiquities, now under the Ministry of Environment.

12. In the same year the Danish Academy of Sciences and Letters offered an essay prize on an archaeological topic: "Compare the prehistoric monuments of Scandinavia, such as burial mounds, dolmens, the objects found in them etc. ... so as to draw conclusions about the earliest origins, migrations, religious worship, culture and domestic life of our Nordic peoples" (Petersen 1938, 14).

13. The visionary enthusiasm of the Committee for Antiquities shows it to be a true child of the Romantic era, as are Nyerup's prophetic visions of the future National Museum, 30 years hence which proved true: "Danish men of honour vie with one another to glorify this Museum; of his own accord each individual offers his mite upon the altar of the National Museum; what was formerly scattered among the private possessions of individuals, hidden to the eye of the student and connoisseur alike, is now brought together as a precious whole. It has taken a long time for the Nyerup vision to be realized, but now that it has been carried out it resembles a proud oak which grows slowly but is in flower so much longer" (quoted in Hermansen 1931, 265).

14. "You know I loathe – what shall I call it – the kind of study of antiquities where you begin with the Celts, proceed to Chinamen and Egyptians, then jump nimbly to Mexico and Florida and thence to the present Kalmucks ... Sound judgment and common sense outweigh quotations and ornate phrases, and conclusions, registers and records may be worked out by the expert, but he sticks to solid facts". (Quoted in Hildebrand 1938, 351).

15. Thomsen summed up his guiding principles in an emotional letter to the young 31-year-old Bror Emil Hildebrand, who – because of a death – had unexpectedly been appointed Keeper of National Antiquities in Sweden in 1837:

"My dear, my beloved friend,
Too much! I exclaimed after reading your letter. Go into your study, pray sincerely to God for wisdom to choose what is right, strength to execute it, and finally humility and love towards others who are happy, I said. Do you know the obligations imposed upon you? They will not appear in your letter of appointment, but an inner voice will tell you that I am right in saying that they are:

1. To order and arrange, according to present scientific knowledge, your native country's collections of antiquities and coins, and work towards the same goal with regard to the historical archives.

2. To open all these collections as far as possible, nay completely, to the public so that not only a few scholars but the whole nation will benefit from them. See that there are regular hours during which the collections can be seen without any kind of prior notice, deference etc. etc., and other hours during which the scholar may use what he wishes to study, or even study-rooms where he can work undisturbed on whatever may interest him at the time.

3. That you promote knowledge by progressing with the times, knowing and using the new discoveries being made; and that you yourself, by serious application, advance the state of knowledge, and make discoveries to this effect, which may enable others to do likewise.

4. That you infuse life and enjoyment into and around the objects entrusted to you and acquire not one, but a couple of able and charming young men who may act as your assistants and, when the time comes, as your successors. As for that, look for people with a natural inclination, reasonable brains and character, so that one may respect them – qualities not easily found together – in that respect I have not been fortunate. Those I have met have either had mediocre intelligence or have been people I could not respect. Wish for me that I may be more successful than before, and a great load will be off my mind.

I can hear you say after this serious address how can I, alone, achieve all this – certainly not at once, but by gradual steps.
You will reverse the question and say, "Has Thomsen achieved this in his own country", and I must reply, "Some, much remains; the will, the intention is there, has always been there, and when I lay my head to rest I hope people will say: he did not work in vain". (Quoted in Hildebrand 1938, 748 f.).

16. Alredy in 1818 the problem of the relationship between provincial collections and the central collection in Copenhagen had arisen when a collection was established at Odense. Thomsen and the Commission had then tried to effect a scheme whereby all newly found antiquities were to be reported to Copenhagen, and the best pieces handed over. However, this plan was not backed up by the Danish Chancellery (Hermansen 1960, 27 ff.).

17. Worsaae wrote in his autobiography about his studies as a young man: "My student days were sustained by the more and more swelling nationalist movements. The new popular spirit sought revival and refreshment in the evocative past, for which Oehlenschläger's poetry had created universal enthusiasm" (Worsaae 1934, 69).

18. Thomsen's "Guide" of 1836 concludes (p. 90): "When ordinary workmen find antiquities, they would do best to contact the vicar, the school teacher or another knowledgeable person who can perceive their context and record what may be desirable to know".

19. The book was published by "The Society for the Proper Use of the

Freedom to Print", and it was "especially intended for educated men of all classes; it is hoped, however, that the first two sections can also be read by less knowledgeable people" (Worsaae 1843, preface). Thomsen correctly remarked in his recommendation of Worsaae's manuscript: "The list of members of the "Free Printing Society" clearly shows that the Society has many members, but that

very few of these belong to the "common people"." (Quoted in Worsaae 1934, 233).

20. This interest in folk culture also manifested itself in many other fields, e.g. in historical research – "The Folk Wave", as Skovmand has termed it (Skovmand 1975). And in the towns young middle-class girls dressed in folk costume (Witt 1977, 11).

REFERENCES

BECKER, C.J. 1966: Johannes Brøndsted, 5. oktober 1890-16. november 1965. Mindetale trykt i *Oversigt over Det Kgl. Vidensk. Selskabs Virksomhed 1965-1966.*

– 1977: De sidste generationers arkæologi. I Politikens Danmarkshistorie, bind 1 (genoptrykt). *De ældste tider indtil år 600* af J. Brøndsted.

BERING LIISBERG, H.C. 1897: *Kunstkammeret.* Dets Stiftelse og ældste Historie. København.

BETÆNKNING NR. 152.

– 1956: *Betænkning om en nyordning af de kulturhistoriske lokalmuseers forhold.* København.

BETÆNKNING NR. 727.

– 1975: *Betænkning afgivet af udvalget vedrørende revision af museumslovene.* København.

BRØNDSTED, J. 1938-40: *Danmarks Oldtid 1-3.* København.

– 1957-60: *Danmarks Oldtid 1-3* (2. à jourførte udgave). København.

– 1962: *Nordische Vorzeit 1-3.* Neumünster.

– 1957: Indledning til *»Danmarks Nationalmuseum«,* redigeret af Aage Roussel. København.

– 1962: Hvor ved vi det fra? Politikens Danmarkshistorie, bind 1: *De ældste tider indtil år 600.* København.

CHRISTENSEN, AKSEL E. 1969: *Vikingetidens Danmark.* På oldhistorisk baggrund. København.

Det kgl. Nordiske Oldskrifts-Selskab 1831: *Om nordiske Oldsager og deres Opbevaring.*

EGGERS, H.J. 1959: *Einführung in die Vorgeschichte.* München.

DYBDAHL, V. 1965: *De nye klasser 1870-1913.* Politikens Danmarkshistorie, bind 12. København.

ENGBERG, J. 1973: *Dansk Guldalder.* Eller oprøret i tugt-, rasp- og forbedringshuset i 1817. København.

FALK, J. & MADSEN, A. 1974: Bønder og Klassekamp. *Marxistisk Antropologi 3-4.* København.

FORCHHAMMER, J. 1866: Om oldnordiske Samlinger, historiske Museer osv. navnlig i Jylland. *Saml. til jydsk Historie og Topografi I.*

GLOB, P.V. 1966: Mindeord om Johannes Brøndsted. *Årbøger for nordisk Oldkyndighed og Historie.*

GRÄSLUND, B. 1974: *Relativ datering. Om kronologisk metod i nordisk arkeologi* (english summary). TOR. Uppsala (also diss. Uppsala).

GRØNDAL, B. 1869: *Breve til og fra Carl Christian Rafn med en biografi.* Kjøbenhavn.

HANSEN, MARTIN A. 1957: *Af Folkets Danmarkshistorie.* København.

HERMANSEN, V. 1931: Oprettelsen af »Den Kongelige Commission til Oldsagers Opbevaring« i 1807. *Årbøger for nordisk Oldkyndighed og Historie.*

– 1934: C.J. Thomsens første Museumsordning. Et Bidrag til Tredelingens Historie. *Årbøger for nordisk Oldkyndighed og Historie.*

– 1953: Baggrunden for oldsagscommissionen (The Background of the Royal Commission for the Preservation of Northern Antiquities). *Årbøger for nordisk Oldkyndighed og Historie.*

– 1954: Fortidsminder og Kuriositeter i Danmarks Middelalder. *Årbøger for nordisk Oldkyndighed og Historie.*

– 1960: *Tredelingen og Odense* (Die Dreiteilung und Odense). Fynske Studier IV.

HILDEBRAND B. 1937-38: *C.J. Thomsen och hans lärda förbindelser i Sverige 1816-1837. Bind I-II.* K.V.H.A.A. Handlingar Del 44:1-2. Stockholm.

HINDENBURG, G. 1859: Bidrag til den danske Archæologies Historie. Særskilt Aftryk af *Dansk Månedsskrift. Ny Række, 1. bind, 2. og 3. Hefte.* København.

JENSEN, C.A. & MØLLER, J.S. 1939: *Danske Kulturhistoriske Museer.* Kortfattet Oversigt udgivet af Dansk Kulturhistorisk Museumsforening. København.

KJÆR, B. 1974: *De første danske, kulturhistoriske provinsmuseers oprettelse omkring midten af det 19. århundrede.* Upubliceret specialeafhandling. Historisk institut. Århus.

KLINDT-JENSEN, O. 1975: *A History of Scandinavian Archaeology.* London.

KNUDSEN, R. 1939: *Håndbog i Hjemstavnsforskning og Hjemstavnskultur.*

KRISTIANSEN, K. 1974a: Arkæologien som Kulturvidenskab. *Kontaktstencil nr. 8.* København.

– 1974b: En kildekritisk analyse af depotfund fra Danmarks yngre bronzealder (periode IV-V). Et bidrag til den arkæologiske kildekritik. *Årbøger for nordisk Oldkyndighed og Historie.*

LARSEN, S. 1935 *Et Provinsmuseums Historie.* Odense.

LÖFFLER, J.B. 1905 *Min Virksomhed ved Nationalmuseet 1868-1900.* Kjøbenhavn.

MACKEPRANG, M. 1929: Fra Nationalmuseets Barndom. *Fra Nationalmuseets Arbejdsmark.* København.

– 1934: Mindeord om Sophus Müller. *Årbøger for nordisk Oldkyndighed og Historie.*

– 1938: Nationalmuseets Bygningshistorie I. Perioden 1880-1917. *Fra Nationalmuseets Arbejdsmark.*

34

– 1939: Nationalmuseets Bygningshistorie II. Perioden 1917-1933. *Fra Nationalmuseets Arbejdsmark.*

MATHIASSEN, Th. 1938: Den nye Fredningslov og de første Forsøg på at praktisere den. *Fra Nationalmuseets Arbejdsmark.*

– 1957: Oldtidsminderne og fredningsloven. *Fra Nationalmuseets Arbejdsmark.*

MONTELIUS, O. 1903: *Die typologische Methode.* Separat aus: Die älteren Kulturperioden im Orient und in Europa. Stockholm. Im Selbstverlage des Verfassers.

MÜLLER, S. 1884: Mindre Bidrag til den forhistoriske Archæologis Methode. *Årbøger for nordisk Oldkyndighed og Historie.*

– 1886: Mindetale over J.J.A. Worsaae. *Årbøger for nordisk Oldkyndighed og Historie.*

– 1897: Udsigt over Oldtidsudgravninger foretagne for Nationalmuseet Årene 1893-1896. *Årbøger for nordisk Oldkyndighed og Historie.*

– 1896-1901: Notice sur les fouilles faites pour le Musee National Copenhague pendant les annees 1893-1896. *Memoires de la Societe Royale des Antiquaires du Nord.*

– 1897: *Vor Oldtid.* København.

– 1898: *Nordische Althertumskunde.* Strassburg.

– 1907: *Nationalmuseet.* Hundrede Aar efter Grundlæggelsen. København.

Nationalmuseet og Provinsmuseerne 1912 *Aarbøger for nordisk Oldkyndighed,* s. 143 ff.

NEERGÅRD, C. 1916: Thomas Bartholin og Oldforskningen i det 17. Aarhundrede. *Ugeskrift for Læger, Nr. 42.*

NIELSEN, V. 1964: Nyere museumslovgivning i Danmark. *Fortid og Nutid. Bind XXII, hefte 5.*

– 1971: Status for den antikvariske lovgivning. *Fortid og Nutid XXIV, 5.*

OLRIK, H. 1913: Lærernes Bidrag til Oldgranskning og Historieforskning. *Lærerne og Samfundet.*

PETERSEN, CARL S. 1938: *Stenalder – Bronzealder – Jernalder.* Bidrag til nordisk Arkæologis Litterærhistorie. København.

PETERSEN, J.M. 1909: *Minder fra min Virksomhed paa Arkæologiens Omraade fra 1845 til 1908.* København.

QUIST, J. 1975: Vorbassedrengene. *Fra Ribe Amt. Bind XIX.*

RIISMØLLER, P. 1971: *Sultegrænsen.* København.

SKOVMAND, R. 1964: *Folkestyrets fødsel.* Politikens Danmarkshistorie. Bind 11.

– 1975: Den folkelige bølge. *Fra Ribe Amt. Bind XIX.*

THOMSEN, C.J. 1836: Kortfattet Udsigt over Mindesmærker og Oldsager fra Nordens Fortid. I *Ledetraad til nordisk Oldkyndighed.* Udgivet af Det kgl. nordiske Oldskriftsselskab, Kjøbenhavn.

– 1837: Kurzgefasste Übersicht über Denkmäler und Alterthümer aus der Vorzeit des Nordens. I *Leitfaden zur nordischen*
Alterhumskunde. Herausgegeben von der königlichen Gesellschaft für Nordische Alterthumskunde.

– 1849: *A Guide to Northern Antiquities.* London.

THORLACIUS, B. 1809: *Bemærkninger over de i Danmark endnu tilværende Hedenolds-Höie og Steensætninger.* Kiöbenhavn.

THORSEN, S. 1979: »Opofrende Venner og farlige Fjender ...« 1890'ernes højplyndringer og et bidrag til arkæologiens socialhistorie. *Fortid og Nutid XXVIII, 2.*

WAD, G.L. 1916: *Fra Fyens Fortid.* Samlinger og Studier. II. Bind. Kjøbenhavn.

WERLAUFF, E.C. 1807: *Udkast til den nordiske Archæologies Historie i vort Fædreland indtil Ole Worms Tid.* Kjøbenhavn.

– 1808: *Bemærkninger i Anledning af den til de nordiske Oldsagers Samling og Opbevaring nedsatte Commission.* Kiöbenhavn.

VIBÆK, J. 1964: *Reform og fallit. 1784-1830.* Politikens Danmarkshistorie. Bind 10.

WITT, T. 1977: *Hvad med museerne?* Wormianum. Århus.

WORSAAE, J.J.A. 1843: *Danmarks Oldtid oplyst ved Oldsager og Gravhöie.* Kiöbenhavn.

– 1844: *Dänemarks Vorzeit durch Alterthümer beleuchtet.* Kopenhagen.

– 1849: *The primeval antiquities of Denmark.* London.

– 1866: Conferentsraadene C.C. Rafn's og C.J. Thomsens Fortjenester af Oldskriftselskabet og af Oldtidsvidenskaben i det hele. *Aarbøger for nordisk Oldkyndighed og Historie.*

– 1875: Tale ved det kgl. nordiske Oldskriftselskabs havtredsindstyveaarige Stiftelsesfest under H. Maj. Kongens Forsæde paa Amalienborg d. 28. jan. *Aarbøger for nordisk Oldkyndighed og Historie.*

– 1877: Om bevaringen af de fædrelandske Oldsager og Mindesmærker i Danmark. *Aarbøger for nordisk Oldkyndighed og Historie.*

– 1872-77: Le Conservation des Antiquites et des Monuments Natiaux en Danemark. *Memoires de la Societe Royale des Antiquaires du Nord.* Nouvelle Serie.

– 1879: On the Preservation of National Antiquities and Monuments in Denmark. Read before Society of Antiquaries 1879. Særtryk.

– 1881: *Nordens Forhistorie efter samtidige Mindesmærker.* Kjøbenhavn.

– 1882: *The Industrial Arts of Denmark.* From the Earliest Times to the Danish Conquest of England. London.

– 1934: *En Oldgranskers Erindringer 1821-47.* Udgivet ved Victor Hermansen. København.

– 1938: *Af en Oldgranskers Breve 1848-1885.* Udgivet ved Victor Hermansen, København.

ØRSNES, M. 1969: Forord til genudgivelse af *Sønderjyske og Fynske Mosefund.* Bind I. Thorsbjerg Mosefund af Conrad Engelhardt.

Legislation Concerning Ancient Monuments in Denmark

by VIGGO NIELSEN

INTRODUCTION

Legislation is part of a cultural and historical pattern of development. The ways in which diverse spheres of society have been organized are reflected in layer upon layer of its own – a kind of stratigraphical series. Naturally, this also applies to the legislation concerning archaeological phenomena, finds or merely old subjects. Different periods have had different perspectives, and this type of legislation in particular has very old roots, which may extend back as far as prehistoric times.

Throughout the ages ancient monuments and antiquities (and hence the relevant statutes) have been regarded from many different angles. As today, attitudes have included elements ranging from reverence to assessment of monetary values, from national sentiment to detached research.

EARLY RULES AND ORDINANCES

In a European context (which may also be relevant to Scandinavian conditions) we observe that in one of the Germanic tribal societies during Merovingian times, the Salic law laid down severe penalties for those who dug up and robbed a buried corpse. Underlying such penalties were ideas of a non-material, magical kind. By contrast, the first known provisions in our part of Europe dealing with archaeological finds (in present-day terminology) are characterized by crass fiscal considerations, as appears from the provisions of the provincial laws (in the Scania Law, King Eric's Law of Zealand, and the Jutland Law). According to these, gold and silver found in the wake of the plough or in mounds belong to the King. These provisions from the first half of the 13th century may reflect the consolidation of centralized royal power in the by now solidly Christian society, but the general principle that ownerless goods belong to the king or chief, may well go back to pre-Christian societies.

It is thus a purely fiscal point of view that, through the transfer of the rules of the provincial laws to Section 5-9-3 of the Danish Code (1683), has significantly formed the basis of the Danish regulations on *the concept of finds* (in what was after 1864 the German part of the Dukedom of Schleswig, the Jutland Law remained valid, which has influenced archaeological and museum activities in Southern Schleswig to the present day). However, as early as the 18th century Section 5-9-3 of the Danish Code was supplemented by regulations – according to the decrees of March 22, 1737 and August 7, 1752 – which, through a socalled "authentic interpretation", represented the viewpoints of early archaeology. The main concern was to ensure that finds of old precious objects were handed over to the royal collections, especially the King's Art Collection. In fact, the decree of 1752 contained special rules regarding the payment of rewards to finders. Further contributions have been made in this century by juridical verdicts and the administrative implementation of the regulations. To a large extent they still have met the demands of modern society and modern research until this year – after 300 years – they have been transferred in a slightly revised form to the Museum Act.

Provisions concerning *prehistoric monuments* or *fixed ancient monuments*, which may not be characterized as finds in the traditional sense of the word but which should be cognizable and visible, reflect quite different sentiments. These monuments, particularly the burial mounds and megaliths, have always been regarded as integral parts of the Danish landscape, which – also because of their significance as ancestral graves – exercised a natural appeal to patriotic sentiments. As such they contributed – both in Denmark and in Sweden – to the national consolidation of the Renaissance and Baroque monarchies. Whereas Sweden as early as 1667 introduced legal protection of ancient monuments, it was to take nearly three centuries before Denmark did likewise. There were many reasons for this, the most important being consideration for farmers and landowners. Even during the absolute monarchy there was immense reluctance to encroach on the utilization possibilities of the landowners and farmers (ideas of acquiring important national monuments under compulsory powers had to be abandoned in 1848). This reluctance was shared by the archaeological administration. The chief concern was to be able to excavate monuments in harmony with the landowners. The wish to retain good relations with the landowners entailed a natural reserve towards legal regulations which they might see as compulsory measures. This on one hand liberal and on the other hand pragmatic attitude meant that most of the efforts to protect ancient monuments concentrated on voluntary, and thus legally weaker, arrangements. In fact, several thousand monuments were protected by voluntary means, but at the same time tens of thousands were destroyed.

LEGISLATION AFTER 1937

Thus it was not primarily a professional archaeological impetus that changed the situation. The decisive factor was the emotionally founded desire to have the landscape protected, not least of all, the megalithic tombs and the Bronze Age barrows as features in the landscape, combined with a feeling of reverence for ancestral graves and of course also an archaeological interest not least among the amateurs in preserving the rapidly dwindling resources in this sphere. The need to protect *in situ*-monuments was given social recognition in the Conservation of Nature Act of 1937. Section two of this act stated that all prehistoric monuments, such as barrows, burial places, dolmens and monoliths, earthworks and similar fortifications, as well as ruins, were to be protected in such a way that no changes were allowed that might damage the monument. After a survey and classification of the monuments the authorities were in a position to exempt those that had lost their significance either archaeologically or as features of the landscape. The owners could then demolish them completely after previous notice to permit excavation.

The chief motive behind this law, i.e. the protection of the landscape and thus an aspect of regional planning, was also the main principle underlying the important supplementary provision of 1961, introducing a protected zone extending up to 100 metres from the monument.

After the discovery of the Viking ships in Peberrenden in Roskilde Fjord there was a need for legislative protection of the historic wrecks. The Protection of Ancient Shipwrecks Act passed in 1963 authorized State confiscation of all objects, including wrecks, found on the sea bed in Danish waters if they were considered to have been lost more than 150 years ago. This law was thus motivated exclusively by archaeological considerations.

The Conservation of Nature Act of 1937 was administered by the prime minister's department; the treasure trove legislation by the Ministry of Education. When the Ministry of Cultural Affairs was established in 1961, a collective framework was created for the administration of laws concerning prehistoric remains. This also provided better opportunities for a co-ordinated approach to the problem of archaeological survey and research and nature conservation.

This remained the administrative framework until the Act of 1937 was revised in 1969. During the preparation of the bill, and above all of the report by the Nature Conservation Commission in 1967, it was again realized that the prehistoric monuments were particularly important as features of the landscape. It was therefore thought preferable to retain the regulations concerning prehistoric monuments within the scope of the Conservation of Nature Act, although their administration involved museum staffs, especially that of the National Museum. In 1970 rapid administrative growth led to the establishment of a special administration of ancient monuments under the Keeper of National Antiquities, the director of the National Museum. Later, when the Ministry of the Environment was set up, this administration together with the other Nature Conservation Administration was transferred to this ministry and amalgamated into one body: Fredningsstyrelsen: *The National Agency for the Protection of Nature, Monuments and Sites*.

The provisions concerning prehistoric monuments in the Conservation of Nature Act of 1969, Part 7, sections 48-53, included an archaeological-cum-juridical catalogue of the various groups of monuments and a classification of the forms and possibilities of protecting them. Apart from direct and unconditional protection in the sections mentioned, the Nature Conservation Act included more conditional methods of protection. For a number of objects Part III of the act offers protection by means of legal proceedings to attach a special conservation regulation or easement against compensation. In addition, ancient monuments may be acquired for the state through private sale. An innovation in this type of legislation was Section 49 dealing with the situation of ancient monuments discovered during construction work and the handing over to museums of associated finds.

The connection between the protection of prehistoric remains and regional planning was logical and the common administrative framework led to excellent results e.g. in the construction of major public works or the establishment of the gas supply network.

There was, however, from the end of the 1950's a remarkable expansion of the local museums and their staffs and a great number of prehistorical archaeologists were employed there. The movement both to undertake excavation and to have a greater influence on their administration led the government to establishing the commission mentioned in note 1. The commission's work resulted first in an administrative transfer of the section (49) of the Conservation of Nature Act from the Ministry of the Environment to the Ministry of Cultural Affairs and later to a revision of the Act, providing that all hitherto unprotected fixed prehistorical monuments and the protection *in situ* of similar submarine objects including ancient shipwrecks be taken care of by the National Agency for the Protection of Nature, Monuments and Sites, while the administration of rescue work and excavation activity is the concern of the Keeper of National Antiquities under the Ministry of Cultural Affairs.

THE PRESENT REGULATIONS

What are the details of the regulations now in force concerning prehistoric monuments and artefacts?

Part VII of the Conservation of Nature Act deals with five groups of prehistoric remains or situations each of which requires special forms of legal protection and special considerations of the owners or authorities involved. For each group there is an exemplary definition of the contents and requirements of the relevant form of protection. Essential for this classification is whether or not the monument is directly visible in the terrain or its protection registered.

Section 48 lists three groups of prehistoric monuments:
1) Barrows, stone cists, castle mounds, defensive structures, ruins or bridges (Subsection 1, item 1), which are either visible in the ground or registered.
2) Menhirs, rock-engraving stones and other stones or sacred runic stones, crosses, milestones etc. (Subsection 2).
3) Other ancient monuments, such as millraces and dams, stone banks, stone rows, canals, and any structure by or in lakes, brooks and holy springs etc. (Sub-

section 2, item 2) provided that they have been registered.

The objects mentioned under 1) and 2) are considered easily recognizable monuments. They therefore come directly under the law but will usually be registered. Recognition of those listed under 3) will, however, often require expert knowledge. They are therefore, as mentioned, protected only when their status as ancient monument is registered in the land certificate.

The Act further mentions in its section 49:
4) Fixed constructions in territorial waters and on the continental shelf up to a distance of 24 m, chiefly ship blockages, harbours and bridges, but also e.g. submerged stone cists, settlements or ruins. Ship blockages may consist of sunken ships or wrecks.
5) Similar protection is given in the same section, subsection 2, to wrecks of ships and their loadings lost more than 100 years ago in the sea or in watercourses or lakes. They must not be damaged, altered or removed without the consent of the Agency. This corresponds to section 28 in the Museum Act, which claims the ownership of the state for such objects and authorizes the Keeper of National Antiquities to decide about excavations and the placing of the objects found. State ownership, also with regard to single finds of objects, does not prevent the Keeper of National Antiquities from granting a reward to the finder.
6) Another group includes remains, which have not previously been known, but are discovered during construction work. This is dealt with in the Museum Act, section 26, in 1984 transferred to this from the Conservation of Nature Act. These objects include graves and burial places, ruins or other fixed remains.

Different forms of protection are stipulated for each of the groups:

As for groups 1) and 3), if the monuments are recorded in the Land Registry they may not be damaged or altered and the area where they are situated may not be divided or parcelled out without the consent of the relevant preservation authorities.

The special character of the monuments in group 2) – isolated, today often removed from their original site – entails a different formulation of protection, viz. that the objects may not be altered or removed without the consent of the relevant preservation authorities.

Group 4) and 5) are special cases, in that entirely different legal conditions apply to territorial waters and to the continental shelf waters. Sovereignty resides in the

State. Regulations concerning parcelling-out, etc. are thus non-applicable. The formulation therefore is that monuments and wrecks etc. in these places may not be damaged or altered without the consent of the National Agency for the Protection of Nature, Monuments and Sites. To make such protection effective, the monuments and the wrecks in question must obviously be recorded.

By virtue of the State sovereignty over territorial waters the sea floor and its fixed constructions could be said to belong to Denmark already when the former Conservation of Nature Act was passed in 1937. But it was an innovation when the former Protection of Ancient Shipwrecks Act in 1963 stipulated that all wrecks and single finds older than 150 years are state property unless anybody can establish the title.

As regards group 6), monuments discovered during construction work, the subject of protection is more complicated and does not necessarily imply preservation. However, at a minimum level the possibility of archaeological excavation is ensured. The law demands that the find is reported at once. It is then decided whether the work may continue or should stop until a professional excavation has been carried out, or until the question of a possible acquisition has been resolved. There is a year's respite in which to arrange for such an excavation. If the construction work is carried out by a public authority, excavation expenses are borne by this public authority; in other cases, by the Keeper of National Antiquities. If the monument is judged to be particularly important, it is possible to make it state property, e.g. by expropriation. The minister decides on such acquisitions.

The protection accorded to prehistoric monuments since 1937 undoubtedly accentuates the temptation of contractors or landowners to turn a blind eye to ancient monuments while construction works are in progress. This situation may to some extent be remedied, as the authorities may demand access to places where construction works are planned or in progress and where archaeological finds are expected. This makes advance surveys possible.

On the whole the major importance of this arrangement is due to the possibilities it offers for undertaking advance surveys and excavations. Many public authorities and private owners would prefer to have the full permission to go through with a construction work once started.

An additional measure of protection is, as mentioned above, given by section 53 through the one-hundred-metre protection zone round most of the categories of monuments (often significant features of the landscape). Within this zone there may not without the consent of the Conservation Board be placed any buildings, sheds, caravans, nor may there be erected any poles, carried out any planting or alterations of the ground by filling in or digging, nor taken any measures which to any appreciable extent might disfigure the monument. In woods and plantations, which were in existence before 1961, replanting may, however, be carried out up to five metres from the foot of the monument. This and similar regulations of the Conservation of Nature Act (e.g. Sections 46 and 47a concerning zones of protection along beaches and fresh waters) are administered by the local Conservation Board (Fredningsnævnet), which, however, must consult the National Agency for the Protection of Nature, Monuments and Sites (Fredningsstyrelsen) before a decision is reached.

Several groups of prehistoric monuments are more or less outside the scope of Part VII and therefore have to be protected under the other regulations of the Conservation of Nature Act. Cases in point are sunken roads, certain traces of field systems, dikes and similar constructions, most of them rather late structures of the Danish agricultural landscape. If such phenomena are to be protected, it will be effected above all by the decision to attach a special regulation or carement to the property in question, with the customary compensation.

The regulations about stray finds on the sea bed have their counterpart on dry land in the *danefæ* provisions mentioned earlier, now in the Museum Act. These also includes rules about rewards to finders, based principally on an assessment of the intrinsic value. The precise scope of *danefæ* regulation is not entirely clear, embracing as it does finds of precious materials or of special scientific or cultural importance. There has been a gradual shift in the practice of the National Museum and the Keeper of National Antiquities. Initially the regulation was applied only to precious metals but nowadays to all kinds of important antiquities. The regulation can probably be interpreted in the light of contemporary needs, thus allowing the Keeper of National Antiquities to demand that any important finds, including those of scientific importance should be submitted. There are no recent interpretations in the form of judicial verdicts.

It is not exclusively the rules governing antiquities that matter when finds are recovered. Other regulations play a direct or indirect role, especially in the field of physical planning. Thus the *Raw Materials Act* regulates the extraction of raw materials from the sea floor and also permits restrictions or bans to be imposed on land. The Act embraces not just common mineral raw materials such as gravel and sand, but also the limited resources of peat, which still remain. Similarly, in the context of excavation it will also be possible to take advantage of the advance designation of development areas to take place according to the *Act of Urban and Rural Development Zones* and the *Municipal Planning Act*. Archaeological surveys and excavations can thus be planned and conducted in advance in co-operation with the municipal authorities and local museums.

CONCLUSION

Part VII of the Conservation of Nature Act with its various restrictive regulations forms a solid basis for the protection of prehistoric remains. Hardly any registered monuments do disappear and in this way the regulations provide a framework for co-operation with public authorities and private citizens planning construction works. Furthermore, if protection cannot be maintained, it is ensured that excavation can take place.

Obviously the restrictive provisions can only be executed if the objects concerned are recorded so that everybody knows when to exercise care. Consequently a comprehensive registration of prehistoric monuments has been carried out, first of the megalithic tombs and the barrows, and later of other groups. Taking as their starting point the national survey, begun in 1873 with its descriptions of the prehistoric remains in all parishes, the staff of the First Department of the National Museum travelled throughout Denmark in the years after 1937 in order to determine which prehistoric monuments were directly encompassed by the provisions. In this connection a considerable number of partially preserved barrows were removed from preservation orders. Most of the recording had been completed by the 1950's. During recent years a systematic surveying has been carried out by the National Agency for the Protection of Nature, Monuments and Sites. Special areas are combed and special groups of remains are taken up, e.g. the prehistoric field systems.

As far as objects from historic times are concerned, the recording of Denmark's castle mounds or earthworks, based on comprehensive surveys of individual localities, has not been completed. Similarly there is still work to be done identifying ruins from churches, monasteries, etc. in old towns.

The monuments by now recorded as worthy of legal protection include: 24,000 barrows – most of them from the Bronze Age – c. 3,000 megalithic tombs, ruins and earthworks, and c. 1,000 other objects, including c. 100 small *areas* containing graves, house sites, field systems etc.

Only for certain groups of remains, such as prehistoric field systems, major advances have been made, in recognizing prehistoric monuments compared with older topographical surveys (the parish records from the 19th century). However, both the legislation of 1937 and that of 1969 have had some significant consequences: in a number of cases where protection has been withdrawn from monuments, it has been possible to carry out professional excavations unhampered by considerations of grants, since the excavations had to be paid for by those who wanted the protection withdrawn.

This illustrates an important legal matter which will always determine archaeological activities, viz. the yearly financial acts defining the scope and context of grants.

The Finance Act reflects the extent of excavation activity as well as the grants and personnel involved. The ordinary appropriations form the primary financial basis, and since 1892 a grant earmarked for National Museum excavations has decisively shaped archaeological research throughout the first half of the 20th century. In addition, extraordinary appropriations have been made, e.g. to finance the extensive bog excavations during and immediately after World War II, besides several other special programmes.

Even the grants from private foundations such as the Carlsberg Foundation for excavations by the National Museum are to be included in the annual Financial Act.

The actual legal basis of the preservation work and of archaeological excavations will be reflected only to a limited degree in the archaeological material; it will make little difference to the statistical material and then only over an extended period of time. In this respect, e.g. the *danefæ* regulations and their interpretations at different times will hardly show up at all. Decisive factors in this respect will be e.g. cultivation of ground untouched in the 19th century or the modern popularity of people's using mine sweepers for treasure hunting.

It is different with regard to ancient monuments because the Conservation of Nature Act of 1937 stopped excavations of the barrows and megalithic tombs, apart from the very few which were exempted: these in turn were subjected to thorough and fairly expensive excavations. Another consequence of this Act after 1937 was the assistance from the National Museum, in connection with the study of the material preserved, in cases where the owner of an unprotected damaged mound wanted it demolished.

As far as the former Protection of Ancient Shipwrecks Act is concerned the material retrieved can be regarded as resulting from a combination of contemporary extraction of raw materials, the development of underwater sports, and the legal regulations ensuring that the museums receive a major part of the newly found material. Systematic surveying has now been launched and is conducted to some degree in cooperation with the National Agency's surveying of raw materials in the sea.

A number of special find groups and excavation programmes, such as settlement studies, have for a long time been relatively independent of the existing legislation, but are now experiencing a remarkable growth in connection with the rescue surveying and excavations in accordance with the law.

The legislation concerning ancient monuments has developed in step with the growing needs of an expanding society to preserve, protect and regulate the exploitation of the landscape and its resources. Ancient monuments are a characteristic and precious feature of the Danish cultural landscape, the future preservation of which is assured by the provisions of the Conservation of Nature Act. Moreover, archaeologists are guaranteed continued access to fresh material through excavations of endangered objects, whether already recorded or according to the Museum Act section 26 newly discovered. The interaction between this legislation and the grants in the Finance Act form the framework and the basis for the archaeological activity administered by the National Agency for the Protection of Nature, Monuments and Sites and the Keeper of National Antiquities, the National Museum, and other museums in Denmark.

Viggo Nielsen,
The National Agency for the Protection of Nature,
Monuments and Sites,
Amaliegade 13,
1256 Copenhagen K.

NOTE 1

The present article has had a bad fate, being originally written in 1978 and dealing with a subject under rapid development.

In the meantime questions about the legal and administrative instruments regulating ancient monuments have been dealt with by a special commission.

The mandate of this commission from 1978 was to make proposals regarding the cooperation between the conservation authorities and the museums, as well as the work done in connection with the administration according to the Conservation of Nature Act and the Preservation of Buildings Act. The report from 1982 of this commission led to immediate administrative changes, the salvage excavations being transferred from the Ministry of the Environment to the Ministry of Cultural Affairs, and the protection of historic wrecks being transferred vice versa. It also resulted in proposals for amendments to the Museum Act, the Conservation of Nature Act, and transfer of the Protection of Shipwrecks Act to the two first mentioned.

These proposals are being dealt with by the Danish parliament in spring 1984, concurrent with the final revision of this article. In the expectation that the Danish parliament will follow the proposals of the government, the author has taken the liberty to anticipate the result so that the article should not be outdated before it has appeared.

Economic Development in Denmark Since Agrarian Reform

A Historical and Statistical Summary

by KRISTIAN KRISTIANSEN

INTRODUCTION

From the end of the 18th century up to the present day Denmark, like a large part of Europe and the U.S., has experienced an economic growth which has no historic parallel, and which has involved fundamental technological, social, and political changes in society.

In Denmark this development – conditioned by special historical circumstances – differed in many respects from that elsewhere in Europe, in that, for example, the development of agriculture preceded that of industry. The establishment of an archaeological National Museum in 1807, and the subsequent early development of prehistoric archaeology as a national field of scholarship, can also be viewed as part of this particular development. The major changes in the traditional cultural landscape, which were the first results of the agrarian reforms of the 1780's (discussed below), meant that archaeological sites were destroyed in their thousands. From dolmens and mounds appeared burial finds, and from bogs, fens and fields came hoard deposits. It became the task of the archaeologist to rescue and keep these finds, and later also to preserve as many of the surviving archaeological sites as possible. The history of archaeology in Denmark is therefore also the history of the transition of Danish society from a relatively static feudal-mercantilistic to a modern dynamic agricultural and industrial society. If we wish to determine the general representativity of archaeological material, which is the aim of this bok, we must consider at the same time the social factors which have determined their discovery. I shall therefore in this paper give a summarized account of economic developments, particularly in agriculture, in Denmark since 1784, and present some statistics selected to illustrate the context in which some of the archaeological material was found. But first a brief account of the period prior to agrarian reform.

THE PERIOD BEFORE 1784

The period before agrarian reform is described by the historian Jens Vibæk as follows (extracts only):

"Little change had taken place in the Danish countryside from the middle of the 15th century until the decades before the major agrarian reforms.

The ratio of cultivated and uncultivated land was almost the same; perhaps in good times they ploughed a slightly longer furrow than in

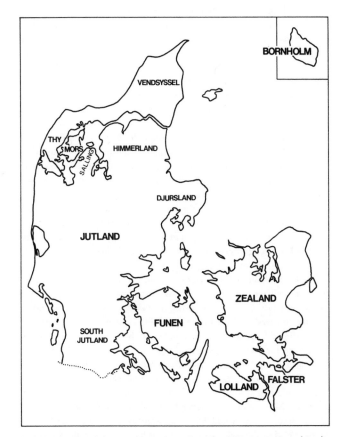

Fig. 1. Names of the most important Danish regions mentioned in the text.

bad, while in lean years they ploughed a shorter. The cultivated fields showed as before like a patchwork in the common wastes. Here and there a village had disappeared to make room for the broad fields of a manor house. The change was not striking, but those changes that had occurred were hardly for the better. The woods had been thinned, and what was left was of poor quality, in many places only scrub and brush. The mighty trees of former ages had been felled for timber and firewood. Here and there towered an old tree mutilated by nocturnal timber thieves. In times of war the heath had spread, and the lost land had not been reclaimed. Spring gales eroded the light soils, and from the coasts advanced a deadly sand drift, not only in Jutland but also in fertile North Zealand. Between Arresø and Kattegat sterile dunes had covered the fertile soil, and whole villages had been forced to flee the sand.

Who were the rulers of this countryside? Three quarters of Denmark's land belonged to *manorial estates,* of which there were 800, but the number of land*owners* was considerably smaller. Many landowners owned several estates, and several owned many. Of the rest of the land the Crown still possessed only a modest share.

Only 13% of the manorial land was worked by the home farm. The rest of the land consisted of tenant farms which the landowners were obliged to rent out. Once it had been desirable for a peasant to become a tenant farmer, but those days were over. Therefore the landowners had arranged it so that they could actually *force* peasants to take on a tenant farm. An important means to this end was *adscription,* which prohibited men of productive age to leave the estate they belonged to.

The landowners' main income from tenant land had originally been *manorial dues.* They were an annual payment in kind, probably averaging 20 to 25% of the yield; this fluctuated around a five to six-fold return. But gradually it became *villeinage,* work for the landowners, which benefited them most and pressed hardest on the tenants. The great majority of peasants were villeins, but there were areas where the peasants simply lived too far from the home farm to be able to work there. Instead these peasants paid a *villein tax.* This tax, however, was regarded as infinitely more lenient than the burden of villeinage; a couple of hundred working days a year was not unusual. In addition, the work load was naturally heaviest in spring and at harvest time, with the result that the peasant's own work was neglected in those very days that were essential for his own economic welfare.

Just as the appearance of the countryside was largely unchanged since the Middle Ages, so farming practice followed the same pattern. Twenty generations of Danish peasants had followed in spring the heavy wheel plough over the stony fields, so that in autumn they could bring home a five to six-fold harvest.

The land adjoining the villages consisted of three elements: the paddocks, the village arable, and the common grazing, of which each had its own function... Each farm owned a *paddock,* which was independent of village ownership. Here the peasant had his kitchen garden; here also were enclosed livestock which had to be watched while grazing. Around the village lay its *arable ploughland.* Usually it was divided into three fields which represented a primitive crop rotation... Each farm was entitled to its share of the arable. [This portion was again divided into a number of small scattered units, determined by the varying fertility of the soil. (My comment)]. Beyond the village arable lay *the common,* which for us today would have appeared as an outstanding natural landscape[1]. For the common lay just as it had been since the forest was felled, perhaps even since the ice withdrew from Denmark... On the common grazed livestock, mostly young animals, sheep and old hor-

ses... If there was forest as part of the common land, this was also used for domestic animals since each farm had its *pannage,* i.e. the right to pasture swine in the forest. This contributed to the constant deterioration of the forests." (Vibæk 1964: 56-67) (Cf. also Falbe Hansen & Scharling 1887, 102-121; Skrubbeltrang 1966, 13-19; and partic. Mathiessen 1942).

To this account we shall add the brief comments of an economist:

"At the beginning of the 18th century Denmark was a primitive country from the economic point of view. The standard of living was extremely low by today's criteria, and there was no question of any visible progress towards greater affluence.

First and foremost development was impeded by the economic 'box system' of the time. There were very sharp divisions between town and country, and between the various trades. In the country, adscription, which from 1733 bound the peasant to his home estate, was the most drastic manifestation of this system. The division between town and country was also reflected in municipal privileges, which with few exceptions gave the towns a monopoly in carrying out trade and crafts. In the towns themselves economic activities were restricted by guild regulations and legislation so severe that we today find it difficult to understand how such a system could function at all.

The possibility of significant economic progress depended on the will to break down these social and institutional barriers which were such a hindrance to a rational employment of the labour force. Such an objective was, however, far removed from the conservative economic policies of the contemporary ruling class, dominated as it was by landowners.

The most important economic activity of the time was agriculture, which employed over 60% of the total population. On peasant farms production was usually only sufficient to cover the necessary expenses and the peasants' own subsistence. A bad harvest year was therefore a serious matter, and the marked fluctuations in crop yield gave rise to sharp alternations between fat and lean years, which affected the death rates and thereby set narrow limits on population increase.

All in all agriculture hardly improved in efficiency until the period of agrarian reform at the end of the century. Until then major technical advances were on the whole confined to the manor farms.

Nor was there any significant increase in urban productivity. The agricultural subsistence economy severely limited the possible outlets of the artisans and manufacturers in the towns.

The Danish overseas trade and shipping, stimulated by frequent wars between the dominant trading nations, were the most evident factors conducive to the economic growth of the period. However, the 'box system' and the large economic sectors that operated within a subsistence economy under the primitive conditions of the time largely prevented this growth from becoming a general one. In this respect Danish society was reminiscent of the dual economy of present-day developing countries, in which modernized economic modules similarly co-exist with primitive economic sectors, with little contact between them.

These conditions are also reflected in the economic policies of the period which emphasized development in the capital city, but was sceptical about the possibility of stimulating provincial economic life, because the inertia factor obstructed the "multiplier effect." (Hansen 1976, 12-13; cf. also Olsen 1967, 24-28)

1784-1813. AGRARIAN REFORM AND THE BEGINNINGS OF GROWTH

A number of radical reforms were carried out after 1784, which laid the basis for a re-structuring of Danish society and created the conditions for the growth of the following century. There was a concurrence of several favourable circumstances in connection with the change in the political and economic system: a *coup*-like change of monarch, supported by a new ruling circle of highly educated and reformist politicians, together with good international trade conditions. The reforms comprised: 1) Agrarian reform (1788), 2) Customs reform (1797), 3) Social legislation (1799 & 1802-03), 4) Fiscal legislation (1802), 5) Forest conservation legislation (1805), and 6) Educational reform (1789 & 1814).

The principles laid down in these laws have been normative right up into modern times. We shall now examine more closely the agrarian reforms and their significance.

Agriculture. As a result of the priority placed on agricultural growth at the expense of trade and industry, there was a geographic dispersal of growth which became decisive for later developments in Denmark. The agrarian reforms entailed: 1) the abolition of adscription, which liberated the peasants and created a more mobile labour market. 2) Villeinage was curtailed or replaced by a cash payment. 3) The abandoning of the open-field system and the dispersal of farms, which had already begun, intensified. 4) Freehold tenure was to be gradually introduced, supported by the government.

Behind this body of laws was not only a general wish to stimulate economic growth at any price. It was also hoped that this growth would benefit the peasants in particular, rather than the landowners. Thus the peasantry was not liberated only to become expropriated and turned into a proletariat by the landowners, as was happening in most of Europe. On the contrary, their land was to be protected from purchase in order to ensure an agricultural system based on a numerous and economically free peasantry, e.g. by prohibiting the abolition of peasant farms and by economic support in connection with the transition to freehold. In other words, this was economic as well as politico-social legislation, and it was based on a political wish to develop the peasantry as a counterweight to the former domination by the landowners (for a discussion of this, see Holmgård 1977).

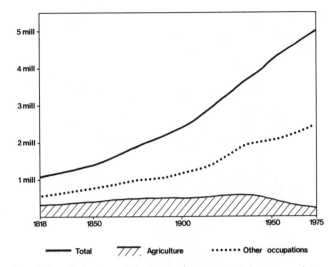

Fig. 2. Population growth in Denmark 1800-1975, in ten-year intervals (after Hansen 1977, table 1).

The consequences of these reforms were seen very quickly. From the point of view of the agricultural economy the *abandoning of the open-field system* was the most important element and that which progressed most quickly: by 1807 2/3 of the land in the Danish islands had already changed from the open-field system, as had half of Jutland. At the same time approx. 25% of the land had become freehold (Larsen 1929, 162). It meant transition from a *communal* to an *individual* system, the amalgamation of each farm's landholdings, the enclosure of fields, and a more varied production. The old *three-field system* gradually ceased and was usually replaced by *crop rotation*[2]. New crops were introduced, such as the potato and red clover. In the period up to 1813 both the number of livestock and cereal production doubled as a result (Nielsen 1933, 338 ff.; Hansen 1976, 80). However, the manor farms still dominated agricultural production, and here, in particular, were introduced agricultural and technical improvements, e.g. crop rotation and the swing plough. Among the peasants old customs and the lack of education were still a handicap as far as a more fundamental progress was concerned, and the actual dispersal of farms also dragged on – for it meant in reality the cessation of a communal way of life that was centuries old.

Socially and demographically agrarian reforms, however, had a profound impact. The growth in production and the improved standard of living gave rise to a great increase in population. During the 18th century the population growth had been very slight (0.3% p.a.), but

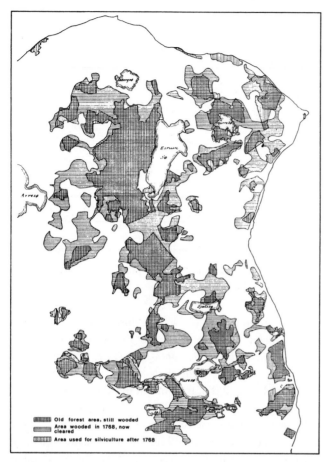

Fig. 3. Area of woodland in North East Zealand before the abolition of the open-field system, and in 1930 (after Grøn 1934, fig. 12).

now it rose to over 1% p.a., a level which was maintained (Falbe-Hansen & Scharling 1885, 419; Nielsen 1933, 341; Hansen 1976, 80) (fig. 2). A large part of this increased population, however, became smallholders, whose number rose appreciably after the reforms. They gradually became the new work force on the estates as villeinage was abolished – a new lower class which grew throughout the century. The number of smallholders around 1700 comprised c. 1/3 of the farmers, after the reforms almost 50%.

The effect on the old cultural landscape of the abolition of the open-field system was that the former common land was incorporated into individual farms for cultivation. Marshland and forest were also shared out, and this meant that a large part of the more open grazing forest was chopped down and brought under cultivation (fig. 3), while the primary forest was preserved. When the legislation to protect forests was introduced, woodlands covered only 4% of the total land area (fig. 4a). In this

way the area under cultivation increased considerably, and it was this, combined with the changes in production, that led to the growth.

1813-1828. AGRICULTURAL DEPRESSION

The coming agricultural depression was heralded by the following historical events: the loss of the Navy to England in 1807, together with the subsequent war inflation and the bankruptcy of the State in 1813. From this time – after the Napoleonic Wars – began a great fall in the price of agricultural goods in Europe. This fall brought to a standstill both the development of reforms and the modernization of agriculture for nearly twenty years (Nielsen 1933, 384; Hansen 1976, fig. V.1). Enfranchisement came to a halt, as did the transition to freehold tenure for lack of capital. In his "Travels" through the Danish kingdom around 1830, the historian Roar Skovmand has given an excellent contemporary sketch of the poor, depressed and stagnating country, where national romanticism flourished in the arts alone (Skovmand 1964, 11-68). Not only patriotic sentiments but also new popular and political movements, harbingers of the future, were in the process of formation.

1828-1857. NEW GROWTH. THE PERIOD OF GRAIN SALES

The economist Sv. Aage Hansen has described the economic growth from the 1820's until 1894 as market-dependent, since the trade conditions in Denmark closely followed those in Europe, and especially in England (Hansen 1976, fig. I.1). The industrialization of Europe, and the steeply rising population, resulted in rising prices for agricultural goods, above all for grain (Nielsen 1933, 419; Hansen 1976, fig. VII.1). The period 1828-57 has therefore been called the period of grain sales, since this was the dominant and most profitable agricultural production. Industrial production was still modest. Progress in this field was closely linked to advances in agriculture, e.g. milling. There was a significant development in trade and transport – in this period particularly the merchant navy – as a result of the growth of foreign trade. Furthermore, the credit market was established and institutionalized (Hansen 1976, table VII. 5). The craft and building sectors advanced considerably – in terms of

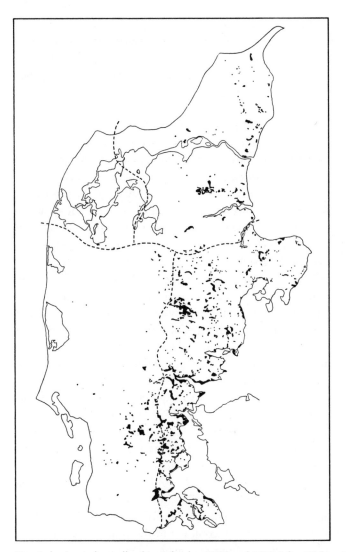

Fig. 4a-b. Area of woodland in Jutland c. 1800 and 1950 (after Nielsen 1953, figs. 7-8).

personnel there was a rise of 6.5% (Hansen 1976, 147), which was related to the establishment of the many new farms and small-holdings. The road network was extended, a task that was begun after the ordinance of 1793 and which was only finished in 1862 (Falbe-Hansen & Scharling 1878, 30 ff.). This work began on the islands, which also received most kilometres of road per county. The extension of most of the main road network took place between 1820 and 1862, terminating in Jutland.

In political terms it was an eventful period, and full of conflict. The peasantry had begun to organize politically, and the popular and national movements were growing. Absolute monarchy was on the decline and was formally abolished with the introduction of the new constitution in

1849. Finally, the war of 1848-51 with Germany strengthened national re-armament and patriotic movements.

Agriculture. During this period agrarian reform continued. Villeinage was almost completely abolished, while the transition to freehold accelerated again. Agriculture began to attract investment, and there were advances in production and technology. Productivity rose significantly, partly through a continued increase in the area under cultivation and in land improvement, partly through new tools and machinery, frequently of iron instead of the former wood.

The improved market conditions meant that the remaining common land was brought under the plough, while the cultivation of marshes and water meadows intensified. This made possible a gradual increase in the number of livestock (Falbe-Hansen 1887, 190), the manure from which was important in the more ruthless and intensive exploitation of arable soil which now took place, which in many areas came close to soil exhaustion. Consequently, there was also a considerable increase in the application of marl. Of particular note among technical advances was the swing plough, which was widely used from the 1840's onwards, together with the newly introduced Swedish harrow. The peasant had now become farmer producing for a market. The cash economy gradually extended into most of the farming sector, which had previously been dominated by a subsistence economy and where production had often been barely sufficient for the maintenance of family and farm (Falbe-Hansen 1889, 263-70). This growth, however, benefited particularly the estates and large farms which had the capital for land improvements and machinery. The steadily growing smallholder class was employed as labour. During the first third of the century one new farm was established for every three new houses; from 1836-73 the proportion was 1:11 (Falbe-Hansen 1887, 238-43). Between 1834 and 1860 the rural population grew from 700,000 to 850,000, of whom most were poor smallholders, since the towns were not yet capable of absorbing surplus labour. In this period the agricultural labour force rose by a total of 20%, the arable zone only by c. 3% (Hansen 1976, 142).

From the 1840's and especially the 1850's the foundations were laid for a change in the economic and political balance between estate owners and peasants, above all by improved standards in peasant education through the establishment of the first "folkehøjskoler" (: folk high schools) and agricultural colleges. But the results of this were only really felt in the following period.

CULTIVATION OF NEW AREAS AND LAND IMRPOVEMENTS 1784-1857

For want of statistical material, regional and chronological variations in the transformation of the old cultural landscape from 1784 until 1857 are difficult to demonstrate. But certain sporadic features can be put forward – as for the period during which the open-field system was abandoned we may refer to Begtrup's account in "*Ager-*

dyrkningens Tilstand i Danmark" (1803-12), and for the 1830's and 1840's there is "*Landhusholdningsselskabets Amtsbeskrivelser*" (1826-44). The following account, however, is based on the summary of Skrubbeltrang, in particular (1966, 44-70)[3].

The Islands. To begin with the initiative for the cultivation of commons and other unused areas came from the landowners, who through the abandoning of the open-field system were often able to establish a more intensive cultivation on large contiguous areas. Among the peasantry, the advances in the agricultural economy made themselves felt most slowly in Zealand, which even in the 'thirties was one of the most backward districts. However, here suppression had also been most ruthless before the reforms. In comparison, Funen and Lolland-Falster were more developed at an early date, with the introduction of enclosure and the new cultivation methods and crops. It seems, however, that most of the common land was cultivated during the period when the open-field system was abandoned, and a large part of the more remote commons were portioned out among smallholder families, the "new colonists". Also a good deal of drainage was carried out. From 1777 to 1797 805 km. of ditches were dug, 236 in Jutland, 233 in Zealand, 34 in Lolland-Falster, and 11 in Langeland (Hansen 1936-43, 30-35). This drainage was only concerned with the most pressing needs in connection with cultivation of the commons (Basse 1939, 362). Also flood protection and diking were begun in Lolland-Falster. According to Begtrup, the use of marl was largely confined to the counties of Hjørring, Thisted, Ringkøbing and Ribe, where it was used particularly on newly reclaimed heathlands.

The more detailed county records from the 1830's and 1840's confirm that it was the commons, in particular, that were brought under cultivation, and that in the extension of the new arable zone, reclaimed fens and swampy soils, lakes and inlets, together with scrub and the light woodland formerly used for grazing, were most important. It appears that this increase in the area under cultivation was still in progress throughout the 1830's and 1840's. At that time there were large uncultivated areas in Holbæk county, above all in the district of Ods, and a good deal of common land remained in Sorø county. In the county of Præstø, on the other hand, few uncultivated areas remained in 1839, and this applied also to Maribo county (in 1844), where there had been large areas not yet cultivated in 1822. In the county of Frederiksborg, the reclamation of bogs and water meadows was begun in the northern districts in the 1820's. In Bornholm the large outlying common of Almindingen (c. 13,750 ha.) lay uncultivated. In Funen, in the county of Odense, in 1843, nearly all parishes contained uncultivated patches: reclaimed bogs, small forest clearings etc., whereas in the county of Svendborg there was little land left uncultivated.

At the time when the county records were written drainage was not very far advanced (with a few exceptions, such as Frederiksborg county and Falster) and was only really developed from the 1850's. All district accounts regret the fact that marl was not applied; the use of marl was almost entirely confined to the estates, and only came into general use on the islands in the 1830's. The spread of marl is probably connected with the improved market conditions and the rising grain production.

On the whole we may conclude that the actual cultivation of new land in the islands was nearly complete around the middle of the 19th century. This impression is confirmed by Baudou's growth curve (fig. 6). However, we know little about the distribution over time of this increase in the area of arable land between 1784 and 1857; it seems reasonably certain that in the main it can be divided into the two periods before and after the agricultural depression. Presumably, the larger expanses of good common land were cultivated in the period before the depression, while the remaining and more remote commons were brought under cultivation in the following period, mainly by the many smallholders. In this later period, however, there was a more intensive exploitation and cultivation of the soil (during the period of grain sales), and a growing proportion of the newly cultivated land consisted of bogs and water meadows reclaimed by the various drainage systems constructed between 1830 and 1850 (Basse 1939, 363).

Jutland. Even after the abolition of the open-field system Jutland remained a land of heath (fig. 5a), formed by the ruthless exploitation of forest and soil since the third millennium B.C. Reclamation had been attempted in the 18th century, but had failed. While the development of the fertile regions of East Jutland, and to some extent also Thisted county, largely resembled that of the islands, it was quite otherwise in the rest of Jutland (cf. Baudou's map). When the heathlands were divided up, with the abolition of the open-field system, many farms received several hundred acres of adjoining heath, which

might stretch several kilometres from the farm. The first cultivation of the heath generally extended from these existing farms. There was still no true colonization of the heath with establishment of new farms on a large scale, although several smallholdings seem to have been set up here and there. Settlements in the heath regions originally lay close to the rivers because of their meadows necessary for cattle husbandry. From here the first cultivation of the heathlands extended like tentacles (Hansen 1975, fig. 9). The cultivation of new areas was both random and individual right up to the middle of the 19th century. It accelerated from the 1850's onwards and became organized from 1870 with the foundation of the Danish Heath Society (1866). We shall discuss this later. Before this time there was no constant practice or purpose in extending cultivation. The most common method was to burn and plough in the heather. Often the soil was exhausted after only a few crops, and the heather returned – from ancient times part of an extensive/intensive method of exploitation of alternating arable and waste. Gradually, interest grew in maintaining soil fertility, and farmers began to use marl and manure, which Begtrup has described as a fairly common practice. It was necessary to do this on the newly established farms in order to survive. It should not be forgotten, however, that traditionally the heath itself played an important role in the economy, like the common lands on the islands. The heather was used as fuel, for house construction, and animal fodder, and the heath peat was also important to the economy (Højrup 1975). Furthermore, large flocks of sheep were kept on the heath for wool (for a social historical account, see Matthiessen 1939).

When the county records were written, Randers and Århus, among the East Jutland counties, had the least extensive uncultivated heathland, whereas there were large heath areas in parts of Skanderborg county and in the west of Vejle county (as much as 9/10 of the latter). There were also considerable areas of heath in Thy and Mors which were gradually being brought under cultivation and fertilized with marl. Generally speaking, heath cultivation seems to have come to a halt during the agricultural depression, and on the whole systematic cultivation of this zone was not possible without organization and state support. The drainage of marshes and swampy areas had not yet begun on a large scale, and the important introduction of meadow irrigation got under way only after 1840. In the following are some converted figures[4] from the period 1837-61, which show the consider-

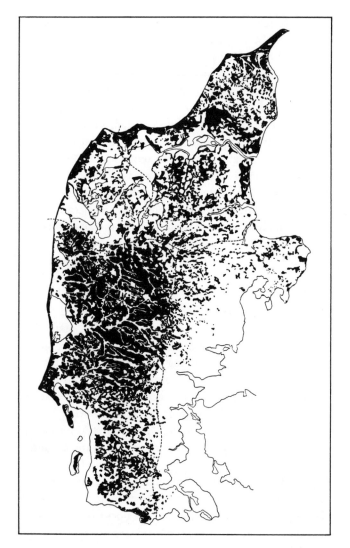
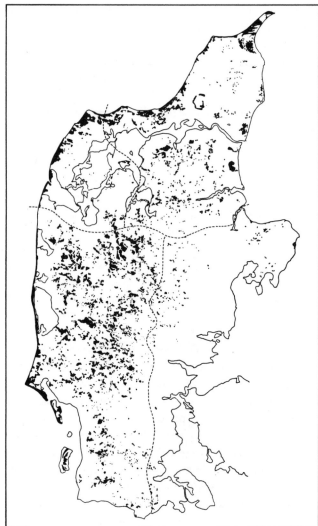

Fig. 5a-b. Area of heathland in Jutland c. 1800 and 1950 (after Nielsen 1953, figs. 4-5).

able increase in the cultivation of new land after the agricultural depression (after Skrubbeltrang 1966, 85):

Cultivation of new land in "tønder land":	1837-61	per annum
North Jutland	84,247	5,123
South West Jutland	174,023	7,251
South East Jutland	117,183	5,508
Total	375,453	24,761

(*Note*: 1 "*tønde land*" (*tdr.*) equals 0.55 hectares)

Skrubbeltrang concludes that the total increase in the area of grain production in Jutland during the same period was 226,000 "*tdr.*", probably larger than in any pre-

vious thirty-year period. In Jutland land reclamation comprised nearly twice as large an area as on the islands where, however, the soil was generally better. In the same thirty-year period the number of livestock (including pigs and horses) rose on the islands by 15% and in Jutland by 41%. This development coincided with a rapid increase in population of between 40% and 60% in South and West Jutland. There was this difference, that in Middle and West Jutland heather still covered most of the region, while on the islands at this time there were only 44,500 "*tdr.*" of common land left. In the latter area the cultivation of new land was nearly completed, in Jutland most had yet to be done.

1857-1894. PROGRESS UNDER FLUCTUATING MARKET CONDITIONS (1857-1876) AND AGRICULTURAL DEPRESSION (1876-1894)

From 1858 till 1873 the export value of agricultural products trebled, which created much of the economic basis for the simultaneous change in infrastructure: the nationwide development of transport and communication systems, and the incipient industrialization – which also included agricultural products – that took place in connection with a gradual shift from plant to animal production during the depression. The years 1876-94 were characterized by a long-term fall in prices (Hansen 1976, fig. IX.1). This was due partly to the growing importation of grain from overseas markets – a result of cheaper and more efficient transport – and partly to the industrial development in Western Europe. In these decades the living conditions of smallholders and workers worsened, and because of population growth there arose a great pool of surplus labour. A large part of this surplus was used in heath cultivation, but there was also a migration of labour from the countryside, which the towns could not yet absorb; some therefore emigrated to the U.S. (especially in the 1880's). This emigration was fairly limited in comparison with Norway and Sweden and the rest of Europe (Hansen 1976, table IX.7).

The development and extension of the transport system perhaps more than anything else transformed the context of economic growth, and constitutes one element in Denmark's integration into the capitalist world market. The merchant navy was enlarged considerably and steamships became more common (Hansen 1976, fig. VIII.2), and train ferries connected the various parts of the country. The main lines of the railway network were laid in the years before 1874 (Hansen 1976, fig. VIII.2), and were afterwards extended into the provinces (Nielsen 1953). This development of the transport system benefited the sales of animal products, which required quick transport, and also linked West Jutland and its heathlands to the market system, a factor of great importance in the further development of this region. In the same period an international telegraph network was established, stamps were introduced, and the mail service was improved. Many new newspapers also emerged.

Industrialization began on a small scale around 1870 (Hansen 1976, fig. VIII.6 & VIII.5) favoured by agricultural exports, which not only stimulated the development of the transport system but also released more mo-

ney for the consumption of industrial goods. So far it represented only 4%-5% of total production. This type of industry originated in trade, and has thus been termed "Trade Capitalism".

The loss of South Jutland loomed large in the national consciousness and gave rise to both Danish and Scandinavian movements. It also influenced the subsequent programme of economic development, which was to benefit Middle and West Jutland. Agriculture was dominant in this period because of its political and economic organization, but workers' trade unions had their beginning in the 1870's and grew in strength in the 1880's and particularly in the 1890's. These decades were characterized by the political and parliamentary conflict between "Left" (the peasantry) and "Right" (landowners, capitalists and the bourgeoisie), in the course of which there was an anti-parliamentarian reaction (the "provisional" government of Estrup 1885-94), before the change of political system in 1901 which at last brought the "Left" into power – on the threshold of the industrial era.

We have more information about the standard of living during this period than that before (Hansen 1976, 254-273). There is a continuing gulf between the social classes, further increased by the growth of capitalism: 3%-4% of the population shared 25% of the income, while 80%-90% shared c. 50% of the income. This latter group, especially the rural and urban workers, lived constantly on the edge of starvation and were therefore vulnerable to disease and had a high death-rate. New social legislation in the 1890's, however, indicated a change in political attitudes.

Agriculture. The years before 1876 had been characterized by steady progress, which resulted in sufficient capital, not only for weathering the depression, but also for investment to effect the change to animal production. At the end of the period Denmark was prepared for a new advance. However, the change was gradual and was primarily motivated by the growing demand for manure (before artificial fertilizers), and secondarily profited from the fall in grain sales. The number of livestock had increased constantly between 1850 and 1900 (Nielsen 1953, tables 27 & 28) and had doubled during this time, while there was a pronounced growth in animal products from the 1850's (Hansen 1976, supplementary table 19). Their value rose from 57% to 75% at the end of the 1870's. The sale of butter and pigs also increased greatly, from 6% and 2% to 33% and 36% respectively in 1875-79 (Hansen 1976, fig. VIII.4).

The gradual change-over to animal production stimulated the impressive scientific and industrial improvement of production. From 1856 this was supported by the foundation of the Royal Veterinary and Agricultural High School, the number of graduates from which rose from 1870 onwards (Larsen 1929, 265). This collaboration of the practical and the scientific has since been fundamental in the advance of agriculture. Its results were conveyed through the many new agricultural colleges established since the 1870's[5], which were soon co-ordinated on a regional and national basis. Agriculture was adjusting itself to the capitalist production of consumer goods. For the last time, however, it was the large estates which led the development, particularly in the field of dairying, but from the 1870's the peasants organized themselves on a large scale and formed co-operative societies to protect themselves against the exploitation of the landowners and commercial capital interests. In the 1880's dairying was organized on a co-operative basis (700 dairies were established in this decade) and with the growing pig production co-operative slaughter houses were set up. The purchase and sale of consumer goods for members was also organized through the establishment of co-operative stores (Hansen 1976, fig. IX.2).

There is hardly any doubt that this development in organization was rooted in the spread among the peasants of agricultural knowhow and political consciousness, disseminated by the now numerous high schools and agricultural colleges much attended by farmers (Larsen 1929, 267)[6].

As for cultivation there was a gradual change to the use of fertilizer or a rapid *crop rotation* of e.g. grain, root crops, grass, grain etc., without a fallow. The soil was exploited with more care and with more use of fertilizer, partly because of the growing number of livestock and partly because of the incipient use of artificial fertilizers around the 1880's and particularly the 1890's. New crops necessary for crop rotation were also introduced, the most important of which were turnips (Nielsen 1953, fig. 11), as were new farming tools and machinery: new improved ploughs which penetrated deeper, harrows and rollers and threshing machines. In combination with the agricultural depression this meant that the labour force stagnated and began to migrate from the countryside. On land with a high valuation there was a tendency for agricultural land to be concentrated in fewer and larger farms. In Jutland, on the other hand, there was an intensification of heath cultivation and the distribution of land into smallholdings (Hansen 1975b, fig. 23), especially after the foundation of the Heath Society and the growing economic involvement of the state. In this way a large part of the population surplus was absorbed, while on the islands it moved to Copenhagen.

The living conditions of the smallholders, however, worsened throughout the period. While the number of farms between 1 and 12 "tdr. htk." only rose from 70,000 to 77,000, the number of smallholdings with or without arable land increased from 110,000 to 212,000 [note: "tdr. htk." = tønder hartkorn: Danish unit of land valuation based on estimated productivity]. This feature, combined with the agricultural depression, explains the lower standard of living and the beginning of migration to the towns. Farms of over four "tdr. htk." cultivated 2/3 of all agricultural land, chiefly with the help of the smallholder and farm labourer class, which in 1905 owned 3/4 of all holdings but only 1/10 of all land (Falk & Madsen 1974, 102 ff., tables 1-7; cf. also Nielsen 1933, 415 & 528). Although in 1905 90% of the land was freehold (Christensen 1925-33, 197), this dispersal of property rights was not identical with the dispersal of arable land and the means of production, a situation which improved somewhat in the following period.

CULTIVATION OF NEW AREAS AND LAND IMPROVEMENT 1857-1894

In all probability the area of agricultural land increased more in these years than in any earlier or later fifty-year period. From 1861 the development can largely be documented by means of figures. It is characterized by two main tendencies with different geographical foci: intensified land improvement (by the use of marl and drainage), especially on the islands and on the good arable land; with the organized extension of cultivation and reforestation on the Jutland heathlands (fig. 6).

The application of marl, and later of lime, began in earnest in the 1840's and probably culminated on the islands in the 1850's and 1860's, but declined during the 1870's. After 1896 marl was seldom used on old agricultural land, but was replaced by artificial fertilizers. On the lime-poor soils of North and West Jutland the use of marl continued and became more intensive after 1896 in connection with the cultivation of heathlands (Hansen 1936, 43-73).

There was a dramatic increase in drainage around 1850 with the introduction of earthenware pipes, especially after 1861, and this became a significant factor in expanding production (cf. Falbe-Hansen 1887, 205, see also table 5):

Area drained in "tdr."	The Islands	Jutland
1861	37,368	22,668
1866	108,270	67,396
1871	242,762	120,766
1876	434,320	210,340
1881	629,320	292,440

A large number of formerly swampy areas could now after drainage be brought under cultivation, as could small patches of bog and marshy depressions in the fields. In the course of this twenty-year period, 20% of the agricultural land was drained. But as can be seen in table 5 this development progressed most quickly on the islands and in East Jutland, where a proportionally larger area had been drained at an early date. In these areas it was mainly the old swamp soils, which could not previously be drained, that were now transformed into arable soils. It was possible, however, to maintain a constant area of wet grazing by draining bogs and fens and converting them into meadowland. The net result was an expansion of arable land. Tables 3 & 4 show a marked fall in the area of wet grazing in the *islands* from 1861-81, and a smaller reduction in the fen and common areas, which does not compensate for the transition of old meadowland to arable. This accounts for the fact that the increase in agricultural land suddenly accelerated between 1866 and 1876, only to fall again.

Expansion of agricultural area in "tdr."

The Islands	
1861-66:	32,000
1866-71:	42,000
1871-76:	39,800
1876-81:	22,200

After 1881 drainage on Zealand slowed down because of the agricultural depression, while the increase continued at a lower rate on Funen and Lolland-Falster until 1896 (table 5).

In *Jutland* we find the opposite trend. Here the meadow and pasture lands were enlarged from 1861-81 (table 4). The main cause of this was a widespread transformation

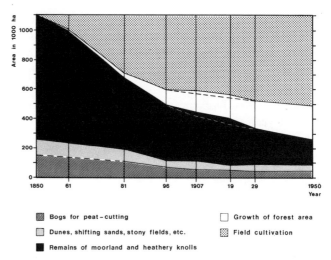

Bogs for peat-cutting

Dunes, shifting sands, stony fields, etc.

Remains of moorland and heathery knolls

Growth of forest area

Field cultivation

Fig. 6. Extention of cultivation and plantations on heathland over 100 years (after Nielsen 1953, fig. 6).

of bogs and fens, continuing right up to 1896 (tables 2-3), together with the meadow irrigation projects of the Heath Society. Thus the tendency in Jutland was to transform bogs and fens into new meadows, while in the islands old meadowland was reclaimed into arable. Between 1881 and 1896 drainage continued to increase in North and West Jutland, but only did so to a minor extent in East Jutland (table 5).

While on the whole the cultivation of new areas was completed on the islands and in East Jutland, it was reaching its maximum in Middle and West Jutland (fig. 6). Here the increase in arable land per capita during this period was exceeded only in the U.S. The following table shows the extent of this increase (after Hansen 1975a, 14-15)[7] (the percentages indicate the proportion of heath in the total area):

Area of heath in ha.	1822	1881	1888	1896
SE-Jutland (Vejle, Århus, Randers county)	108,500 (15%)	50,570 (7%)	40,000 (5.5%)	36,200 (4.8%)
N-Jutland (Ålborg, Hjørring, Thisted county)	130,800 (17%)	99,750 (13%)	86,700 (11.5%)	79,170 (10.5%)
SW-Jutland (Viborg, Ringkøbing, Ribe county)	418,900 (39%)	317,860 (30%)	272,900 (25%)	228,620 (21.4%)
Central Jutland	658,200 (26%)	468,180 (18%)	399,600 (16%)	342,990 (13.4%)

There is a very large reduction between 1822 and 1881 (of c. 190,000 ha., or c. 30%). As the earlier figures showing the reduction in 1837-61 suggested, it only began in earnest at this time and probably continued with growing intensity up to 1881. This impression is confirmed if we trace the development from 1861 until 1881 in successive five-year periods (after Falbe-Hansen 1887, 180):

Increase of agricultural area in "tdr.". Jutland

1861-66:	41,000
1866-71:	151,000
1871-76:	163,000
1876-81:	199,000

We notice that the cultivation of the heath only really commenced after 1866, the year in which the Heath Society was founded. Its activities were decisive in many of the advances that now occurred. The cultivation of heathland was now systematized. Before 1870 it was particularly the more fertile isolated hills that were cultivated, but afterwards the initiative was spread over a wider front. On areas with no agricultural potential conifer plantations were planted: from 1870-95 the plantation area of the Heath Society rose from 4,410 to 62,738 "tdr.". As time went by, the fields were enclosed by windbreaks, which prevented the drift of earth and sand. Projects for irrigating water meadows were also begun early: by 1891 391 km of irrigation canal had been constructed, but afterwards this work largely ceased. Of great importance for the actual cultivation was the location of marl deposits in lime-poor Middle and West Jutland, together with the organization of its distribution, by means of e.g. marlpit tracks. On the other hand, the cultivation of bogs – through the drainage and reclamation of the large fen and swampy areas – only gained momentum in the 1890's, which was to continue. The figures reflect this progress: from 1881 to 1907 the heathlands decreased by c. 160,000 ha. (34%), more than in the period 1822-81. However, in South East Jutland most heath came under cultivation between 1822 and 1881, and a similar tendency can be seen in North Jutland, which corresponds to the earlier observation that cultivation of heathlands first spread from the more fertile areas.

After 1850 there was also a growth in rural population, and in the number of new farms and smallholdings, in step with that of the agricultural area (Nielsen 1953, tables 9, 12 & 13). The increase in the number of farms and houses came to a temporary halt in 1885-95 due to the depression. In contrast, the islands showed no particular increase neither in rural population, and the number of farms and houses, nor in the cultivated areas. And at the end of the period the figures begin to fall. The increase here took place in the first half of the 19th century (Nielsen 1953, tables 8, 10 & 11). This illustrates very well the differing tempo of development in the two regions: land reclamation on the islands was prior to 1860, improvement of soils largely later, simultaneously with land reclamation in Jutland.

1895-1950. ACCELERATING GROWTH (1895-1920). RESTRICTION OF GROWTH IN THE INTERWAR PERIOD (1921-39). WAR AND RECONSTRUCTION (1940-50).

This fifty-year period of fluctuating market trends saw the development carried through for which the growth of infrastructure at the end of the 19th century had created the basis and framework.

Agriculture as well as industry enjoyed considerable progress during this period of accelerated growth, resulting in investment and modernization of the productive apparatus. There was also a marked growth in provincial areas. Altogether there was a general expansion comprising nearly all sectors – including artisans and small manufacturing industries (Hansen 1976, table XI.4). A further major factor in development was the new technological discoveries, such as the spread of electricity, the diesel engine, and in the smaller enterprises the electric motor.

As a result of the development of industry, it began to approach agriculture in economic importance (Hansen 1976, fig. XII.1). Throughout the 1920's they struggled for supremacy until in the following decade industry became dominant. Meanwhile agricultural production stagnated and there was an increase in migration to the towns. Part of the rural population growth could be kept in agricultural production by dividing landholdings and by intensifying heath cultivation.

Politically the first part of this period was characterized by alternating Labour and Agricultural Party governments until the Social Democrats (= Labour) became the dominant parliamentary party. This led to a strengthening of state power from the 1930's, which pointed towards the more tightly controlled growth after World War II. The uneven distribution of incomes from the end of the previous century was only slightly adjusted and was only to be redressed later by progressive taxation. In 1933 all previous social legislation was integrated into a simplified and reformed body of laws, which, as their effects became felt, gave greater social security to large sections of society. In the field of education we should mention the Education Act of 1914, which introduced comprehensive schooling and which in principle democratized the educational system, and very gradually raised the general level of education – an important precondition for a continued broadening of economic growth.

After the war industry very soon established its increase in productivity, partly by recruiting a larger labour force. To a certain extent agriculture changed its investment from building and land improvement over to labour-saving machinery, particularly tractors. This was due to the migration to the towns from 1945-50 of 100,000 farmhands, c. 20% of the labour force. The industrial labour force rose correspondingly from 180,000 to 250,000. This gave the development of the 'thirties an added impetus and formed the basis for the very large changes in the composition of labour force and population characteristic of the 1950's and 1960's.

Agriculture. In the 1890's began a new economic expansion, which was to last until 1920. The restricted growth of the interwar years did not really affect agriculture until the world depression in the 1930's, whereas the war and the subsequent reconstruction produced renewed progress, though not of the kind as in the first part of the period.

During the period of progress from 1896 to 1920 the reorganization of agriculture began to bear fruit; from 1903 and during the following decade there was heavy investment in new buildings (for the many cattle) and in new machinery (Larsen 1929, 288). A favourable interplay arose between investment, increased production, and rising prices (Hansen 1976, fig. XI.3). This period marks a provisional peak in the improvement of agricultural efficiency. The continued development of the co-operative societies was a contributing factor (Larsen 1929, 262) – particularly the building of slaughter-houses and the establishment of co-operative fodder societies. The improvements in production were gradually disseminated to the whole farming community by means of agricultural advisers, agricultural colleges, technical journals, meetings etc. (cf. notes 5-6). Crop rotation be-

came dominant with the increased production of rootcrops (Nielsen 1953, table?), and field fallow disappeared. In 1896 there were still 195,000 ha. in fallow; in 1937 18,000 ha. (Hansen 1925-33, 145). There was also reduction in the area of pastures and meadows (Nielsen 1953, table 11).

It was now the turn of the smallholders to assert themselves through their organizations[8], and since the advance in agricultural technology also made the smallholdings profitable, a political basis was formed for improving the conditions of this group, although there was always some antagonism between the organizations of smallholders and farmers – reflected politically in, for example, the breaking away of the "Radical Left" from the "Left" party. After the political change of 1901 the state supported a land policy designed to provide sufficient land to the smallholders to ensure their livelihood. Legislation was passed in 1919-20 which reduced the size of estates and released glebes and public land for distribution – altogether c. 53,000 ha. This led to the establishment of new smallholdings, aided by cheap state loans. It was widely believed at the time that smallholdings were the most efficient agricultural units. 10,000 new holdings were established in 1920-30, and this tendency continued into the 1930's (Kamp 1959, 59-82 and fig. 31-50).

Progress in production is particularly marked until 1930, after which there is only a slight and fluctuating increase until 1950. By 1930 the number of cattle doubled for the last time (Nielsen 1953, tables 27-28) and the number of pigs increased five-fold (Nielsen 1953, table 29). Animal production was, moreover, improved considerably by cattle and pig breeding. The continued growth of crop yields was particularly a result of the greater application of artificial fertilizers and the full adoption of crop rotation. The use of artificial fertilizer increased fifty times from 1897 till 1950, and grain production trebled (Nielsen 1953, fig. 12 & table 25). The labour force grew in the 1920's but declined during the depression of the 'thirties, while the number of pigs and cattle fell, especially in the islands. Technologically, there was at the same time a saving of labour by the now general use of machines for sowing, harvesting and threshing at the beginning of the period, and towards the end of the period by the spread of milking machines and tractors. The redundant labour force was set to work in the 1920's and 1930's on land and soil improvements (stone clearance, drainage etc.), which, as already mentioned, slowed down in the 1940's.

54

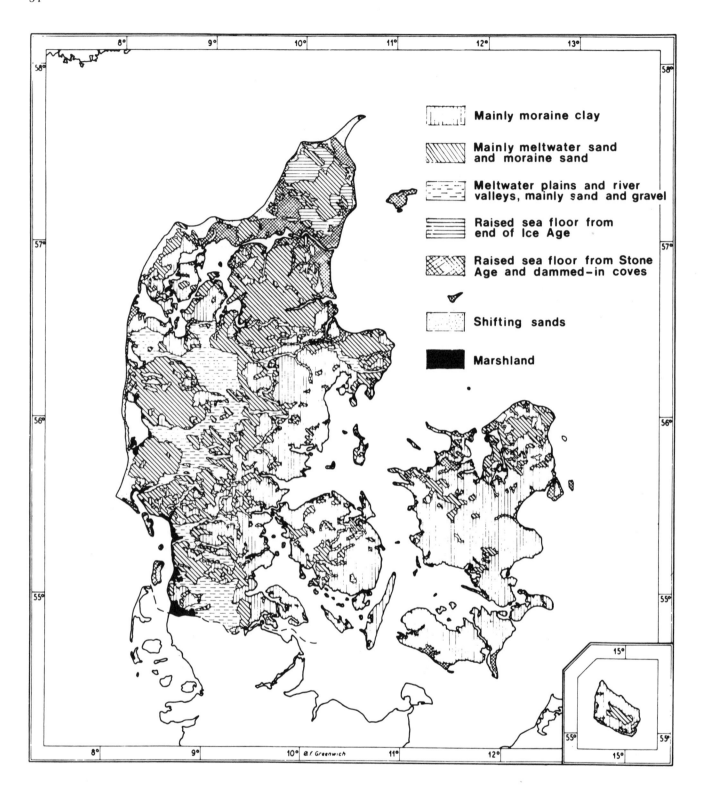

Mainly moraine clay

Mainly meltwater sand and moraine sand

Meltwater plains and river valleys, mainly sand and gravel

Raised sea floor from end of Ice Age

Raised sea floor from Stone Age and dammed-in coves

Shifting sands

Marshland

Fig. 7. Soil map of Denmark.

CULTIVATION OF NEW AREAS AND LAND IMPROVEMENT 1895-1950

The pattern of the former period continued. In *Jutland* the tempo of heath reclamation fell somewhat from 1896 until 1920 – under favourable market conditions – by which time the better soils had come under cultivation. After the new land legislation of 1919, however, reclamation resumed again, and the heathland was reduced considerably, both in SE-NW & SW Jutland, until 1950. Although the area was reduced by a total of c. 50%, this was less than in the period 1850-1896 as the following table shows (after Hansen 1975a):

Heath area in ha.	1907	1919	1929	1951	1961
South East Jutland	33,780	32,360	25,650	14,800	13,420
North Jutland	72,400	78,000	55,050	41,290	38,460
South West Jutland	203,010	198,340	147,860	96,090	63,400
Central Jutland	309,190	308,700	228,560	152,180	115,280

The reclamation now proceeded very systematically with extensive use of marl and artificial fertilizer – around 1927 most of Jutland was covered by a complex network of marlpit tracks (Skrubbeltrang 1966, 461) – and from the 1930's tractors were regularly used for deep ploughing. In the beginning the depth of furrow was c. 40 cm, but from 1947 it began to reach 80 cm, deep enough to break the hard pan. The other activities of the Heath Society continued, and by 1950 large areas were covered with conifer plantations (fig. 4b). Altogether, heath reclamation can be considered complete by 1950, with the exception of South West Jutland (fig. 5b & 6).

In the decades between 1881 and 1907 extension of the drainage system slowed down over the whole country, except in North and West Jutland. However, it received a new impetus from initiatives undertaken by the government in 1919 and 1921 to support land improvement – there was particular progress in North and West Jutland. This development accelerated after new land improvement legislation was passed in 1932-3. This meant that until the middle of the 1950's there was a dramatic growth in drainage area (table 6)[9].

If we next consider the changes in the area of bog, fen grazing, and water meadows given in tables 2-4, we notice a marked growth in the area of fen grazing between 1896 and 1919, and a fall in that of water meadows. This was not because water meadows deteriorated into fens in

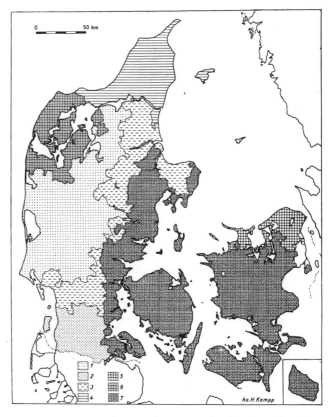

Fig. 8. The division of Denmark into agricultural regions (after Kamp 1959, fig. 1) according to production diversity and production output, increasing from 1 to 7 (see Kamp 1959, 7-54, figs. 12-30).

a period with a rising number of cattle. Rather these changes reflect a conversion of water meadows into arable and swamps into fenland, since the reduction in bog area equals the increase in fenland (tables 2-3). In the decade 1919-1929 there followed a considerable reduction in fenlands. These were probably converted into water meadows as a result of extensive drainage, in that the reduction of water meadows was only half that of fenland – i.e. the reclamation of new water meadows (from fen) was somewhat greater than the conversion of old meadowland to arable. The subsequent rise in the area of both meadowland and fen from 1930-40 reflects a marked drainage of large areas of swamp. From 1940-50 therewas a continuous reduction of meadow as well as fen by the extension of drainage.

In Jutland the general tendency from 1896-1950 was a reduction in meadowland (apart from the period 1930-40), while the area of fenland fluctuated according to the extent of swamp drainage. This can be seen from the rise during World War II in connection with more intensive peat cutting.

On *the islands* there was a gradual loss of agricultural land to towns, roads etc., but it increased again from 1919-29. This was due to the new land legislation, and more intensive drainage. Table 4 shows a marked reduction in water meadows from 1919-29 (replaced by arable), and (as in Jutland) a new increase from 1929-40, a period dominated by the intensive reclamation of swamps and fens into water meadows. The area of fenland thus declined from 27,000 to 17,000 ha. until 1950.

On the islands the years 1907-50 were also characterized by large-scale reclamation – first of old water meadow into arable (re-drainage), then of swamps and fens into new meadowland (new drainage). In contrast to Jutland this process continued until 1950, the fens diminishing steadily while meadowland remained stable.

By approx. 1950 the differences between Eastern and Western Denmark in terms of cultivation and land improvement had almost vanished. To a large extent regional differences were now due to variations in agricultural production based on local land potential (figs. 7 & 8).

1950-1975. GROWTH AND THE WELFARE SOCIETY. CULMINATION AND CRISIS

The period was dominated politically by the Social Democrats who favoured greater state intervention. Until 1957 there was a low rate of growth in spite of good international market conditions. From 1957 legislation was passed to stimulate industry, which, combined with a favourable world market, ushered in an economic expansion without parallel, establishing a new eve of growth. Until 1957 economic growth depended on the recruitment of a very great labour force into industry (extensive capital accumulation) – from 1950 to 1960 an increase of 250,000, of whom agriculture contributed 100,000. After 1960 expansion focussed on the process of industrialization itself (intensive capital accumulation). In the same period the social changes were greater than in any corresponding quarter century, comparable with the progress in infrastructure during the later part of the previous century. The great mobility radically altered the social structure in terms of the relationship between town and country, and between those publicly and privately employed. Wages, provision of services, and consumption increased greatly during the period 1957-73.

Agriculture in the same years suffered a gradual economic decline caused by huge rises in production costs. The rate of return fell from 9% to 3.7% in 1957. The response was a vigorous increase in production, primarily by means of improved breeding and mechanization, in order to make up for the drift of labour into industry – a reduction of manpower from 400,000 in 1948 to 275,000 in 1957. During this period the use of tractors became universal. The agricultural depression worsened in the 1960's when productivity reached a provisional peak. Mechanization and rationalization continued at a rapidly growing rate under increasingly adverse conditions caused by the falling rate of return, and then gradually slowed down. The labour force diminished to 173,000 in 1970. Thousands of agricultural holdings were now abandoned: their number fell from c. 200,000 in 1960 to 130,000 in 1975. After entry into the EEC there was renewed progress and mechanization.

CULTIVATION OF NEW AREAS AND LAND IMPROVEMENT

In the course of the 1950's these activities declined and remained at their lowest ebb till the end of the period. The agricultural area was now shrinking constantly because of urbanization – a development which had already begun to characterize the eastern part of Denmark from around the turn of the century, but which now accelerated greatly throughout the country. Improvements were carried out mainly in the form of more advanced methods of cultivation (crop breeding, full mechanization) and more intensive soil utilization (artificial fertilizers and above all the introduction of insecticides and weed-killers). Remaining uncultivated areas were set aside as nature reserves on a large scale. This period is characterized by a more intensive crop production and a reduction in the area of grazing, as the number of cattle fell. From 1974-75 further land improvement was carried out – replacement of old drainage systems and to a lesser extent the drainage of new areas.

Altogether, the period is characterized by a significantly deeper and more intensive tilling of the soil. The cultivation of new areas comes to a halt, and there is now a constant reduction in area. The labour force continues to decrease as mechanization advances (the rural population comprises today 8.5% of the total). These tendencies will undoubtedly also hold true in the future.

Kristian Kristiansen,
The National Agency for The Protection of Nature,
Monuments and Sites,
Amaliegade 13,
1256 Copenhagen K.

NOTES

1. In Jutland and Funen there was little common land, and this was usually covered with woods and scrub. Wooded common was also found in North East Zealand (in Hornsherred), in Central Zealand and the area around Vordingborg. Otherwise commons in Zealand were normally in open grassland (Christensen 1925-33, 105 ff.; for a general discussion, see Matthiessen 1942).

2. The three-field system comprised three fields which were successively in rye, barley and fallow (Christensen 1925-33, 95-11). Crop rotation was introduced from Schleswig-Holstein and Mecklenburg. The land was divided into 6-10 fields or enclosures. In these were cultivated e.g. cereals for 4-5 years, then grass for 4-5 years, and finally a fallow. Crop rotation was essentially a form of cereal cultivation (Hansen 1925-33, 139-145).

   Re: fencing. Although as early as 1695 a decree was issued which ordered that stone walls should replace wattle fencing in order to conserve woodlands, by 1794 wattle fencing was used nearly everywhere. Farmers were now rewarded for laying out living hedges and stone walls, and within forty years c. 407 km of living hedge was planted, particularly on Funen, while 530 km. of stone wall was built. The objective was to encourage the cultivation of new areas by clearing stones from the fields. This type of fencing was eventually replaced by a wire-fence, and many hedges were cleared in connection with the reorganization of fields, while some of the stone walls were used for road-filling and the construction of railways. Three factors thus led to the rising use of stones after 1784: fencing, the construction of roads, and later of railways. The decree of 1793

regarding road construction permitted the removal of stones from dolmens, a practice which was abolished in 1887.

3. The areal distribution of arable, bog, forest, heath etc. was calculated on the basis of the National Survey carried out by the Danish Scientific Society, published in a series of 1:120,000 maps between 1768 and 1805. However, since the commons were included with the arable and since it was these in particular that were brought under cultivation, this material cannot be used as a basis for comparison with later statistics of the area cultivated. (Calculations according to county published in Hansen 1936-43, 7).

4. The size of the areas was based on the quantity sown and therefore must be treated with caution.

5. The first agricultural societies were founded in the 1840's; in 1870 there were approx. fifty, and in 1900 102 such societies with 60,000 members (Larsen 1929, 256).

6. In 1861 there were four agricultural colleges with 70 students, and in 1891 thirteen with 707 students. After the turn of the century the increase was even more marked: in 1927 there were 25 agricultural colleges with 2,897 students.

7. The figures from 1850 given in fig. 6 are considerably higher than those given here for 1822, but we must subtract South Jutland, as well as swamps and sand dunes, which in 1881 covered nearly 1/3 of the area. In the same year the area of hilly heathland covered an estimated 492,000 ha., and if we subtract South Jutland it corresponds with the figures given here. This is not true of the 1822 data. If we similarly subtract from the 1850 data given in fig. 6, we are still left with a figure exceeding that of 1822. These old estimates are therefore fairly unreliable.

8. In the year 1900 there were 100 smallholders' associations. In 1928 there were 1,220 with 85,000 members (Larsen 1929, 256).

9. The lower figures for Jutland reflect a lower overall need for drainage. The extension of drainage is fairly uniform on a national scale.

10. The classification of swamp and fen is often problematical. Small-scale variations in their relative area is of little significance.

County	1850	1861	1871	1881	1896	1907	1919	1929	1940	1950
Vejle	134	146	153	170	174	172	170	173	167	163
Århus-Skanderb.	140	153	164	177	179	176	173	174	167	162
Randers	131	144	152	168	175	174	172	178	170	167
Aalborg	107	118	133	164	183	184	182	202	195	193
Hjørring	107	118	132	161	180	182	182	192	187	182
Thisted	71	78	80	89	97	97	97	109	99	105
Viborg	123	135	150	182	202	201	199	210	204	211
Ringkøbing	119	131	146	186	224	229	235	257	266	274
Ribe	93	102	119	142	163	163	164	181	189	189
Haderslev			100	100	94	92	97	104	103	95
Aabenraa	246	(271)	56	56	53	53	51	55	55	55
Sønderborg			35	34	35	35	34	35	34	34
Tønder			89	87	80	79	72	80	80	84
Jutland	1271	1396	1509	1716	1839	1837	1828	1950	1916	1914
Islands	900	924	977	1004	1007	1002	984	990	958	947
Total Denmark	2171	2320	2486	2720	2846	2839	2812	2940	2874	2861

Table 1. Cultivated area (in 1,000 ha.) (after Nielsen 1953, table 16).

	1881	1896	1907	1919	1929	1950
Heath	492	363	327	324	239	174
Swamps for peatcutting	105	66	52	43	41	45
Dunes and stony areas	75	58	65	35	46	(40)
Σ	672	485	444	402	326	259

Table 2. Distribution of major non-exploited zones (in 1,000 ha.) (after Nielsen 1963, table 5).

County	1861	1871	1881	1896	1907	1919	1929	1940	1950
Vejle	3	3	3	3	4	5	4	4	2
Århus-Skanderb. .	5	4	3	2	3	4	4	4	2
Randers	11	10	8	8	9	10	8	12	7
Aalborg	24	20	16	15	20	20	9	11	6
Hjørring	37	29	21	12	12	11	6	14	11
Thisted	16	21	13	8	11	13	4	11	11
Viborg	18	16	11	9	9	11	4	11	6
Ringkøbing	18	22	14	13	16	16	8	12	9
Ribe	14	12	8	7	8	9	5	7	6
Haderslev		8	8	8	8	8	5	3	3
Aabenraa	32	7	7	7	7	7	4	2	3
Sønderborg		2	2	2	2	1	1	1	0
Tønder		16	15	14	14	13	7	6	2
Jutland	178	170	130	108	123	128	68	98	68
Islands	27	24	22	16	22	28	27	22	17
Total Denmark	205	194	152	124	145	156	95	120	85

Table 3. Fen and common etc. (in 1,000 ha.) (after Nielsen 1953, table 18).

County	1861	1871	1881	1896	1907	1919	1929	1940	1950
Vejle	12	12	11	11	10	10	8	9	7
Århus-Skanderb. .	11	10	11	11	11	10	9	10	8
Randers	18	18	21	18	17	18	13	17	11
Aalborg	27	24	25	22	22	23	19	22	23
Hjørring .	24	22	24	21	18	18	16	14	15
Thisted	7	9	10	9	9	9	8	7	7
Viborg	15	16	20	19	19	20	18	19	15
Ringkøbing	36	33	39	37	36	36	31	29	21
Ribe	22	25	27	27	26	26	23	22	19
Haderslev		9	9	9	9	9	8	8	7
Aabenraa	30	7	7	6	6	6	5	7	6
Sønderborg		2	2	2	2	2	1	2	1
Tønder		25	25	23	23	20	20	16	19
Jutland	202	212	231	215	208	207	179	182	159
Islands	68	59	54	52	54	51	34	41	41
Total Denmark	270	271	285	267	262	258	213	223	200

Table 4. Area of water meadows (in 1,000 ha.) (after Nielsen 1953, table 17).

	Area drained in each of years given. Ha.						% of agricultural area.			
	1861	1871	1881	1896	1907	1929	1861	1881	1907	1929
Zealand	11200	75510	195560	224490	234780	259930	2.2	34.9	41.8	44.9
Bornholm	80	4880	14620	17610	18600	21360	0.3	38.2	47.2	52.1
Lolland-Falster	3150	18220	56680	79470	85560	95190	2.6	42.9	63.4	66.0
Funen	6190	35610	80290	107610	109200	122530	2.3	29.3	40.4	42.7
Islands	20620	134220	347150	429180	448140	499010	–	–	–	47.5
E. Jutland	8710	51300	109680	125350	126820	148170	2.0	21.3	24.0	25.9
N. Jutland	1190	4230	18260	29680	33400	60210	0.4	4.4	7.3	10.7
W. Jutland	2600	11080	33370	48430	51060	80050	0.7	6.5	8.6	10.8
S. Jutland	–	–	–	–	–	17350	–	–	–	5.3
Jutland	12500	66610	161310	203460	211280	305780	–	–	–	13.9
Total Denmark	33120	200830	508460	632640	659420	804790	1.6	20.8	25.5	24.8

Table 5. Area drained in Denmark 1861-1929 (after Hansen, K. 1936-43, 38).

County	% of area drained				Total
	before 1920	1921-32	1933-50	1951-72	
N. Jutland. N	2	9	15	10	36
N. Jutland S	2	3	10	9	24
Viborg	8	7	14	10	39
Ringkøbing	3	3	17	11	34
Ribe	4	5	13	9	31
Århus	8	7	18	12	45
Vejle	9	12	17	9	47
S. Jutland	6	6	32	18	62
Funen	16	8	20	11	55
W. Zealand	36	9	11	22	78
E. Zealand	31	8	15	11	65
Storstrøm	34	8	28	11	81
Bornholm	26	6	17	9	58
Total Denmark	12	7	18	12	49

Table 6. Area drained in Denmark before 1920 up to the present day, based on a 1 % random sample (after Skriver & Hedegård 1973, table e).

APPENDIX: BOGS AND PEAT CUTTING

Bogs can be divided into two main categories: low-level and raised. Low-level bogs are generally found in river valleys, while raised bogs are mainly found on poor soils. Agriculturally, most of the swampland, particularly low-level bogs, has been used over thousands of years for grazing and hay-cutting. These are distinguished in the text as water meadows (= meadowland = wet grazing) and fen. In Jutland they have been of particular impor-

tance for livestock production. Raised bogs, on the other hand, have to a larger extent lain unused. Both categories have also been used for the production of fuel. However, it is extremely difficult to provide a systematic account of peat cutting and its geographic variation and historical development because of the lack of numerical data. The statistics of peat production are only known from 1902 (table 9). Before this time the information is sparse and

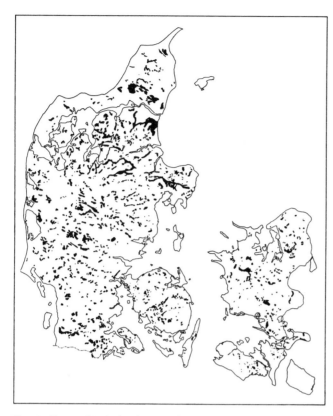

Fig. 9. Geographical distribution of swamps over 5 ha, based on Heath Society survey carried out between 1924-1940. (After Thøgersen 1942).

incidental. As for Jutland, we can follow the reduction of bog areas (table 5 in the article), although this is not only due to peat cutting but also to drainage. Furthermore, we have a number of statistics on the extent of bogs and fens. One of the earliest shows these areas at the beginning of the 19th century (table 7), while a map based on the more reliable and detailed surveys carried out by the Heath Society is reproduced in table 8. Finally there is ethnological and historical information on regional variations in the technology and historical development of peat cutting. In the following I shall give a brief account of the various sources of information.

There is considerable regional variation in the extent of bogs and fens. Data from the Scientific Society's map series (1768-1805) show that the area of water meadow, fen, bog and lake covers 5%-18% of the total area of Jutland. The highest proportion is in the counties of Aalborg and Hjørring with 18% and 12%, respectively. The other counties of Jutland have between 5% and 8%. On

the islands the largest area is in North Zealand, in Frederiksborg and Holbæk counties with 9% and 5%. The other counties have between 3.5% and 5% (Hansen 1936-43, 7). Bergsøe gives the areas of bog and fen (table 7), and these show the same distribution: on the islands the highest figure is for Holbæk county, in Jutland for Aalborg county. The first systematic survey was undertaken by the Heath Society in the interwar years (Thøgersen 1942) with a view to possible industrial exploitation. The study included only bogs larger than 5 ha. and more than 30 cm deep. The bogs were classified into four groups according to their potential productivity. Both the geographical distribution (fig. 9) and the statistics (table 8) show the same general tendency as the earlier statistics, although the area is naturally somewhat smaller. Few bogs are still found in South West Zealand, South West Lolland, East Funen and Bornholm. In Jutland Aalborg county still dominates, while Ringkøbing and Hjørring lag behind.

Peat has probably been cut for local fuel consumption and for smithies since the Iron Age (Becker 1948; Hove 1971), but only from more recent historic times is there sufficient information to describe it in detail (Schmidt 1948). Village regulations which have survived from the 17th and 18th centuries contain a large number of rules concerning peat cutting: how much could be cut by private individuals, how much by the manor (peat cutting was included in villein-service), how much for sale etc. There were also rules governing procedure, drainage etc. (Schmidt 1948, 26 ff.). Normally each village owned a bog, in which each peasant had his share. This meant that peat cutting was very unsystematic – a large number of small individual cuttings, as can be seen on the old maps (Rise Hansen & Axel Steensberg 1951, map plates). The depth of cuttings was limited by the fact that drainage was usually poor. New peat cuttings were frequently opened, and the old ones allowed to fill in. Peat could be cut again from the latter some decades later. Several factors contributed, however, to the fact that peat cutting assumed a different character and a different extent in the various parts of Denmark.

It must be assumed that peat cutting increased with woodland clearance, which reached its climax around 1800 when only 4% of woods were left. In *Jutland* people in all the heath areas used heather peat, which burned better than bog peat (Højrup 1975; Lerche 1969). A single farm would use in a year between 60 and 100 cartloads, c. 4-8 ha. Peat cutting only intensified with the

County	Ha.	County	Ha.
København	1165	Hjørring	34588
Frederiksborg	3312	Thisted	9573
Holbæk	6933	Viborg	33124
Sorø	2378	Århus	5774
Præstø	3441	Skanderborg	
Bornholm	1365	Randers	17538
Odense	4362	Ribe	17295
Svendborg	3452	Ringkøbing	38672
Maribo	3028	Vejle	11973
Aalborg	52157		

Table 7. Swamp and Fen. (After Bergsøe 1843, 156-ff.)

heath reclamation during the 19th century – particularly the later part. The uneven geographical distribution of bog areas meant that in *the islands* during the 19th century a large part of the bogs had already been cut so that people had to cut into the deeper, wetter layers. Long-handled tools, often shaped like a racket, were used for this (Schmidt 1948, 96). The peat was macerated and mixed, and then shaped (Schmidt 1948, 75 ff.; Rasmussen 1969, fig. 1). In Jutland, however, cut peat was most common because the level of bog exploitation was lower and the areas larger (Schmidt 1948, 55 ff.).

The uneven geographical distribution of bogs also entailed a certain amount of trade in peat (Schmidt 1948, 147 ff.), while towns, too, were important customers – particularly Copenhagen. Cartloads of peat were brought in from the whole of North Zealand, and this was an essential extra income for the peasants. In 1756 Zealand peasants delivered 24,850 cartloads (c. 12,000 metric tons) to Copenhagen, in 1851 70,000 loads. With the growth of industrialization and urbanization at the end of the 19th century, coal and coke began to replace peat. This meant that the country was vulnerable to a suspension of supplies, as happened in both world wars. This explains the boom in peat production characteristic of the years around the two world wars (table 9). During World War I the manual production of cut peat was still dominant, while in World War II most production was mechanized.

Today the peat has been removed from most of the small bogs, and the large bog areas suitable for cultivation have been drained. Bogs and peat cutting no longer play a significant role in either the social economy or archaeology.

County	Total	Ha.	Mill. ton
Aabenraa-Sønderborg	76	4262	5.146
Aalborg	138	27586	45.829
Aarhus	112	4834	4.676
Haderslev	31	1547	1.087
Hjørring	56	10333	12.550
Randers	149	10934	12.154
Ribe	118	7834	7.859
Ringkøbing	166	13785	8.239
Thisted	25	1527	0.990
Tønder	40	4429	3.711
Vejle	80	5220	6.116
Viborg	109	15929	16.721
Total Jutland	1100	108220	125.078
Frederiksborg	56	1969	2.502
Holbæk	48	5155	6.484
København	46	1147	1.336
Præstø	61	3469	5.563
Sorø	43	1813	3.858
Bornholm	4*)	85	0.265
Maribo	83	2476	3.856
Odense	97	3304	3.525
Svendborg	87	3113	3.969
Total Islands	525	22531	31.358
Total Denmark	1625	130751	156.436

*) +4 Swamps below 5 ha.

Table 8. Swamps over 5 ha, based on Heath Society survey carried out between 1924-1940.(After Thøgersen 1942.)

		1921	846	1941	4674	1961	113
1902	100	1922	623	1942	4824	1962	61
1903	105	1923	434	1943	5976	1963	48
1904	107	1924	356	1944	5815	1964	36
1905	122	1925	395	1945	5685	1965	12
1906	118	1926	386	1946	3705	1966	9
1907	114	1927	338	1947	5168		
1908	118	1928	326	1948	3617		
1909	140	1929	336	1949	1416		
1910	156	1930	357	1950	902		
1911	175	1931	337	1951	2014		
1912	185	1932	312	1952	1627		
1913	194	1933	348	1953	574		
1914	187	1934	384	1954	545		
1915	195	1935	336	1955	712		
1916	285	1936	384	1956	706		
1917	1307	1937	480	1957	734		
1918	2259	1938	432	1958	385		
1919	1493	1939	420	1959	420		
1920	2085	1940	2513	1960	170		

Table 9. Total peat production 1902-66. 1000 metric tons. (After Hove 1983).

REFERENCES

BASSE, N. 1939: Grundforbedring og Opdyrkningsarbejder. *Tidsskrift for Landøkonomi 6.* København.

BECKER, C.J. 1948: Tørvegravning i ældre jernalder. *Fra Nationalmuseets Arbejdsmark.* København.

BEGTRUP, G. 1803-12: *Beskrivelse over Agerdyrkningens Tilstand i Danmark.* København.

BERGSØE, A.F. 1843: *Den Danske Stats Statistik.* Kjøbenhavn.

CHRISTENSEN, O. 1925-33: Jordens Besiddelse og Brug. In Hansen, K. *Det danske Landbrugs Historie, Bind I* (p. 75-240). København.

DYBDAHL, V. 1965: *Danmarks historie 1870-1913.* Politikens Danmarkshistorie, bind 13. København.

FALBE-HANSEN, V. & SCHARLING W. 1878-87: *Danmarks Statistik. Bind 1-3.* Kjøbenhavn.

FALBE-HANSEN, V. 1887: Landbrugets Udvikling. In Falbe-Hansen & Scharling *Danmarks Statistik, Bind 2* (p. 195-271). Kjøbenhavn.

FALK, J. & MADSEN, A. 1974: Bønder og klassekamp. *Marxistisk Antropologi 3-4.*

GRØN, A.H. 1934: Skoven og Mennesket gennem de vekslende Tider. *Dansk Natur.* København.

HANSEN, K. (ed.) 1925-33, 1936-43: *Det danske Landbrugs Historie. Bind 1-4.* København.

HANSEN, K. 1936-43: *Bind 2: Planteavlen.* I. Landbrugsarealet II. Opdyrkning III. Grundforbedringer. København.

HANSEN, K. & SIGGÅRD, N. 1936-43: Landbrugsarealet. From *Det danske Landbrugs Historie,* II. Bind. København.

HANSEN, Sv.Aa. 1976: *Økonomisk vækst i Danmark. Bind 1, 1720-1914.* Københavns Universitet. Institut for økonomisk historie.
– 1977: *Økonomisk vækst i Danmark. Bind 2, 1914-1975.* Københavns Universitet, Institut for økonomisk historie.

HANSEN, V. 1975a: Hedens Bebyggelse. *Danmarks Natur, bind 7.* København.
– 1975b: Hedens opståen og omfang. *Danmarks natur, bind 7.* København.
– 1975c: Bebyggelsens historie. *Danmarks Natur, bind 9.* København.

HOLMGÅRD, J. 1977: Landboreformerne – drivkræfter og motiver. *Fortid og nutid. Bind XXVII, hft. 1.* København.

HOVE, TH. TH. 1971: Tørvegravning i Oldtiden. *MIV 1.* Viborg.
– 1983 *Tørvegravning i Danmark.* Herning.

HØJRUP, O. 1975: Hedens udnyttelse. *Danmarks Natur, bind 7.* København.

JØRGENSEN, B.S. 1975: Hedens opdyrkning og beplantning. *Danmarks Natur, bind 7.* København.

KAMP, AA. 1959: *Landbrugsgeografiske studier over Danmark* (some Agro-Geographical Investigations of Denmark). Kulturgeografiske Skrifter, Bd. 6. København.

LARSEN, O.H. 1929: *Landbrugets Historie og Statistik.* København.

LERCHE, G. 1969: Cutting of Sod and Heather Turf in Denmark. From *The Spade in Northern and Atlantic Europe* (ed. A. Gailey & A. Fenton). Belfast.

MATTHIESSEN, H. 1939: *Den sorte Jyde.* Tværsnit af Hedens Kulturhistorie. København.
– 1942: *Det gamle Land.* Billeder fra Tiden før Udskiftningen. København.

NIELSEN, E. 1933: *Dänische Wirtschaftsgeschichte.* Jena.

NIELSEN, N.C. 1953: Udviklingen gennem 100 Aar. In *Hedens Opdyrkning i Danmark* (ed. H. Skodshøj). København.

OLSEN, E. 1967: *Danmarks økonomiske historie siden 1750.* København.

RASMUSSEN, H. 1969: Peat Cutting in Denmark. From *The Spade in Northern and Atlantic Europe* (ed. A. Gailey & A. Fenton). Belfast.

RISE HANSEN, C. & STEENSBERG, A. 1951: *Jordfordeling og Udskiftning.* Undersøgelser i tre sjællandske landsbyer. Det Kgl. Danske Vid. Selsk. Hist.-Filologiske Skrift. Bind II, Nr. 1. København.

SCHARLING, W. 1878: Samfærdselsmidlerne. In Falbe-Hansen & Scharling: *Danmarks Statistik.* København.

SCHMIDT, A.F. 1948: *Moser og Tørv* (et stykke Bondehistorie).

SKODSHØJ, H. (ed.) 1953: *Hedens opdyrkning i Danmark.* Mindebog udgivet ved oprettelsen af Kongenshus-Mindepark for hedens opdyrkere. København.

SKOVMAND, R. 1964: *Danmarks historie 1830-70.* Politikens Danmarkshistorie, bind 11. København.
– 1966: *Det indvundne land.* København.

SKRIVER, K. & HEDEGÅRD, J. 1974: Undersøgelse over danske jorders dræningstilstand. In Olesen, J. (ed.) *Planteavlsarbejdet i Landbo- og husmandsforeningerne 1973.*

SKRUBBELTRANG, F. 1938: *Den danske Bonde 1788-1938.* København.

THØGERSEN, F. 1942: *Danmarks Moser* (Beretning om Hedeselskabets systematiske Eng- og Moseundersøgelser).

VIBÆK, J. 1964: *Danmarks historie 1784-1830.* Politikens Danmarkshistorie, bind 10. København.

Archaeological Source Criticism and the History of Modern Cultivation in Denmark

by EVERT BAUDOU

INTRODUCTION

When analysing find data for material used in a study of the Late Bronze Age in Scandinavia (Baudou 1960), it was quite clear that recent cultivation had significantly influenced the find frequency and the pattern of distribution. On the one hand, cultivation within an area with numerous prehistoric remains may produce many finds which are handed over to a local museum or kept at home, and which gradually become known and registered. On the other hand, cultivation within an old and fertile agricultural zone may have destroyed prehistoric remains long before any museums were set up and before anybody took an interest in preserving finds. In both cases, though in opposite ways, cultivation affects the representativity of the remaining prehistoric material. In a country with such widespread agriculture as Denmark, cultivation – both in prehistoric and historic times – may constitute a serious source of error in archaeological research. It is therefore very important to study how cultivation affected the *representativity* of different types of prehistoric phenomena, and how this in turn affects our interpretation of prehistoric conditions. This is one kind of archaeological source criticism. There are many similar sources of error which may influence the representativity of the find frequency and the distribution pattern, e.g. recent socio-economic developments such as road building, and peat and gravel digging. However, this paper will deal only with the role of cultivation in archaeological research in Denmark.

My work on cultivation and Bronze Age mounds and finds was carried out in 1962-63[1]. Unfortunately, other tasks prevented me from completing the work for publication. The subject was discussed, however, in a publication on ancient monuments in northern Sweden (Baudou 1968, 112-114 and 118-120).

PROBLEM, MATERIAL AND OBJECTIVE

Problem: Is it possible to specify the degree to which cultivation in Denmark has affected the representativity of find frequencies of ancient monuments as well as finds in different parts of the country?

The general outline of cultivation changes in Denmark can be determined by means of the statistics available since 1682. My discussion of archaeological material is based on the large burial mounds and grave finds of the Bronze Age. Other types of prehistoric monuments and finds present other variations of the representativity problem in connection with destruction caused by cultivation. The purpose of this paper is to present the relevant data and discuss the following points:

A. To determine and map the extent of the cultivated area at different times after 1682; to calculate the increase and differential fertility of cultivated land during different periods. To establish the relation between cultivation and soil types.

B. Listing of known large Bronze Age burial mounds and also damaged or demolished mounds from the same period.

C. Discussion of the relation between recent cultivation and the destruction of large Bronze Age mounds. The significance of the intensity of cultivation.

D. An attempt to determine the cultivated area during the Middle Ages.

E. Discussion of the connection between recent cultivation and the distribution of Bronze Age grave finds and large mounds.

There is no intention in this paper to study the quaternary geological background for cultivation or for Bronze Age settlements. In several cases squared maps giving the numerical basis for the isometric maps are included in order to facilitate other types of calculations. The material which formed the basis for the mapping of cultivated area parish by parish in the four years chosen is far too comprehensive to be published here.

CULTIVATED AREA IN DENMARK, 1682-1955

My starting-point is the land holding registers from the years 1682, 1866, 1907 and 1955. The register from 1682 is the first that can be used in this context in Denmark. The register concerned is that of King Christian V, the most important parts of which were published by H. Pedersen in 1928. The register includes the extent of cultivated land and the number of so-called *hartkorn** (cf. discussion below of figs. 10-11) parish by parish for the greater part of present-day Denmark. Proper agricultural statistics began in 1861 and continued until 1912 with registrations approximately every five years (Hansen 1943, 9). After 1915 there was an annual census. The choice of the yars 1866, 1907 and 1955 was motivated by the wish to compare the growth of finds in the museum collections with changes in the extent of agriculture. The purpose was to attempt an assessment of the representativity of museum collections at different points in time. The first museum collections, above all those of the National Museum in Copenhagen, had already been established by 1866. The year 1907 saw a great increase in Copenhagen but also in many provincial museums. The year 1955 was the last year when agricultural statistics were available since the data for this paper were processed in 1962-63. I never had the time to finish this study of the representativity of museum collections.

Begtrup's work on Danish agriculture (1803-1812) has not been used, since my primary purpose was not to study the recent history of cultivation. Moreover, a later comparison of Begtrup's figures for each county (Hansen 1943, 7f.) reveals that his concept of *Agerland* (: arable land) includes not only the actual cultivated area but also most of the common land. The latter has been left out in this paper. If we compare Begtrup's figures with those in Table I for the cultivated area in 1866, it appears that on the islands Begtrup's figures are up to 16% higher and in Jutland up to 18% higher.

Apart from the statistics covering the cultivated area, the data on *hartkorn* for 1682 and 1866 have also been used (cf. discussion below of figs. 10-11).

The administrative divisions in Denmark have undergone certain changes between 1682 and 1955. What matters in this context is that the division into counties and parishes changed somewhat between the various land surveys. Relevant corrections have been made to ensure that the figures are comparable[2]. The southernmost part of Jutland, which was formerly outside the Danish frontier, is not included in the statistics. When comparing the different years it is essential that our concept of "cultivated area" remain constant. For 1682 the figures under "cultivated area *tønder land**" literally signify *only* the actual cultivated area. The corresponding columns for 1866 and 1907 have been converted to equivalent figures[3]. In 1963 the Statistical Dept. of the Office for Agricultural Statistics in Copenhagen obligingly placed at my disposal the corresponding figures for the actual cultivated area in the year 1955, i.e. arable land, plough land, and crop rotation areas. Thus I have made the figures comparable as far as possible.

Figures 1-4: Maps of the cultivated area in 1682, 1866, 1907 and 1955. In each map the presence of cultivated fields is indicated in 20% intervals by means of five different colours. In the respective years the extent of cultivation in those parts of Denmark covered by the maps is 28.4%, 53.8%, 66.4%, and 66.1%.

In 1682 the most widespread cultivation is found in North and West Zealand, in North and Central Funen, in East Central Jutland and in the western Limfjord area in North-West Jutland. In these regions the interval of 40-60% cultivated fields is dominant. In adjacent areas and in North Jutland and on the islands to the south the interval is 20-40%.

The extent of cultivation in 1682 closely reflects the different soil types. Two main types of soil predominate in Denmark: brown earth and podsol. The cultivation map for 1682 coincides fairly closely to the map of the two types of soil, *fig. 5*. In Jutland the correspondence is striking. The two concentrations of cultivated land, in eastern Central Jutland and in the western Limfjord area, are both within the brown earth zone. In Djursland the band of podsolics extending from north to south has a lower proportion of cultivated area. West Jutland, which is heavily podsolized, makes up the greater part of the area with the lowest percentage of cultivation. Part of this largely uncultivated area tapers off to a point towards the east in Skanderborg county. The same pattern recurs in the distribution of podsolics.

By 1866 the cultivated area in Denmark had nearly doubled, with an increase from 28.4% to 53.8% in the area under cultivation. However, the map in fig. 2 shows

Fig. 1. Cultivated area in 1682. Calculated according to parish as percentage of total area.

0%–20%	green	>60%–80%	blue
>20%–40%	yellow	>80%	red
>40%–60%	grey		

Fig. 2. Cultivated area in 1866. Calculated according to parish as percentage of total area.

0%–20%	green	>60%–80%	blue
>20%–40%	yellow	>80%	red
>40%–60%	grey		

Fig. 3. Cultivated area in 1907. Calculated according to parish as percentage of total area.

0%–20%	green	>60%–80%	blue
>20%–40%	yellow	>80%	red
>40%–60%	grey		

Fig. 4. Cultivated area in 1955. Calculated according to parish as percentage of total area.

0%–20%	green	>60%–80%	blue
>20%–40%	yellow	>80%	red
>40%–60%	grey		

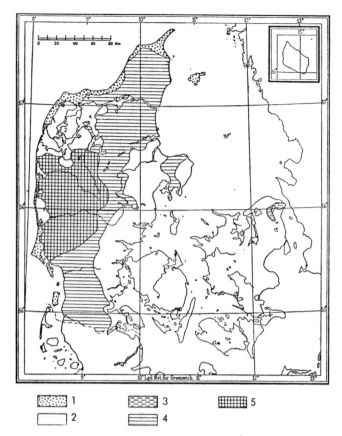

Fig. 6. Increase in percentage of cultivated area, 1682-1866. The mean value for the increase in all parishes is 25.3.

>2 M	>50.6%	red
>3/2M–2 M	>37.9%–50.5%	blue
>M–3/2 M	>25.3%–37.9%	grey

Fig. 5. Map showing areas of podsol and brown earth in Denmark (Hansen 1973, fig. 5). 1. Shifting sands. 2. Brown earth. 3. Lightly podsolized. 4. Podsolic. 5. Heavily podsolized.

the same general trends as before. The proportion of cultivated fields shows a very marked rise within the entire brown earth zone, both on the islands and in Jutland, and is now within the two highest intervals, i.e. above 60%. In North Jutland, in the counties of Hjørring and Ålborg, a steady increase in cultivation also extends into the podsolic zone. There is still a noticeably lower degree of cultivation in part of Djursland. The most heavily podsolized part of West Jutland remains lightly cultivated.

The maps from 1907 and 1955, figs. 3-4, are similar in broad outline. This was to be expected, since the overall percentage of cultivation in Denmark remained practically unchanged, 66.4% and 66.1%. They differ from that of 1866 in the pronounced increase in cultivation in North and West Jutland.

Figures 6-7: Maps of the increase in cultivation, 1682-1866 and 1866-1907. The best way to illustrate the differences between the two periods 1682-1866 and 1866-1907 is to

Fig. 7. Increase in percentage of cultivated area, 1866-1907. The mean value for the increase in all parishes is 12.4.

>2 M	>24.8%	red
>3/2M – 2M	>18.6%–24.8%	blue
>M–3/2M	>12.4%–18.6%	grey

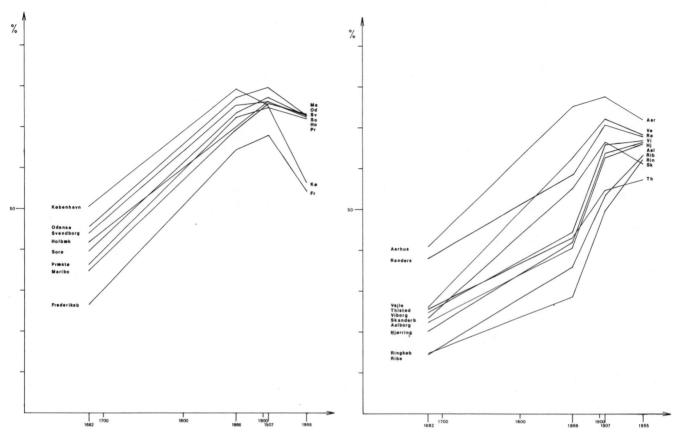

Fig. 8. Diagram of cultivated area in percentages for each county on the Danish Islands, 1682-1955.

Fig. 9. Diagram of cultivated area in percentages for each county in Jutland, 1682-1955.

map the increase in cultivation. The maps are based on the increase in cultivation in the whole of Denmark, 25.3% during the first period and 12.4% during the second. (The figures vary slightly from those in Table I because of minor differences in area calculations). These values are taken as the mean (M) for the increase in cultivation in the parishes of Denmark. The two maps published here indicate the three highest intervals: above M to 1.5 M; above 1.5 M to 2 M; above 2 M. The same colours have been used as in figs. 1-4. Maps giving intervals below M have been prepared, but are not published here.

Figure 6 shows clearly that right until 1866 the greatest cultivation increase was in brown earth zones. Only in North Jutland, in parts of Hjørring and Ålborg counties, was there a significant rise within the podsol area. It should be noted, however, that the cultivated area also increased in the other regions of Denmark. The increase there is, however, below 25.3%. The map in fig. 7 for

1866-1907 shows the opposite picture. Practically all increases over 12.4% are within podsol zones. Even in the heavily podsolized area to the west the rise in cultivation is within the highest interval. Similarly, the cultivation increase within the band of podsols in Djursland is above the M-value. Even in this period new land was also brought into cultivation in the rest of Denmark, though on a comparatively minor scale. It should be noted that in map 7 the value 2 M equals 24.8%, i.e. almost the same as the value M = 25.3% in map 6.

Similarly, in the period 1682-1866 the value 0.5 M equals 12.7%, but only 6.2% in the period 1866-1907. In large parts of the podsol zones there is an even increase in cultivation, calculated in percentages during the two periods. The great contrast between the maps is because the relative increase is accentuated.

The percentages of cultivated land for each county in the four years appear from figs. 8-9, based on Table I. The counties on the islands (fig. 8) saw a very marked

County	Total area Tønder land	Cultivated area %			
		1682	1866	1907	1955
Frederiksborg	246408	26.6	64.5	68.0	54.3
København	225550	50.7	79.3	75.6	56.3
Holbæk	312109	43.5	69.9	76.2	72.5
Sorø	268357	39.7	73.4	77.2	72.8
Præstø	306900	36.4	72.4	74.7	72.0
Bornholm	106510	–	54.1	67.9	64.8
Maribo	324720	34.8	69.3	75.7	73.1
Odense	327992	45.6	77.2	79.6	72.8
Svendborg	301814	44.0	75.3	76.1	72.8
Hjørring	517133	20.3	42.0	63.8	66.4
Thisted	322390	26.4	43.3	54.9	57.4
Aalborg	531620	22.4	40.7	62.6	66.1
Viborg	554280	24.8	44.6	65.8	66.9
Randers	445986	38.1	58.6	70.7	67.9
Århus	145647	40.9	75.2	77.6	72.1
Skanderborg	309439	23.4	55.2	66.5	61.1
Vejle	426048	26.1	62.7	73.2	69.3
Ringkøbing	836849	14.7	28.7	49.6	60.2
Ribe	554620	14.2	36.1	53.5	63.2
Total	7064372	28.4	53.8	66.4	66.1

Table I. Cultivated area in Denmark 1682, 1866, 1907, and 1955.

Fig. 10. Crop yields in 1682 indicated in "specific *hartkorn*".

1201–	red
801–1200	blue
401–800	yellow
0–400	green

increase between 1682 and 1866, followed by a levelling off and subsequent decrease between 1866 and 1907. For the counties in Jutland the great rise occurred between 1866 and 1907. Århus county is an exception, and follows the pattern of the islands. After 1907 the four counties with a maximum of cultivation experience a decline, while the others continue to increase their cultivated areas.

Figures 10-11: Maps of crop yields in 1682 and 1866. The unit of taxation in the year 1682 was one *tønde hartkorn*. The principle was that "a certain number of *tønder land* of a certain quality, sown with certain cereals, would yield one *tønde* (: barrel) of *hartkorn* (: hard grain, i.e. rye or barley) as manorial dues" (Aakjær 1928, 16). All types of land were assessed in this manner: arable land, hay meadows, pastures, and woodland. "Thus it would be possible to draw up a soil map of Denmark at that time; the lower the index figure, the better the soil" (Aakjær 1928, 23).

In 1877 C. Meldahl published an isometric map of the "specific *hartkorn*" in Denmark. By "specific *hartkorn*" is meant the number of *tønder* of field and water meadow *hartkorn* which correspond to one geographical square

Fig. 11. Crop yields in 1866 indicated in "specific *hartkorn*".

1201–	red
801–1200	blue
401–800	yellow
0–400	green

mil*, calculated for each parish (Meldahl 1877, LXV). In this calculation forest reserves have been deducted from the total parish area. Meldahl's map is based on the land register of 1844.

The maps in figs. 10-11 show the distribution of the "specific *hartkorn*" in Denmark in 1682 and 1866. Forest reserves have not been deducted in the maps. This does not affect the overall picture. For 1682 Pedersen's published *hartkorn* figures had to be corrected because of a conversion that took place by Royal decree in 1690 (Aakjær 1928, 23 f.). In Funen and Langeland this decree added an extra 1/12 to the established *hartkorn* figures, and in Jutland an extra 1/16. These additions are included in Pedersen's *hartkorn* table (1928). The published *hartkorn* figure for Funen and Langeland has therefore been multiplied by a factor of 0.92 and for Jutland by 0.94 so as to reduce it to the original assessment.

All three maps, figs. 10-11 and Meldahl 1877, LXV, are very similar. The three groups with higher values in these maps are clearly related to the distribution of brown earths, and the lowest values to the podsol areas (fig. 5). This is to be expected from an agricultural economy which on the whole was the same type in 1682 and in 1866.

THE LARGE BRONZE AGE MOUNDS

The source material for the lists and maps of Bronze Age burial mounds is the archives in the parish records of the National Museum in Copenhagen. Each mound was recorded with the appropriate parish record number and marked in archaeological maps of Denmark (1:100,000). This work was carried out by Svend E. Albrethsen and

County	Large mounds	Large mounds per 1000 tnd. land	Demolished Bronze Age mounds		Former large mounds		Now low Bronze Age mounds		Damaged large mounds	
	Total			%		%	Total	%		%
Frederiksborg	523	2.1	83	15.9	22	4.2	50	9.6	155	29.6
København	477	2.1	39	8.2	26	5.5	47	9.9	112	23.5
Holbæk	605	1.9	104	17.2	40	6.6	81	13.4	225	37.2
Sorø	215	0.8	31	14.4	14	6.5	12	5.6	57	26.5
Præstø	434	1.4	66	15.2	38	8.8	17	8.5	64	32.0
Bornholm	200	1.9	35	17.5	12	6.0	9	3.4	46	17.5
Maribo	263	0.8	13	4.9	24	9.1	9	3.4	46	17.5
Odense	157	0.5	29	18.5	26	16.6	34	21.7	89	56.7
Svendborg	143	0.5	21	14.7	15	10.5	26	18.2	62	43.4
Hjørring	1226	2.4	38	3.1	27	8.2	21	1.7	86	7.0
Thisted	1690	5.2	115	6.8	71	4.2	147	8.7	333	19.7
Ålborg	2237	4.2	30	1.3	198	8.9	25	1.1	253	11.3
Viborg	2810	5.1	60	2.1	446	15.9	177	6.3	683	24.3
Randers	1239	2.8	18	1.5	249	20.1	18	1.5	285	23.0
Århus	146	1.0	9	6.2	31	21.2	11	7.5	51	34.9
Skanderborg ...	926	3.0	54	5.8	156	16.9	93	10.0	303	32.7
Vejle	580	1.4	23	4.0	97	16.7	88	15.2	208	35.7
Ringkøbing	2111	2.5	24	1.1	337	16.0	60	2.8	421	19.9
Ribe	1247	2.2	71	5.7	212	17.0	93	7.5	376	30.2
Haderslev	477	2.6	39	8.2	53	11.1	42	8.8	134	28.1
Tønder	164	1.1	6	3.7	22	13.4	7	4.3	35	21.3
Åbenrå	169	1.7	14	8.3	5	3.0	53	31.4	72	42.6
Sønderborg	91	1.5	9	9.9	5	5.5	9	9.9	23	25.3
Denmark	18130	3.5	931	5.1	2126	11.7	1136	6.3	4193	23.1
Denmark except Haderslev-Sønderborg	17229	4.1	863	5.0	2041	11.9	1025	5.9	3929	22.9

Table II. Large mounds in Denmark.

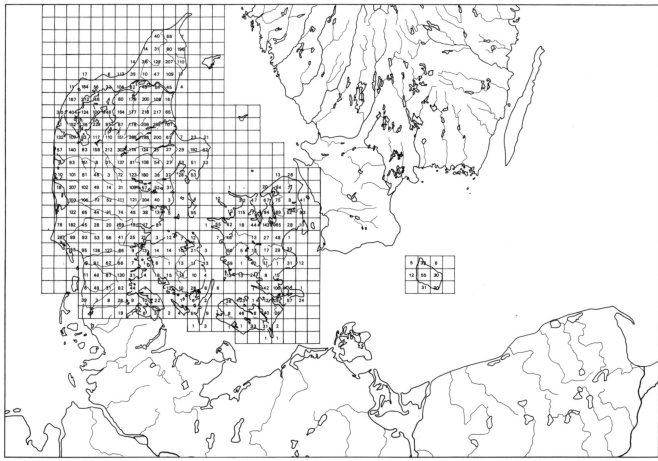

Fig. 12. Large mounds in Denmark. Each square equals c. 109 km².

Erik Bendixen in 1962-63. Around this time E. Aner and K. Kersten had begun their comprehensive work of publishing finds from the Early Bronze Age in Denmark, but part one appeared in print only in 1973. I have made no revisions here in the light of this work.

In this paper a large mound refers to a round mound with a height of 2 m or more. This definition was used by the Prehistoric Section (Department I) of the National Museum when Denmark's prehistoric monuments were registered (Mathiassen 1957, 9 f.). These large mounds belong primarily to the Early Bonze Age, but a few are from the Iron Age and some may contain unrecognized megalithic graves from the Late Stone Age. Experience shows that large mounds from periods other than the Bronze Age are few compared to the known Bronze Age mounds. It would be possible to work out, through a study of the records, the probable percentage of large mounds from other periods, but this has not been done in

this paper. Also long barrows were recorded. About ten of these in Jutland with Bronze Age finds are included here.

The tables and maps include demolished large mounds and also damaged mounds reported to have been at least 2 m high before damage was inflicted. Furthermore, there is a group of damaged Bronze Age mounds, now of reduced height, which cannot with absolute certainty be assigned to the group of large mounds. These categories of damaged mounds are listed according to county in Table II.

Figures 12-13: Maps of large mounds in Denmark. In the squared map in fig. 12 each square indicates the number of large mounds. Each square corresponds to c. 109 km². The map may serve as a basis for statistical comparisons with similar maps of different groups of Bronze Age finds. Figure 13 shows the large mounds per 1,000 *tønder land*, according to parish. The value for Denmark as a whole, as defined by the frontiers after 1682, is stated as 2.6/1,000 *tønder land*, which is regarded as the mean value (M) for the parishes. Parishes are then divided into the following groups: >2 M, >M – 2 M, >0.5 M – M, and – 0.5 M. Due to some variation in area calculation, M has in some cases been given as 2.5, which does not affect the results.

There is a marked predominance of mounds in Jutland, as appears from the maps and Table II. A quick comparison with earlier maps gives the impression that the mound distribution map in fig. 13 is an inversion of the cultivation maps for 1682 and 1866 (figs. 1-2). The distribution of large mounds in Jutland is in general agreement with the distribution of podsolics in fig. 5 but also penetrates deeply into the heavily podsolized area of West Jutland. The brown earths in Thisted county also have a high density of mounds.

CULTIVATION AND THE DISTRIBUTION OF LARGE MOUNDS

The disparity between the distribution of large mounds and the subsequent pattern of cultivation may be interpreted in one of two ways:

A. The people who built the grave mounds exploited the most fertile land, i.e. the brown earths, to a very limited extent compared to the contemporary exploitation of podsolics.

B. The prolonged and increasingly widespread cultivation in subsequent periods has removed the greater part of the large mounds which at one time existed also on brown earths.

In order to determine the correlation between destruction of mounds and the development of cultivation I have used Spearman's rank correlation formula:

$$r = 1 - \frac{6 \, \Sigma \, d^2}{n(n^2 - 1)}$$

The two sets of values to be compared are ranked so that the cultivation percentage for each county is placed in descending order; the density of mounds is arranged likewise. *n* refers to the number of units, *d* to the difference between two rank numbers. There are 18 counties involved. If we take as a basis the number of large mounds per 1,000 *tønder land* in each county (Table II) and compare

Fig. 13. Large mounds in Denmark per 1,000 *tønder land*.

>2 M	>5.2	red
>M–2 M	>2.6–5.2	blue
>M/2–M	>1.3–2.6	yellow
0–M/2	0–1.3	green

County	Large mounds per 1.000 tnd. land rank	% cultivated area in 1682 rank	d	d²
Thisted	1	11	-10	100
Viborg	2	13	-11	121
Ålborg	3	15	-12	144
Skanderborg	4	14	-10	100
Randers	5	7	-2	4
Ringkøbing	6	17	-11	121
Hjørring	7	16	-9	81
Ribe	8	18	-10	100
Frederiksborg	9	10	-1	1
København	10	1	9	81
Holbæk	11	4	7	49
Præstø	12	8	4	16
Vejle	13	12	1	1
Århus	14	5	9	81
Maribo	15	9	6	36
Sorø	16	6	10	100
Odense	17	2	15	225
Svendborg	18	3	15	225
Σ			0	1586

Table III. Calculation of rank correlation according to Spearman. Large mounds and percentage of cultivated area.

them to the percentage of cultivated land in each county in the year 1682 (Table I), we get the results in Table III. With the values 18 and 1586 inserted in the formula the rank correlation is −0.64. Similarly, for the years 1866, 1907 and 1955 the rank correlation works out at −0.76, −0.82 and −0.73, respectively. This is a marked negative correlation, i.e. a high density of mounds corresponds to a low degree of cultivation. The negative correlation is greatest in 1866 and 1907 and somewhat less marked in 1682.

If we use the figures for damaged mounds, we get instead a positive correlation. The total percentage of damaged Bronze Age mounds listed in Table II is used as a basis, after which the counties are ranked according to the number of mounds and the cultivated area; the two are then compared. The rank correlation for 1682, 1866, 1907 and 1955 becomes 0.48, 0.56, 0.57, and 0.36, respectively.

Changes in the amount of land under cultivation between the chosen years can also be used for comparison with the number of damaged burial mounds. For the periods 1682-1866 (fig. 6), 1866-1907 (fig. 7) and 1907-1955 the values are 0.51, −0.59 and −0.60, respectively. The increase in the cultivated area between 1682 and 1866 thus proves to be correlated to the distribution of damaged mounds, while the increase after 1866 appears to bear no such correlation. This result agrees with those mentioned previously.

However, the time factor also plays a role. A high level of cultivation operating over a long period would involve greater damage to ancient monuments than if an equally high level of cultivation operated over a short period. For this reason I have introduced the term *cultivation intensity* to illustrate further the relationship between cultivation and damage to ancient monuments. Cultivation intensity here means percentage of cultivated area over a certain period of time multiplied by the number of years of the period. The percentage of cultivated land is represented by the mean value of the percentage during the first and last year of the period. According to Table 1 the cultivation intensity for Frederiksborg County during the years 1682-1866 is: $185(0.266 + 0.645) \div 2 = 84.267$. According to Table 4 we get the values 0.53, 0.55 and 0.48 for the periods 1682-1866, 1866-1907 and 1907-55, respectively.

Table 4 also shows that with one exception all counties remain in approximately the same relative position in terms of cultivation intensity in relation to damaged large mounds throughout the period 1682-1907. There is a marked change in the county of Copenhagen after 1907 when urban development clearly takes up much arable land. There were other, smaller changes in the period 1907-55. However, this uniform tendency throughout the period for which figures are available makes it probable that the counties which consistently show the highest cultivation intensity and nowadays have the highest percentage of damaged large mounds would also previously have been most vulnerable to such damage. This means that the four counties with probably the greatest total damage are Odense, Svendborg, Holbæk and Århus. The county of Copenhagen may also be included here. All these counties lie within the brown earth zone (fig. 5). Probably the counties of Ringkøbing, Hjørring, Ålborg and Thisted had the least damage. Of these Thisted lies mainly in a brown earth zone, the others on podsol.

It is likely that other and more advanced methods of calculation may provide a more varied picture of the correlation between cultivation, disturbance of ancient monuments and soil type. The differences within individual counties may also be considerable.

The results of the four correlations we have carried out can be summarized as follows:

1. In view of the negative correlation between the presence of large mounds and the extent of land under cultivation, which is at its highest in 1907 when cultivation reached its maximum, and lowest in 1682 when the extent of land under cultivation was considerably lower, it is probable that cultivation completely changed the original pattern of distribution of Bronze Age mounds. Interpretation B is probable.
2. The correspondence between the present-day distribution of damaged mounds and the extent of land under cultivation shows the degree of destruction that can still be measured. Interpretation B applies.
3. The greatest spread of correlation values (1.11) is obtained by comparing the distribution of damaged mounds with the increase in cultivated area (1682-1866 = 0.51; 1907-55 = −0.60). As the increase in cultivated area between 1682 and 1866 applies mainly to brown earth zones, it follows that interpretation B is more probable than A.
4. If the time factor is taken into consideration by introducing the concept of cultivation intensity, the spread in correlation values becomes only 0.07, with a clear relationship between the distribution of damaged

mounds and cultivation intensity. In that case the greatest disturbance would probably have occurred in the counties of Odense, Svendborg, Holbæk, Århus and Copenhagen, all within the brown earth zone. Interpretation B is more likely than A.

As far as the Danish Bronze Age is concerned this source-critical analysis means that areas with brown earth were more sought after during the Early Bronze Age than the distribution of large mounds would suggest. Whether in later times brown earth zones were exploited more for cultivation than for grazing can only be determined by pollen analyses in different parts of Denmark.

CULTIVATED AREAS DURING THE MIDDLE AGES

If we compare figs. 1-4 with a map of Danish parishes, it appears that parishes with a small area have a high proportion of cultivated land, while parishes with a large area have a low proportion of cultivated land. The formation of parishes must have depended on the size of the population, which in its turn depended on the number of farms the fields could support. The agricultural conditions at the time when parishes were formed must thus have been much the same as in 1682 and later. If this is the case, we would have a map of the relative distribution of cultivated land during the Middle Ages for comparison with the maps for 1682-1955. The map in *fig. 14* is based on 4,107 *tønder* total area as the average for Denmark's 1,720 parishes (towns included), according to the land register of 1682. The total area of Denmark at this time has been put at 7,064,372 *tønder land*, according to the register of 1907.

The map in fig. 14 shows the expected general agreement with the map of the percentages of cultivated area in 1682 (fig. 1), except in North Jutland and in small areas of Central Jutland. In much of the counties of Ål- borg, Randers and Viborg there are far more small pari- shes than the cultivation figures of 1682 would lead us to expect. On a smaller scale the same is true of an area along the Central Jutland ridge in the counties of Skan- derborg and Vejle. There is a similar lack of agreement with the map of "specific *hartkorn*" in 1682, fig. 10. The small parishes in these parts of North and Central Jut- land are the only large continuous area with small pari- shes outside the brown earth zone (fig. 5). What causes this discrepancy?

The formation of parishes was nearly completed in the

Fig. 14. The relative size of parishes. The mean value for Denmark is 4,107 *tønder land*.

>2 M	>8214	red
>M–2 M	>4107–8214	blue
>M/2–M	>2054–4107	yellow
0–M/2	0–2054	green

middle of the 13th century (Christensen 1938, 16 ff.). A map published by A.E. Christensen showing Roman- esque churches, *fig. 15*, i.e. pre-13th century, is in close agreement with the map showing the relative size of pa- rishes (fig. 14). The discrepancy in North Jutland is no- ticeable. However, Christensen also indicates (1938, 20) that surprisingly many churches in North Jutland had been closed down before 1536-1600. There are 111 aban- doned churches in Jutland, i.e. 10.4% of all mediaeval churches in Jutland. In the islands the corresponding figures are 24 and 3.6%. A map of the changing numbers of churches (Christensen 1938, fig. 3) shows that chur- ches were built and abandoned in different regions of Jutland. Churches were closed down mainly within the parts of North and Central Jutland which are characteri- zed by a large number of small parishes on podsolized soil. If we compare the distribution of abandoned me- diaeval churches in Jutland with the distribution of brown earths and podsols, we find that out of 66 chur- ches closed down before 1536, approximately 75% are on podsols and approximately 25% on brown earths. In the first place this means that there was a decrease in cultiva-

74

Fig. 15. The distribution of settlements in Denmark during the 13th century (Christensen 1938, fig. 4).
● Parishes during the Romanesque period
+ Rural monasteries in the 13th century
⬤ Towns in the 13th century

tion in Jutland during the Late Middle Ages, which is already well known. Secondly, it is clear that the decline occurred above all in areas with – for the Midde Ages – an unusually heavy exploitation of podsols.

During the period 1536-1600 a further 44 churches were closed down in Jutland. However, c. 65% of these were on brown earths and c. 35% on podsols. The new churches did not counter-balance those abolished within the same area. The economic and demographic depression in Jutland first affected severely the podsolized areas, but also reached the fertile brown earth zones to the east.

The result of this analysis of the map in fig. 14, showing the relative size of Danish parishes, can be summarized as follows:

1. The map can be used to indicate the relative distribution of cultivated land around 1250 when the forma-

tion of parishes stabilized and the Romanesque churches were built.

2. The cultivated area on the islands around 1250 corresponds largely to that of 1682. In Jutland the cultivated area around 1250 has a more extensive distribution in parts of North and Central Jutland than in the year 1682. The cultivated area there does not increase significantly until after 1866. This is particularly noticeable in Ålborg county (except in the district of Kær).

3. During the Late Middle Ages and the early Renaissance cultivation declined in large parts of Jutland, especially in regions with podsols, which are less fertile than the brown earths. In 1682 the relationship between the relative distribution of cultivated land and the relative proportion of podsols and brown earths stabilized. This also appears from the soil fertility maps for 1682.

Thus the destruction of prehistoric monuments caused by cultivation can be traced on the maps back to approx. 1250, i.e. more than seven centuries. The constantly high level of cultivation on the islands and the easternmost part of Jutland *may* explain the absence of Bronze Age mounds in these regions. The brief increase in cultivation during the Middle Ages in parts of North and Central Jutland could not have affected the number of monuments in the same way. In this context it would also be possible to apply the concept previously used in this paper, viz. "cultivation intensity = percentage of cultivated land during a certain time, multiplied by the number of years of the period." We then use an estimated value for the year 1250. For the period 1250-1682 we get the multiplier 433, which results in a very high degree of cultivation intensity for this period, no matter what reasonable value we accept as the percentage of cultivated area in 1250. This result confirms the impression of the heavy dependence of the number of ancient monuments on the distribution and intensity of cultivation in historic times. The probability of the above hypothesis B thus increases, i.e. prolonged and increasingly widespread cultivation removed most of the large mounds that once existed on brown earths.

This presupposes, however, that other factors did not impede the proposed destruction of prehistoric remains through cultivation. Such impeding factors may be superstition and inefficient cultivation methods (Kristiansen 1984). Surveys of the distribution of cultivation and damaged prehistoric monuments are therefore not sufficient. It is also necessary to examine whether the surviving mounds and other types of prehistoric remains stood in the old cultural landscape, in arable land, common land, heath, or woods (Kristiansen 1984). Such examinations presuppose detailed studies of limited areas.

But the indirect conclusions which might be drawn from all such studies are not entirely satisfactory. A direct answer to the question of the distribution of Bronze Age settlements within an area where the present remains are few would, on the other hand, be provided by a series of pollen analyses, e.g. of the brown earth areas in East Jutland.

CULTIVATION AND BRONZE AGE GRAVE FINDS

Figures 16-17: Maps of Early Bronze Age grave finds, listed in Broholm's *Danmarks Bronzealder* I (: Denmark's Bronze Age) (1943). The isometric map is based on the squared map. The figures in the latter can be compared to the figures for known large mounds on the map in fig. 12. A statistical comparison has not been made in this paper. Such a comparison should be carried out on the basis of

Kersten and Aner's comprehensive study. The isometric map in fig. 17 may, however, be compared for an overall view with the map of large mounds per 1,000 *tønder land* according to county, fig. 13. The correspondence is excellent in North-West Jutland and in the interior of Central Jutland, as well as in North Zealand. In Ålborg county and to the south of Ringkøbing county the finds are under-represented. This can be explained by the low degree of cultivation in the two counties, in Ålborg until 1866 and in Ringkøbing until 1907. Both counties belong to the group which has the lowest cultivation intensity and the lowest percentage of damaged large mounds (Table IV). In Haderslev county, on the other hand, finds are over-represented in comparison with mounds. An exceptionally great number of archaeological investigations have influenced the distribution pattern in this county.

Figures 18-19: Maps of Late Bronze Age finds, from Baudou (1960). The squared map indicates objects from known grave finds from Montelius, periods IV-VI, as well as single finds of such objects. These types of objects, when of known provenance, are always from graves. Single finds of these artefacts must therefore mark the site of destroyed graves. They include knives, razors, pincers, pins, buttons, all of specifically Jutland types

County	Damaged large mounds		1682-1866 number for comparison		1866-1907 number for comparison		1907-1955 number for comparison	
	%	rank		rank		rank		rank
Odense	56.7	1	113.590	2	32.928	1	37.338	1
Svendborg	43.4	2	110.352	3	31.794	4	36.481	4
Holbæk	37.2	3	104.895	5	30.681	7	36.432	6
Vejle	35.9	4	82.140	11	28.539	9	34.913	8
Århus	34.9	5	107.393	4	32.088	3	36.677	3
Skanderborg	32.7	6	72.705	12	25.557	12	31.262	14
Ribe	30.2	7	46.528	17	18.816	17	28.592	16
Frederiksborg	29.6	8	84.267	10	27.825	10	29.964	15
Præstø	27.6	9	100.640	7	30.891	6	35.942	7
Sorø	26.5	10	104.618	6	31.626	5	36.750	2
Viborg	24.3	11	64.195	14	23.184	13	32.512	10
København	23.5	12	120.250	1	32.529	2	32.316	11
Randers	23.0	13	89.448	9	27.153	11	33.957	9
Ringkøbing	19.9	14	40.145	18	16.443	18	26.901	18
Thisted	19.7	15	64.473	13	20.622	16	27.514	17
Maribo	17.5	16	96.293	8	30.450	8	36.456	5
Ålborg	11.3	17	58.368	15	21.693	15	31.532	13
Hjørring	7.0	18	57.628	16	22.218	14	31.899	12

Table IV. Basis for the calculation of rank correlation according to Spearman. Percentage of damaged large mounds, and cultivation intensity during different periods.

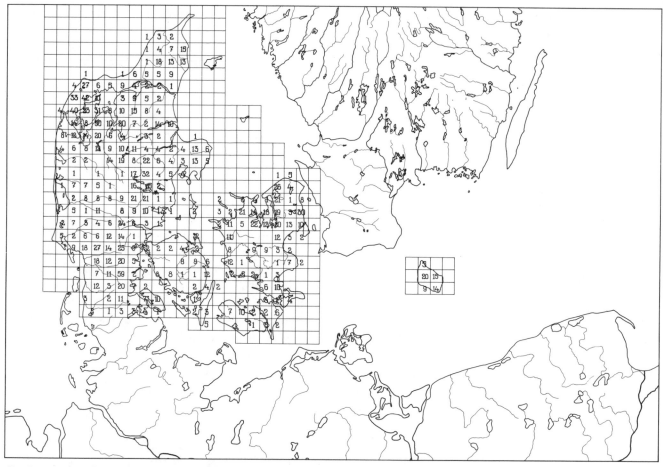

Fig. 16. Number of Early Bronze Age grave finds, Montelius, periods I-III.

(Baudou 1960). The graves are predominantly secondary graves in large mounds. A small number of graves are on level ground, especially those from period VI in South Jutland and Bornholm (Broholm 1949). Small mounds with period VI finds are, however, more common throughout Denmark (Broholm 1949, 94).

If settlements during the Late Bronze Age had the same distribution as during the Early Bronze Age, the maps in figs. 18-19 should be in close agreement with the mound distribution maps in figs. 12-13. In North Jutland and North Zealand there is, indeed, a better correspondence than between the distribution of Early Bronze Age grave finds and mounds. This closer correspondence is found particularly in Ålborg county. This is undoubtedly because cultivation there increased greatly between 1866 and 1907. At this time there was a fast growing interest in the past, and several collections acquired much material. The southern part of Ringkøbing county may be strongly under-represented on account of the low degree of cultivation as late as 1907, whereas Haderslev county – because of the many archaeological excavations – tends towards over-representation, as is the case with Early Bronze Age grave finds. If one takes such considerations of source critical conditions into account, one gets the impression that there is a close correspondence between the distribution of settlements in Denmark during the Early and the Late Bronze Ages.

Such a comparison is, however, far too crude. It is necessary to follow the changes period by period. That would take us too far from the subject of this paper. It also presents certain problems, e.g. as regards the dating of a number of artefact types. Even more problematical are the many graves lacking grave offerings. What is the proportion of datable graves to the total number of graves within any one period? Has this proportion changed from one period to the next? This is a representativity

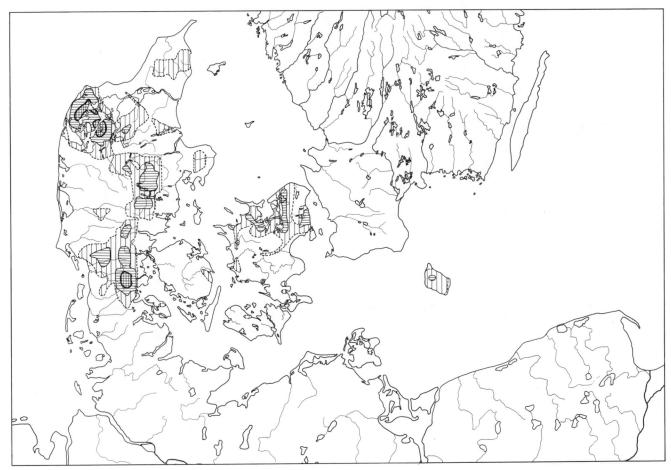

Fig. 17. Isometric map showing the number of Early Bronze Age finds Montelius, periods I-III. Thin line delimits M = 18. Thick line delimits 2 M = 36. Hatched line delimits M/2 = 9.

problem of a kind which is important for archaeological studies of settlements but falls outside the scope of this paper.

SUMMARY

The study of the representativity of surviving prehistoric monuments is an essential form of archaeological source criticism. Among the factors affecting the quantity of prehistoric remains, cultivation during historic times is probably the most important.

Material and analysis

1. The distribution of cultivated areas in Denmark has been mapped, on the basis of statistical data, in percentages for each county for the years 1682, 1866, 1907 and 1955.

2. A map of the relative size of parishes shows the relative extent of the cultivated area at the time when parishes were formed. The parish divisions were completed when the building of the numerous Romanesque churches ended around 1250.

3. The maps showing cultivation between 1250 and 1955, cultivation increase, and soil fertility are compared to a map showing the distribution of podsol and brown earth areas.

4. The large mounds, which are predominantly from the Bronze Age, have been mapped. Damaged or demolished large mounds have been indicated and correlated to the development of cultivation.

5. Early and Late Bronze Age grave finds have been mapped and compared to the distribution of the large mounds.

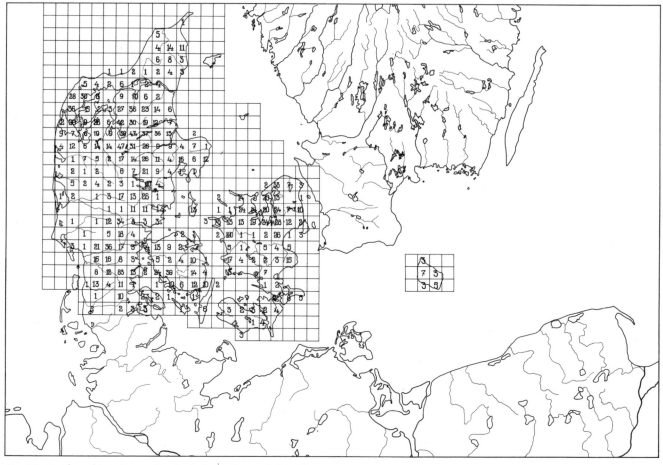

Fig. 18. Number of Late Bronze Age finds, Montelius, periods IV-VI.

Results

1. *Cultivation* around 1250 covers primarily the brown earth areas on the islands, in East Jutland and in Thisted county but also parts of the podsol areas in North and Central Jutland. There is a marked decline within the podsol zone during the Late Middle Ages. In 1682 the broad outlines of cultivation are in close agreement with the distribution of brown earths and podsols. Up to 1866 there is a great increase in the already large cultivated area on the islands and in East Jutland. The common lands are probably brought into cultivation. By contrast, from 1866 to 1907 the greatest cultivation increase occurs in Jutland's podsol area. From 1907 to 1955 the pronounced increase continues in the counties of Ringkøbing and Ribe, which are the most heavily podsolized zone. The cultivated areas of Copenhagen and Frederiksborg counties are greatly reduced, whereas the other counties remain fairly stable.

2. The *destruction* of large Bronze Age mounds, as measured in terms of damaged and demolished mounds, is correlated with intensive cultivation. The connection between damage and cultivation increase is particularly noticeable on the islands and in East Jutland, 1682-1866. The tendency is increased if we introduce the concept of "cultivation intensity", which incorporates a time factor. This would suggest that prolonged and increasingly widespread cultivation has removed most of the large mounds that once existed in brown earth zones. Detailed studies of mound destruction on a different basis may question this result. A series of pollen analyses should provide more reliable information on the distribution of Bronze Age settlements.

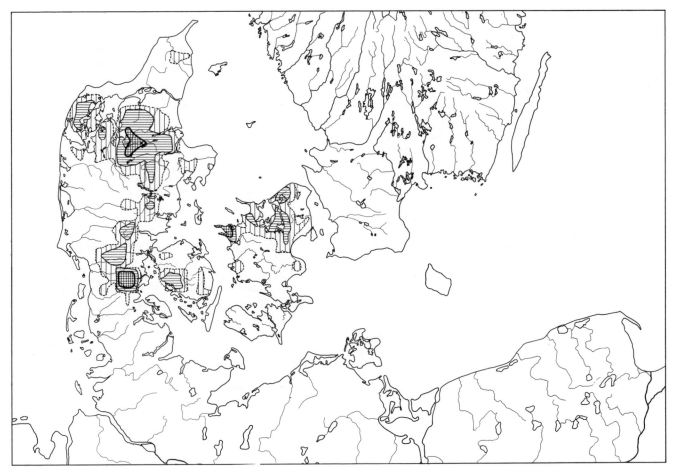

Fig. 19. Isometric map showing the number of Late Bronze Age finds Montelius, periods IV-VI. Thick line delimits 2 M = 10. Thin line delimits M = 20.5. Hatched line delimits M/2 = 41.

3. *The distribution of Early and Late Bronze Age grave finds* can be adjusted to make a pattern which is probably representative of the distribution of mounds if we take into consideration the influence of cultivation, collecting activities, and the extent of archaeological excavations.

4. *The problem concerning the representativity of Bronze Age finds and monuments* is very evident. All interpretations which start from factors concerning spatial distribution will be precariously based as long as the source-critical research has not taken the influence of recent cultivation into consideration.

Evert Baudou,
Department of Archaeology,
Umeå University,
90187 Umeå,
Sweden

Hartkorn: Danish unit of land valuation based on estimated productivity.

Tønder land: Danish measure of land equal to c. 0.55 hectares or 1.36 acres.

Mil: 1 Danish *mil* equals 4.68 statute miles, or 7.532 km.

NOTES

1. The maps in figs. 1-4, 6-7, 12 and 16-19 and the diagrams in figs. 8-9 in this paper were presented in a lecture given to the Royal Society of Northern Antiquaries in Copenhagen on January 21, 1964. A large part of the results and the discussion in the following pages were given then. Until March 1966 I revised the problem and results in lectures given to the archaeological institutes at the universities of Bergen, Göteborg and Oslo, the Institute of Cultural Geography at the University of Stockholm, and the Geographical Society in Stockholm.

2. In 1682 the land was measured in Zealand square *alen* (Pedersen 1928, 15). One thousand Zealand *alen* equalled 1,007 *alen* in later statistics, i.e. 1,000 Zealand square *alen* equals 1,014.049 square *alen* in later statistics (1 *alen* = 0.6277 m). I have multiplied all figures for 1682 (Table I, column 8 in Pedersen 1928) by 1.014 to make them comparable to the figures for the total parish area. As a standard measurement for parish and county areas I have used the figures for 1907 (cf. *Statistisk Tabelværk* 1909, 10).

3. *Statistisk Tabelværk* of 1868 states: "Total area exploited (sown fields, land used for pasture, hay meadow, fallow, water meadow and common land)". The three types of field, pasture, hay and fallow, are included in the arable land, while common lands and water meadows are not. In order to get values comparable with 1682 I have used only the figures for the first three types of field, *not* the figures for "total area exploited". The same has been done with the statistics of 1907 (*Statistisk Tabelværk* 1909, Table I). The figures for the total area have been reduced by land other than cultivated fields, i.e. columns Nos. 37 (meadow), 38 (water meadow), 39 (common land) and 40-48 (gardens, woods, roads, building sites and farmyards, expanses of water etc.).

REFERENCES ·

AAKJÆR, S. 1928. Indledning. Pedersen 1928:5*-62*.

ANER, E. – KERSTEN, K. 1973. *Die Funde der älteren Bronzezeit des Nordischen Kreises in Dänemark, Schleswig-Holstein und Niedersachsen.* Band I. Frederiksborg und Københavns Amt. Neumünster.

BAUDOU, E. 1960. Die regionale und chronologische Einteilung der jüngeren Bronzezeit im Nordischen Kreis. *Acta Universitatis Stockholmiensis. Studies in North-European Archaeology* 1. Stockholm.

– 1968. Forntida bebyggelse i Ångermanlands kustland. Arkeologiska undersökningar av ångermanländska kuströsen. *Arkiv för norrländsk hembygdsforskning* XVII:1-209. Örnsköldsvik.

BEGTRUP, G. 1803-1812. *Beskrivelse over Agerdyrkningens Tilstand i Danmark.* Kjøbenhavn.

BROHOLM, H.C. 1943. *Danmarks Bronzealder* I. Samlede Fund fra den Ældre Bronzealder. København.

– 1949. *Danmarks Bronzealder* IV. Danmarks Kultur i den Yngre Bronzealder. København.

CHRISTENSEN, A.K. 1938. Danmarks befolkning og bebyggelse i middelalderen. *Nordisk Kultur* II:1-57. Stockholm-Oslo-København.

HANSEN, K. 1943. Planteavlen. *Det danske Landbrugs Historie* II:5-279. København.

HANSEN, S. 1973. Geologische Einleitung. Aner, E. – Kersten, K. 1973: XV-XXXIV.

KRISTIANSEN, K. 1984. Early Bronze Age Burial Finds. (This volume).

MATHIASSEN, Th. 1957. Oldtidsminderne og fredningsloven. *Fra Nationalmuseets Arbejdsmark* 1957:5-14. København.

PEDERSEN, H. 1928. *De danske Landbrug fremstillet paa Grundlag af Forarbejderne til Christian V.s Matrikel 1688.* København.

MELDAHL, C. 1877. Bemærkninger om Hartkornskaartet. *Statistisk Tabelværk.* 3. Række, Bind 32: LXV-LXVII. Kjöbenhavn.

Statistisk Tabelværk. 1868. 3. Række, 11. Bind. Tabeller over Störrelsen af det besaaede Areal og Udsæden i Kongeriget Danmark den 16de Juli 1866. Udgivet af det statistiske Bureau. Kjöbenhavn.

Statistisk Tabelværk. 1877. 3. Række, 32. Bind. Tabeller over Hartkornets Fordeling i Kongeriget Danmark den 1ste April 1873. Udgivet af det statistiske Bureau. Kjöbenhavn.

Statistisk Tabelværk. 1909. 5. Række, Litra C Nr. 3. Arealets Benyttelse i Danmark den 15. juli 1907. Udgivet af Statens statistiske Bureau. København.

Late Paleolithic Finds

by ANDERS FISCHER

INTRODUCTION

At the height of the Weichsel Glaciation, ice covered the larger part or perhaps the whole of the area now called Denmark[1]. It has not yet been established with any certainty when the ice sheet retreated again from the various parts of the country. However, it seems certain that the whole country became ice-free before the Bölling period, i.e. before 11,000 B.C. (Berglund 1976, 37-38). The subject of this paper is the time between the disappearance of the glaciers and the beginning of the present warm period (c. 8,300 B.C.) (Tauber 1970, table 2). Until recently this period, covering several millennia, has been an almost unknown part of Danish prehistory.

A few years ago C.J. Becker published the single find of a flint point (Becker 1970, see also Tromnau 1974, fig. 3), which indicated that people of the "Hamburg Culture" may have moved into the Danish region shortly after the disappearance of the ice cap[2]. Definite evidence of man's presence, in the form of settlement finds, is however, not available until the "Tanged Point Technocomplex", scientifically dated to the Allerød and Younger Dryas periods (Fischer 1978).

This paper is a source critical consideration of the Danish material from the latter group. This preliminary investigation is limited to the two most frequent and most intensively studied categories of finds, viz. the settlements and the single finds of tanged points. I shall first put forward some observations concerning the general representativity (cf. Kristiansen 1976:124) of these categories. I shall then assess the information value of the finds in relation to a set of specific problems: to what extent is the horizontal distribution of the objects – at the regional and local level and internally with regard to the individual settlements – representative of the original pattern of distribution?

WHICH FINDS BELONG TO THE LATE PALEOLITHIC TANGED POINT COMPLEX?

The first and fundamental question of this study is: which finds are Late Paleolithic? Only a few finds can be assigned to the period by means of scientific dating. It appears from the literature that a number of specialists in the Old Stone Age have believed it possible to assign to this period finds which are not scientifically dated (e.g. Mathiassen 1946, 164 ff.; Taute 1968, 95 ff.; Becker 1971). In all these cases the dating has been based on purely typological criteria. Unfortunately, it has not so far been clearly defined which finds can be regarded as definite or probable Late Paleolithic. Taking the scientifically dated settlement finds as basis, it appears that most Late Paleolithic flint types can hardly be clearly distinguished in size, shape and method of manufacture from those known from other periods.

The most characteristic of the Late Paleolithic flint types is the tanged point (for a general description of this type see Taute 1968, 11). This shows considerable variation in shape and size throughout the period in question. It is most easily distinguished from other related tool forms from previous and subsequent periods during the earliest and latest parts of the Tanged Point Complex. The Appendix contains a provisional definition of the indubitable Late Paleolithic tanged points from the earlier part of the complex. Only those tanged points which conform to this definition are included in the following discussion. Where the other flint types (cores, flakes, scrapers and burins)[3] are single finds, they cannot usually be assigned with any certainty to the Tanged Point Complex. Such single finds are therefore not included in the following discussion. Settlements from the Tanged Point Complex are, however, discussed in the paper. A settlement, in this paper, refers to a site where more than

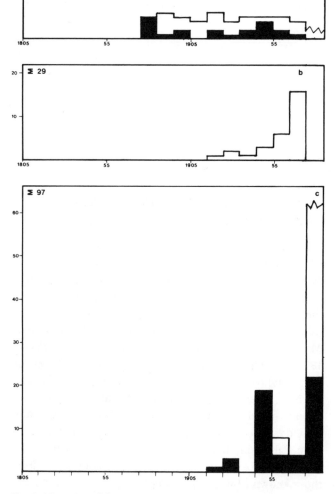

Fig. 1. Histogram of the year of registration, year of discovery and year in which single finds of tanged points are reported in the literature.
a. Year of registration of tanged points belonging to public museums. Those in the National Museum are represented by shading.
b. Year of discovery of tanged points in private ownership (no information on fifteen examples).
c. Year in which the tanged points are first mentioned in the literature (Jessen & Nordmann 1915, 52-55; Ekholm 1925, 4; Mathiassen 1946, 167-170; 1959, 20 and 142-145; Johansson 1964, 265-267; Taute 1968, 95; Magnussen 1976, 3-13; plus the present paper). Finds in public museums are shaded.

three artefacts which can be typologically assigned to the Tanged Point Complex have been found within an area at most 30 metres in diameter.

GENERAL REPRESENTATIVITY

Both the tanged points discovered as single finds and most of the artefacts found in settlements are made of

flint. This raw material is so durable that in practical terms we can assume that all the artefacts produced have been preserved until today. The only problem therefore is how much of the surviving material has been found, and how much of that found is available for systematic examination.

The unspectacular nature of these finds is clearly its most important negative source critical factor. Experience shows that most people in Denmark would not notice anything unusual if they walked over a place where many Late Paleolithic flints were lying clearly visible on the ground. Actually, it is only people who have already learnt to distinguish man-made flints from natural stones who have found the tanged points and settlements mentioned in this paper.

None of the thirty Late Paleolithic settlements now known has been found in connection with "ordinary" economic activities. Archaeological surveys account for 28 of the sites. These were all found in areas where the ground was not covered by vegetation – 26 on cultivated ground, one on a beach and one in shallow water near a beach. Of the remaining two settlements, one was discovered during the professional excavation of a passage grave, while all we know of the other is that it was "found on the fields of Fjellerup". Similar conditions apply to the single finds of tanged points. Of the total of 51 such artefacts, with adequate find data, 47 were found on cultivated ground.

Relatively few square metres of the Danish ploughland have been so intensively surveyed by flint experts that any visible tanged points have been identified and collected. Furthermore, only a small percentage of the tanged points would have been visible on the surface of the top soil at the time of the survey. Finally, some of the existing tanged points doubtless lie beneath the depth of ploughing. All things considered this means that only a very small part of the surviving tanged points have yet been found. Much the same is true of the settlements.

Even when a Late Paleolithic artefact has been found and incorporated into a public or private collection, it does not follow that it is easily available for study. The absence so far of clear definitions by which to distinguish Late Paleolithic artefacts from similar types from other periods has meant that the true age of many Late Paleolithic finds has not been recognized. As a result, we may assume that some of the finds have been stored in such a way that they are difficult to find in amateur and museum collections. This assumption seems confirmed by a survey of material in the store rooms of the National Museum in Copenhagen. This indicates that only about half of this museum's accessions of single finds of tanged points of undoubted Late Paleolithic age are to be found in the appropriate boxes. The remainder are found in boxes with single finds of other flint types or are in cases with various surface collections of flint artefacts. The same is probably the case of most of the other collections in Denmark.

A great many public and private collections contain finds from the Tanged Point Complex. There was not sufficient time during the present study to permit the search of all public collections where one might expect to find relevant material[4]. Furthermore it is probable that a very lengthy examination of the archives in the museums visited would provide information on a number of definite Late Paleolithic tanged points in private ownership. However, such an examination has not been carried out and the following registration of finds in private ownership is therefore based primarily on the author's personal contact with a small number of the many Danish amateur archaeologists. For this reason it may be expected that the number of finds in private ownership is markedly underrepresented compared to finds in public museums. It should also be mentioned that the author knows of a number of possible Late Paleolithic finds which for various reasons were not available for the present investigation. The finds analysed in this paper thus comprise a very small proportion of the Late Paleolithic source material which has survived up to the present day. How much material has survived altogether cannot be judged from the available data. Nor is it possible to decide, therefore, the proportion of the available material to that originally deposited.

Figures 1 & 2 show that a future increase in Late Paleolithic source material may be expected. Figure 1a indicates that the combined accessions of single finds of tanged points to all museums have been fairly constant from the 1870's onwards. In the periods 1875 to 1885 and 1945 to 1965 the National Museum acquired most of the tanged points recorded in this paper, while in the other decades most went to local museums. It appears from fig. 1b that the find group is far from exhausted. In recent decades private collections have been augmented by a steadily rising number of tanged points. Furthermore, it appears from fig. 1c that until now only a very small proportion of tanged points in private ownership has been mentioned in the literature.

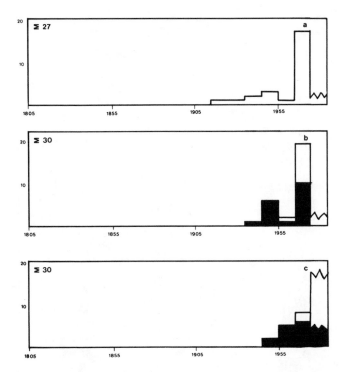

Fig. 2. Histogram showing year of discovery, year of identification, and year in which reported in the literature of Late Paleolithic settlements.
a. Year of discovery (where known).
b. Year in which individual settlements were recognized as being of Late Paleolithic age. Finds in public museums shaded.
c. Year in which settlements were first mentioned in the literature (Berg 1941; Mathiassen 1946, 121 ff. and 168; 1959, 20; Johansson 1964, 265; Andersen 1970 and 1977; Becker 1971; Rasmussen 1972; Holm 1973; Fischer 1976; plus the present paper). Finds from settlements owned partly or wholly by public museums are shaded.

The number of settlement finds is also increasing. The first definite Late Paleolithic settlement (Fjellerup Mark) was registered in 1890, and in the period from 1920 until 1940 three further settlements with tanged points were found (fig. 2a), but their chronological position was not recognized. Erik Westerby who found the Bromme settlement in 1944 was the first to realize that sites with these artefacts were of Late Paleolithic age (Westerby 1946). Since then the number of settlements from the Tanged Point Complex which have been found and recognized as such has increased rapidly during two periods: in the decade 1945-1955, and from 1965 to the present day (fig. 2b). These two peaks reflect periods when the Late Paleolithic has received particular attention from archaeologists and when highly trained personnel have carried out special surveys to find such sites.

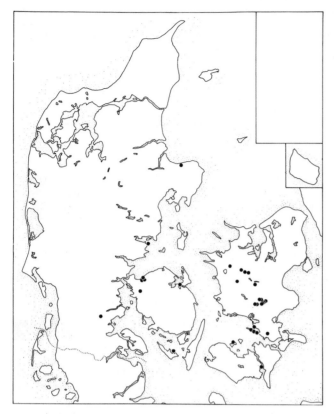

Fig. 3. Distribution of Danish settlements from the Late Paleolithic Tanged Point Complex.

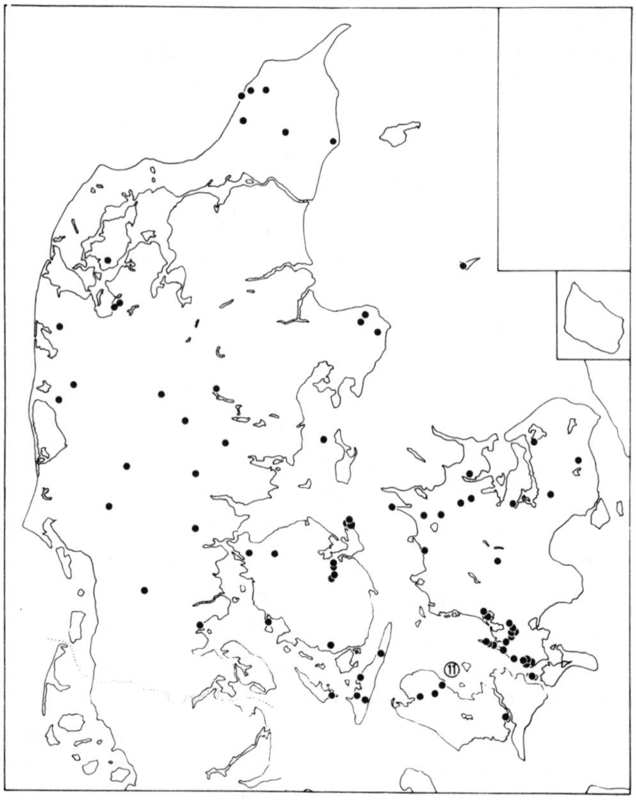

Fig. 4. Distribution of single finds of tanged points from the Danish Late Paleolithic (only finds which conform to the definition in the Appendix are included).

SPECIFIC REPRESENTATIVITY

Regional Distribution of Finds

Practically all the finds mentioned here were collected by people with expert knowledge of flint artefacts. Although this special group of people has been busy in many different parts of Denmark, their collecting activities are unlikely to have been evenly spread over the whole country. It should therefore be born in mind that the number of finds in each region is not necessarily proportional to the number of artefacts originally left there. Since the author's main contact has been with museums and private collections in East Denmark, it must be assumed that the sample discussed in this paper is not geographically representative. Thus the number of finds per region can hardly be taken as a measure of how intensively Late Paleolithic populations exploited different areas.

The settlement finds indicate that Late Paleolithic populations at least exploited the Danish islands and East-

ern Jutland (fig. 3). It is less certain whether the single finds of tanged points can be used to map the presence of Late Paleolithic peoples. Tanged points probably functioned as points to hunting weapons, so we cannot exclude the possibility that these artefacts may have been carried a considerable distance from the place they were used, in the body of a wounded animal. In practice, however, tanged points would seldom have ended up more than a few kilometres from the spot where man used them. Moreover, there are indications that many of the places where there have been so-called single finds of tanged points may prove to be definite settlements from the Tanged Point Complex after more intensive surveying. If we exercise some caution, we can assume single finds of tanged points to be evidence of the presence of Late Paleolithic peoples in the close vicinity of their place of discovery. If that is the case, fig. 4 would indicate that already during the period of the Tanged Point Complex, the northern limit of human habitation was north of present-day Denmark. However, the source material available cannot clarify the actual structure of the regional distribution of Late Paleolithic settlement.

Local Distribution of Finds

There is, however, a greater chance that distribution patterns are representative of the original situation if we look at the distribution of finds in particular parts of Denmark. This applies, for instance, to the area around Holmegård Bog and the adjacent swampy basins in Southern Mid-Zealand. In recent years the stretches of cultivated ground bordering on this bog complex have several times been systematically surveyed with a view to mapping local Stone Age settlements (Fischer, Grønnow & Petersen 1978). In this connection it has been registered how frequently and intensively the different parts of the area have been surveyed. In this way it should be possible to provide a relatively accurate estimate of how representative is the observed distribution pattern of finds with respect to the total number of Late Paleolithic flint artefacts in the farmland topsoil of the area. Since the surveys are not yet completed, there are as yet no final results. However, it is likely that the distribution of presently known sites will be roughly representative of the total Late Paleolithic settlement in this former lake area. It can immediately be seen from fig. 5 that the finds are not evenly distributed along the former lake shores. All sites lie on the edge of the largest lake basin. There is, furthermore, a clear tendency for most, and apparently also the richest, sites around the basin to cluster near the inlet and outlet of the Suså River. Similar conditions, incidentally, apply to the location of Late Paleolithic settlements in other intensively surveyed bog areas – e.g. Åmose, West Zealand (cf. table 1). It seems likely, therefore, that this distribution of lake-side settlements will prove to be representative of the original situation.

Assuming that settlements were located primarily with a view to maximizing the output from the subsistence activities carried out from them, this distribution pattern would seem to indicate that fishing played a major role in the Late Paleolithic subsistence strategy.

Intra-settlements Distribution

If the perspective is narrowed further to observe the internal distribution of artefacts within settlements, there is an even greater chance of establishing a representative

distribution pattern. This is possible because a large proportion of the known Late Paleolithic settlements have been excavated. Most excavations have been carried out within the present decade, and their results have therefore only been published to a limited extent as yet. In this respect, the fact that the excavations have been carried out relatively late can be seen as a distinct advantage from the source critical point of view. In contrast to earlier excavations (e.g. at Bromme) it has been widely realized in recent years that the horizontal distribution of artefacts in settlements may contribute valuable information on the prehistoric way of life. As a result, there has been considerable emphasis on excavating as large a part of the sites as possible. Moreover, in most cases there has been a deliberate effort to eliminate sampling errors by sieving all excavated earth through finemeshed sieves. Finally, all objects found have been brought back and stored, together with its relevant data, so that the initial artefact classification can always be checked and if necessary extended or altered.

When studying Late Paleolithic settlements it should be borne in mind that artefacts may have been removed from their original context by periglacial soil movement. It has long been known that the horizontal distribution of artefacts may be disturbed by solifluction (Mathiassen 1946, p. 128), and more examples of this kind have since been added. Excavations in recent years have also revealed cases where objects have been pushed up into higher,

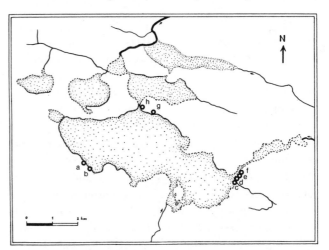

Fig. 5. Distribution of Tanged Point settlements at Holmegård Bog and adjacent swampy basins (no single finds of tanged points known from this area).
a. Fensmark Skydebane, b. Trollesgave, c. Stoksbjerg Vest, d. Stoksbjerg Syd, e. Stoksbjerg Bro II, f. Stoksbjerg Bro I, g. Sømose, h. Broksø.

Status of finds as of 16 October 1978		Distance from former lake less than 100 m, distance from former stream greater than 100 m.	Distance from former lake greater than 100 m, distance from former stream less than 100 m.	Distance from former lake less than 100 m, distance from former stream less than 100 m.	Distance from former lake greater than 100 m, distance from former stream greater than 100 m	Topographic context unknown.
Single finds of tanged points	Number	9	5	2	14	67
	% of total number with known topographic context	30.0	16.7	6.7	46.7	
Settle-ments	Number	9	2	10	7	2
	% of total number with known topographic context	32.1	7.1	35.7	25.0	

Table 1.
Topographic position of single finds of tanged points and of settlements of the Tanged Point Complex from the Danish Late Paleolithic. Determination of the topographic situation for most finds is based only on modern 1:20.000 maps. It cannot be assumed that all lakes and streams of that period can be demonstrated from these maps. It should therefore be pointed out that the sites may have been more »water-associated« than appears from the table.

more recent deposits. Large objects have been particularly prone to such vertical displacement. If the higher levels contain no artefacts from later settlements, this type of frost disturbance entails no serious problems in the study of the lay-out of the settlements. Indeed, in some ways such displacements may be regarded as a positive source critical factor. Several of the best preserved settlement deposits from the Danish Late Paleolithic were identified solely because a few, but large and characteristic, artefacts lay in the cultivated topsoil, whereas the rest of the culture layer was found, well-protected, up to several decimetres below the bottom of the ploughzone.

From publications so far it appears that the different types of flint artefact have by no means a random distribution in Late Paleolithic settlements (Andersen 1973, fig. 10-17; Fischer & Mortensen 1976, fig. 3, 1977, fig. 4-7, and 1978, fig. 2-5). It can therefore be expected that the horizontal distribution of artefacts in settlements will prove a valuable basis for the testing of hypotheses on the economic activities, group size etc. of Late Paleolithic peoples.

Anders Fischer,
The National Agency for the Protection of Nature,
Monuments and Sites,
Amaliegade 13,
1256 Copenhagen K.

Acknowledgments

The author wishes to express his appreciation towards the people and institutions who have made available finds and data for this study. Special thanks for valuable information on finds in private ownership are due to Professor C.J. Becker (Copenhagen), Museum Assistant J. Holm (Tullebølle), Teacher A.D. Johansson (Lundby), Teacher J. Rasmussen (Ringsted), Stud.mag. F. Rieck (Aller), and Lecturer E.B. Petersen (Copenhagen). I should also like to thank Stud.mag. Bjarne Grønnow (Copenhagen) for information on Neolithic blade arrowheads. Finally, I wish to thank the governing body of Japetus Steen-strup's Awards for a contribution to the travel expenses incurred during this study.

NOTES

1. Until now it has been believed that during the last glaciation ice covered the whole of Denmark with the exception of South West Jutland. Recently it has been claimed, however, that this region too was covered by ice (Marcussen & Østergård 1977).
2. According to the latest pollen analyses, the "Hamburg Culture" should probably be assigned to the Bølling period (Ussinger 1975, 123 and 136).
3. *Federmessers* and similar small points with backing retouch are only present in such small numbers in Denmark (cf. Petersen 1974 and Andersen 1977, 24-26) that they are not considered in this paper.
4. In connection with this study the author has been in contact with the following public museums: Danmarks Nationalmuseum (Copenhagen), Forhistorisk Museum – Moesgård (Århus), Fyns Stiftsmuseum (Odense), Holbæk Museum, Kalundborg og Omegns Museum, Langelands Museum (Rudkøbing), Lolland-Falsters Stiftsmuseum (Maribo), Jens Hansens Søfartsmuseum (Marstal), Næstved Museum, Ringkøbing Museum, Silkeborg Museum, Svendborg og Omegns Museum, Sydsjællands Museum (Vordingborg) and Vendsyssels Historiske Museum (Hjørring).

APPENDIX

The Late Paleolithic Tanged Point – a Preliminary Definition

By no means all Late Paleolithic tanged points can at present be distinguished with reasonable certainty from similar types from earlier or later periods. Some of the probable "chronologically unmixed" settlement deposits from the earlier part of the Tanged Point Complex (see Fischer 1978) have yielded a few tanged points which in form and size approach the range of variation for certain Mesolithic and Neolithic tool types (Mathiassen 1948, Nos. 17, 23 & 24; Glob 1952, No. 260). Similarly, in settlements from the middle and recent parts of the Tanged Point Complex may be found points which approach the range of variation for either "Hamburgian" shouldered points (Tromnau 1975, 35-41), or oblique arrowheads of the "Kongemose Culture" (Petersen 1977, 152-53) or "Pitted Ware" blade arrowheads (Becker 1951, 188-89; Malmer 1969, 45-50).

I regard as Late Paleolithic tanged points those flint tools which conform to the following criteria:

1. Retouch on both edges of the tang and any retouch of the point should be carried out from the bulb-side of the flake.
2. The shortest tang retouch should be longer than the longest tang retouch divided by 1.5 ($x > y/1.5$, see fig. 6).
3. The length should be equal to or larger than double the shortest tang retouch, and equal to or smaller than four times the shortest tang retouch ($2 x \leqq L \leqq 4 x$, see fig. 6).

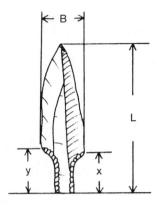

Fig. 6. Schematic representation of tanged point showing the measurements used in the definition.

4. The flake used for making the tanged point should not have been struck off with a "soft" percussion implement (see fig. 7).
5. If it cannot be shown that the flake was removed by using a "hard" percussion implement (see fig. 7) the length should be at least 8.0 cm, or the width should be at least 2.2 cm, or the weight should be at least 6.5 grammes ($L \geqq 8.0 \vee W \geqq 2.2$ cm $\vee$ Wgt $\geqq 6.5$ g). If the flake has definitely been struck off with a "hard" implement, then the length need only be at least 6.0 cm ($L \geqq 6.0$ cm).

It should be emphasized that this definition does not claim to demarcate all tanged points of the Tanged Point Complex from all other flint tools. On the contrary, it is already clear that several tanged points from "chronologically unmixed" settlement deposits (particularly those from the later part of the Complex) do not fulfil all the criteria given here. What matters

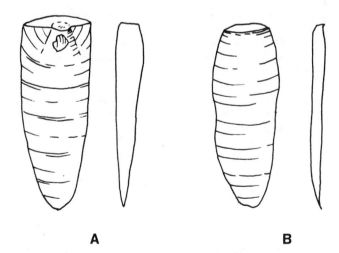

A　　　　**B**

Fig. 7. Idealized representation of characteristics showing the use of a "hard" percussion implement, e.g. quartzite (A), and a "soft" percussion implement, e.g. antler (B) (cf. Crabtree 1972, 44).

is that those artefacts which meet these requirements can be assigned with reasonable certainty to the Late Paleolithic Tanged Point Complex.

REFERENCES

ANDERSEN, S.H. 1970: Senglaciale bopladser ved Bro. *Fynske Minder*. Odense. 1970.

– 1973: Bro. En senglacial boplads på Fyn. *KUML* 1972. Århus.

– 1977: En stenalderboplads i Jarup Mose. *Nordslesvigske Museer* Bd. 4.

BECKER, C.J. 1951: Den grubekeramiske kultur i Danmark. *Aarbøger 1951*. København.

– 1970: Eine Kerbspitze der Hamburger Stufe aus Jutland. In Gripp, J. & K.R. Schütrumpf & H. Schwabedissen (eds.): *Frühe Menscheit und Umwelt*, Teil I, Archäologische Beiträge. (Fundamenta Rh. A, Bd. 2). Köln.

– 1971: Late Palaeolithic Finds from Denmark. *Proceedings of the Prehistoric Society*. Cambridge.

BERG, H. 1941: Stenaldersfund fra Porsmosen. *Årbøger for Historisk Samfund for Præstø Amt*. Næstved.

BERGLUND, B.E. 1976: The Deglaciation of Southern Sweden. *University of Lund Quarterly Geology*. Report 10.

CRABTREE, D.E. 1972: An Introduction to Flintworking. *Occasional Papers of the Idaho State University Museum*. No 28. Pocatello, Idaho.

EKHOLM, G. 1925: Die erste Besiedlung des Ostseegebietes. *Wiener Prähistorische Zeitschrift*. Jahrgang XII.

FISCHER, A. 1976: Senpalæolitisk bosætning i Danmark. *Kontaktstencil* nr. 12. Turku.

– 1978: På sporet af overgangen mellem palæolitikum og mesolitikum i Sydskandinavien. *Hikuin* nr. 4.

FISCHER, A. & MORTENSEN, B.N. 1976: ARCADY. En programkæde for computer-analyse af stenalderbopladser. *Kontaktstencil* nr. 11. Lund.

– 1977: Trollesgave-bopladsen. Et eksempel på anvendelse af EDB inden for arkæologien. *Nationalmuseets Arbejdsmark*. København.

– 1978: Report on the Use of Computers in the Treatment of Data from an Archaeological Excavation. In Kristiansen, K. & Paludan-Müller, C. (eds.): *New Directions in Scandinavian Archaeology*. København.

FISCHER, A. & GRØNNOW, B. & PETERSEN, C. 1978: En bosættelsesarkæologisk undersøgelse ved Holmegård Mose. Et projektoplæg. *Kontaktstencil* nr. 15. Umeå.

GLOB, P.V. 1952: *Danske Oldsager II, yngre stenalder*. København.

HOLM, J. 1973: Istidsjægere på Ærø. *Fynske Minder* 1972. Odense.

JESSEN, A. & NORDMANN, V. 1915: Ferskvandslagene ved Nørre Lyngby. *Danmarks Geologiske Undersøgelse*, II. Række, Nr. 29.

JOHANSSON, A. 1964: Sydsjællands oldtidsbebyggelse. En foreløbig meddelelse. *Årbog for Historisk Samfund i Præstø Amt*. Næstved.

KRISTIANSEN, K. 1974: En kildekritisk analyse af depotfund fra Danmarks yngre bronzealder (Periode IV-V). Et bidrag til den arkæologiske kildekritik. *Aarbøger* 1974. København.

MAGNUSSEN, F. 1976: Lidt om skafttungepile og et Brommefund fra Østrup. *Egnshistorisk Forening i Gundsø, Årsskrift*.

MALMER, M.P. 1969: Gropkeramikboplatsen Jonstorp. RÄ. *Antikvarisk Arkiv* 36. Stockholm.

MARCUSSEN, J. & ØSTERGÅRD, T.V. 1977: Danmark i sidste istid. *Naturens Verden*.

MATHIASSEN, T. 1946: En Senglacial boplads ved Bromme. *Aarbøger*. København.

– 1948: *Danske Oldsager I, ældre stenalder*. København.

– 1959: Nordvestsjællands Oldtidsbebyggelse. *Nationalmuseets Skrifter*. Arkæologisk Række, Nr. VII. København.

PETERSEN, B.F. 1974: Senpalæolitiske flækkespidser fra Knudshoved Odde, Sydsjælland. *Aarbøger* 1973. København.

PETERSEN, P.V. 1977: Vedbæk Boldbaner – endnu engang. *Søllerødbogen*. Søllerød.

RASMUSSEN, J. 1972: Æskebjerg – en rensdyrjægerboplads på Knudshoved Odde. *Aarbøger for Historisk Samfund i Præstø Amt* 1969-70. Næstved.

TAUBER, H. 1970: The Scandinavian Varve Chronology and C-14 Dating. In Olsson, J.U. (ed.): *Nobel Symposium 12. Radiocarbon Variations and Absolute Chronology*. Stockholm.

TROMNAU, G. 1974: Zur jungpaläolithischen Fundstelle der Hamburger Kultur im Dörgener Moor, Kr. Meppen. *Die Kunde*, Neue Folge 25.

– 1975: Neue Ausgrabungen im Ahrensburger Tunneltal. *Offa-Bücher* Bd. 33. Neumünster.

USINGER, H. 1975: Pollenanalytische und stratigraphische Untersuchungen an zwei Spätglazial-Vorkommen in Schleswig-Holstein. *Mitteilungen der Arbeitsgemeinschaft Geobotanik in Schleswig-Holstein und Hamburg*, Heft 25. Kiel.

WESTERBY, E. 1946: Da Danmarks ældste stenalderboplads blev fundet. *Unpublished manuscript*.

Grave Mounds, Battle Axes and Pottery of the Single-Grave Culture from South-West Jutland

by MOGENS HANSEN

INTRODUCTION

Among the find groups from Danish prehistory which have been recovered chiefly as a result of large-scale, systematic excavation programs covering *a large geographical area* are the grave mounds of the Single-Grave culture in Central and West Jutland. Most of the find material from these mounds appeared in the decades around the turn of the century through the extensive excavation programs conducted by archaeologists from the National Museum under the supervision of Sophus Müller (Glob 1944, 7 ff.). Such a find group obviously presents special source-critical problems, as stressed by, for instance, Malmer (Malmer 1962, 776).

These problems may have contributed to the fact that the material has not been much used except in investigations of the chronology and origins of the culture. To pave the way for other investigations we shall carry out in this paper a number of source-critical examinations which, by means of quantitative methods of analysis, may help to clarify the general representativity of some of the most important groups of artefacts from the Single-Grave culture.

We shall follow the main lines of the archaeological source criticism as systematised by Kristian Kristiansen (Kristiansen 1974). We shall, however, develop the statistical analyses as well as the analyses of the find frequencies for the subregions of South-West Jutland in order to study regional differences in the impact of source-critical factors. Since an analysis such as the following depends on a time-consuming collection of material and the use of slightly problematical statistical calculations, the investigation has been confined to a small part of the Single-Grave area in Jutland, so as to assess both the source material and the method before larger areas of Jutland are analysed.

The aims of this paper are as follows:
1. To present a regional division which will facilitate comparisons of spatial distribution by statistical means.
2. To attempt to uncover the factors which have determined the discovery of the prehistoric material.
3. To calculate the relative amount of material originally deposited.
4. To examine whether the actual find material is representative of the material deposited in prehistoric times.

REGIONAL DIVISION OF JUTLAND

The regional division of Jutland presented here is based on an unpublished study by Carsten Boisen, Århus (Boisen 1976)[1]. Our division has been carried out in accordance with the following principles: 1) It must follow the parish boundaries (TRAP Danmark, 5th ed.). This enables us to use a good deal of data with no other information on provenance than the parish concerned, e.g. the extent of land under cultivation; the number of mounds; a great many single finds as well as finds from published find catalogues, for which there is usually no other localizing factor than the parish. Considerable difficulty and uncertainty would be involved if these data were to have only a UTM co-ordinate as reference, or were to be placed in a hexagonal division as done by Malmer and others (Malmer 1957 and 1962, 697 ff.).

2) The regions must be approximations to squares of nearly the same size and exclude large expanses of water. Great variations in area may distort the data employed and thus have an unfortunate influence on the results of the statistical calculations.

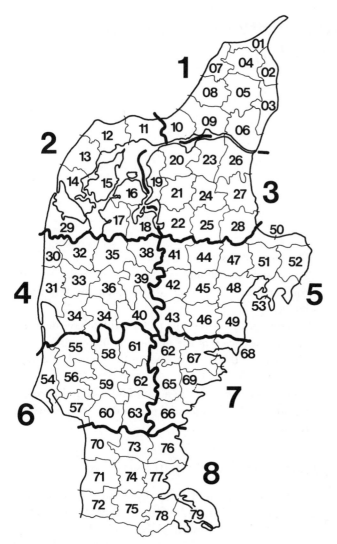

Fig. 1. Division of Jutland into regions and zones.

others in Salling, or for one region to comprise only 100-120 km² owing to large expanses of water. If the UTM grid lines are consistently adhered to, there will be several cases of this kind with, according to point 2, an unfortunate distribution of land and water, especially in the Limfjord region, in North Jutland, and along the west coast of Jutland. Consequently, in these areas it has been necessary to disregard the UTM grid in several cases and instead amalgamate parishes with a view to standardizing regional size, and in such a way that expanses of water that form natural boundaries are taken into account. It has not been possible to make sections of exactly the same size because of the great variations in parish area. The average size and standard deviation of the sections constitute 370 ± 65.5 km², with a total of 79 sections. These regions are then combined into 8 approximately square zones (fig. 1).

SINGLE-GRAVE MATERIAL FROM SOUTH-WEST JUTLAND

I shall now return to the subject of this paper, i.e. the Single-Grave culture in South-West Jutland. In the following, South-West Jutland is defined as zone 6 of the regional division, comprising regions 54-63 (fig. 2). Today the Single-Grave culture is represented by a number of artefact groups of stone, pottery and amber, which in South-West Jutland come predominantly from grave mounds. Only part of the artefacts can definitely be as-

3) The regions must be of a certain minimum size to avoid zero-observations in the interests of the statistical calculations.

To fulfil these conditions we have initially superimposed on a map of Danish parishes (the Geodetic Institute map of counties, municipalities and parishes, 1:500,000) sections of 20 times 20 km that follow the UTM grid (Buchwaldt 1973). We have then attempted to fulfil the conditions in 1) and 3) by adjusting the boundaries of the squares.

The UTM grid cuts across large expanses of water and other dividing lines that may conceivably have affected cultural diffusion in prehistoric times. It would therefore be meaningless to join a single parish on Mors to ten

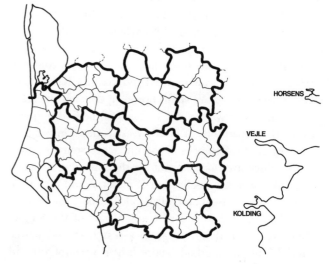

Fig. 2. Regional division of South-West Jutland (zone 6).

	Excavated axes.	Single finds of axes	Σ axes.	Excavated clay vessels.	Single finds of clay vessels.	Σ clay vessels.	Excavated mounds.
1865-69		1	1				
1870-79		4	4		1	1	
1880-89		16	16				10
1890-99	161	20	181	56	9	65	278
1900-09	84	55	139	41	2	43	190
1910-19	63	17	80	15	1	16	83
1920-29	1	15	16	1		1	13
1930-39	5	4	9	7	1	8	8
1940-49	5		5		2	2	10
1950-59	16	7	23	8	2	10	42
1960-69	5	1	6	3	3	6	20
1970-75	5		5	6		6	19
Total	345	140	485	137	21	158	673

Table 1: The number of registered excavated battle axes and clay vessels; registered single finds of battle axes and clay vessels; excavated mounds; total of these per ten-year interval.

signed to the Single-Grave culture, viz. battle axes, clay vessels, certain amber ornaments, and some less frequent groups of objects. Since flint axes, flakes (Højlund 1974, 190), and many of the amber ornaments cannot be distinguished with complete certainty from similar material from a number of other periods, the following analyses will concentrate on mounds, battle axes, and clay vessels.[2] In contrast to find groups like e.g. hoards (Kristiansen 1974), which have been recovered mainly as a result of socio-economic factors, the recovery of grave finds from the Single-Grave culture – like other grave mounds – is conditioned by a complex interplay of research-related factors and socio-economic factors (agriculture, urban growth, and mound looting). These factors affect both the number of registered mounds and the potential finds in them. To assess the general representativity of Single-Grave material, the investigation is for practical reasons divided into the following sections:
a) Influence of physical factors.
b) Influence of socio-economic and research-related factors on the number of registered mounds.
c) Influence of research-related factors on the amount of prehistoric material recovered.
d) Influence of socio-economic factors on the amount of prehistoric material recovered.

Physical source-critical factors

These factors are largely irrelevant for artefacts like battle axes and clay vessels, which are not subject to physical destruction in the mounds, irrespective of soil conditions etc.

Influence of socio-economic and research-related factors on the number of registered mounds

In this context the socio-economic factors can be divided into agriculture and urban growth. The research-related factor is the registration of mounds during local field visits in the period 1890-1910. Of decisive importance in this respect is the length of the period between the time when large parts of the agricultural area was brought into cultivation and the time of the local field trips. The size of particular towns at the time of the relevant field trips also determines the number of mounds demolished before registration could take place.

The agricultural factor can be measured in terms of the extent of cultivation (the proportion of cultivated area in relation to total area)[3]. The diagrams in fig. 3 illustrate the extent of cultivation in the period 1861-1907 for each region in South-West Jutland. In general they

92

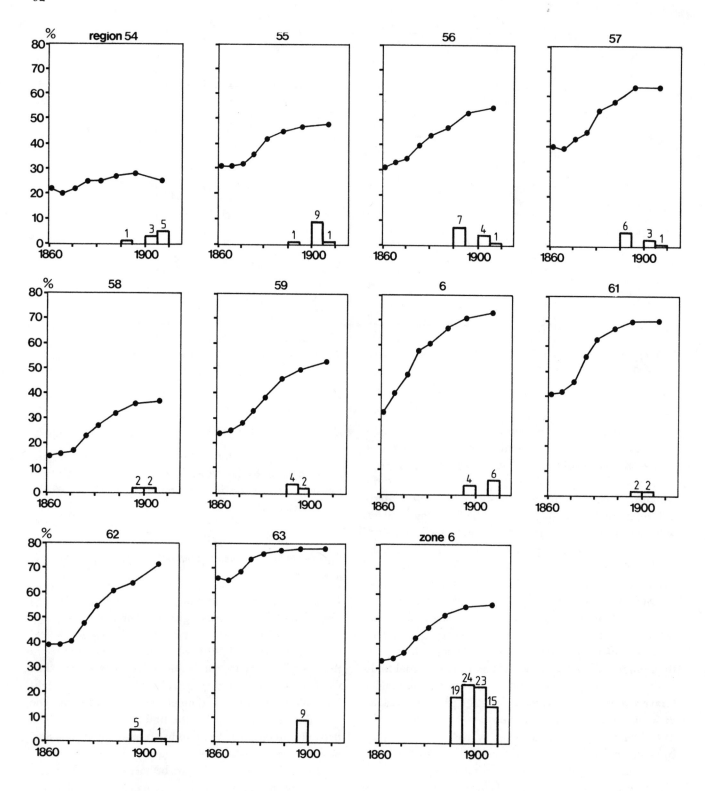

Fig. 3. Extent of cultivation (curves) expressed as percentage of cultivated land in relation to total area. Years of local field visits (columns); figures above columns indicate the number of parishes visited in each five-year period.

show a high degree of uniformity. The largest area of land was brought into cultivation during the 1870's, and the curves level off around 1900 because of the decline in new cultivation areas. On the average there is an increase in cultivated land from 33% in 1861 to 56% in 1907. However, regions 54 and 63 deviate somewhat from this picture. Thus region 54 shows a difference of only 3% over the period and a cultivated area of 25% in 1907. In region 63 there is a difference of 12% between 1861 and 1907, but a cultivated area of 78% in 1907. The situation in region 54 does not affect the number of registered mounds, whereas the great extent of cultivation in region 63, which extends further back in time than in the other regions, may mean that this region has seen more mounds demolished that were never registered than other regions.

The times of local field visits (column diagrams in fig. 3) indicate that in general the mounds of South-West Jutland, in contrast, for instance, to East Jutland and the islands, were registered only a few decades after this area was brought into cultivation (Baudou's article)[4]. This means that mound demolitions caused by agricultural activities before the field visits must have been very limited, especially compared to East Denmark, although a few very early demolitions can, of course, be documented also in South-West Jutland (Andersen 1973). Local visits to the towns of the area (Esbjerg, 1891, and Varde, 1904) took place while they were still very small (TRAP, 4th and 5th eds.).

We may conclude that, except for region 63, the number of mounds registered in South-West Jutland must be very close to the original number.

Influence of research-related factors on the amount of prehistoric material recovered

The amount of research can be measured by the number of excavated mounds. The diagram in fig. 4a illustrates the number of mounds excavated per decade. The hatched area indicates mounds excavated by the National Museum. The remaining mounds were excavated for the Antiquarian Collection at Ribe (by A.P. Madsen during the period 1889-1909), Esbjerg Museum and *Forhistorisk Museum*, Moesgård (1930 onwards). The large-scale excavation programs initiated by the National Museum are very clearly reflected in the period 1890-1920. A maximum during the first decade is followed by a very steep decline; the decline continues until 1950 when – especial-

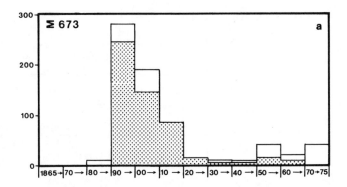

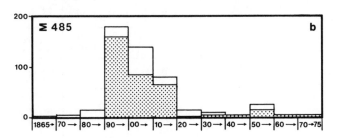

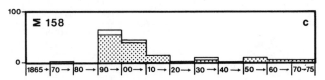

Fig. 4. a) Year of excavation of mounds. The National Museum – shaded, local museums – not shaded. b) Year of registration in South-West Jutland of battle axes. Excavated battle axes – shaded, single finds of battle axes – not shaded. c) Year of registration in South-West Jutland of clay vessels. Excavated clay vessels – shaded, single finds of clay vessels – not shaded.

ly in the 1950's and the first half of the 1970's – there is a new outburst of excavation activity, directed mainly by the Esbjerg Museum.[5]

The diagrams showing finds of battle axes (fig. 4b) and clay vessels (fig. 4c) reveal almost the same distribution. There is, however, a clear tendency for single finds of battle axes to reach their peak in the decade 1900-1909. These distributions can be illustrated in a scatter diagram and their mutual correlation computed (product-moment correlation: r).[6] If we consult Table VI in Clarke 1971, we can ascertain whether the correlation coefficient is significant at a 1% significance level.

As expected the calculations reveal an excellent correlation between the number of excavated mounds and the number of excavated clay vessels (r = 0.99), and between the number of excavated mounds and the number of

	54	55	56	57	58	59	60	61	62	63
1	43715	40917	45171	29544	43253	44401	40981	38135	39031	37371
2	25	48	55	64	37	53	73	70	72	78
3	278 (304)	804 (822)	1169 (1320)	1640 (1211)	345 (373)	745 (827)	1034 (1059)	1055 (1006)	1030 (1005)	791 (739)
4	129 (141)	279 (285)	308 (348)	303 (224)	164 (177)	159 (176)	207 (212)	211 (201)	249 (243)	86 (80)
5	46	35	26	18	47	21	20	25	24	11
6	54	65	74	82	53	79	80	75	76	89
7	24 (26)	18 (18)	81 (91)	261 (193)	31 (33)	32 (36)	24 (25)	120 (114)	55 (54)	84 (78)
8	8.6	2.2	6.1	15.9	8.8	4.4	2.4	11.3	5.4	10.6
9	15.6 (17)	4.9 (5)	51.4 (58)	203.1 (150)	24.0 (26)	23.4 (26)	18.5 (19)	89.2 (85)	47.1 (46)	45.0 (42)
10	10.1 (11)	3.9 (4)	38.1 (43)	157.1 (116)	13.9 (15)	23.4 (26)	14.6 (15)	54.5 (52)	33.8 (33)	31.0 (29)
11	12.8 (14)	33.2 (34)	60.2 (68)	138.1 (102)	10.2 (11)	114.4 (127)	124.0 (127)	93.4 (89)	154.7 (151)	100.6 (94)
12	22.9 (25)	37.1 (38)	98.3 (111)	295.2 (218)	24.0 (26)	137.8 (153)	138.6 (142)	147.9 (141)	188.6 (184)	131.6 (123)
13	0.42	0.22	0.47	0.60	0.45	0.72	0.60	0.46	0.61	0.37
14	0.046	0.041	0.052	0.081	0.029	0.154	0.120	0.110	0.150	0.127
15	180	640	867	1269	200	745	816	645	739	244
16	6.4 (7)	1.0 (1)	8.0 (9)	40.6 (30)	3.7 (4)	5.4 (6)	9.8 (10)	35.7 (34)	16.4 (16)	13.9 (13)
17	0.9 (1)	2.0 (2)	4.4 (5)	2.7 (2)	1.8 (2)	10.8 (12)	6.8 (7)	19.9 (19)	25.6 (25)	11.8 (11)
18	7.3 (8)	2.9 (3)	12.4 (14)	43.3 (32)	5.5 (6)	16.2 (18)	16.6 (17)	55.6 (53)	42.0 (41)	25.7 (24)
19	114	164	182	328	53	172	548	422	359	244

Table II:

1. Area of the regions in hectares (10,000 m²).
2. Extent of cultivation in 1907 as percentage of total area (cf. fig. 3).
3. Quantitative distribution (expressed per 40,000 ha) of all registered mounds. Figures in parentheses indicate the absolute number in the region.
4. Density of protected mounds.
5. Percentage of protected mounds in relation to the total number of mounds.
6. Percentage of demolished mounds in relation to the total number of mounds.
7. Density of excavated mounds.
8. Percentage of excavated mounds in relation to the total number of mounds.

9. Quantitative distribution of dated mounds (cf. note 11).
10. Quantitative distribution of excavated battle axes.
11. Quantitative distribution of single finds of battle axes.
12. Quantitative distribution of all finds of battle axes.
13. Number of excavated battle axes per excavated mound.
14. Number of single finds of battle axes per mound.
15. Calculated distribution of battle axes originally deposited.
16. Quantitative distribution of excavated clay vessels.
17. Quantitative distribution of single finds of clay vessels.
18. Quantitative distribution of all finds of clay vessels.
19. Calculated distribution of clay vessels originally deposited.

All densities/quantitative distributions are expressed in number per 40,000 ha. Absolute numbers are given in parentheses below the densities.

excavated battle axes (r = 0.98). On the other hand, the calculations show that the correlation between excavated mounds and single finds of battle axes is not significant (r = 0.68). In other words, single finds are not dependent on the amount of research carried out.

If we look at the frequencies of excavated battle axes per excavated mound in individual regions (Table II, No. 13), the correlation between excavated mounds and excavated battle axes is not self-evident. We shall therefore compare the intensity of research to the quantity of finds within each of the ten regions in the area (fig. 5a-5e).[7] It appears that the correlations between the density of excavated mounds and a) the quantitative distribution of excavated battle axes (r = 0.98) and b) the quantitative distribution of clay vessels (r = 0.89) are significant at a 1% level. By contrast, the remaining two correlations are not significant as the correlation coefficient between density of excavated mounds and c) single finds of battle axes and single finds of clay vessels is 0.45 and 0.025, respectively. The variations in find frequency are therefore sufficiently low to indicate that the number of excavated artefacts is directly dependent on the number of excavated mounds.

From Table II, Nos. 7 and 8, it appears that the excavated mounds are unevenly distributed, in that the proportion of excavated mounds in relation to the total in the regions varies from 2.2% to 15.2%, with 7.9% as the mean value. This variation does not appear to be directly related to either the density of mounds or any socio-economic factors. It may reflect, however, a certain degree of previous looting, since regions with the lowest percentage of excavated mounds also have the highest number of single finds. This variation means that the distribution of excavated axes and clay vessels cannot be representative of the distribution of the artefacts originally deposited.

Influence of socio-economic factors on the amount of prehistoric material recovered

These factors fall into three groups, viz. 1) demolition of mounds without preceding excavation in connection with urban development; 2) systematic looting of mounds to procure antiquities for sale; 3) agricultural activity, reflected mainly in the ploughing under of mounds, whereby monuments are destroyed and artefacts ploughed up.

Urban development in Esbjerg does not seem to have caused demolition of mounds without preceding archaeo-logical excavation on a larger scale than in the rural parishes. For instance, many of the excavations carried out by the Esbjerg Museum were occasioned by road building and other construction work around the town of Esbjerg itself.

Plundering of mounds is a phenomenon of long standing, but probably did not occur on a large scale until the second half of the 19th century, when it became possible to sell antiquities to private collectors and local museums at a handsome profit. It appears from the excavation reports that 90%-100% of all excavated grave mounds in South-West Jutland have suffered looting. This is confirmed by material systematically collected from all mounds in seven parishes of the area (Kvist 1975). There is no reason to suppose that the degree of looting in the rest of the area differs from the 90%-100% mentioned above. Furthermore, without excavation it is difficult to register the fact and extent of plundering. The holes made by the looters may have been filled in prior to the field visit, or the looting may have taken place after the visit. Parish reports often contain no or only dubious information on what had been looted.

The extent of cultivation, as quantified in the diagrams in fig. 3, expresses a generalised picture, which it would be possible to supplement with detailed investigations. Additional information such as parish reports, aerial photographs, old maps, and other potential sources would enable us to isolate and date more closely the impact of socio-economic factors on the various mounds. This is outside the scope of the present work. However, on a general level it is still possible to examine whether destruction of mounds is related to the extent of cultivation. The degree of destruction can be expressed by the percentage of demolished mounds (i.e. ploughed under or entirely removed) in relation to the total number of mounds (TRAP, 5th ed.). The degree of destruction can be compared to the extent of cultivation in 1907[8] by means of the scatter diagram, fig. 6. The correlation coefficient (r = 0.89) is significant at a 1% level. This would seem to indicate that cultivation extent is a useful expression of the impact of agriculture on the mounds.[9] The correlation between the number of single finds per mound and cultivation extent in 1907 (about the time when the frequency of single finds reached their peak – cf. fig. 4b) is not significant at a 1% level (r = 0.67) (fig. 7). It is therefore not the extent of cultivation alone that determines the number of registered single finds. It is curious that in fig. 7 only two regions (54 and 59) fall

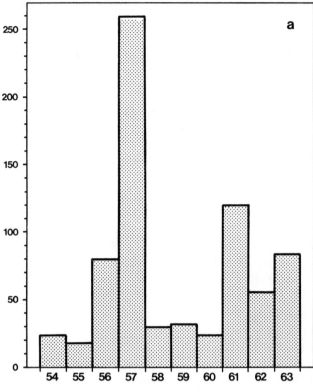

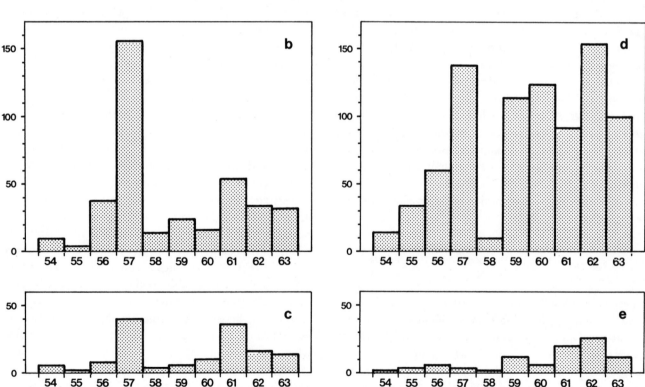

outside the linear distribution.[10] A closer study might show whether special conditions have caused exceptionally many finds to be submitted to the museums, or whether during field visits more attention was paid to registering earlier single finds here than in the other regions.

For the recovery of single finds, looting and agriculture are without doubt the most important factors. However, the material collected does not enable us to isolate the specific influence of these factors on the recovery and registration of single finds. Nevertheless, the results suggest that fluctuations in the cultivated area have been more significant than plundering, which seems to have affected the area in a fairly uniform fashion.

AN ESTIMATE OF THE RELATIVE QUANTITY OF MATERIAL DEPOSITED AND THE REPRESENTATIVITY OF THE ACTUAL NUMBER OF FINDS

In the preceding pages we have attempted to demonstrate which factors have determined the recovery of materi-

Fig. 5. Density (number per 400 km²) of excavated mounds (a), excavated battle axes (b), excavated clay vessels (c), single finds of battle axes (d), and single finds of clay vessels (e) in each region.

al, viz. looting, which seems to have had a fairly uniform effect throughout the area, and the levels of excavation and cultivation, which have affected the various regions differently, irrespective of the number of mounds and the quantity of material originally deposited.

Figure 5 shows that in some regions with many single finds of axes, only a few axes (and a few mounds) have been excavated (regions 55, 59, 60 and 62). This might suggest that single finds and excavated finds supplement each other and, taken together, constitute a representative sample of the original deposition of artefacts in the mounds. To analyse whether this is the case, we have worked out the correlation between the total number of battle axes and the total number of registered mounds. This gives a correlation coefficient of 0.81, which is significant at a 1% level.

As already mentioned, the find frequency per mound may vary somewhat. Similarly, the proportion of Single-Grave mounds to the total number of registered mounds cannot be supposed to be the same in all regions. By making allowances for these sources of error we can calculate the relative number of battle axes and clay vessels originally deposited in each region. The results can then be compared to the total number of battle axes and clay vessels found.

As a result of extensive excavation it is possible to work out how much would have been found if all registered mounds had been excavated before they were ploughed under.

The mounds excavated by the National Museum around the turn of the century were often selected because they were fairly well preserved (offering a good chance of making finds) and because they were in danger of being destroyed by cultivation or plundering (Müller 1898, 157 f.). To some extent the mounds had been selected during the local field visits and were marked as "suitable for excavation" in the parish reports. They were then sometimes protected for ten years. This means that excavations generally took place in mounds that were less destroyed by, for instance, cultivation than most mounds in the area. This can be documented by illustrating (fig. 8) the find frequency (number of excavated axes per mound per region) as a function of the extent of cultivation. The correlation coefficient, r, is calculated as 0.27, which is not significant at a 1% level (compare fig. 7).

We may therefore assume that a calculation according to region of the amount that would have been found if all

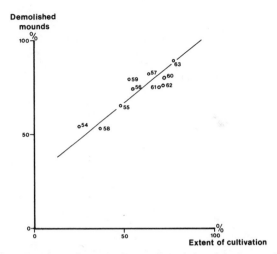

Fig. 6. Correlation between the number of demolished mounds (as percentage of the total of registered mounds) and extent of cultivation in 1907. r = 0.89.

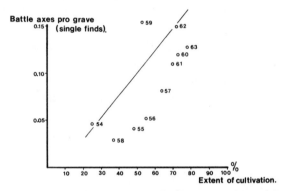

Fig. 7. Correlation between extent of cultivation in 1907 and the number of single finds of battle axes per mound in the regions. r = 0.67.

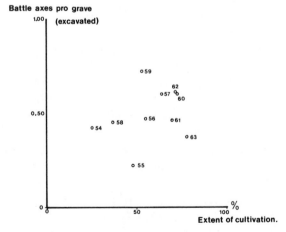

Fig. 8. Correlation between extent of cultivation in 1907 and the number of excavated battle axes per mound. r = 0.27.

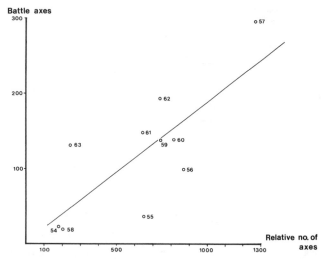

Fig. 9. Correlation between the quantitative distribution of the relative number of originally deposited battle axes and that of clay vessels found in the regions. r = 0.77.

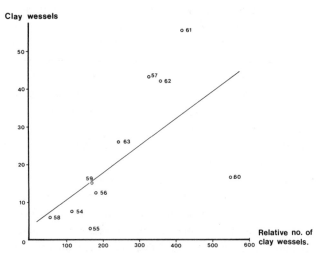

Fig. 10. Correlation between the quantitative distribution of the relative number of originally deposited clay vessels and the number of clay vessels found in the regions. r = 0.63.

mounds had been excavated, is a representative sample of the battle axes and clay vessels originally deposited.

The relative number of battle axes originally deposited can be calculated according to region by means of the following formula:

$$M_{reg} \quad x \ \frac{M_{SG}}{M_{dat}} \ x \ \frac{A_{exc}}{M_{SG}} = \ M_{reg} \ x \quad \frac{A_{exc}}{M_{dat}}$$

The following abbreviations have been used in the formula:

M_{reg} : total number of registered mounds.

M_{SG} : number of mounds which, when excavated, were assigned to the Single-Grave culture.[11]

M_{dat} : number of mounds where it was possible to date the primary grave by excavation.

A_{exc} : number of battle axes found by excavation.

(V_{exc} : number of clay vessels found by excavation).

$M_{reg} \ x \ \dfrac{M_{SG}}{M_{dat}}$ equals the total number of Single-Grave mounds, while

$\dfrac{A_{exc}}{M_{SG}}$ is the find frequency, i.e. number of axes per Single-Grave mound.

By substituting V_{exc} for A_{exc} the relative quantity of originally deposited clay vessels can be calculated.

Evidently, the problems surrounding the representativity of such data are centred upon M_{reg} and M_{dat}. We

have previously expressed reservations regarding the number of registered mounds in region 63. As for M_{dat}, only region 55 appears to be underrepresented, in that there are only five dated mounds from this region. It is also the only region where less than 1% of all registered mounds have been dated.

The results of these calculations are shown in Table II, Nos. 15 and 19. By means of the scatter diagram in figs. 9 and 10 the computed original number of battle axes and clay vessels is compared to the actual number of finds. The calculations show that the correlation between the calculated number of battle axes and the axes actually found is significant at a 1% level (r = 0.77), whereas the correlation between the calculated number of clay vessels and the vessels actually found is not (r = 0.63). However, it appears from fig. 10 that only region 60 falls outside the linear distribution, so that the clay vessels may be more representative than the calculation indicates.

Figure 9 shows that the two critical regions, 55 and 63, deviate most from the expected values. It is therefore natural to assume that the representativity in region 55 is lower than in the other regions, while the deviation in region 63 probably means that the number of registered mounds is not representative of the original number.[12]

With reservations concerning regions 55 and 63, the actual number of battle axes found seems to be representative of the quantity originally deposited. The clay vessels seem to be repreentative except in region 60.

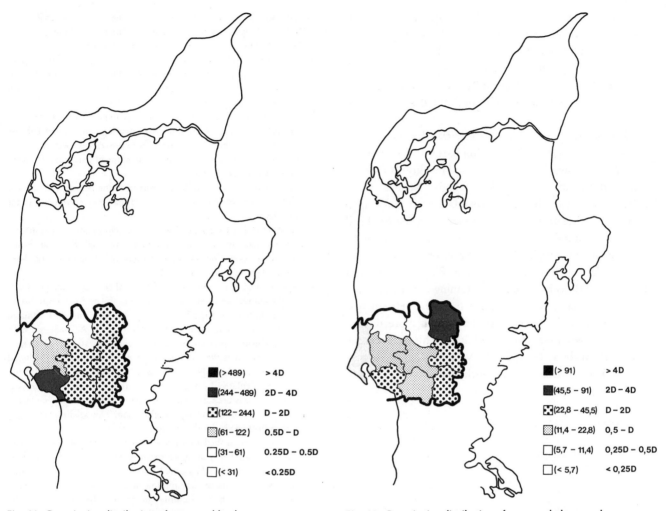

Fig. 11. Quantitative distribution of recovered battle axes.

Fig. 12. Quantitative distribution of recovered clay vessels.

SUMMARY AND CONCLUSION

By separating excavated artefacts from single finds it has been possible to document that the quantity of excavated material is a direct function of the intensity of research.

The single finds, however, present a number of problems which we were unable to solve. There is, for example, some uncertainty regarding the relation between registered single finds and those actually found. It has proved impossible to isolate, quantify and analyse the effects of cultivation and looting as separate factors. The analyses suggest, however, that plundering was a fairly uniform factor throughout the area, so that variations in the number of single finds can be attributed to cultiva-

tion. The results clearly indicate the necessity of analysing chronological as well as regional relationships.

On the basis of the results from the preceding analyses we calculated the relative quantity of material originally deposited. When comparing this figure with the material actually found, it appeared that (except for region 55) the battle axes and (except for region 60) the clay vessels are representative of the material originally deposited.

It also appeared that it is necessary to supplement calculations of correlation coefficients with the more visual representation given by the relevant scatter diagrams. This clearly shows the limitations of the method.

Figure 11 illustrates the quantitative distribution of battle axes. As in Malmer (Malmer 1962, 698 ff.) the mean, D, is taken as a basis. The map shows that the greatest density of finds is in the south-western part of the area, with a lower density towards the south and east; the lowest is in the north-western part of the area.

Figure 12 shows the quantitative distribution of clay vessels. They are most densely distributed in the north-east of the area.

It has not been possible to establish what prehistoric factors determined this distribution pattern. We have calculated the following correlations: soil fertility/number of finds, and marsh area/number of finds. None of these analyses show any significant correlation. It is an open question whether this is because modern estimates of soil fertility and marsh areas cannot be compared to conditions during the Single-Grave culture, or whether other economic factors have played a role. Finally, we should bear in mind that the mounds containing battle axes may have been located some distance from the settlements. The location of the latter must have been more dependent on the resources they exploited. This is a classic discussion (Malmer 1962, 780 ff., with references); unfortunately, half its basis, i.e. the settlements, is on the whole still conspicuous by its absence.

Mogens Hansen,
Sillevadvej 9
Gundestrup
DK — 9600 Års

NOTES

1. I wish to thank Carsten Boisen for his permission to present and use this division.
2. The empirical material used has been obtained by a systematic study of registers, excavation reports, parish reports and the topographical archives in Section I of the National Museum, as well as registers and reports in the Antiquarian Collection at Ribe, and the museum at Koldinghus Castle, Kolding. Only the pottery was studied primarily in the storerooms of the respective museums.

   The assignation of the other prehistoric material to the Single-Grave culture depends exclusively on archival data and information in Glob (Glob 1944). I am grateful to the curators of the museums visited for their assistance while I collected the material, and for permission to use it. Numbers of protected and demolished grave mounds are from TRAP Danmark, 5th ed., vols. 21, 22, 23 and 24. Lack of time prevented a visit to the Esbjerg Museum, but as the Museum's excavations are chiefly of fairly recent date, the information required can be found in the National Museum archives. All data used are listed in Tables I and II.
3. Cultivated area refers to the portion of agricultural land that is put under plough for longer or shorter intervals. This area can be calculated according to parish on the basis of *Statistisk Tabelværk* 1865-1909, which contains information from the years 1861, 1866, 1871, 1876, 1881, 1888, 1896, 1901 (not used) and 1907. I am grateful to Bodil Ølholm for carrying out these calculations.
4. Exceptions are the three South Jutland parishes of Lintrup (region 60), Skrave and Skodborg (region 63). They were included in the local field visits of 1925-30. They were part of Germany when the other parishes were visited.
5. This pronounced excavation activity is undoubtedly related to a very active local museum and urban development around Esbjerg. In recent years there have also been improved prospects for financing excavations that come within the scope of paragraph 49 of the Preservation Act of 1969.

   For reasons of comparability finds from the periods 1865-69 and 1970-75 have been multiplied by 2, so that they correspond to the other ten-year intervals.
6. I wish to thank Carsten Boisen for his help in choosing statistical methods and carrying out calculations. Although the product-moment correlation is not ideal for this type of calculation, it has been used for lack of a better method.
7. As mentioned, the regions are not of equal size (cf. Table II, No. 1) (for the ten regions in South-West Jutland the mean value and standard deviation are $402.52 \pm ... $ km^2). We have therefore adjusted the original data to form comparable entities. As such, we have chosen density expressed in number of units per 400 km^2. However, each diagram lists the absolute number of units involved. It should be pointed out that when the finds in the diagrams are added up, the sum calculated by region exceeds that calculated by ten-year interval. This is because some finds have information only on locality, not on year of discovery or registration. This applies, for instance, to collections in local museums.
8. There is no published information on the extent of cultivation in individual parishes from more recent times. The number of single finds, however, reached its peak between 1900 and 1909 (cf. fig. 4b).
9. This result contests the assumption that the protected mounds are representative of the total number of mounds (Bekmose 1978). The correlation coefficient between the total number of registered mounds and the number of protected mounds in the region works out at 0.63, which is not significant at a 1% level. Bekmose's assumption therefore is invalid in South-West Jutland.
10. If we exclude regions 54 and 59, the correlation coefficient for extent of cultivation/single finds of battle axes becomes 0.85, which is significant at a 1% level.
11. When registered the mounds were divided into the following categories: Mounds with:
    1. Securely dated primary graves; these are subdivided into:
       1a. Graves belonging to the Single-Grave culture.
       1b. Graves belonging to later periods. (The number of demonstrated monuments from the TRB-culture is negligible and is left out of the calculations, except for mounds with primary TRB and secondary Single-Grave constructions. These are classified under 2b).
    2. Insecurely dated primary graves of the Single-Grave culture; these are subdivided into:
       2a) Single graves containing only flint axes, amber beads, flakes etc. that *may* belong to other Neolithic cultures although they are far more likely – particularly in this area – to belong to the Single-Grave culture.

2b. Graves other than primary graves that can be assigned to the Single-Grave culture.

3. Possible primary graves from later periods, i.e. graves that can be confidently given a more recent date than the Single-Grave culture, but cannot be classified as definite primary graves.

4. Undated primary graves.

In the calculations, category 4 is disregarded. Among Single-Grave mounds (M_{SG}) we have included 1a, 2a and 2b, while 1b and 3 are regarded as more recently constructed mounds. M_{dat} thus comprises 1a, 1b, 2a, 2b and 3.

12. If we exclude region 60, the correlation coefficient for the relative quantity of originally deposited clay vessels/ the sum total of recovered clay vessels becomes 0.96. A corresponding calculation for battle axes excluding regions 55 and 63 gives a coefficient of 0.91. In both cases the results are significant at a 1% level.

REFERENCES

ANDERSEN, V. 1973: Landvindinger og oldtidsminder. *Fra Ribe Amt.* 18. bd. p. 341-42.

BEKMOSE, Jens 1977: Megalitgrave og megalitbygder. *Antikvariske studier*, p. 47-64.

BOISEN, C. 1976: Skitse til kvantitativ sammenligning af udbredelse af arkæologiske fund. Århus. Unpublished.

BUCHWALDT, F. 1973: UTM-nettet. Opbygning og anvendelse. Geodætisk Institut, København

CLARKE, G.M. 1971: *Statistics and Experimental Design.*

GLOB, P.V. 1944: Studier over den jyske Enkeltgravskultur. *Aarbøger for Nordisk Oldkyndighed og Historie.* København.

HØJLUND, F. 1974: Stridsøksekulturens flintøkser og -mejsler. *Kuml* 1973-74, p. 179-196 Århus.

KRISTIANSEN, K. 1974: En kildekritisk analyse af depotfund fra Danmarks yngre bronzealder (periode IV-V). *Aarbøger for Nordisk Oldkyndighed og Historie*, p. 119-160. København.

KVIST, J. 1975: Vorbassedrengene. *Fra Ribe Amt.* Bd. 19 p. 151-52.

MALMER, M.P. 1957: Pleionbegreppets betydelse för studiet av förhistoriska innovationsförlopp. *Finska Fornminnesföreningens Tidskrift* 58 p. 160-184.

– 1962: *Jungneolitischen Studien.* Lund.

MÜLLER, S. 1898: De jyske Enkeltgrave fra Stenalderen. *Aarbøger for Nordisk Oldkyndighed og Historie.* København.

STATISTISK TABELVÆRK. 1865-1909. København.

TRAP Danmark, 4th and 5th edition.

Neolithic Hoards from Denmark

by POUL OTTO NIELSEN

INTRODUCTION

The neolithic hoards from Denmark comprise a type of archaeological material which has been very incompletely preserved and recorded. Nevertheless, in this paper we propose to give a survey of the amount and geographical distribution of the existing material, and also attempt to illuminate the particular source problems relevant to this type of material. The purpose of this article is to discuss the *general* representativity of the material, in accordance with the guide-lines for this and the other contributions. An examination of the general representativity is a necessary preliminary for assessing the more specific questions of interpretation regarding this type of find (cf. Müller 1886, Petersen 1890, Müller 1897, Brøndsted 1938, 149ff., 191, Becker 1947, 282, Brøndsted 1957, 198f., Nielsen 1977b).

FIND CATEGORIES

There has been no comprehensive review of the material from neolithic hoards since 1886 (Müller 1886), though sections of the material have been discussed (Becker 1952, Lomborg 1973, Ebbesen 1975, Nielsen 1977a & b). This survey deals with the material from a total of 678 hoards. Demarcation of the material largely follows the work of S. Müller of 1886 so that amber and metal finds and pottery found in bogs are not considered. For such finds the reader should consult the specialized studies available (Becker 1947 & 1957). Hoards containing thick wide flakes with steep retouch are not dealt with either, since a number of finds indicate that they are from the Bronze Age. Even this delimitation does not avoid the possibility of overlap with the early Bronze Age. This is true of a number of hoards with late flint daggers, flint axes, and symmetrical flint sickles. It would be artificial to exclude these finds when the material is viewed as a totality. – For practical reasons only hoards with two or more objects are included.

Table A shows the categories of artefacts found. It is only a minimal classification for the purpose of clarity, and it should be pointed out that the groups of objects overlap more than the survey would indicate.

Table A.

Thin-butted flint axes	. 230 finds
Thick-butted flint axes alone or in combination with thin-bladed axes, point-butted adzes, thick-butted adzes, chisels etc.	. 79 finds
Thick-butted adzes only	. 48 finds
Wide-edged axes	. 35 finds
Flint axes, form not specified	. 34 finds
Flint daggers	. 70 finds
Flint sickles	. 97 finds
Flint daggers and axes	. 7 finds
Flint daggers and sickles	. 7 finds
Scrapers	. 8 finds
Flint sickles and scrapers	. 3 finds
Flint blanks	. 25 finds
Other, including shaft-hole axes, flakes, bone chisels etc.	. 35 finds
Total	. 678 finds

Table B gives a comparison with Müller's categories from 1886. Müller limited his material to 'finds which contain a greater or lesser number of *morphologically similar* objects' because of the interpretation model he proposed. In reality, several of the available hoard finds consisted of multiple forms, and it must now be regarded as an artificial procedure to disregard these in a comprehensive analysis of hoard finds. In table B are listed finds with several types of artefact according to the types that dominate in the single finds.

Table B.

	1886	1978
Thin-butted flint axes	38 finds (37%)	230 finds (34%)
Thick-butted flint axes and adzes (including wide-edged axes)	18 finds (17.6%)	162 finds (24%)
Flint sickles (Müller's 'semi-circular flint saws')	24 finds (23%)	100 finds (14.5%)
Flint daggers	9 finds (8.7%)	87 finds (12.8%)
Scrapers	3 finds (3%)	8 finds (1.2%)
Other	11 finds (10.7%)	91 finds (13.5%)
Total	103 finds (100%)	678 finds (100%)

In spite of the increase in the number of finds (575) from 1886 to 1978, there is a striking correspondence in their composition. For this reason it could well be argued that Müller's analysis and characterization was based on material as varied and representative as that available today.

However, this does not settle the question of representativity. Connected to this group of finds are a number of problems concerning provenance, which will be discussed in the following.

FIND FREQUENCY

As a first step in the investigation of the representativity of the finds we have prepared a frequency diagram, figure 1. It shows the number of registered finds within ten-year intervals. At the same time it illustrates the number of finds in the museum collections which (a) originate direct from the finder, possibly through an intermediary, and (b) which have been acquired from provincial museums for the National Museum, from private collections or through dealers. The diagram is further divided so that the upper section shows the year of discovery for finds that are still privately owned. Information concerning finds in private collections and their year of discovery is based throughout on data in the parish records and topographical archives in the National Museum. Thus the upper figures in the diagram tend to show to what extent the National and provincial museums have collected information on privately owned material rather than how much material is actually in private ownership. With regard to both museum and privately owned material the number of finds with information about the year of discovery is lower than the number of

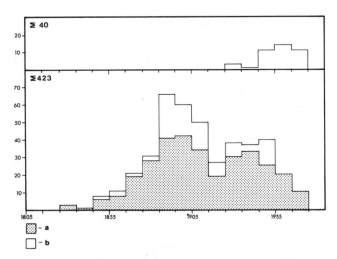

Fig. 1. Year of registration for all hoards. The upper section shows year of registration for finds in private ownership, the lower section shows year of registration for finds in museums – a: finds with known year of discovery or finds registered immediately after discovery. b: finds acquired from a small museum, dealers, or as part of a large private collection

actual finds. Thus figure 1 includes only 463 finds out of a total of 678. Material without information about the year of discovery is particularly common in provincial museums and private collections. In figure 2 the frequency diagram is divided into two parts, 'Zealand' and 'Jutland and Funen'. 'Zealand' comprises throughout the Zealand island group including Bornholm and Lolland-Falster. 'Jutland and Funen' consists of Jutland and the Funen islands with Langeland. This geographical division divides the material into two nearly equal parts. A

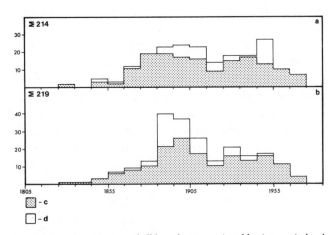

Fig. 2. Year of registration of all hoards on a regional basis. – a: Jutland & Funen, b: Zealand, c: finds with known year of discovery or finds registered immediately after discovery, d: finds acquired from a small museum, dealers, or as part of a large private collection.

comparison of the two diagrams in figure 2 shows that the number of finds has grown at much the same rate in the two areas. As for the Zealand islands, the frequency culminates in the period 1885-95, which is due to the acquisition of a large private collection, the Classen collection, by the National Museum. Similarly, the slight fluctuation in Jutland/Funen during the period 1945-55 was because a large Jutland private collection, Reffsgaard's No. 2 collection, was acquired by the National Museum. Both these collections contained a large number of neolithic hoards. If these factors are disregarded, it appears that Jutland/Funen is one decade ahead of the rest of the country. The peak in Jutland/Funen for finds registered directly in the museums was reached in 1875-85, while in the Zealand group this only happened in 1885-95. The difference, however, is slight. In both diagrams there is a marked decrease in the period 1915-25, after which the frequency increases in the years around World War II. Towards 1975 the amount of material found declines in both areas. If we compare with figure 1, and add the finds registered in private collections, the fall in frequency is less marked.

A comparison of the diagrams showing the dates when neolithic hoards were found (figures 1-2) with the corresponding diagrams for hoards from the early Bronze Age (Kristiansen 1974, fig. 1 ff.) reveals a striking difference. The Bronze Age finds increase at a steady rate from the period 1815-20 until the frequency reaches a peak around 1855-75. Some connection has been demonstrated between this frequency curve and a number of factors regarding research and economic geography (Kristiansen 1974, 126ff.). For another group of metal hoards from the German Iron Age (cf. Fonnesbech, fig. 1), the frequency rises in a nearly identical way from around 1815-20, culminating in the period 1865-75. By contrast, the frequency of neolithic hoard finds at first increases slowly and gradually in the collections after c. 1850, and the rate of discovery is at its height as late as 1885-1905. We therefore have to investigate whether the factors regarding research and economic geography that played a role in the discovery of finds from the Stone Age and Metal Age, respectively, are different, or whether there are special reasons for the 'deferment' of Stone Age finds.

RESEARCH FACTORS

The map in figure 3 shows that neolithic hoards are not evenly distributed over the whole of Denmark. The same impression is given by the diagram in figure 4, where the number of finds is given from each county, both the museum finds and those in private ownership. The richest source of finds in the Zealand island group are the counties of Præstø, Holbæk and Copenhagen, in that order. In the Jutland/Funen region Hjørring county comes first, both on a regional and a national basis, followed by the counties of Ålborg, Viborg and Randers. It is noteworthy that West and South Jutland have very sparse collections.

The distribution largely follows the most densely populated areas in the Neolithic, and can be explained in this manner. Important find areas also coincide with natural sources of flint in chalk zones. This is particularly true of Stevns and Møn, Vendsyssel and Himmerland (the latter two areas bordering on the chalk deposits in the Ålborg district), together with Djursland.

If we disregard the counties where less than 20 finds are registered, there are two counties which have a special place, viz. Ringkøbing and Holbæk. Here the National Museum carried out, in the 1940's and 1950's, respectively, two large archaeological surveys (Mathiassen 1948 & 1959). As a result of these field-programmes there was a marked increase in find material, and many finds in private ownership were registered. The number of finds in museums from these two counties is, however, not particularly large compared to the counties where intensive surveys have not taken place. On the other hand, the registered number of hoard finds in private collections is larger in the counties of Ringkøbing and Holbæk, nearly 3/4 of the material in the museums. That gives some basis for estimating how many finds would probably be registered if a correspondingly comprehensive registration were carried out in the rest of the country. It is estimated that the result would be c. 250 extra finds, or an increase of 37%. It is probable, however, that certain regions are under-represented because of the still somewhat uneven museum coverage of the country. It is therefore possible that there exists, or has existed, a much larger number of finds than it is possible to assess on this basis.

The accessions policy of the museums is shown in figs. 1-2. In the period 1845-85 there is a steady rise in acquisitions, especially as regards finds obtained direct from the finders, or obtained shortly after their discovery. The number of private collections with neolithic hoards is slight, as is the number procured from dealers. From around 1885 there is a significant increase in the number

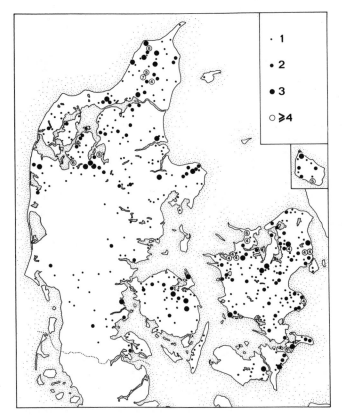

Fig. 3a. Distribution of neolithic hoards in Denmark.

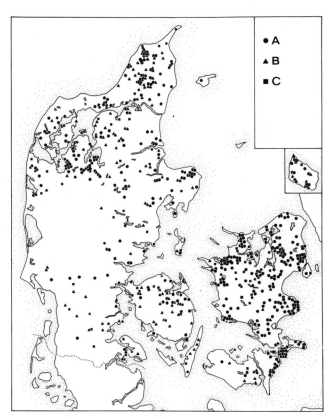

Fig 3b. Distribution of neolithic hoards in Denmark. – A: finds in the National Museum. B: finds in provincial museums. C: finds in private ownership.

of finds acquired both directly and indirectly. At this time especially we seem to encounter a change in the accessions policy of the National Museum, whereby finds are incorporated regardless of whether they originate direct from the finder, from a private collector, or from a dealer. As a rule finds are paid for with a sum fixed by the museum staff, and the practice is begun of sending out questionnaires to supplement information about the finds. This period coincides with the circulation in local districts of museum personnel, who thereby come into more direct contact with regions which otherwise had rarely been touched by the activities of the institution. Some places where neolithic hoards were found were registered in the parish records of the National Museum in connection with these visits by museum people, but the finds do not figure in the frequency diagram because the year of their discovery is mostly unknown. It is also in the period 1885-1915 that the National Museum makes use of its authority to procure from the provincial museums

finds considered of outstanding scientific value, among them several neolithic hoards.

The driving force behind the National Museum's intensive acquisition of finds and information concerning finds in this period was Sophus Müller, who became Inspector at the then 'Royal Museum for Nordic Antiquities' in 1885, and became Director of antiquities when the National Museum was established in 1892. It was also Müller who published, *inter alia,* the first scientific analysis of the neolithic hoards (Müller 1886), 20 years after J.J.A. Worsaae had presented his work on the Bronze Age hoards (Worsaae 1866), and 23 years after the publication of the first large Iron Age sacrificial find (Engelhardt 1863-65, cf. ibid. 1867-69, and Worsaae 1867). The scientific analysis of Stone Age hoards thus occurred with a significant delay compared to that of hoards from the Metal Age. The recognition of the neolithic hoards as a separate find group was also somewhat delayed. In fact, only 12 hoard finds (with known year of discovery) were

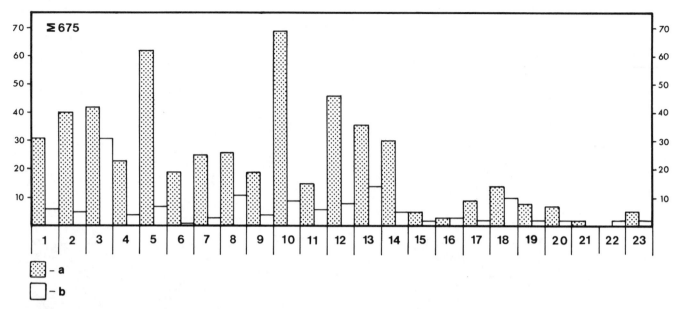

Fig. 4. Distribution of finds according to county. For numbers on the horizontal axis, refer to key p. 248 ff. a: hoards in museums, b: hoards in private collections.

registered before 1855. The most likely explanation for this is that this type of find did not attract sufficient attention for the objects to be kept as associated finds and incorporated as such into private and museum collections. An examination of Vedel Simonsen's large collection acquired by the Royal Museum for Nordic Antiquities in 1854 confirms this. In the catalogues of the collection are recorded not a few single flint artefacts said to have been found with several others of the same kind. The originally associated finds have been separated, and the objects have been lost, sold, or gone into other collections. The first large private collection which contains neolithic hoard finds as originally associated is the Classen collection, which was procured by the Royal Museum in 1887, and which mainly contains finds from Lolland and Falster.

A total of 176 finds were obtained by the museums in the period 1885-1915, i.e. 42% of all finds with known year of registration or discovery. After this there is a marked decline. If we are to point to any significant research factor, it is most likely to relate to the general abatement of the National Museum's activities in the 1920's.

For the following decades up until the present day it is difficult to single out particular research-related factors. It is, of course, important that collecting activities intensified during the last war to keep pace with the peat cutting in bogs, from which came a large number of finds. The hoard find frequency also increases in these years, without approaching that of Sophus Müller's time.

Nor has the recent growth in museum services caused the frequency to rise. On the other hand finds in private collections are now registered more often (fig. 1). There is no doubt that we are more restrained today in acquiring neolithic material for museums. One of the reasons for this is that we are less eager to obtain objects that are already heavily represented in the museum. In this field there has been a gradual change in the accessions policy of the museums, which for instance means that single finds of flint axes etc. are seldom reported. The number of purchases is also greatly reduced, while large sums now go to the museums' excavation activities. Several provincial museums consistently refuse to buy antiquities. This development may be significant for the type of find discussed here, which is very seldom encountered in archaeological excavations.

Another factor, which is more difficult to control, is the worth of flint artefacts as objects for collection. They continue to be much more common in private collections than metal hoards. There is little widespread appreciation among laymen of the special value of closed finds, including those of flint and stone. There are many cases of large hoard finds being divided among several owners before an archaeological institution has been notified of the find.

SOCIO-ECONOMIC FACTORS

For only 343 of the whole 678 hoards do we have any information about how the find occurred, i.e. what activities – cultivation, digging, building etc. – which led to the dicovery. The fact that the circumstances of only about half the finds are known is doubtless because many finds were acquired through dealers, or purchased from private collections etc.

An examination of the circumstances of the finds is, however, necessary in order to judge the extent to which socio-economic factors affect the number of finds. Table C lists the nine types of economic activity which have resulted in the discovery of this category of find, together with a tenth group comprising 10-14% of the finds, which includes more specialized or not precisely defined activities.

It can be seen that cultivation, peat cutting, and land improvement in the form of drainage, in that order, are the most frequent means by which these finds are made. Of all the other activities only building and construction work have played any part. It will be noticed that the number of finds originating from archaeological excavations is quite insignificant. Moreover, a considerable number of the finds listed under the heading 'other' should presumably be distributed under the headings 'drainage work' and 'peat cutting', but the scarcity of information has not justified placing some of the finds in a definite category.

There are some striking similarities to be seen in different parts of the country as regards the cause of discovery; but there are also differences. While the agricultural activity in the three areas has provided approximately the same number of finds, more material has been discovered from drainage in the Zealand island group than in Funen and Jutland. Conversely, while peat cutting is the most frequent means of discovery in Jutland, in Funen it has been of equal importance with agricultural work, but in Zealand it has led to the discovery of nearly 1/5 of the finds. Building and construction work has been most important in the Zealand islands, twice as important as in Jutland.

As for drainage, the difference in numbers reflects the fact that this form of land improvement was practised more intensively in the islands than in Jutland from around 1860 (see the article: Economic Development, table 5).

It is more difficult to explain why peat cutting has

Table C.

	Zealand	Funen	Jutland
Cultivation	29.0%	28.5%	29.0%
Drainage work	20.0%	19.0%	14.0%
Building & construction work, & maintenance of waterways and canals	13.5%	0.0%	6.5%
Peat cutting	21.5%	28.5%	32.0%
Marl digging	1.5%	5.0%	2.0%
Gravel digging	1.0%	5.0%	3.0%
Other industrial activity	1.0%	0.0%	0.5%
Gardening & forestry	1.5%	0.0%	1.5%
Archaeological excavations	0.5%	0.0%	1.5%
Other (including unspecified digging)	10.5%	14.0%	10.0%
Total	100.0%	100.0%	100.0%

played a lesser role as a means of discovery in Zealand than in the rest of the country. Perhaps this is because archaeological material had already been found at an early stage in the Zealand peat bogs (compare e.g. Late Bronze Age hoards, Kristiansen 1974, fig. 5), and because many layers containing finds had already been removed by the time the registration of Stone Age hoards began in the middle of the 19th century.

Table D.

Topography of sites:	Zealand (166 finds)	Funen & & Jutland (231 finds)
bog	50.0%	58.0%
edge of bog	5.4%	3.9%
slope or elevation near bog	3.0%	1.3%
elevation in bog	0.6%	1.3%
Total bog finds	59.0%	64.5%
water meadow or damp depression	10.9%	14.1%
spring, lake or watercourse	5.4%	3.1%
large stones in bog, water meadow or lake	1.8%	1.3%
Total finds in bogs and wet soils	77.1%	83.0%
gravel or sand	4.8%	3.1%
clay	3.0%	0.0%
elevation	1.8%	3.1%
large stones	12.1%	9.5%
in or near burial mound	1.2%	1.3%
Total	100.0%	100.0%

108

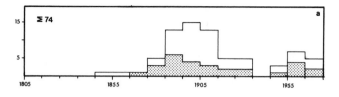

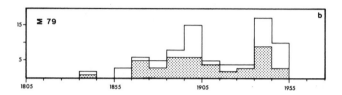

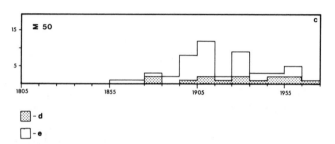

☒ - d

☐ - e

Fig. 5. Year of registration for hoard finds resulting from (a) cultivation, (b) peat cutting and (c) drainage and ditch digging. d: Jutland, e: Zealand & Funen.

The information on the circumstances of finds is supplemented in table D with data on the topography of sites. We only have information about the topography of a total of 397 finds.

Together with table C, table D helps to define the typical topography for a large proportion of the neolithic hoards: bogs, water meadows, and other wet soils. Four fifths of all finds of which the topography is known originate from soils of this kind. Funen and Jutland together have a slightly larger proportion of finds from wet soils than Zealand. This corresponds with the observation made above that there are fewer finds from peat bogs in Zealand than in the rest of the country.

The indications of the year of dicovery (figure 5 a-c) must be interpreted in the light of the information about the conditions and circumstances of the finds given in the two tables just mentioned. The upper section of the diagram (5a) shows how little material resulted from agricultural work until c. 1870. The steep rise in frequency from 1875 till the turn of the century doubtless reflects the improvement of agricultural techniques carried out

in this period, especially the introduction of new types of plough. If we compare the activity in Jutland in bringing large areas of heath as well as commons and stretches of meadow into cultivation, it is remarkable that Jutland has little share in the growth towards the turn of the century. As we can see from the map in figure 3, it is not the light soils which have yielded most finds. It is probably the deep ploughing from 1947 onwards that causes the slight increase in the frequency of finds which can be seen around this time in figure 5a.

As the preceding discussion has indicated, peat cutting first played a role as a cause of discovery in the second half of the 19th century. The histogram in figure 5b shows clearly that there are two significant peaks, one in the 1890's, and the other in the years around World War II. After 1950 peat exploitation ceased, except for some harrowing of Sphagnum from the surface of the raised bogs.

The last diagram showing year of discovery (figure 5c) indicates that drainage and ditching were the latest causative factors: the main feature is the drainage of the meadow and bog areas reclaimed in the 1890's. Although drainage of cultivated · areas has today been largely completed in Denmark, there is still some maintenance work required on the drainage system, being a potential source of finds.

We have information on the find depth of only 184 out of 678 finds, which is insufficient to give a precise picture. The histograms in figure 6a-b are based on the available information. It will be noticed that there have been more bog finds at a greater depth in Jutland/Funen than in Zealand.

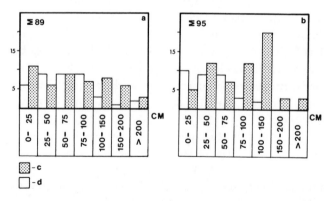

Fig. 6. Depth of finds. a: Zealand, b: Jutland & Funen, c: finds from bogs and watermeadows, d: finds from dry soils.

If we are to look for a cause for the marked decline in the total frequency of finds in the last 20-25 years, without regard to possible research factors, it must be the cessation of peat cutting in the years just after World War II, which removed this rich source of material, cf. figure 5b. Another factor to be considered is that efforts for nature conservation tend more and more to protect bog and meadow stretches for animal life and to maintain the natural landscape. The cultivation of low-lying swampy areas has practically ceased. Old peat cuttings lie idle as small lakes and gradually fill in. They become a refuge for the increasingly hard-pressed wild flora and fauna, and are protected for that reason. One factor for which modern soil-utilizaton techniques are responsible is the gradual soil movement which covers up the peat deposits in the small depressions in open fields, and with them the finds that might have been placed there.

The development in the areas mentioned has considerable significance for neolithic hoard finds, and therefore one can hardly conclude that the decrease in finds means that hoard finds are exhausted. It seems more likely that it is modern agricultural practice, the discontinued use of peat for fuel, and the changed attitude to the natural landscape, which in large part account for the decrease in finds.

Poul Otto Nielsen,
The National Museum,
1st Department,
Frederiksholms Kanal 12,
1220 Copenhagen K.

NOTE

The author is indebted to Klaus Ebbesen for information concerning finds in private ownership.

The manuscript was completed in 1978. Works published later have not been referred to in the text. A greater part of the finds discussed here were treated in a recent study: M. Rech, "Studien zu Depotfunden der Trichterbecher- und Einzelgrabkultur des Nordens". Offa-Bücher, Band 39. Neumünster 1979.

REFERENCES

BECKER, C.J., 1947: Mosefundne Lerkar fra yngre Stenalder. *Aarbøger for nordisk Oldk. og Hist.*

– 1952: Die nordschwedischen Flintdepots. *Acta Archaeologica XXIII.*

– 1957: Die frühneolithischen Bernsteinfunde Dänemarks. *Abramiceo zbornik II (Abramic-Festschrift II).* Vjesnik za arheologiju i historiju dalmatinsku LVI-LIX/2, 1954-57 (Bulletin d'archeologie et d'histoire dalmate LVI-LIX/2, 1954-57).

BRØNDSTED, J., 1938: *Danmarks Oldtid* I, Stenalderen. Københ.

– 1957: *Danmarks Oldtid* I, Stenalderen. Københ.

CULLBERG, C., 1968: On Artifact Analysis. *Acta Arch. Lundensia,* Ser. 4°, 7. Lund.

EBBESEN, K., 1975: Die jüngere Trichterbecherkultur auf den dänischen Inseln. *Arkæologiske Studier* II, Københ.

ENGELHARDT, C., 1863-65: *Sønderjyske Mosefund* I-II, Københ.

– 1867-69: *Fynske Mosefund* I-II, Københ.

KRISTIANSEN, K., 1974: En kildekritisk analyse af depotfund fra Danmarks yngre bronzealder (periode IV-V). *Aarbøger f. nord. Oldk. og Hist.*

LOMBORG, E., 1973: Die Flintdolche Dänemarks. *Nordiske Fortidsminder,* Ser. B: 1, Københ.

MATHIASSEN, Th., 1948: Studier over Vestjyllands Oldtidsbebyggelse. *Nationalmuseets Skrifter, Arkæol.-hist. Rk.* II, Københ.

– 1959: Nordvestsjællands Oldtidsbebyggelse. *Nationalmuseets Skrifter, Arkæol.-hist. Rk.* VII, Københ.

MÜLLER, S., 1886: Votivfund fra Sten- og Bronzealderen. *Aarbøger f. nord. Oldk. og Hist.*

– 1897: *Vor Oldtid.* Københ.

NIELSEN, P.O., 1977(a): De tyknakkede flintøksers kronologi. *Aarbøger f. nord. Oldk. og Hist.*

– 1977(b): Die Flintbeile der frühen Trichterbecherkultur in Dänemark. *Acta Archaeologica* vol. 48.

PETERSEN, H., 1890: Hypotesen om religiøse Offer- og Votivfund fra Danmarks forhistoriske Tid. *Aarbøger f. nord. Oldk. og Hist.*

WORSAAE, J.J.A., 1866: Om nogle Mosefund fra Broncealderen. *Aarbøger f. nord. Oldk. og Hist.*

– 1867: Om Betydningen af vore store Mosefund fra den ældre Jernalder. *Oversigt over det Kgl. danske Videnskabs Selskabs Forhandlinger.* København.

Neolithic Settlements of the TRB Culture

by KARSTEN DAVIDSEN

INTRODUCTION

In an earlier publication the author stated that TRB settlement sites should be regarded as representative of the total occupation, whereas other types of find have special circumstances rendering them unsuitable for any assessment of the extent of settlement (Davidsen 1978, p. 158). This opinion was based on the four following assumptions: 1) A settlement site always produces remains which are demonstrably living remains. The total number of (known and unknown) sites must therefore be expected to give an accurate reflection of the occupation. 2) For the time being it is impossible to determine the proportion of habitation and other finds (single finds, burials, sacrificial deposits and hoards). 3) Relatively few Stone Age settlements have been lost, while it is impossible to estimate the number of burials, sacrificial deposits and hoards lost. 4) The available material from TRB settlements is a representative sample.

It is the last of these assumptions which we shall examine in this paper. For this end the author has collected data on a total of 400 settlements containing TRB pottery. Only definite settlement finds are included, i.e. the pottery is associated with flint tools probably related to settlement, or associated with a settlement deposit (shell midden, rubbish pit, culture layer). The reason why only sites containing pottery are included is partly because a total recording is impracticable, and partly because minor flint assemblages as a rule cannot be assumed with any certainty to represent TRB settlements (for example, a flint axe could have been brought to the site or shaped at a later date). It often happens that several recorded finds originate from the same settlement. In such cases only the first find with definite TRB pottery is taken into account (except fig. 2-3). Furthermore, the practice has been followed that where a find is classified as a result of a museum survey it is included even if only a single sherd was found and even if some of the material remained in private collections. However, this practice has not been followed in the cases where a private find was made many years before a museum survey and did not give rise to it. These principles mean that the activities of private (amateur) archaeologists do not receive enough attention, and therefore it should be pointed out that most museum investigations are occasioned by the efforts of amateur archaeologists or other interested people.

Another problem is to delimit each settlement. In the relatively few doubtful cases this has been done by assuming a minimum distance of 2-300 metres between different settlements. When sites have a natural limit (as in Åmose), this figure can be smaller. In practice there have been few problems of this kind, and in nearly all cases it has been possible to isolate settlements as in the parish records of the National Museum.

The material discussed was recorded in the National Museum and nearly all the larger provincial museums. The National Museum collections have been examined several times, and practically all this material has been recorded (NM VIII lists only finds described in the literature). It can be provisionally assumed that about half the material in the other museums has not been analysed (this is true mainly of more recent finds). We have also made use of published references and information in the National Museum about finds in private collections and local museums. In this connection we have covered systematically the files of site reports, topography and private collections. It is therefore reasonable to assume that there has been a balanced assessment of the material.

ANALYSIS

The diagram in fig. 1a shows the year of discovery for TRB settlements. In this diagram the finds are divided into three main groups, those made by the National Museum, by other museums and by private individuals.

This division is based on the recorded ownership of artefacts directly after excavation (or collection). This procedure has the advantage of being objective, and has been used because it is not always possible to determine when an investigation is scientific or amateur.

Figure 1b-c is the same diagram divided into two parts. One of these (fig. 1b) comprises finds that wholly or in part have been discovered by excavation, while the other (fig. 1c) shows the finds known only as collected material. The number of 'private' finds is the same in the two diagrams, while fig. 1c clearly shows that museums have taken very little interest in collecting finds.

If there had been a standard practice for collecting material, we could probably expect a steadily rising curve, and the irregularities can be easily explained by reference to the history of research. The oldest of the finds (from 1824) was only recognized as a settlement long afterwards (Becker 1950, p. 179), so that the true beginning must be set at 1851 when J. Steenstrup found TRB pottery in three shell middens (Forchhammer et al. 1851-56, p. 60 ff.). After this there are two decades during which the National Museum does not account for a single find. This lack of interest is apparently due to a feeling that the problems have already been solved. A new burst of activity takes place around the turn of the century in connection with the work of the Second Kitchen Midden Commission. With the completion of this project there is another falling off. After this there is a steady growth of find material, which continues till 1954. The dedicated work of T. Mathiassen is clearly reflected in the diagrams during the period 1935-54.

In the period 1955-64 there is a pronounced decline, which is probably a reaction to the former intensive research – a phenomenon we have observed twice before. Doubtless another significant cause is the changing nature of the National Museum's relationship with amateur archaeologists. Figure 1a shows that the years 1945-54 are characterized by a marked increase in the number of private finds. This was a deliberate policy. The task was too great, and part of the work was delegated to private collectors and amateurs who were in close touch with the museum. The result was that settlement finds increasingly became collectors' objects, and also attracted the interest of amateurs not in contact with the museum. This could well have resulted in fewer reported finds. We can also assume that the National Museum's interest in surface finds was very slight in these years because of the widespread collection of such material in previous deca-

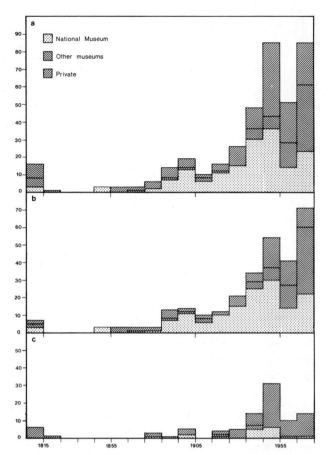

Fig. 1. Year of registration for settlements with TRB pottery, a: total finds, b: excavated finds, c: collected finds.

des. As a result, the museum knew much less about the work of the amateurs, and many finds were not registered. This still seems to be a weak point, and more registration of private collections is highly desirable.

Another factor became important in the years 1955-64: in this period the National Museum's share of the finds has fallen sharply, but at the same time the activities of the other museums increase, so that these two groups are now equally important. This development becomes more pronounced from 1965 to 1974, and will doubtless become a lasting phenomenon.

Figure 2 shows the year of discovery for shell middens, pits, and culture layers, respectively. A single locality may figure in two or three diagrams, sometimes with different years of discovery. First and foremost one is struck by the early discovery of shell middens. This is a direct consequence of the history of research. Already in the 1880's it was realized that definite neolithic settle-

112

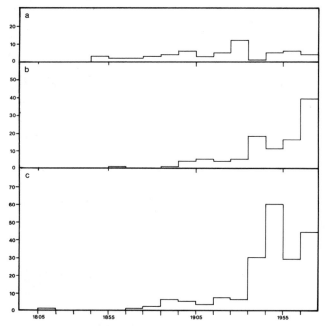

Fig. 2. Year of registration for a: shell middens, b: pits, and c: culture layers with TRB pottery.

ments existed, but in the next five decades there was little interest in investigating such finds. On the contrary, many mesolithic settlements were excavated, mainly shell middens. It is also noticeable that most of the shell middens were found between the years 1925 to 1934, while the following decade, during which the so-called Third Kitchen Midden Commission was in operation, marks the lowest point on the curve for shell middens (i.e. few new sites were excavated).

Another interesting detail in fig. 2 is the relationship between pits and culture layers in the most recent finds. A growing proportion of the collected material is from pit finds. This is doubtless the result of the steadily increasing depth of ploughing, which destroys the culture layers. This is made more significant by the fact that the destruction of the culture layers permits the mechanical exposure of larger areas.

Figure 3 indicates the duration of the excavations by the National Museum (as far as this is known). The material used here comprises all excavations of Stone Age settlements with TRB pottery, and also includes a few cases where a settlement features twice in the diagrams. As far as the early excavations are concerned these diagrams cannot illustrate the extent of the efforts invested in examining neolithic settlements. This is be-

cause about 2/3 of the investigations before 1935 took place at sites which were either shell middens or were mainly from the mesolithic period. This is compensated for by the fact that not one of the finds from after 1954 can be described as an intrusive element in a mesolithic settlement.

One of the most characteristic features of the graphs are the many short field-programmes in the period 1935-44 (fig. 3a). This led to a decline in the number of more extended field-programmes (fig. 3c). It must have been the new interest in settlement archaeology which necessitated this policy. Perhaps the renewed decline in short field-programmes from 1945 to 1954 was due to a greater dependence on the work of amateur archaeologists.

In recent years the tendency has been either to undertake a survey that can be completed in a day, or to have an extended excavation. This procedure may have unfortunate consequences for future settlement studies because the material which results from a survey is often insufficient for an accurate dating. Probably some of the more expensive excavations could profitably be replaced by several minor field-programmes.

The significance of socio-economic factors is shown in fig. 4, which gives the cause of discovery of the various settlements. It has not been possible to get this information for 48 of the sites. The most important factor is

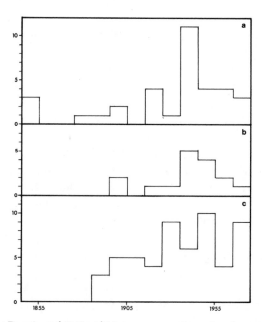

Fig. 3. Duration of National Museum excavations of settlements with TRB pottery, a: 1-2 days, b: 3-6 days, c: over 6 days.

ploughing, which has invariably resulted in the identification of many settlements from surface finds (fig. 4a). Surface finds have also been revealed by natural phenomena, and the next diagram (fig. 4b) comprises sites that have been found as a result of marine erosion, fallen trees or sand drift. Furthermore, this group includes a few finds that were recognized during a surface examination of places not under the plough.

Among the various sorts of artificial soil disturbance which can lead to the discovery of settlements, only peat cutting and gathering of peat litter are limited to a certain period, this restriction on the other hand being very marked (fig. 4c). By far the largest proportion of these finds are from Åmose.

However, the other digging activities are very evenly distributed during the last 100 years. Gravel digging has played a certain role (fig. 4d), whereas clay digging has been less important (fig. 4e). This may have given rise to a certain distortion in the registration of material, so that the light soils have been over-represented, but this is probably of minor importance. The other fairly common factors leading to the discovery of sites are ditch-digging (fig. 4f), road building (fig. 4g), and house construction (fig. 4h). To this must be added several other types of earth work that have been combined into a single group (fig. 4i). This includes activities such as the dredging of rivers, fencing, levelling of grounds, gardening etc. This group also comprises a few finds which have been exposed by explosions.

At the bottom of the diagram (fig. 4k) is a large group which includes all the finds that have been accidentally discovered in connection with the excavation of types of find other than Stone Age settlements. If we had also included excavations primarily designed to investigate a settlement from the Older Stone Age, the group would have been much larger. There have, however, been too many instances where it cannot be distinguished whether the main purpose of the excavation was to investigate the Mesolithic or the Neolithic. The excavated features mentioned in fig. 4k are very diverse, and extend chronologically from the Paleolithic to the Middle Ages. It is important that this group of finds is so large because we can be fairly certain from this that the areas shown on the distribution maps as poor in archaeological material really are so.

Since there is no account of the total activities of the museums from year to year, the group of neolithic settlements that have resulted from the excavation of other

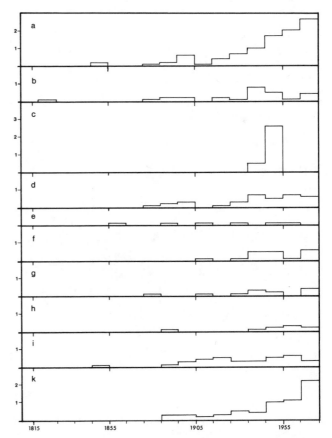

Fig. 4. Cause of discovery of sites with TRB pottery.
a: field collection (30%), b: natural phenomena (8%), c: peat cutting (9%), d: gravel and sand digging (11%), e: clay and marl digging (2%), f: ditch digging (6%), g: road building (3%), h: house construction (2%), i: other earth work (10%), k: excavation of find groups other than Stone Age settlements (19%).

material is the best basis to assess how high a priority has been placed on the excavation of neolithic settlements. over time. In the period 1935-44 we find the lowest percentage (9%) of these finds (calculated in proportion to the total number of settlements from the decade in question). This corresponds well with the general impression that this was a time when there was considerable emphasis placed on the study of Stone Age settlements. As at this time many short-term excavations took place (fig. 3a), this may have contributed to the low figure. The percentage rises in the following three decades and has never been as high as now (1965-74: 26%). This is likely to be because research on neolithic settlements has a particularly low priority at present. The longer duration

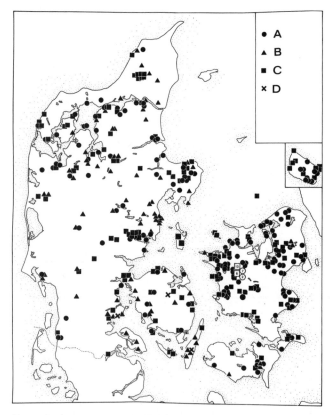

Fig. 5. Settlements containing TRB pottery. A: The National Museum, B: Other museum, C: Private collections, D: Unknown.

of excavations has probably had little effect on the percentage since it applies equally to all other find groups.

The flint content of Stone Age sites means that these are hardly ever destroyed. There may be some exceptions, such as shell middens, which are occasionally removed because of the economic value of the shell, and settlements in peat. But the decisive question in assessing the representativity of Stone Age settlements will always be, how many sites have been found. The percentage lost is so small that we can disregard it. This is a crucial advantage over other sites such as burials and hoards, and we can assume in advance that it is possible to obtain a very high degree of representativity. Only if there has been a varying intensity in collection activities in different districts, can it be claimed that the settlements are not a random sample. All the evidence indicates that interest in collecting settlement material has had an even

geographic distribution. Only in a few areas is it clear that investigations have been particularly numerous (Åmose) or few (parts of South Jutland). The finds originating from the excavation of other find groups presumably have a completely random distribution. This is probably also true of the large group of finds discovered as a result of different kinds of earth working. At any rate, there is a very large body of people who volunteer information about such finds, while surface finds are made largely by amateur archaeologists. There seems to be a relatively even number of these amateurs in different parts of the country if we take into account that we are considering a period of over 100 years. There appears to be no type of landscape where the finds are difficult to locate, and it can be mentioned that there are also several finds from forest and urban zones.

Moreover, it is fortunate that the conditions which cause an uneven collection of material operate to different effect. In this respect it is particularly interesting that areas which were earlier neglected to some extent by the National Museum (Funen and parts of Jutland) have experienced a very marked increase in the material found in recent years, as a result of the development of local museums in these areas. In Bornholm the situation is reversed. Here there is a clear preponderance of old finds, and with the exception of a period during the 1950's there are almost no additions from our century. There is a similar compensation if we look at the different types of finds. Pit finds were underrepresented in early discoveries, while the destruction of culture layers in recent times has made the finding of neolithic settlement pits a common occurrence. The shell middens are a particularly clear example since, as mentioned above, they are heavily overrepresented in finds from before c. 1935. On the other hand it appears that in recent decades there has been a deliberate avoidance of shell midden excavation. The pattern of shell midden distribution is independent of any particular research programme: these sites have been found in exactly the same manner as other settlements.

Although to a great extent shell middens have been registered in the parish records of the National Museum (unlike other types of site), finds of the kind discussed here rarely occur in connection with this registration. We cannot be sure whether the present percentage of shell middens (14%) corresponds to that originally found, but their geographic distribution has been established with certainty.

CONCLUSION

We may conclude from the previous discussion that the material from TRB settlements is fairly representative, and suitable for statistical analysis if the areas involved are sufficiently large. But this applies only to the present situation. Only thirty or forty years ago a statistical analysis was impossible because shell midden finds were over-represented.

Statistical assessment is not yet possible on one important point. There is no hope of calculating the original number of settlements because we lack a sufficiently large area where the total number of sites has been established by exhaustive field work. Admittedly, Åmose is an exception, but conditions here are not typical and Mathiassen's investigations in North-West Jutland and North-West Zealand were not sufficiently intensive to serve as a starting point for such studies (Thrane 1974, p. 308).

This problem can be resolved, however, by further field-programmes in settlement archaeology.

Karsten Davidsen,
Folkets Alle 10,
2000 Copenhagen F.

REFERENCES

BECKER, C.J., 1950: Den grubekeramiske kultur i Danmark. *Årbøger for Nordisk Oldkyndighed og Historie*, p. 153-263. København.

DAVIDSEN, K., 1978: *The Final TRB Culture in Denmark*. Arkæologiske Studier V. København.

FORCHHAMMER, G., STEENSTRUP, J. & WORSAAE, J., 1851-56: Undersøgelser i geologisk-antiqvarisk Retning. København.

THRANE, H., 1974: Bebyggelseshistorie – en arkæologisk arbejdsopgave. *Fortid og Nutid* XXV, p. 299-321. København.

Early Bronze Age Burial Finds

by KRISTIAN KRISTIANSEN

INTRODUCTION

Burial finds from the Early Bronze Age almost all come from barrows which have been exposed from the beginning to looting, damage or demolition. A distinction must be made, however, between looting and demolition.

A number of well documented examples show that, to a limited extent, the *looting of barrows* already occurred during the Bronze Age. And up through history digging has taken place from time to time in the hope of finding gravegoods. Testimony to this from the Viking Age, for instance, is given by the name Thorstein Haugabriotr (barrow breaker), and there are scattered references to treasure hunts of this nature through the ages (Werlauff 1807, 12ff.; Hermansen 1954). Yet archaeological investigations seem to support the assumption that it has never been a question of systematic plundering.

The first organized effort to record prehistoric monuments began in the Renaissance with Ole Worm's: Danicorum Monumentorum Libri Sex, published in 1643 (Klindt Jensen 1975, 18ff.), but it was not followed up by any excavations. The cabinets of curiosities which now became fashionable among royal collectors in Europe only included a few random archaeological relics. This also applied to Ole Worm's collection and later collections (Neergård 1916). The number of private collections continued to be fairly limited, as collecting was a prestigious hobby cultivated by the aristocracy. Werlauff only knows of the loss of eight private collections in 1808 (Werlauff 1808, 44-49), none of which contained any archaeological relics to speak of. There seem to be two reasons why relatively little digging for treasure occurred. Firstly, rich graves were rarely discovered because those digging rarely reached the central grave, yet there are often references to burial urns, cinerary vessels, etc. – i.e. later graves with only a few artefacts. Secondly, the peasantry generally regarded barrows with considerable superstition, so barrows were left undisturbed for fear of desecrating the dead and arousing the wrath of the spirits of the underworld. Many examples of these superstitions are known far into the 1800's, just as they are revealed by barrow names and legends (Hald 1969, 59ff.).

A slight change, however, seems to become apparent in the course of the 18th century. Bircherod thus relates in 1701: "Even a few years ago the Peasantry considered the ancient artefacts found by chance to be so much rubbish and they were thrown away. But after some sagacious people have begun to scrutinize the relics, and to question the peasants, as well as to promise them rewards for what they bring in, these things begin to come to light, indeed they seem to rise from their graves" (quoted after Müller 1892, 162). This type of excavation occurred in Funen, for example, but a number of papers published in the 18th century show that it was more common in Schleswig-Holstein and Mecklenburg (Tanderup and Ebbesen 1979).

The *destruction of barrows,* on the other hand, is a phenomenon about which extremely little is known because – as opposed to treasure hunting – it could be justified from an agricultural point of view, and carried out whenever a barrow obstructed farming. In general, though, barrows seem to have remained unmolested, and their systematic ploughing out did not begin until later on. Many old field names recorded in Christian V's land register (1681-83) reveal the existence of barrows, dolmens and passage-graves (Hald 1969, 13ff.), and records from later parish inspections show that they were still preserved. Yet a study of megalithic monuments has shown that in Funen about 50% had vanished in the span of time between 1681-83 and the inspection of parishes two hundred years later (Kousgård Sørensen 1964). Nevertheless, when approaching 60,000 ancient monuments in Denmark have survived thousands of years of agriculture (Mathiassen 1956), it ought to be possible to pinpoint some concrete reasons for this.

There can be little doubt that methods of cultivation

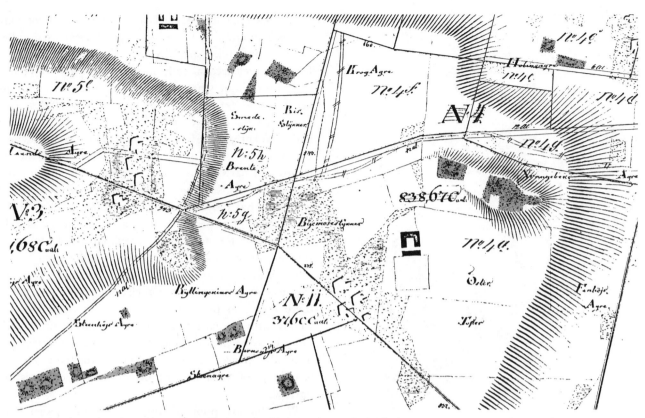

Fig. 1. Detail of a cadastral map from 1816 with Asnæs parish in North-west Zealand. The many ancient monuments on arable land are marked with the reference for common. Touched up here by dark stippling (after Thorsen 1980,4).

have decided to what extent barrows are preserved today. In this context a decisive factor has been the unchanging farming and settlement patterns from the Middle Ages until the 18th century. Only between 20% and 30% of the land was under the plough, with regional variations (cf. Baudou's article), the remaining unwooded land was common, heath or meadow. Barrows often contributed to production as land where a cow or a couple of sheep could be put out to graze, or where grass was cut for hay. For example, a number of published enclosure maps of Zealand from the end of the 18th century show that most ancient monuments served as patches of pasture amid arable land (fig. 1). Many barrows stood in groups[1] which were too difficult to remove, instead the land round them was worked, while the ancient sites themselves were left as pasture. The destruction of lone barrows was probably more common. Steensberg gives examples of the disappearance of single barrows in Jutland in 1616 and 1638 (Steensberg 1969, 530). These isolated cases of destruction have naturally had a more serious effect in areas with only a few scat-

tered barrows. Barrows on manor lands were probably more systematically destroyed than those on peasant holdings because estates were more effectively farmed. However, truly landed estates were only a small percentage of the total amount of farmland, but because of a certain geographical variation it may be noticeable in the number of barrows destroyed (fig. 2). The biggest estates were on the Danish islands where they owned between 10 and 15% of the land. In Jutland less than 10% was under estates. The concentration of manors on the islands was highest in South Zealand, Lolland, and Funen; in Jutland it was particularly in the north (Bergsøe 1847, 27ff. and 60ff.).

To form a reliable impression of the extent to which barrows were destroyed prior to 1800 in different parts of Denmark, it is necessary to investigate systematically where the preserved barrows have stood in the old cultural landscape, taking a representative number of parishes throughout the country – whether on arable land, common, heath, or in woodland. Although in depth studies cannot be made in the present paper, certain general

Fig. 2. Map showing landed estates c. 1940 (after Mathiassen 1943).

which saw the felling of the last great forests. Barrows are not as numerous in these old forested areas as in other parts of Jutland, especially West Jutland where much forest was cleared already in prehistoric and early historic times, and where place-names linked with forests are few and far between. In areas where afforestation post-dates the barrows, trees have grown up round them and frequently served as protection. The extent to which barrows have been destroyed can be assessed by the number of barrows recorded in forests, and the number recorded in fields. If most of the barrows are in woodland it means that barrows in fields were levelled before the time of parish inspections. The sheet maps for vols. I-II in Aner and Kersten, show considerable differences on the islands. For example, in Lolland and Falster by far the greatest number of barrows is in woodland, thus indicating widespread destruction elsewhere. Yet in Zealand there seems to be far more barrows in fields than in woods, with the exception of Præstø county ("amt") with more barrows in woodland. In Funen most barrows are in fields. However, most surviving woodland on the islands is of such ancient origin that it contains no barrows.

With the exception of land under manors, therefore, the systematic levelling of barrows seems to have been rare in early times. Due in part to superstition, in part to ineffective methods of cultivation which left countryside with common, heath and woodland intact. There is evidence to suggest that a more systematic destruction of barrows commenced earlier in Lolland, Falster, and Præstø county (in Zealand), than elsewhere in Denmark. These conclusions seem also to comply with the few bronzes known to have been recovered prior to 1805. The question, then, is at what period did the systematic and widespread destruction of barrows in earnest begin?

There can be little doubt that the first phase set in with the land reforms and abolition of the open-field system. Even though these measures may not have immediately given rise to improved methods of cultivation, they were instrumental in bringing commons under the plough. The disappearance of the open-field system and villeinage likewise encouraged the peasantry to farm more effectively. The Royal Commission for the Preservation of Northern Antiquities, "Den Kongelige Comission til Oldsagers Opbevaring" set up in 1807, was a direct result of the increase in the destruction of barrows which followed the land reforms. Both Nyerup and Münster speak of the imminent threat to ancient monuments

trends can be outlined. For instance, there is little doubt that the widespread heaths of Central and West Jutland acted as a protection for barrows far into the 19th century, and are one of the main reasons why so many barrows are recorded in these areas. The same applies to the common on the islands, particularly Zealand's wide tracts of common on which there are preserved more barrows than among the rest of the islands[2]. On the other hand, the absence of barrows in East Jutland is presumably because there have never been any (Randsborg 1974, 40), and the considerable number of dolmens and passage-graves preserved in the area would seem to confirm this. In the Bronze Age much of this part of Jutland was probably covered by forest. Research by Dalgas into the ancient forests of Jutland has demonstrated that the frequency of old forest placenames, and the number of barrows per square mile (Danish, 4½ × 1 statute mile) are complementary (Dalgas 1883-84). Far into the Middle Ages there were dense forests up through Central Jutland, in east Himmerland, and mid-Vendsyssel. The most intensive clearance presumably began in the Middle Ages and continued into the 17th and 18th centuries,

(Hermansen 1953). Admittedly only few reports on the destruction of barrows date from before 1807. The first systematic insight into the ancient monuments of Denmark is given in B. Thorlacius's antiquarian work, "Bemærkninger over de i Danmark endnu tilværende Hedenolds Høie og Steensætninger" published in 1809, and which was based on reports to the commission from 700-800 priests in various parts of the country. It reveals a story of widespread destruction. For example, there is the report of a barrow with 50-60 urns, and a footnote about urns in general: "According to their reports, urns are broken in their thousands, or if brittle they simply crumble away" (Thorlacius 1809, 37). A description is given of the rich number of barrows in Thisted county, North Jutland, and also of the areas with plentiful barrows on the islands: the counties of Roskilde, Sorø and Holbæk in Zealand, for example. But of Funen it is written, "Of the Danish provinces, Funen insofar as barrows are concerned, seems to be least noteworthy, partly because there is no great number, partly and noticeably because the expansion of cultivation has destroyed them" (Thorlacius 1809, 25). This agrees well with our knowledge of agricultural development in Denmark. About 1830 Zealand was described as conservative and backward, Funen underwent a far higher degree of development and modernization: fields were enclosed, swing ploughs used, and the soil was marled. The last mentioned activity cost barrows. Lolland, Falster and Møn developed equally efficiently (Politikens Danmarkshistorie, vol. 11, p. 30ff.).

The systematic destruction of barrows has therefore begun at the close of the 18th century, particularly in Funen, Lolland, Falster, and Præstø county in Zealand. The mid-19th century boom followed a period of agricultural crisis, and it brought about new farming methods and the impetus to improve the exploitation of land; all of which presumably accelerated the destruction of barrows throughout the country. This was the period, too, which saw the organized reclamation commence of Jutland heathland. And how this course of development is reflected by the frequency of finds after 1805 will now be looked into more closely[3].

THE DANISH ISLANDS

Figs. 3 and 4 show the frequency of finds from barrows excavated in Zealand either professionally (by antiqua-

Counties	A	B	C	D	E	F	G	H	J
Frederiksborg	144	26	45	46	60	41	231	34	1841
København	158	27	15	67	89	57	282	48	1114
Holbæk	163	46 (73)	92	117	132	63 (102)	343	76	2351
Sorø	52	16	28	39	43	24	115	33	659
Præstø	57	20 (23)	17	59	70	37 (49)	153	28	1690
Bornholm	90	14 (25)	2	14	19	23 (37)	127	0	1120
Maribo	57	7	3	61	71	17	135	19	2003
Odense	68	30	15	90	121	69	227	61	645
Svendborg	64	23	15	67	75	34	165	49	1006

TABLE 1

The different categories of finds on the Danish islands.
A. Documented burial finds, minus graves with no visible monument.
B. Probable burial finds in the category classed as indeterminable.
C. Missing finds on the basis of the National Museum's topographical descriptions of parishes. (Included in Kersten's tables).
D. Hoards on the basis of Kersten's tables.
E. Hoards on the basis of the present author's classification, including probable hoards with no firm documentation.
F. Indeterminable finds on the basis of Kersten's tables. Brackets denote finds solely localized as to county or herred. Also for C.
G. Total number of recorded finds according to Kersten's tables, minus missing finds (C).
H. Finds acquired from private collections.
J. Number of recorded barrows on the basis of Kersten's tables.

rians) or unprofessionally (by farmers or farm labourers mainly). The finds excavated unprofessionally were recovered in the process of demolishing barrows. The rocketing curve as from 1825 is unlikely to reflect a corresponding rise in the number of barrows destroyed – this was presumably well under way. It is sooner due to the population's greater awareness of the value of the finds, and of the existence of a new museum in Copenhagen. In the upper ranks of society and in official circles it was an interest and hobby, and among the peasantry delivering finds was encouraged by the payment of rewards. As already mentioned, the highest frequency of finds coincides with improved farming methods. A slight drop after 1865 may to some extent be due to the many private collections formed at this time, but it is more a reflection of the increasing number of official excavations and parish inspections which helped to spread information and propaganda about the protection of ancient monuments. It is worth noting that excavations by antiquarians first began at a point when the quantity of finds recovered unofficially had reached its peak. Most of the earliest professional excavations were carried out under the

120

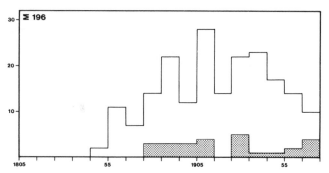

Fig. 3. Recorded recovery dates for burial finds from professionally excavated barrows in Zealand. The dotted area indicates Præstø and Sorø counties.

auspices of King Frederik VII. Not until the 1860's did an enlarged team of professional antiquarians on the staff of the National Museum begin more systematic excavations, often in connection with their inspections of parishes. The abrupt decrease in the frequency of professional finds after 1895 is undoubtedly because the destruction of barrows had dropped sharply. Agriculture had evidently become consolidated within the framework planned for it a century earlier. The trend is constant until 1945, apart from a rise between 1925 and 1935, as shown in all diagrams. The drop after 1945 is unquestionably due to the effect of the new conservation legislation passed in 1937.

The frequency of the professional excavation of barrows cannot be directly related to changes in the frequency of those done unprofessionally. The number of professional excavations seems rather to be more a reflection of the changing activities and interests of the National Museum. The drop in the decade between 1895 and 1905 coincides with the single-grave campaign in Jutland, whereas an increase in the period between 1925 and 1945 should presumably be seen as the result of some new appointments, and the inspections preceding the protection of ancient monuments which led to an increasing number of notifications. Afterwards a lower level has been maintained until today, although an increase is to be expected after a clause to provide funds for rescue excavations was passed in the legislation of 1969. South Zealand seems by and large to have lain outside the National Museum's sphere of interest (fig. 7). North Zealand, however, has been more closely followed, although this may be because notifications in this area were more numerous, i.e. a greater number of barrows.

If we turn to Lolland, Falster, Funen and Bornholm

(figs. 5 and 6), a somewhat different picture emerges (fig. 5). As in the case of hoards, the rise after 1805 in these areas is more gradual than in Zealand, due to the lack of contact between those parts of the country and the National Museum during the first half of the 19th century. The great rise from 1835 to 1895 is largely absent, only the last part of the increase is reflected by the figures. It should be added, though, that missing finds have not all disappeared. Vedel Simonsen's collection from Funen begun about 1807, and given to the National Museum in 1857-58, contains a large part of these finds, but without information as to years of acquisition. Frederik VII was also extremely active on Funen. As far as Bornholm, Lolland and Falster are concerned, a certain amount of finds recovered at this period must have disappeared. As in Zealand, the frequency of finds falls after 1895, and the low level has largely been maintained up to the present day. Fig. 6 is nicely complemented by the frequency of professionally excavated finds given in fig. 5, in that they start at the point when unprofessional finds reached their height – apart from a slight increase on Bornholm in 1820 with Lieutenant Jensen's excavations for the Commission. The explosion of professional excavations in the decades preceding the turn of the last century is due to a handful of "amateurs": Sehested on Funen, Amtmand Vedel on Bornholm, assisted by Messrs. Jørgensen and Petersen (see fig. 7). Taken together, figs. 5 and 6 reveal a

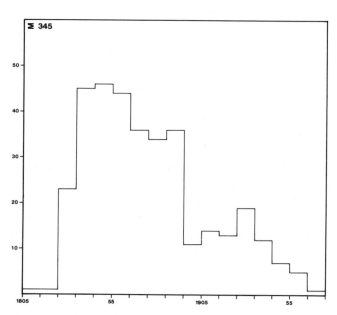

Fig. 4. Recorded recovery dates for burial finds from barrows unprofessionally excavated in Zealand.

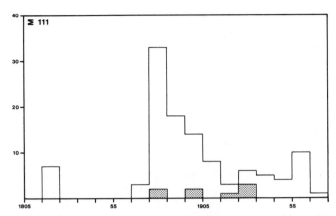

Fig. 5. Recorded recovery dates for burial finds from professionally excavated barrows in Lolland, Falster, Funen and Bornholm. The dotted area indicates the National Museum's excavations in Funen.

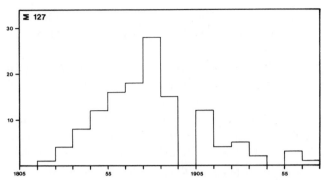

Fig. 6. Recorded recovery dates for burial finds from barrows unprofessionally excavated in Lolland, Falster, Funen and Bornholm.

characteristic frequency; an even rise, a brief culmination, followed by an even fall. Common to all these areas was the high level of private activity around the close of the 19th century, and it has wholly determined the results shown in the graphs, as well as assuring that burial finds were preserved at a period when the National Museum and local museums played a more passive role.

The present analysis of the frequency of finds from both professional and unprofessional excavations on the Danish islands gives an insight into the interplay between the development of agriculture and museums. The regional differences which can be observed, are primarily the result of how museums have evolved. The early increase in finds in Zealand reflects the proximity of the National Museum, whereas on the other islands early finds either disappeared or ended up in private collections. Later on the National Museum's efforts in these parts of the country were still sporadic. The general fall in the frequency of finds after 1895 was evidently a manifestation of agricultural stability, in that the improvement of land by levelling barrows had abated[4], at the same time professional excavations were increasing in number and have since remained at a constant level; unprofessional finds have fallen since the conservation legislation of 1937. Generally speaking the frequency of excavation and of recording seems to have been higher in Zealand than the other islands, as reflected by the number of burial finds: 541 as against 238. Other factors, however, must be taken into consideration when assessing representation, and it is first and foremost the number of excavated finds in relation to the total number of

barrows (virtually all barrows on the islands date from the Early Bronze Age).

We begin by assuming that the number of barrows recorded in the course of parish inspections is representative of the original number of barrows. We then assume that under the parish inspections carried out at the close of the 19th century it has still been possible – with the help of oral tradition – to trace most of the barrows which were ploughed away since the 1780's. We also accept that prior to this the systematic levelling of barrows had not yet become practice. The representativeness of burial finds may therefore be gauged in relation to the number of barrows; this is done county by county ("amt") in fig. 8. It shows that the counties of Copenhagen and Odense have the highest proportion in relation to barrows (more than 10%). Not surprising in Copenhagen county in view of the National Museum being nearby, but there seem to be other reasons in Odense county – and these

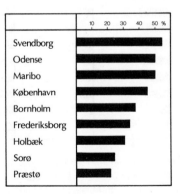

Fig. 7. Percentage of barrows professionally excavated in relation to the total number of burial finds.

we will return to. There then follows a big middle group where the percentage is slightly less than 10% but stable. There are two counties with remarkably low percentages, namely Præstø and Maribo with less than 5%. Known but missing finds are given to complete the picture, and here Frederiksborg, Holbæk and Sorø counties occupy a special place with a large number of missing finds, which would have enhanced the ratios in these areas quite considerably. The explanation for the large amount of missing finds lies partly in the prolific number of barrows in these three counties, the many missing finds are concentrated in precisely those districts (called "herred"s) with a great many barrows; in Holbæk county, Ods herred, in Frederiksborg county, Holbo herred, and in Sorø county, Slagelse herred. Information about the missing material was largely collected during parish inspections, obviously the earlier the date of the visitation the better were the chances of recollecting the past destruction of barrows. It is possible to follow the find-frequency of these missing finds when the year of the find is recorded (fig. 9), and on the whole it corresponds to the frequency of unprofessionally excavated finds in Zealand. Thereby supporting the assumption that the frequency here is indeed proportional to the number of barrows destroyed – with the exclusion of the first couple of decades in the last century. The reason why in fig. 9 a low frequency is also shown for these decades, presumably indicates that informants were unable to recall more than one (or two) generations back in relation to the time the parish was visited, and it modifies our calculations. However, the later drop in the curve is genuine enough; it coincides with the rise in professional excavations and the fall in

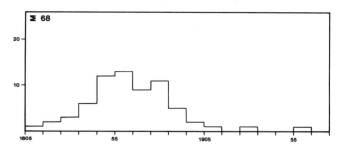

Fig. 9. Missing burial finds with recorded recovery date, i.e. when barrows were levelled, etc., but which never reached a museum. Most of the finds in this category are from Zealand.

unprofessional ones (figs. 3-6). It is unlikely that many finds eluded records after 1900 (compared with pre-1900). Naturally, the recorded number of missing finds in figs. 8 and 9 constitutes only a fraction of the great quantity of finds which vanished upon the destruction of barrows. Like the recorded burial finds, they should be regarded as a test sample.

Many of the missing finds were probably incorporated in private collections, later a large number ended in museums but without details of provenance. There is, then, a great number of finds of uncertain provenance from private collections in Ods herred, the same applies to the counties of Holbæk and Sorø, where finds of this nature make up a high percentage in relation to burial finds (exceeded only in Præstø and Odense counties). If we consider only the uncertain or the likely burial finds in fig. 8 (i.e. burial finds without details of provenance but which, because of their composition must be from a destroyed grave), they present a picture which in general resembles the frequency of missing burial finds and finds

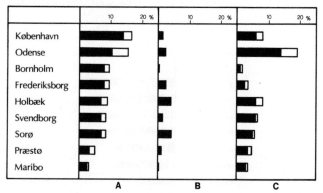

Fig. 8. A. Percentage of burial finds from excavated barrows in relation to the total number of barrows. Hatched: documented burial finds. Blank: probable burial finds. B. Missing burial finds as a percentage of all barrows. C. Hoards as a percentage of all barrows. Hatched: hoards after Aner and Kersten. Blank: authors classifikation, (cf. table 1).

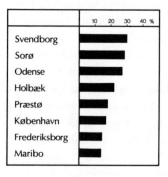

Fig. 10. Finds acquired from private collections, or in private collections as a percentage of the total accumulation of finds (cf. table 1).

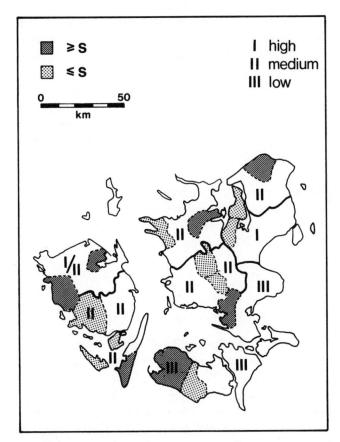

Fig. 11. The geographical representation of burial finds in accordance with fig. 8. Herreds (administrative districts) with an either notably high or low degree of representation are hatched. S = standard deviation.

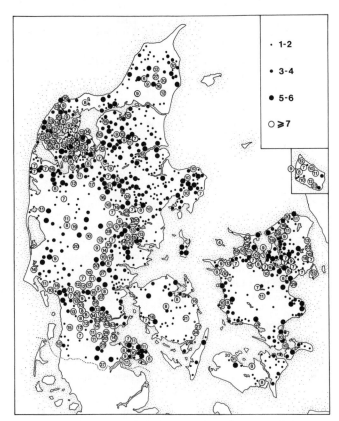

Fig. 12. Distribution of burial finds from the Early Bronze Age.

from private collections. Svendborg and Odense counties (Funen), and Sorø, Præstø and Holbæk counties (Zealand) lead the field with the greatest number of uncertain burial finds in relation to the number of fully identified burial finds. And more than 50% of all uncertain burial finds without details of provenance come from private collections.

If we go one step further and try to ascertain how many finds of this kind have been acquired from private collections in relation to the total number of finds, it could well shed light on the relationship between private acquisition and museum collections. Fig. 10 clearly shows that on Funen one third of all finds have been acquired from private collections. The amount ranges between a steady 15-20% for the other islands, with two exceptions: Sorø county, with almost one-third, and Bornholm county, where private collections have played no role. These observations agree fairly well with the

conclusions of the frequency analyses in figs. 3-6. The high proportion in Funen is due first and foremost to the persistence of private collectors, namely Vedel Simonsen, Sehested and the Mikkelsen family. That Sorø county has had the same high percentage is astonishing, it cannot be ascribed to one person, and is presumably the sum total of the activities of numerous collectors.

Therefore we conclude that Zealand does not have a better representativity in relation to barrows than the other islands. On the contrary, the ratio between recorded burial finds and recorded barrows is fairly constant, taken county by county. On the basis of fig. 8 it is possible to divide the Danish islands into three representativity zones (fig. 11), and we will at present consider zone 2 to be representative of "the normal" ratio between burial finds and barrows. In fig. 12 this zonal division can be compared with the distribution of all burial finds (plotted parish by parish). But the division into zones raises the

Counties	Rank-order	Product-moment
Frederiksborg	0.88	0.40
København	0.14	0.14
Holbæk	0.81	0.74
Sorø	0.81	0.71
Præstø	0.36	0.64
Bornholm	0.36	0.56
Maribo	0.29	0.26
Odense	0.34	0.64
Svendborg	0.74	0.71

TABLE 2

Correlation coefficients (r^2 converted from r) for the rank-order of barrows and burial finds (Spearman rank-order), and the ratio of barrows to burial finds (Pearson product-moment) calculated district by district in each county. If the figures are multiplied by 100 it gives in per cent what part of the variations are in accordance with the relation between the two variables.

question of whether all areas within a zone are equally representative? If not, what is then the smallest area suitable for consideration as a representative geographical unit? Parish units are too small, there is no stable relation between the number of barrows and the number of burial finds in a parish – it varies at random. Yet if the "herred" is considered as a unit, we find that in these districts many chance trends correct themselves, so that comparisons between herreds within a county shows a regular trend: the more barrows, the more burial finds (table 2). In other words, the herred is the smallest satisfactory unit for statistical/quantative analyses. One or two herreds stand out because of their extremely low representativeness in relation to the average for the county in question. In fig. 11 the herreds are hatched when the average is either higher or lower than the standard deviation. In some cases the low representation is due to the existence of large private collections; for example in Voldborg herred with the Ledreborg Manor collection. In other herreds a lack of local interest can be the only explanation – the reverse cause. It ought to be mentioned in this context that the two counties with the lowest correlation coefficient (table 2) are respectively the best and worst represented county according to fig. 11. In Copenhagen county the correlation is destroyed by overexcavation in one or two herreds, in Maribo by too little. Apart from the hatched herreds in fig. 8, there are also one or two herreds which are fairly low in relation to the county average; e.g. Horns, Ars and Ods herreds in Zealand, and Skovby and Vends herreds in Funen.

It is possible to conclude provisionally, therefore, that the numerical representation of burial finds is a fairly steady c. 10% of the recorded number of barrows (zone 2), but with two counties having a higher percentage (zone 1), and two counties with a considerably lower percentage (zone 3). Moreover, the herred can be judged as the smallest representative, geographical unit. A precondition of these conclusions is that the number of recorded barrows represents a steady, representative yardstick of the original number of barrows. It would, however, be reassuring to be able to test this assumption. An attempt to do this follows, and this leads to the comparison and correlation of results yielded by the analyses of hoards and burial finds.

HOARDS AND BURIAL FINDS ON THE DANISH ISLANDS. SOME CONCLUSIONS

In the preceding pages we have assumed that the number of recorded barrows is a firm yardstick of the original number of barrows. Yet, as shown in the introductory remarks about the destruction of barrows prior to 1805, this supposition needs to be modified because more barrows were presumably destroyed in Funen, Lolland, Falster and in Præstø county than elsewhere. We will therefore try to test this by means of an independent factor, i.e. hoards. It has been established that their geographical representation is more or less constant, although slightly lower in Funen, and more so in Lolland and Falster in comparison with Zealand. This we will try to offset by increasing the number of deposits by 20% in these areas[6]. We will then suppose that the hoards represent a constant value in relation to which the representation of barrows and burial finds can be measured (fig. 8C).

Let us first consider hoards expressed as a percentage of barrows. If barrows were destroyed with more or less the same intensity in all counties, the proportion of hoards in relation to barrows (in %) is expected to be constant (withen a reasonable margin). If one side preponderates over the other it infers an imbalance in the representation of barrows. If the percentage is too high more than the average number of barrows have been destroyed, if too low more than the average number are preserved. But it is difficult to decide what is too low and what is too high. If, however, the standard deviation is calculated (S=3.72/, with the "increased" counties 4.55), and respectively added to or deducted from the mean value (M=5.33/5.83), some marginal values of 9.05/ 10.38 and 1.61/1.28 are established, which means that Odense falls outside with too many demolished barrows, and so does Bornholm with very few demolished barrows (this statistical treatment is previously used in fig. 11). The result for Odense supports the earlier assumptions about the destruction of barrows in Funen. Yet if we look at the distribution within the marginal values, both Præstø and Maribo counties are conspicuously low. This could either mean that not many hoards were deposited in the Bronze Age, or that hoards are very under-represented in these counties because, as already mentioned, there is little doubt that many barrows were destroyed before the time of parish inspections. The high figure for Svendborg county, on the other hand, harmonizes with the trend for Funen.

In most counties, therefore, hoards support our earlier conclusions reached by other means, concerning the demolition of barrows, although there are descrepancies in some counties (Maribo and Præstø).

The next step is to include burial finds. First the ratio of hoards to barrows is calculated, then the ratio of hoards to burial finds. These values are then plotted into a system of coordinates (fig. 13). In this way we register both the representation of barrows and burial finds in relation to hoards. If the number of barrows and number of burial finds balance we can expect a linear correlation. Too many or too few barrows/too many or too few burial finds will worsen the correlation. The correlation coefficient is low ($r^2=0.40$) in all counties. The best correlation ($r^2=0.99$) is in counties 1,3,4,6 and 9; the next best ($r^2=0.91$) in counties 1,2,3,6 and 8, which suggests that the future level will probably lie here.

It is not possible on the basis of fig. 13 to decide whether the deviation is because of few or many burial finds or due to few preserved barrows. Fig. 13 is therefore only a guide. Here our earlier analyses have shown that the primary cause of county 2's deviation is the large number of excavated barrows, in county 8 also in conjunction with the small number of preserved barrows. In counties 5 and 7 it is caused by the small number of excavated barrows. Thus by taking hoards as the yardstick of representativeness we can corroborate a number of variations in the representation of burial finds and barrows, which have earlier been ascertained by other methods. In conclusion, we will attempt to calculate the size of the population, and population density in settle-

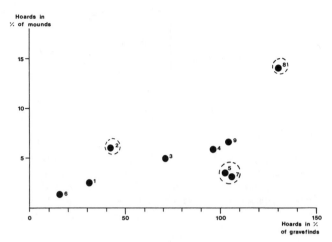

Fig. 13. The ratio of hoards to barrows and to burial finds (cf. table 1).

ment areas, as well as the amount of bronze in circulation.

In calculations of the size of the population our point of departure is the number of recorded barrows, and as the greatest number of these are in Zealand we will restrict ourselves to that area. The number of barrows preserved here is 7,635. It can be estimated that on the average 5 adults have been interred in each barrow[6], amounting to 38,175 persons in all. By far the greater part of these burials is from period II-III, the span of which we set at 500 years. The number of adults alive contemporaneously can then be calculated on the basis of the following formula:

$$\frac{\text{number of burials x average age}}{\text{length of period}} = \text{number of contemporary adults alive}$$

Before this can be done, however, the problem of the average life expectancy of the population has to be solved. In the Middle Ages it was about 27 years; in the Early Iron Age (Hamfelde cemetery) the average age (for men) was about 29; this is probably too high, due to the absence of infants in the figures (Gebühr 1976). It appears that children were relatively rarely buried in the Early Bronze Age, therefore the average age of buried adults must be adjusted. To return to the Hamfelde find, the average expectation of life for men, after surviving the first 14 years, would be 33 years. On this basis, then, the average life expectancy in the Bronze Age will be set at 33 years.

Before calculating the contemporary population a

Counties	Population Size
Frederiksborg	5035 - 6707
København	4240 - 5648
Holbæk	5565 - 7413
Sorø	4505 - 6001
Præstø	6890 - 9178

TABLE 3

The size of population in counties 1-4 calculated on the basis of two alternative estimates as to the original number of barrows (respectively one-third and one-half levelled before the earliest parish inspections). The density pr. km² in counties 1-4 is respectively 4.53 and 6.04.

correction has to be made to allow for the number of barrows demolished from the Iron Age onwards, until the beginning of the 19th century. A minimum and a maximum estimate are given below.

A. The recorded number of barrows constitutes two-thirds of the original number, the latter then must have amounted to 11,452, containing 57,260 dead. This gives an average of 115 burials and 23 new barrows each year. According to this estimate, the number of contemporary adults to expect burial amounts to 3,779.

B. The recorded number of barrows amounts to one half of the original number, the latter then must have amounted to 15,270, containing 76,350 dead. This gives an average of 153 burials and 31 new barrows each year. The number of contemporary adults to expect burial amounts to 5,039.

Clearly these figures for the contemporary population which would expect burial do not correspond to the total population. Sources of error lie, for example, in the fact that women's graves are under-represented, amounting to 44% of men's graves, and of all sex-determined burial finds only about 30% are female. In other words, women's graves are 56% short (according to Randsborg 1974, fig. 5). The under-representation of women's graves corresponds to 39% of all graves. Children (up to 14 years) must then be added. If we again base our calculations on the large Iron-Age cemeteries (Gebühr 1976) about 50% of the population was under 14. In A: the minimum population is 3,779 + 1,474 (missing women) multiplied by 2 (children) = 10,506. In B: 5,039 + 1,965 (missing women) multiplied by 2 (children) = 14,008. That is to say, on the basis of the two alternative estimates of the original number of barrows, the provisional size of the contemporary population would have been between c.

10,000 and 14,000. But these figures are also probably too small, because of the unlikelihood that all male adults would have been interred in barrows. It has probably been a question of social rank, just how large or small the group has been is a matter of judgement. If we assume that only about 40% of the male population was buried in barrows the total population arrived at for A: = c. 26,000, and for B: 35,000, of which the number buried amounts to c. 14%. If we assume that only about 20% of the male population was buried in barrows, the figures for the total population increase correspondingly, namely A: 53,000 and B: 70,000, of which the number of buried amounts to c. 7%. If the areas of settlement are added together (parish with one or more barrows), we are able to calculate the density of settlement (table 3). For the whole of Zealand (male 40 %) it is between A: 4,5 and B: 6,0 persons per km². It can be seen that marked fluctuations occur within the individual counties. Densely settled areas have a higher number of persons per km² than the county average.

By taking the established upper and lower limits for the number of burials in Zealand we will try to calculate the amount of bronze in circulation. Firstly, the average amount of bronze per grave: on the basis of Randsborg's table of weights (Randsborg 1974, fig. 5), the approximate weight of bronze in men's graves is 378 g per grave, in women's graves 170 g. Burials without bronze must be deducted. Test sampling well-excavated barrows with several graves has revealed that almost 50% are without bronze. The average, then, can be reduced to 200 g bronze per grave. The reason why the amount is not reduced by 50% is because barrows with multiple graves are often poorer than barrows with one or two central graves, and the latter have not been included. If we suppose that there was 200 g bronze per grave, the result for Zealand is that the average amount of bronze deposited as grave-goods annually amounted to between A: 23 kg and B: 31 kg. To this must be added 2 to 3 hoards of bronze every year, estimated at c. 2 kg each. The final figures for the annual deposition of bronze are then between 25 kg and 35 kg, which corresponds to the minimum import demand. The amount of bronze in circulation at one time may be calculated at A: 755 kg and B: 1008 kg. These figures are based on the assumption that only the buried were in the possession of bronze, and then only an average of 200 g. The latter figure, though, is too low in that bronze grave-goods only represent a selection of the bronze in circulation. The most important among which would have been spearheads and axe blades – normally only recovered in hoards. If we assume that all buried persons also possessed a further 200 g of bronze, the amount of bronze in circulation increases to between 1,510 kg and 2,016 kg. And, moreover, these figures are probably too low. Only relatively small quantities of bronze would be needed to maintain the level in circulation in relation to this amount. This probably means that melting down bronze for re-use was very usual. It was thus far more difficult to work up this amount of bronze than to maintain it. In this period there was not enough bronze in circulation to allow for depositions in graves, because apart from a constant annual import there would have to have been some to take out of circulation for the purpose. In the Early Bronze Age (SN C and period I) deposits only represented an annual loss of 2-3 kg, as against 30-40 kg in the latter part of the Early Bronze Age (periods II-III), when bronzes were also laid in graves. We may conclude, too, from the above, that hoards reflect some unique event, in that 2 to 3 deposits a year cannot be construed as a common custom.

The purpose of these calculations of population and quantities of bronze is to demonstrate that by laying down a number of alternatives it is possible to derive from them some calculations of probability which can be more closely defined by future research.

The most uncertain factor in regard to population figures is obviously the question of how many men had the expectation of being buried in a barrow. On the basis of pollen analysis and the spread of barrows it is possible to calculate the extent of open country in settlement areas, and this supports a low estimate of 20% of all males (giving higher population figures). Some areas were virtually without forests. In other words, extensively exploited countryside and closely settled. The problem of population can be approached from a third angle, by setting out a number of prerequisites for agricultural production. For example, the amount of arable land/pasture needed in relation to the number of livestock and human beings. In this way a corrective is reached as to the number of persons per km^2 (Poulsen 1980). Finally, within small thoroughly investigated areas, it should be possible to arrive at very precise calculations on the basis of the number of settlements and where they lay (e.g. Myhre 1982; Edgren & Herschend 1982). There is a vast research potential in calculations of cause and effect or simulation, especially in

countries like Denmark, where the representation of finds is so large that margins of uncertainty can be considerably reduced by deductive methods.

Kristian Kristiansen
National Agency for the Nature
Monuments and Sites,
Amaliegade 13
1206 Copenhagen

Acknowledgements

Without the superlative help of Professor Karl Kersten, this work could not have been carried out. Professor Kersten placed without condition the unpublished parts of his great catalogue of finds of the Early Bronze Age at my full disposal, both the completed catalogues and the cards over the areas yet to be written up, sending me the county reports as they were completed. For this generosity I wish to convey my thanks.

The 1st Department of the National Museum, whose collections and archives I have worked in for long periods since 1971, have always shown me great hospitality. This also applies to the many Danish provincial museums which have willingly opened their collections and archives and responded to my enquiries.

For private hospitality and friendship during my visits to Schleswig, I thank Michael Gebühr and Karl Kersten.

Finally, special thanks to my wife Lotte Hedeager for her help with the completed work on the extensive grave find material from Jutland, the final presentation of which has unfortunately had to be postponed until a later publication.

NOTES

1. As shown by barrow names such as "three barrows" and "seven barrows". (Aner and Kersten 1977, 217ff).
2. Several kinds of damage to barrows are covered by the word "destruction". Sometimes it means total obliteration, in others partial demolition, and then ploughing over – often by degrees. If the latter, a barrow will be detectable for at least a century, possibly longer. Generally speaking, very little is known about the representativeness of the barrows recorded during parish inspections in relation to the original number of barrows. In some well examined areas it can be established that it was in the region of 50% (Knudsen 1982), but big variations are to be expected (Ebbesen in press).
3. The following criteria for classification are used in the analyses:
   A. Only burials *found in barrows* are included. As in the German summary in Aner and Kersten, where the most usual expression is: "in Grabhügel sb.nr. ...", uncertain barrow finds are termed "Unbestimmbar", and they are described according to the categories "Wahrscheinlich, vermutlich and vielleicht (Grab)", in increasing degrees of uncertainty.
   B. A distinction is made between *professional* and *unprofessional* excavations of barrows. Excavations are termed "professional" when there is a report from the excavator giving a description of the burial as a whole (information as to the construction of the

grave, the position of artefacts etc.). The level of documentation, and thereby the definition of "professional" is assessed according to its time. For example, several of Jansen's excavations on Bornholm are included in this category, as well as several by Frederik VII, when reports have been written. A report by an archaeologist (in connection with an inspection, or a secondary excavation) after an unofficial excavation has taken place, is only accepted as professional when a reconstruction of the find has been possible.

C. When counting the number of recorded finds per decade, *a barrow counts as one unit*. For example, if during one excavation 4 barrows in one field have been excavated they count as 4. All finds acquired from *private collections are excluded* from these counts if the year in which the find was originally made is not given. Most of the 'uncertain' category of burial finds have come from private collections, or from local museums with no archaeologist on the staff (but which have often acquired a certain amount of burial finds from private collections). In a large number of cases the information published by Aner and Kersten has been supplemented by archival studies, which have resulted in the addition of finding dates in a number of cases.

4. A comparison between fig. 2 and fig. 3 in the article on hoards, reveals how the frequency of deposits markedly increases, when the frequency of burial finds falls. It is evidently the result of changing farming methods, away from tilting and clearing of new land towards more intensive land utilization, draining wetlands to increase arable land – just the activities which cause hoards to be discovered.

5. Cf. note 5 in the article on deposits.

6. A test sampling of thoroughly investigated barrows in Lolland, Falster and Bornholm produced an average of 6.6. Only one or two burials are known from most barrows. This is presumably because only the richest burial finds were sent to the museum after many of the early unprofessional excavations.

REFERENCES

BERGSØE, A. F. 1847: *Den Danske Stats Statistik*. Copenhagen.

DALGAS, E. 1883-84: Fortids og Fremtidsskovene i Jyllands Hedeegne. *Hedeselskabets Tidsskrift 4.de Aarg*. Aarhus.

EBBESEN, K. in press (1984) *Fortidsminderegistreringen i Danmark*. Fredningsstyrelsen, Copenhagen.

EDGREN, B. & HERSCHEND, F. 1982. Arkeologisk ekonomi och ekonomisk arkeologi. Ett försök till beskrivning av det öländska jordbrukets förutsättningar under äldre järnålder. *Fornvännen*, vol. 77, I. Stockholm.

GEBÜHR, M. 1976: Das Gräberfeld Hamfelde, Kr. Hzgt. Lauenbung – Grösse und Altersaufbau der bestattenden Bevölkerung. *Die Heimat 83. Jahrgang, Heft 11*. Neumünster.

HALD, K. 1969: *Stednavne og kulturhistorie*. Copenhagen.

HERMANSEN, V. 1953: Baggrunden for Oldsagskommissionen. *Aarbøger for nordisk Oldkyndighed og Historie*. Copenhagen.

– 1954: Fortidsminder og Kuriositeter i Danmarks Middelalder. *Aarbøger for nordisk Oldkyndighed og Historie*. Copenhagen.

KLINDT-JENSEN, O. 1975: *A History of Scandinavian Archaeology*. London.

KNUDSEN, S. AA. 1982: *Landskab og oldtid. Atlas over Søllerød og Lyngby-Taarbæk kommuner*.

MATHIASSEN, TH. 1943 (ed.) *Herregårdene og Samfundet*.

– 1956: Oldtidsminderne og fredningsloven. *Fra Nationalmuseets Arbejdsmark*.

MÜLLER, S. 1897: Udsigt over Oldtidsudgravninger foretagne for Nationalmuseet i Årene 1893-96. *Aarbøger for nordisk Oldkyndighed og Historie*.

MYHRE, B. 1982: Beregning af folketall på Jæren i yngre romertid og folkevandringstid. Fra *Hus, Gård og Bebyggelse*. Föredrag från det XVI nordiska arkeologmötet, Island 1982. Ed. G. Olafsson.

NEERGÅRD, C. 1916: Thomas Bartholin og Oldforskningen i det 17. Århundrede. *Ugeskrift for Læger Nr. 42*.

POULSEN, J. 1980: Om arealudnyttelsen i bronzealderen: Nogle praktiske synspunkter og nogle synspunkter om praksis. In *Bronzealderbebyggelse i Norden*, edited by Henrik Thrane, Odense University Press.

RANDSBORG, K. 1974: Social Stratification in Early Bronze Age Denmark: A Study in the Regulation of Cultural Systems. *Praehistorische Zeitschrift 49. Band*. Berlin – New York.

STEENSBERG, A. (ed.) 1969: *Dagligliv i Danmark i det syttende og attende århundrede, 1620-1720. Part I*. København.

TANDERUP, R. & EBBESEN, K. 1979: *Forhistoriens historie*. Wormianum.

THORLACIUS, B. 1809: *Bemærkninger over de i Danmark endnu tilværende Hedenolds-Höie og Steensætninger*. Kiøbenhavn.

THORSEN, S. & ANDERSEN, TH. 1980: *Pleje af fortidsminder – et pilotprojekt i Storstrøms amt*. Fredningsstyrelsen Rapport B3, Copenhagen.

WERLAUFF, E. C. 1807: *Udkast til den nordiske Archeologies Historie i vort Fædreland indtil Ole Worms tid*. Kjøbenhavn.

– 1808: *Bemærkninger i Anledning af den til de nordiske Oldsagers Samling og Opbevaring nedsatte Commission*. Kiøbenhavn.

Bronze Hoards from the Late Neolithic and Early Bronze Age[1]

by KRISTIAN KRISTIANSEN

INTRODUCTION

Hoards are set apart by the fact that they cannot be sought out and plundered like barrows. Their discovery is therefore entirely dependent on factors relating to land use, and it is the effect of these which will be examined in the following, as far back in time as possible[2]. A major watershed in this connection is the year 1807, when The Royal Commission for the Preservation of Northern Antiquities was formed, and a systematic registration and preservation of antiquities inaugurated.

We have only a limited possibility of establishing how many hoards had been discovered before 1805, but an attempt will nevertheless be made, since such information has a bearing on the evidential value of the analyses after 1805.

Only very few hoards from the Late Neolithic and Early Bronze Age found prior to 1805 are now extant, since most of the finds are single finds, mainly massive flanged axes and palstaves which were presumably normally melted down on account of their large content of bronze and their ordinary form. From the Late Bronze Age, however, considerably more hoards found before 1805 are extant, first and foremost »showpieces«: gold, lures, etc., which are more numerous in this period. I have in a previous article used these finds to estimate how many of these hoards were found and lost before 1805, and will cite the relevant passage, since I believe the conclusions are also valid for the bronze hoards from the Late Neolithic and Early Bronze Age.

Hoards found before 1805. It is of great importance to know how many finds were made before the foundation of The Royal Commission for the Preservation of Northern Antiquities in 1807 (Hermansen 1953). This question, however, is not quite as unanswerable as one would immediately think.

The five bronze age finds from before 1805 consist of valuable or remarkable objects, so-called "magnificent specimens". They date back to the seventeenth century, that is to the time of the "Collections of Curiosities", when interest in the traces of antiquity first arose. This period is marked by the discovery of the first of the two famous gold horns in 1639, the publication of Ole Worm's volume on the Danish relics of antiquity: "Danicorum Monumentorum Libri Sex" in 1643, and the foundation of King Frederik III's "kunstkammer" (art cabinet) in 1653 (Bering Liisberg 1897,18). There among other things "danefæ" (treasure trove) was delivered and displayed. Prior to this "danefæ" was considered an income source for the king and was melted down. For this reason there are no known antiquities from before the time of King Christian IV (Hindenburg 1859,24 f.; Kjær 1926,25 ff.). From 1650 until 1805 the "magnificent finds" survived due to the treasure trove law and the interest taken in rarities by the nobility.

If one then compares the number of "magnificent finds" from before 1805 with those from after 1805 there appears to be a remarkable difference. Thirty-six are known from the period 1805-1975, while only 5 from the previous period of the same length. The 36 finds make up c. 8% of the entire number of hoards from this period. If this percentage is applied to the period before 1805 it seems that approximately 60 "ordinary" hoards have been lost between the Renaissance and 1805. If we go further back to the introduction of the wheel plough in the Middle Ages (Steensberg 1968, 332 ff.) the number will exceed 200. These calculations assume that the "magnificent finds" may be regarded as a variable independent of the extension and development of museums and popular knowledge of archaeology so that they may represent a reasonable yardstick for the intensity of finds before as well as after 1805.

If these calculations hold true hoards must have been found far more seldom before 1805 than after. This is explained by the fact that Danish agriculture had remained largely unaltered since the Middle Ages. Large areas lay waste as commons or heaths, and the agricultural tools were primitive (Vibæk 1964, 55-57; Steensberg 1960,41 ff.). The wheel plough was the most important tool, but the plough-share did not go as deep down as more recent ploughs and therefore did not reach down to the depth where most of the hoards were to be found. Furthermore the moist places where hoards are usually deposited were not arable in those days.

Peat-cutting, which has been done since the Iron Age, must also be considered (Becker 1948; Jørgensen 1956,120 ff.; Hove 1971). In the Iron Age as well as later in historic times, however, the easily available, dry upper layers were mainly cut, whereas the lower, waterbearing layers where the Bronze Age hoards were located did not invite direct

130

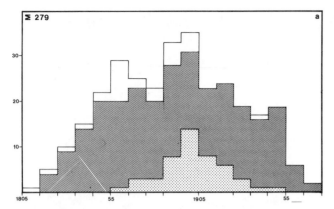

Fig. 1a. Find frequency for all hoards from Zealand (hatched = 279). Hoards lacking information on find circumstances are shown unhatched. The dotted signature indicates finds obtained through purchasing agents.

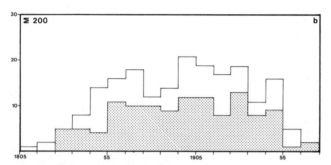

Fig. 1b. Find frequency for field hoards from Zealand. The dotted signature indicates finds made on damp ground.

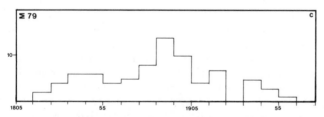

Fig. 1c. Find frequency for bog hoards from Zealand, normally found during peat cutting.

cutting and were generally avoided. Furthermore, peat-cutting must be seen in relation to the availability of other kinds of fuel. Peat-cutting has probably increased with the deforestation, which reached its climax around 1800 when only 4% of the country was covered with forest (Nielsen 1969, 9-64). Like agricultural activities, turf-cutting was probably not intensified until after 1805.

I have now briefly shown that the entire number of hoards found since 1805 make up a major and representative part of the finds made since the Iron Age. Explanations of irregularities of the survival of hoards should therefore not be sought in the period prior to 1805, but in

the period after. Consequently, a source-critical analysis of finds from that period of time is decisive for a determination of the general representativity of the material.

I will then proceed to a regional analysis of the representativeness of the bronze hoards after 1805. The information subjected to statistical treatment comprises find frequency since 1805, method of discovery, and depth of find (figs. 1 and 2).

THE DANISH ISLANDS

The find frequency for all hoards found on the islands (figs. 1a and 2a) follows a characteristic, regular course: a gradual rise, consolidation, a brief climax, consolidation again, and finally a relatively steep fall. If we take Zealand as model, Lolland-Falster, Funen, and Bornholm may be said to lack the first consolidation phase, but the similarities between the two curves are obvious, and the question arises as to whether they actually manifest the discovery, exploitation and exhaustion of an archaeological find group. In order to establish this, we have to investigate which factors have produced figs. 1a and 2a through an analysis of the effects of land utilization. We do this in the first instance by dividing the hoards into field finds and bog finds.

Field hoards

In general, the field hoards manifest themselves earlier in Zealand than on the other islands (figs. 1b and 2b), and reach an earlier climax. The former circumstance can hardly be due to anything other than the nearness of the National Museum, for there was little difference between the two areas in respect of land utilization. Some of the "missing" finds from Lolland-Falster and Bornholm were lost; others found their way into private collections, especially on Funen (Vedel Simonsen's) – hence our lack of knowledge of year and circumstances of find.

The rapid advance of land drainage after 1855 shows clearly in both diagrams in an increase in the number of hoards found on damp soils. On Lolland-Falster, Funen and Bornholm, these finds already culminate before the turn of the century (52.6% before 1895, 47.4% after), whereas on Zealand they continue to increase until 1935 (46.3% before, 53.7% after). This is due partly to the fact that development here was slower, but also to the circumstance that on Zealand a number of major land and bog reclamation projects were started after 1900. The damp areas were also of greater extent there than on the other islands (cf. fig. 19).

Thus figs. 1b and 2b show that the hoard finds to a great extent coincided with the start of the more intensive utilization of agricultural land (inclusion of previously uncultivated areas, drainage, and deeper ploughing) – activities which all accelerated from the mid-19th century. This is further corroborated by the fact that regional differences in these activities are reflected in the find frequency.

Figs. 3 and 4 throw further light on find circumstances. The rather few well documented finds must be treated as a sample, presumably representative, since the pattern is the same for both figures (an x^2 test showing no significant difference). We must, however, reckon with a certain general skew in the evidential value of the figures. Figs. 3 and 4 thus record the cases where the exposure and discovery of a hoard coincided, which most often occurs with digging, whereas most finds were probably exposed by plough and harrow and were only later found lying on the surface, so that they are poorly documented and have been excluded from the statistics. This method of find is, however, documented in 11 and 16 cases, respectively, some of them with beet-hoeing. With digging, the commonest activity on damp ground is the digging of drainage ditches. On dry ground, activities are more scattered, comprising excavation for beet clamps, the digging of holes for planting, gardening, and various unspecified digging in fields. The grubbing up of large stones in fields is also featured. Hoards found by machinery during ploughing or harrowing occurred especially on damp ground. It is frequently stated that ploughing over a newly drained bog or meadow was involved. In a large number of cases where we lack such information, bog patina (frequently over green patina) and find topography reveal that the find was made in a damp depression in the field.

All in all, the many hoards recovered from damp ground show that it was the inclusion of areas which had not previously been actively cultivated (but perhaps used for hay and grazing), which yielded the majority of finds. First draining was carried out, which yielded a number of finds, then ploughing and harrowing over the newly reclaimed areas, turning up the rest. Hoards found on damp ground thus comprise on Zealand 60.5% and on Lolland-Falster, Funen and Bornholm 57.6% (according

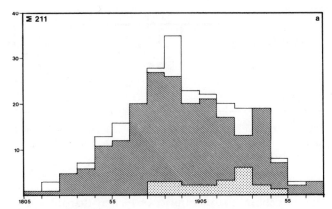

Fig. 2a. Find frequency for all hoards from Funen, Lolland-Falster and Bornholm (hatched = 211). Signatures as for fig. 1a.

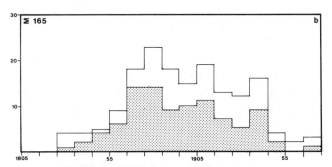

Fig. 2b. Find frequency for field hoards from Funen, Lolland-Falster and Bornholm. The dotted signature indicates finds made on damp ground.

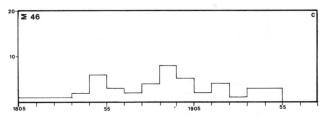

Fig. 2c. Find frequency for bog hoards from Funen, Lolland-Falster and Bornholm, normally found during peat cutting.

to figs. 2a and 2b). The corresponding figures according to figs. 3 and 4 are 61.7% and 57.1% respectively, which also emphasizes the value of figs. 3 and 4 as a sample.

The preponderance of hoards from damp areas does not necessarily mean that the finds from the dry areas are underrepresented to any significant extent. Although dry areas are more extensive and mainly comprise the old arable land, it would have been natural in the Bronze

132

	Dry	Wet	Total
Machinery	11	28	39
Digging	25	30	55
Total	36	58	94

Fig. 3. Recorded find circumstances for field hoards from Zealand, finds made during construction work excluded. 16 finds picked up on the surface are also recorded.

	Dry	Wet	Total
Machinery	7	13	20
Digging	17	19	36
Total	24	32	56

Fig. 4. Recorded find circumstances for field hoards from Funen, Lolland-Falster and Bornholm. 11 finds picked up on the surface are also recorded.

Age to deposit hoards in places which at that time, too, were not under cultivation, so that the dominance of finds from damp areas by and large represents a reality. We do have to reckon with a lower representation for the old cultivated areas, but, as mentioned in the introduction, not much lower.

After this examination of the circumstances pertaining to field finds, we return to figs. 2a and 2b and try to explain why the find frequency suddenly falls – on Zealand from 1955, on the other islands from 1945. We have shown that the frequency is largely determined by the development of agricultural land utilization, working on

the assumption that archaeological interest and the level of museum activity were fairly constant factors. The question is, therefore, whether agricultural activities changed after 1945.

It can be shown unequivocally that the fall in find frequency largely coincides with the mechanization of agriculture – the adoption of tractors and large machines. Whereas the farmer previously followed the plough, he now rides a tractor. But here it should not be forgotten that he has not yet lost his direct contact with the earth. Until 10-15 years ago (but not much longer), most root crops were taken up by hand and every square metre of

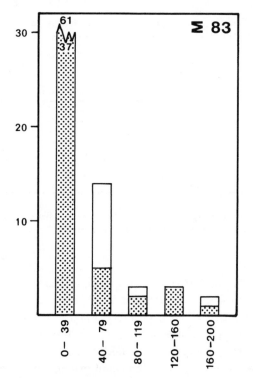

Fig. 5. Recorded find depths for field hoards from Zealand. Hoards found on damp ground are dotted.

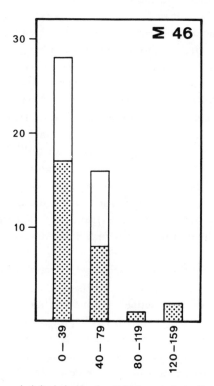

Fig. 6. Recorded find depths for field hoards from Funen, Lolland-Falster and Bornholm. Hoards found on damp ground are dotted.

Depth	≤ 1890	> 1890
0 – 80	6	0
> 80	5	17

a

Fig. 7a. Depth of bog hoards from Zealand before and after 1890.

Depth	≤ 1890	> 1890
0 – 80	3	3
> 80	1	6

b

Fig. 7b. Depth of bog hoards from Funen, Lolland-Falster and Bornholm before and after 1890.

ground gone over every few years in beet-hoeing. The farmer also regurlarly inspects his fields, and many finds have been made in just this fashion: picked up while walking across the field or hoeing beet. The depth of ploughing has also gradually increased with tractor ploughing, but without yielding more finds. We can thus not explain the fall in find frequency by referring to the mechanization of agriculture, because after this there were still activities which should have led to the discovery of any new finds. An explanation should rather be sought in the consolidation of agricultural activities which has occurred. There is now little land to reclaim, nearly all land being either cultivated or built on. The soil is also well drained and the fields cleared of stones, etc. The paucity of new finds deriving from the growth of the towns and the explosive development of construction works over the last ten years is due not merely to their being lost because big machines were used: it is to an equal extent due to the fact that the land used has already been cultivated and has thus already yielded its finds.

The last factor which shall be investigated is the depth of deposition of the hoards, since they reveal their accessibility in relation to the activities which expose them. Here figs. 5 and 6 show that the quantity of finds is in inverse proportion to depth of find, which was also the case with the Late Bronze Age hoards (Kristiansen 1976, fig. 9). The question as to whether this reflects the prevailing depth of deposition in the Bronze Age or the prevalent economic activities was then answered with a yes and no for both, though with a bias towards deposition depth. It is, however, remarkable how few deep finds there are. Does this not mean that the earth conceals a large number of deep hoards? To this we can reply in the negative. A comparison with find depths for Early Iron Age graves reveals that deep finds are discovered if they are present (see Lotte Hedeager's article). It is furthermore remarkable that the majority of deep finds are from

damp ground. There are practically none from dry ground deeper than 80 cm. This, too, marks a difference in relation to the Late Bronze Age (see fig. 20).

The constancy of agricultural activity in relation to the fall in find frequency therefore most probably means that the earth has yielded most of the bronze hoards once deposited in what are now cultivated fields. This group will thus largely be exhausted.

Bog hoards

This group is rather sparse. The find frequency nevertheless shows certain similarities between fig. 1c and fig. 2c. There is a hump in the first half of the 19th century, slightly later and more short-lived on Lolland-Falster, Funen, and Bornholm than on Zealand. There follows a minor fall, before the frequency moves towards a maximum in the decades up to 1905. Again, this maximum is stronger and longer-lived on Zealand. The increased peat production of the war years is only slightly evident – an increase in the period 1915-1925, then an abrupt fall in both diagrams, before a small increase in connection with the production of the forties. We can thus establish that find frequency falls in a period where peat production increases enormously, while the maximum is reached in a period with relatively limited peat cutting in relation to later periods.

In a previous study of bog hoards from the Late Bronze Age, it was held that the reason for this was that the Bronze Age surface was reached before the turn of the century (Kristiansen 1976, 141). This was tested in a comparison with finds from the Neolithic and Iron Age, which revealed that the Neolithic hoards, which were found especially after the turn of the century, were well represented on Zealand, where they normally lay deeper than the Bronze Age finds, while Iron Age hoards higher up in the peat in the so-called "dog's meat" were ex-

134

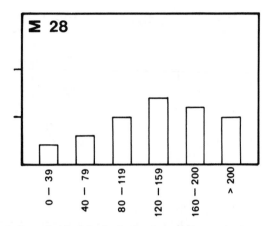

Fig. 8. Recorded find depths for bog hoards from Zealand.

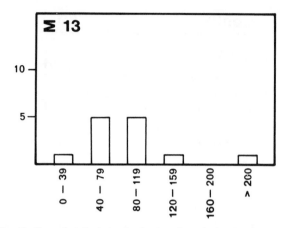

Fig. 9. Recorded find depths for bog hoards from Funen, Lolland-Falster and Bornholm.

tremely few on Zealand. It was assumed that they had been cut away before 1805 and were therefore lost. A comparison with bog hoards from the Late Bronze Age and Late Neolithic/Early Bronze Age respectively does not show, however, the similarity expected, the centre of gravity for the hoards from the Late Bronze Age lying around the first hump in figs. 1c and 2c (Kristiansen 1976, fig. 5), while the later maximum before 1900 is absent. There can be several reasons for this. Thus it emerges that some of the bog hoards from the Late Neolithic and Early Bronze Age were placed or cast into a then open lake which only later became marshy, several of them being found at the base of the peat. This contrasts with the majority of the hoards of the Late Bronze Age. Nor should it be forgotten that 500 to 1000 years separate these groups of finds, during which time the growth of peat may have been considerable. We shall therefore assume that a larger part of the finds from the Late Neolithic and Early Bronze Age lay deeper in the bogs than the case was for the finds from the Late Bronze Age, and the find maximum is therefore first reached at the end of the 19th century.

If there is such a correlation between find depth and frequency, the deepest finds in figs. 1c and 2c should have been found later than finds lying higher up in the peat. This has been tested in fig. 7. In the case of Zealand there is no doubt about the tendency: there is a clear correlation between find depth and year of find before and after 1890. In the other islands there are fewer deep hoards. For hoards found deeper than 80 cm the tendency is clear enough though, while hoards found deeper than 80 cm are also common after 1890. We have thus confirmation

that there is a positive correlation between find depth and year of find. But what implications does this have for the representativeness of the bog hoards?

In figs. 8 and 9 all recorded depths have been systematized. Despite the quite few observations, a difference between Zealand and the other islands, which entirely lack deep finds, is obvious. On this basis we must assume that only on Zealand did peat cutting reach the depths which yield finds from the Late Neolithic and Early Bronze Age, while these and the Early Neolithic finds are for a large part still to be found in the bogs of Lolland-Falster, Funen and Bornholm. This accords well with the rather limited knowledge we have on the history of peat digging in Denmark (cf. the appendix on this in the article on economic development). In the first place, the bogs are larger on Zealand than on the other islands, but probably more important is the fact that the Zealand bogs supplied peat to Copenhagen for fuel. In older times this affected mainly the nearest areas (northern Zealand). The farmers simply drove in with a load of peats. But later, larger parts of Zealand were probably involved, and at one point in the early 19th century a plan to obtain peat from Jutland was even considered, but shelved. This is merely to indicate the size and importance of the production. These historical circumstances probably explain the many deep finds from Zealand, where many peat cuttings were almost depleted, which was apparently not the case on the smaller islands, even during the wartime production. Therefore Lolland-Falster, Funen and Bornholm must as far as bog finds are concerned be considered under-represented in relation to Zealand, where the majority of the bogs have been exploited.

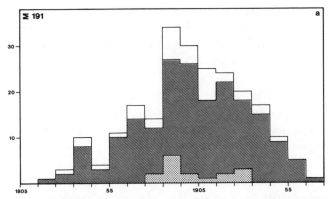

Fig. 10a. Find frequency for all hoards in northern Jutland including Ålborg, Hjørring, Thisted, Viborg and Randers county (hatched = 191). Hoards lacking information on find circumstances are shown unhatched. The dotted signature indicates finds obtained through purchasing agents.

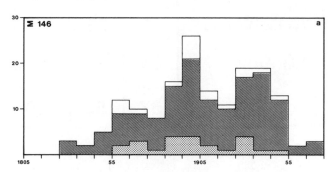

Fig. 11a. Find frequency for all hoards from southern and central Jutland (hatched = 146). Signatures as for fig. 1a.

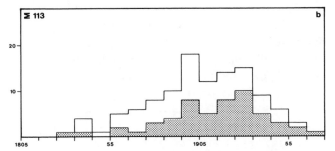

Fig. 10b. Find frequency for field hoards from northern Jutland including Randers county. The dotted signature indicates finds made on damp ground.

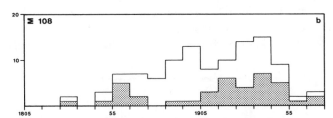

Fig. 11b. Find frequency for field hoards from southern and central Jutland. The dotted signature indicates finds made on damp ground.

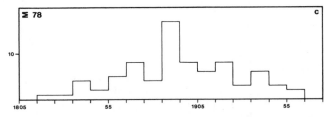

Fig. 10c. Find frequency for bog hoards from northern Jutland including Randers county, normally found during peat cutting.

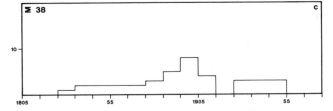

Fig. 11c. Find frequency for bog hoards from southern and central Jutland, normally found during peat cutting.

JUTLAND

The find frequencies for the Jutland hoards from northern, southern and central Jutland follow more or less the same pattern (figs. 10a and 11a), and the curves also show marked similarities to the corresponding curves for the islands – namely a 20-year climax from 1885 to 1905,

followed by a gradual fall, especially after 1945-55. As for Funen, the left half of the curve is considerably lower than the right one: in Jutland the increase begins in 1855.

For Jutland, too, the factors governing the general shape of the curves will be examined by in the first instance dividing them up into field and bog finds.

	Dry	Wet	Total
Maschinery	22	23	45
Digging	35	29	64
Total	57	52	109

Fig. 12. Recorded find depths for field hoards from Jutland, finds made during construction work excluded.

Field hoards

The field finds first begin to occur in large numbers from 1855, at a time when the first museums were established in Jutland, and reclamation, especially of the moors, was intensified. But reclamation up to 1855 must also have produced a number of finds, which were lost or ended up in private collections to partly explain the skew in the find frequency. It must be remarked, however, that drainage did not really get under way until after the turn

of the century (cf. the article on economic development) and reached a climax from the 1930s on to the 1950s, which is also clearly reflected in the diagrams (figs. 10b and 11b). The curve for finds on damp ground is thus almost certainly representative. Only on the better soils of eastern Jutland had drainage already been started in the 18th century. That this resulted in only a few finds, in the southern and central parts, supports the belief that eastern Jutland was only sparsely populated in the Bronze Age (Randsborg 1974).

In contrast, moor reclamation does not seem to have manifested itself particularly strongly in the hoard diagrams, unlike the grave finds. A climax can be demonstrated, however, in the decades around the turn of the century, which undoubtedly has a connection not only with the moor reclamation, but with the whole intensivation of arable cultivation in these decades. The paucity of hoard finds in the 19th century relative to the 20th is thus doubtless due to the circumstance that those factors of agricultural development which brought hoards to light did not really come into their own until the end of the last century. And this means first and foremost draining,

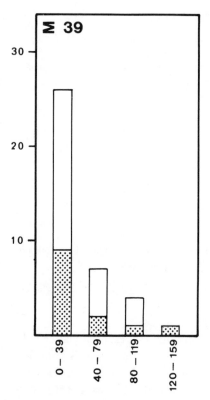

Fig. 13. Recorded find depths for field hoards from northern Jutland. Hoards found on damp ground are dotted.

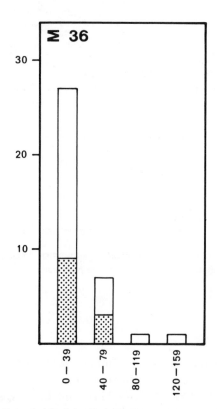

Fig. 14. Recorded find depths for field hoards from southern and central Jutland. Hoards found on damp ground are dotted.

Depth	≤ 1890	> 1890
0 - 80	1	1
80 - 200	8	9
> 200	1	3

a

Depth	≤ 1890	> 1890
0 - 80	1	3
> 80	3	1

b

Fig. 15. Depth of bog hoards before and after 1890 for a) northern Jutland, and b) southern and central Jutland.

loaming, tree planting, etc. To illustrate this further, fig. 12 has been drawn up. This shows the same pattern as the islands with respect to the relation between machines and digging, whereas the damp ground finds are predominant on the islands. The balanced relation between wet and dry ground in Jutland is, however, not entirely confirmed by figs. 10b and 11b, where dry finds dominate in southern and central Jutland.

Let us now examine the find frequency's abrupt fall after 1955 in southern and central Jutland, and in northern Jutland already from 1945. As was the case with the islands, this fall cannot be attributed solely to the mechanization of agriculture, but must be due to an actual depletion of the number of hoards. Also fig. 14 over the prevalent hoard depths shows by and large the same picture as the islands, and the same conclusions can be drawn. But fewer finds have been made on damp ground in Jutland.

We can thus draw the same conclusion for Jutland as for Zealand, that hoard finds are largely exhausted on dry soils.

Bog hoards

This group of finds is very rare in southern and central Jutland, but more common in northern Jutland, which also contains by far the larger part of the bog areas of the peninsula (cf. the appendix to the article on economic development). The two diagrams thus show similarities in the form of a climax just before the turn of the century, as on the islands. And as on the islands, the increased wartime production is only slightly apparent, and we can draw the same conclusion for Jutland, namely that the layers with Bronze Age hoards had already been cut away and utilized by that time. For the islands this was confirmed in fig. 7; fig. 15 makes the test for northern

Jutland and central and southern Jutland respectively. Central and southern Jutland show a disparate tendency, and the material must be considered too small to have any evidential value. As far as northern Jutland is concerned, deep finds have been made both early and late, but if finds made deeper than 2 m are scrutinized, they turn out to have been made late. In relation to the islands, hoards have by and large not been found in the upper layers, and we must therefore conclude that the Bronze Age hoards lie generally deeper in Jutland, and that the bogs may still conceal several finds from the Early Bronze Age and Late Neolithic.

There is also the possibility that the later development of peat cutting in Jutland means that the depths given there are related to the original surface in contrast to Zealand, where the upper layers had presumably already been cut away by the beginning of the 18th century. Fig. 15 confirms that deeper finds are absent in central and southern Jutland, and that they are possibly still to be found in the bogs. It should be remembered, however, that bog finds as such are rare in the Early Bronze Age

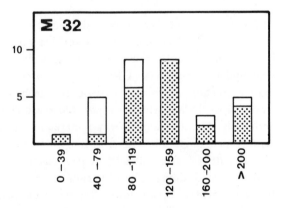

Fig. 16. Recorded find depths for bog hoards in Jutland. Northern Jutland is dotted.

	Zealand		Funen, Bornholm Loll.–Falster		N–Jutland		Central– & S–Jutland	
Agriculture	**41,6**	(48,8)	**44,7**	(52,9)	**39,6**	(43,1)	**35,0**	(45,6)
Ditching/Drainage	**13,9**	(7,8)	**18,1**	(9,4)	**9,9**	(5,3)	**16,3**	(8,1)
Constuction	**9,6**	(5,4)	**8,6**	(4,5)	**11,7**	(6,2)	**7,4**	(3,8)
Peat – cutting	**21,1**	(30,2)	**13,3**	(25,2)	**28,8**	(40,2)	**26,3**	(35,0)
Marl – taking	**1,2**	(0,7)	**0**		**1,8**	(1,0)	**0**	
Gravel – taking	**5,4**	(3,1)	**2,9**	(1,5)	**6,3**	(3,3)	**3,8**	(1,9)
Forestry/Gardening	**4,8**	(2,7)	**8,6**	(4,5)	**0,9**	(0,5)	**6,2**	(3,1)
Misch.	**2,4**	(1,3)	**3,8**	(2,0)	**0,9**	(0,5)	**5,0**	(2,5)
Total	**129**	(295)	**97**	(202)	**111**	(209)	**80**	(160)

Fig. 17. Regional survey of the relation between different find modes in per cent, based on specific find information. The bracketed percentages are those obtained when indirect information on find circumstances, such as "found in the field", etc., are included, and doubtless give the most accurate picture. This broader method of assessment yields 295 hoards for Zealand and 202 for the other Danish islands. For a good half of these there is specific information, for the rest indirect information deriving from cultivation or peat cutting. For Jutland the corresponding figures are 191 (specific) and 369 (indirect included).

and Late Neolithic in southern and central Jutland, like hoard depositions in general. The few hoards thus no doubt also reflect regional variations in deposition practices.

CONSPECTUS

We will finally carry out a synoptic analysis of the regional variations in the find circumstances. For this purpose fig. 17 has been produced, to show the most commonly occurring find circumstances. The figures are based on reported circumstances, while the distribution in brackets includes those finds in which it is possible to ascertain them indirectly. The diagram shows a remarkable agreement with respect to circumstances, with agricultural activities clearly dominating, followed by peat cutting and ditch-digging and draining. The few regional variations may be easily explanied: the lower frequency for peat cutting on Funen, Bornholm and Lolland-Falster is thus due to the relative lack of exploitation of bogs there;

forestry and horticulture are not particularly widespread in northern Jutland, while horticulture is centred on Funen.

We may thus draw the general conclusion that those factors which led to the appearance and discovery of hoards have largely worked in the same manner on a national basis, but with different chronological courses, as apparent from the frequency diagrams. On account of the strong decline after 1945 compared with the constancy of agricultural activity, we must conclude that the earth has yielded most of those hoards which were deposited in the Late Neolithic and Early Bronze Age, and conclude further that the picture we have today of their regional distribution and intensity is by and large historically representative.

Let us finally see for how many hoards information on find circumstances is available, in relation to the total number of hoards (fig. 18). Firstly, it is apparent that the custom of depositing hoards was associated with the Danish islands and far less widespread in Jutland in the Late Neolithic and Early Bronze Age. Deposition density

Region	⋜ Hoards	Registrated	Private collections
Zealand	409	309 (75,6%)	90 (23%)
Other Islands	310	242 (78,1%)	51 (16,5%)
Northern Jutland	280	226 (80,7%)	44 (15,7%)
Central-& S-Jutland	280	161 (57,5%)	72 (25,7%)

Fig. 18. Relation between the total number of hoards, hoards with year of registration, and hoards from private collections. The rest are undocumented hoards in museums.

Region	⋜ Hoards		Area in Ha.	
Zealand	89	(63,6%)	13.553	(60,2%)
Other Islands	51	(36,4%)	8.978	(39,8%)
Northern Jutland	84	(60%)	66.309	(60,9%)
Central-& S-Jutland	56	(40%)	41.911	(39,1%)

Fig. 19. Relation between number of bog hoards (including finds without year of registration) and area of bog around 1944, calculated separately for the islands and Jutland.

per sq.km was far greater on the islands than in Jutland (see further the distribution map fig. 21). Of the total amount of finds we have information on registration year for 75-80%, with the exception of southern and central Jutland which are right down to 57.5%. If these figures are compared with the figures for finds from private collections, there is in most areas a clear connection. A large number of finds from private collections corresponds to few finds with information.

One of the questions which has been frequently discussed in connection with the interpretation of the hoards is the choice of site: field or bog. In fig. 19 the number of finds from bogs in the different regions is correlated with bog area. It is apparent from this that there is a clear relation between the number of finds and total bog area. We may conclude from this that finds from bogs are regionally representative, but also that the deposition of finds in bogs was first and foremost determined by whether any bogs were available. Where there were fewer bogs, more finds were deposited in fields. This means that it is not legitimate on the basis of deposition in a bog alone to make culture historical and religious interpretations.

Another question which has a bearing on both the representativeness and the interpretation of the depositions is the depth of field deposition. Fig. 20 compares the Late Neolithic/Early Bronze Age and the Late Bronze Age. A clear difference is apparent, in that deeply deposited finds are more prominent in the Late Bronze Age than in the Early Bronze Age/Late Neolithic. It has apparently been more important to secure the deposited valuables in the Late Bronze Age by burying them deeper. This presumably also means that there are still a number of deeply buried finds from the Late Bronze Age, which have not yet been discovered, since the chance of encountering deeply buried objects is naturally less than for finds lying at ploughing depth.

CONCLUSION

We have now concluded the analysis of the representativeness of the field and bog hoards and reached for both categories the conclusion that it was geographically even within the respective areas. This means that the hoards from the Late Neolithic and Early Bronze Age are randomly distributed within the areas in which it was customary to deposit hoards. Lolland-Falster, Funen and Bornholm's numerical representation was lower than Zealand's, however. This is due partly to the fact that a late start was made in reporting finds, and that the peat diggings are still not exhausted. How representative the number of finds is in relation to the originally deposited number of hoards is more uncertain. In the case of the Late Bronze Age, it was estimated to lie between 15 and 25%. Taking 25%, we arrive at a figure for the Late Neolithic and Early Bronze Age of about 1200 hoards deposited on Zealand and about 980 on the other islands (844 plus 16%, cf. note 3). Spread over 600 years (from Late Neolithic C up to period III), this gives respectively 2.0 and 1.6 depositions per year. These figures are the lowest possible, since they have been calculated from figs. 1 and 2. If hoards without date of find are added, the figures must be increased by about 9%. If we take 15% as our starting point, the figures become: Zealand

Depth in cm	E.B.A.	L.B.A.
0 – 39	142 (70,3%)	47 (54,7%)
40 – 79	44 (21,8%)	26 (30,2%)
80 – 160	16 (7,9%)	13 (15,1%)
Total	206 (100%)	86 (100%)

Fig. 20. Burial depths for field hoards in the Early and Late Bronze Age respectively. (The lower number from LBA is due to the fact that only hoards with two or more objects were recorded).

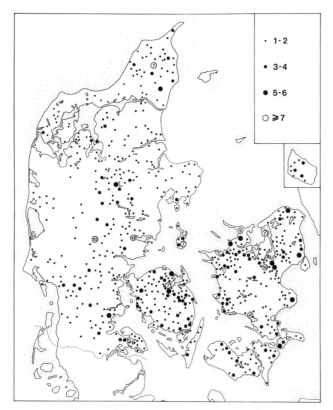

Fig. 21. Distribution of bronze hoards with one or more objects from Late Neolithic/Early Bronze Age.

2000/3.3 depositions per year, the other islands 1600/2.7 depositions per year. Even if we go further down in representation level, there will at all events only be an extremely restricted number of depositions. In relation to the amount of bronze in circulation it cannot have been very much – how much is discussed in the article on representativeness of grave finds. (p. 134-146 in this volume).

Kristian Kristiansen,
National Agency for the Nature,
Monuments and Sites,
Amaliegade 13,
1256 Copenhagen

Acknowledgements

Without the superlative help of Professor Karl Kersten, this work could not have been carried out. Professor Kersten placed without condition the unpublished parts of his great catalogue of finds of the Early Bronze Age at my full disposal, both the completed catalogues and the cards over the areas yet to be written up, sending me the county reports as they were completed. For this generosity I wish to convey my thanks.

The 1st Department of the National Museum, whose collections and archives I have worked in for long periods since 1971, have always shown me great hospitality. This also applies to the many Danish provincial museums which have willingly opened their collections and archives and responded to my enquiries.

For private hospitality and friendship during my visits to Schleswig, I thank Michael Gebürh and Karl Kersten.

Finally, special thanks to my wife Lotte Hedager for her help with the completed work on the extensive grave find material from Jutland, the final presentation of which has unfortunately had to be postponed until a later publication.

NOTES

1. This analysis has been primarily based on Aner and Kersten's catalogue of finds of the Early Bronze Age, (1973-76) including its unpublished parts from Jutland.

   With respect to the period 1965-74, the following situation obtains. The north Jutland counties of Ålborg, Hjørring, Thisted and Viborg were finished by Professor Kersten c. 1969-70, the other counties of Jutland after 1975. I have done my best to supplement the material with more recent finds, but the decade 1965-1974 is hardly complete.

   The manuscript was completed in the summer of 1977, with adjustments and a few additions in 1980.

2. The following considerations apply to the analysis:

   A. To *hoards* are assigned all documented finds made in field or bog and unassociated with a barrow, including single finds. A number of finds without specific information on mode of discovery are classified as hoards when they consist of objects traditionally never found in graves, first and foremost flanged axes and palstaves, and which based on indirect information (see B) must also be classified as hoards. Objects which can occur in both graves and hoards are classified as hoards only when find circumstances indicated this.

   B. Assignment to *field, bog and damp ground* is based on present circumstances. If, for example, a find is made during harrowing of a field in a drained bog, it is classified as a "field find on damp ground", even though a culture-historical interpretation would rather place it among bog hoards. This means that many hoards termed "Moordepot" in Aner and Kersten (based on deposition circumstances) are on the basis of the original documentation assigned to "field finds on damp ground" (based on find circumstances). When specific information on provenance (field or bog) is lacking, patina is used as criterion, but with certain reservations. Green patina = field find. Bog patina superimposed on green patina, (a common phenomenon) = damp ground, because it shows that the object, although originally deposited dry, perhaps in a hollow in the field, was later subjected to bog conditions. Hoards found in a field, but with bog patina = damp ground. Bog patina without other information has been left out of the calculations but been shown unhatched in the complete find frequency diagram.

C. Most finds lack specific information on mode of find: *machines, digging, picked up*. Normally, the only indication is "found in the field", or "found during field work". Finds of this nature are not assigned to a category: this requires that specific information be available. When there are no indications of field state (damp/dry), the definitions of B have been followed.

D. Only when *find depth* is specifically indicated is it employed in calculation, with the exception that all finds found directly during ploughing have been assigned to the 0-40 cm group.

E. Finally it should be remarked that all finds deriving from private collections have been omitted from the counts. In a number of cases the information in Aner and Kersten has been supplemented with archive studies, whereby a number of finds, in particular from provincial museums in Jutland, have had *year of registration* appended. Kersten has been consistent in stating *year of find* only. The interval between year of registration and year of discovery will normally be under 10 years, when finds from private collections are excluded. And since most of the finds in the provincial museums record year of registration only, it was decided to include these on grounds of representativeness.

F. Information on all counted finds have been recorded on data sheets, and find lists can be produced by computer. Further information may be obtained from the author.

3. To the 5 "showpieces" mentioned should be added 3 bronze shields received from *Kunstkammeret*, where they were as early as 1737. This affects the basis of calculation slightly. The 36 fine pieces found between 1805 and 1974 comprise 11.8% of the total of 304 finds, which is rounded up to 12%. The number of finds lost between 1650 and 1805 thus becomes 66, and from the Middle Ages and on 264. Iron Age agriculture is not thought to have played any important role, but some finds will naturally have been made, and we therefore round up to 400. Further, it should be assumed that a number of hoards have been lost since 1805, too, but hardly many, to judge by the parish inventories. On Zealand, the recorded number of lost hoards from the Late Neolithic and Early Bronze Age thus comprises 4.5%. If we therefore increase the number to 100,

this is a liberal estimate. To arrive at a figure for the original number of hoards, we must finally add the number still buried: 300 is a liberal estimate (cf. Kristiansen 1976, 148). There should thus have been deposited 1100 hoards with 2 or more objects in periods IV and V of the Bronze Age, of which the amount recorded today comprises 25% or more. If the deposition period is put at 400 years, this gives 2.75 depositions per year on a national basis. The estimates employed in this calculation are, as stated, liberal, apart from the number of lost finds in the Iron Age. But even if this is increased by, for example, 300, it lowers the level of representativeness only to 20%. The same result is obtained if it is assumed that, in addition to the 8 preserved "showpieces" found between 1650 and 1805, a further 8 have been lost, which is scarcely unrealistic. If we to this then add the further 300 lost finds from the Iron Age, we come down to about 17.5%. Taken together, we may conclude that the level of representation of hoards may with considerable confidence be said to lie between 15 and 20% in the Late Bronze Age.

4. If one supposes that as many finds were made in the period 1825-1875 as in the period 1895-1945, a difference of 34 finds is obtained, comprising 15%.

REFERENCES

ANER, E. & KERSTEN, K. 1973-1976. *Die Funde der älteren Bronzezeit des Nordischen Kreises in Dänemark, Schleswig-Holstein und Niedersachsen*. Band 1-3. Neumünster & Copenhagen.

KRISTIANSEN, K. 1976. En kildekritisk analyse af depotfund fra Danmarks bronzealder (periode IV-V). Et bidrag til den arkæologiske kildekritik. *Årbøger for nordisk Oldkyndighed og Historie*. Copenhagen.

RANDSBORG, K. 1974. Social Stratification in Early Bronze Age Denmark. A Study in the Regulation of Cultural Systems. *Praehistorische Zeitschrift*. 49.

Bronze Age Settlements[1]

by HENRIK THRANE

INTRODUCTION

While Bronze Age graves and hoards have been recognized in Denmark since the Renaissance, and their variations fairly well established by 1900, nothing was known about the actual settlements till 1909. In this year Carl Neergaard began his excavations of the Voldtofte settlement, which continued with some interruptions up to 1921. It was not until Sophus Müller published the first account of 12 settlement finds in 1919 that the nature of the material became known. The Bronze Age settlements could not be as easily found as the "Køkkenmøddinger" of the Stone Age, but they were no less conspicuous than the Iron Age settlements, published in 1906 by Müller. Bronze Age and Iron Age settlements were represented only by pits, hearths and refuse layers (culture layers) and could be dated by their pottery, bronzes and characteristic poor-quality flint work.

The main sites published by Müller were Voldtofte and Hasmark, both in Funen, Bulbjerg in Jutland, and Abbetved in Zealand. They showed environmental as well as geographical diversity, since Hasmark and Bulbjerg were coastal sites while Voldtofte and Abbetved were inland sites. This was clearly reflected in the fauna found in the pits and refuse layers (Winge 1919).

Müller's pioneering work was not continued, except that Carl Neergaard carried out excavations in the Lejre area, where an amateur archaeologist found several new sites (Broholm 1949, 181). The odd pit was found occasionally, but nobody considered serious research on the ·problem. It may have been felt that Müller had exhausted the potential of this field. The lack of house plans was a continuous source of concern, and several claims of such plans were made during the 1920's. V. la Cour (1927, 310 f) in his treatment of Bronze Age settlements (1927, 292 ff) found proof of round houses in the circle of postholes excavated by the brilliant excavator Rosenberg at Vesterlund. Although others agreed with his interpretation (Brøndsted 1939, 132: Mortuary houses or proper

houses), Gudmund Hatt (1941, 161 ff) produced the correct interpretation: posts enclosing a barrow (Thrane 1967). Another house from Birknæs, Østbirk in Jutland (la Cour 1927, 300 ff, 206 fig. 3; Berglund 1973) turned out to be insecurely dated (Broholm 1949, 186). The Sonnerup house (la Cour 1927, 308 f) has also disappeared from later literature.

There only remained the two postholes from Nexø on Bornholm (Müller 1906, 195; la Cour 1927, 309 f).

As long as houses were rare from other periods, this lack of Bronze Age houses was not conspicuous. But after the discoveries in the 1920's (Kraghede house as early as 1906, Müller 1912, 113) of a series of complete Iron Age houses (Kjær 1928) and even Stone Age houses (Winther 1935) the absence of Bronze Age houses appeared rather noticeable, especially considering the technological stage of the Bronze Age.

An explanation of the lack of houses was proposed by G. Hatt (1936, 97 ff): If the Bronze Age people were herdsmen they had to move fairly often, so that no substantial remains would be left for the archaeologists to find (Hatt 1937, 134; Mathiassen 1959, 45, 1948, 97 ff, Thorvildsen 1960, 69 f).

The official settlement excavation technique of the National Museum was taken over from Stone Age settlement excavation (Køkkenmøddinger), whereby the sites were excavated in separate square metres. This method did not favour the observation of house structures. I think it may even be called prohibitive in this respect. It is significant that the only well-documented structures were found under barrows which were excavated in planes e.g. Vesterlund and Svenstrup (Aner & Kersten 1976, no. 1010), Norddorf on Amrum (Struve 1955), Ballermosen (Lomborg 1956, fig. 8) and recently Trappendal in south east Jutland (Neumann 1975).

Not until after World War II were larger areas excavated in Bronze Age settlements – when the methods evol-

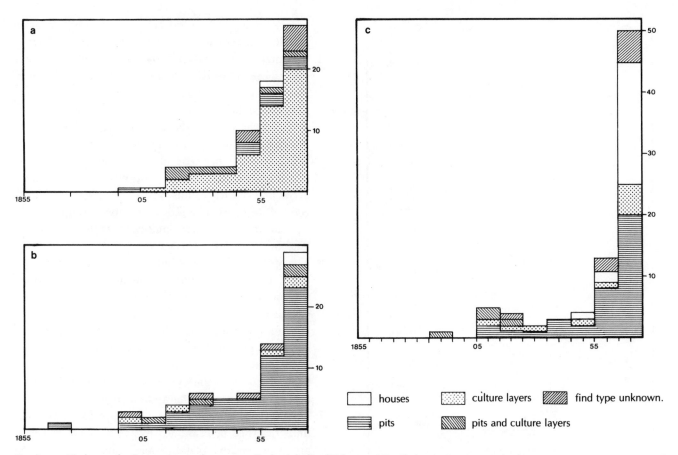

Fig. 1. a-c. Find types for Bronze Age settlements. a: Zealand, Lolland-Falster and Bornholm, b: Funen, c: Jutland.

ved in digging Iron Age houses by Hatt and Steensberg had proved succesful.

As early as 1927 Vilhelm la Cour had pointed out that when only rubbish layers were excavated, the chances of finding houses were slight (1927, 292 ff).

In his first major survey of Danish prehistory, J. Brøndsted (1939, 255-258) mentioned no more than 29 sites characterized by rubbish pits, citing only Müller's examples of more extensive settlements. Houses were unknown, but Brøndsted was confident that they would appear. He saw the lack of settlements as a result of a lesser emphasis on agriculture related to the arrival of the Battle Axe people (1939, 130).

Even if Broholm (1949, 179-192) gave the settlements a more extensive treatment and better documentation, his list was the same as that of Brøndsted. Broholm sought an explanation for the absence of houses in the destruction caused by later (recent) agricultural activities (1949, 186), as also proposed by Hatt.

When Brøndsted revised his "Danmarks Oldtid" (1959, 302 f), the 3 houses from Fragtrup in 1955 (Thorvildsen 1960, 68) were added to the list.

However, nothing was changed in the text.

The small house under the Ballermosen barrow (Lomborg 1956) was not clearly identified as a living house, mortuary house (Glob 1970, 104) or cult house (Brøndsted 1959, 126).

Considering Brøndsted's superficial treatment in 1959 of the problems and the means of solving them, it is a relief to find a clear statement of ways and means, and above all a precise summary of the lack of sufficient information for current problems, in Jørgen Jensen's paper (1967 a).

STATISTICS

The statistics illustrate some factors operating in the discovery of Bronze Age settlements in modern times.

144

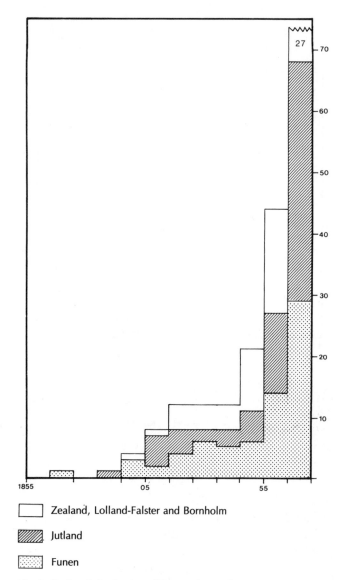

Fig. 2. Regional distribution of Bronze Age settlements.

Legend:
- ☐ Zealand, Lolland-Falster and Bornholm
- ▨ Jutland
- ▦ Funen

1. The rate of accession remained fairly constant over 75 years. This situation changed only in the 1950's, when the whole society became mechanized – cf. fig. 6.

   The result was an enormous increase in the number of observations and excavations.

   At no stage was the ratio of excavations to observations greater than in the 1960's and 1970's.

2. The part played by agricultural activities has remained fairly constant when seen in relation to the number of finds at any given stage.

3. Various deep non-archaeological excavation activities have taken place over a long period, starting around the turn of the century, but remained at a low level compared to agricultural activities. These excavation activities have however risen since the late 1950's.

4. The majority of known Bronze Age settlements have never been subjected to planned excavation. The normal procedure involves simply the salvage of enough material to date the site, plotting on maps, and for the more energetic, the excavation of the pit involved, or perhaps even more than one pit.

5. The knowledge of houses depends upon large area excavations, i.e. the stripping of areas of several hundreds or even thousands of m². The digging of areas wanted for construction or extraction purposes should present important opportunities for more work of this kind in the future (cf. Lomborg 1977).

6. The geographical distribution seems haphazard, cf. fig. 4. The concentrations on the map normally reflect the activities of local amateur archaeologists. The excavations in W. Jutland (Becker 1968 etc. and Jensen 1967 c) have shown that the distribution of grave finds known at present is not to be trusted as an indication of the distribution of Bronze Age settlements. (It may be doubted how reliably the maps (Broholm 1949) reflect the present-day latent knowledge[2]).

7. Up to 1955 (but in Funen already before 1940) the finds recorded or examined by the National Museum are representative of the whole country, although no attempt was made to provide an explicitly representative sample or to increase the knowledge acquired before 1919 by new, planned field work. The activities of the local museums after 1955 remain uncontrolled and guided by unknown factors. No policy of research has been laid down. The statistics cannot show how representative are the data recorded in the central archives of the National Museum. There is no way of checking how much remained unreported, except by periodic revision of the individual museum archives. The amateur archaeologists represent a weak point even more than the local museums although – like all other citizens – they are obliged to report any new find, according to the Preservation Law of 1969.

8. The statistics show – when compared to the published statements – that the archaeological material always had a greater potential than was apparent from the literature. This gap between stored knowledge and used knowledge has widened steadily since 1919. The revival of interest in the Bronze Age settlements caused by the accidental discovery of houses in West Jutland is no exception. So far only a fraction of the

material has been published even in preliminary form, and until today no Bronze Age settlement has been finally published, i.e. with complete documentation of finds and observations and their interpretation.

Only a dozen excavations out of the 123 field observations made since 1964 have been mentioned in more than a few lines (Becker 1968, 1972, 1976; Jensen 1967 c; Kristiansen 1972; Lomborg 1976, 1977; Neumann 1975; Thrane 1971, 1979; Wortmann 1971).

As long as the gap between field observations and publication is allowed to widen, no genuinely planned excavation can be undertaken. Without an exhaustive knowledge of the problems involved and the material already available elsewhere it will be impossible to organize new research (rescue or planned) in a sufficiently economic way to ensure the optimal retrieval of observations. Because of the history of the discovery of the Bronze Age settlements, this situation may be worse for this group of archaeological remains than for others with a more traditional history of recovery. The long fallow period followed by the sudden burst of house excavations in the late 1960's may have led to a bottle-neck of publication potential.

FIND CATEGORIES

The character of the Bronze Age settlements does not differ radically from that of the Neolithic or Early Iron Age settlements. The main archaeological elements are: A. surface indications, B. subterranean features, viz: 1. cooking pits, 2. refuse storage pits, 3. rubbish layers, 4. houses or parts of houses. A. may be specified by excavations. B. will in different degrees appear as A. under normal Danish and Scanian conditions, i.e. on intensively cultivated land. Each group presents its own problems.

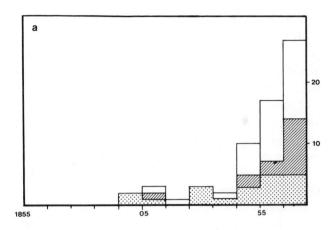

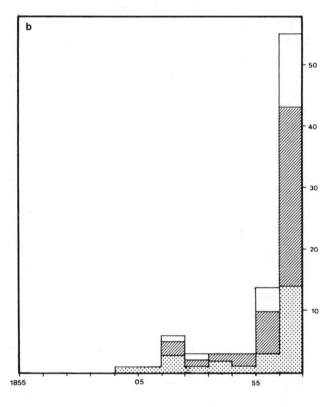

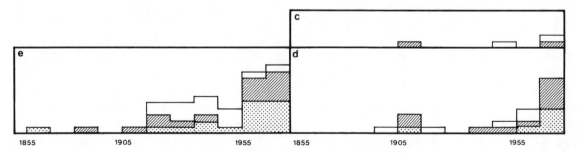

Fig. 3 a-e. Find causes for Bronze Age settlements, signatures cf. fig. 2. a. Construction incl. drainage, sewage, marl digging and levelling. b. Farming and gardening incl. stone removal and surface survey. c. Nature. d. Excavations for other purposes. e. Unspecified.

A. *Surface indications*

Only sites with pottery have been included in the present paper, since they have a better dating potential than aceramic sites. It is extremely difficult to distinguish between LN and EBA flintwork, and LBA flint is traditionally included in the Stone Age sections of the museum store-rooms so that they tend to be forgotten or ignored (perhaps also because of the poor technique, since not many amateurs will collect such low-quality material).

This selection means a distortion in the total number of settlements known. However the exact degree of this distortion is unknown.

A look at the regional surveys of Therkel Mathiassen will give an idea of the nature of this problem.

The survey of NW Jutland was completed in 1945, and Mathiassen (1948, 97) listed 171 LN settlements, 223 Neolithic and Bronze Age settlements characterized solely by flints, plus a further 281 flint sites so small that they were labelled "flint spots", i.e. sites without tools or other datable objects. These flint scatters may belong anywhere within the span of the Stone Age and the Bronze Age.

Mathiassen finished his NW Zealand survey in 1954. It produced 13 settlements with Bronze Age flint only (Mathiassen 1959, 94) (out of a total of 23 Bronze Age settlements), 151 LN/EBA sites (ibid. 40) and an additional 1312 flint scatters (ibid. 43).

The presence of so many flint scatters seen against a total of 859 settlements from the entire Stone Age, including LN, calls for a comment.

Mathiassen (1948, 97) interpreted the flint scatters partly as evidence of short stays by smaller groups. This may, of course, be true for some of the sites, but it is more likely that we are mistaking size conditioned by function for size as the expression of sampling technique.

The size of a sample from a given site depends upon the intensity and quality of the survey. Although these factors are mentioned by Mathiassen (1948, 33) they are of paramount importance in the use of survey material as such, and especially in this case, for both the aceramic and ceramic sites, but most of all for the flint scatters. I have no new material from NW Jutland, but experience from Funen and NW Zealand has convinced me that the size of the sample as well as its quality above all depends upon the intensity of the survey.

Walking once over a field, or during one season, is not enough if a valid impression of the inherent qualities of a site is to be obtained.

Factors such as the time of the year, the state of the field, farming methods, the intensity of rainfall and frost, the distance between the walking lines, the speed and experience of the observer, are decisive.

There are two standard situations connected with the surface observations of archaeological material itself.

I. If the same plough layer has been cultivated for several generations, the less resistant objects, such as metal and pottery, will disappear from the topsoil, leaving flints and stones.

II. Only when the ploughing depth is increased will layers with new contents of pottery etc. be churned up. Each year some of these will be destroyed by weathering until the original situation is restored.

Situation I has existed in most parts of Denmark since the Viking Age, which explains why so few sites with pottery were found during Mathiassen's surveys.

Situation II now dominates after the introduction of deep ploughing during the 1950's – for how long, nobody knows.

I have tried to demonstrate the relevance of these phenomena for Odsherred, the NW-corner of NW Zealand (Thrane 1971, 163 with map fig. 19).

If the number of datable ceramic settlements is compared to the number of flint sites (aceramic) it becomes evident that pottery sites are rare. There are 389 flint scatters plus 48 LN/EBA sites, compared to 8 pottery sites – all discovered after 1954 (3 after 1971). This discrepancy can only mean that a large part of the flint sites are prospective pottery producers, robbed by situation I of their pottery. Situation II will, with repeated surveys, no doubt in many cases produce pottery which eventually may permit a division into LN, EBA and LBA settlements.

This position prevails everywhere else, most drastically in NW Jutland where Mathiassen's survey failed to produce a single ceramic Bronze Age site.

The line of reasoning followed here implies that it is impossible to assess the representativity of the extant pottery sites in a given region without knowing the history of the archaeology of that region. NW Zealand and NW Jutland are both atypical for Denmark as a whole, since they are the only areas which have been systematically surveyed. The regrettable fact that the surveys took place in situation I, before deep ploughing set in, means that both areas are atypical in relation to the situation in the Bronze Age (Eggers 1951, 24).

The typical Danish landscape has never been subjec-

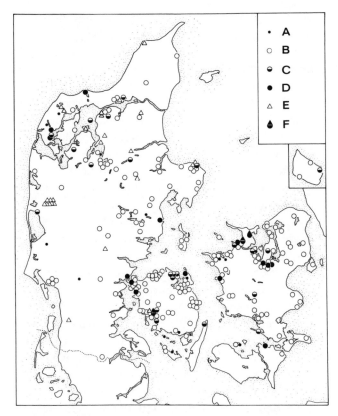

Fig. 4. Bronze Age settlements according to their find type, A: Unspecified settlement indicators, B: Pits, C: Culture layer, D: B plus C, E: Houses resp. postholes indicating houses, F: E plus C or D.

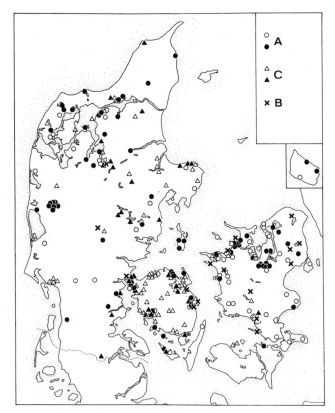

Fig. 5. Bronze Age settlements according to their archaeological treatment, by: A. the National Museum (incl. Copenhagen University), B. local museums, C. private persons. Open symbols indicate registration, filled symbols indicate excavations. Finds reported to museums are listed under the respective museums.

ted to systematic survey, which means that even flint sites are hardly known, or only slightly better known than pottery sites.

The obvious implication of this is that the Bronze Age settlements known at present cannot be representative of the situation in antiquity, the Grøntofte area being as clearly overrepresented as the rest of Denmark is underrepresented.

Our knowledge is dependant upon several factors:

a. The local presence of interested persons.

b. Various non-archaeological activities such as construction work and farming.

c. The difficult accessibility will limit our possibilities of observation much more than grave finds and so the relationship between graves and settlements will be out of proportion to what it was in antiquity, we will observe more graves than settlements.

d. Only fresh regional studies can determine what the relationship between sites with pottery and sites with

only flint should be, whether there is a real difference and what this difference means.

e. Future surveys and accidental discoveries will produce many new sites of both categories and presumably provide a better basis for an understanding of the character of the Bronze Age settlement.

f. Many vital aspects including the internal organisation of individual settlements, settlement patterns, production patterns etc. are still insufficiently known – the range of new discoveries made since 1964 shows this very clearly.

g. A sufficient basis for selecting sites or groups of sites for complete excavation is still not available anywhere in Denmark.

B. *Subterranean features*

1. *Cooking pits* have been examined in great numbers in recent years and have been noted so frequently over

the whole South Scandinavian area that registration is nearly impossible. They are easily recognized by non-archaeologists because of their black earth and the firecracked stones, but have been disregarded by archaeologists because they very rarely contain datable finds. This situation has now changed, since C 14-dates may be produced from the charcoal at the bottom of the pits, thermoluminescence or TL-dates made directly on the stones. This is important for the inclusion of isolated groups of pits in a regional context (settlement pattern) (Thrane 1974). The majority of the cooking pits (types Seeberg 1969 fig. 8; Thrane 1971 and 1974) may belong to the Bronze Age, but they certainly continue into the Iron Age (Thrane 1976 b) and up to the Viking period. Ethnographic parallels and practical experiments show that the pits are very efficient in roasting meat (or baking?) (Lerche 1969). The use of section digging shows that the cooking pits were always disturbed, by taking out the finished product. The stones from cooking pits have been used as indicators of the location of the settlements in West Jutland which are otherwise difficult to recognize (Becker 1976), and thus have great potential in the study of Bronze Age settlements.

2. Pits, normally called *refuse pits* (Müller 1919), constitute the most common type of settlement remains which can be dated by archaeological material alone. The term may be unfortunate since their use as rubbish dumps was clearly a secondary one. As the primary purpose of the pits has not been completely settled, the term may however be used here. Some pits were dug to procure raw materials, others presumably as storage holes, while yet others have been interpreted as pit houses (Salomonsson 1970) which is not a valid suggestion for more than a very few pits.

Be that as it may, the pits have served the purpose of producing information on the fauna, pottery and flint-work of LBA, and for many years remained the only source available for this kind of information (Müller 1919; Winge 1919). The concept that flint work continued as an integral part of Bronze Age technology all through the Bronze Age was one of the contributions of the pits. The level of knowledge reached in 1919 has not been much improved by later discoveries, because of the thorough analysis then made, and perhaps also due to an *a priori* pessimistic attitude towards renewed study.

Section digging has however improved the knowledge of the filling process of the pits and proved that the rubbish fill was secondary.

New techniques for the sampling and extraction of faunal and floral remains have not been applied to any great extent. The large area excavations in Jutland and NW Zealand have shown that the cooking and other pits tend to cluster in certain parts of the settlements (cf. Schindler 1960 Abb. 32) outside the houses. If only the areas immediately adjacent to the pits (cooking or refuse) are examined, no houses will be found – this explains why the houses were so late in appearing.

Future pit excavators should consider the possibility of identifying the primary purpose of the pits through various methods.

3. *Refuse layers* (normally called culture layers in Dan. arch. terminology) have, of course, the same potential as the pits, and Müller leaned heavily on the Voldtofte layers for his study (1919). The distribution of artefacts and the character of the more than 1 m thick deposit made it clear that it was a midden (Müller 1919, 40 *et al.*). It was not deposited in or around houses. This cannot however be true everywhere, since other sites have been found with thinner culture layers on level ground with house remains in situ, and refuse was not dumped away from the houses (Thrane 1971, 158). New excavations at Voldtofte have shown: a) that the thick layers are found at the bottom of slopes while the houses presumably stood at the top; b) that thinner layers with postholes etc. were found on level ground. The large area excavations at Jyderup Skov (Thrane 1971) and Skamlebæk (Lomborg 1977) (both NW Zealand) and Egehøj in East Jutland (Boas 1977) have not yet been analysed so that information on the distribution of different types of artefact in relation to cooking activity areas, houses etc. is not yet available. For the culture layers on level ground this is a promising field.

The lack of culture layers in some parts of Denmark may be due to the agricultural exploitation of the sites which took place in antiquity, certainly during the Iron Age (Becker 1971, 99 ff) if not as early as the Bronze Age itself (Lomborg unpubl. data for EBA Vadgård).

It seems at our present level of knowledge that culture layers of some depth (0.20-1.0 m) are found on the islands and perhaps in East Jutland, but not in West Jutland. The soil type cannot be a determining factor, since the Jyderup and Skamlebæk settlements and also Voldtofte are situated on light sands. An explanation may be found in the exploitation pattern of different regions (see below), but is more likely to be found in future excavations.

4. The first definite Bronze Age *house plans* did not become available until the settlement at Fragtrup was found by an amateur archaeologist and excavated by E. Thorvildsen in 1957-58. (Fyrkat was excavated in 1954-55 but remained unknown till 1971 (Jensen 1971)). Unfortunately the Fragtrup houses have not played any significant part in the subsequent discussion as they have remained unpublished. The preliminary date quoted by Brøndsted (per. VI) was no doubt influenced by the strong resemblance to Iron Age houses, but the pottery is earlier (per. IV, or with Jensen 1967a, 98 per. V). The houses caused considerable surprise. Not only did they belong to the main Iron Age tradition, but their orientation, construction, size, and interior arrangement, even down to the stable in the east end, corresponded closely to the Iron Age houses from Jutland.

Although a stable does not seem to be a current feature in the Bronze Age houses found since 1960, other instances are now known (Jensen 1967c).

During the last ten years the number of house plans recovered in the course of normal excavation, e.g. under barrows, has increased steadily, but the growth rate has been much less than that of houses found during large scale mechanized excavations in West Jutland (Becker 1968, 19).

These large area excavations have revealed some 100 houses from seven different sites all within an area measuring some 7 × 10 km, lying 16 km inland from the present shore line (Becker 1976; cf. also Müller-Wille 1978). These houses were found when digging Stone Age graves and Iron Age houses, but gradually the focus was switched to the Bronze Age settlements. The more recently found sites were located by two factors, their position on the highest ground in the landscape and the presence of fire cracked stones (cooking stones).

The first step towards a better understanding of the evolution of the Bronze Age house is to have all excavated houses published, until which time a policy cannot be laid down.

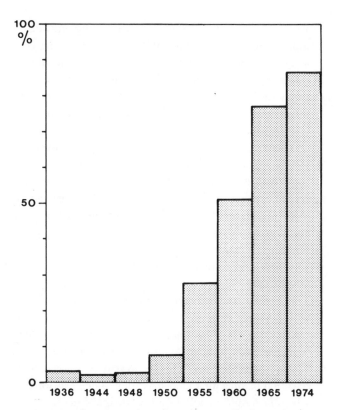

Fig. 6 Import of tractors excl. garden cultivators. The import is seen as a reflection of the intensity of the mechanization of agriculture, although some tractors may have been used for other purposes. The number of independent farms with more than 5 hectares was 184,433 in 1950, 155,922 in 1959. The variations in the later part of the diagram presumably reflect the renewal of worn out tractors and the increasing use of more than one tractor per farm.

CONCLUSION

This brief survey may be summarized as follows:

1. The material available up to 1955 was in many ways misleading, insofar as only the simpler categories of archaeological sites, such as pits and culture layers, were represented. The only planned excavations antedated 1919, and were carried out with inadequate digging techniques so that much information is simply not available.

2. No Bronze Age settlement has ever been finally published. This deplorable fact not only obscures a clear recognition of the actual evidence but prevents an overall view of the *status quo* and a reasonable planning of future field work. This is very serious in view of the present wholesale destruction of archaeological evidence everywhere in Denmark.

3. Recent excavations have been guided by uncontrolable factors such as accidental finds made during construction work, farming, or during excavations undertaken for other purposes. The conscious intention to excavate Bronze Age sites has rarely been a determining factor. Even in the Grøntofte area the objective was restricted to finding houses.

There have been virtually no attempts to examine the overall character and pattern of settlements, with the possible exception of Jyderup Skov. The long-term rescue excavations at Skamlebæk prior to construction work (Lomborg 1977) may also provide the basis for studying a site as a total entity rather than as a set of separate elements.

4. The sites now known and dated by their pottery cannot be representative of the situation in antiquity. There is a strong overrepresentation of excavated sites with posthole structures but devoid of culture layers in restricted parts of Jutland, and a corresponding underrepresentation of East Danish sites with houses.

5. There is a strong need at the present time for careful selection of sites for total excavation. The basis for this selection should ideally be a knowledge of the situation in a given region, so that the structure of the individual settlement may be seen in the context of local settlement patterns known from survey and sampled by excavation (Thrane 1973 and 1982).

Henrik Thrane,
Fyns Stiftsmuseum,
Hollufgård,
DK – 5220 Odense SØ

NOTES

1. The material for this paper has been collected over a number of years ending in 1976. Total coverage cannot be expected except in the case of the National Museum and *Fyns Stiftsmuseum*. I have analysed the topographical archives of the National Museum, the find records of the NM and FSM, the material in their store-rooms as well as the annual reports published by some local museums and *"Nyt og Noter"*. Due to the reluctance of some local museums to report to the NM archives or *"Nyt og Noter"* much has no doubt not been covered. Amateur archaeologists may also possess finds which have not been reported to any museum. The statistics presented here deviate on some points from previously published data (Thrane 1971 and 1973), because supplementary data have appeared. The manuscript was revised in 1979, only a few references have been added in 1984.

2. Latent knowledge means: the information available in different archives, private and public. Ideally they should have been included in the published knowledge, i.e. the inventories and statements appearing in the publications. It seems inevitable that a gap between the two categories of knowledge should exist, but the narrowing of the gap should be a chief objective of research.

ABBREVIATIONS

NM Arbm.: Nationalmuseets Arbejdsmark
Aarb.: Aarbøger for nordisk Oldkyndighed og Historie,
J.D.A.: Journal of Danish Archaeology,
Acta Arch.: Acta Archaeologica.

REFERENCES

ANER, E. & K. KERSTEN 1976, *Die Funde der älteren Bronzezeit* II.
BECKER, C. J. 1966, Ein früheisenzeitliches Dorf bei Grøntoft Westjütland. *Acta Arch.* XXXVI, 209-222.
– 1968, Bronzealderhuse i Vestjylland. *NM Arbm.* 1968, 79-88.
– 1971, Früheisenzeitliche Dörfer bei Grøntoft, Westjütland. *Acta Arch.* XLII, 79-110.
– 1972, Hal og hus i yngre bronzealder. *NM Arbm.* 1972, 5-16.
– 1976, Bosættelsesformer i bronze- og jernalder, H. Thrane ed., *Bebyggelsesarkæologi*, 70-83. Skrifter fra Institut f. Historie og Samfundsvidenskab no. 17, Odense.
– 1980, Bebyggelsesformer i Danmarks yngre bronzealder, set i forhold til ældste jernalders landsbysamfund. *Skrifter fra Historisk Institut*, Odense Universitet no. 28, 127-141.
BERGLUND, J. 1973, Fund af meldrøjer i yngre bronzealder. *Holstebro Museums Årsskrift* 1972-73, 67-70, Holstebro.
BOAS, N. A. 1977, Egehøj bopladsen. Hovedfagspeciale Århus Universitet, unpubl., cf. *J.D.A.* 2, 1984.
BOKELMANN, K. 1975, Wohnungen der Toten. *Kölner Römer-Illustrierte* 2, 66-67, cf. *Offa* 34, 82-89.
BROHOLM, H. C. 1949, *Danmarks Bronzealder* IV, København.
BRØNDSTED, J. 1939, *Danmarks Oldtid* II, København.
– 1959, *Danmarks Oldtid* II, København, 2nd ed.
EGGERS, H. J. 1951, *Der römische Import im freien Germanien*. Beiheft zum Atlas der Urgeschichte, Hamburg.
GLOB, P. V. 1970, *Højfolket* (The mound people). København.
HATT, G. 1936, Oldtidens Landsby i Danmark. *Fortid og Nutid*, 97-129, København.
– 1937, *Landbrug i Danmarks Oldtid*, København.
– 1941, Forhistoriske Plovfurer i Jylland, *Aarb.* 1941, 155-165.
HVASS, S. 1976, Das eisenzeitliche Dorf bei Hodde, Westjütland. *Acta Arch.* 46, 142-158.
JENSEN, J. 1967a, Voldtofte-fundet. *Aarb.* 1967, 91-154, København.
– 1967b, Zwei Abfallgruben von Gevninge, Seeland, *Acta Arch.* XXXVII, 187-202.
– 1967 c, Rammen. *Skalk*, Århus, 1967.
– 1971, Et bronzealder anlæg fra Fyrkat. *Aarb.* 1970, 78-93.
KJÆR, H. 1928, Oldtidshuse ved Ginderup i Thy. *NM Arbm.* 1928, 7-20, København.

KRISTIANSEN, K. 1972, Løgstrup, nogle affaldsgruber fra den yngre bronzealder. *MIV* 2, 62-67, Viborg.

lA COUR, V. 1927, *Sjællands ældste Bygder*. København.

LERCHE, G. 1970, Kogegruber i New Guineas Højland. *Kuml* 1969, 195-210, Århus.

LOMBORG, E. 1956, En Højgruppe ved Ballermosen. *Aarb.* 1956, 144-204.

– 1973, En landsby med huse og kultsted fra ældre bronzealder. *NM Arbm.* 1973, 5-14.

– 1976, Vadgård, Ein Dorf mit Häusern und einer Kultstätte aus der älteren nordischen Bronzezeit. *Pittioni Festschrift*, 414-432, Wien.

– 1977, Bronzealderbopladsen på Skamlebæk radiostation. *Antikvariske studier*, 123-130, København.

MATHIASSEN, T. 1948, *Studier over Nordvestsjællands Oldtidsbebyggelse*. Nationalmuseets skrifter, arkæol. hist. række II, København.

– 1959, *Nordvestsjællands Oldtidsbebyggelse*. Nationalmuseets skrifter, arkæol. hist. række VII, København.

MÜLLER, S. 1906, Bopladsfundene fra den romerske Tid. *Aarb.* 1906, 93-224.

– 1912, Vendsysselstudier III. *Aarb.* 1912, 84-142 (113).

– 1919, Bopladsfundene fra Bronzealderen. *Aarb.* 1919, 31-105.

MÜLLER-WILLE, M. 1977, Bäuerliche Siedlungen der Bronze- und Eisenzeit in den Nordseegebieten. H. Jankuhn, R. Schützeichel & F. Schwind ed., *Das Dorf der Eisenzeit und des frühen Mittelalters*, 153-219, Göttingen.

NEUMANN, H. 1975, Udgravningen ved Trappendal. *Sønderjysk månedsskrift* 51, 225-226 cf. *J.D.A.* 2, 1983.

SALOMONSSON, B. 1970, Malmötraktens förhistoria. *Malmö Stadshistoria* I, 15-170.

SCHINDLER, R. 1960, *Die Bodenaltertümer der Freien und Hansestadt Hamburg*. Hamburg.

SEEBERG, P. 1968, Hvolris. *Kuml* 1968, 111-136.

STRUVE, K. W. 1955, Der erste Grundriss eines bronzezeitlichen Hauses von Norddorf auf Amrum. *Offa* 1954, 35-40, Neumünster.

THORVILDSEN, E. 1960, *Bronzealderen*. København.

THRANE, H. 1968, En broncealderhøj ved Vesterlund. *Kuml* 1967, 7-31.

– *1971*, En broncealderboplads ved Jyderup Skov i Odsherred. *NM Arbm.* 1971, 141-164.

– 1973, Bebyggelseshistorie – en arbejdsopgave. *Fortid og Nutid* XXV, 299-321.

– 1974, Hundredvis af energikilder fra broncealderen. *Fynske Minder* 1974, 96-114, Odense.

– 1976 a, Bebyggelsesarkæologi som arbejdsmethode. *Skrifter fra institut for historie og samfundsvidenskab* no. 17, 5-17, Odense.

– 1976b, Nyt fra et dunkelt afsnit af Odsherreds fortid. *Fra Holbæk Amt* 1975, 21-40.

– 1979, On painted daub from the Bronze Age Settlement on Kirkebjerg. Voldtofte. *Skalk*. Cf. Berglund, *J.D.A.* 1, 1983.

– 1981, Continuity of the Rural Prehistoric Settlement on Southwest Funen. V. Hansen (ed.), *Collected Papers of the Permanent European Conference for the Study of Rural Landscapes* 1979, 45-50.

– 1982, Towards a Research Policy for Bronze Age Settlements. *Journal of Danish Archaeology*, Vol. 1.

WINGE, H. 1919, Dyreknogler fra Bronzealderens Bopladser. *Aarb.* 1919, 93-101.

WINTHER, J. 1935, *Troldebjerg*. Rudkøbing.

WORTMANN, A. 1971, Sjælden karform fra Sønderjyllands yngste bronzealder. *Haderslev Museum* 13, 62-66, Haderslev.

Grave Finds from the Roman Iron Age

by LOTTE HEDEAGER

INTRODUCTION[1]

Burial customs during the Roman Iron Age show a diverse pattern of inhumation and cremation graves, primary and secondary burials beneath grave mounds, and graves in level ground – lying either singly or clustered in small or large grave-yards. There is marked local variation in spite of certain regional characteristics. The prospects for discovering or destroying graves have therefore differed between different regions and different grave types, as have the factors which brought burials to light.

Grave mounds can be compared with other mounds for frequency of demolition, while graves in level ground should be compared to hoards, with the difference, however, that cremation graves are an unobtrusive find group, often revealed as a collection of potsherds or slightly blackened soil which does not usually attract the farmer's attention. The antiquarian value of such finds is on the whole realised only by professional archaeologists and those interested in archaeology. The percentage of urn burials lost – compared to e.g. hoard finds –

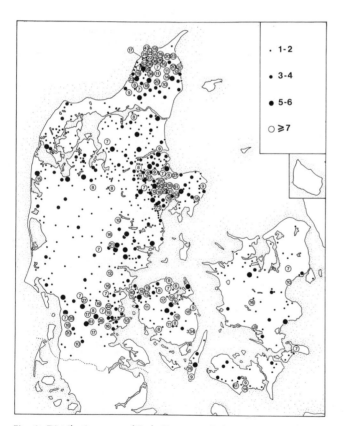

Fig. 1. Distribution map of Early Roman period graves, Denmark.

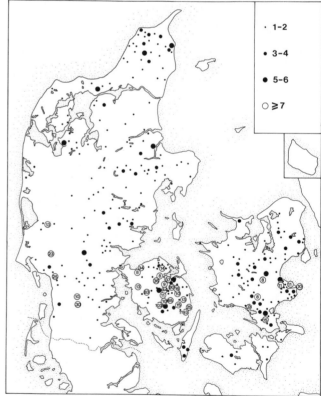

Fig. 2. Distribution map of Late Roman period graves, Denmark.

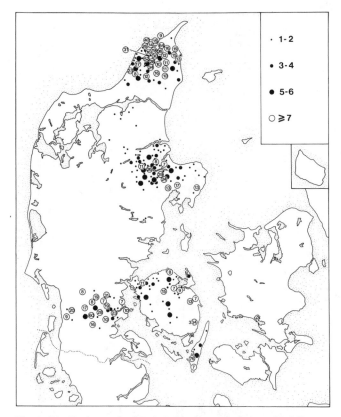

Fig. 3. Distribution map of Early Roman grave finds from the following museums: *Fyns Stiftsmuseum*; Haderslev Museum; *Kulturhistorisk Museum*, Randers; and *Vendsyssel historiske Museum*.

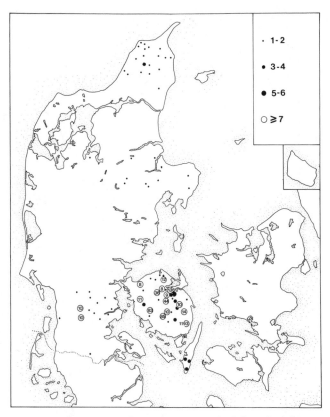

Fig. 4. Distribution map of Late Roman grave finds from the following museums: *Fyns Stiftsmuseum*; Haderslev Museum; *Kulturhistorisk Museum*, Randers; and *Vendsyssel historiske Museum*.

increased further because as secondary burials beneath a mound they were the first to be ploughed over and destroyed. It appears from Thorlacius' account that this occurred thousands of times even around 1808 (Thorlacius 1809, 31). Iron Age cremation burials have thus been much more vulnerable than inhumation graves and primary burials beneath mounds (especially in Jutland), whose discovery is in part related to other economic factors, and the general representativity of cremation graves must therefore be lower.

An analysis of the representativity of graves must attempt to answer the following questions:

1. Does the distribution of graves reflect their original distribution, or have e.g. present-day economic factors and museum influence had a decisive impact on the picture we see today?
2. Will future finds disturb or alter the analytical basis – or is the present number representative?

EASTERN DENMARK
(Zealand, Lolland-Faster)[2]

In Zealand throughout the Roman period graves consisted mainly of dispersed inhumation burials on level ground. There are also occasional cremation graves. 29 burials, particularly of skeletons, were found when mounds were demolished. These are particularly concentrated around Frederiksborg county, but are also found scattered throughout Eastern Denmark, where they comprise 12.5% of the total finds. A detailed analysis is not relevant to this paper.

On Lolland-Falster cremation graves – either single or clustered in fairly large grave-yards – are the dominant burial type in the Early Roman period. Some inhumation graves are known. There are few Late Roman graves in this area, and they include both inhumation and cremation burials.

If we look at the distribution of graves from the Early

154

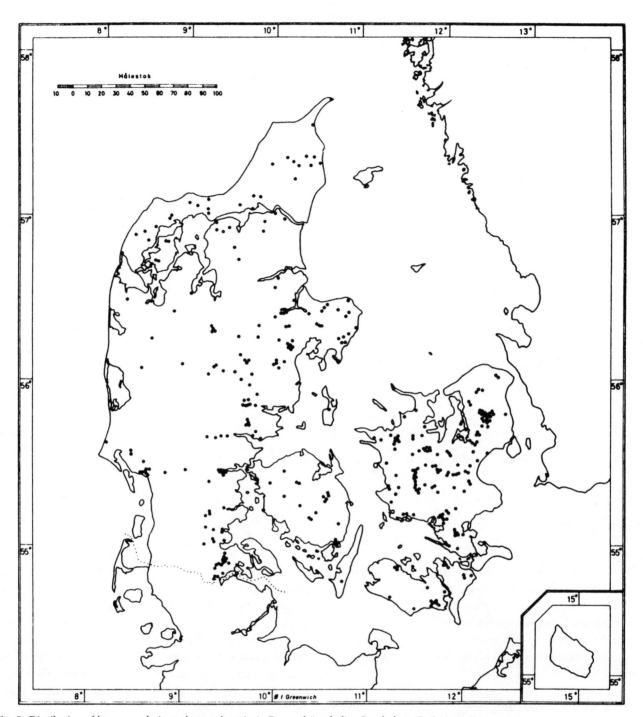

Fig. 5. Distribution of large gravel pits and stone deposits in Denmark (excluding Bornholm). (D.G.U. 1963).

and Late Roman periods respectively, shown in figs. 1 and 2, there is an uneven geographical distribution with some marked concentrations. We shall therefore examine the extent to which these regional differences are due to economic activities.

A considerable part of Roman period burials have been found as a result of gravel digging. The question is whether the concentration of graves in certain areas can be ascribed to more intensive gravel exploitation. Fig. 5 shows gravel deposits in Zealand. There is no apparent correlation between gravel deposits and grave clusters. Fig. 6 gives burial sites from the two periods, which were found in association with gravel. It can be seen that the distribution is random, since it follows neither the regional clustering of graves nor the parts of Zealand most heavily used for gravel digging. We must therefore conclude that although gravel exploitation has played a part in revealing some of the graves, it has not determined their pattern of distribution.

Some of the rich inhumation graves from the Roman period have been found at depths over 1.5 m. It might be supposed that the distribution of this group in particular would be connected to gravel digging, which reaches such depths. The histograms in fig. 7 show the find depth of inhumation burials in gravel and other soil types. If we compare 7a and 7b it appears that in both cases the graphs have two peaks and are fairly similar. The deepest graves are equally well-represented (13 over 1.5 m in both 7a and 7b). This registration shows that the possible discovery of the deepest graves is not solely connected to gravel digging, but also to other economic aspects. Among these marl digging can be singled out as a frequent factor in discovery, though other kinds of earth removal, such as drainage, may also produce deep finds.

This leads on to the more general factors which may have affected the representativity of distribution maps. First agriculture: has the pattern of agricultural exploitation been uniform in Zealand, or have certain kinds of land improvement been more pronounced in one region than another? In ecological terms Eastern Denmark must be regarded as a uniform region, with the same needs and the same possibilities for land improvement. Both marling and drainage have been general practice everywhere, but during the last century there was also an expansion of local construction work in the form of roads, farm-houses, railways etc., using local gravel deposits.

Fig. 6. Burial sites in gravel.

On the whole, therefore, this factor is geographically uniform and does not affect the distribution of groups of finds originating from gravel digging.

A third factor which may have affected the geographical representativity of registered grave material is the existence of museums. However, all finds from Zealand and Lolland-Falster are registered in the National

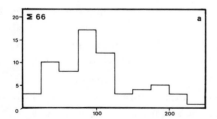

Fig. 7a. Find depth of inhumation graves (not in gravel). Eastern Denmark.

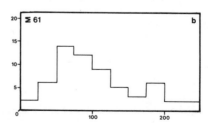

Fig. 7b. Find depth of inhumation graves (in gravel). Eastern Denmark.

156

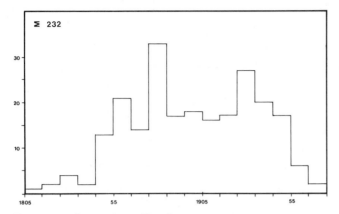

Fig. 8. Year of registration of burial sites. Eastern Denmark.

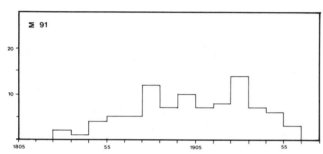

Fig. 9. Year of registration of burial sites found in gravel. Eastern Denmark.

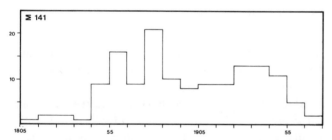

Fig. 10. Year of registration of burial sites not found in gravel. Eastern Denmark.

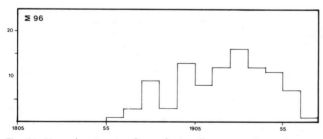

Fig. 11. Year of registration for professionally excavated sites. Eastern Denmark.

Museum in Copenhagen, which functions as Denmark's principal museum. Furthermore, no local museums contain noteworthy finds from Roman period graves. The material in Copenhagen can therefore be regarded as representative.

From the analysis of the geographical distribution of graves we may provisionally conclude that the pattern does not seem to be influenced by special economic factors or by museum activities.

The second question: will future finds disturb or alter to any significant extent the numerical basis of this paper? – can best be answered by a registration of find frequency since 1805 (fig. 8). The course of the graph for graves found in gravel and graves found elsewhere is largely the same, and can therefore be treated together initially (figs. 9 and 10). The following observations can be made: firstly, there is a sudden rise in the number of registered finds from around 1845. Secondly, the distribution has two peaks (the 1870's and 1880's, and from the middle of the 1920's till the middle of the 1940's). Thirdly, registrations fall sharply after 1955 and practically cease after 1965.

The question now arises: to what extent does this graph show the discovery, exploitation, and exhaustion of an archaeological find group? To decide this, the factors determining the discovery and registration of the finds must be analysed for the same period, to show whether they have been constant throughout, or whether they have fluctuated along with the curve of the graph.

The steeply rising number of finds from the 1850's onwards may be due to several causes. An important factor is the agrarian reforms. They made it possible to bring new areas into cultivation. From the 1840's there was more intensive exploitation of agricultural land, and land improvement in the form of marling and drainage gathered momentum from the 1850's , when both private and public construction work also increased. The two histograms (figs. 9 and 10) seem to reflect this tendency, since graves from gravel deposits reached their peak slightly later (around the 1880's) than graves found in other contexts (beginning in the 1850's, they also culminated in the 1880's). The latter frequency diagram reflects rather the more intensive exploitation and extension of agricultural areas in former times.

These economic factors alone are hardly sufficient to account for the sudden increase in Roman period graves in the National Museum collections. The scientific developments in archaeology and the growth of museums

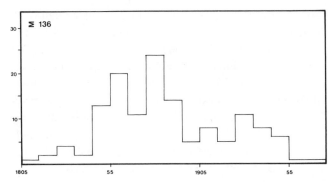

Fig. 12. Year of registration for amateur excavations. Eastern Denmark.

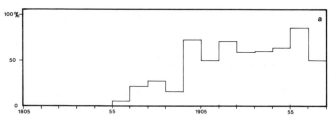

Fig. 13a. Professionally excavated sites as percentage of total sites (per decade). Eastern Denmark.

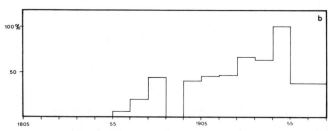

Fig. 13b. Professionally excavated sites as percentage of total sites (per decade). Funen, Langeland.

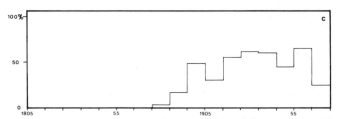

Fig. 13c. Professionally excavated sites as percentage of total sites (per decade). Jutland.

and popular archaeological interest also played a part. The commencement of real archaeological investigation and the first local field visits only began at the end of the nineteenth century (fig. 11). These museum activities can therefore hardly be the original reason for the increased frequency of finds, but became more important from the middle of the 1890's, when accessions from professional archaeological investigations began to outweigh those from amateurs (figs. 11, 12, 13). Until the end of the 19th century the National Museum and the other museums must be regarded as a passive factor. They registered and preserved finds, the discovery of which was primarily the result of Denmark's socio-economic development. It is hardly accidental that museum activities began in earnest at a time when both economic developments and find frequencies reached their peak. It is also apparent that the apex of the 1920's and 1930's cannot be explained only by the increased work of the National Museum, but must be due to other causes as well (fig. 8). One factor may be the many public works started for the unemployed in the economic depression of the 1920's and 1930's.

As already mentioned the curve falls abruptly after 1955, and there is an insignificant registration of new finds after 1965. The emphasis on mechanization in agriculture as well as building is doubtless an important reason for this – and one that will not change in the future. However if we take into consideration the development of museums and the popular appeal of archaeology, the decline in finds seems too radical to be accounted for by mechanization alone. Such effective inroads have probably been made into Roman period graves since 1805 that only a small number remains today.

FUNEN (including Langeland)[3]

In contrast to the Zealand graves those from Funen are often clustered into large grave-yards. Thus the 184 cemetaries discussed here do not indicate to the same extent as those in Zealand anything like the actual number of graves. The distribution map of graves shows Funen's numerical superiority (a total of 1225 graves + c. 1525 at Møllegårdsmarken).

Furthermore, cremation graves are the dominant form in contrast to the Roman period graves in Zealand; but the find situations do not seem to differ between the two regions, which are also ecologically similar.

Graves in level ground predominate, and they are often found in connection with gravel digging (fig. 14). In comparison with Zealand (fig. 9), there are only half as many (graves found in Funen as a result of gravel digging

158

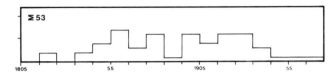

Fig. 14. Year of registration for burial sites in gravel. Funen, Langeland.

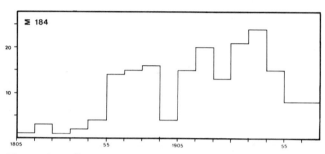

Fig. 15. Year of registration for burial sites. Funen, Langeland.

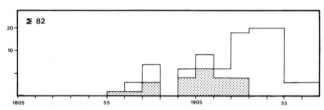

Fig. 16. Year of registration for professionally excavated sites (National Museum excavations hatched). Funen, Langeland.

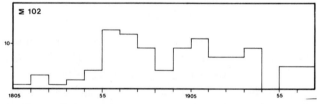

Fig. 17. Year of registration for amateur excavations. Funen, Langeland.

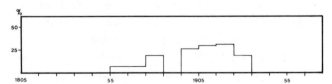

Fig. 18. National Museum excavations as percentage of total sites. Funen, Langeland.

constitute c. 29% as compared to 39% in Zealand). A comparison of the two histograms shows a high degree of overlapping with a few exception.

In 1855-64 finds from Funen increased more than those from Zealand, with a subsequent steeper fall from 1865-74. The two peaks which appear in the histogram for Eastern Denmark (1875-84 and 1925-34) are not, however, reflected in the Funen material. In the preceding pages we attempted to explain the two peaks in terms of increased public and private construction work, including the major unemployment work schemes in the 1920's and 1930's. Since large gravel deposits are much more common in Zealand than in Funen, sites found in gravel in Zealand will to a greater extent reflect the increased exploitation.

Other socio-economic and museum-related factors have influenced the find diagram of Funen, shown clearly in fig. 15 (1855-85), as have the increased activities of the 1920's and 1930's. From 1955 there is a sharp fall in the registration of new sites. As already mentioned with regard to Zealand, this is partly due to an increase in mechanization and partly, we may assume, to the near depletion of the archaeological find group.

Before we draw any final conclusion we shall have to consider the impact of museum-related factors.

The frequency diagram for professionally excavated sites is shown in fig. 16, together with the remaining sites (fig. 17). In contrast to the sites of Eastern Denmark (fig. 11), a greater proportion of the material has been examined by professionals (Funen 45%, Eastern Denmark 41%), and in 1925 the number of professionally excavated sites rose to double the number of sites excavated by non-professionals. In Zealand this did not happen until after 1955. Generally speaking the Roman period graves from Funen are thus at least as well documented as those from Zealand. Funen's first museum, the *Fyns Stiftsmuseum*, was established in Odense in 1860, and *Langeland's Museum* was founded in 1900. A large number of competent archaeologists (most of them 'amateurs') have over the years been associated with Funen and Langeland. Among them we may mention: from the middle of the 19th century the land-owner N. F. B. Sehested; from the end of the century the merchant J. Winther, Langeland, and the apothecary K. Mikkelsen; from the 1920's the apothecary P. Helweg Mikkelsen; and from 1941 the Museum Curator E. Albrectsen.

National Museum staff have also over the years sur-

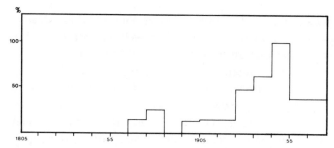

Fig. 19. Funen museums excavations as percentage of total sites. Funen, Langeland.

veyed and excavated in Funen. The professionally excavated sites thus reflect the work of several institutions. Fig. 16 isolates sites investigated by the National Museum. From 1895 to 1925 the activity of the National Museum was greater than that of Funen museums, but around 1925-35 a change occurred: National Museum excavations retained their *status quo* (though the proportion of total find material was smaller), while the activity of Funen museums increased considerably, and became predominant after 1935. This situation can be seen even more clearly in figs. 18 and 19 (cf. fig. 13 b). A comparison with the corresponding diagram for Eastern Denmark (fig. 12, cf. fig. 13 a) reveals the following:

From 1895 to 1925 the sites excavated by the National Museum contributed approximately the same percentage of total find material (c. 30%), with a subsequent fall in 1925-34 (to 19%), after which time the National Museum excavations ceased entirely.

The corresponding curve for museums in Funen shows a rise in 1925-34 (from 15% to 48%), which is especially due to the efforts of P. Helweg Mikkelsen. The appointment of Erling Albrectsen as Curator of the *Fyns Stiftsmuseum* in 1941 is also reflected in fig. 19 (Between 1945-54 all Roman period graves had been professionally excavated). On the other hand the percentage of professionally investigated sites fell after 1955. This is likely to be related to the excavations at Møllegårdsmarken, where c. 2000 graves were uncovered in the period 1959-66 (Albrectsen 1971). It is natural that such extensive excavations should monopolize time as well as money and man-power at the expense of the *Fyns Stiftsmuseum*. However, this does not explain the fall in find material that began between 1945-54 and became especially pronounced after 1955 (fig. 15).

Few other areas in Denmark have been as thoroughly investigated for Roman period graves as Funen during

the last 80 years, and much of this can be credited to Albrectsen's special interest and great efforts. This probably explains why the find material has not, after all, decreased as markedly as in Zealand (fig. 8) (the 1955-74 graves in Zealand comprise 3% of the total find material; in Funen 9%). The reason find material nevertheless decreased to an all-time low during the last twenty years can only be because, as in Zealand and Lolland-Falster, most of the Roman period graves have already been found.

We thus arrive at the second question: the geographical representativity of graves. Figs. 1 and 2 show the distribution of graves from the Early and Late Roman periods, respectively. A certain regional variation is known to occur: in the Early Roman period graves are found dispersed, though with a certain concentration to the north-west and in Southern Langeland. In the Late Roman period, however, there is an increase in the num-

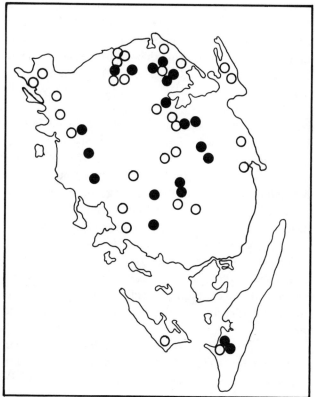

○ ER
● LR

Fig. 20. Sites found in gravel. Funen, Langeland.

ber of graves with a concentration around the middle of Funen, away from the coast.

Funen (and Langeland) can be regarded as an ecological unit, like Eastern Denmark. This means that the pattern of land exploitation (e.g. the use of marl and drainage) is also geographically uniform. Various kinds of local construction work have, as mentioned above (cf. fig. 12), determined the exploitation of gravel deposits. We shall now examine to what extent this pattern of exploitation has affected the geographical and numerical representativity of graves.

Fig. 20 shows grave sites from the Early and Late Roman periods found as a result of gravel digging. In spite of the limited number of sites there is a certain overlap (the distribution also agrees with fig. 5). In comparison with the overall distribution of graves (figs. 1 and 2) there seems to be a random distribution of graves found in gravel. Clusters of graves and cemetaries (cf. also Albrectsen's Map 1, 1956 and 1968) have no counterparts among the sites found in gravel.

We can thus conclude that socio-economic factors have hardly influenced the present distribution pattern of graves. As mentioned above, these factors have been geographically uniform. Since the grave types – and thus the possibility of registering them – are the same in both the Early and Late Roman periods, changes in the distribution of graves must be seen as historically conditioned.

Finally, let us consider the geographical factors in relation to museums. The Early Roman period in Funen is represented by 771 graves. Of these, 476 (62%) are found at *Fyns Stiftsmuseum* in Odense. Their number and distribution is shown in the map (fig. 3). If this map is compared to the overall distribution map of graves (fig. 1), we notice that the material from the *Fyns Stiftsmuseum* and the National Museum shows the same distribution in Odense county. In Svendborg county there is a slight tendency for the *Fyns Stiftsmuseum* to be under-represented, with the exception of Møllegårdsmarken (Gudme parish and district), all the material from which is in Odense.

There are 1982 grave finds from the Late Roman period, of which 1693 (85%) are in the *Fyns Stiftsmuseum*. If we compare the two distribution maps (figs. 2 and 4), it appears that Odense county is again evenly represented between the two museums. The only exception is the parish of Seden in the Åsum district near Odense. A concentration of grave finds from this place is in the

Odense museum. With the exception of Møllegårdsmarken, Svendborg county is less well-represented in the total find picture than the National Museum.

The general tendency is thus for grave finds from both the National Museum and the Funen museum to be geographically representative in Odense county. In Svendborg county (Langeland excepted) the National Museum grave finds provide a more varied distribution pattern. Here, apparently, the *Fyns Stiftsmuseum* has not been very active.

JUTLAND[4]

In Jutland grave types are more heterogeneous than on the islands, and their find situations also differ somewhat. Most characteristic in Jutland are the many grave mounds (secondary burials in older mounds are the most common type), which are not generally found on the islands. On the other hand graves found in gravel are more unusual. From a total of 849 registered finds (in the National Museum), 299 (c. 35%) were found when mounds were destroyed, only 74 (9%) were found as a result of gravel digging. The latter are above all concentrated in the counties of Randers (15), Vejle (10), and Ribe (11) (cf. fig. 5), but make up such a small proportion of the total finds that they are not dealt with in this analysis.

More important in representativity analysis are the graves found in mounds (fig. 21). It appears that the destruction of mounds (or at any rate the registered finds from them) rose to a peak in 1895-1904, falling evenly to either side. The period 1845-54 was a minor exception in that there seems to have been an increase in finds from mounds, especially from the northern counties of Hjør-

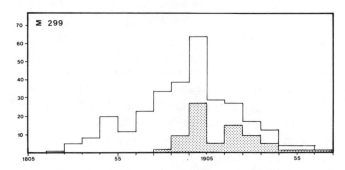

Fig. 21. Year of registration for National Museum graves in mounds (professionally excavated mounds hatched). Jutland.

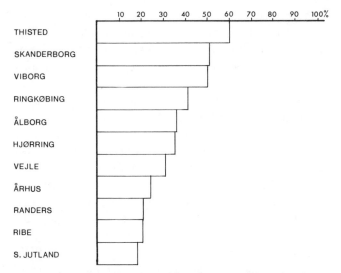

Fig. 22. National Museum mound burials as percentage of total sites (according to county). Jutland.

ring (5) and Ålborg (6) (cf. Appendix). The first professional excavations of burial mounds did not occur until 1875-84, and have therefore not affected the pattern of finds (cf. fig. 21). The destruction of mounds increased during the 19th century along with the extension and heavier exploitation of agricultural land. Various kinds of construction work have also affected the find curve. The stones from dolmens were excellent filling material in the construction of roads and railways, and the earth from mounds was used to improve agricultural land. By the time of the Preservation Law of 1937, most of the mounds had already been demolished, and the tendency for demolitions to decline, as seen in the histogram, shows no pronounced drop after this time.

Graves in burial mounds are not spread evenly over Jutland, but fluctuate between 60% and 18% of total sites calculated by county. In fig. 22, sites in Jutland are arranged in order of precedence according to county. Thisted has the highest percentage of burial mound graves (60%), followed by Skanderborg and Viborg with 50%. In terms of absolute numbers Skanderborg, Hjørring, Viborg and Ålborg have the most (c. 40), while Thisted has only 30 mound finds. Southern Jutland has the lowest representation (18%), and with Århus is the county where mounds are most scarce (8 and 11, respectively) (cf. also Appendix).

Mound burials are far from being the only grave type in Jutland. Inhumation and cremation graves in level ground are more common. As with Funen material, all

types are represented: single graves; a few graves together; and large cemeteries with several hundred graves. But they share a lack of visible traces on the ground surface, so that in the following their find situations can be discussed as a whole and compared directly to those in the islands.

Fig. 23 shows year of registration of these sites (which are combined with burial mound sites in fig. 24). The number did not increase significantly until 1865. The next major increase took place in 1895 to a level which remained unchanged for the next 40 years. From 1935 the curve drops steadily until 1965, when from 1965-74 there was an absolute minimum of three finds. The graph is thus quite different from that for the islands, although the same economic factors as discussed above operated in Jutland.

The intensification of agriculture, which involved the digging of marl and drainage, and the cultivation of new areas, began and ended later in Jutland than in the islands. Around - or a little before - the middle of the 19th century, the number of registered finds from the islands gradually began to increase (cf. figs. 8 and 15), while in Jutland this did not happen until a few decades later. This delay alone does not explain the high level of finds between 1895 and 1934. A comparison with mound burials (fig. 21) shows a rise in finds throughout the 19th century, corresponding to that in level-ground finds, until 1905. The registration of new finds fell everywhere in Denmark from the end of the 1930's.

Up to this point, we may assume that agricultural and economic factors have had a significant influence on the find frequency of graves in Jutland, as they did in the islands. Certain differences in the course of the frequency

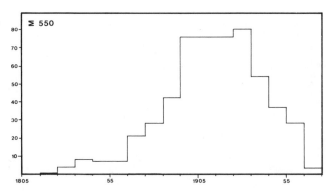

Fig. 23. Year of registration for National Museum graves in level ground. Jutland.

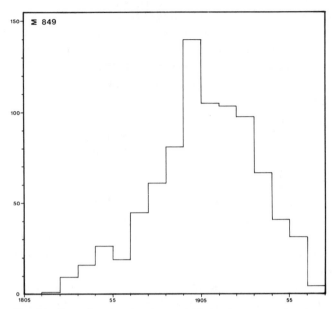

Fig. 24. Year of registration for total National Museum sites from Jutland.

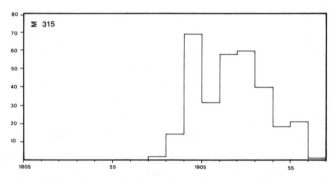

Fig. 25. Year of registration for professionally excavated sites in Jutland (in the National Museum).

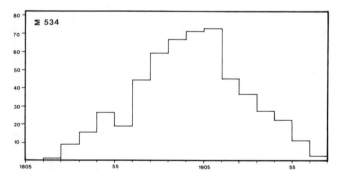

Fig. 26. Year of registration for amateur excavations in Jutland (in the National Museum).

diagrams should however be examined more closely: what causes the marked rise from 1895 with a subsequent period of stability lasting 40 years (fig. 23)? And why does the amount of find material fall so heavily after 1965?

The National Museum collection of Roman period graves from Jutland numbers 1847, of which 849 are represented in the sites discussed here; 316 of these were professionally excavated. The frequency graph for these sites is shown in fig. 25, together with the remaining sites (fig. 26). Even more than on the islands there was a very sudden rise in the number of professionally excavated sites from 1895, and from 1915 these outweighed the number of sites excavated by amateurs. However, they both followed the same falling curve. In the decade 1965-74 the National Museum excavated only one of a total of four sites in Jutland.

As fig. 26 shows, the number of non-professionally excavated sites rose by only four between 1885-94 and 1895-1904, while those professionally excavated rose by 55 (fig. 25). This sudden growth coincided with the beginning of local field visits in Jutland from the National Museum staff (and with the Single-Grave Project).

These doubtless contributed to the increase in finds by professionals around the turn of the century and some decades afterwards. However, this factor alone does not account for the course of the graph showing professional excavations. Other factors must have contributed.

In the period up to the middle of the 1930's, the National Museum was by and large the only institution in Denmark to carry out excavations. Not all parts of the country received the same attention from archaeologists in Copenhagen. Fig. 27, which classifies all counties according to their percentage of professional excavations, shows that Århus and Randers are the best studied Jutland counties, with 62% and 42%, respectively. In both counties the graves are concentrated into large level-ground cemetaries (the so-called urn burials, inhumation and cremation graves), which were excavated in the period 1895-1932 by the Museum Curator Neergaard in co-operation with two local amateur archaeologists, the school teacher Andersen in Djursland (Randers county), and Christen Christensen from the Lisbjerg district (Århus county).

The decrease in the number of professional excavations in the years 1905-14 may be a distortion arising from the methods of counting, by which a site was registered only once and only according to the year in which

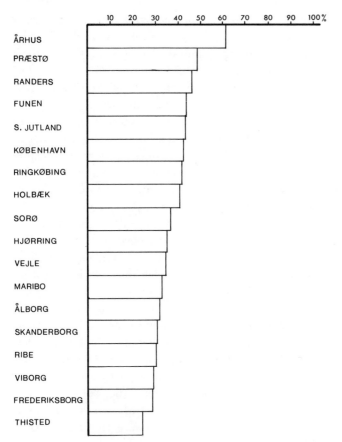

Fig. 27. Professional excavations (National Museum) as percentage of total sites, according to county. Jutland.

excavations were begun. In several cases however Neergaard's excavations extended over a number of years, e.g. Virring 1900-1909 and Bulbjerg 1900-1906. Other large sites were excavated at the same time, and this naturally means that they do not show up as clearly on the frequency graphs as many small sites would have done.

In spite of the falling number of professional excavations up to the present day, their proportional contribution calculated per decade (fig. 13 c) remains fairly constant from 1895 till 1964 (50%-60%, with 1905-14 as an exception). In comparison with the corresponding graphs for Funen and Eastern Denmark (fig. 13 a & b). Jutland differs partly in the relative constancy of its percentage compared to the rise in the islands, partly in the markedly greater decline during the last decade, 1965-74.

The preceding analysis of the Roman period material in Jutland is intended as a preliminary to answering the two main questions: 1) Are we dealing with an

archaeological find group that is nearly exhausted? and 2) Are the graves geographically representative?

Of fundamental importance in answering both questions is an examination of the material in terms of its museum representativity. In the preceding pages we have come across a frequency diagram that seems to suggest that future finds of Roman period graves will be few in number. But does the course of the registration graph simply reflect a decrease in the activities in Jutland of the National Museum? If this is so, we might expect the frequency graph for provincial museums to follow the reverse course.

And with regard to geographical representativity: are our distribution maps more an expression of the activities of the National Museum than a true prehistoric differentation, on the assumption that economic factors have not altered the picture to any marked degree?

Most museums in Jutland include Roman period grave finds in their collections. A complete registration of all this material has not been feasible at this point. The analysis is therefore focused on the three provincial museums with the largest collections from Roman period graves: Haderslev, Randers and Hjørring. We shall discuss them one by one.

Haderslev Museum[5]

Haderslev Museum was founded in 1887. Until recent years the museum's activities were geographically limited to Haderslev county. The museum houses finds from c. 350 Roman period graves, representing 99 sites, whose year of registration is shown in fig. 28. It can be seen that the decade 1885-94 differs from the otherwise very low rate of registration until 1925. This can be related to the period around the founding of the museum, when several large (German) private collections were

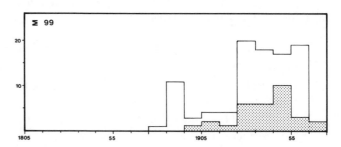

Fig. 28. Year of registration of burial sites from Southern Jutland, Haderslev Museum (hatched: professionally excavated).

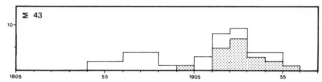

Fig. 29. Year of registration of burial sites from Southern Jutland, the National Museum (hatched: professionally excavated).

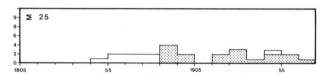

Fig. 30. Year of registration of burial mounds from Southern Jutland, National Museum and Haderslev Museum (hatched).

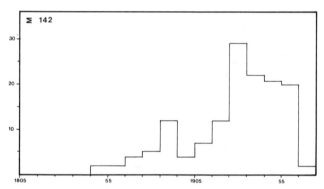

Fig. 31. Year of registration of burial sites from Southern Jutland, National Museum and Haderslev Museum.

acquired. Until 1925 the accession of new finds was minimal. During the 1920's and early 1930's find material increased five-fold, and retained this level almost unaltered until the middle of the 1960's. In the period 1965-74 there were almost no new finds entering Haderslev Museum. To evaluate the frequency graph we must examine the following questions:

1. What is the pattern of National Museum finds in the same area?
2. How do Haderslev Museum's activities compare to those of the National Museum?
3. What factors, economic or otherwise, have led to the discovery of the graves?

1. First the frequency graph of the National Museum finds. Fig. 29 shows the find frequency for graves from Southern Jutland (i.e. graves from Haderslev, Tønder and Sønderborg counties). The total of 43 sites show two small peaks, 1865-84 and 1915-34, and thus largely follow the find frequency of the islands. This histogram bears only a little similarity to fig. 28. In both of them there is a maximum in 1925-34 and an almost total absence of new finds after 1965. It can also be seen that the number of finds in 1935-64 declines in contrast to the number of finds in Haderslev Museum. Only a few finds went to Copenhagen, and after 1955 almost none.

2. From 1864 to 1920 Southern Jutland, and therefore also Haderslev Museum, belonged to Germany. Not until 1920 did the National Museum begin its field work (fig. 29, hatched), which included local district visits from 1920-29. If the re-union of North Schleswig with Denmark in 1920 had been equally important for Haderslev Museum, we should expect an increase in the find frequency at this time, but this did not happen until a decade later (1925-34). The sudden rise in the number of finds and in professional excavations carried out by Haderslev Museum (fig. 28, hatched) is related rather to the fact that a Museum Curator was appointed at Haderslev at an early date (1936). Moreover, the museum possessed a car.[6]

Figure 29 also shows how few finds excavated by amateurs entered the National Museum after 1915. From the middle of the 1930's professional excavations decreased as Haderslev Museum's own activities increased, and they ceased completely after 1965. However, the Haderslev Museum's excavations were also reduced after 1955, although the number of finds remained the same until 1965.

3. The third factor to be examined concerns the find situations. Graves in Southern Jutland include both inhumation and cremation graves (predominantly the latter), in burial mounds as well as large and small flat-field cemetaries. 17 graves from Haderslev Museum came from burial mounds (fig. 30), i.e. 17 % of all sites, which is very close to the National Museum material (fig. 22: 18 %). Thirteen sites were found as a result of gravel digging. These comprise 13 % of the total, a little more than the average for Jutland (9 %). Otherwise the find situations do not differ from those we have analysed in Jutland as a whole. In this respect the National Museum material is apparently representative.

It is otherwise with the graphs showing find frequencies (figs. 28 and 29). The finds in the National Museum reach a peak in 1915-34 (in actual fact from 1920). Not until 1925-34 does the find frequency for Haderslev Museum reach a stable level, at which it remains for 40 years, until 1964. After this the find frequency for Haderslev Museum falls to an unprecedentedly low level. The total frequency diagram for Haderslev county (fig. 31) shows the actual find frequency of the area, heavily dominated by the finds made by Haderslev Museum. The period of maximum finds in 1925-34 and the very marked decline in new sites after 1964 show up even more clearly.

The surprising decrease in finds in recent years is probably not due to a lower level of museum activity (cf. note 6) (in the years 1955-64 there were very few professional excavations, without the number of finds being affected). It is more likely to be caused by an actual decline in the number of new Roman period graves.

The second question to be examined concerns the geographical representativity of the graves. Are grave finds from the National Museum geographically representative, i.e. does their distribution correspond to that of graves from the Haderslev Museum?

The 135 grave finds in the National Museum are geographically distributed over Southern Jutland. Of the approximately 110 graves from the Early Roman period, most are along the west coast of Jutland, in Tønder county. Only a few scattered graves are known from Haderslev county, with the exception of one large cemetary. Of the 25 graves from the Late Roman period 20 are concentrated in a single cemetary in Haderslev county. If the Haderslev Museum graves are transferred to the distribution maps, the picture changes (figs. 1 and 2 compared with figs. 3 and 4). The relatively "empty" county of Haderslev now fills up. The pronounced difference in the distribution of Early and Late Roman sites thus becomes even clearer in the map, and is now in agreement with the general picture for Jutland.

The activities of the National Museum have apparently been concentrated *outside* the county of Haderslev. In the few instances where the National Museum collections contain finds from Haderslev county, they originate from the Museum's own large-scale excavations (Neergaard and Broholm, among others, excavated there). We must conclude that the National Museum material is *not* geographically representative, but rather reflects the activities of the National Museum in Southern Jutland.

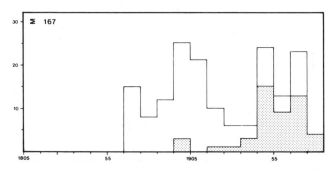

Fig. 32. Year of registration of burial sites from Randers county, Randers Museum (professional excavations hatched).

"Kulturhistorisk Museum", Randers[7]

The Randers Museum was established in 1872. Today it contains finds from approx. 315 Roman period graves representing 167 sites (fig. 32).

The find frequency graph has two peaks: the period 1895-1914 and the two decades 1945-54 and 1965-74. The decade of the founding of the museum (1865-74) is represented by a higher find frequency than in subsequent decades (till 1895). From 1915-44 the find frequency is very low. The same is true of the period after 1974.[8]

To assess the significance of this graph, we must examine the same questions as for Haderslev:

1. What is the frequency curve of the National Museum for Randers county?
2. How do the activities of the Randers Museum compare to those of the National Museum?
3. What factors, economic or otherwise, have led to the discovery of graves?

1. The frequency curve of the National Museum for Randers county is shown in fig. 33. The total of 132 sites show a marked rise from 1885 (local field trips took place in 1874-94); during 1895-1904 the frequency rate reached its maximum, followed by an abrupt decline in 1905-14. With the exception of the following decade (1915-24), the number of finds remained fairly constant until 1954. The decade 1955-64 is represented by only three finds. After this the accession ceased of new finds from Randers county into the National Museum.

If we compare this with the frequency graph for Randers Museum (fig. 32), we notice some important differences. The most striking is the heavy representation of the period 1915-24 in the National Museum graph, and the many finds from Randers Museum in

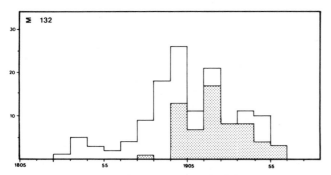

Fig. 33. Year of registration of burial sites from Randers county, the National Museum (professional excavations hatched).

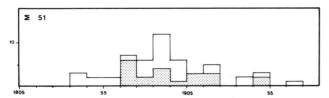

Fig. 34. Year of registration of burial mounds from Randers county, the National Museum and Randers Museum (Randers Museum hatched).

1945-74. Both curves reach a maximum in 1895-1904 with a subsequent fall in find material, which occurred for the National Museum as early as 1955 and for Randers probably from 1975.[9] However, the graph for National Museum sites in the county of Randers and the total frequency graph for Jutland (fig. 24) largely follow the same course.

2. The activities of Randers Museum compared to those of the National Museum are further illustrated by the figures showing professionally excavated sites from the two museums (figs. 32 and 33, hatched). The *National Museum* excavations were most important during the period 1895 to 1944, particularly in the two decades 1895-1904 and 1915-24. From 1895 to 1932 Neergaard, in particular, excavated a very large number of Roman period sites in Randers county, together with the school master Andersen from Djursland and others. The sites included e.g. Virring in 1900-1909, Langkastrup in 1903-05 and Hvilsager in 1912-13 and in 1919.[10]

Professional excavations show another pattern with regard to *Randers Museum*. As already mentioned, from the middle of the 1920's local museums were permitted to conduct independent excavations. However, this

situation is not reflected in the frequency graph for Randers Museum (fig. 32). A group of competent amateur archaeologists (including some of the Museum management committee) affected very clearly the frequency graph (especially through the many surveys and supplementary excavations). In 1962 the first professional archaeologist was appointed to Randers Museum, and the many professional excavations continued (in the period 1965-74 these contributed 57% of the find accessions). From 1975 the museum itself has been wholly responsible for the discovery of the – by now fairly few – Roman period graves.

3. The third question concerns find situations. The graves in Randers county are primarily inhumation burials. The county of Randers is divided into two "culture zones" ["kulturprovinser"] (Lysdahl 1971): one north of the Gudenå river with massive stone cists (like those of Vendsyssel and Himmerland), and one to the south with urn burials often collected into large grave-yards (very common in Århus county).

Ordinary inhumation and cremation graves are known from the whole county, sometimes as secondary burials in ancient mounds. 13%, i.e. 22 graves, were found in connection with mound demolition (fig. 34). This is less than the National Museum material from Randers county (29 sites or 22%, cf. fig. 22).

Fourteen sites were found as a result of gravel digging. These comprise 8% of the sites from Randers Museum, and correspond to the average percentage for Jutland (9%). Finds resulting from mound demolition and gravel digging thus contribute a total of 21% of the material. Most of the remaining sites were found during agricultural work, especially ploughing.

The find situations of material from Randers county in the National Museum are fairly similar. In this respect the National Museum material would seem to be representative. It is otherwise with the frequency graphs (figs. 32 and 33). Whereas the National Museum finds diminish from 1924 onwards, those from the Randers Museum increase after the Second World War.

The aggregate frequency graph for Randers county (fig. 35) shows the actual find frequency of the area, with an evenly rising curve from 1865 till 1894 (the period of local field visits); a great increase between 1895 and 1904 followed by a decline till 1944. In the period 1945-54 the number of finds rose markedly and then began to fall again, most clearly from 1975.

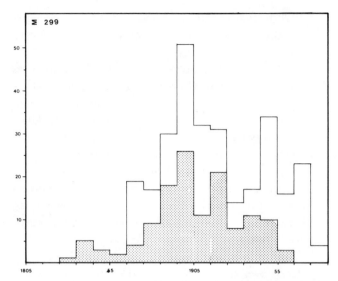

Fig. 35. Year of registration of burial sites from Randers county, the National Museum and Randers Museum (National Museum hatched).

An active National Museum, an active local museum, and in addition a circle of enthusiastic local amateur archaeologists have no doubt had a great influence on the course of the frequency graph. The marked decline in finds during the last few years can hardly be attributed to excavation priorities, but is more likely to reflect a real reduction of new Roman period finds. In contrast to Haderslev, for example (fig. 31), the decline occurred about ten years later.

The geographical representativity. The total number of graves from the county of Randers is 677 (644 from the Early Roman period, 33 from the Late Roman). Their distribution covers nearly all parishes in Randers county, although with considerable variation in numbers.

The areas richest in finds are the Sønderhald district, including the parishes of Virring, Lime, Hørning, Hvilsager and Marie Magdalene; and the Øster-Lisbjerg district including the parishes of Thorsager and Hornslet. Does this distribution pattern reflect a higher level of museum activity within Randers county, rather than a true geographical differentiation?

As mentioned before, the National Museum carried out many excavations in the Sønderhald district in the beginning of this century, where Neergaard and Andersen excavated a large number of sites.

However, these sites alone do not make up the whole concentration of finds. The grave finds from Randers Museum are distributed over the same areas, although

they were discovered and excavated often long after the National Museum graves (figs. 1 and 2 compared with figs. 3 and 4).

The only area which shows a distinct difference between the two museums is the Støvring district, where Randers Museum acquired most of the finds. There is little doubt that this is due to its geographical proximity to Randers town: for one thing there is more construction work near a large town (Randers parish has the highest number of finds), and for another the distance to the Randers Museum is smaller – and the contact presumably closer.

We can thus conclude that regional variations in the pattern of distribution for the county of Randers only reflect to a very limited extent factors associated with museums. In most cases we must assume that the distribution pattern expresses the true geographical distribution. The National Museum finds can thus be considered representative of the total pattern of finds in the district.

The "Vendsyssel historiske Museum", Hjørring.[11]

Hjørring Museum was founded in 1889. It houses today an outstanding collection of finds from 715 Roman

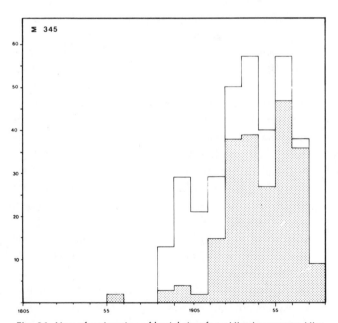

Fig. 36. Year of registration of burial sites from Hjørring county, Hjørring Museum (professional excavations hatched).

168

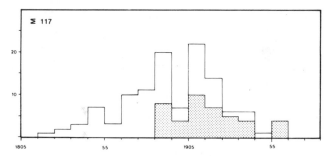

Fig. 37. Year of registration of burial sites from Hjørring county, the National Museum (professional excavations hatched).

period graves, representing 345 sites.

The frequency graph (fig. 36) shows the first increase to be in the years 1895-1904. The majority of finds were made from 1925-44 and from 1955-64. From 1965 the frequency falls.[12]

To assess the graph we must examine the same three question as in the previous analyses:

1. What is the frequency curve of the National Museum for Hjørring county?
2. How do the activities of the Hjørring Museum compare with those of the National Museum?
3. What factors, economic or otherwise, led to the discovery of graves?

1. The find frequency graph for National Museum graves from the Roman period in the county of Hjørring includes 117 sites found over the years 1815 to 1964 (fig. 37). The find frequency rises evenly up to 1884 (with an isolated exception in 1855-64). The years 1885-94 and 1905-14 are the two periods with maximum finds. From 1915 the number of newly found sites diminishes, and nearly ceases after 1964.

If we compare this frequency graph with that for Hjørring Museum (fig. 36), we notice important differences. The fact that finds began 70 years earlier at the National Museum than at Hjørring is obviously because of the later date of founding of the Hjørring Museum (which among other accessions also received a few finds from an earlier private collection in 1855-64). There is a striking inverse correlation in increase and decline between the two museums: whereas the National Museum experienced a fall in find material (1895-1904 and 1915-64), the Hjørring Museum had an equivalent – or greater – increase in new finds; and whereas the turning-point for the National Museum was at the end of the 19th century and the beginning of

the 20th, that for Hjørring was from the mid-twenties and after. Both frequency graphs however share a decrease in finds during the last 10-15 years.[13]

The frequency graph for National Museum sites from the county of Hjørring (fig. 37) largely follows that for finds from Jutland in the National Museum (fig. 24), with the exception of 1895-1904 when Hjørring county had a fall in find material, while Jutland as a whole (and the grave finds in Hjørring Museum itself) show a very rapid growth.

2. The other factor to be examined is the relationship between the activities of the two museums, where the distribution of professionally excavated sites is particularly relevant (figs. 36 and 37, hatched).

The excavation work of the National Museum extends over the period 1885-1944, besides a very few excavated sites in the period 1955-64. Altogether 36% of the sites are professionally excavated, and the county of Hjørring is thus placed tenth (out of 18) on the National Museum "activity scale" (fig. 27). It is lower than other counties in Jutland, such as Århus, Randers, Southern Jutland (including Haderslev), and Ringkøbing. This situation probably reflects the higher rate of local activity in Hjørring rather than any neglect of Vendsyssel by the National Museum.

As early as 1915-24, professional excavations contributed half of the period's finds at Hjørring Museum, and in subsequent years this proportion rose steadily (fig. 36). Altogether 222 sites out of a total of 345 were professionally excavated. This constitutes 64% and is higher even than the activities of the National Museum itself in the county of Århus (fig. 27). This is due above all to the immense contribution of the dentist Holger Friis throughout his long life. From 1910, when he excavated his first major site, until the end of the 1960's, his excavations brought a large number of Roman period finds into Hjørring Museum. In 1959 the first museum curator was appointed, who,

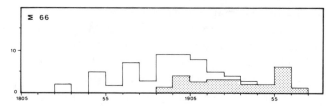

Fig. 38. Year of registration of grave mounds from Hjørring county, the National Museum and Hjørring Museum. (Hjørring Museum hatched).

although an architect by training, carried out many major excavations. In 1974 the first professional archaeologist entered the museum. In the last 25 years, 92 out of a total of 104 sites (88%) have been professionally excavated.

3. The third factor relevant to an assessment of the frequency graph is the find situations. The graves from Hjørring county are predominantly inhumation burials, either in large stone cists or in open ground. The inhumation graves, particularly those in open ground, may be clustered into large cemeteries. Cremation graves, mainly cremation patches, are also known from burial sites (cf. Lysdahl 1971, 88). Secondary burials in mounds also occur. There are only a few cases of primary mound burials. 24 sites were found as a result of mound demolition. These are 7% of all sites, a marked difference from the National Museum material, where there are 42 burial sites beneath mounds, i.e. 36% (cf. fig. 22). As the graph shows (fig. 38), the National Museum burial mounds occur much earlier: from the middle of the 19th to the beginning of this century. The later and fewer mound finds remained in Hjørring Museum. There is a noticeable sudden rise in mound finds in the period 1955-64, which is probably due to the ploughing under of mounds.

19 sites were found as a result of gravel digging. They comprise less than 6% of the sites and are thus fewer than the average figure for Jutland of 9% (National Museum finds).

Together the sites from gravel digging and mounds make up approx. 12% of the total. Most of the remaining sites were found during ploughing. In this respect the stone cists are particularly easy to find (the plough hitting against stones), but nonetheless they contribute no more than half of the total number of graves (a little more when calculated on the basis of sites), since ordinary inhumation and cremation burials are found mainly in grave-yards).

The situations in which the material now in the National Museum and in the Vendsyssel Museum was found are fairly similar. If we except the sites found beneath mounds, the material from the National Museum appears to be representative.

It is otherwise with the frequency graphs (figs. 36 and 37). The periods of maximum finds at the National Museum are 1885-94 and 1905-14, while at the Hjørring Museum it is the period from 1925 to 1974.

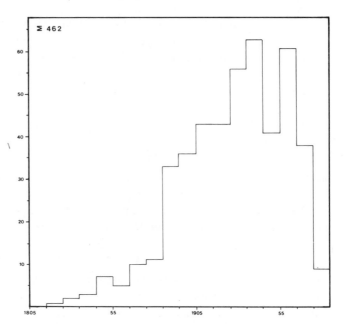

Fig. 39. Year of registration of burial sites from Hjørring county, the National Museum and Hjørring Museum (Hjørring county).

The total frequency graph for the county (fig. 39) shows the actual find frequency for the area. In the period 1815-84 the increase is slow and gradual. The years 1885-94 are marked by a very rapid growth, which can be attributed partly to the establishment of the Hjørring Museum, partly to the local field visits of the previous period (1881-84 in the districts discussed here). In the following 40 years there is again a moderate increase in finds, and a steep rise in 1925-34. The curve reaches its peak in the next decade, 1935-44, and maintains almost the same level in 1955-64. After this the find rate dwindles.

This find graph, apart from the economic factors outlined earlier, first and foremost reflects the great contribution of the Friis family, especially Holger Friis. He carried out his first major excavation in 1910, and in 1921 became Director of the Vendsyssel Museum, carrying out numerous excavations until the late 1960's. In 1959 Palle Friis became the first Museum Curator, and has since conducted many archaeological excavations. The combination of Holger Friis' extensive excavation work and Palle Friis' competence in excavation and maintenance of archival records has resulted in an outstanding collection of Roman period grave finds at the Vendsyssel Historical Museum.

The decrease in find material after 1964, and above all after 1974, cannot be attributed to any falling off in interest or activity on the part of the museum. During the last 15 years only two out of a total of 47 grave finds have been acquired without a preceding survey or excavation by the museum. As for Randers Museum, the greatest decline has taken place over the last few years.

Geographical representativity. There are a total of 885 graves[14] from the county of Hjørring, 828 from the Early Roman and 57 from the Late Roman period.[15]

Their distribution covers nearly all parishes in the districts of Børglum, Dronninglund, Vennebjerg, and Horns (with the exception of the northernmost parishes in Horns district: Skagen and Tversted). The district richest in finds is Vennebjerg, with the parishes of Horne, Bjergby, Sindal, Astrup, Skt. Olai and Skt. Hans. The following places also have many finds: Bindslev and Flade in the Horns district, and Vrejlev in the district of Børglum.

To assess the geographical representativity we have to compare the distribution pattern of the many finds from the Vendsyssel Museum (Early Roman period: 683 finds) with the much fewer finds from the National Museum (Early Roman period: 145) (figs. 1 and 2 compared with figs. 3 and 4). This will tell us whether the areas most heavily represented at the Hjørring Museum show corresponding concentrations of finds in the National Museum material. If so, we may consider the National Museum material under consideration as geographically representative, and also establish whether 683 finds and 145 finds show the same distribution pattern – in other words whether in this instance the 145 finds can be considered representative of the pattern.

The National Museum grave finds come mainly from the same four districts, in which nearly every parish is represented by one or more finds. In the districts the concentrations of finds overlap: Vennebjerg has most, followed by the districts of Horns, Børglum, and Dronninglund, in that order. On a parish level there are certain similarities and differences. Several parishes recur with large quantities of find material, whereas others are heavily represented in only one of the distribution maps.[16] The large number of finds in the immediate vicinity of Hjørring (in the parishes of Skt. Olai and Skt. Hans, besides the town of Hjørring) probably reflects the increase in construction work (building of roads, excavation of building sites, etc.), and also the closer and easier

contact with the museum. These concentrations are not found in the distribution of National Museum finds.

We can thus conclude that the regional variations in the distribution pattern for Hjørring county reflects only to a limited extent differences in the activities of the two museums. The overall distribution pattern can be regarded as representative of the true geographical differentiation of find material, and on a district level the National Museum material is representative.

Summary. Jutland

The introductory discussion of Roman period grave finds from Jutland in the National Museum closed with the following two questions:
1. Are we dealing with an archaeological find group that is nearly exhausted?
2. Are the graves geographically representative?

In both cases we had to examine first whether the results primarily reflected the activities of the National Museum. To illustrate this the three largest Roman period collections, from *Haderslev Museum,* the *Randers Kulturhistorisk Museum,* and the *Vendsyssel historiske Museum,* were analysed individually.[17]

In fig. 40 the find frequencies of the three local museums are indicated on the graph for the total number of registered Roman period finds in Jutland. A comparison between the frequency graph and the separate diagram for the National Museum (fig. 24) gives the following results. The two graphs take the same course until the period 1885-94, at which point the local museum collections grow more rapidly than those of the National Museum. In the subsequent decade 1895-1904 the increase at the National Museum is considerably higher. This is largely due to the increased activity by the National Museum (fig. 25), combined with the levelling of many mounds (fig. 21) (cf. above). This sudden expansion of National Museum material within a single decade is followed by a lower find frequency which maintains a stable level from 1905 to 1935. Local museums also experience a slight fall in accessions, but otherwise there is a fairly constant increase in new finds until 1964.

The sudden fall in find material experienced by the National Museum in the middle of the 1930's was also felt by local museums approximately thirty years later, in the mid-1960's, when the total increase in new finds was lower than at any time since 1885.

As mentioned above, most Roman period graves are

level-ground burials, i.e. the sites are found *accidentally* and are recognized by potsherds, slightly darker soil or stones. The drop in find material is probably due to a lower priority given by the museums to excavating Roman period graves. Vendsyssel can serve here as a control area: more than half the graves are large stone cists. The commonest report of the means of discovery is "plough striking against stones", and it is museum practice *invariably* to survey and examine such sites. We may thus assume that the museum has responded to all find reports. Nevertheless the amount of find material fell in 1965-74, and the drop has accelerated in the last few years. We can therefore exclude the possibility that deliberate excavation priorities have caused the decline in material which is seen in all frequency diagrams with minor chronological variations.

Various kinds of earth working – from ploughing with a tractor to excavation with large earth-moving machines – reduce the prospects of discovering graves. Is this the reason for the fall in find frequency? Hardly. If so, the large stone cists in Vendsyssel would also be destroyed unnoticed during ploughing or digging. Considering their size, this is hardly the case.

For Jutland as a whole it would seem that the fall in find frequency expresses an actual decrease in the *possibilities* of making new finds.

The second point in our discussion concerns the geographical representativity of the graves. The four distribution maps show the total find material from the Early and Late Roman periods, and also the share of the local museums in this pattern (figs. 1-4).

Approximately 90% of Roman period graves in Jutland are dated to the Early Roman period. If we compare the geographical distribution of finds from the major local museums with those of the National Museum, we get an impression of the extent to which the finds from the National Museum, although fewer and earlier, show the same pattern of distribution as those in local museums. The results of the previous analyses can be briefly summarized as follows:

The finds from the Haderslev Museum and the National Museum are complementary, which means that the National Museum grave finds are not representative of the total pattern. The changing national boundaries of Southern Jutland gives this region a special position.

In Randers county the find concentrations overlap, at least on a district level. The only exception is the Støvring district, where Randers Museum has more finds.

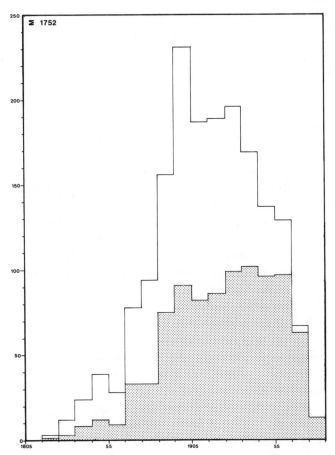

Fig. 40. Year of registration of burial sites in Jutland (Haderslev Museum, Randers Museum and Hjørring Museum hatched).

The location of the town of Randers and its museum in this district is doubtless the cause of the uneven geographical distribution.

In the county of Hjørring there is a similar overlap of find concentrations on a district level. The only exceptions are the parishes around Hjørring town and its museum, where the concentration of finds is not reflected in National Museum material.

The few scattered Late Roman Age finds show the same distribution pattern everywhere. There is no clustering of finds from this period around museums and towns. The only exception is Southern Jutland, where the distribution of the two museums remains complementary.

The conclusion to be drawn on the geographical situation is that the National Museum material appears to be representative of the total material on a district level, except in Southern Jutland.

The overall distribution pattern can be assessed as representative of the original distribution of Roman period burials. Where there are many, many will be found.

CONCLUSION

We shall finally consider briefly the two questions with which this paper has been chiefly concerned:

1. Does the distribution map reflect the original distribution of the graves, or have, for instance, present-day economic factors and museum activities influenced the pattern we see today?
2. Will future finds disturb or alter the basis for analysis, or are those known at present representative?

Economic factors (e.g. gravel digging) could not be demonstrated to have had any selective influence on the geographical representativity of burial sites.

Graves beneath burial mounds have been found primarily in the old Bronze Age areas. However, their numbers vary from county to county. This variation is determined more by the use of mounds for secondary burials, and by Roman period settlement compared to Bronze Age settlement, than by any regional fluctuations in the degree – and intensity – of mound demolition.

Museum-related factors have rarely had an effect on the distribution maps extending beyond the parish as a geographical unit. On a district level possible fluctuations in the representativity of the distribution pattern seem to have become neutralized, so that new finds conform with the present pattern of distribution.

Apart from the question of regional representativity, the distribution of Roman period graves also involves the question of numerical representativity between the Early and Late Roman periods. The Late Roman grave material comprises c. 50% of the total grave material in Zealand, Lolland and Falster, 70% in Funen and Langeland, but only 10% in Jutland. The regional analyses of the number of finds in local museums (assuming the same burial customs) make it likely that this numerical proportion is determined by actual prehistoric factors.

The other point to be assessed is the statistical representativity of grave finds, i.e. the possible relationship between discovered and undiscovered graves.

The find graphs from 1805 to the present day show to what extent the find frequency for Roman period graves has been due to economic factors. Despite regional differences between the find frequency for graves in the islands (Zealand, Lolland-Falster, Funen, Langeland) and those in Jutland, the tendency remains the same: an increase in the number of newly discovered sites from the middle to the end of the 19th century is followed by a period of stability which is interrupted only by a slight rise from the middle of the 1920's to the middle of the 1930's. Eventually there is a fall in find material, which begins in the middle of the 1950's in the islands and in the mid-1960's in Jutland (cf. figs. 8, 15 and 40).

The general picture today is that the increase of new finds in all parts of Denmark is at a lower ebb than at any time since the first half of the 19th century. There are three possible explanations for this: 1) The remaining graves are so deep that present-day economic activities will not bring them to light. 2) Graves are uncovered but not recognized as such because of the high level of mechanization. 3) Grave finds are in fact nearly exhausted.

As suggested in the preceding pages, the last explanation seems most plausible, and at the present time it is impossible to indicate any economic or other factors likely to make the find frequency rise again.[18]

Lotte Hedeager
University of Copenhagen
Center for Historical Anthrorology,
Kejsergade 2,
1155 Copenhagen K.

NOTES

1. The grave material is analysed partly in terms of sites (containing one or more graves), partly in terms of individual graves. In the frequency graphs burial *sites* are used, while the distribution maps are based on the total number of *graves*. In some areas and periods (Zealand in the Early Roman period – shown as ÆR – and Late Roman (YR), Jutland in the Late Roman period (YR)), the grave finds and sites coincide. In other areas (Lolland Early Roman (ÆR), Funen Early and Late Roman (ÆR, YR) and Jutland Early Roman (ÆR)), there are large cemeteries which tend to distort the actual quantity of graves.

   Professionally excavated sites include those surveyed and/or completely excavated by a museum.

   The latest years of registration are as follows:

   Zealand, Lolland, Falster (National Museum): 1974

   Jutland (National Museum): 1976

   Haderslev Museum: 1977

   Kulturhistorisk Museum, Randers: 1979

   Vendsyssel historiske Museum: 1979

   At the present time it has not been possible to include Bornholm in the analysis.

2. I wish to thank the Director of Department I, Assistant Curator Dr. Mogens Ørsnes, for permission to use the wealth of find material at the National Museum in Copenhagen.

A catalogue of Roman period graves in Eastern Denmark is published (Hedeager 1980). Problems concerning the relationship between graves and settlement are also discussed elsewhere (Hedeager 1978).

3. The Funen material is taken exclusively from Albrectsen, *Fynske Jernaldergrave* II-V, 1956-73.

4. I am grateful to the Director of Department I, Dr. Mogens Ørsnes, for permission to record the Jutland Roman period grave finds in the National Museum. – Unless otherwise stated, all material discussed is from the National Museum.

5. For permission to record Roman period grave finds in Haderslev Museum, and for assistance while doing so, I should like to thank the former Curator Hans Neumann and the Museum Instructor Stine Wiell.

6. The professionally excavated sites are more difficult to assess than the National Museum excavations. In many cases Haderslev Museum surveyed or excavated sites without leaving a record in the archives or making a report. The active role of the Museum in obtaining finds has therefore no doubt been greater than is suggested by the histograms.

7. I should like to thank Museum Curator Bjørn Stürup for permission to record the Roman period graves at the *Randers Kulturhistorisk Museum.*

8. I visited the *Kulturhistorisk Museum* in Randers in 1979, which is why the semi-decade 1975-79 is included.

9. If the find material of four sites from the semi-decade 1974-79 is doubled into a whole decade, the resulting eight sites still represent a marked fall in find material.

10. Large sites are not as conspicuous as many small sites in the frequency graphs. This may be a reason for the low frequency of professionally excavated sites in the period 1905-14. This is also the case during the same period for Jutland as a whole (fig. 25).

11. I wish to thank the Museum Curators Palle Friis and Per Lysdahl for permission to record the comprehensive grave find material at the *Vendsyssel historiske Museum.* I am especially grateful to Per Lysdahl for his kind assistance, which included placing at my disposal an unpublished catalogue of all Early Roman period graves found in Vendsyssel.

12. The period 1975-79 has been included because of its recent registrations. Sites excavated several times at intervals over ten years are regarded as new finds in the total figures.

13. If the nine finds from the semi-decade of 1975-79 are doubled into a whole decade, as was done for Randers, the resulting 18 finds still constitute a smaller number than any shown on the graph since 1895.

14. Stone cists sometimes contain two or more burials from the Early as well as the Late Roman periods. When counting the total such stone cists have been included once for each period to which they contributed finds, since it is rarely possible to establish the actual number of burials.

15. I am indebted to Museum Curator Jens-Henrik Bech for help in establishing the finer chronological divisions between the Pre-Roman Iron Age and the Early Roman Period.

16. Since the maps show the number of grave finds, not sites, a few large grave-yards can easily distort representativity on a parish level. Cf. also Lysdahl 1971, fig. 1: grave-yards and single graves from the Early Roman period in Vendsyssel.

17. P. Lysdahl has kindly informed me of the approximate number of Early Roman period graves at around 1970 in the following museums: Ålborg 55, Års 65, Thisted 20, Hobro 20, Viborg c. 30; a total of c. 190 graves, in contrast to Haderslev 310, Randers 302, Hjørring 683; a total of 1295 graves. To these can be added a considerable number of private collections, which it has not yet been possible to record.

18. The major earthworks connected with the proposed gas-pipe network over Denmark may offer an important control factor.

REFERENCES

ALBRECTSEN, E. 1956 *Fynske Jernaldergrave II. Ældre Romersk Jernalder.* København.

– 1968 *Fynske Jernaldergrave III. Yngre Romersk Jernalder.* Odense.

– 1971 *Fynske jernaldergrave IV, 1-2.* Gravpladsen på Møllegårdsmarken ved Broholm. Odense.

– 1973 *Fynske Jernaldergrave V.* Nye Fund. Odense.

HEDEAGER, L. 1978 Bebyggelse, social struktur og politisk organisation i Øst-Danmarks ældre og yngre romertid. *Fortid og Nutid, bd. XXVII, hft. 3.*

– 1980 Besiedlung, soziale Struktur und politische Organisation in der älteren und jüngeren römischen Kaiserzeit Ostdanmarks. *Praehistorische Zeitschrift.* 55:1.

LYSDAHL, P. 1971 Vendsyssel som lokalgruppe i ældre romersk jernalder. *Brudstykker. Festskrift Holger Friis.* Historisk Samfund for Vendsyssel.

THORLACIUS, B. 1809 *Bemærkninger over de i Danmark endnu tilværende Hedenolds-Høie og Stensætninger.* Kiøbenhavn.

Amt:	1	2	3	4	5	7	8-9	10	11	12	13	14	15	16	17	18	19	20
1805-14	–	–	–	1	–	–	1	–	–	–	–	–	–	–	–	–	–	–
1815-24	–	–	–	2	–	–	3	1	–	–	–	–	1	–	–	–	–	–
1825-34	–	2	–	–	2	–	1	2	1	2	1	1	–	–	–	2	–	–
1835-44	–	1	–	1	–	–	2	3	2	1	2	5	–	2	–	1	–	–
1845-54	1	3	2	1	4	2	4	7	–	8	2	3	1	1	2	2	1	2
1855-64	4	3	2	3	8	1	14	3	1	1	1	2	2	2	1	1	3	2
1865-74	1	1	2	2	6	2	15	10	2	2	4	4	1	3	7	3	3	4
1875-84	5	2	2	7	14	4	16	11	11	5	3	9	1	4	3	6	6	4
1885-94	–	1	2	2	8	2	4	20	6	7	7	18	1	5	3	7	6	1
1895-04	1	2	3	–	6	7	15	7	4	25	8	26	5	21	21	11	10	1
1905-14	–	2	5	–	4	5	20	22	3	13	16	11	9	9	5	3	11	3
1915-24	–	2	3	5	4	3	13	14	3	10	15	21	13	5	4	5	4	8
1925-34	2	3	5	2	11	4	21	6	10	9	10	8	8	12	8	6	11	9
1935-44	–	7	4	1	4	4	24	6	3	9	8	11	3	8	3	6	6	4
1945-54	2	6	1	2	6	–	15	1	1	1	4	10	–	3	2	8	7	4
1955-64	–	2	1	1	3	2	8	4	3	4	–	3	–	3	3	4	7	1
1965-74	1	–	–	–	–	–	8	–	–	1	–	–	–	–	1	1	1	–

Regional distribution of burial sites (in the National Museum).

Amt:	10	11	12	13	14	15	16	17	18	19	20-23
1805-14	–	–	–	–	–	–	–	–	–	–	–
1815-24	–	–	–	–	–	1	–	–	–	–	–
1825-34	2	1	–	1	–	–	–	–	1	–	–
1835-44	–	1	1	1	3	–	1	–	1	–	–
1845-54	5	–	6	2	2	1	–	2	–	1	1
1855-64	2	1	–	1	2	1	2	–	1	1	2
1865-74	7	2	2	1	1	1	3	3	1	–	2
1875-84	3	9	2	2	4	–	3	–	4	4	2
1885-94	8	3	4	5	8	–	3	1	4	2	–
1895-04	5	4	8	6	4	1	17	10	5	4	–
1905-14	6	3	5	6	–	1	4	.1	1	2	–
1915-24	2	2	3	10	2	3	–	–	4	1	–
1925-34	1	3	1	4	–	2	3	2	1	–	–
1935-44	1	–	3	2	2	–	2	–	3	–	–
1945-54	–	–	–	–	1	–	1	–	1	–	1
1955-64	–	1	1	–	–	–	1	–	–	1	–
1965-74	–	–	–	–	–	–	–	1	–	–	–

Regional distribution of year of registration of burial mounds (in the National Museum).

Amt:	1	2	3	4	5	7	8-9	10	11	12	13	14	15	16	17	18	19	20-23
1805-14	–	–	–	–	–	–	–	–	–	–	–	–	–	–	–	–	–	–
1815-24	–	–	–	–	–	–	–	–	–	–	–	–	–	–	–	–	–	–
1825-34	–	–	–	–	–	–	–	–	–	–	–	–	–	–	–	–	–	–
1835-44	–	–	–	–	–	–	–	–	–	–	–	–	–	–	–	–	–	–
1845-54	–	–	–	–	–	–	–	–	–	–	–	–	–	–	–	–	–	–
1855-64	–	–	–	1	–	–	1	–	–	–	–	–	–	–	–	–	–	–
1865-74	–	–	–	1	2	–	3	–	–	–	–	–	–	–	–	–	–	–
1875-84	1	–	–	1	7	–	7	–	1	–	–	1	–	–	–	–	–	–
1885-94	–	1	–	1	1	–	–	8	–	–	–	–	1	2	–	3	–	–
1895-04	1	1	1	–	6	4	6	4	–	10	5	13	5	7	11	8	5	1
1905-14	–	1	3	–	2	2	9	10	–	–	5	7	4	1	2	–	3	–
1915-24	–	2	2	3	2	3	6	7	2	5	6	17	8	2	–	5	1	5
1925-34	1	1	3	1	8	2	14	5	5	5	3	8	8	8	4	2	5	7
1935-44	–	6	2	–	3	1	15	4	2	8	4	8	2	2	2	3	2	3
1945-54	1	2	1	2	5	–	15	–	–	–	1	4	–	2	1	5	3	2
1955-64	–	2	1	1	3	–	3	4	2	4	–	3	–	–	1	2	4	1
1965-74	1	–	–	–	–	–	3	–	–	–	–	–	–	–	1	–	–	–

Regional distribution of professionally excavated sites (in the National Museum).

Hoard Finds from the Early Germanic Iron Age

by ELIZA FONNESBECH-SANDBERG

INTRODUCTION

In the following paper hoards refer to finds deposited in fields, bogs, lakes, rivers or the sea which do not originate from either graves or settlements. According to this definition hoards may thus include both sacred and secular deposits containing one or more objects.

The Early Germanic Iron Age covers the period c. 400-525/550 A.D. Its beginning is defined by the appearance of the Søsdala style with animal heads in profile and cruciform fibulae, and its close is characterized by the disappearance of solidi and bracteate hoards.

Most of the available material from the Early Germanic Period consists of hoard finds. Apart from the large bog deposits, which are often interpreted as sacrifices after war, and apart from three large silver finds, the hoards contain mainly objects worked in gold, e.g. rings for neck, arm and finger, bracteates and other pendants, fibulae, beads, solidi and gold used for payment, in various associations. The hoards vary considerably with regard to the number of objects and their weight. It is the general representativity of these gold hoards which we shall now examine in detail.[1]

As Malmer has shown, the national distribution in percentages of the different types of bracteates found by 1850 was largely the same as the present distribution (Malmer 1963, 183 ff). Since the intervening years have not altered the proportional distribution to any important extent, the number and composition of the finds may be taken to be historically representative. The question now is whether this is also true of the geographical distribution of finds and of the various types of finds (dry fields/bog). In the following this will be examined more specifically by comparing the find frequency of the different hoard categories during the last 175 years with the factors which brought the finds to light. However, the discussion is not limited to bracteate hoards, but includes all hoards which can with some certainty be attributed to the Early Germanic Period.[2]

HOARDS FOUND BEFORE 1805

In contrast to e.g. grave mounds, which are clearly visible in the landscape, the discovery of a hoard find is completely independent of the desire for archaeological or pecuniary benefit. On the other hand, whether hoards are preserved after their discovery is closely dependent on how widespread is the knowledge and appreciation of the antiquarian value of artefacts. Thus it was decided as early as the first half of the 13th century in King Erik's Law of Zealand that *"danefæ"* – gold and silver found in the ground – should belong to the king. In the Jutland Law of 1241 (Book 2, Chapter 113) it was further specified that *"danefæ"* was gold or silver found after ploughing or in burial mounds, which suggests that even at this time there was an awareness of prehistoric remains (Hermansen 1954, 224; Werlauff 1807, 23 f). This provision was made statutory however for purely economic reasons, since all gold and silver obtained was melted down.

This clause was repeated in the Danish Law of 1683 (5-9-3), and the right to *"danefæ"* was also granted to counts of the realm as part of their privileges of 1671 (Hindenburg 1859, 24). However, at least some of the *"danefæ"* sent to the king after the Chamber of Arts was established in the middle of the 17th century was preserved. Furthermore the *"danefæ"* legislation was extended with an ordinance passed in 1737, which included metal and other treasure, in addition to gold and silver, and also withdrew the privileges of the counts. From 1752 onwards a sum was paid to the finders equivalent to the metal value of the objects found (Hindenburg 1859, 24 f). This provision, as it turned out, stimulated the handing over of hoards (Worsaae 1879, 4)[3], but it was not really until the 19th century that antiquities began to come into the Museum in large numbers.[4] By lucky chance it was also the time when a fairly large number of hoards were beginning to come to light as a result of agrarian reforms in the 1780's and the resulting cultivation of common lands. The question now is whether one can arrive at any notion of how many finds were lost – either from ignorance or by being melted down – before the intensification of agriculture with its accompanying hoard finds began in the 19th century.

In addition to the gold objects a small number of bronze and even fewer silver pieces are found. Bronze objects were not even mentioned before 1737, and it is doubtful whether they were later assigned antiquarian value and handed in – apart from finds of exceptional splendour. This only occurred during the 19th century with the growing knowledge about the past (Hindenburg 1859, 25). Many small bronze objects are so covered in verdigris that it would have been uneconomic to melt them down, and their incorporation into private collections also in the 19th century – especially the less impressive objects like cruciform fibulae – probably indicates that they were not generally considered *"danefæ"*.

The situation with regard to gold and silver objects is rather different. These metals have an intrinsic value and people were usually aware of this. There are several reports that parts of the hoard submitted had been sold beforehand to an itinerant vendor, and some find reports mention earlier discoveries of gold in the area. The Else-hoved hoard, which was dug up in the years around 1830, was first reported to have been found in Scania. The seller obviously knew about the existing *"danefæ"* legislation, and therefore passed the find off as foreign – notwithstanding the similar Swedish legislation (Breitenstein 1942, 90 ff).

To summarize, we can say that as long as there was no widespread popular knowledge of archaeology there was probably a steady loss of bronze objects, while at least a good proportion of gold finds were handed in as a result of the *"danefæ"* regulations and, after the Chamber of Arts was founded, these finds were preserved (cf. the later comparison with the situation obtaining for Late Bronze Age hoards). Normally, therefore, neither gold nor silver entered into private collections.

The gold objects which were preserved, and which were found before the establishment of the commission for Antiquities in 1807, are, apart from the gold horns, not particularly large but they nevertheless represent a certain value in metal and rarity. They comprise 30-35 gold bracteates, for over half of which we have no information on the find spot; some may belong to the same find. We also have information on some solidi and *"guldgubber"* (:embossed gold plates figuring human

beings). However so-called ring gold or gold for payment has not been preserved, though some seems to have been sent to the Chamber of Arts, e.g. from Sorte Muld (Breitenstein 1944, 65). As a general rule ring gold is common in bracteate hoards, so there is reason to suppose that some of the early bracteates were found in such association. There may be some coins and bracteates missing from the period before 1805; at any rate no pre-1805 ring gold has been preserved.

Silver is a fairly rare metal in the hoards in question, and as far as we know there were no silver objects from the Early Germanic Period in the Chamber of Arts collection.

HOARDS FOUND AFTER 1805

If we turn to hoards found after 1805, the graph (fig. 1) indicates a marked increase in the number of finds until 1875, from 4 to 74 per decade, after which the curve declines almost as steeply again to 17 finds per decade in 1905. Subsequently, the number of finds per decade remains virtually constant until 1965 when finds decrease to seven in the next ten years. It would seem therefore as if the source of finds is nearly exhausted. In order to ascertain whether the graph in fig. 1 reflects a general tendency applicable to all of Denmark or whether various factors have influenced the quantitative and geographical distribution of finds, we shall now analyse the hoards according to region and type of environment.

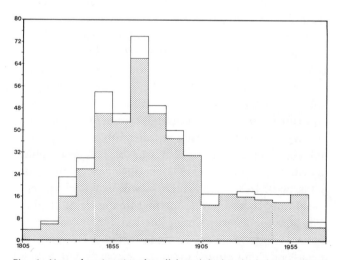

Fig. 1. Year of registration for all hoard finds. Shaded area – total number of hoards. Area not shaded – later discovered supplementary objects, belonging to hoards previously registered.

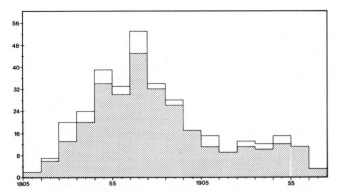

Fig. 2. Year of registration for field hoards. (Signatures – cf. fig. 1).

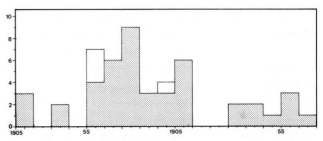

Fig. 3. Year of registration for hoards from wet land/water meadow/former bog. (Signatures – cf. fig. 1).

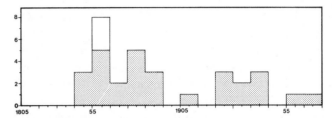

Fig. 4. Year of registration for gold/silver hoards from bogs. (Signatures – cf. fig. 1).

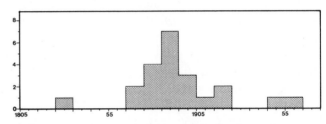

Fig. 5. Year of registration for bronze hoards from bogs. (Signatures – cf. fig. 1).

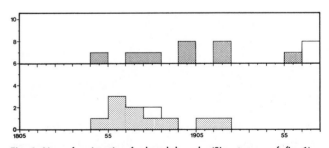

Fig. 6. Year of registration for beach hoards. (Signatures – cf. fig. 1).

Fig. 7. Year of registration for hoards from rivers or the sea. (Signatures – cf. fig. 1).

The total number of hoards found between 1805 and 1975 comprises 418 finds (cf. fig. 1, shaded area)[5]. When sites were classified according to their environment, hoards lacking such information were excluded. The finds can be divided into five groups according to the type of site: field finds – dry land; bog finds; field finds – wet land/water meadow/former bog; beach finds; river or sea finds.[6] The find frequency for these groups is given in histograms (figs. 2-7). It should be noted that bog finds are divided into gold/silver hoards (which may include bronze) and hoards with bronze only, which in this context means single finds of bronze objects. The reason this distinction between the metals used has not been applied to the other groups is because their bronze hoards are so few as to exert no decisive influence on the find frequency. It is however otherwise with bog finds, where bronze hoards constitute between one third and one half of the total number.

In the case of some hoards a greater or smaller part was found initially, and supplementary objects discovered later. Such later find additions are shown by open signature in the histograms. From figures 2-7 it appears that this is a rare occurrence in bog hoards. This is related to the manner of their discovery. Practically all bog finds have been made during peat-cutting, which means that either the whole hoard is found at once, or some may be lost since one cannot normally return to the finding place later and continue the search. In one of the few cases involving later additions to a bog find, the supplementary objects were found in peat cut from the same bog in the same year. However, these objects were found only when the peat was to be burnt.

The reason why find additions from the same hoard occur more frequently in other environments is because the find matrix is not removed. For instance, in the case of various field finds made while ploughing etc., a single object was often discovered first, while the remainder of the hoard appeared later as a result of repeated ploughing or other farm work. As for the number of later find additions, fig. 1 shows that this is c. 2½ times greater in the period 1805-84 than in the period 1885-1964. That the number is falling is undoubtedly because the finders have become more careful about examining the site, possibly as a result of the spreading knowledge of archaeology.

Figures 6-7 show that there are few finds from rivers, the sea, or beaches. Among the beach finds, information on the manner of discovery is available for only one hoard: it was spotted during a walk and led to an archaeological investigation. The discovery of beach hoards is too accidental to use in representativity analysis. River and sea finds have resulted from fishing, digging for blue clay, and crossing of fords. Their appearance must also be regarded as accidental; though related to commercial activities, these are not systematic (the sea floor, for instance, is not examined systematically and regularly). It is therefore not possible to analyse their representativity.

It is the three large find groups – field, dry land; field, wet land; and bog – which we shall analyse in some detail.[7]

The investigation will cover the following points:

A. The relationship between find frequency and active socio-economic factors.

B. The possible regional dependence of find frequency on the presence of people with a special knowledge of antiquities.

C. The relationship between Early Germanic and Late Bronze Age hoards as regards representativity (gold and bronze).

A. The relationship between find frequency and active socio-ecomonic factors.

In figures 8-10 field finds, finds from wet fields/water meadow/former bog, and finds from bogs are shown according to regional distribution in Zealand and its smaller islands, Bornholm, Funen and its smaller islands (including Lolland-Falster), and Jutland.

Field hoards

The histograms of the four regional groups show a very uniform development with few chronological variations.[8] Thus the curves begin in either 1805 or 1815 with a fairly steep rise and reach a peak around the middle of the century, after which they fall equally sharply until 1895, 1905 or 1915; the curves then climb again on a lower level than before and stabilize over a number of years before their final decline from the middle of the 20th century. Generally speaking the maximum number of field finds is to be found between c. 1825/35 and 1905/15 but with different peaks according to region. The curves for Zealand and Bornholm start only in 1815, whereas those for Funen and Jutland indicate finds already from 1805. On the other hand, Zealand and Bornholm culminate first, between 1855 and 1865, while Funen and Jutland reach their peaks between 1865 and 1875. Jutland's period of maximum finds contains some fluctuations, e.g. between 1845-55 and 1905-15 (the latter only if later find additions are included), just as Bornholm's rising curve shows a sudden peak in 1825-35. The dip of the curves around the turn of the century occurs in Bornholm and Jutland as soon as 1895-1905, in Zealand between 1905-15, and in Funen not until 1915-25. After 1965 neither Zealand, Bornholm, nor Funen has supplied any field finds, while the curve for Jutland remains at the low level of the previous decade.

The rise in find frequency after 1805 coincides with the reclamation of common land and heath which, with different degrees of intensity, began throughout the country after the open-field system was abandoned as a result of the agrarian reforms of 1788.

Figure 11 lists various types of agricultural work leading to the discovery of hoards. As in Kr. Kristiansen's investigation of Late Bronze Age hoards (Kristiansen 1974) a distinction has been made between those activities carried out manually and those carried out with the use of machinery. Manual farm work includes activities such as gardening, peat-cutting on heathlands, digging in/clearing of woods, digging in/removal of burial mound, removal of stones, earthing potatoes, lifting beets etc. Farm work with the use of machinery includes ploughing, harrowing, and rolling.

Figure 11 shows that apart from Zealand most finds have been made during farm work using machinery. This can probably be attributed to the depth at which finds are located. Some field finds lack information about the activity resulting in their discovery, but there is a group of finds reported to have been discovered in fields or during unspecified field work. These were probably ploughed/harrowed up and, lying about in the field, were found later during manual field work. The group involved is made up of 41 finds.

Figure 13 indicates the find depths of field hoards. Information is available for only a small number of hoards. This is because, as already mentioned, some of the hoards were found in fields, in or just beneath the top soil, and were probably ploughed up from their original depth.

It will be seen from the figure that the group of 10-30 cm has supplied by far the most finds. This depth is the normal ploughing depth in fields. The number of shallow finds is supplemented by many of the hoards found during ploughing (without indication of depth), in the top soil (without indication of activity), or probably ploughed up and only found later.

Deep ploughing was first used on heathlands in the 1920's, with depths reaching 40 cm and from the 1940's reaching 80 cm. This may have affected the discovery of deep finds after 1920. Among the finds in question, discovered during ploughing at an unspecified depth, there are not many after 1920 (17 as opposed to 100 before 1920), but those from heathlands may have been found at a greater depth than the normal ploughing depth.

The appearance of other deep hoards is due partly to digging activities during manual field work, partly to such activities as gravel-digging and construction work.

Apart from showing the dependence of the find frequency on agricultural expansion in the 19th century, the diagrams in fig. 8 also reflect the construction work which took place during the 19th century, involving the extension of the road system, especially between 1820 and 1862, and the building of the main railway lines before 1874. Hoards which have appeared during gravel-digging are also most frequent during the 19th century, culminating between 1845 and 1855 and then declining until 1915. These facts are documented in fig. 15, which classifies hoards according to the type of activity and year of registration. The description: "found during other activity on dry land" includes e.g. archaeological excavation and subsequent examination of sites. If the curves in fig. 15a and 15b are added up, it will be seen that several hoards appearing in fig. 8 are missing; they are the ones lacking any indication of the type of activity leading to their discovery.

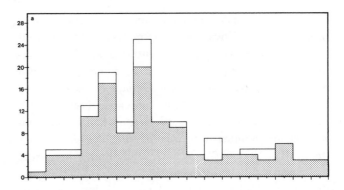
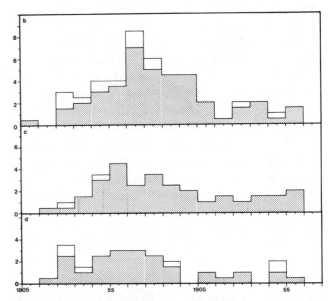

Fig. 8. Year of registration for field hoards, according to region. a: Jutland, b: Funen with islands, c: Zealand, d: Bornholm. (Signatures – cf. fig. 1).

As so few deep hoards have been found despite continued construction work in this century (the building of motorways etc.) – which is also due to the fact that much construction work takes place on land already brought under cultivation – and as overall find frequencies are declining, this would indicate that Early Germanic field hoards were not usually deposited much below the ground surface. This observation corresponds with the prevailing theory about Early Germanic hoards as treasures deposited for later retrieval.

If we attempt to sum up the relationship between find frequency and economic activities, and also look at the fluctuations in the Danish islands and Jutland, respectively (fig. 8), we get the following result:

The Islands: The common lands had largely been brought under cultivation by the middle of the 19th century, and efforts were then concentrated on soil improvement, followed by the removal of stones and burial mounds (cf. Kr. Kristiansen's chapter on economic developments). Although land cultivation became more and more intensive during the second half of the 19th century, the number of hoards found in the islands after the peak in 1855/65/75 declined until around the turn of the century. The subsequent slight increase means that there were still hoards left in the ground, but fewer than before, since there was no diminution of economic activity. As no new land was brought into cultivation, it was the hoards remaining in areas already cultivated which appeared until 1965, probably because of e.g. deep ploughing. That no more finds were made thereafter must mean that they have been largely exhausted in the islands, and that the fields have now yielded the hoards that were originally deposited in them. There are no areas of major significance in the islands that have not been brought under cultivation. Woods, for instance, cover only 11% of the land area in present-day Denmark and this percentage was even smaller earlier, so that there cannot be may finds left there. There is hardly any open ground which has not been cultivated or dug up in some other way during the last few centuries, e.g. in connection with construction work.

Jutland: Heath reclamation proceeded in an unsystematic fashion until the Danish Heath Society was established in 1866, which explains the fluctuations in the find curve. Between 1835-55 there was obviously some reclamation, after which the curve declined over the next decade. Following the establishment of the Heath Society it suddenly reached a maximum in the decade 1865-74. The decline of the curve after 1895 was due to two factors: partly that a major part of the hoards deposited had presumably been discovered during heath reclamation in the 19th century, partly that there was a falling off in reclamation between 1896 and 1920. After the new land legislation in 1919 and the consequent resumption of heath reclamation the number of field finds rose slightly – from 1945-55 probably because of deep ploughing. Field finds in Jutland have not yet ceased, but seem to be on the point of doing so. The remaining heath area is not large, and there cannot be many finds left. As for woodlands, the situation is the same as in the islands. In the areas under cultivation agricultural activities proceed as before, so that it is not a diminution of these which has caused a decline in finds. It must be simply an actual reduction in the hoards remaining.[9]

Hoards from wet fields/water meadow/former bog

These hoards have been grouped together because they are all likely to originate from areas which used to be bog/lake or wet depressions in fields. As find details are often fairly incomplete, we have had to make our own assessment as to type of environment. Thus all finds made while ditching have been assigned to the hoard group in question. While some finds from this category may have been registered under field finds, a few field finds may have been included in this group. We shall disregard this possibility, since the likelihood is that such small overlaps counter-balance each other.

A comparison of the histograms of the different regional groups (fig. 9) shows that those of the islands are fairly similar, while the graph for Jutland is rather different. Bornholm has supplied only one find from drained land, appearing in 1869. The maximum finds were made in the islands between 1845 and 1875/85, the peak being reached between 1865 and 1875 if we disregard later additions to previously found hoards. There were a few finds around the turn of the century and after that a few finds scattered through this century. In Jutland, however, a peak was reached as early as 1855-65, while the greatest concentration of hoards was in the decades

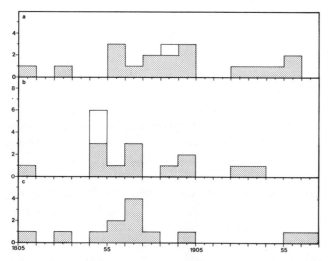

Fig. 9. Regional distribution of year of registration for hoards found in former bogs. a: Jutland, b: Funen with islands, c: Zealand. (Signatures – cf. fig. 1).

between 1875 and 1905 with a second peak between 1895 and 1905. There was a gap between 1905 and 1925, and then a resumption of finds ending in 1955/65. The regional distribution of hoards found on wet land thus shows a delayed maximum in Jutland as compared to the islands.

This late maximum is in complete accord with the tempo of drainage in Jutland (cf. Kr. Kristiansen's chapter on economic developments). Drainage happened considerably later in Jutland than in the islands. In this respect the period 1861-81 was particularly significant in the islands (and East Jutland), as is reflected in the diagrams of fig. 9. After 1881 drainage still increased in North and West Jutland, but decreased elsewhere. It is this continued draining activity which is reflected in the high point of the diagram representing Jutland's hoards from former bogs, while the corresponding diagrams of the islands show falling curves at this time.

Figure 12 contains an account of hoards found during agricultural work carried out manually or with the use of machinery. Hoards found during manual work include those resulting from ditching and draining, i.e. activities connected with the drainage of swamps. Hoards found while using machinery include those resulting from ploughing and harrowing. Most finds from wet fields/water meadow/former bog have resulted from the manual activities. Their discovery is due to the extensive drainage work which took place especially in the 19th century, whereas hoards found while using machinery reflect the subsequent cultivation of the areas.

After the fall in drainage activities, which began around the turn of the century and is reflected in all diagrams, they were resumed in the 1920's, particularly in Jutland, following new government directives. This is in accordance with the pattern shown in the graphs, in that finds from Funen and Jutland begin again around 1925 – mainly in Jutland – after a complete stop between 1905 and 1925. However, there is nothing like the same number of finds from drained land in this period as in the 19th century, despite the fact that there was most land drained in Funen and Jutland after 1920 (cf. Kr. Kristiansen's chapter on economic developments, table 6). This must be because the large-scale drainage work after 1920 concentrated on areas already under cultivation, from which many new finds obviously could not be expected.

The two finds from Zealand between 1955 and 1975 reflect the greatest drainage work in Zealand during the 20th century, which occurred in this very period.

Our examination of hoards from drained areas has shown that their discovery is closely related to socioeconomic factors. Although there was an extension of drainage activities in the 20th century, few new finds were made, and the areas must be assumed to have yielded their hoards.[10]

Bog finds

Figure 10 shows regional diagrams indicating year of registration for single finds of bronze objects (b) and other hoards (a). Bornholm has supplied only one bog hoard, found in 1866 and containing bronze and iron objects. From Funen there are two finds in category b: one discovered between 1885 and 1895, and one between 1945 and 1955. In category a there are two hoards found between 1845 and 1855 and one find addition from the same decade. There are two bronze hoards from Zealand bogs from the period 1875-85. These groups with few finds have not been represented in diagrams.

Gold/silver bog finds: The number of bog finds is very small in Funen and Zealand, and not significantly larger in Jutland when we consider the size of Jutland in relation to the islands. But despite the scarcity of finds we

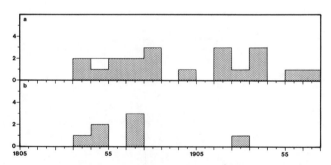

Fig. 10a. Regional distribution of year of registration for gold/silver hoards found in bogs. a: Jutland, b: Zealand. (Signatures – cf. fig. 1).

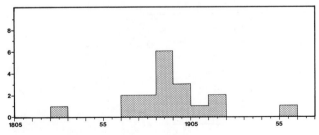

Fig. 10b. Year of registration for bronze hoards from bogs in Jutland. (Signatures – cf. fig. 1).

	a	b	Σ
ZEALAND	17	15	32
BORNHOLM	9	14	23
FUNEN WITH ISLANDS	21	30	51
JUTLAND	20	41	61
total	67	100	167

Fig. 11. Regional distribution of hoards found during agricultural work: a) manual, b) using machinery.

	a	b	Σ
ZEALAND	10	1	11
BORNHOLM	1	0	1
FUNEN WITH ISLANDS	6	6	12
JUTLAND	7	7	14
total	24	14	38

Fig. 12. Regional distribution of hoards found during agricultural activities on wet land/water meadow/former bog: a) manually, b) using machinery.

notice that gold/silver hoards in Zeeland were found in the second and third quarter of the 19th century; the two hoards from Funen appeared between 1845 and 1855, while the find curve for Jutland is divided into two peaks: one starting around 1835 and ending in 1885 with the highest point between 1875 and 1885; another between 1915 and 1945 with peaks in 1915-25 and 1935-45.

If we compare these histograms of gold/silver hoards with the information we have concerning the develop-

ment of peat-cutting, it appears that the Jutland find curve in particular corresponds with this development.

Jutland: The production of bog peat only really began as heath reclamation proceeded during the 19th century because in former times heath peat had been the major source of fuel. This steady encroachment on bogs for peat-cutting is clearly reflected in the first peak of the curve for Jutland. The near absence of finds between 1885 and 1915 coincides with the almost complete sub-

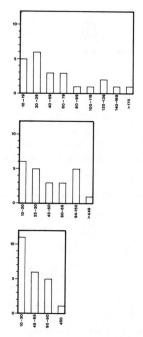

Fig. 13. Find depths of field hoards.

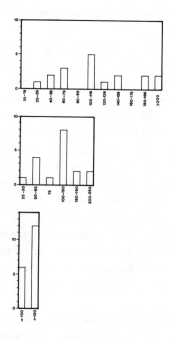

Fig. 14. Find depths of bog hoards.

stitution of peat for coal and coke as a source of energy. The other peak in Jutland also coincides with the immense increase in peat-cutting during the Second World War as a result of the halt in fuel imports. After the War peat-cutting diminished again and gradually ceased almost entirely. The question now is whether the hoards deposited in Jutland are nearly depleted, i.e. the bogs contain no more finds, or whether the reduction in finds is due only to the stop in peat-cutting.

Considering the immense increase in peat-cutting during World Wars I & II, the resulting quantity of finds is not large (Det Statistiske Departement 1959, table 10). It is no larger than during the period 1875-85 in spite of a considerably greater exploitation of peat reserves (c. 9 and 19 times greater – calculated on the basis of figures in the Statistical Dept. 1959 and Humlum 1943 with an estimated national production during this decade of 1,000,000 metric tons; Jutland's share of this is estimated at 75%). Although it must be assumed that several hoards have been lost because of the increasing mechanization of peat production (Andersen and Woel 1940, 12 ff; Humlum 1943, 24 ff.), the total number of finds from the war periods does not equal that of 1875-85 when the extent of peat production is taken into consideration. We must therefore conclude that despite the graphic impression of a culmination during the world wars there was in fact a significant proportional decline in finds. This is also true even though it gradually became possible to penetrate deeper levels in the bogs because of improved drainage and mechanized peat-cutting, so that also the deepest finds were recovered.

As peat-cutting in Jutland only started in earnest after 1850 and as drainage also began only in the 19th century, it is unlikely that many gold/silver finds from Jutland bogs will have been lost because of failure to appreciate their value; on the other hand a few finds may have been lost because of the increasing use of machinery in peat-cutting. In view of the above it is reasonable to assume that few gold/silver hoards remain in Jutland's bogs.

The Islands: In Zealand peat production played a major role quite early, according to Kr. Kristiansen (1974, 140), since peasants from many parts of the island supplied a steadily increasing amount of peat to be used for fuel in Copenhagen during the 18th and 19th centuries. This early production explains why the bog finds remaining after peat-cutting in the 18th century reach their maximum already between 1835 and 1875. As Kr. Kristiansen has suggested, it is probable that Iron Age

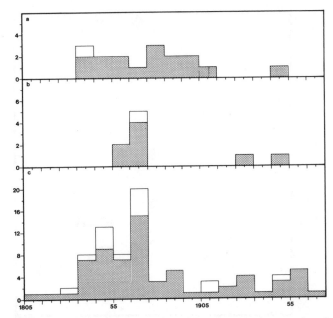

Fig. 15a. Year of registration for field hoards, according to type of activity: a) gravel-digging, b) construction work, c) manual field work. (Signatures – cf. fig. 1)

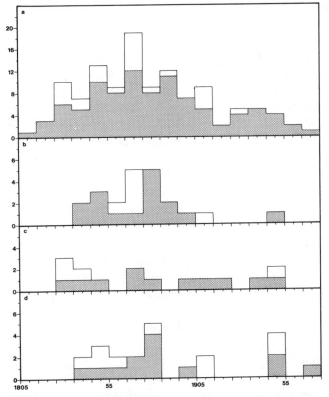

Fig. 15b. Year of registration for field hoards, according to type of activity: a) ploughing/harrowing, b) probably ploughed up from original deposit and found later during other work, c) unspecified agricultural work, d) other activities. (Signatures – cf. fig. 1)

184

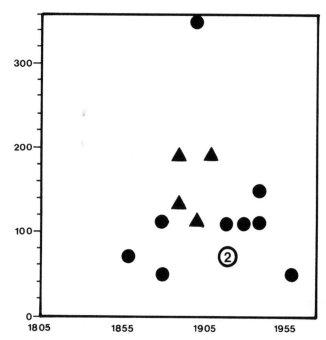

Fig. 16. Year of registration for finds from bogs in Jutland (x-axis) related to find depths (y-axis): ● = gold/silver, ▲ = bronze.

hoards have been lost as a result of the early peat exploitation as they must have been deposited at a higher level than Bronze Age hoards, whose find layers were probably exploited only in the 19th century. Gold/silver finds from Zealand bogs show the same tendency as hoards from drained areas, in that there are few finds after 1875. Considering the extent of land drained in Zealand (except South Zealand and Møn) – by 1972 c. 72% of the agricultural area – and considering the large-scale peat-cutting during the world wars – up to 40% of the total peat production took place in Zealand during the Second World War – it must be assumed that there are very few hoards left in Zealand bogs.

In Funen peat-cutting must also have intensified during the 19th century after wood reserves were exhausted and before coal was imported. Production must have started earlier than in Jutland because of the lack of heath peat. On the other hand the exploitation was hardly as great as in Zealand as the population was smaller. This may explain the near absence of finds during peat-cutting in Funen, whereas drainage has produced several finds. It should also be noted that East Funen and South West Lolland had few swampy areas. Although Funen must be somewhat under-represented

as regards gold/silver bog finds because peat-cutting probably happened early, the island undoubtedly shows a higher degree of representativity than Zealand, since bogs were less heavily exploited in the 18th century than was the case in Zealand. By 1972 81% had been drained of the total agricultural area in Lolland-Falster, Møn and South Zealand, and 55% in Funen, while peat production still remained at 5-6% of the national total in 1942. The fact that no gold/silver finds have been made during peat-cutting after 1855 in Funen and the other islands, while finds from drained areas have also come to a halt, can only mean that the finds have been exhausted.

Bornholm has not seen much peat-cutting; yet by 1972 an area had been drained corresponding to 58% of the island's total agricultural land. There has only been one find from drained land and one bog find, which would suggest that in Bornholm the deposition of hoards in bogs was not very common during the Early Germanic Period.

Bronze finds in bogs: If we compare the diagrams of gold/silver hoards from bogs (fig. 10 a) with those for bronze finds (fig. 10 b), we observe a remarkable difference: the course of the curves for bronze finds is clearly delayed and therefore rather different from the curves for hoards containing precious metals. Thus bronze finds from Zealand occur between 1875 and 1885, those from Funen between 1885 and 1895 and again between 1945 and 1955, while those from Jutland occur especially from 1865 till 1925, culminating between 1885 and 1895. There may be several reasons for this: 1. bronze finds generally lie deeper than the earliest finds of gold; 2. because of the unimpressiveness of the bronzes – usually single finds of cruciform, more or less eroded, fibulae – people did not notice and collect them, despite the *"danefæ"* legislation and the early storage of antiquities in museums, until the knowledge of archaeology became more widespread during the 19th century; 3. their distribution was so limited that they did not appear continuously, but only when peat was being cut in the very areas where bronzes had been deposited.

To illustrate the question of the depth of deposition, the depths of hoards from bogs are shown in fig. 14. It will be seen that there are twice as many finds from depths greater than 99 cm as from depths between 10 and 99 cm. However, when hoards are separated into gold/silver and bronze it appears that six hoards of the former category have been found at a depth less than 100 cm and eight hoards at a greater depth – i.e. no signifi-

A

DEPTH	BEFORE 1885	AFTER 1885
0 - 99	2	3
> 99	1	5

B

DEPTH	BEFORE 1885	AFTER 1885
0 99	0	0
> 99	0	4

Fig. 17. Relative distribution of shallow and deep finds from bogs in Jutland discovered before and after 1885: A) gold/silver, B) bronze.

cant difference – whereas the four find depths for bronze are all greater than 99 cm.

A study of Late Bronze Age hoards seems to demonstrate that the depth of deposition in bogs was generally lower in the islands than in Jutland (Kr. Kristiansen 1974, 141). It is a reasonable assumption that the same applies to Early Germanic hoards as they must necessarily have been deposited above the Bronze Age hoards due to the accumulation of peat. The following part of our analysis will therefore be made on a regional basis:

Jutland: Figure 16 shows the two-dimensional distribution of find depths for Jutland's hoards in relation to their year of registration. The four bronze finds with indication of depth are all from Jutland and were discovered after 1884, while the gold/silver finds include both deep and shallow finds before and after 1884 (fig. 17). All things considered the deepest hoards are unquestionably the more numerous after 1884. Even though information on find depths before 1885 is available for only three gold/silver hoards, of which two were found at less than 100 cm – we are thus dealing with very small figures on which to base anything – it is not unreasonable to think that the hoards found high up in the peat would appear first, once peat-cutting got under way in Jutland in the 19th century. This does not, however, support an assumption about a general, deep deposition of bronze hoards, since bronze hoards have in fact been discovered before 1885. Even if bronze finds may have been deposited about 100 years earlier than most gold finds, the accumulation of peat cannot have been so great in those years as to explain a possible difference in the deposition depths of gold and bronze finds. Besides, there are also some deep gold finds, which makes it improbable that only bronze hoards should be deeply imbedded while gold/silver is found at different depths. Consequently, the absence of bronze finds from Jutland during the first half of the 19th century probably means that they have been lost. The apparently deep level of deposition for bronze

hoards is thus fictitious and is caused by the loss of shallow hoards. This means that the first hypothesis is unlikely, whereas the second seems to be verified as far as Jutland's finds are concerned. The third hypothesis may be one of the reasons why bronze hoards largely ceased after 1925, whereas gold/silver hoards from bogs continued to appear. Another contributory factor may be that gold glitters more and is probably easier to detect than bronze, and that the gold objects are often bigger. When peat production became more mechanized, gold objects were therefore more easily spotted.

The Islands: As already mentioned hoards were probably lower deposited in the islands than in Jutland, and the bog finds nearest the surface were probably dug up before the 19th century in Zealand. Though deep finds were not prevalent in Zealand, the one gold find we have with an indication of depth – found in 1849 at a depth of 3 metres – shows that they did exist. The fact that bronze hoards were found only after the middle of the 19th century in the islands is best explained by the growing awareness among the population of the antiquarian value of these objects. For this reason relatively more bronze than gold/silver hoards must have been lost also in the islands.[11] As with gold/silver finds from bogs, we must suppose that practically all bronze hoards deposited in the islands have appeared.

Our discussion of finds from bogs, former bogs and water meadows has shown that the number of hoards deposited in these areas was small compared to the number of hoards from fields. Jutland's gold/silver hoards must be regarded as fully representative and even if we add estimated number of lacking bronze hoards, the final figure is still well below that for field finds. Apart from the fact that the number of hoards deposited in swampy soil is relatively modest, the distribution in Jutland, particularly of bronze hoards within this find group, is limited to certain areas, above all North and West Jutland. Furthermore, bog finds from the islands must in

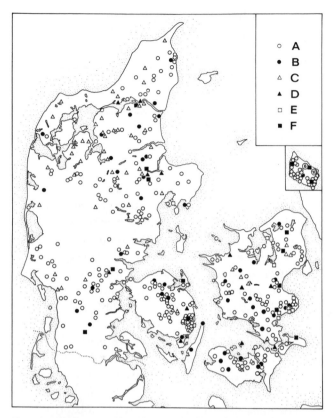

Fig. 18. Distribution of hoards according to environment: A) field, B) former bog/wet land, C) bog, D) river, sea, E) beach, F) unspecified environment.

general be regarded as under-represented in relation to those from Jutland.

Having analysed bog hoards in full, we must oppose Geisslinger's claim that numerous hoards may still be expected from Danish bogs (Geisslinger 1967, 24 ff). On the contrary, peat soil must now be regarded as almost depleted of Early Germanic hoards.

During our discussion of hoards according to type of environment we have noted their inter-relation with socio-economic factors and have also mentioned which groups are depleted, which groups may still be expected to yield finds, and which groups are under-represented. Before we proceed to a conclusion, it is necessary to analyse the possible connection between the find picture and the presence of people with a special knowledge of antiquities. Moreover the representativity of hoards will be assessed in relation to hoard finds from the Late Bronze Age.

B. The possible regional dependence of find frequency on the presence of people with a special knowledge of antiquities

It might be supposed that as long as there was no widespread appreciation of the value of archaeological remains, their recovery would depend on the presence around the country of people with a special knowledge of antiquities. It has already been argued, however, that at least part of the gold hoards were submitted at an early stage due to the *"danefæ"* legislation. Furthermore, we can illustrate this question by looking at the find distribution of Early Germanic hoards (fig. 18). There are clusters of finds particularly in East Funen and in Bornholm. As it happens, at one time these regions did have people with an active interest in archaeology. For instance, it was the Court Chamberlain Sehested of Broholm who prevented the great Broholm gold treasure from being scattered to the four winds when it was ploughed up in 1833; and in Bornholm the Prefect Vedel and later the Schoolmaster Jørgensen from Ibsker helped to ensure that some finds were submitted between 1866 and the turn of the century. The question is however whether similar people were not equally active in other parts of the country, perhaps at other times. In fact, all the early finds were submitted via public officers, while later on teachers etc. took over this function (as in Bornholm). It is an open question whether these other people's contributions did not balance those of Sehested and Vedel.

If regional find curves had been decisively influenced by certain people, we should expect there to be regional fluctuations not explicable by reference to socio-economic factors. This is not the case. We have examined the relative distribution of field finds in the counties of Svendborg and Odense, since economic activities in these counties were probably similar during the period when Sehested was particularly active in Svendborg county (it seems unlikely that he should have supervised the appearance of all hoards throughout Funen)[12]. During the years 1825-84, i.e. the period when Sehested might have influenced the find frequency, the ratio between the two counties' field finds is as follows: Svendborg 63.63% – Odense 36.36%. During a subsequent period of corresponding length the ratio is: 60% – 40%. Thus there is only a slight dominance of finds in Svendborg county during the period 1825-84 in relation to Odense county and in relation to the two counties' share of field finds in Funen during the subsequent period.

On the basis of this analysis we must conclude that the distribution shown by the find map is not very dependent on particularly active people.

C. *The relationship between Early Germanic and Late Bronze Age hoards as regards their level of representativity*

The purpose of the following analysis is to examine whether the survival of finds has been influenced by the fact that Early Germanic hoards (gold) are intrinsically more valuable than Late Bronze Age hoards (bronze). As already mentioned the major part of Early Germanic bronze hoards – bog finds from Jutland – were not discovered till late in the 19th century. In order to be in a position to examine and compare groups found under similar conditions applying from around the year 1800, we have chosen to compare Early Germanic gold hoards with bronze hoards from the Late Bronze Age.

We have already ascertained that Early Germanic field hoards are found fairly high up in the ground, as is the case with Late Bronze Age hoards (Kristiansen 1974, fig. 9). However, hoards deposited in bogs differ from this pattern in that Iron Age finds were probably deposited at a higher level than Bronze Age finds. An analysis of the level of representativity of the two periods can therefore be limited to finds from fields. As for bog finds, it is immediately apparent that Bronze Age hoards must be more representative than Iron Age hoards in Zealand and Funen.

As Kr. Kristiansen's diagrams for Late Bronze Age field finds contain hoards found on wet land, we have had to include them in our analysis. Furthermore, Kristiansen has grouped Lolland-Falster with Zealand, and we have had to do likewise.

The visual impression one gets by comparing find frequencies from the Early Germanic Period (fig. 19) with the Late Bronze Age (Kristiansen 1974, fig. 5) is that in the case of Funen and Zealand the curves start rising later for Late Bronze Age hoards than they do for Early Germanic ones. As far as Jutland is concerned, the number of Bronze Age hoards seems on the whole to lag behind during the 19th century without the distinct peak seen for the Early Germanic Period.

Figure 20 shows in percentages the number of field finds per decade, as well as the aggregate number in percentages. This diagram indicates that our conclusions based on visual impressions are fairly accurate. It also emphasizes some points which were not immediately

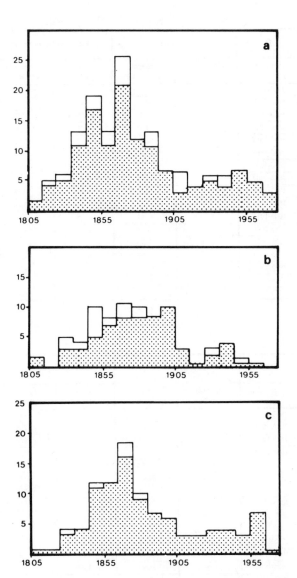

Fig. 19. Regional distribution of year of registration for hoards found in dry and wet fields. a: Jutland, b: Funen, c: Zealand and Lolland-Falster. (Signatures – cf. fig.1).

apparent from the graphs. For example, while it is true that to begin with Funen shows a greater increase in Early Germanic hoards than in Late Bronze Age ones, the aggregate figure for the latter period begins to catch up with that for the Early Germanic Period already around 1835. They meet around 1855 and then develop along the same lines. In Zealand the aggregate number of Late Bronze Age hoards is greater during the first twenty years (however, the figures are too small to carry much significance); then Early Germanic hoards are in the lead almost until the end of the 19th century. In

a	Late Bronze Age		Early Germanic Period	
Interval	Number in %	Aggregate number in %	Number in %	Aggregate number in %
1805-1814	0	0	1,30	1,30
1815-1824	0	0	3,25	4,55
1825-1834	2,27	2,27	3,90	8,45
1835-1844	11,36	13,63	8,44	16,89
1845-1854	9,09	22,72	12,34	29,23
1855-1864	9,09	31,81	8,44	37,67
1865-1874	6,82	38,63	16,88	54,55
1875-1884	2,27	40,90	7,79	62,34
1885-1894	11,36	52,26	8,44	70,78
1895-1904	11,36	63,62	4,55	75,33
1905-1914	6,82	70,44	4,55	79,88
1915-1924	4,55	74,99	2,60	82,48
1925-1934	11,36	86,35	3,90	86,38
1935-1944	2,27	88,62	3,90	90,28
1945-1954	6,82	95,44	4,55	94,83
1955-1964	4,55	99,99	3,25	98,08
1965-1974	0	99,99	1,95	100,03

b	Late Bronze Age		Early Germanic Period	
Interval	Number in %	Aggregate number in %	Number in %	Aggregate number in %
1805-1814	0	0	2,44	2,44
1815-1824	2,13	2,13	0	2,44
1825-1834	4,26	6,39	6,10	8,54
1835-1844	8,51	14,90	4,87	13,41
1845-1854	4,26	19,16	12,20	25,61
1855-1864	19,15	38,31	9,76	35,37
1865-1874	6,38	44,69	13,41	48,78
1875-1884	19,15	63,84	12,20	60,98
1885-1894	4,26	68,10	9,76	70,74
1895-1904	8,51	76,61	12,20	82,94
1905-1914	6,38	82,99	3,66	86,60
1915-1924	2,13	85,12	1,22	87,82
1925-1934	6,38	91,50	3,66	91,48
1935-1944	4,26	95,76	4,87	96,35
1945-1954	0	95,76	2,44	98,79
1955-1964	4,26	100,02	1,22	100,01
1965-1974	0	100,02	0	100,01

c	Late Bronze Age		Early Germanic Period	
Interval	Number in %	Aggregate number in %	Number in %	Aggregate number in %
1805-1814	2,22	2,22	1,0	1,0
1815-1824	2,22	4,44	1,0	2,0
1825-1834	2,22	6,66	4,0	6,0
1835-1844	2,22	8,88	4,0	10,0
1845-1854	4,44	13,32	12,0	24,0
1855-1864	11,11	24,43	12,0	35,0
1865-1874	20,00	44,43	18,0	54,0
1875-1884	11,11	55,54	10,0	64,0
1885-1894	8,89	64,43	7,0	71,0
1895-1904	11,11	75,54	6,0	77,0
1905-1914	4,44	79,98	3,0	80,0
1915-1924	4,44	84,42	3,0	83,0
1925-1934	6,67	91,09	4,0	87,0
1935-1944	4,44	95,53	4,0	91,0
1945-1954	2,22	97,75	3,0	94,0
1955-1964	2,22	99,97	7,0	99,0
1965-1974	0	99,97	1,0	100,0

Fig. 20. Regional distribution of year of registration for hoards found in dry and wet fields. Number of hoards and aggregate number in percentages. a: Jutland, b: Funen, c: Zealand and Lolland-Falster.

Jutland the aggregate number of Late Bronze Age hoards only catches up with that of Early Germanic hoards around 1925. There is thus a general shift in the curves and their maximum between Early Germanic and Late Bronze Age as well as a regional shift.

One explanation of the *regional difference* between the curves is that hoards from wet field/former bog are included in the diagrams. Finds from wet land appeared primarily as a result of drainage work, which was first intensified in the islands (after 1850) and later in Jutland (especially after 1900). The reason why Bronze Age hoards catch up with hoards from the Germanic Period before the turn of the century in the islands, but only after the turn of the century in Jutland, may be because considerably more Bronze Age hoards were deposited in wet land than in dry (a historically conditioned situation). The conditions for expecting a parallel development in find frequencies for Bronze Age and Germanic hoards existed until drainage was intensified; subsequently there was a faster increase in the discovery of Bronze Age hoards. The "lead" until this time of hoards from the Germanic Period probably reflects a more *general situation*, viz. that more gold than bronze finds survived at the beginning of the 19th century, when the appreciation of the archaeological value of antiquities was limited. This consideration was also relevant in connection with Early Germanic bronze hoards.

This explanation fits the cases of Jutland and Zealand and the earliest finds from Funen. However, in Funen Bronze Age hoards caught up with Early Germanic hoards at an early stage. This may be because certain people with a knowledge of antiquities did influence the recovery of bronze hoards there. This also means that Early Germanic bronze hoards were not common in Funen, for in that case they would have been found.[13]

CONCLUSION

The increase in the number of hoards registered after 1805 is closely related to the intensification of land cultivation, peat-cutting, and construction works in the 19th century, and to the foundation of the National Museum and the Commission for Antiquities, combined with a growing popular awareness of the value of archaeological remains. The fall in all find curves during the 20th century to about zero today would seem to indicate that the hoards deposited have been depleted. The fields yield hardly any more finds despite continuing agricultural and construction work. As for bogs, we have seen that the immense production of peat during the world wars did not increase the find frequency to the level of former times with a lower peat production.

The degree of representativity for hoards varies somewhat on a regional basis from one type of environment to another. Finds from dry land seem to be fully representative. Though some gold hoards may be missing from the old fields, these areas are not noticeably under-represented in comparison with areas newly brought into cultivation. Firstly, some gold has probably also disappeared from the new areas which were cultivated first. Secondly, the swing plough was in common use only from the 1840's, so it was not until this time that farm machinery penetrated to a depth where hoards were presumably most numerous. Thirdly, it may be pointed out that even if the old cultivated areas may be somewhat under-represented this has not significantly influenced the total number of finds. The distribution map (fig. 19) indicates that e.g. Svendborg and Præstø counties, which are old agricultural areas, have produced a great many finds, while counties like Ribe and Ringkøbing in Jutland, which have had the greatest augmentation of cultivated land over the past century, have not produced as many hoards.

Our examination of hoards from bogs and former bogs/wet fields showed that before 1805 some shallow finds have probably been lost during peat-cutting in Zealand and Funen. In addition bronze hoards were in general under-represented until the second half of the 19th century. Gold/silver hoards from Jutland must be regarded as representative on account of the late start of peat production – except perhaps for finds that may have been lost where production was most highly mechanized. They show that deposition was far less common in bogs than in fields during the Early Germanic Period.

Eliza Fonnesbech – Sandberg,
Søllerød Kommunes Museum,
Søllerødvej 25,
2840 Holte.

Acknowledgements

I wish to thank Departments 1 and 6 of the National Museum for permission to examine the material and for their kind assistance in removing finds from exhibition.

I am grateful to Bjarne N. Mortensen of the Niels Bohr Institute, for his help in processing the data.

NOTES

1. Finds have been registered according to parish of discovery, i.e. finds which are located only as to county, district or region are not included here. In general, objects have been excluded from our analysis if there is no information on find category or type of environment. This applies e.g. to some cruciform fibulae which are as likely to originate from a grave as from a hoard. However, objects lacking information on find context which are assumed to belong to hoards (because they have often been found in hoards but not in graves or settlements) are included among hoard finds. Bracteates and solidi are cases in point. Objects not registered but with information which enables us to infer that they must come from a hoard are analysed accordingly. This is the case, for instance, with objects from bogs.

2. Geisslinger has previously analysed the representativity of hoards (Geisslinger 1967, 20 ff), but the following analysis differs from his in some significant respects. Firstly, Geisslinger's examination comp.ises all hoard finds from the Germanic Period, whereas ours is confined to Early Germanic hoards. One consequence of this is that the material under investigation is particularly rich in gold objects while Geisslinger's catalogue contains quite a number of hoards with bronze objects on account of the extensive use of this metal in the Late Germanic Period. This distinction between gold/silver and bronze is, as we shall see later, fairly important. Secondly, in Geisslinger's histograms of the year of registration for hoards he has used 25-year intervals. This however obscures the possibly close connection between find intensity and socio-economic factors. We have therefore used 10-year intervals.

   It should be added that for this source-critical examination we have undertaken a complete definition and dating of Early Germanic hoard material. Thus Geisslinger's dates have not been used.

3. Rewards for finds had been paid before – e.g. for the gold horns.

4. The Commission for Antiquities was directed to propose "how the common people could best be instructed about the value of antiquities regularly dug out of the earth, which are usually destroyed because nobody realizes their potential use." (Werlauff 1808, 23 ff).

5. In most cases there is coincidence of year of discovery and year of registration, i.e. the year the find was made and the year it was registered in the museum. Where bronze finds from private collec-

tions are involved there may be a difference of several years between the discovery of the find and its incorporation into the museum collection. However, there are only a few cases where year of discovery is lacking for bronzes from private collections – those of King Frederic VII and the veterinary Thomsen. Such finds therefore have little influence on the graphs.

6. There are no hoards from lakes.

7. The distinction between finds from dry fields and finds from wet fields has been made because most hoards from wet fields come from places that were formerly a bog or possibly a lake; with regard to environment representativity they should therefore be classified as bog finds rather than field finds. The reason this has not been done is because the economic activities that led to their discovery are not the same for bog finds as for finds from wet land/water meadow/former bog; and one of the objects of our analysis is to investigate the influence of such economic factors.

8. As far as field finds are concerned we cannot rule out the possibility that some of the single finds which are of a type that may belong to either the Late Roman or the Early Germanic Period may come from unrecognized graves on level ground. Most of the objects in question are spiral rings the size of finger rings. When these hoards were separated from the rest, it appeared however that the graphs for the two groups developed fairly similarly. This is obviously because grave finds which are found at the same depth as hoards are as likely to be ploughed up as objects from hoards. Even though the diagrams may thus include some objects from graves, the graphs are affected in absolute but hardly in relative terms.

9. The number of finds from dry land may be too high since we have included finds with no information on soil conditions other than "found in field", "found while ploughing" etc. If we compare the regional distribution of dry field finds (fig. 8), the course of the curves shows no marked difference. However, find frequencies for wet land do vary, which suggests that the curves for field finds are unlikely to be much affected by a possible intrusion of finds from wet land.

10. Out of 18 hoards resulting from drainage in Jutland only two contain bronze, while peat-cutting has produced 18 bronze hoards compared to 20 gold/silver hoards. This may be because bronze hoards have a limited distribution and are found mainly in areas which have experienced intensive peat-cutting in the 19th century, for which reason none was found during later drainage.

No find depth is given for hoards found in wet land as the soil (peat) collapses when drained, which makes depth indications unreliable. Furthermore, peat may also have been cut in an area which was subsequently drained, and this makes depth indications even more useless.

11. It is possible that bronzes were less common in the islands than in Jutland. For instance, among the fairly sparse grave finds there are somewhat more cruciform fibulae from Jutland than from the islands. Cruciform fibulae make up the greater part of bronze hoards.

12. It is not worthwhile comparing finds from other environments as their number is relatively small.

13. According to what has previously been stated the fact remains that this influence didn't concern the gold hoards and it didn't influence the find curves since the value of the gold was known to the public.

REFERENCES

ANDERSEN, C. H., WOEL, CAI M., 1940: *Om tørv.* Nyttebøger No. 7. København.

BREITENSTEIN, NIELS 1942: De romerske møntfund fra Gudme Herred. *Nordisk Numismatisk Årsskrift.*

– 1944: De romerske møntfund fra Bornholm. *Nordisk Numismatisk Årsskrift.*

GEISSLINGER, HELMUT 1967: Horte als Geschichtsquelle, dargestellt an den völkerwanderungs- und merowingerzeitlichen Funden des südwestlichen Ostseeraumes. *Offa-Bücher,* Band 19. Neumünster.

HERMANSEN, VICTOR 1954: Fortidsminder og Kuriositeter i Danmarks Middelalder. *Aarbøger for Nordisk Oldkyndighed og Historie.* København.

HINDENBURG, C. 1859: Bidrag til den danske Archæologis Historie. Særskilt Aftryk af *Dansk Maanedsskrift.* Ny Række, 1ste Bind, 2det og 3die Hefte. København.

HUMLUM, J. 1943: *Danmarks minedrift.* København.

KRISTIANSEN, KRISTIAN 1974: En kildekritisk analyse af depotfund fra Danmarks yngre Bronzealder (periode IV-V). *Årbøger for Nordisk Oldkyndighed og Historie.* København.

MALMER, MATS P. 1963: Metodproblem inom järnålderns konsthistoria. *Acta Archaeologica Lundensia.* Series in 8°. No. 3.

DET STATISTISKE DEPARTEMENT 1959: *Danmarks energiforsyning 1900-58.* Statistiske Undersøgelser 2.

WERLAUFF, E. C. 1807: *Udkast til den nordiske Archæologies Historie i vort Fædreland, indtil Ole Worms Tid.* Skandinaviske Litteratur-Selskabs Skrifter, 1ste Bind.

– 1808: *Bemærkninger i Anledning af den til de nordiske Oldsagers Samling og Opbevaring nedsatte Commission.* København.

WORSAAE, J. J. A. 1879: *On the Preservation of National Antiquities & Monuments in Denmark.* København.

Iron Age Settlements

by STEEN HVASS

INTRODUCTION

Iron Age settlements with their houses, farms and villages are one of the best known aspects of Danish prehistory. Iron Age houses are now also being reconstructed in many parts of the country so that those interested in social history can get an impression of living conditions in the Iron Age.

Iron Age settlements are characterized by their easily recognizable rubbish pits, often containing large quantities of pottery. These sites are by far the most frequently reported to Danish museums, and are also those first described in the archaeological literature, e.g. the middens at Broholm on Funen excavated by F. Sehested in the 1870's and published in 1878.

In 1906 Sophus Müller published 35 settlements from the Roman period. These finds had been largely investigated by officials from the National Museum between 1877 and 1905. The sites were found all over the country, but particularly in Jutland. The various types of sites were: midden deposits on a slope, clay pits used for rubbish, middens on the ground surface (cultural layer), midden deposits in natural depressions, small pits and hearths as well as hut floors and post holes. One of the finds from Brørup in Hjortlund parish, Ribe county, was excavated in 1877 and described as follows: "In an area c. 22 metres long and 5 metres wide were found twenty rounded depressions, some large, more than 2 metres wide, containing up to 300 potsherds, but most small, only 30-60 cm wide and with no or few potsherds. The depth of the former was 1.5 metres or more, of the latter 1 metre or slightly more." There can be no doubt that this refers to a complete Iron Age long house with roof post holes and some pits, although the actual house type was not clear to the excavator. This is the oldest excavated Iron Age house known to me from Denmark. In the same survey of Iron Age settlements was published a shell midden from Eltang bay near Kolding fiord, which, to the excavator's surprise, turned out to be Iron Age. The

same publication also described the two largest finds of bones from any Iron Age site, one from Borgbjerg on Sejerø with 20,000 bones, the other from Veileby on Lolland with more than 30,000 bones.

No later settlement find has surpassed this number of bones. In his publication Sophus Müller established the most common types of settlement, except that his hut sites were in fact houses.

In 1906 at Kraghede in southern Vendsyssel two Iron Age houses were identified for the first time, during the investigation of a large burial place (O. Klindt-Jensen 1949). In 1922 the excavation of a large Roman Iron Age settlement at Ginnerup in southern Thy, which contained several extremely well preserved long houses, was begun. Even when only a few long houses had been excavated, this site attracted considerable attention, both in Denmark and abroad (H. Kjær 1928). Since then the excavation of Iron Age houses has gathered momentum in Denmark (G. Hatt 1935, 1938, 1957, 1960; A. K. Rasmussen 1968; N. Thomsen 1959, 1964, 1965), and in recent decades whole villages have been revealed. However, 99% of the excavations have taken place in Jutland and in Himmerland. On the other hand, almost no houses have been excavated from eastern Jutland or from Funen, Zealand, or the other Danish islands.

STATISTICS

In order to examine the distribution of finds in Denmark the parish records of the National Museum were studied by the author in March and April 1978. These records cover the whole country and should contain reports of all registered finds in Denmark. Such a study will reveal when finds were registered. This is necessary to form an impression of the representativity of Danish find material, and how it can be used to assess Iron Age settlements in various parts of the country.

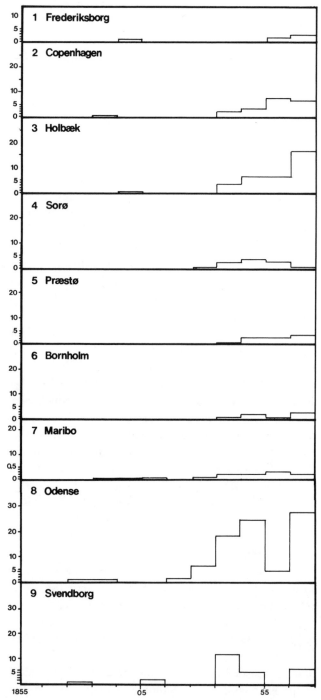

Fig. 1-9. Registration of Iron Age settlements in the counties from 1855-1975.

To begin with, we should be aware that not all known Iron Age settlements have been reported to the National Museum, but its parish records are so comprehensive and cover such a wide area that the picture they give should be representative of this type of site.

A total of 900 sites are registered in the parish records. These range from pits or cultural layers with Iron Age pottery, charcoal etc., cultural layers with houses (these only where there have been excavations) to surface collections. Finally, some sites are registered as settlements without further details.

In figs. 1-23 these sites are shown in bar graphs according to county and decade up to 1975. Finds registered after 1975 are not included.

The counties of eastern Denmark: Frederiksborg, Copenhagen, Holbæk, Sorø, Præstø, Bornholm and Maribo (figs. 1-7) show surprisingly little material, representing only 103 sites. Most finds are registered after 1935, and only in Holbæk county does registration increase until 1975. Otherwise, the figures show that the registration of Iron Age settlements in this area is uniformly small from 1935 to 1975 and is largely due to chance. In this large area of eastern Denmark there must be numerous Iron Age settlements that have not been registered.

The two counties in Funen, Svendborg and Odense, show a marked difference. In the county of Svendborg little material is registered, and that was mainly found between 1935 and 1955. There is a fairly large amount of material registered from Odense county: registrations were numerous between 1935 and 1955, and even more so between 1965 and 1975, with a further increase after this date. In the years 1935 to 1955 Erling Albrectsen was Assistant Curator at the Funen Stiftsmuseum and was particularly careful about registering all reported finds, visiting most sites in person. The registrations show, however, that settlements are clearly less numerous than burials (E. Albrectsen 1954, 1956, 1968). The finds registered between 1965 and 1975 (1978) are also due to major activity by the Funen Stiftsmuseum, including e.g. the organization of comprehensive site surveys.[1]

There is great variation in the registration of Iron Age settlements in the counties of Jutland. The oldest registrations go back as far as 1875 and stay at a fairly low level until 1925-35, after which finds increase. In the three counties of North Jutland, Ålborg, Thisted and Hjørring, registrations show a marked increase from 1955, and particularly from 1965.

In the counties of mid-Jutland, Randers, Viborg, Skanderborg and Ringkøbing, there is also an increase in registration from 1955 and particularly from 1965, but

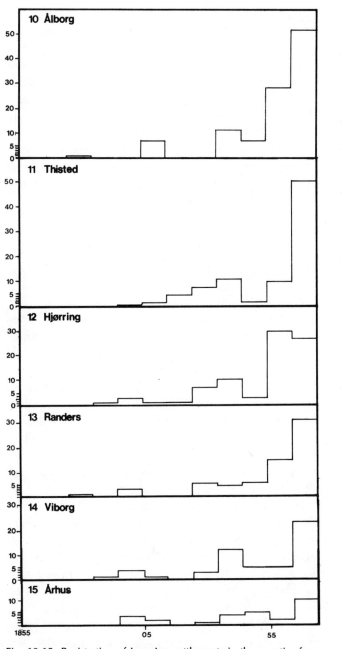

Fig. 10-15. Registration of Iron Age settlements in the counties from 1855-1975.

this is not nearly as marked as in the three northern counties. Århus county has a uniformly low registration, perhaps reflecting the small size of the county and the dense urbanization around the city of Århus. Vejle county shows a great increase in 1905-15 due to the survey work done by G. Sarauw during his local visits at this time.

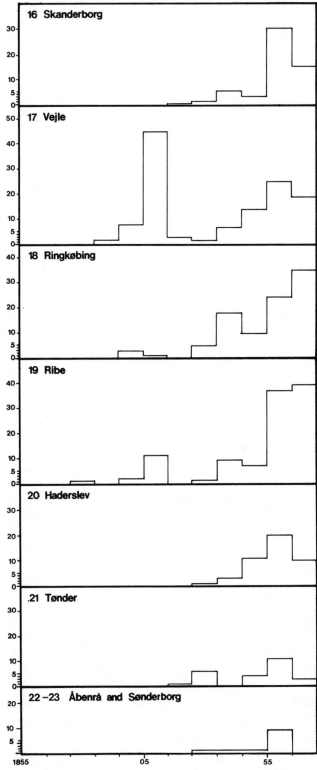

Fig. 16-23. Registration of Iron Age settlements in the counties from 1855-1975.

194

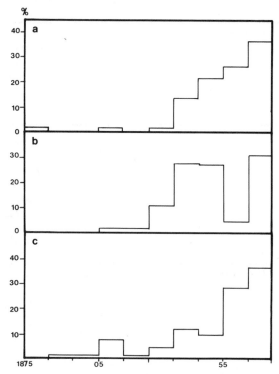

%

Fig. 24. Distribution of registered Iron Age settlements from 1855-1975 in percent. a: Zealand, Møn, Lolland-Falster and Bornholm; b: Funen and surrounding islands; c: Jutland.

Among the counties of South Jutland, Ribe, Haderslev, Tønder, Åbenrå and Sønderborg, there is considerable registration in Ribe county from 1955 to 1975. This is the result of the intensive search for Iron Age settlements especially around Esbjerg, where Esbjerg Museum has been very active. On the other hand, there has been surprisingly little registration in the rest of southern Jutland.

This division of registrations by decade according to county shows very clearly that where provincial museums employ professional archaeologists who take an interest in Iron Age settlements, there is a marked increase in registrations up to 1975, Odense county being a particularly good example. By contrast, in counties lacking professional archaeologists not many Iron Age settlements have been registered. In such counties there may be several Iron Age settlements still to be registered. The registration of Iron Age settlements in Denmark and our knowledge of their representativity is almost completely dependent on whether the various provincial museums employ professional archaeologists.

Figs. 24 a, b, c indicate the percentage of Iron Age settlements per decade on Zealand (including Møn, Lolland-Falster and Bornholm) (a), Funen (b) and Jutland (c). This shows clearly a general increase in the registration of Iron Age settlements up to 1975. Funen differs somewhat from the other regions, but this is because of the activity mentioned above by the Funen Stiftsmuseum between 1935 and 1955 concerning the Iron Age in Funen, which is reflected in fig. 24 b. Figs. 24 a, b, c show an increasing number of Iron Age settlements registered in Denmark up to 1975, and that this type of find is therefore far from exhausted, in that a large number of settlements are still to to be found.

REGISTRATION AND SETTLEMENT INDICATORS

During settlement excavations in recent decades it has become apparent that several new settlements are found near the habitation sites where excavations are carried out over several years (Becker 1966, 1968, 1971, 1972; S. Jensen 1976; S. Hvass 1977, 1979; G. Kossack *et al.* 1974). These areas registered in more detail give an impression of how many settlements from different Iron Age periods are to be found within small, clearly defined habitation areas and how closely they were situated. This must certainly be taken into account when considering areas in Denmark where only single, more scattered settlements have been registered (fig. 25).

Figure 26 shows the percentage of the different types of site: pits, cultural layers and houses, surface collections, and unspecified finds. This is shown for Zealand (including Møn, Lolland-Falster and Bornholm) (a), Funen (b), North Jutland (Hjørring, Thisted and Ålborg counties) (c), and the rest of Jutland (d). Nearly everywhere the most common sites are settlement pits with pottery, except in North Jutland, where cultural layers and house sites are most common. For Jutland as a whole the category of unspecified settlements constitutes a fairly large percentage of sites found, so this distribution in Jutland must be treated with some reservation.

Figure 25 indicates all the settlements registered in the National Museum parish records up to March-April 1978. This is almost the same material as used in figs. 1-23. It is clear from the map that settlement finds are strongly under-represented in Zealand, Møn, Lolland-Falster and Bornholm. Only when we come to Odense county does there seem to be a reasonable distribution of settlements, except in those areas which also lack grave finds. This is particularly true of Vissenbjerg, which seems to have been always forested and uninhabited.

In Jutland the registration of settlements varies somewhat from region to region. In Vendsyssel and Thy it probably reflects fairly accurately the original settlement pattern, just as the absence of settlements in the more sandy areas of mid-Jutland probably also reflects a sparser population. On the other hand, those areas in the rest of Jutland (Himmerland, East, West and South Jutland) with concentrations and relative absence of settlements no doubt show more active collecting in the former case, and in the latter the lack of archaeological effort in registering local Iron Age settlements.

Most of the sites are dated by pottery to the Early Iron Age. Some are described as Iron Age settlements, but in all cases they are assigned to the Iron Age on the basis of their pottery. If we consider this in the light of the excavated settlement material, where we know the quantity of pottery from the different periods, it appears that those with most pottery are the Late Pre-Roman and Early Roman Iron Age.

The sites in the parish records whose pottery is dated more precisely also belong mainly to the Late Pre-Roman/Early Roman Iron Age, from which period come most of the registered sites.

The settlements from the Early and Middle Pre-Roman Iron Age do not contain as much pottery as those a little later. Settlements from the Late Roman and Early Germanic Iron Age have only been identified in the few cases where proper excavations have been carried out, since the quantity of pottery is very small compared to the Early Roman Iron Age sites. These settlements are seldom found by means of surface collections, and the known habitation pits contain very little pottery. For example, in the excavation of the Late Roman / Early Germanic Iron Age settlement at Vorbasse (S. Hvass 1979) surface collections were carried out in the fields before excavation started without finding a single piece of pottery. However, under the topsoil in the same fields, excavation revealed numerous Late Roman/Early Germanic Iron Age houses.

In the same excavated settlement area the pits found also turned out to contain few potsherds. At any rate, pottery was so scarce that such sites will be identified only exceptionally, in the event of excavation occurring by chance in the same area, e.g. construction work etc., together with surveying. The same applies to the pre-

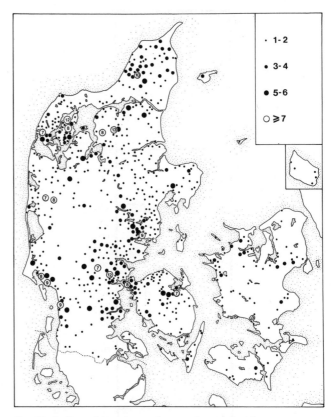

Fig. 25. Registered Iron Age settlements in each parish.

sence of settlements from the Late Germanic Iron Age and the Viking period.

We can conclude from this that our present knowledge of Danish Iron Age settlements is very inadequate. In some areas there has been only occasional registration, and in others the lack of professional archaeologists has meant that only a few sites have been registered, e.g. in Zealand, Lolland-Falster and Bornholm, where the number of burials shows clearly that there must be many Iron Age settlements yet to be registered (U. Lund Hansen 1976; L. Hedeager 1978). Furthermore, settlements from several periods are very difficult to recognize without excavation. Only in a few small, clearly defined areas has there been sufficient registration of settlements to give us a reasonable knowledge of their extent.

That many sites still remain to be found is shown by e.g. the occasional aerial photography carried out in Jutland (fig. 27). By this means 47 new settlements were found during an average of one week's aerial photography over Jutland each summer in the years 1966 to 1970, carried out by the English archaeologist, Dr. J. K. St. Joseph of Cambridge University.[2] Some of these aerial

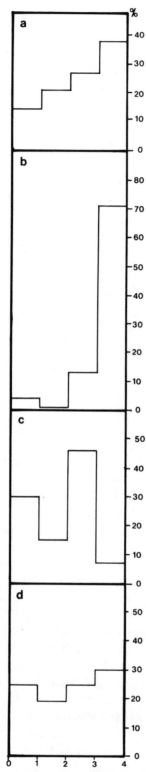

Fig. 26. Distribution af different find types in percent; 1: Finds without further information; 2: Surface collections; 3: Culture-layers and houses; 4: Pits. a: Zealand, b: Funen, c: Northern Jutland (Hjørring, Thisted and Ålborg counties), d: remaining Jutland.

photographs are so distinct that the plan of the whole village is clearly visible, e.g. at the eastern part of Limfjorden, where several houses can be distinguished in various sites (J. Lund 1976). The same is also true of the many clearly visible settlements discovered along the south-west coast of Jutland, where even the house type can be distinguished and where later excavations of two sites have shown that observations from aerial photographs are in complete accordance with the excavated house plans (E. Thorvildsen 1972; S. Hvass 1975). The aerial photographs of several of these south-west Jutland sites show that the house types belong to the end of the Late Roman/Early Germanic Iron Age, i.e. the very period from which settlements are very difficult to recognize from surface collections and occasional construction work.

Systematic aerial photographing of Jutland would provide a number of new Iron Age settlements and, what is of particular importance, would also be a means of discovering settlements from the Late Roman and Germanic Iron Age and Viking period so difficult to distinguish in surveys. However, it is obvious that aerial photography is particularly suited to Jutland, and especially West Jutland, because of the handier substratum and thinner topsoil which provide special growing conditions for cereals in very dry summers.

Another aspect of Iron Age settlement which can tell us how much of the total archaeological material has been registered and how much may remain to be registered, are field complexes. The basic work in this area was carried out by Gudmund Hatt and published in 1949, and recorded 116 field complexes in Jutland. Aerial photography has also been used in this field and a considerably larger number of field complexes has already been registered (N. R. Jeansson 1963; R. M. Newcomb 1971). In aerial photography covering the whole country (Basic Cover 1954), in which c. 80% of the photographs were taken between the 7th-12th May, and the 24th-29th May 1954, Major P. Harder Sørensen (1972-73) confirmed most of Hatt's 116 field complexes in Jutland and discovered up to 300 new ones. They range in size from traces of boundary walls or a small part of the sides of fields to large contiguous field complexes of more than 100 ha. A study of soil conditions shows that apparently only drifting sand and marsh lack traces of ancient fields. More comprehensive and specialized aerial photographs may reveal a considerable number of traces of old field boundary walls. A more detailed study of Vendsyssel (P.

Harder Sørensen 1972-73) has so far revealed more than 100 new field systems apart from those shown on the photographs of May 1954. The distribution of field complexes in Vendsyssel and the registration of Iron Age settlements show much the same pattern and supplement each other.

A study of the aerial photographs now available, together with any new ones, may increase quite considerably our knowledge of ancient field systems and the intensity of land use in the Iron Age. It is particularly important when studying settlements to remember that field complexes with boundary walls have so far been dated only to the Iron Age.

A detailed study with a view to registration of field complexes at Angel in South Schleswig has revealed several examples (summary in M. Müller-Wille 1965). The evidence from Angel suggests the possible number of field complexes still to be identified in the woods of East Jutland, Funen, Zealand, and Bornholm. Some have already been registered, e.g. in the Næsbyholm woods and the woods at Broby Vesterskov in mid-Zealand, and at Geelskov in North Zealand (V. Nielsen 1970).

CONCLUSION

The preceding study of the representativity of Iron Age settlements in Denmark shows very clearly that only a modest part of this material is known, and that a substantial number of sites remain to be found in the future. Only at a few sites have there been large contiguous area excavations with the aim of investigating a whole village community (Becker 1966, 1968, 1971; Hvass 1975, 1977; Lund 1976; Voss 1976). These largescale excavation projects have shown that only with complete area excavation is it possible to form a total picture of village communities. They have also shown that much additional information can be had which is not otherwise obtainable. It will be on the basis of such total excavation of village sites that the remaining scattered and fragmentary material from settlements must be assessed in future.

Modern industrial societies today make increasing spatial demands for urban development and road building (particularly the large motorway projects) and prehistoric sites are consequently destroyed on an unprecedented scale. The large Iron Age sites are particularly endangered because of their size and because they have not been registered.

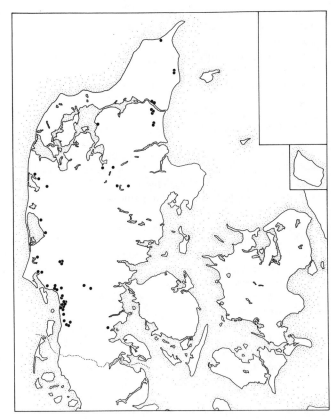

Fig. 27. Settlements with house plans recorded by aerial reconnaissance.

Steen Hvass,
Vejle Kulturhistoriske Museum,
Flegborg 18,
DK – 7100 Vejle

NOTES

1. Vejledning i arkæologisk recognosceringsteknik (: Guide to archaeological survey techniques), Fyns Stiftsmuseum 1977. Odense.
2. I wish to thank P. Kjærum, Curator of the Forhistorisk Museum, Moesgård, Århus, for permission to examine the aerial photographs.

   In fig. 27, three sites at Hodde were not found by Dr. J. K. St. Joseph of Cambridge, and two sites, Sjælborg near Esbjerg and Grønhedens Mark near Sæby, were known from earlier excavations of Iron Age houses.

REFERENCES

ALBRECTSEN, E. 1946: Fyns bebyggelse i den ældre jernalder. *Årbøger.*
ALBRECTSEN, E. *Fynske jernaldergrave:*

– 1954: Bind I. Førromersk jernalder.
– 1956: Bind II. Ældre romersk jernalder.
– 1968: Bind III. Yngre romersk jernalder.
– 1970: Den ældre jernalders bebyggelse på Fyn. *KUML*, 123 f.

BECKER, C. J. 1966: Ein früheisenzeitliches Dorf bei Grøntoft, Westjütland. *Acta Arch.* XXXVI, 209-222.

– 1968: Das zweite früheisenzeitliche Dorf bei Grøntoft, Westjütland. *Acta Arch.* XXXIX.

– 1971: Früheisenzeitliche Dörfer bei Grøntoft, Westjütland. *Acta Arch.* XLII.

– 1976: Bosættelsesformer i bronze- og jernalder, (H. Thrane ed. *Bebyggelsesarkæologi*). Skrifter fra Institut for Historie og Samfundsvidenskab no. 17. Odense.

FRIIS P., JENSEN, P. L. 1966: En jernalderhustomt med kælder på Grønhedens Mark. *KUML.*

HARDER SØRENSEN, P. 1972-73: Jysk Oldtidsagerbrug. Lokaliseret efter luftfotografering. *Kulturgeografi* 120, 337 ff.

HATT, G. 1935: Jernalderbopladsen ved Ginderup i Thy. *Nationalmuseets Arbejdsmark.*

– 1938: Jernalders bopladser i Himmerland. *Årbøger.*

– 1949: *Oldtidsagre.* Kgl. Dan. Vid. Sel. Ark. Kunst.

– 1957: *Nørre Fjand.* Arkæol. Kunsthist. Skr. Dan. Vid. Selskab 2. no. 2.

– 1958: A Dwelling Site of early Migration period at Oksbøl, Southwest Jutland. *Acta Arch.* XXIX.

– 1960: The Roman Iron Age Dwelling Site at Mariesminde Vestervig. *Acta Arch.* XXXI.

HEDEAGER, L. 1978: Bebyggelse, social struktur og politisk organisation i Østdanmarks ældre og yngre romertid. *Fortid og Nutid.* XXVII, 3.

HVASS, S. 1975: Das eisenzeitliche Dorf bei Hodde, Westjütland. *Acta Arch.* 46.

– 1977: Udgravningerne i Vorbasse. *Fra Ribe Amt.*

– 1979: Die völkerwanderungszeitliche Siedlung Vorbasse, Mittel-Jütland. *Acta Arch.* (I tryk)

– 1977: Jernalderlandsbyens udvikling i Hodde og Vorbasse. (H. Thrane ed.) *Kontinuitet og bebyggelse.* Skrifter fra Institut for historie og samfundsvidenskab nr. 22. Odense.

JEANSSON, N. R. 1963: Fossila åkrar i Himmerland. En flygbildsinventering. *Svensk Geografisk Årsbok*, 39, 111.

JENSEN, S. 1976: Byhøjene i Thy. *MIV* (Muserne i Viborg amt) 6.

KJÆR, H. 1928: Oldtidshuse ved Ginderup. *Fra Nationalmuseets Arbejdsmark.*

KLINDT-JENSEN, O. 1949: Foreign influences in Denmark's early iron age. *Acta Arch.* XX.

KOSSACK, K., HARCK, O., REICHSTEIN, J. 1974: Zehn Jahre Siedlungsforschung in Archsum auf Sylt. *Bericht der Römischen Kommission* 55. II.

LUND, J. 1976: Overbygård – En jernalderlandsby med neddybede huse. *KUML.*

LUND HANSEN, U. 1976: Das Gräberfeld bei Harpelev, Seeland. *Acta Arch.* 47.

NEWCOMB, R. M. 1971: Celtic Fields in Himmerland, as revealed by vertical Photography, at a Scale of 1 : 25,000. *Photogrammetria* 27. Elsevier, Publishing Company. Amsterdam.

NIELSEN, V. 1970: Agerlandets historie. *Danmarks Natur* Bd. 8.

MÜLLER, S. 1906: Bopladsfundene. Den romerske tid. *Årbøger.*

MÜLLER-WILLE, M. 1965: Eisenzeitliche Fluren in den festländischen Nordseegebieten. *Siedlung und Landschaft in Westfalen* 5. Münster.

RASMUSSEN, A. K. 1968: En byhøj i Thyland. *Nat. Arbejdsmark.*

SEHESTED, F. 1878: *Fortidsminder og Oldsager fra Egnen omkring Broholm*, p. 234f.

THOMSEN, N. 1953: Om en vestjysk stald. *KUML.*

– 1959: Hus og kælder i romersk jernalder. *KUML.*

– 1964: Myrthue. Et gårdsanlæg fra jernalderen. *KUML.*

– 1965: Nye landsbyer. *Mark og Montre.* Fra sydvestjyske museer.

THORVILDSEN, E. 1972: Dankirke. *Nat. Arbejdsmark.*

VORTING, H. C. 1973: Endnu en bopladsforekomst fra germansk jernalder i Esbjerg. *Mark og Montre.*

VOSS, O. 1957: Trælborg. *SKALK* 4.

– 1976: Drengsted. Et bopladsområde fra 5. årh. e.Kr.f. ved Sønderjyllands vestkyst. *ISKOS* I.

Prehistoric Wheeled Vehicles

by PER OLE SCHOVSBO

INTRODUCTION

In spite of the prominence of large and very large wooden objects[1] in museum storerooms throughout the country, they have received little attention in historic and prehistoric research. The reason for this unfortunate state of affairs is that it has not been possible to date the wooden objects with the necessary degree of certainty, since they have resisted the typological analyses applied to other artefacts. The problem is that the preparation and construction of wooden objects incorporates timeless elements and is less influenced by style and period than artefacts of pottery, metal or glass. Furthermore, the wooden objects have undergone drastic changes in size and shape in connection with their excavation and storage in museums. The wooden objects are usually fragments of larger units, pieces of spoked wheel rims which belonged to a cart with two or four wheels and also with a body, shafts, axles and perch. When reconstructing the units of which the wooden objects are fragments it is therefore difficult to achieve the degree of certainty desirable if the subject is to attract the attention of researchers.

BOG FINDS

By far the greater part of the material[2] has been found in bogs, lakes and large streams. This is predictable since wooden objects from places without the same conditions of preservation have not survived[3].

But in connection with the deposition of wooden objects in water-logged areas, some factors must be considered which have so far not been adequately discussed in the archaeological literature.

1. First the factors concerning the density and hydrostatic properties of the wood as a sediment. The density of wood is usually much less than that of water and mineral sediments, and as a result the sedimentation of wooden objects takes place differently. Interpretation of the stratigraphic evidence is therefore usually open to question – too little is yet known about the speed with which different sorts of wood become water-logged and form a sediment. Most water-deposited sediments are sorted according to density and volume, the lighter overlying the heavier. The larger sediments are more liable to be carried by water movement away from the place of deposition than the smaller and perhaps more compact ones.

   In addition, wooden objects are not always deposited in open water or on a swampy surface. In many cases wooden objects have been deposited in peat-cuttings under potsherds, stones or under the foundations of causeways and bridges. In several cases the object has been pushed well below the original surface – either to get rid of it or because it was needed as a tethering stake or as a hand-hold when walking over boggy ground. When deposited in open water wooden objects have also sunk into the silt layer at the bottom of the basin.

2. The second problem concerns ploughs, ards, and fragments of vehicles found in water-logged areas. The use and maintenance of wooden artefacts depend on the ability to control moisture as well as destructive attacks of bacteria, fungi and insects. Until recent times dried-out wooden tubs and barrels have been placed to soak in the village pond, just as wooden carts have been driven into water so that the wheels would not dry out and fall apart. Every spring the clinker-built offshore fishing boats had to be caulked and lie some time in water before they could be used. Wooden spades in some areas are kept under water to remain pliable[4]. A possible explanation of the many finds of prehistoric ards is that they were placed in water so that they could be used in the spring ploughing[5]. Wheels were also submerged so that they would not

dry out completely. The problem of warping and shrinking caused by the drying out of wood seems to have been particularly pronounced in the case of the massive disc wheels, and was solved by placing them under water for some time. This is perhaps part of the reason why the many disc wheels are found in pairs or groups of four – unaccompanied by other parts of the vehicle.

3. Furthermore, before and during the working of wood it should be seasoned in such a way as to give the finished product the most suitable qualities. Freshly cut wood was seldom used. Wood for the hubs of spoked wheels was traditionally soaked in water for up to five years before further work took place[6]. Among the finds there are, therefore, many hubs in a preliminary stage of manufacture. Wood for rims was also seasoned in water. This is not known in modern times, but can be attributed to the fact that prehistoric rims, unlike recent ones, were hardly ever bound by metal tyres. Part of the other wood found in bogs – planks and other indeterminate pieces – may thus have been deposited for purely practical reasons. The finds may be hoards, wood hoards, which represent not only the temporary storage of useful goods, but perhaps even more represent lost stages in the total manufacturing process of wooden artefacts[7].

We may therefore conclude that in only a few instances can we rule out a purely practical and rational purpose in connection with the deposition of wooden artefacts in prehistoric times.

VEHICLE REMAINS

A preliminary examination of approx. 600 finds of vehicle remains from a large part of Europe reveals that in March 1977 there were 225 registered Danish finds, of which 129 were actual vehicle remains – the others were wood finds containing large and very large wooden objects[8]. The majority of the vehicle remains (83%) are from bogs, lakes and large streams, while the remaining material (17%) comes from other localities, such as graves, urban deposits, castle mounds and settlements. The date of the finds will be discussed in another context[9]. It is sufficient here to state that most of the Danish material is prehistoric, while a small part is mediaeval and later.

Context and Depth of Finds

Of the vehicle remains in bogs, found in 107 different localities in Denmark (fig. 1), we have information on the locality of 99 (92%), and the year of discovery of 82 (77%). For only 33 finds (31%) do we know the depth beneath the surface of the bog. Furthermore, in most cases the find depth is only known with such uncertainty that it has little systematic value[10]. No constant relationship can be seen between the find depth and year of discovery[11]. The upper and presumably latest finds have not been registered before the lower and therefore earlier finds, according to current stratigraphic theories. Apart from the fact that information on find depth is open to doubt (see above), this absence of anticipated regularity is because peat-cutting in the areas concerned was primarily a private activity, and therefore restricted to small strips of ground. Most of the localities are in Jutland, where people worked deep cuttings rather than stripping peat from an extensive horizontal surface, which would have uncovered the contents layer by layer in an almost systematic way.

Several of the areas in question are the small Jutland raised bogs which are not large enough for extensive surface cutting. Since the industrial peat production of Jutland did not become largescale until relatively late[12], the methods used were crude and hurried. Soft wooden artefacts do not reveal their presence in the same way as stone, pottery or metal, which interfere with the machinery. This sharply reduced the possibility of careful and systematic archaeological observations. It is ironic that in the very years when the archaeological material increased in quantity, there was an unusual decline in quality.

Distribution and Find Frequency

The geographic distribution of finds covers the whole country with the exception of Bornholm and the smaller islands. The situation in Jutland is characterised by a sparse distribution of finds in the Limfjord region and East Himmerland, their absence in South East Jutland, and a concentration of finds around Herning. There are several reasons for this. The accessions policy of the various museums has been far from uniform because not all archaeologists were eager to bring back wood finds to already overburdened museum storerooms and conservators. Furthermore, the present study is not complete, and therefore a certain deviation from the actual pattern of finds must be expected, even if it is probably not of major significance (fig. 1).

The surprisingly few finds east of Funen must be ascribed to a combination of two separate factors. Firstly, large-scale peat-cutting occurred somewhat earlier east of Funen than in the west[13]. Secondly, wooden parts of vehicles were not recognized as artefacts worth keeping until fairly late – around 1885-90. By this time the layers containing wood finds east of Funen may have been largely removed with the peat[14].

However, a systematic examination of the archives in provincial museums and the parish records of the National Museum may supplement the distribution map which is based on the study of stored wooden artefacts.

The bar graph, which shows the number of finds listed according to year of discovery, contains 99 vehicle finds, 83 of these from bogs, to which should be added two finds from 1975, Risby and Edslev[15]. The unexpected sequence in the diagram must mean that parts of wooden vehicles were not regarded as artefacts by peat cutters and were thrown away – unless there were very special circumstances connected with the finds. Apart from the presence of an expert, these special circumstances may have been an unusually large number of wooden artefacts found in the same place, artefacts found together with pottery, metal objects, bodies or bones – or the special circumstances may have been the individual's unusual knowledge or observation[16].

The large number of finds in the years 1935 to 1955 are mainly due to the field trips by the National Museum in the years of intensive peat-cutting during and just after World War II. The number of finds culminates in the decade before 1955, and the subsequent decline is chiefly due to the marked decrease in peat production as conditions after the war went back to normal[17], but also because wooden artefacts did not attract the attention from archaeologists one might have expected. This was obviously because there was no clear chronology for wooden artefacts, but even more because other material found in bogs during the war required professional attention of a kind likely to prove more valuable to Danish archaeology. As late as 1964 precious material was being lost[18].

If, however, we compare the bar diagram (fig. 2) with other find groups, it appears that the majority of wooden artefacts have presumably been lost. The registration of Late Bronze Age hoard finds from bogs, found under the

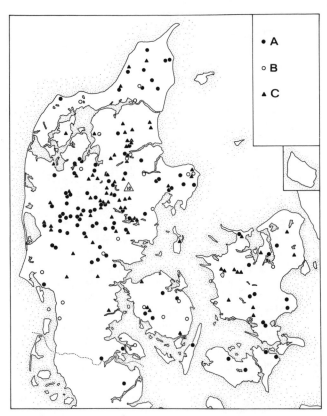

Fig. 1. Map showing geographical distribution of 208 Danish finds of large and very large wooden artefacts and vehicle remains (out of the total of 225 such finds registered in March 1977).
Key: A: vehicle remains from bogs (99)
       B: other vehicle remains (22)
       C: large and very large wooden artefacts from bogs (87)

same circumstances as wooden artefacts but regarded to a much larger extent by both finders and museum personnel as worth keeping, culminated 80 years earlier[19].

History of Finds

The oldest surviving Danish vehicle find was excavated in 1817 at Skerne in Falster[20]. Like another early find of 7 kg. of bronzes from Egemosen in Funen[21] it was only in 1969 that it was professionally studied by an archaeologist and published[22]. In 1823 we hear for the first time about a Danish find from the previous year of a wooden vehicle, namely a "whole waggon with wheels which fell to pieces when exposed to the air"[23], found together with metal artefacts in Kragehul Mose (Funen), which was to become so widely known. A few years later were found the two well-known wooden collars from a Viking period

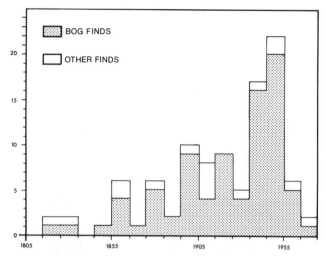

Fig. 2. Bar graph of Danish prehistoric and mediaeval vehicle finds (March 1977), showing locality of find and year of discovery or registration. The number culminates in the decade before 1955, and if compared with other artefact groups gives an impression of how many bog finds have been lost over time. The number of Late Bronze Age hoards from bogs, recognized as worth keeping by finders and museum personnel to a much greater extent than vehicle remains, culminates in the decade before 1875, i.e. 80 years earlier (Kristiansen 1976, fig. 2, 128).

The diagram shows 83 bog finds (to which should be added 2 from 1975) and 16 other finds. Total 99 (101).

grave at Møllemosegård in Funen[24]. They were found together with a mounting for a cart body of the type presumed to have been found among grave goods in the burial chamber of the northern barrow at Jelling[25]. The type is best known from the waggon found at Oseberg[26]. The first part of a wooden vehicle to be published in Denmark is from Thorsbjerg Mose in Schleswig[27]. It is a rim fragment which is probably the same age as Late Iron Age artefacts from the same site, and apparently a good many vehicle remains were found during the excavation[28]. Conrad Engelhardt, the excavator, refers in his publication to a similar vehicle found in Nydam Engmose[29], but not until the publication of Vimose in 1869 was a well-preserved spoked wheel presented in an Iron Age context[30], though not with complete certainty since "even in our day such wheels are used in the heath areas of Jutland"[31]. The situation was not improved by the discovery of a wheel of apparently the same type at Danevirke — presumably much more recent[32]. The uncertainty became even more pronounced with Herbst's

dating of the disc wheel from Fårup Mark in Viborg county[33] and the vehicle find from Tranbær Mose south of Vejle[34]. Both finds were thought to be from the Middle Ages. The Fårup wheel has been dated by C-14 to the Late Neolithic and the Tranbær find to the Early Iron Age[35]. Right up to the 1880's bog finds of vehicle remains could not be assigned with any confidence to the prehistoric period, and only when the Oseberg deposit was found and published at the beginning of this century[36], was there material available as evidence for the interpretation of those Viking graves containing iron chains, rivets, angle irons and collars like those in vehicle finds. This possibility, however, was not exploited until a few years ago[37]. All in all these circumstances have meant that the recognition and preservation of vehicle finds have in certain periods been completely dependent on the recent initiative of professional archaeologists, and of individual amateurs who have been steadily collecting wooden artefacts regardless of the ambivalent attitude of established research[38] – cf. fig. 2. A turning point occurred when in 1878 Frederik Sehested of Broholm, a Court Chamberlain, published a grave find from Langå Mark in Funen and interpreted its contents of iron and bronze fittings as pieces of a four-wheeled waggon[39]. This interpretation met with strong opposition from professional archaeologists, but chance favoured Sehested and a few years later some peat cutters found an almost identical waggon near Ringkøbing. The site was in a glebe fen at Dejbjerg and contained pieces of wood with bronze fittings which revealed themselves when the spades hit the metal, rather than the wood, since wood was very common in local peat-cuttings. Henry Petersen travelled at once to Dejbjerg after having ascertained that the bronze fittings from Dejbjerg were identical with those from Langå[40]. In a few days Petersen had retrieved two wheels with bronze-mounted hubs, boards from a waggon and several other parts. In the following year Petersen excavated several vehicle remains from Tranbær Mose[41], where he also found weapons, ropes and other objects which had a strong similarity with the finds from Vimose and Thorsbjerg – and with regard to the vehicle remains, a strong similarity to those found at Dejbjerg[42]. 1883 was an even better year. Petersen returned to Dejbjerg and excavated the rest of waggon No. 2, together with the two missing wheels from the first waggon. In 1888 appeared Petersen's publication of the two ceremonial four-wheeled waggons from Dejbjerg, the first of which is identical with the Langå waggon and those found this century at Kraghede[43] and Fredbjerg[44]. After 1888 there was no activity in this field by professional archaeologists until in 1907 Sophus Müller published the disc wheel from Dystrup Mose and on very slight evidence dated it to the Neolithic[45]. In 1920 Müller published the disc wheel from Tindbæk Mose near Skjern[46]. As late as 1957 Johannes Brøndsted described the two wheels as Neolithic – although with reservations[47]. The Dystrup wheel has since been dated by C-14 to the Early Iron Age[48] and we can probably expect a similar dating for the Tindbæk wheel[48a]. In the years up till the preliminary report in 1950 of the wheel find from Rappendam at Jørlunde in Zealand[49], the archaeological literature in Denmark made almost no mention of Danish vehicle finds[50], although the find material increased steadily in these years. Meanwhile the European literature discussed Danish finds other than Langå, Kraghede and Dejbjerg, which in 1949 were placed in an archaeological context by Ole Klindt-Jensen[51].

The extensive collections of wooden vehicle remains thus lay untouched in museum storerooms, and to all intents and purposes archaeologists knew only the ceremonial waggons with bronze fittings and the disc wheels from Dystrup and Tindbæk which, moreover, had been placed in the wrong chronological context. A new turning point occurred in 1964 with J. D. van der Waal's publication of several disc wheels from North West Europe[52]. These were placed in a social and cultural context by means of stratified settlement finds and scientific dating. This study also contained an unpretentious discussion of the Danish material, and the typology of disc wheels was put into a sensible and still largely valid chronological framework, though it has since turned out that disc wheels are particularly difficult to date by typological means[53]. Georg Kunwald's publication in 1970 of the find from Rappendam continued the same approach[54], while Torben Witt in his publication of 1969 adopted a completely different perspective[55]. The latter paper gave a fairly representative sample of Danish prehistoric and early mediaeval spoked wheels based on technical and socio-economic principles[56]. A new branch of research was introduced which by analysing the structure of wood and using other scientific methods may lead to new knowledge and solve those immensely difficult technological and chronological problems which more traditional archaeological methods have not been able to deal with.

CONCLUSION

The history of vehicle remains and other large wooden artefacts from bogs is the history of an artefact group which no one knew what to do with in time, while there was still a large amount of material available. Probably most of the bog finds have now been retrieved, and the archaeologist must turn his attention to other areas which can provide supplementary material. There are many well-dated stretches of road and wheel-tracks which when precisely measured can provide valuable supplementary evidence to the fragments of vehicles known from bog finds. Wider studies of prehistoric and early mediaevel settlement layers can provide both actual vehicle remains and evidence of the siting of roads and their traffic. This in turn enables us to understand the significance of vehicles for everyday use, as a means of transport and as a means of indicating social status. Prehistoric trade and trade routes have long been discussed, but little attention has been paid to the purely physical aspects of trade: siting of roads and means of transport. New light is being cast on sea transport by the study of sea-going ships and natural harbours[57], and in view of the number of amateur divers wrecks may in future exceed the existing capacity of museums, just as large and very large wooden artefacts have done.

The small amount of vehicle remains still available must be registered, preserved and scientifically studied before it is too late, so that the evidence they provide on prehistoric and mediaeval wood-working technology will not be lost.

Per Ole Skovsbo,
Nyringen 58,
DK – 8240 Risskov

Acknowledgements

In writing this paper the author has had the benefit of detailed discussions with Grith Lerche, Dept. III of the National Museum; Peter Wagner, Botanisk Centralbibliotek; Ole Crumlin-Pedersen, Skibshistorisk Laboratorium; and Ole Klindt-Jensen, Jørgen Lund and Kristian Kristiansen, all of Moesgård.

For economic support in a fairly costly study I should like to thank Den Hjelmstierne-Rosencroneske Stiftelse and the Faculty of Humanities at Århus University.

The papers is intended as an introduction to the future presentation of the research results of recent years. In 1982-84 we have reconstructed five different vehicles at Danish museums. Now the Dejbjerg group (6-6 waggons) is to be analysed and reconstructed at Fyens Stiftsmuseum and Historisk Værksted in Odense (Funen). In more than ten papers since 1979 the author har discussed the Danish finds.

Tranbær Mose (bog) south of Vejle 1882. Unpublished lithograph by Magnus Petersen 1883 (National Museum Topographical Archives).

NOTES

1. "Large and very large wooden objects" is here used in accordance with the National Museum storage groups 8 and 9.
2. The material registered up to March 1, 1977 is found in 25 Danish museums – to which should be added the material abroad, which is not included here.
3. See B. Brorson Christensen 1970 and 1971-72.
4. Grith Lerche has kindly drawn my attention to areas in New Guinea, where wooden ploughs and spades are still used and are kept in water. See Grith Lerche 1977, 111-124 and Grith Lerche and Axel Steensberg 1973, 87-104.
5. See note 4, and also Glob 1951, 102 ff. for a rather different point of view.
6. See e.g. T. Tobiassen Kragelund 1940 and 1952.
7. See Henry Petersen 1890, in which nearly every bog find is regarded as a hoard – in controversy with the interpretation advanced by Engelhardt and Worsaae of weapon deposits as offerings of war booty, a theory still defended today.
8. Large and very large wooden objects comprise several main groups: 1) timber from roads and bridges, 2) other building timber, 3) boat timber, 4) ship's timber, 5) timber from vehicles, 6) wood from ploughs, 7) wooden yokes, 8) other large wooden implements, 9) carved wood. Some of these groups are discussed in the archaeological literature. See e.g. (early articles) Feddersen 1881, 363 ff. (carved wood), Müller 1900a, 223: Vognaag til Trækdyr (: waggon yokes for draught animals), and 1900b: Oldtidens Plov (: Prehistoric ploughs) et al.
9. A research project is planned in connection with the history of Henry Petersen's investigation of early vehicle remains. The material will be presented in catalogues, and the Tranbær find will be published. These articles will discuss the chronology of the material, and will also attempt to deduce technological data, functional interpretations etc. See Schovsbo 1977.
10. Kristian Kristiansen 1976, 139ff., fig. 10 – which gives find depths for Late Bronze Age hoards found in bogs while peat-cutting. Kristiansen's find depths differ considerably from the impressions left by wooden objects found in bogs: the find depth of pre-Iron Age objects is 2-4 m below the surface of the bog. Because of the many unknown factors involved it is questionable whether find depths can be used in any systematic way.
11. Cf. Kristian Kristiansen 1976, 141 ff.
12. Cf. Kristian Kristiansen 1976, 139 ff.
13. Cf. Kristian Kristiansen 1976, 140.
14. Cf. Kristian Kristiansen 1976, 142.
15. The Risby find, see Mogens Schou Jørgensen 1976, 170-171. The Edslev find is unpublished, Forhistorisk Museum, Moesgård, cat. No. 1974.
16. A large number of the wooden objects stored in Danish museums originate from private collections. The Silkeborg Kulturhistoriske Museum has some of the Hammer collection, Forhistorisk Museum, Moesgård, has some of the Balslev collection – in both cases these comprise a major part of the two museum collections of wood material from bogs. See Ulrik Balslev 1940, 3 ff.; H. P. Hansen 1942, 80 & 84, et al.
17. Cf. Kristian Kristiansen 1976, 128, fig. 2, which shows a similar pattern for Bronze Age hoards found in bogs.
18. The find from Fløjstrup, Kulturhistorisk Museum, Randers, cat. No. 11/65. The find was investigated in 1964 by the Kulturhistorisk Museum in collaboration with Dept. II of the National Museum. Three spoked wheels and five rim pieces in a preliminary stage of

manufacture were found. These were associated with a large amount of unworked wood that seemed to be fixed with stakes driven into the soft peat. – The find, which appears to be a close parallel to the Risby find, is described in the archives of the Kulturhistorisk Museum, to which Museum Inspector Bjørn Stürup kindly drew my attention. The reason for considering these to be comparable finds is that in both cases there are scattered vehicle remains found in or near the foundations of causeways or swampy areas. The vehicle parts may have been lost while these causeways were being constructed, just like the vehicle remains found between 1906 and 1916 in the foundations of the manor farm of Borringholm, which was built on soft ground around the year 1400 (Dept. II of the National Museum, no number). Vehicle remains found near roads may also have been deposited later as discarded material. The finds at Varpelev and at Sjellebro Bridge have both produced vehicle remains. See e.g. Hajo Hayen's numerous short articles on the roads built with wood which were excavated near Oldenburg and contained numerous vehicle remains. – Hayen 1965, 1971, 1975 et al. See also Mogens Schou Jørgensen 1977, 147-162.

19. Cf. Kristian Kristiansen 1976, 128, fig. 2 – compare note 17.
20. Mus. No. III – Oldnordisk Museum, now Dept. I of the National Museum.
21. NM I B-1269-1301.
22. Jacob-Friesen 1969, 122 ff. A similar find was discovered in a Bronze Age burial mound in Funen – see Henrik Thrane 1976, 17-32.
23. Antiqvariske Annaler IV 1823, 567.
24. Antikvarisk Tidsskrift 1864, 16-22.
25. See Finn Magnussen 1823, 35; Jacob Kornerup 1875, Table XIV and p. 22; Else Roesdahl 1977, 83 ff., together with an analysis of grave cists by Peter Wagner, ibid., 84 ff. We may also refer to Else Roesdahl and Jørgen Nordquist 1971, 15-33, et al. The identification of the waggon bodies from Møllemosegård, Jelling and Oseberg, and of the shaft from Edslev is my own, and is based on the presence of angle irons, carry-rings, and rivets, and on the chief dimensions 1×2 m and the rounded base. The matter has been discussed with Peter Wagner and Else Roesdahl, who have referred to further grave finds from Jutland and some Schleswig finds. A similar discovery has been made in Søllested in Funen. Rapidly Else Roesdahl published these aspects in Skalk 1978, 9-14. Late Iron Age grave finds contain what are probably two-wheeled carts. See Gustafsson 1974, and note 37. However, the two-wheeled carts are not proved by these finds and now (June 1984) I prefer to see the "waggon bodies" as real cists instead of parts of vehicles.
26. Sigurd Grieg 1928, 3 ff.
27. Conrad Engelhardt 1863 Pl 16.2.
28. Conrad Engelhardt 1863, 56.
29. Conrad Engelhardt 1863, 56, note "4".
30. Conrad Engelhardt 1869 Pl. 15.28 – NMI C-27774, doubtless contemporaneous with some of the weapon finds. Engelhardt (1867, p. 9, note 1 & p. 29) mentions that "several waggon wheels and fragments of vehicles" were found in later excavations at Vimose. It is hardly remarkable that vehicle remains have been found in major bog excavations. The most recent is the discovery of a well-preserved axle, together with several dug-out canoes, at the excavation by the Forhistorisk Museum of the weapon deposit at Illerup Ådal near Skanderborg.

31. Conrad Engelhardt 1869, 25, note "1".
32. Conrad Engelhardt 1869, 25, note "1", NMI No. 20456, of Late Iron Age type.
33. NMII D-996.
34. NMII D-949.
35. Fårup – see Tauber 1966, 109: C-14 dated to 1510 B.C. (K-989) Tranbær – C-14 dates are still unpublished. Information from Tauber: C-8800 dated to A.D. 200 (K-2415) C-4967 dated to A.D. 140 (K-2416) – all C-14 dates are uncalibrated ± 100 years.
36. Sigurd Grieg 1928, 3 ff.
37. See note 25 – and Müller-Wille 1974, 175 ff. and Jan Helmer Gustafsson 1974, et al.
38. See note 16.
39. Sehested 1878, 172 ff.
40. Henry Petersen 1888, 3 ff.
41. NMI C-4966-4992, the find is being prepared for publication by the author.
42. Henry Petersen 1883 and 1890. See also Schovsbo 1979, where Henry Petersen's research into early vehicles is evaluated in the light of unpublished archaeological and archival material.
43. NMI C-13245.
44. Forhistorisk Museum, Moesgård, cat. No. 1602.
45. Sophus Müller 1907, 75 ff. – NMI A-22214.
46. Sophus Müller 1920, 90 ff. – NMI B-10749.
47. Johannes Brøndsted 1957, 177.
48. Tauber 1966, 110, C-14 dated to 470 B.C. (K-823) – uncalibrated ± 100 years.
48a. The Tindbæk wheel has been C-14 dated to 360 ± 80 B.C. (K-2895), Rostholm 1977, 207 & note 142.
49. Georg Kunwald 1950, 13-18.
50. The vehicle remains without fittings are mentioned as curiosa and in passing in the many publications of material discovered while peat-cutting during the war years – e.g. Glob 1951, Margrethe Hald 1950, Gösta Berg 1935.
51. Ole Klindt-Jensen 1949, discusses Danish ceremonial waggons with bronze fittings. Material without fittings is not included in his discussion.
52. J. D. van der Waals 1964.
53. Karl W. Struve 1973, 205-218, gives 5 disc wheels with fixed hub, Waals' Neolithic type "1", C-14 dated to the Late Iron Age.
54. Georg Kunwald 1970, 42 ff.
55. Torben Witt 1969, 111 ff.
56. The material discussed by Torben Witt is based exclusively on Departments I & II of the National Museum, Copenhagen. See also the unpublished report (April 1978) by the author of vehicle material in Dept. II (in Archives of Dept. II).
57. See Ole Crumlin-Pedersen 1968 & 1977.

REFERENCES

The bibliography is not comprehensive and includes only references mentioned in the paper. Some of the European literature also discusses Danish vehicle finds, particularly the Dejbjerg find which is famous throughout Europe.

ANTIQUARISKE ANNALER Bd. IV 1823. København.
ANTIQUARISK TIDSSKRIFT 1864. København.

BALSLEV, ULRIK, 1940: Nye østjydske Mosefund. *Østjydsk Hjemstavn*, vol. V, p. 3-8.

BERG, GÖSTA, 1935: *Sledges and Wheeled Vehicles*. Nordiska Museets Handlinger 4, Stockholm.

BRØNDSTED, JOHANNES, 1957: *Danmarks Oldtid*, bd. I, 2nd edition, København.

CHRISTENSEN, B. BRORSON, 1970: *The Conservation of Waterlogged Wood in the National Museum of Denmark*. København.

– 1971-72: Lectures on wood and conservation of wood (unpublished).

CRUMLIN-PEDERSEN, OLE, 1968: *Træskibet. Fra langskib til fregat*. Træbranchens Oplysningsråd. København.

– 1977: *Træskibet. Sømand og Købmand*. Træbranchens Oplysningsråd. København.

ENGELHARDT, CONRAD, 1863: *Sønderjydske Mosefund* Bd I. Thorsbjerg Fundet. København.

– 1867: *Fynske Mosefund* Bd I. Kragehul Fundet. København.

– 1869: *Fynske Mosefund* Bd II. Vimose Fundet, København.

FEDDERSEN, A. 1881: To Mosefund. *Aarbøger for Nordisk Oldkyndighed og Historie* p. 363 ff.

GLOB, P. V., 1951: *Ard og Plov i Nordens Oldtid*. Jysk Arkæologisk Selskabs Skrifter Bd I, Århus.

GRIEG, SIGURD, 1928: *Osebergfundet*, Bd II (p. 3 ff.). Oslo.

GUSTAFSSON, JAN HELMER, 1974: *Körredskap och färdväger*. Uppsats för grk C 1 vid seminariet för Arkeologi, Uppsala (unpublished).

HALD, MARGRETHE, 1950: *Olddanske Tekstiler*. Nordiske Fortidsminder bd V, København.

HANSEN, H. P., 1942: *Herning Museum 1892-1942*. Herning.

HAYEN, HAJO, 1965: Menschenförmige Holzfiguren neben dem Bohlenweg XLII im Wittemoor. *Oldenburger Jahrbuch*. Bd 64 p. 1-25.

– 1971: Möglichkeiten und Forderungen der Moorarchäologie. *TELMA* Bd I p 31-36. Hannover.

– 1975: Neue Untersuchungen am Bohlenweg I im Legener Moor Sommer 1973 und 1974. *Mitteilungen der Arbeitsgruppen der ostfriesischen Landschaft* 1975 Hft I p. 12-20.

JACOB-FRIESEN, GERNOT, 1969: Skjerne und Egemose. Wagenteile südlicher Provenienz in Skandinavischen Funden. *Acta Archaeologica* vol. XL p. 122 ff. København.

JØRGENSEN, MOGENS SCHOU, 1976: Risby-vej og -vogn fra vikingetid. *Nationalmuseets Arbejdsmark* p. 170-171.

– 1977: Veje af træ. *Antikvariske studier tilegnet Knud Thorvildsen* p. 147-162. København.

KLINDT-JENSEN, OLE, 1949: Foreign Influences in Denmark's Early Iron Age. *Acta Archaeologica* Vol XX, København.

KORNERUP, JACOB, 1875: *Kongehøjene i Jelling og deres Undersøgelse efter Kong Frederik VII's Befaling i 1861*. København.

KRAGELUND, T. TOBIASSEN, 1940: Arbejdsvognen. *Fra Ribe Amt*, bd X. København.

– 1952: Hjulet og værktøj til fremstilling af hjulet. *Sprog og Kultur* Bd XIX, Århus.

KRISTIANSEN, KRISTIAN, 1976: En kildekritisk analyse af depotfund fra Danmarks yngre bronzealder. *Aarbøger for Nordisk Oldkyndighed og Historie* p. 119-152. København.

KUNWALD, GEORG, 1950: Nogle offerfund fra nordsjællandske Moser. *Frederiksborg Amts historiske Samfunds Aarbog* 1949.

– 1970: Der Moorfund im Rappendam auf Seeland. *Prehistorische Zeitschrift* Bd 45 p. 42 ff.

LERCHE, GRITH AND AXEL STEENSBERG, 1973: Observations on Spade-cultivation in the New Guinea Highlands. *Tools & Tillage*, vol II,2. p. 87-104. København.

– 1977: Double Paddle-spades in prehistoric contexts in Denmark. *Tools & Tillage*, vol III,2 p. 111-124.

MAGNUSSEN, FINN, 1823: *Efterretninger om Mindesmærkerne ved Jellinge og de derved i Aarene 1820 og 1821 foretagne Undersøgelser*. København.

MÜLLER, SOPHUS, 1900a: Vognaag til Trækdyr. *Aarbøger for Nordisk Oldkyndighed og Historie* p. 223 ff.

– 1900b: Oldtidens Plov. *Aarbøger for Nordisk Oldkyndighed og Historie* p. 203 ff.

– 1907: Nye Fund og Iagttagelser fra Sten-, Bronze- og Jernalderen. *Aarbøger for Nordisk Oldkyndighed og Historie* p. 75 ff.

– 1920: Nye Fund og Former. *Aarbøger for Nordisk Oldkyndighed og Historie* p. 88 ff.

MÜLLER-WILLE, MICHAEL, 1974: Ein Reitergrab der jüngeren Wikingerzeit aus Süderbrarup (Angeln). *Festgabe Kurt Tackenberg*, p. 175 ff. Bonn.

NORDQUIST, JØRGEN – see *Else Roesdahl* 1971.

PETERSEN, HENRY, 1883: Beretning om mødet i Det Kongelige Nordiske Oldskriftselskab – published in Berlingske Tidende 31. January 1883. København.

– 1888: *Vognfundene i Dejbjerg Præstegaardsmose ved Ringkøbing*. København.

– 1890: Hypothesen om religiøse Offer- og Votivfund fra Danmarks Forhistoriske Tid. *Aarbøger for Nordisk Oldkyndighed og Historie* p. 209 ff.

ROESDAHL, ELSE AND JØRGEN NORDQUIST, 1971: De døde fra Fyrkat. *Nationalmuseets Arbejdsmark* p. 15 ff.

ROESDAHL, ELSE, 1977: Fyrkat. En jysk vikingeborg. II. Oldsagerne og gravpladsen. *Nordiske Fortidsminder*, Serie B, bd 4.

ROSTHOLM, HANS, 1978: Neolitiske skivehjul fra Kideris og Bjerregårde i Midtjylland. *Kuml* 1977 p. 185-222. Århus 1978.

SCHOVSBO, PER OLE, 1977: Hjulnav (fra Randers by). *hikuin* nr. 3, p. 118.

– 1983: Henry Petersen og vognfundene fra den ældre jernalder. En forskningshistorisk undersøgelse. *Aarbøger for Nordisk Oldkyndighed og Historie*. 1983. København.

SEHESTED, NIELS FREDERIK BERNHARD VON, 1878: *Fortidsminder og Oldsager fra Egnen om Broholm* .

STEENSBERG, AXEL – see Grith Lerche 1973.

STRUVE, KARL W., 1973: Hölzerne Scheibenräder aus einem Moor bei Alt-Bennebek, Kr. Schleswig. *Offa*, 30 p. 205-218.

TAUBER, HENRIK 1966: Danske kulstof-14 dateringer af arkæologiske prøver II. *Aarbøger for Nordisk Oldkyndighed og Historie* p. 102 ff.

THRANE, HENRIK, 1976: Lusehøj ved Voldtofte. *Fynske Minder* p. 17-32.

WAALS, J. D. VAN DER, 1964: *Prehistoric Disc Wheels in The Netherlands*. Groningen.

WITT, TORBEN, 1970: Egerhjul og vogne. *Kuml* 1969 p. 111 ff. Århus.

Wooden T-Shaped Spades and Double Paddle-Spades

by GRITH LERCHE

INTRODUCTION

Wooden artefacts have been neglected by archaeologists, not only because of the problems of conservation and storage but also because of difficulties in interpretation and dating. Thus wooden artefacts used as tools have often been referred to in the literature, whereas little effort has been made to describe their functions in a prehistoric context. Social conditions, kinship, and social relationships are important aspects, but do not tell us everything about daily life in a human society. Descriptions of cultural remains, their design and function, are essential components in the interpretation and understanding of human daily life in a distant past or a strange world. Collaborative work across several research disciplines would be useful, for instance, when interpreting the use and proper context of archaeological finds.

PEAT SPADES

In many local museums in Denmark and in all three Danish departments of the National Museum in Copenhagen there is a type of wooden object shaped like a T, or rather like a sword. These objects have two sharp edges and a wooden handle fastened crosswise with a peg to the upper end (fig. 1). This group of artefacts has been kept in museums without attracting much attention, as have many other wooden objects, such as double paddle-spades.[1]

The T-shaped objects must be interpreted as tools. The people who found them and the staff of museums usually interpreted them as peat spades. In an article in the *Nationalmuseets Arbejdsmark* in 1948 C. J. Becker described an excavation at Nørre Smedeby in the parish of Bov, only a few kilometres north of the German frontier, where several bog pits were found containing interesting remains. It was obvious that the pits were the result of peat digging. Since there were several earthenware vessels and potsherds which dated the peat cutting to the Pre-Roman Iron Age, it is probable that the T-shaped spade found there also dates from this period, although its position in the bog was not quite certain.[2] The discovery of a wooden hoe and several wooden troughs and scoops gives some indication of how the peat cutting was carried out. The Nr. Smedeby find thus provides us, in one site, with the tools necessary for the simple production of kneaded peat. The work may have taken place in the following way: The heatherturf or sod was cut away with a wooden hoe until the black, decomposed sphagnum peat was reached, which was as easy to cut as butter. The thin T-shaped peat spade may have been used to make vertical cuts in the peat. Vertical slices

Fig. 1. Peat spade from Asferg bog, Asferg parish, Nørhald district, Randers county. Length 50 cm, width 8 cm, length of handle 45,5 cm. Mariager Museum. Photo G.L.

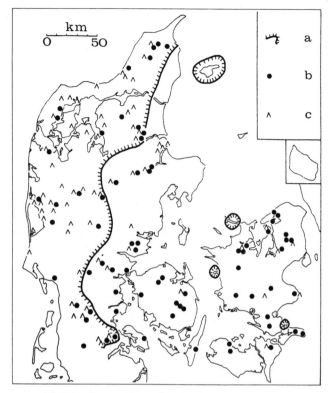

Fig. 2. Peat and turf working in Denmark. a: limit of turf cutting, b: peat kneading, c: peat cutting (after H. Rasmussen, 201).
(N.B. *Peat* is the soft decomposed, compacted vegetal matter in the bog, while *turf* is the fibrous, matted roots and incorporated earth just under the vegetation cover – also called *sod*).

of peat were cut away and placed in the trough. The scoop may have been used for adding water so that the peat could be kneaded by hand.[3]

Among the many kinds of peat spades used during the 19th and the first half of the 20th century it is the spades used for cutting peat in the bank (stikspade) with which the T-shaped tools must be compared functionally (Hove 1971,78; Hove 1983, 81, fig. 105-107; Rasmussen 1970, 206).[4]

Peat cutting and peat kneading was known in almost all parts of Denmark during the last 100 years, but the kneading process was predominant during that period in eastern Denmark. In most Jutish bogs peat could still be cut at the end of the 19th century and even later where peat had to be brought up wet from a considerable depth. They were kneaded and moulded in peat moulds before drying. Cf. the distribution map (fig. 2) (Rasmussen 1970, 201).

One marked difference between more recent peat spades and the T-shaped ones is that the latter do not

have a long handle. It is therefore clear that the T-shaped spade was not used as a shovel.[5]

Neither on any of the Danish spades found nor in the information about finds is there any indication of a longer handle. Only one find description mentions that a stick found together with a T-shaped spade from around the beginning of the Christian era might have belonged to it (Hingst 1959, 394, Table 133 No. 3; Hove 1983, 44).

Geographical distribution (fig. 3)

Altogether there are now a total of 245 T-shaped peat spades recorded in Denmark. These are kept in the National Museum, local museums, and in private collections.

There are no finds from Funen and Zealand or the area north of Limfjorden (Jutland), but a marked concentration is seen in the areas around Herning, Skive, Silkeborg and Hobro. One find is known from Thy, but the find information is inaccurate and it is therefore not included in fig. 3. Two finds are known from the Maribo Museum, but only one is shown, since one has been lost. It indicates, however, that the region is not devoid of finds.

The explanation for this distribution can probably be found not only in the prehistoric context but in a number of other factors described elsewhere in this book. There have been different accession policies in various museums, and some spades offered to the National Museum were rejected because of the large collection already in existence. In Zealand extensive bog areas are less frequent than in Jutland, and in many bogs the upper layers were removed at an early date, before the awakening of historical interest and the development of museums. This may account for the lack of finds in the area. The contribution of alert local amateur archaeologists in other regions, e.g. around Hobro, should also be taken into account. In spite of the many factors which may have influenced the present find frequency, archaeologists should examine more closely what may have produced the concentration in western Denmark. Who lived here, and what patterns of settlement, way of life, etc. did the people have here which differed from other regions in Denmark? The distribution of T-shaped spades should thus be compared with the equivalent maps of other find groups.

It should be mentioned in this connection that the distribution of T-shaped spades does not coincide completely with that of double paddle-spades (fig. 6). It seems unlikely therefore that these implements were used for the same type of work. The T-shaped spade has been found in Lolland, Funen, Langeland, and southern Jutland, where the double paddle-spade is not known. Moreover, at least five T-spades are known from Schleswig-Holstein (Kersten 1951, 99, 284 and Abb. 70 Nos. 2 and 3; Hingst 1959, 65, 394 and Table 133 No. 3; Tensbüttel – unpublished, but on display in the Nydamhalle in the museum of Gottorp Castle in Schleswig).[6] A Scania item is in Landskrona Museum (Mus. No. LM 790).

Frequency, Context and Depth of Finds

Of the total of 245 finds of T-shaped spades from Denmark, 139 (c. 57%) have a known year of discovery (fig. 4). The diagram shows when the finds were made, and also whether they were found in bogs or not. One hundred and ten spades (79%) are in fact from bogs, while the remaining 29 (21%) were found elsewhere.

The very active peat cutting around the Second World War to replace imported fuels resulted in many finds, and museum staff were favourably disposed towards bog finds. Strangely enough there is no particular concentration of finds shown on the bar graph around the time of the First World War. This may be related to the depth of finds and the methods of peat cutting used.

Only 47 out of all the finds (19%) have information on the find depth. Information on find depth can seldom be regarded and used as an accurate statement of depth in relation to the original ground surface, since it was probably given by the finder in terms of depth below the then surface of that part of the bog. Sometimes after several years of cutting peat in one part of a bog, the area is left undisturbed for some years before cutting is resumed. The ground surface at the second peat cutting may be 0.9-1.5 metres lower than it was originally. The following extract from the records of Herning Museum may serve as an example: "... the area was then dug for a second time. It [the spade] lay in the mire". (Mus. No. 29/42). "It was dug for the third time" (Mus. No. 115/30); or the bog is "14 klyne (peats) deep, [the spade] lay at a depth of 10 klyne (peats)" (Mus. No. 83/34); or "c. 1.5 metres deep, and some way from the bottom, [it] lay almost on its side" (Mus. No. 18/42).

In 12 cases the find depth is given as 1.2-1.5 m, but in some cases this is also the bottom of the peat bog: "c. 1.5 metres deep on the sandy bottom". Three finds are

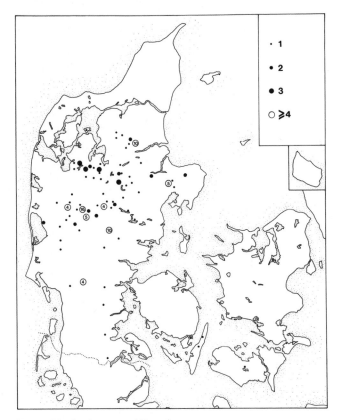

Fig. 3. Distribution map of T-spades.

recorded to have lain higher in the bog, i.e. c. 1 m down, while only a few lay from 2 to 4 m. Descriptions such as "deep in the bog"; "in one metre of mire"; "lay deep in the mire"; "c. 1 metre deep in funnel-shaped holes"; "c. 1.8 metres deep in peat bog"; "in mire on top of the sandy bottom under the peat"; "near the sandy bottom", etc. show that the artefacts were often found at a considerable depth.

In 16 cases there is information that the T-shaped spade was lying on the "sandy bottom" (the sandy layer that formed the bottom of the peat bog). But the statement: "there was c. 7 feet of bog, but the spade lay near the surface" (Mus. No. 47/43, Herning), shows that discoveries can occur at little depth, and makes it likely that the tool entered the bog while the latter was still being formed. We must also bear in mind that the method of peat cutting was not so systematic in earlier times that people in fact began at one end of the bog and carried on to the other end. Moreover, tools may have been left behind either on the bottom of the pits from which peat had been taken, or perhaps in the bank of the peat cutting.[7]

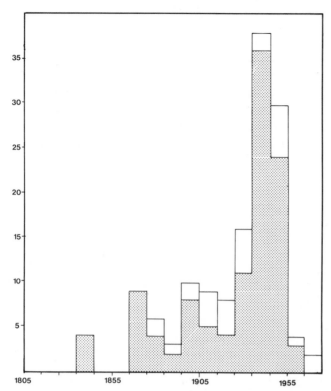

Fig. 4. Find frequency of T-spades, spades found in bogs – shaded.

DOUBLE PADDLE-SPADES

There is a large group of wooden objects with a rounded shaft in the middle and a narrow, oval blade at both ends, which have so far been interpreted by Danish archaeologists as double paddles used in dug-out canoes.[8]

When these were examined more closely, it was seen that some of the paddle-shaped blades on the so-called double paddles preserved in Danish museums bore distinct marks of sharpening and use. Furthermore, the blades were not always the same length, which makes them unsuitable for paddling. It is therefore more likely that the tools were used to dig into an element harder and more compact than water.

The "double paddles" found in Denmark in a prehistoric context are interpreted by the present author as spades with a blade at both ends, so that the spade could be turned around when one end became too blunt or worn. The tools will therefore be referred to in this paper as *double paddle-spades* (fig. 5) (for a more detailed discussion see Lerche 1977).

They are all carved from one piece of wood, in most cases oak.[9] Most of the spades are between 0.9 and 1.6 m long, and the length of the blades, when not of equal length, usually varies between 2 and 9 cm. The shaft between the blades has a length ranging from 12-40 cm (Lerche 1977, 114-115). With regard to blade length we must bear in mind that a hand tool is as personal a possession as one's clothing. It must have the right height and the right strength (see also Lerche 1977, 115-116). In other words we cannot assume a theoretical original length for them all. Most are either little worn, or have become very worn and have had the edge re-sharpened, while others are completely worn down.

The use of both double and single paddle-spades has a much wider geographical and chronological range than would appear from the fairly limited distribution of Danish prehistoric material, although this has a strong numerical representation[10]. It should be mentioned that the Danish double paddle-spades fit into the general picture of the many different kinds of prehistoric digging activities such as in ancient fields (balks and ditches), house- and fencebuilding (wall foundations and post

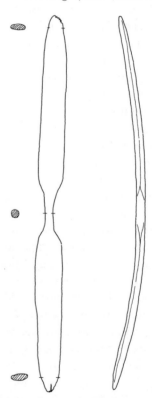

Fig. 5. Double paddle-spade Nat. Mus. No. C 25742. Scale 1:10, from Fly bog and parish, Fjends district, Viborg county. One of four spades from the same place.

holes), turf cutting (for houses and burial mounds), etc. revealed by archaeological excavations. These testify that the ancestors of the Danish people must have made use of many different kinds of tools for their digging activities, including spades, hoes and digging sticks (Lerche 1976, 110ff; Lerche 1977, 122-123; Lerche 1980, 57).[11]

The pronounced wear on many of the double paddle-spades suggests that they were used to dig moraine soils containing gravel and pebbles, and not for digging soft peat.

A couple of double paddle-spades have been reconstructed, and now function excellently in connection with the activities of the Iron Age village at the *Historisk-Arkæologisk Forsøgscenter* (:Historical-Archaeological Research Centre) in Lejre. Naturally those using the tools had to be instructed how to handle them properly when working with them, after which the impression that they are awkward to work with soon vanished (Lerche 1977, 120-121) and ditches for new fences were dug by double paddle-spades in 1979.

Geographical Distribution

At the finish of the investigation there were 281 double paddle-spades registered in Denmark.[12] The map in fig. 6 shows all finds for which the place of discovery is known. The finds are surprisingly concentrated. Not only are they limited to Jutland, but there are large areas with no finds in southern and East Jutland. There is a clustering of finds in Himmerland and westwards past Viborg and Skive down along the west coast of Jutland. They are not found south of a line from Nymindegab to Horsens. A few finds are known from Vendsyssel and Djursland and the more easterly parts of Jutland. One double paddle-spade is kept at Samsø Museum, and may have been found on the island, but since there is no information on the find situation it is not shown on the map.

Some museums outside the area where finds are concentrated have a few double paddle-spades in their collections, but according to their records these invariably turned out to have been found in Jutland. The two double paddle-spades (Mus. No. A 2959) in the Langelands Museum, for example, came from a bog near Viborg. They were donated by J. Winther in 1905. A specimen in the Antiquarian Collection in Ribe is also described as having been found in a bog near Viborg (Mus. No. 2091), but the other three in this collection (Nos. 8230, 8232, 8233) "have lain in the museum from

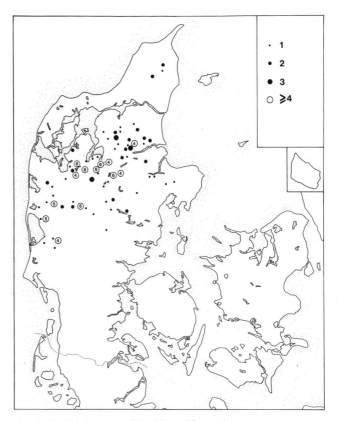

Fig. 6. Distribution map of double paddle-spades.

an early time", for which reason the statement that they were probably found in the river did not permit their inclusion on the map.

We may wonder why there is such a striking distribution in Denmark and not in Scandinavia as a whole. Apart from Jutland only one prehistoric double paddle-spade is so far known in Scandinavia.[13] This is a specimen made of oak, of the same type as the Danish examples, 169 cm long, with one blade 64.5 cm and the other 45 cm long, and a shaft of 59.5 cm. It was found during peat cutting in 1926 in the parish of Öja near Gemla in Småland, Sweden, and is now in the collections of Växjö Museum (Mus. No. 3672). The circumstances of the find were the same as in Denmark, i.e. it was lying horizontally on the bottom of a bog. It is thought to belong to the Celtic Iron Age (Kjellmark 1936, 364-370).

As mentioned with reference to T-shaped spades, there may be several reasons for the distribution of the two types of wooden tool, and their distribution must naturally be compared to the map showing other archaeological phenomena which will be analysed in this volume. If we compare the distribution of T-shaped peat

14*

212

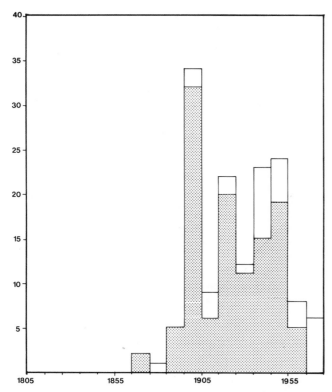

Fig. 7. Find frequency of double paddle-spades found in bogs – shaded.

spades and double paddle-spades, it appears from the maps that their distribution does *not* coincide completely. Peat spades are found in Lolland, Funen, Langeland, southern Jutland, Schleswig-Holstein and Scania, i.e. in areas where there are no reports of finds of double paddle-spades. It is therefore unlikely that the two types of tool were used for the same kind of work (Hove 1971, 1978). The material available has not provided a wholly satisfying explanation for this distribution. A broader archaeologically based interpretation may provide answer in the future.

Dating

All double paddle-spades found in Denmark are assumed to be prehistoric. Three of the implements have been dated by C-14 to the Pre-Roman Iron Age. The double paddle-spade at Ringkøbing Museum (Mus. No. G 747), found at Rybjerg bog in Velling parish, Ringkøbing county, has been dated to 330 b.c. (415 B.C. calibrated). The other double paddle-spade in the Ringkøbing Museum from Holmegårds bog, Sønder Lem parish, Ringkøbing county, is dated to 220 b.c. (240-355 B.C.

calibrated). A third one in the 1st department of the National Museum (Mus. No. A 31066) is dated to 180 b.c. (185 B.C. calibrated). It was found in peaty soil in Østrup village, Aalborg county. But a double paddle-spade also in the 1st department of the National Museum (No. C 25478) found in Ålestrup bog has recently been dated to 770 b.c. (945 B.C. calibrated), i.e. to the Bronze Age. It is a considerably long period to find an unchanged tool type.

The idea of giving a hand tool two working-ends has been used also for digging sticks. A rather big and straight stick without the slightest paddle shape has also been C-14 dated to the Bronze Age 710 b.c. (810 B.C. calibrated). It is not only from the same period as the famous Døstrup ard (890 B.C. calibrated) but also from the same bog.[14]

Frequency, Context and Depth of Finds

As mentioned above, 281 double paddle-spades have been registered. This total includes specimens from the National Museum's three Danish departments, from local museums, and a few private collections, including that of Regnar Pedersen in Nysum. Approximately 95 of the total number are found in the National Museum.

Only 34 specimens (12%) have no information on the place and circumstance of discovery, while it is stated for 163 (c. 58%) that they were found in bogs – most of these, of course, as a result of peat cutting. Eighty-four double paddle-spades (30%) were discovered by other means (while ploughing, digging ditches etc.).

All finds for which the year of discovery is known are shown on the bar graph in fig. 7. It appears from this that the year of discovery is known for 115 (c. 70%) of all spades found in bogs. The year of discovery is known for only 31 examples (37%) of spades not found in bogs. The diagram shows clearly that the rate of discovery has been high in certain periods, including both World Wars, when the need for indigenous fuels resulted in an increase in peat production. It is perhaps somewhat surprising that the find frequency was so high up to 1955, since in its last phase peat extraction was more mechanized. No satisfactory explanation seems possible for the very large number of finds in the period 1895-1905. About half of all the double paddle-spades in the National Museum for which the year of discovery is known were found during this period. Was there a general interest in wooden objects at the Museum at that time, which later was lost?

There were also many newly established local museums throughout Denmark to house artefacts.

Double paddle-spades are usually found in bogs. As a rule more than one spade was found at the spot, or it was associated with other wooden objects and pottery. Sometimes it was found with a T-shaped spade. However, one double paddle-spade of known find-context was found beside a dug-out canoe.[15] Double paddle-spades are often found lying horizontally on the sandy layer at the bottom of bogs; or less than one metre above the bottom; or between 1.3 m and 1.8 m beneath the surface.[16]

CONCLUSION

In this paper I have drawn attention to two types of wooden object which deserve the attention of the archaeologist, both because of their unusual distribution pattern and the very large number of finds. What other groups of wooden artefacts have been preserved in such numbers? This may reflect their importance in everyday life during the period to which they belong. Until recently all the evidence indicated that both tool types belonged to the Pre-Roman Iron Age; but the recent C-14 datings show that the span of time is much longer from late Bronze Age to late Pre-Roman Iron Age and because of the unchanged shape for both tool types, we may assume that they had well adapted shapes for the many digging purposes which were common in prehistoric man's daily life. Their function as peat spades and digging spades, respectively, has only been touched on here but is described elsewhere (Lerche 1977; Hove 1983). But in the future more attention should be given to the types of implements that were used by prehistoric man to carry out such work as soil cultivation, digging holes, ditches, building mounds, banks, cutting turf for house building and peat for fuel etc. These are all activities which archaeological excavations demonstrate have taken place.

Grith Lerche,
The National Museum, Brede,
International Secretariat for Research on the History of Agricultural Implements,
DK – 2800 Lyngby

NOTES

1. In connection with a study of double paddle-spades, the T-shaped peat spades were also recorded. In 1971 the *Kgl. danske Videnskabernes Selskabs Kommission til Udforskning af Landbrugsredskabernes og Ager-* *strukturernes Historie* (:Royal Danish Academy of Sciences and Letters Commission for Research on the History of Agricultural Implements and Field Structures) sent out a questionnaire to the Scandinavian and North German museums of cultural history about whether T-shaped were found in their collections.

2. Unfortunately the chapter *Dating* has dropped out in the last proof. The first C-14 datings of this tool-type are quite recent. All T-shaped spades were assumed to be from the late Pre-Roman Iron Age, e.g. the finds from Schleswig-Holstein as well as one of the spades from Langeland (Mus.No. C591), but a scoop from the Nørre Smedeby find is now C-14 dated to 340 b.c. (420 B.C. calib.) and two finds from Ringkøbing county, West Jutland, have also been C-14 dated to earlier periods respectively to 430 b.c. (475 B.C. calib.) and to 500 b.c. (600 B.C. calib.) (see Lerche 1983,216). The time of *use* might well be 40-200 years later, but the datings widens the time span for the use of such tools to include the latest Bronze Age.

3. In 1946-48 in Rüde bog south of the town of Satrup, Kreis Schleswig, several Iron Age peat cutting pits were found, 3-5 m long, 2-3 m wide and 0.6-1.2 m deep. Some were divided into two, with a bank of peat left standing. Several pieces of Iron Age pottery, votive dishes etc. were recovered, and peats (10×6×4.5 cm) with a high calory rating.

4. There need not have been a separate implement for each function in prehistoric peat cutting. The T-shaped spade was presumably used to cut off columns of soft peat from the back of the banks from top to bottom in the bog. The implement can be pushed down or pulled upwards with both hands on the cross-bar. Whether it cuts into the peat horizontally or vertically is thus irrelevant; it remains a cutting implement with no device for lifting.

5. It may be noted that bare hands can always be used as a shovel, and such a "shovel" was probably often used in prehistoric times, as can be seen today in several primitive societies (see e.g. *Tools and Tillage* III:2, 1977, 117-; and *Tools and Tillage* II:2, 1973, 87 ff., which discusses digging in New Guinea). The T-spade has only a cross-bar handle fastened with a peg, 4-6 cm wide and only c. 7 cm long, in the upper end of the blade. A wooden pin through a hole in the peg keeps the handle in place.

6. The T-spades were found in Koberg, Damendorf, Rethwisch, and Tensbüttel. The implement was recognized as a peat spade by the prehistorians in Gottorp, but not by the Museum's ethnological staff. However, an *"Armbohr"* (:"Arm drill") is recorded of the same size (73.5 cm, length of handle 35.0 cm) and nearly the same shape as the T-shaped peat spade, but the cross-handle of the *Armbohr* was fastened with five nails, and the implement was made of beech and hazel wood. Information from Dr. A. Lühning on the use of the *Armbohr* is far removed from any interpretation of its function as a peat-cutting implement. The *Armbohr* was apparently used to cut through a thatch roof so that a man could thrust his arm in and thereby pull cord and stakes through more easily to sew the thatch on firmly. Only this one specimen is known. Dr. Lühning's interpretation has not received much support, but we have mentioned it because it cannot be ruled out that the implement had another function than cutting peat. However, the peat spade interpretation does seem more plausible (Alan Hjorth Rasmussen: *Strâtage* (:Thatch Roofs). Copenhagen 1966).

7. That several of the implements were in fact used is shown by, for example, marks left on the handle by the pressure of the wooden

peg. In the best preserved specimens the edge of the blade may be a little worn, and sometimes there are visible marks of a knife used to sharpen and fine down the edge of the blade. Where the type of wood is identifiable, only oak has been used.

The degree of preservation of these tools varies a great deal. Some of the examples in Department I of the National Museum were unfortunately preserved in the 1930s. Many have dried out, and others have deep cuts, made by the blades of modern iron spades when they were found; some have been cut right through. As mentioned above, the cross-handles have often been lost.

8. Double paddles of a similar shape used in canoes are known among the Canadian Eskimos, and in Greenland, Northern White Russia, and several East Slavonic countries (K. Moszynski: *Kultura Ludowa Slowian*. Swedish ed. 10234, 673). A similar type used for the same purpose is also known in South America (e.g. Hans Dietrich Disselhoff: *Alltag im alten Peru*. Munich 1966, 92). But the paddle-spade is known in South America and often registered as oar or digging stick in museum collections.

Other interpretations have been proposed. The double-bladed implement may have been a bow, a weapon, a ladle used in e.g. stirring boiling tar, or a fishing float. None of these interpretations are very convincing.

9. When wood identification tests were applied to 102 examples, it appeared that 59 were of oak, while only 12 could with some uncertainty be identified as ash, elm, willow or pine. It was difficult to identify the type of wood in the other specimens because of their conditions of preservation. Light wood gives good oars, hard wood strong spades.

10. This chronological and geographical range is expressed in several articles (Best 1925, Kramer 1966, Lerche and Steensberg 1973, Lerche 1977, Raum 1977, Gorecki 1978, Steensberg 1980).

11. A double digging stick found in Døstrup, same parish, Ålborg county, North Jutland, has now been radiocarbon-dated to 710 b.c. (890 B.C. calibrated) (Lerche 1983, 57). Known to me is also a nicely shaped digging stick found at the Muldbjerg site in Åmosen, Zealand, belonging to the earliest phase of the Funnel beaker culture c. 3000 b.c. (2800-3900 B.C. calibrated).

12. This was the number reached on June 1, 1977. In spite of the questionnaire and visits to most museums in order to trace double paddle-spades, new items will probably turn up after publication of this paper. Not all objects were accessible in the museum store-rooms, and some may have remained unregistered after they were excavated. Furthermore, certain museums with a large collection of double paddle-spades (registered as "double-oars") have declined to accept any more. Consequently, these implements have either been discarded or may eventually turn up in a private collection.

13. The collection of data on double paddle-spades began 16 years ago during a study of digging tools in Danish provincial museums.

As mentioned in the section on T-shaped peat spades, the two types of wooden implements were recorded at the same time, and all Danish museums of cultural history besides museums in Sweden, Norway, Finland, and Northern Germany were sent a questionnaire asking whether such implements were found in their collections. The spade from Växsjö was the only positive response concerning double paddle-spades outside Denmark.

14. The C-14 sample number of the Rybjerg spade is K-1252. The C-14 sample number of the Holmegård find is K-1251. The age of the latter can be given only as an interval, since the C-14 scale is uncertain in this period. The C-14 date may therefore represent a slightly different absolute age within the interval given, according to information from H. Tauber, Jan. 1979. The C-14 dating of the Østrup and the Ålestrup double paddle-spades (K-3267 and K-3268) and the Døstrup digging stick (K-3266) are published in *Tools and Tillage* Vol. IV:1, 1980 p. 57, 58 and in Lerche and Steensberg 1980 p. 82, 86.

15. Mus. No. A 17059, Dept. I, National Museum. It was found in Stokholm bog, Vebbestrup parish, in the Ålborg district. Another has been exhibited with a dug-out canoe in Grenå Museum.

16. The horizontal position was the most common, except for three double paddle-spades – Mus. Nos. A 20185, A 20186, and A 20187, Dept. I, National Museum – which were found together in 1902 in Kvolsted bog near Hjarbæk fiord, Taarup parish, Fjends district, formerly in Viborg county; and one which was found in 1897 in Gassum bog, Gassum parish, Nørhald district, formerly in the county of Randers. These four items were found standing in a sloping or nearly vertical position (Lerche 1977, 113).

REFERENCES

Best, Elsdon: 1925, *Maori Agriculture*. Wellington.

Gorecki, P. P.: 1978, Further Notes on Prehistoric Wooden Spades from the New Guinea Highlands, in: *Tools and Tillage* III:3, 185-190.

Hingst, Hans: 1959, *Vorgeschichte des Kreises Stormarn*. Neumünster, p. 394 and plate 133 No. 3.

Hove, Th. Th.: 1983, *Tørvegravning i Danmark*. Fra håndgravning til moseindustri. Udvikling og vilkår. (Ed. Grith Lerche). Herning.

– 1971, Tørvegravning i Oldtiden. *MIV* No. 7. Viborg.

Kramer, Fritz: 1966, *Breaking Ground*. Sacramento. California.

Kersten, K.: 1951, *Vorgeschichte des Kreises Herzogtum Lauenburg*. Neumünster, p. 99, 284 and fig. 70 No. 2 and 3.

Kjellmark, Knut: 1936, Fund och Föremål i Svenska Museer. En förhistorisk paddelåra funnen nära Gemla i Småland, in: *Fornvännen* Vol. 31, 364-370.

Lerche, Grith: 1976, The Spades from Dannevirke and Jelling, in: *Folk and Farm*. Ed. C.Ó. Danachair. Dublin.

– 1977, Double Paddle-Spades in Prehistoric Contexts in Denmark, in: *Tools and Tillage* III: 2, 111-124.

– 1975, 1980, 1983, The Radiocarbon dated Implements, in: *Tools and Tillage* Vol. II:4, IV:1 and IV:4. Copenhagen.

Lerche, Grith and Steensberg, Axel: 1973. Observations on Spade-Cultivation in the New Guinea Highlands, in: *Tools and Tillage* II:2, 87-104.

– 1980, *Agricultural Tools and Field Shapes*. Copenhagen.

Rasmussen, Holger: 1970, Peat cutting in Denmark, in: *The Spade in Northern and Atlantic Europe* (ed. Gailey and Fenton). Belfast, 200 ff.

Raum, O. F.: 1977, The Culture Historical Significance of the Xhosa Spade, in: *Tools and Tillage* III:2, 99-110.

Schwabedissen, Hermann: 1951, Torfstiche mit Opfergefässen der Eisenzeit aus dem Rüder Moor, Kreis Schleswig, in: *Offa* Vol 9, 46-52.

Steensberg, Axel: 1980, *New Guinea Gardens*. London.

Ship Finds and Ship Blockages A D 800-1200

by OLE CRUMLIN-PEDERSEN

INTRODUCTION

In registering archaeological discoveries on land one can usually without much trouble have the site identified, surveyed and measured in relation to an established measuring system by means of ordnance and cadastral maps, but with marine finds one is in a much more difficult position.

Visibility in Danish waters is seldom more than a few metres and in many places is less than half a metre. This, together with currents, wave action and the cold water etc., can make a survey of underwater sites extremely difficult even for trained divers. In addition, the parish and property boundaries known inland do not continue out into the sea. Here quite different methods of fixing the position must be used, which at best may be very accurate, but which are based on technical knowledge and equipment not normally found in Danish museums. Therefore, the information required for exact location of the position is rarely registered for marine finds acquired by museums, even in cases where the finder possesses such data, e.g. in the form of bearings or Decca-readings. There is therefore no exaggeration in claiming that in Denmark we are a hundred years behind in the registration of underwater archaeological finds, compared to the situation on land. This obviously affects the possibilities of using the material in interpreting the past. If two of the underwater archaeological find groups – blockages and wrecks – are nevertheless discussed here, it is primarily because the material exists and is highly deserving of the archaeological attention which may help to ensure that the necessary registration and surveying will be carried out on a sound basis. At the same time this provides an opportunity for a brief discussion of a number of the socio-economic factors which, through the past registration activity of the Institute of Nautical Archaeology of the Danish National Museum, has proved to lead to the discovery of underwater archaeological finds.

SOURCE-CRITICAL FACTORS

In the following we shall use the term "nautical archaeology" for the archaeological activity concerned with sites which are connected with the use by prehistoric societies of the sea, rivers, and lakes for transport, economic exploitation, warfare etc. The term has the advantage over "underwater archaeology" that it delimits the field of activity to exclude the investigation of Stone Age settlements that by the movement of land and sea have been covered by water. Furthermore, it does not confine the researcher to working under water, but allows for the investigation of relevant finds on dry land.

The most important find groups in nautical archaeology are various fixed constructions connected with shipping, fishing, maritime defence etc. (e.g. harbours, ship blockages, canals, navigation marks, fixed fishing equipment etc.), as well as moveable finds (e.g. ships, components or cargoes of ships, anchors, fishing tackle etc.). Legislation in theory provides full protection for these find groups. In practice, however, it extends only to finds in so far as they are known and can be kept under control with respect to diving and other activities.

Sites in nautical archaeology are, of course, concentrated in the boundary between land and sea, rather than in deep water or on dry land. Landing stages, bridges etc. were built on the beaches while in the shallow water off the coast were found ship blockages, natural harbours, fishing tackle etc. Wrecks are concentrated along the dangerous coasts and bars or in the "ships' graveyards" near old harbours. It is therefore very important to have a detailed knowledge of changes in the coastline over time.

Over the last 1,000 years in Denmark there do not seem to have been major *changes in sea level* in relation to the land surface. We can probably count on a maximum difference of one metre from the present level as a result of some periodic minor changes. In future nautical archaeology will probably be able to contribute to a more detailed knowledge of this.

Of far greater influence on the character of the coastal area has been the *erosion* of projecting parts of the coast and especially the *deposition of material* where the coast is indented. In many places this has radically altered the coastline and its navigation potential. Dutch studies of sand dunes (S. Jelgersma *et al.* 1970, p. 147) have shown that in the North Sea since the 12th century there seems to have been an increased frequency of storms from the west and north-west, which may explain the probable closure of Limfjorden to the west in the 12th century. This also means that the Danish west coast may have changed its character radically since the Viking Period, if the process of coastal adjustment only began in earnest at this time. This process seems to have taken place on the east coast at an earlier period, judging from the Hasnæs wrecks. Remains of these were found in 1961 when digging gravel from the wide beach ridge plain Øer Hage, built up by material from the east coast of Djursland. The site containing wreckage from the 6th century A. D. lay c. 160 metres inland from the present coastline, whereas parts of a ship from c. 1,000 A. D. lay scattered along a beach ridge only 50 metres inland. Here deposition has extended the coastline by 110 metres in the first 5 centuries, but by only 50 metres in the following 9-10 centuries. There may have been special conditions involved in this case, but the example shows the potential value of nautical archaeology in throwing light on prehistoric coastal and climatic conditions, in collaboration with geology.

The closure of previously navigable areas has also been furthered by *shifting sand* and material deposited by rivers and streams, together with the growth of marsh plants. At Ellingå north of Frederikshavn in 1968 a medieval wreck was excavated, which lay two to four metres below the surface of the field, 800 metres inland from the present coastline. A geological examination showed that the ship when wrecked lay in a small bay or lagoon, which was the northernmost natural harbour on the east coast of Jutland. This has since been completely silted up by shifting sand and river-borne sediments.

Only in very rare cases will mediaeval or earlier shipwrecks etc. be preserved unless they are imbedded in marine deposits of sand, mud etc. In Danish seas exposed wood will be attacked by fungi and bacteria, which soften its outer layers. In this way the wood automatically becomes vulnerable to wear and to boring moluscs and crustaceans, which make large and small holes in it, whereas speedy and almost total destruction results from the attack of ship worms. These are common in Danish seas, except in the brackish waters of the Baltic.

This means that finds of early wrecks and blockages are usually only made when early marine deposits are disturbed by natural or human activity. Such disturbances may occur in connection with changes in winds and currents caused by either climatic changes or by floods and gales. Special conditions, such as the worldwide epidemic of grass-wrack *(Zostera)* which hit in Denmark in 1932, may also produce increased erosion on the sea bed. The great activity in recent years with the extraction of sand and gravel in Danish waters for the building industry (c. 10,000,000 m³ p.a.), together with oyster shells for agriculture (c. 100,000 m³ p.a. in Roskilde fiord), give rise to considerable displacements on the sea floor. Whilst gravel-digging on land threatens only those prehistoric remains directly involved, the construction of jetties, bridges etc. and the excavation of marine deposits may affect conditions of deposition several kilometres from the place of actual activity. This is because of reduced friction between particles in suspension and because water currents have a great capacity for carrying sediments.

It is primarily in connection with the actual digging in older sea bed deposits that wrecks and ship blockages are found. This happened, for instance, in the drainage work as part of the many *reclamation* schemes carried out in the period 1840-1920 in order to increase the area of agricultural land, and since 1950 to provide land for industry, oil refineries and purifying plants. The digging of foundations in areas long ago filled in, e.g. large parts of inner Copenhagen, can also produce many finds. The construction of harbours and the dredging of channels over the years since the 1830's in the Danish fiords have also in many cases led to contact with ship blockages and wrecks, and data on these are often available in archival sources on Danish harbours.

Dredging and Harbour Construction

The development of Danish harbours is closely connected with *the socio-economic development*. Before 1800 most provincial towns in Denmark had no proper harbour, but only a simple landing stage for the loading and unloading of ships. In many cases ships had to lie at anchor some distance from the town and unload into lighters, which carried the goods over the shoals to the town. In the decades around 1800 many towns began to study the possibilities of improving harbour facilities, partly to ensure the sale of the increased agricultural production. Generally the first step was to survey the harbour entrance. Thus in 1813 P. J. Hjorth conducted the first detailed survey of Roskilde fiord. With its many channels and blockages the fiord can be seen as an underwater cultural landscape which today is in parts changed beyond recognition by dredging and the digging for oyster shells.

With the state bankruptcy of 1813 and the agricultural depression that lasted till 1828 many of the planned *dredging schemes* were delayed, but were set in motion from around 1830, e.g. in Roskilde fiord 1833-36, while Haderslev fiord was first dredged in 1830-46, and again in 1856-59. In both fiords stake barriers were encountered during the work. These had to be partly removed to clear the fairway (Crumlin-Pedersen 1966, 1975 & 1978). Additional dredging was required in Haderslev fiord in 1899-1902 and in 1922-23 to provide a depth of 6.5 metres for the new steamships and motor vessels, while Roskilde was unable to dig the channel through its fiord deeper than the 3.0 metres that had been achieved by dredging operations in the 1870's.

Generally the harbours made a point of providing good conditions for steamships. Of the 64 harbours in 1871 which had registered shipping, 54 increased their depth in the period up to 1901. In the same period only 5 harbours had not extended their depth af the quays, and 5 others were more or less left to silt up, usually because they had lost their importance as ports, e.g. Ribe and Næstved (Flagbogen 1871 & 1901).

In the same period a number of *new harbours* were built (e.g. Fakse Ladeplads 1862-64 and Esbjerg 1868-74). Similarly, many landing stages were built in connection with the cultivation of sugar beet, which was introduced in the 1870's.

Harbour extension continued after 1900, and new types of harbour were introduced when special *ferry ports* were built for the many new ferry routes to serve motor traffic in the 1950's and 1960's. These were usually built on parts of the open coast where there had not previously been any appreciable maritime activity. Long jetties of large stones were constructed to protect the ports. In a few places, e.g. in Marstal, these were built mainly of field stones, including megaliths, but were otherwise usually constructed from stones from the sea bed. The collection of such stones took place wherever large stones were found on the littoral near the ports, or in the sea at depths of up to c. 10 metres, which included a few blockage constructions. In 1906 it became necessary to stop such activity by means of coastal preservation legislation passed to protect coastal areas against the increasing erosion.

The increased leisure and greater affluence, which in the 1960's was expressed in widespread building of summer cottages, resulted in the 1970's mainly in a large increase in the number of pleasure boats. The necessary harbour facilities are now being developed at a tremendous pace, and in contrast to commercial and ferry ports, which have moved from the old seafaring centres to deeper and more open waters, *yachting harbours* are largely situated according to criteria similar to those which determined the location of military and trading ports etc. in the Viking Period and the Middle Ages. In this way situations continuously occur where work on new harbours for pleasure boats produces nautical archaeological sites. Unless these finds are registered and examined immediately, invaluable evidence for our interpretation of the area's prehistory may be lost. If these problems are to be dealt with in a proper way, grants must be made over a number of years for a systematic registration of archaeological finds and constructions on the sea bed. In this way archaeological interests can be taken into account during the planning of harbour projects, and costly work stoppages avoided.

Diving Techniques

A decisive technical precondition for work on the sea floor has been the technical development in diving. This can be divided into two periods: that of *heavy* diving equipment unchallenged for about 100 years from around 1840, and that of *light* diving equipment since the Second World War. During the period of heavy equipment, staying and working under water was confined to a small number of professional civilian and military divers, and salvagers of stones and wrecks etc. An outstanding exception was the investigation of a mediaeval shipwreck in Kolding fiord in 1943-44, when amongst others the then director of the National Museum, Poul Nørlund, played an active part as diver. Since the mid-1950's light diving equipment has become so widespread that there are now an estimated 5-10,000 active amateur divers in Denmark, while diving is also now gaining a foothold as a natural aid in marine science and nautical archaeology.

The many amateur divers, most of whom belong to the Danish Amateur Divers' Association (DSF), are a heterogeneous group. The majority of them do not have the farming or teaching background which has traditionally characterized many amateur archaeologists on land in Denmark. Since 1971 courses have therefore been arranged, in cooperation with the DSF archaeological committee for amateur divers with an interest in archaeology, to ensure that over the whole country there will be people who can assist the museums in their registration of marine finds and give the other club members an increased understanding of the necessity to protect antiquities on the sea bed from destruction.

Summing up, we may say that finds of wrecks and ship blockages from the Viking Period and Middle Ages are mainly associated with the contemporaneous littoral zone and narrow fairways, and that socio-economic developments since 1830 have affected several underwater sites. However, most of the finds were made at a time when there was little tradition or technical possibility of carrying out archaeological investigations at the site. If information about the finds can be traced at all, it must be in newspaper articles and in archival sources (e.g. port registers) that are not archaeologically orientated, but may contain technical data of considerable interest.

We may expect that the intensive construction of yachting harbours along the Danish coasts in recent years will bring many new finds to light. It is of the greatest importance that the museums and relevant authorities should be provided in time with the necessary means for registration and investigation.

SHIP FINDS A D 800-1200

At first sight it may seem impossible to include ship finds in any representativity analysis of Danish archaeological find groups. This is partly because of the complexity and relatively small number of ship finds, partly because ships by their very nature are mobile and often end up far from their home ports. A ship may also change its home port several times, and objects may be found on board about which it is impossible to decide without further evidence whether they are part of the cargo or personal property of the crew. Moreover, the crew may have included many nationalities. Consequently, ship finds cannot be compared methodologically to house sites, burials, votive offerings, hoards, or loose finds – they comprise a distinctive group of their own.

When subjected to critical analysis which takes account of the special circumstances of this find group, ship finds may, however, directly and indirectly increase our knowledge of some of the important factors which have determined the development of prehistoric cultures and have been the driving force behind their changes. Furthermore, ship finds may contribute significantly to dating techniques, in that a wreck with its contents is a closed find, in which everything has been "deposited" at the same time.

It is therefore essential that the analysis and interpretation of ship finds should be carried out on such a methodical basis that the conclusions, both specific and general, drawn from the material can be understood and evaluated outside the narrow circle of specialists in this field. If this succeeds, ship finds may gradually provide important information on the level of technology and the economic and social structure of prehistoric cultures. Similarly, knowledge of the size and type of ship is essential for evaluating the interplay between navigation and patterns of settlement and fortification which have shaped decisively the Danish cultural landscape.

Context of Ship Finds

The situation which has led to the preservation up to today of a particular ancient vessel or significant parts of it, may have come about in different ways. The vessel found may have been:

1. *Sacrificed* a) as a grave offering, deposited burnt or unburnt in the grave,
   b) as an offering of war, deposited whole or broken in a bog.
2. *Sunk* a) in warfare, rammed, or as a fire-ship,
   b) as an offensive blockage of the enemy's exit routes,
   c) as a defensive blockage of one's own approach routes,

d) as a foundation for filling-in,

e) on shallow water for breaking up.

3. *Wrecked* a) sunk in a natural harbour or in sheltered waters,

b) wrecked on the open coast,

c) sunk in open waters.

Furthermore, parts of ships can be found re-used as building material on land or in other ships, and detached parts of ships can be found which do not necessarily reflect the shipwreck or sinking of the ship itself (e.g. timbers deposited for seasoning or detached rudders).

One may expect certain definite relations between the circumstances of the find and the vessel's type, age etc. For instance, it may be assumed that the grave ships from around Oslo fiord reflect local traditions in the building of vessels for war or travel, possibly in a particularly refined form. The vessels found as war offerings in bogs, on the other hand, have ended up there precisely because they represent the enemy rather than the local population. We cannot, therefore, assume that they represent local methods of construction.

Ships sunk on purpose will primarily be those which are worn out, provided they are not hostile ships sunk in war or to blockage the enemy. On the other hand, wrecked ships can be expected to include both newly built and older ships of all normal kinds.

Loose Finds

Shipwrecks from the period 800-1200 in Danish waters have so far provided few loose finds of cargo, equipment etc. This is probably because all the known wrecks are from shallow waters where either the ships were sunk after being emptied of everything that could be used elsewhere, or it was possible to salvage those parts of the cargo that had not surfaced of their own accord after the shipwreck.

We know of several cases where soapstone vessels and other cargo have been found in deeper waters along the east coast of Jutland, with no proof of shipwreck (Crumlin-Pedersen 1960). This does not exclude the possibility, but for the time being we know of no wrecks of this period sunk with their cargo in open water. The context of their deposition will be characterized by the possibility of repeated accumulation and removal of sand, and the risk that secondary material may have been dragged to the wrecks by drifting seaweed, fishing nets etc.

The boats found in graves or as votive offerings in

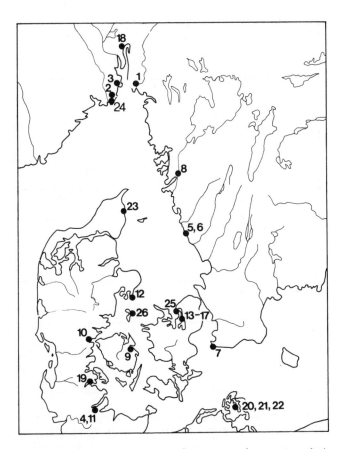

Fig. 1. Ship finds (800-1200) according to year of excavation, (finds not excavated are shown according to the year of first archaeological registration).

		recorded/excav.			recorded/excav.
1	Tune	1867/1867	14	Skuldelev 2	1957/1962
2	Gokstad	1880/1880	15	Skuldelev 3	1957/1962
3	Oseberg	1903/1904	16	Skuldelev 5	1959/1962
4	Hedeby G	1907/1908	17	Skuldelev 6	1959/1962
5	Galtabäck S	1928/1928	18	Sjövold	1960/1964
6	Galtabäck N	1928/	19	Egernsund	1966/1967
7	Falsterbo	1932/1932	20	Ralswiek 1	1967/1967
8	Äskekärr	1933/1933	21	Ralswiek 2	1967/1967
9	Ladby	1934/1935	22	Ralswiek 3	1968/1968
10	Eltang	1943/1947	23	Ellingå	1922/1968
11	Hedeby W	1953/	24	Klåstad	1893/1970
12	Hasnæs 2	1961/1961	25	Lynæs	1975/1975
13	Skuldelev 1	1924/1962	26	Kyholm	1977/

bogs, like the other objects sacrificed, conform with the system of beliefs which induced the people of that time to select these particular objects for sacrifice there, whereas there is no certainty of a functional connection between these. For instance, it is obvious that the wagon, sledges and beds found at Oseberg were for use on land and not on board ship; but this point of view should be applied

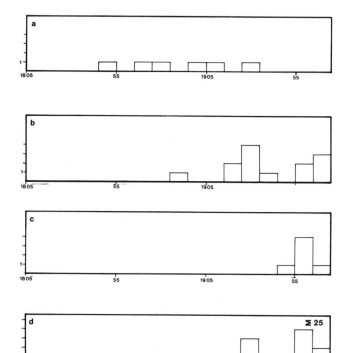

Fig. 2. Distribution of ship finds (800-1200) according to year of registration, a: in graves (> 12 m), b: "dry", c: by diving, d: total.

the year of first archaeological registration). Before 1860 only a single find is known in the area that conforms with the criteria of selection given above. This was a 17 metre long ship burial, excavated in 1850 during road construction at Borre near the Oseberg mound. This find has not been preserved or described in detail, and is therefore included only in figs. 2 and 3.

Figure 1 does not include salvaged detached pieces from ships of that time, such as rudders and mast partners; nor does it include re-used ship components like those known from Hedeby, Lund and other places. The figure thus only lists finds where sufficient material has been preserved to give a reasonably good impression of the vessel's structure, type, and size.

It also does not include grave finds with boats less than 12 metres long, since the primary aim of the analysis is to discuss the larger sea-going ships. This 12 metre limit agrees approximately with the traditional West Scandinavian distinction between "boat" and "ship", and in order to ensure an unambiguous classification we shall use the following terms for size categories of Scandinavian vessels in the period 800-1200:

consistently to the find material, so that only proper ship equipment is assumed to belong to the ship (and even some of this was newly made or brought from elsewhere to the burial place, see Osebergfundet I, 316).

Survey of Ship Finds

This article includes finds from all coastal areas bordering on the western part of the Baltic, the Sound, the waters of the Belts, Kattegat and Skagerak. This follows naturally from the fact that ships might end up far from the place where they were built, so that to discuss Danish ship finds one must have suitable comparative material. The map in fig. 1 shows 26 ship finds, all of which were registered 1860-1977 and belong to the period 800-1200.

The individual finds will not be described in detail. The reader is referred to the two German registers by Müller-Wille 1970 and Ellmers 1972, and also Crumlin-Pedersen 1979.

Figure 1 lists the ship finds according to year of excavation (finds not excavated are shown according to

Group	Category	Total length	Find no.
Boat	small	up to 3 m	
	medium	3-9 m	19
	large	9-12 m	17, 21, 22
Ship	small	12-15 m	5, 6?, 7, 15, 20, 23
	medium	15-24 m	1, 2, 3, 4, 8, 9, 10, 11, 12, 13, 16, 18, 24, 26
	large	over 24 m	14, 25

It appears that four of the wrecks listed in fig. 1 (Egernsund, Skuldelev 6 and Ralswiek 2 & 3) do not reach the 12 metre limit.

The reason for selecting the period 800-1200 is because in these centuries the role of shipping was particularly important in the Scandinavian countries, but above all because in this period there is an abundance of diverse ship finds without parallel in Nordic prehistory, or indeed in the whole of Northern Europe before 1500. An analysis of the representativity of the material is therefore appropriate at this point.

REPRESENTATIVITY

The analysis of the socio-economic factors which might lead to ship finds indicated that it was particularly in the decades after 1830 with the first deepening of fiords, and in the last decades of the 19th century with the deepening and reclamation of harbours, that there were good prospects of ship finds. If we compare this with figs. 2 and 3, which show the distribution of ship finds according to year of registration and of excavation, quite a different tendency is clear despite the small number of finds: before the 1920's only *ship burials* were registered as archaeological objects and were promptly excavated after discovery. The exception is the Klåstad wreck, which was examined in 1893 because of the soapstone and whetstone found there, but which was not excavated till 1970. The *wrecks* which must have turned up in the same period as a result of reclamation and dredging were simply not recognized as archaeological objects in Scandinavia and have consequently not been registered. In comparison we may mention that in the Danzig area from 1894 to 1906 five vessels from this period were found during drainage work. These were excavated, and stored in local museums. We have accounts of still more wreck finds from the same area which, however, were lost before they came to the knowledge of the museums.

In the beginning of the 1920's a blockage of ships (Skuldelev) and a wreck on a silted-up site (Ellingå) were registered, but none of these vessels was excavated at the time. In 1928 two wrecks were found in a sanded-up inlet at Galtabäck near Varberg, at the site of Gamla Köpstad, and one of these was excavated and preserved. The work on this wreck by the ethnologist Humbla eventually resulted in an increased interest in wreck finds, but still outside the circle of professional archaeologists. This was reflected in the excavations in 1933 of the Äskekärr ship and in 1947 of the Eltang ship, while the Falsterbo ship, salvaged from the beach on the south coast of Skåneøret in 1932, was not examined in detail until 1947 and was published in 1952, following Harald Åkerlund's excavation of several mediaeval wrecks in Kalmar harbour in the 1930's and their publication in 1951.

Between 1961 and 1970 thirteen wrecks were excavated, of which the Institute of Maritime Archaeology of the Danish National Museum (Roskilde) conducted the excavation of eight, the Kulturhistorisches Museum in Stralsund of three, and Oslo University's Oldsaksamling of two. Apparently, this is consistent with the increased building activity after 1950 and the growth of amateur diving in the same period, but of the eight ships excavated by the Danish National Museum only two were actually new finds (Hasnæs and Egernsund, found dur-

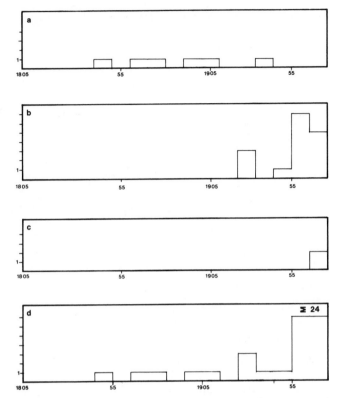

Fig. 3. Distribution of ship finds (800-1200) according to year of excavation, a: in graves (> 12 m), b: "dry", c: by diving, d: total.

ing gravel digging and bridge building, respectively). Only after 1975 did finds by amateur divers begin to have an impact, to which category the Lynæs and Kyholm ships belong.

To summarize, it can be stated that ship finds are in no way representative of the number of wrecks affected by the socio-economic development of the past 150 years, let alone of the total number of ships wrecked in the period 800-1200. The diagram of find frequencies reflects different research traditions and also the small number of researchers engaged in this field, and the limited technical and economic means at their disposal. However, this does not exclude the possibility of drawing some more general conclusions from the material, provided these are supported by a close analysis of the relationship between individual vessels and the context of their discovery.

CONTEXT ANALYSIS

If ship finds are divided according to context and the criteria given above, the following picture emerges (numbers in brackets indicate that place of deposition is secondary or uncertain):

Context		Find no.
1a	(grave find)	1, 2, 3, 4, 9
1b	(war offering)	.
2a	(sunk in battle)	11
2b	(offensive blockage)	
2c	(defensive blockage)	13, 14, 15, 16, 17
2d	(filling in)	
2e	(broken up for salvage)	(8), (12), (13), 18, 20, 21, 22
3a	(wrecked in sheltered waters)	5, 6, 7, 8, 10, (11), (18), 19, 23, 24, 25, 26
3b	(wrecked on open coast)	12
3c	(sunk in open waters)	

In this table the three Ralswiek wrecks (Nos. 20, 21, 22) are placed in group 2e (breaking up), since all three are old vessels used for repairs from which parts have clearly been removed for use elsewhere. The excavator, on the other hand, regards the ships as sacrifices because of the surrounding bone finds (Herfert 1973).

It is immediately apparent from the table that apart from the grave ships, all vessels were sunk or wrecked in sheltered waters, with the exception of No. 12, Hasnæs Wreck 2, found in beach ridge deposits on the open coast with strong indications that the ship was partly broken up after being wrecked. It may therefore be useful to analyse this situation in more detail. If we exclude the five grave ships, the five ships used for blockages, and the single beach find, there are fifteen vessels remaining, which can be divided as follows:

Location:	Primary cause of sinking:		
	shipwreck	age/breaking up	war activity
Ferry crossing	19		
At former settlement/ trading place	5, 6, 7, 25	18?, 20, 21, 22	11
Natural harbour apparently without former settlement	10, 23, 24?, 26		
Other		8	

It appears from the above table that only one of the fifteen wrecks (the Äskekärr ship on the bank of the Göta river) cannot be connected with a former settlement, a natural harbour, or a ferry. Nine of the vessels seem to have been wrecked, while four or five seem to be old ships

which were allowed to sink into the mud after some of the ships' timber had been removed for re-use.

It may seem remarkable that eight of the vessels found were wrecked while they lay in a natural harbour or at a trading place, but this is natural enough if we relinquish the modern concept of a harbour. The locations described as natural harbours were suitable anchorages which were relatively well sheltered from the prevailing winds and had a modest depth of water; here ships could usually lie sheltered over night or if need be for several days to trade or wait for better weather. None of the harbours, however, could provide shelter against winds from all directions, and the ships were very dependent on the ability of the ground tackle to hold the ship fast while lying at anchor. The ships also required frequent bailing out, since the building techniques which made them flexible also made them liable to leak around the nails for the frames. It is not surprising, therefore, that a small number of the many ships which used these harbours and anchorages over 400 years did not find sufficient shelter there to avoid shipwreck.

The risk of shipwreck at that time was fairly great, but that is hardly reason to expect a correspondingly large number of wrecks surviving into the present, since in a storm crew, cargo and ship might be saved by sailing the ship directly up onto the coast ("sigla til brots"). Even if the ship was damaged by this (the Hasnæs 2 find may be the remains of such a wreck), in many cases it could be repaired and continue the voyage. If the ship was swamped without being heavily loaded, it would stay afloat because of the buoyant hull. Only ships containing a heavy cargo or ballast would sink at once, and thus enable posterity to find wreckage surviving on the spot.

Ships, which after long use were so worn out that it was not worthwhile repairing them any more, were not discarded, but either the whole or parts were re-used. The five Skuldelev ships were all worn out when they were chosen for use in the blockage, and Skuldelev 5 was even built with planks from another ship. Several re-used planks and beams from ships have been found in wharves, roads, houses, even in graves, of the time. There is little reason, therefore, to give every find of ships' nails in Viking Period graves a religious significance. Apparently, the breaking-up of old ships often took place by grounding them on the beach in a sheltered inlet near a settlement, and one should be particularly alert to the possibility of such finds at the towns and trading centres of the time.

Before we conclude the discussion of the context of ship finds, it should be related to the types of ship, as presented in the following table:

Relationship between ship type and find context:

Primary function of vessel		Grave find	Blockage war activity	Wreck	Breaking-up
Transport of people in open water (»war ships«)		1, 2, 3, 4, 9	11, 14, 16	12	20, 21, 22?
Transport of cargo in open water (»cargo ships«)			13, 15	5, 6, 7, 10, 23, 24, 25, 26	8?, 18
Other	Fishing		16?		
	Ferry			19	

It appears that the two main groups of finds which occur frequently: vessels for carrying people and cargo, respectively, in open water (or in brief: "war ships" and "cargo ships"), show a marked difference in distribution among the various find groups.

In the "cargo ship" group there is a total of twelve ships comprising eight wrecks, two partly broken up, and two used for blockages, while not one is found as a grave ship. Among the "war ships" there are five grave ships, three sunk as blockages or in battle, one wrecked on the open coast, and three partly broken up, a total of twelve.

Is there any reason to assume that this distribution reflects a genuine tendency, in that we may expect to find cargo ships wrecked primarily in natural harbours? It was not only cargo ships, but occasionally also ships for war and travel, which used these anchorages, even if the war ships probably mainly used a smaller number of strategically placed harbours, at any rate in connection with the assembling of large fleets.

Nevertheless, there would have been a greater probability of shipwreck among the relatively heavy-draught cargo ships, which needed a certain quantity of ballast or heavy cargo on board when sailing and therefore sank if they were swamped, than among the war ships, which were built and manned to cope with landing at short notice. Consequently, the conclusions we can draw from ship finds on the frequency of various types of wrecks in natural harbours are supported by other data.

The tendency indicated in the above table for cargo ships to be absent from graves seems likewise to be soundly based. Only chiefs or local kings whom we can suppose to have owned their own ship, for personal

transportation, seem to have been buried with ships larger than 12 metres. It is possible that a comparatively large percentage of the (relatively few) ships of this particular kind were buried in graves together with their male and female owners before the introduction of christianity. Any hypothetical figure for this sub-group of ship-finds is, however, irrelevant in estimating the relative frequency, let alone the absolute number, of vessels of different types in the area or its various regions in the period 800-1200. This can never be obtained only from analyses of the number of ship finds and the find context, as the relationship between the original number of ships of different types and the relatively few ship finds is far too uncertain. On the other hand, the study of ship design and choice of materials, even with a small number of finds, may take us a long way towards defining the function of individual ship types and their geographical distribution. In this way the finds may help to illuminate changes in the relative strengths of maritime trade and war at sea, based on the development of ship construction in the area.

SHIP BLOCKAGES

Only in recent years have ship blockages attracted the attention of archaeologists. As with shipwrecks, bridges, and wooden road and canal constructions, it is the recent possibilities for dating organic material which enable us to establish a chronology for the blockages, and thereby facilitate proper archaeological treatment.

The study of ship blockages is still at an early stage, and this survey is based necessarily on a small number of partly investigated constructions and a larger number which are known, but have not been studied in detail or dated.

In the same way as walls and ditches have been used for centuries to regulate and protect land traffic, ship blockages reflect the regulation or blocking of sea traffic to large or small areas of importance at the time.

The technical design was partly dependent on the construction and draught of the ships. Coastal engineering techniques, the materials available, and not least local topographic conditions also affected the choice of blockage components.

Some examples from abroad can provide information on different ship blockage designs. As defence against Viking raids up the rivers of Western Europe, various blockages were built, e.g. in the form of a bridge complete with fortifications on the river banks, in France at Pitres (864) and Paris (886), and in England at Ware (895) and in London (1013-16). They were intended to prevent attacks on the towns, but also to halt further penetration into the country, and the places suitable for the construction of blockages were often also the best for bridge-building. Existing bridges were therefore extended into blockages, or new bridges were built for the dual purpose.

The Danish historian Sakse describes how at the Slavonic town of Wolgast the inhabitants tried to protect themselves against the Danish raids in the 1170's, partly by sinking ships and stones in the channels, partly by fixing many stakes in a circle around the town fortifications. Here we see a combination of closure of the actual sailing routes into the area and reinforcement of the local defensive works by an additional protective ring facing the sea. A similar system can be seen at Slien, where the sea route to Hedeby and Slesvig was probably controlled by various constructions, including twin fortifications at Kielfoth and a stake barrier at Stexvig-Palör. The harbour at Hedeby was protected with a palisade in the bay in continuation of the semi-circular wall on land, and possibly also by a row of piles over the mouth of the bay (Wåhlin 1964, Crumlin-Pedersen 1969).

In the Swedish archipelago around Hellerumsviken in Blekinge, Viking Period stake barriers have been found. There has been found no trace of permanent settlement on the spot, but the concentration of Viking Period grave finds and place names implies that this area was an important stop on the route between Birka and Hedeby, which needed protection from attack (Atterman 1967 & 1969; Frykman 1974).

As a final example of actual harbour defences from the Middle Ages we may mention a number of caissons filled with stones and built of heavy timber, found at the edge of Kalmar's mediaeval harbour (Åkerlund 1951); Norwegian sources also describe how in 1135 Bergen's harbour was blocked by logs and iron chains across the entrance.

These examples show that ship blockages could protect a large area against invasion or sacking, or could serve as protection of an important town or harbour against conquest, destruction or pillage. Blockages were constructed in the form of bridges, rows of piles, stone caissons, submerged ships, floating booms, or combinations of these.

However, not every row of piles or stone caisson on the sea floor is a sign of an old ship blockage. From the late Middle Ages to the present day it has been customary to build stone caissons or fix groups of piles to which large ships could be moored when laid up for the winter, or from which ships could be hauled through narrow passages. Eel weirs and other fixed fishing equipment have also left many stumps of piles in the sea bed, and the same is true of old jetties etc. In these cases, however, topographic conditions and the nature of the stakes will usually exclude the possibility that they functioned as a blockage.

However, it can sometimes be difficult to decide whether some of the rows of piles which could have been used for either bridge or blockage should be assigned to one category or the other, or whether they served both purposes.

The earliest Danish reports on ship blockages come from the first decades of the 19th century when, as already mentioned, the seaward approaches to several Danish towns were surveyed with a view to dredging them. A number of blockages were registered in this connection. Local fishermen had doubtless known of them for centuries, but only now did they become known publicly. The next set of reports on blockages came around the turn of this century, when a new dredging program was begun as the ships using provincial harbours grew in size.

In the 1930's some further finds were reported, including those from Roskilde fiord mentioned in the introduction, and in 1933 the first archaeological excavation of a ship blockage was carried out. This was a stake barrier at the *Hominde* entrance to Rødby fiord, which appeared during drainage of the fiord, and was excavated by C. G. Schulz from the National Museum. In 1935 and 1946 the Langelands Museum investigated a blockage in *Henninge Bay*, but otherwise it was not until 1962, the year of the Skuldelev excavation, that registration gathered momentum. During 1962-63 there proved to be no less than four different blockage constructions around Skuldelev in Roskilde fiord. Using these as a starting point Vagn Wåhlin undertook a survey of topographic sources etc. to find information about other ship blockages (Wåhlin 1964). In this way he became aware of a Swedish study on the relationship between place names containing the words "stok", "stäk" and "pål" [stake, pile] and the presence of stake barriers (Bolin 1933). Two of these place names have already been mentioned in connection with the entrance to Hedeby and Slesvig, where the two sites of *Palör* and *Stexvig* are located opposite each other where Slien narrows just east of Slesvig.

The survey of Danish material brought to light a number of earlier finds of ship blockages and indicated a number of places where the name *Steg* occurred at places strategically suitable for the construction of blockages. This is not surprising since the name derives from old norse "stika" = stake, and generally indicates a narrow sailing passage blocked by rows of piles. This applies to the town of *Stege* at the entrance to the bay on Møn, *Stegehoved* by Skælskør fiord, *Stige* at the entrance to Odense river and *Store* and *Lille Stigø* at Bogense. Here the name is attached to places where it would be natural to build a blockage to protect the country inland, although none has yet been definitely shown to exist on these locations.

At Vordingborg, however, a blockage has been found, called *"Queen Margrethe's Stiger"*, stretching across the bay which was a naval base in the 12th century. Similarly, in northern Als a proper rampart has been found extending towards the *Steg* farm, which is situated by the narrow passage into what was formerly a very extensive system of small connected bays. In Kolding fiord a blockage has been located at Kidholm by *Stegenav*. Finally, *Stikshage* stretches out into the mouth of Haderslev fiord where the outermost of the three blockages known from this fiord is connected with the shore.

As appears from the map in fig. 4, blockages are also found in many places where they have left no echo in the place name. This map shows the locality of 28 known constructions of stakes, stones and earth-works, which are presented in the table on p. 245. As we can see, there are C-14 dates available for only ten of these; two are from the 2nd-4th century A. D.; eight are from the 10th-11th century (one of these also with a 3rd century dating); and one is dated, according to samples submitted, to the 16th-17th century. In this survey the dates will not be examined in detail; we shall merely mention that not all are from the outermost growth rings of the stakes, and it should be noted that the dates given are uncalibrated.

It appears from the frequency diagrams in fig. 5 that we could reasonably expect several more discoveries of blockages in the coming decades when this archaeological material is better known, and more museums are able to carry out investigations. So far most of the work of registration and examination has been done by the Institute of Maritime Archaeology of the Danish National

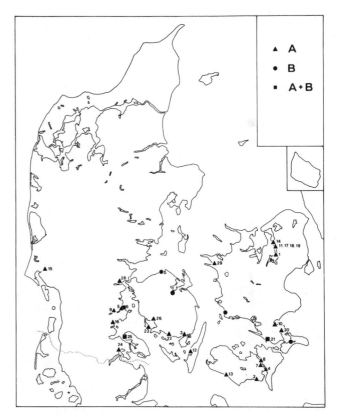

Fig. 4. Ship blockages, A: known ship blockages, B: Steg-, Stig- place names near sailing entrances.

Museum, which is also where the Wåhlin archives about blockages are kept. The only investigations of blockages that have been published so far are those in Roskilde fiord (especially No. 11 and 14), Haderslev fiord (Nos. 5 and 6), and Hominde and Helnæs (Nos. 13 and 23) (Crumlin-Pedersen 1966, 1974, 1975, 1978; Olsen & Crumlin-Pedersen 1969, 1978; Schulz 1936).

Figure 4 shows a marked concentration of ship blockages in the areas facing the western part of the Baltic. The only group of blockages outside this area are those from Roskilde fiord. There is a striking absence of blockages from Limfjorden or from the Jutland fiords north of Kolding. There was similar dredging activity here as elsewhere in the 19th century to provide adequate sailing depth up to the market towns. We must therefore, provisionally, accept that there were few or no ship blockages in the northern part of the country compared to the many in the south.

This broad pattern can be tentatively divided into several sections if we use the available dates in the analysis. First of all a picture emerges of active construction

226

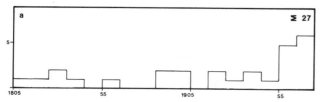

Fig. 5a. Blockages registered 1805-1974.

Fig. 5b. Blockages excavated 1805-1974.

work in the 10th and 11th centuries, to which phase belong the blockages at Skuldelev (Nos. 11, 17, 18, 19), Hominde (No. 13), Helnæs (No. 23), Æ Lei (No. 5) and Egernsund (No. 24).

These are blockages with sunken ships, floating caissons and booms, and rows of piles, which individually or collectively served to protect a particular hinterland rather than a town alone. Several undated blockages seem to be of a similar kind, e.g. Frederikssund (No. 14), Henninge (No. 12), Nakkebølle (No. 22), Nabben (No. 26), Kidholm (No. 27), and Slivsøen (No. 16).

Two constructions have a restricted function similar to the palisade at Hedeby bay outside the semi-circular rampart, viz. the harbour blockages at Vordingborg (Queen Margrethe's Stiger, No. 21) and Kalundborg (Houget, No. 28). Until further knowledge is available, it seems reasonable to associate these places with their use as bases for the war fleet in the Middle Ages.

The blockages in Guldborg Sound (Nos. 4, 7 & 8), two of which are called "The Swedish Bridge", may have served partly to regulate shipping, partly as a bridge. The same is also true of the row of piles called "Old Bridge" between Eskildsø and Hornsherred (No. 1) in Zealand, and a similar row of piles at Jungshoved (No. 20).

All these blockages fit the picture of a troubled period in Denmark towards the end of the Viking Period, and the subsequent period when the Wends were raiding in the south. It would be worthwhile studying their presence in more detail in relation to the other indications of fortification and settlement in the areas.

Outside this pattern fall the two blockages at the

mouth of Haderslev fiord dated to the 3rd century A D (Nos. 5 & 6). At least one of these has a later period of use in the 11th century. These were blockages of Roman Iron Age date of the sea route to a major settlement area, separated from a similar area on Sundeved by Olmer Dike, dated to the same period. The study of Danish ship blockages has only just begun, and the broad outline given here on the basis of the evidence at hand around 1978 is not necessarily representative of the situation as it will develop in ten or twenty years, when we may hope for results from large-scale systematic surveys of the interplay between navigation, settlement, and fortification. These should be conducted by archaeologists, historians, place-name researchers and natural scientists in close co-operation, who will thus be able to give maritime factors a more prominent position than in previous research on the archaeology of Iron Age and Mediaeval Denmark.

Ole Crumlin-Pedersen
The National Museum,
Institute of Nautical Archaeology,
Frederiksborgvej 63,
4000 Roskilde

Ship-finds (Denmark + S. Norway + W. Sweden + NE. Germany) 1805-1974.

Interval	Grave-ships	Wrecks »dry«	Wrecks »wet«	Ships total
1805-14	0	0	0	0
1815-24	0	0	0	0
1825-34	0	0	0	0
1835-44	0	0	0	0
1845-54	1	0	0	1
1855-64	0	0	0	0
1865-74	1	0	0	1
1875-84	1	0	0	1
1885-94	0	0	0	0
1895-1904	1	0	0	1
1905-14	1	0	0	1
1915-24	0	0	0	0
1925-34	0	3	0	3
1935-44	1	0	0	1
1945-54	0	1	0	1
1955-64	0	7	0	7
1965-74	0	5	2	7
	6	16	2	24

No.	Locality	Water	Registr./ excavated	Type	Dating (uncalibrated)
1	Eskildsø	Roskilde fj.	1813/	B? S?	
2	Nysted	Østersøen	1822/	H? S?	
3	Svendborg	Svendborgsund	1826/	H?	
4	Hasselø	Guldborgsund	1828/	S	
5	Æ Lei	Haderslev fj.	1843/1969	S	290±100/1030±100
6	Margr. Bro	Haderslev fj.	1859/1969	S	240±100/260±100
7	Pandebjerg	Guldborgsund	1893/	B? S?	
8	Ejegod	Guldborgsund	1893/	B? S?	
9	Snævringen	Haderslev fj.	1899/	B? S?	
10	Præstø	Præstø fj.	1899/	H?	
11	Peberrenden	Roskilde fj.	1924/1957-62	S	980±100
12	Henninge	Lindelse nor	1924/35-46	S	
13	Hominde	Rødby fj.	1933/1933	S	930±100
14	Fr.sund	Roskilde fj.	1935/	S	
15	Varde	Varde å	1937/	H	
16	Slivsøen	Lillebælt	1958/	S	
17	Jydedybet	Roskilde fj.	1962/	S	1080±100
18	Vesterrende	Roskilde fj.	1962/	S	1010±100
19	Vimmelskaft	Roskilde fj.	1962/	S	1070±100
20	Jungshoved	Bøgestrømmen	1963/	B? S?	
21	D. M.'s stiger	Masnedsund	1964/1978	H	
22	Nakkebølle	Nakkebølle fj.	1965/	S	
23	Helnæs	Lillebælt	1965/1972	S	1060±100
24	Egernsund	Flensborg fj.	1967/1967	S?	1070±75
25	Steg	Lillebælt	1967/1967	S	1550±70/1670±70?
26	Nabben	Lillebælt	1972/	S	
27	Kidholm	Kolding fj.	1973/	S	
28	Houget	Kalundborg fj.	1975/	H	

Known ship blockages in Danish waters.
B = bridge,   H = harbour blockage,   S = ship blockage of area or passage.

REFERENCES

ATTERMAN, INGEMAR, 1967. Kring Hallarumsviken. *Blekingeboken* 1967, Karlskrona.
– 1969. Rapport från Bussevikspärren. *Blekingeboken* 1969, Karlskrona.
BOLIN, GUNNAR, 1933. *Stockholms uppkomst*, Uppsala 1933.
BRØGGER, A. W. & HAAKON SHETELIG, 1951. *The Viking Ships*. Oslo 1951.
CHRISTENSEN JR., ARNE EMIL, 1964. Et middelalderskip i Asker. *Viking* 1964, Oslo.
– 1968. The Sjøvollen Ship. *Viking* 1968, Oslo.
– & G. LEIRO, 1976. Klåstadskipet. *Vestfoldminne* 1976, Tønsberg.
CRUMLIN-PEDERSEN, OLE, 1960. Sideroret fra Vorså. *Kuml* 1960.
– 1966. En kogge i Roskilde. *Handels- & Søfartsmuseet på Kronborg, årbog* 1966.
– 1969. *Das Haithabuschiff*. Berichte über die Ausgrabungen in Haithabu 3. Neumünster 1969.

– 1974. Helnæs-spærringen. *Fynske Minder* 1973. Odense 1974.
– 1975. "Æ Lei" og "Margrethes Bro". *Nordslesvigske Museer* 2, Tønder 1975.
– 1978. Søvejen til Roskilde. *Historisk årbog fra Roskilde amt* 1978. Roskilde 1978.
– 1979. Skibsfund fra danske farvande fra perioden 600-1200. *Handels- & Søfartsmuseet på Kronborg, årbog* 1979.
ELLMERS, DETLEV, 1972. *Frühmittelalterliche Handelsschiffahrt in Mittel- und Nordeuropa*. Neumünster 1972.
ENQVIST, ARVID, 1929. *Skeppsfyndet vid Galtabäck*. Kulturhistoriska studier och uppteckningar. Halmstad 1929.
FISCHER, CHR., 1969. Skibet skal sejle – (Ellingå-skibet). *Skalk* 3/1969.
FLAGBOGEN 1871. Schneider, A.: *Danmarks Handelsflaade i Aaret 1871*. Kbh., u. å.
FLAGBOGEN 1901. Registrerings- og Skibsmaalings-Bureauet: *Danmarks Handelsflaade i Aaret 1901*. 15. udg. Kbh. 1901.

228

FRYKMAN, JONAS & JAN SANDSTRÖM, 1974. Vikingatid ur annorlunda perspektiv. *Blekingeboken* 1974, Karlskrona.

HANSEN, KNUD E., 1944. Kolding Skibet. *Handels- & Søfartsmuseet på Kronborg.* Aarbog 1944.

HERFERT, P., 1968. Frühmittelalterliche Bootsfunde in Ralswiek, Kr. Rügen. *Ausgrabungen und Funde.* Bd. 13. 1968.

– 1973. Ralswiek. Ein frühgeschichtlicher Seehandelsplatz auf der Insel Rügen. *Greifswald-Stralsunder Jahrbuch.* Bd. 10, 1972/73.

HINGST, H. & K. KERSTEN, 1955. Die Tauchaktion vor Haithabu im Jahre 1953. *Germania* 33, Heft 3, 1955.

HUMBLA, PH. & H. THOMASSON, 1934. Äskekärrsbåten. *Göteborgs och Bohusläns fornminnesförenings tidskrift,* Göteborg 1934.

HUMBLA, PH. & L.VON POST, 1937. Galtabäcksbåten och tidigt båtbyggeri i Norden. *Göteborgs kungl. vetenskaps- och vitterh.-samh. handlinger* 5A- 6/1. Göteborg 1937.

JELGERSMA, S. et al., 1970. The costal dunes of the western Netherlands; Geology, vegetation history and archaeology. *Mededelingen Rijks Geologische Dienst,* Nieuwe Serie No. 21, 1970.

MÜLLER-WILLE, MICHAEL, 1970. Bestattung im Boot. *Offa* 25/26, 1968/69. Neumünster 1970.

– 1976. *Das Bootkammergrab von Haithabu.* Berichte über die Ausgrabungen in Haithabu, 8, Neumünster 1976.

NICOLAYSEN, N., 1882. *Langskibet fra Gokstad ved Sandefjord,* Kristiania 1882.

OLSEN, OLAF & OLE CRUMLIN-PEDERSEN, 1958. The Skuldelev Ships (I). *Acta Archaeologica* 29, København 1958.

– 1968. The Skuldelev Ships (II). *Acta Archaeologica* 38, København 1968.

– 1969. *Fem vikingeskibe fra Roskilde fjord.* Roskilde 1969.

– 1978. *Five Viking Ships from Roskilde Fjord.* Copenhagen 1978.

SCHETELIG, HAAKON, 1917. *Tune-Skibet.* Norske Oldfund 2, Kristiania 1917.

SCHETELIG, H., A. W. BRØGGER & HJ. FALK, 1917. *Osebergfundet,* Bind 1, Kristiania 1917.

SCHULZ, C. G., 1936. Hominde og Pæleværket i Vestre Skarholmsrende. *Lolland-Falsters historiske Samfunds Aarbog* 1936.

SKOV, SIGVARD, 1944. Skibsfundene i Kolding fjord. *Vejle Amts Aarbog* 1941-44.

– 1952. Et middelalderligt skibsfund fra Eltang Vig. *Kuml* 1952.

THORVILDSEN, KNUD, 1957. Ladbyskibet. *Nordiske Fortidsminder* VI, 1, København 1957.

WÅHLIN ANDERSEN, VAGN, 1964. Skuldelevskibene i perspektiv. *Skalk* 4/1964.

ÅKERLUND, HARALD, 1942. Galtabäcksbåtens ålder och härstamning. *Göteborgs och Bohusläns fornminnesförenings tidskrift,* Göteborg 1942.

– 1948. Galtabäckbåtens ålder och härstamning II. *Sjöhistorisk årsbok,* Stockholm 1948.

– 1951. *Fartygsfynden i den forna hamnen i Kalmar.* Uppsala 1951.

– 1952. Skeppsfyndet vid Falsterbo 1932, *Sjöhistorisk årsbok,* Stockholm 1952.

Appendix 1

Place Name Register

PREFACE

The following classification and numbering of Danish counties, districts and parishes have been carried out by Dept. I of the National Museum to facilitate topographical registration of archaeological material.

The work is based on: "Traps Danmark", "Fortegnelse over købstæder samt herreder og sogne på landet" (:list of provincial boroughs, districts and parishes) (published by the Land Registry Office in 1954), the maps of the Geodetic Institute, the numbered topographical registers of the Folk Museum, the parish records of the National Museum, Dept. I, and the Place-Name Committee's register of place names, approved by the Government.

Counties are listed in the same *order* as that used in "Traps Danmark". Within each county the districts, and within each district the parishes and boroughs, are listed in alphabetical order. Within boroughs no distinction has been made between individual parishes, and in the district of Sokkelund we have chosen (in accordance with the latest edition of "Traps Danmark") a division into rural districts that corresponds to the old parishes.

Spelling follows present-day usage, and alphabetization is in accordance with the rules of alphabetization of the Danish Standardization Board. We wish to call attention to the following: compound names are treated as one word and alphabetized according to the first part of the name, e.g. *Kirke*-Helsinge, *Nørre*-Bjert; the letter "å" replaces "aa" throughout and is the last letter of the alphabet.

The purpose of giving each place a number is to set up a simple number code for topographical units; the division of the country into counties, districts and parishes or boroughs is regarded as a system of units of descending order which are classified in a decimal system. The counties are numbered consecutively in the order mentioned above. Within each county the districts are numbered, and within each district the parishes or boroughs. The number given to a parish may be rendered as e.g.

14.07.11, in which 14. indicates the county, .07 the district, and .11 the parish. The number may also be rendered as 140711, as long as it is borne in mind that the numbers of districts and parishes should always contain two digits, e.g. 07. The designations are unambiguous and can be used for topographical registration in punchcard files. When sites are numbered consecutively within individual parishes (as in the parish records), the parish record number (e.g. No. 4) is added immediately after the place number, e.g. 14.07.11,4 or 140711,4.

Finds that can be assigned to a particular area without further details on locality are numbered according to the county, district or parish number of the area in question. For example, finds from Bornholm are numbered under Bornholm County (6), from Vendsyssel under Hjørring County (10), from Møn under Mønbo District (5.05).

Single finds that are assigned merely to "Denmark" or large areas are numbered according to a special list of numbers given under DANISH COUNTIES.

In the list of place numbers several parishes or boroughs have added parentheses. These indicate special registration procedures in the parish records of the National Museum, Dept. I: for a very long time sites within two or more parishes may have been numbered consecutively on a single list which is filed under one of the parishes. This is because subsequent parish divisions have taken place or because two areas, e.g. a borough and a parish, have been regarded as a natural unit. In such cases there are additions like:

10.02.02 Aså-Melholt (part of .03)

      .03 Dronninglund (including .02).

Thus a description of sites in the parish of Aså-Melholt will be found in the parish records filed under Dronninglund, which comprises both parishes.

Where parishes are intersected by the boundary of a district there is a different kind of supplementary parenthesis. In such cases the whole parish has been included numerically within one of the two districts, and the parish is referred to without a number within the other district, with supplementary information on where it is filed and numbered, e.g.:

12.04.06 Ove
  – Ravnkilde Ø (added to 12.08.10)
  .07 Rostrup.

Finally it should be mentioned that occasional *revisions of the list of place numbers* are necessary. After all, the division of Denmark into parishes is not final, but subject to periodic changes of a major or minor kind. As long as these are confined to divisions of existing parishes, the revision need include only additions like that mentioned above (Aså-Melholt and Dronninglund). If the changes include the incorporation of existing parishes or parts of these into other parishes or boroughs, a more radical revision is required, since old parish boundaries will be omitted from the maps on which the parish division (and the parish record numbers) is based. When new maps begin to be used it is therefore essential to check carefully whether the parish boundaries have been altered in relation to the maps previously used.

The National Museum, March 1961.

Olfert Voss   Mogens Ørsnes

00.   Denmark
00.01 Zealand
00.02 Funen
00.03 Jutland
00.04 North Jutland
00.05 South Jutland

DANISH COUNTIES

1-9	1. Frederiksborg
The	2. København
Islands	3. Holbæk
	4. Sorø
	5. Præstø
	6. Bornholm
	7. Maribo
	8. Odense
	9. Svendborg
10-23	10. Hjørring
Jutland	11. Thisted
	12. Ålborg
	13. Viborg
	14. Randers
	15. Århus
	16. Skanderborg
	17. Vejle
	18. Ringkøbing
	19. Ribe
	20. Haderslev
	21. Tønder
	22. Åbenrå
	23. Sønderborg

1. Frederiksborg County

1.01 Holbo
1.02 Horns
1.03 Lynge-Frederiksborg
1.04 Lynge-Kronborg
1.05 Strø
1.06 Ølstykke

1.01 *Holbo District*

1.01.01 Annisse
  .02 Blistrup
  .03 Esbønderup
  .04 Gilleleje
  .05 Græsted
  .06 Helsinge
  .07 Mårum
  .08 Nødebo
  .09 Ramløse
  .10 Søborg
  .11 Tibirke
  .12 Valby
  .13 Vejlby

1.02 *Horns District*

1.02.01 Dråby
  .02 Ferslev
  .03 Gerlev
  .04 Krogstrup
  .05 Kyndby
  .06 Selsø
  .07 Skibby
  .08 Skuldelev
  .09 Vellerup

1.03 *Lynge-Frederiksborg District*

1.03.01 Frederiksborg Slotssogn
  .02 Frederikssund
  .03 Græse
  .04 Gørløse
  .05 Hillerød
  .06 Jørlunde
  .07 Lillerød
  .08 Lynge
  .09 Nørre-Herlev
  .10 Oppe-Sundby
  .11 Sigerslevvester
  .12 Slangerup
   – Ude-Sundby, now: .02
  .13 Uggeløse
  .14 Uvelse

1.04 *Lynge-Kronborg District*

1.04.01 Asminderød (including .09)
  .02 Birkerød
  .03 Blovstrød
  .04 Egebæksvang
  .05 Grønholt
  .06 Hellebæk (part of .08)
  .07 Helsingør
  .08 Hornbæk (including .06)
  .09 Humlebæk (part of .01)
  .10 Hørsholm
  .11 Karlebo
  .12 Tikøb

1.05 *Strø District*

1.05.01 Alsønderup
  .02 Frederiksværk (part of .10)
  .03 Kregme
  .04 Lille Lyngby
  .05 Melby
  .06 Skævinge
  .07 Strø
  .08 Tjæreby
  .09 Torup
  .10 Vinderød (including .02)
  .11 Ølsted

1.06 *Ølstykke District*

1.06.01 Farum
  .02 Ganløse
  .03 Slagslunde
  .04 Snostrup
  .05 Stenløse
  .06 Veksø
  .07 Ølstykke

2. Københavns County

2.01 Ramsø
2.02 Smørum
2.03 Sokkelund
2.04 Sømme
2.05 Tune
2.06 Volborg

2.01 *Ramsø District*

2.01.01 Borup
  .02 Dåstrup
  .03 Ejby
  .04 Gadstrup
  .05 Højelse
  .06 Kimmerslev
  .07 Køge
  .08 Nørre-Dalby
  .09 Rorup
  .10 Syv
  .11 Ølsemagle
  .12 Ørsted

2.02 *Smørum District*

2.02.01 Ballerup
  .02 Brøndbyøster
  .03 Brøndbyvester
  .04 Glostrup
  .05 Herstedvester
  .06 Herstedøster
  .07 Høje Tåstrup (including .14)
  .08 Ishøj
  .09 Ledøje
  .10 Måløv
  .11 Sengeløse
  .12 Smørum
  .13 Torslunde
  .14 Tåstrup Nykirke (part of .07)
  .15 Vallensbæk
  .16 Værløse

2.03 *Sokkelund District*

2.03.01 Dragør (part of .09)
  .02 Gentofte
  .03 Gladsakse
  .04 Herlev
  .05 Hvidovre
  .06 København including Frederiksberg
  .07 Lyngby-Tårbæk
  .08 Rødovre
  .09 Store-Magleby (including .01)
  .10 Søllerød
  .11 Tårnby

2.04 *Sømme District*

2.04.01 Fløng
  .02 Glim
  .03 Gundsømagle
  .04 Herslev
  .05 Himmelev
  .06 Hvedstrup
  .07 Jyllinge
  .08 Kirkerup

.09 Kornerup
.10 Roskilde (including .11)
.11 Roskilde Domkirkes lds.
  (part of .10)
.12 Skt. Jørgensbjerg
.13 Svogerslev
.14 Vor Frue
.15 Ågerup

2.05 *Tune District*

2.05.01 Greve
.02 Havdrup
.03 Jersie
.04 Karlslunde
.05 Karlstrup
.06 Kildebrønde
.07 Kirke-Skensved
.08 Reerslev
.09 Snoldelev
.10 Solrød
 − Torslunde S.
  (added to 2.02.13)
.11 Tune
.12 Vindinge

2.06 *Volborg District*

2.06.01 Allerslev
.02 Gershøj
.03 Gevninge
.04 Kirke-Hvalsø
.05 Kirke-Hyllinge
.06 Kirke-Sonnerup
.07 Kirke-Såby
.08 Kisserup
.09 Lyndby
.10 Osted
.11 Rye
 − Soderup (added to 3.03.08)
.12 Sæby
.13 Særløse

3. Holbæk County

3.01 Ars
3.02 Løve
3.03 Merløse
3.04 Ods
3.05 Samsø
3.06 Skippinge
3.07 Tuse

3.01 *Ars District*

3.01.01 Kalundborg
.02 Lille-Fuglede
.03 Raklev
.04 Rørby
.05 Røsnæs
.06 Store-Fuglede
.07 Svallerup
.08 Tømmerup
.09 Ubby
.10 Årby

3.02 *Løve District*

3.02.01 Bakkendrup
.02 Buerup (including .14)
.03 Drøsselbjerg
.04 Finderup
.05 Gierslev
.06 Gørlev
.07 Hallenslev
.08 Havrebjerg
.09 Kirke-Helsinge
.10 Reerslev
.11 Ruds-Vedby
.12 Skellebjerg
.13 Solbjerg
.14 Sæby (part of .02)
.15 Ørslev

3.03 *Merløse District*

3.03.01 Butterup
.02 Grandløse
.03 Holbæk
.04 Kirke-Eskilstrup
.05 Kvanløse
.06 Niløse
.07 Nørre-Jernløse
.08 Soderup
.09 Stenlille
.10 Store-Tåstrup
.11 Sønder-Asmindrup
.12 Sønder-Jernløse
.13 Søndersted
.14 Søstrup
.15 Tersløse
.16 Tølløse
.17 Ugerløse
.18 Undløse
.19 Ågerup

3.04 *Ods District*

3.04.01 Asnæs

.02 Egebjerg
.03 Fårevejle
.04 Grevinge
.05 Højby
.06 Hørve
.07 Nykøbing S
.08 Nørre-Asmindrup
.09 Odden
.10 Rørvig
.11 Vallekilde
.12 Vig

3.05 *Samsø District*

3.05.01 Besser
.02 Kolby
.03 Nordby
.04 Onsbjerg
.05 Tranebjerg

3.06 *Skippinge District*

3.06.01 Avnsø
.02 Bjergsted
.03 Bregninge
.04 Føllenslev
.05 Holmstrup
.06 Jorløse
.07 Sejerø
.08 Særslev
.09 Viskinge
.10 Værslev

3.07 *Tuse District*

3.07.01 Frydendal
.02 Gislinge
.03 Hagested
.04 Hjembæk
.05 Hørby
.06 Jyderup
.07 Kundby
.08 Mørkøv
.09 Orø
.10 Skamstrup
.11 Stigs-Bjergby
.12 Svinninge
.13 Tuse
.14 Udby

4. Sorø County

4.01 Alsted
4.02 Ringsted
4.03 Slagelse
4.04 Vester-Flakkebjerg

4.05 Øster-Flakkebjerg

4.01 *Alsted District*

4.01.01 Alsted
  .02 Bjernede
  .03 Bromme
  .04 Fjenneslev
  .05 Gyrstinge
  .06 Kirke-Flinterup
  .07 Lynge
  .08 Munke-Bjergby
  .09 Pedersborg
  .10 Slaglille
  .11 Sorø
  .12 Stenmagle
  .13 Vester-Broby

4.02 *Ringsted District*

4.02.01 Allindemagle
  .02 Benløse
  :03 Bringstrup
  .04 Farendløse
  .05 Freerslev
  .06 Haraldsted
  .07 Haslev
  .08 Høm
  .09 Jystrup
  .10 Kværkeby
  .11 Nordrupøster
  .12 Ringsted (including .13)
  .13 Ringsted landsogn
     (part of .12)
  .14 Sigersted
  .15 Sneslev
  .16 Teestrup
  .17 Terslev
  .18 Valsølille
  .19 Vetterslev
  .20 Vigersted
  .21 Øde-Førslev
  .22 Ørslev
  .23 Øster-Broby

4.03 *Slagelse District*

4.03.01 Boeslunde
  .02 Gerlev
  .03 Gudum
  .04 Hejninge
  .05 Hemmeshøj
  .06 Kindertofte
  .07 Kirke-Stillinge
  .08 Korsør

  .09 Lundforlund
  .10 Nordrupvester
  .11 Ottestrup
  .12 Skt. Mikkels landsogn
  .13 Skt. Peders landsogn
  .14 Slagelse
  .15 Slots-Bjergby
  .16 Sludstrup
  .17 Sorterup
  .18 Sønderup
  .19 Tårnborg
  .20 Vemmelev

4.04 *Vester-Flakkebjerg District*

4.04.01 Agersø
  .02 Eggeslevmagle
  .03 Flakkebjerg
  .04 Fårdrup
  .05 Gimlinge
  .06 Holsteinborg
  .07 Hyllested
  .08 Høve
  .09 Hårslev
  .10 Kirkerup
  .11 Magleby
  .12 Omø
  .13 Skælskør
  .14 Skørpinge
  .15 Sønder-Bjerge
  .16 Sørbymagle
  .17 Ting-Jellinge
  .18 Tjæreby
  .19 Venslev
  .20 Ørslev

4.05 *Øster-Flakkebjerg District*

4.05.01 Fodby
  .02 Fuglebjærg
  .03 Fyrendal
  .04 Førslev
  .05 Gunderslev
  .06 Haldagerlille
  .07 Herlufsholm
  .08 Hyllinge
  .09 Karrebæk
  .10 Krummerup
  .11 Kvislemark
  .12 Marvede
  .13 Tystrup
  .14 Vallensved

5. Præstø County

5.01 Bjæverskov
5.02 Bårse
5.03 Fakse
5.04 Hammer
5.05 Mønbo
5.06 Stevns
5.07 Tybjerg

5.01 *Bjæverskov District*

5.01.01 Bjæverskov
  .02 Endeslev
  .03 Gørslev
  .04 Herfølge
  .05 Himlingøje
  .06 Hårlev
  .07 Lellinge
  .08 Lidemark
  .09 Sædder
  .10 Tårnby
  .11 Valløby
  .12 Vollerslev
  .13 Vråby

5.02 *Bårse District*

5.02.01 Allerslev
  .02 Beldringe
  .03 Bårse
  .04 Everdrup
  .05 Jungshoved
  .06 Kalvehave
  .07 Mern
  .08 Præstø (including .09)
  .09 Præstø landsogn (part of .08)
  .10 Skibinge
  .11 Snesere
  .12 Udby
  .13 Vordingborg (including .14)
  .14 Vordingborg landsogn
     (part of .13)
  .15 Ørslev
  .16 Øster-Egesborg

5.03 *Fakse District*

5.03.01 Alslev
  .02 Fakse
  .03 Hylleholt
  .04 Karise
  .05 Kongsted
  .06 Roholte
  .07 Spjellerup
  .08 Sønder-Dalby

.09 Tureby
.10 Ulse
.11 Vemmetofte
.12 Øster-Egede

5.04 *Hammer District*

5.04.01 Hammer
.02 Holme-Olstrup
.03 Kastrup
.04 Køng
.05 Lundby
.06 Mogenstrup
.07 Næstelsø
.08 Rønnebæk
.09 Sværdborg
.10 Toksværd
.11 Vejlø
.12 Vester-Egesborg
– Vordingborg: Knudshoved
(added to 5.02.13)

5.05 *Mønbo District*

5.05.01 Bogø
.02 Borre
.03 Damsholte
.04 Elmelunde
.05 Fanefjord
.06 Keldby
.07 Magleby
.08 Nyord
.09 Stege (including .10 and .11)
.10 Stege landdistrikt (part of .09)
.11 Stege landsogn (part of .09)

5.06 *Stevns District*

5.06.01 Frøslev
.02 Havnelev
.03 Hellested
.04 Holtug
.05 Højerup
.06 Lille-Heddinge
.07 Lyderslev
.08 Magleby Stevns
.09 Smerup
.10 Store-Heddinge (including .11)
.11 Store-Heddinge landsogn
(part of .10)
.12 Strøby
.13 Varpelev

5.07 *Tybjerg District*

5.07.01 Aversi

.02 Bavelse
.03 Fensmark
.04 Glumsø
.05 Herlufmagle
.06 Næsby
.07 Næstved
.08 Rislev
.09 Sandby
.10 Skelby
.11 Tybjerg
.12 Tyvelse
.13 Vester-Egede
.14 Vrangstrup

6. Bornholms County

6.01 Bornholms Nørre
6.02 Bornholms Sønder
6.03 Bornholms Vester
6.04 Bornholms Øster

6.01 *Bornholms Nørre District*

6.01.01 Allinge-Sandvig (part of .05)
.02 Hasle (including .03 og .06)
.03 Hasle landdistrikt
(part of .02)
.04 Klemensker
.05 Olsker (including .01)
.06 Rutsker (part of .02)
.07 Rø

6.02 *Bornholms Sønder District*

6.02.01 Bodilsker
.02 Neksø
.03 Pedersker
.04 Povlsker
.05 Åker (part of .06)
.06 Åkirkeby (including .05)

6.03 *Bornholms Vester District*

6.03.01 Knudsker
.02 Nyker
.03 Nylarsker
.04 Rønne
.05 Vester-Marie

6.04 *Bornholms Øster District*

6.04.01 Christiansø
.02 Gudhjem (part of .05)
.03 Ibsker
.04 Svaneke
.05 Øster-Larsker
(including .02)

.06 Øster-Marie

7. Maribo County

7.01 Falsters Nørre
7.02 Falsters Sønder
7.03 Fuglse
7.04 Lollands Nørre
7.05 Lollands Sønder
7.06 Musse

7.01 *Falsters Nørre District*

7.01.01 Brarup
.02 Eskilstrup
.03 Gundslev
.04 Kippinge
.05 Lillebrænde
.06 Maglebrænde
.07 Nørre-Alslev
.08 Nørre-Kirkeby
.09 Nørre-Vedby
.10 Stadager
.11 Stubbekøbing
.12 Tingsted
.13 Torkilstrup
.14 Vålse
.15 Ønslev

7.02 *Falsters Sønder District*

7.02.01 Falkerslev
.02 Gedesby
.03 Horbelev
.04 Horreby
.05 Idestrup
.06 Karleby
.07 Nykøbing F
.08 Nørre-Ørslev
.09 Skelby
.10 Systofte
.11 Sønder-Alslev
.12 Sønder-Kirkeby
.13 Væggerløse
.14 Åstrup

7.03 *Fuglse District*

7.03.01 Askø
.02 Bandholm
.03 Bursø
.04 Errindlev
.05 Fejø
.06 Femø
.07 Fuglse

.08 Hillested
.09 Holeby
.10 Krønge
.11 Nebbelunde
.12 Olstrup
.13 Ringsebølle
.14 Rødby
.15 Skørringe
.16 Sædinge
.17 Tirsted
.18 Torslunde
.19 Tågerup
.20 Vejleby
.21 Østofte

7.04 *Lollands Nørre District*

7.04.01 Birket
.02 Branderslev
.03 Halsted
.04 Herredskirke
.05 Horslunde
.06 Købelev
.07 Løjtofte
.08 Nakskov
.09 Nordlunde
.10 Sandby
.11 Utterslev
.12 Vesterborg
.13 Vindeby

7.05 *Lollands Sønder District*

7.05.01 Arninge
.02 Avnede
.03 Dannemare
.04 Gloslunde
.05 Græshave
.06 Gurreby
 – Halsted SØ (added to 7.04.03)
.07 Kappel
.08 Landet
.09 Ryde
.10 Skovlænge
.11 Stokkemarke
.12 Søllested
.13 Tillitse
.14 Vestenskov
 – Vesterborg S
 (added to 7.04.12)

7.06 *Musse District*

7.06.01 Bregninge
.02 Døllefjelde

.03 Engestofte
.04 Fjelde
.05 Godsted
.06 Herritslev
.07 Hunseby
.08 Kettinge
.09 Majbølle
.10 Maribo (including .11)
.11 Maribo landsogn (part of .10)
.12 Musse
.13 Nysted (including .14)
.14 Nysted landsogn (part of .13)
.15 Radsted
.16 Sakskøbing (including .17)
.17 Sakskøbing landsogn
 (part of .16)
.18 Slemminge
.19 Toreby
.20 Tårs
.21 Vester-Ulslev
.22 Vigsnæs
.23 Våbensted
.24 Øster-Ulslev

8. Odense County

8.01 Bjerge
8.02 Båg
8.03 Lunde
8.04 Odense
8.05 Skam
8.06 Skovby
8.07 Vends
8.08 Åsum

8.01 *Bjerge District*

8.01.01 Agedrup
.02 Birkende
.03 Dalby
.04 Drigstrup
.05 Kerteminde
.06 Kølstrup
.07 Marslev
.08 Mesinge
.09 Munkebo
.10 Revninge
.11 Rynkeby
.12 Stubberup
.13 Viby

8.02 *Båg District*

8.02.01 Assens

.02 Barløse
.03 Bågø
.04 Dreslette
.05 Flemløse
.06 Gamtofte
.07 Helnæs
.08 Holevad
.09 Hårby
.10 Kerte
.11 Kærum
.12 Køng
.13 Orte
.14 Sandager
.15 Skydebjerg
.16 Søby
.17 Søllested
.18 Sønderby
.19 Tanderup
.20 Turup
.21 Vedtofte
.22 Ørsted

8.03 *Lunde District*

8.03.01 Allese
.02 Hjadstrup
.03 Lumby
.04 Lunde
.05 Norup
.06 Otterup
.07 Skeby
.08 Østrup

8.04 *Odense District*

8.04.01 Bellinge
.02 Brylle
.03 Brændekilde
.04 Dalum
.05 Fangel
.06 Næsbyhoved-Broby
.07 Odense
.08 Pårup
.09 Sanderum
.10 Stenløse
.11 Tommerup
.12 Trøstrup-Korup
.13 Ubberud
.14 Verninge
.15 Vissenbjerg

8.05 *Skam District*

8.05.01 Bederslev
.02 Grindløse

.03 Klinte
.04 Krogsbølle
.05 Nørre-Højrup
.06 Nørre-Nærå
.07 Skamby
.08 Uggerslev

8.06 *Skovby District*

8.06.01 Bogense
.02 Ejlby
.03 Guldbjerg
.04 Hårslev
.05 Melby
.06 Nørre-Sandager
.07 Ore
.08 Skovby
.09 Særslev
.10 Søndersø
.11 Veflinge
.12 Vigerslev

8.07 *Vends District*

8.07.01 Asperup
.02 Balslev
.03 Brenderup
 − Bågø N: Brandsø
  (added to 8.02.03)
.04 Ejby
.05 Fjelsted
 − Fænø = .14
.06 Føns
.07 Gamborg
.08 Gelsted
.09 Harndrup
.10 Husby
.11 Ingslev
.12 Kavslunde
.13 Middelfart (including .14)
.14 Middelfart landsogn: Fænø
  (part of .13)
.15 Nørre-Åby
.16 Rorslev
.17 Rørup
.18 Strib-Røjleskov (part of .20)
.19 Udby
.20 Vejlby (including .18)
.21 Ørslev

8.08 *Åsum District*

8.08.01 Allerup
.02 Davinde
.03 Fraugde

.04 Højby
.05 Nørre-Lyndelse
.06 Nørre-Søby
.07 Rolsted
.08 Rønninge
.09 Seden
.10 Sønder-Nærå
.11 Åsum

9. Svendborg County

9.01 Gudme
9.02 Langelands Nørre
9.03 Langelands Sønder
9.04 Sallinge
9.05 Sunds
9.06 Vindinge
9.07 Ærø

9.01 *Gudme District*

9.01.01 Brudager
.02 Gislev
.03 Gudbjerg
.04 Gudme
.05 Hesselager
.06 Langå
.07 Oure
.08 Ringe
.09 Ryslinge
.10 Svindinge
.11 Vejstrup
.12 Øksendrup

9.02 *Langelands Nørre District*

9.02.01 Bøstrup
.02 Hov (part of .07)
.03 Rudkøbing
.04 Simmerbølle
.05 Skrøbelev
.06 Snøde
.07 Stoense (including .02)
.08 Tranekær
.09 Tullebølle

9.03 *Langelands Sønder District*

9.03.01 Fodslette
.02 Fuglsbølle
.03 Humble
.04 Lindelse
.05 Longelse
.06 Magleby
.07 Tryggelev

9.04 *Sallinge District*

9.04.01 Allested
.02 Avernakø
 − Bjørnø = .07
.03 Brahetrolleborg
.04 Diernæs
.05 Espe
.06 Fåborg (including .07)
.07 Fåborg landsogn
  (part of .06)
.08 Gestelev
.09 Heden
.10 Herringe
.11 Hillerslev
.12 Horne
.13 Hundstrup
.14 Håstrup
.15 Jordløse
.16 Krarup
.17 Lyø
.18 Nørre-Broby
.19 Sandholts-Lyndelse
.20 Svanninge
.21 Sønder-Broby
.22 Ulbølle
.23 Vantinge
.24 Vejle
.25 Vester-Hæsinge
.26 Vester-Skerninge
.27 Vester-Åby
.28 Øster-Hæsinge
.29 Åstrup

9.05 *Sunds District*

9.05.01 Bjerreby
.02 Bregninge
.03 Drejø
.04 Egense
.05 Kirkeby
.06 Kværndrup
.07 Landet
.08 Lunde
.09 Ollerup
.10 Skårup
.11 Stenstrup
.12 Strynø
.13 Svendborg
.14 Thurø
.15 Tved
.16 Øster-Skerninge

9.06 *Vindinge District*
9.06.01 Avnslev
.02 Bovense
.03 Ellested
.04 Ellinge
.05 Flødstrup
.06 Frørup
.07 Hellerup
.08 Herrested
– Hjulby = .11
.09 Kullerup
.10 Nyborg (including .11)
.11 Nyborg landsogn (part of .10)
.12 Refs-Vindinge
.13 Skellerup
.14 Søllinge
.15 Sønder-Højrup
.16 Ullerslev
.17 Vindinge
.18 Ørbæk
.19 Årslev

9.07 *Ærø District*
9.07.01 Bregninge
.02 Marstal
.03 Marstal landsogn
.04 Rise
.05 Søby
.06 Tranderup
.07 Ærøskøbing

10. Hjørring County
10.01 Børglum
10.02 Dronninglund
10.03 Horns
10.04 Hvetbo
10.05 Læsø
10.06 Vennebjerg
10.07 Øster Han·

10.01 *Børglum District*
10.01.01 Brønderslev
.02 Børglum
.03 Em
.04 Furreby
.05 Hæstrup
.06 Jerslev
.07 Lyngby
.08 Rakkeby
.09 Sejlstrup
.10 Serreslev

.11 Stenum
.12 Tise
.13 Tolstrup
.14 Tårs
.15 Vejby
– Vester-Brønderslev, now: .01
.16 Vrejlev
.17 Vrensted
.18 Vrå
.19 Øster-Brønderslev

10.02 *Dronninglund District*
10.02.01 Albæk
.02 Aså-Melholt (part of .03)
.03 Dronninglund (including .02)
.04 Hallund
.05 Hellevad
.06 Hellum
.07 Hørby
.08 Karup
.09 Skæve
.10 Sæby
.11 Torslev
.12 Understed
.13 Voer
.14 Volstrup
.15 Ørum

10.03 *Horns District*
10.03.01 Bindslev
.02 Elling
.03 Flade
.04 Frederikshavn
.05 Gærum
.06 Hirsholmene
.07 Hørmested
.08 Lendum
.09 Mosbjerg
.10 Råbjerg
.11 Skagen (including .12)
.12 Skagen landsogn (part of .11)
.13 Skærum
.14 Tolne
.15 Tværsted
.16 Årsted

10.04 *Hvetbo District*
10.04.01 Alstrup
– Brovst Ø (added to 10.07.03)
.02 Gøl
.03 Hune
.04 Ingstrup

.05 Jetsmark
.06 Saltum
.07 Vedsted
.08 Vester-Hjermeslev

10.05 *Læsø District*
10.05.01 Byrum
.02 Hals
.03 Vesterø

10.06 *Vennebjerg District*
10.06.01 Asdal
.02 Astrup
.03 Bjergby
.04 Harreslev
.05 Hjørring
.06 Horne
.07 Jelstrup
.08 Mygdal
.09 Mårup
.10 Rubjerg
.11 Skt. Hans
.12 Skt. Olai
.13 Sindal
.14 Skallerup
.15 Tornby
.16 Uggerby
.17 Ugilt
.18 Vennebjerg
.19 Vidstrup

10.07 *Øster-Han District*
10.07.01 Aggersborg
.02 Bejstrup
.03 Brovst
.04 Haverslev
.05 Lerup
.06 Skræm
.07 Torslev
.08 Tranum
.09 Øland
.10 Øster-Svenstrup

11. Thisted County
11.01 Hassing
11.02 Hillerslev
11.03 Hundborg
11.04 Morsø Nørre
11.05 Morsø Sønder
11.06 Refs
11.07 Vester-Han

11.01 *Hassing District*

11.01.01 Bested
  .02 Grurup
  .03 Harring
  .04 Hassing
  .05 Hvidbjerg
  .06 Hørdum
  .07 Hørsted
  .08 Lodbjerg
  .09 Skyum
  .10 Snedsted
  .11 Stagstrup
  .12 Sønderhå
  .13 Villerslev
  .14 Visby
  .15 Ørum

11.02 *Hillerslev District*

11.02.01 Hansted
  .02 Hillerslev
  .03 Hjaremål
  .04 Hunstrup
  .05 Kåstrup
  .06 Nors
  .07 Ræer
  .08 Sennels
  .09 Tved
  .10 Vester-Vandet
  .11 Vigsø
  .12 Østerild
  .13 Øster-Vandet

11.03 *Hundborg District*

11.03.01 Hundborg
  .02 Jannerup
  .03 Kallerup
  .04 Nørhå
  .05 Sjørring
  .06 Skinnerup
  .07 Skjoldborg
   – Stagstrup N
    (added to 11.01.11)
  .08 Thisted
  .09 Thisted landsogn
  .10 Tilsted
  .11 Torsted
  .12 Tvorup (part of .13)
  .13 Vang (including .12)

11.04 *Morsø Nørre District*

11.04.01 Alsted
  .02 Bjergby

  .03 Dragstrup
  .04 Ejerslev
  .05 Erslev
  .06 Flade
  .07 Galtrup
  .08 Jørsby
  .09 Sejerslev
  .10 Skallerup
  .11 Solbjerg
  .12 Sundby
  .13 Sønder-Dråby
  .14 Tødsø
  .15 Øster-Jølby

11.05 *Morsø Sønder District*

11.05.01 Blidstrup
  .02 Elsø
  .03 Frøslev
  .04 Hvidbjerg
  .05 Karby
  .06 Lødderup
  .07 Lørslev
  .08 Mollerup
  .09 Nykøbing M
  .10 Ovtrup
  .11 Rakkeby
  .12 Rested
  .13 Tæbring
  .14 Vejerslev
  .15 Vester-Assels
  .16 Ørding
  .17 Øster-Assels

11.06 *Refs District*

11.06.01 Agger
  .02 Boddum
  .03 Gettrup
  .04 Helligsø
  .05 Heltborg
  .06 Hurup
  .07 Hvidbjerg
  .08 Jegindø
  .09 Lyngs
  .10 Odby
  .11 Søndbjerg
  .12 Vestervig
  .13 Ydby

11.07 *Vester-Han District*

11.07.01 Arup
  .02 Gøttrup
  .03 Hjortdal

  .04 Kettrup
  .05 Klim
  .06 Kollerup
  .07 Lild
  .08 Tømmerby
  .09 Vestløs
  .10 Vester-Torup
  .11 Vust
  .12 Østløs

12. Ålborg County

12.01 Fleskum
12.02 Gislum
12.03 Hellum
12.04 Hindsted
12.05 Hornum
12.06 Kær
12.07 Slet
12.08 Års

12.01 *Fleskum District*

12.01.01 Dall
  .02 Ferslev
  .03 Gudum
  .04 Gunderup
  .05 Klarup
  .06 Lillevorde
  .07 Mou
  .08 Nørre-Tranders
    (including .14)
  .09 Nøvling
  .10 Romdrup
  .11 Sejlflod
  .12 Storvorde
  .13 Sønder-Tranders
  .14 Vejgård (part of .08)
  .15 Volsted

12.02 *Gislum District*

12.02.01 Alstrup
  .02 Binderup
  .03 Durup
  .04 Farsø
  .05 Fovlum
  .06 Gislum
  .07 Grynderup
  .08 Kongens Tisted
  .09 Lovns
  .10 Rørbæk
  .11 Stenild
  .12 Strandby

.13 Ullits
.14 Vognsild

12.03 *Hellum District*

12.03.01 Blenstrup
.02 Bælum
.03 Fræer
.04 Gerding
.05 Komdrup
.06 Lyngby
.07 Nørre-Kongerslev
.08 Siem
.09 Skibsted
.10 Skørping
.11 Solbjerg
.12 Store-Brøndum
.13 Sønder-Kongerslev
.14 Torup

12.04 *Hindsted District*

12.04.01 Als
.02 Astrup
.03 Døstrup
.04 Hadsund (part of .13)
.05 Hørby
.06 Ove
  – Ravnkilde Ø
    (added to 12.08.10)
.07 Rold
.08 Rostrup
  – Rørbæk Ø
    (added to 12.02.10)
.09 Skelund
  – Solbjerg S
    (added to 12.03.11)
.10 Store-Arden
.11 Valsgård
.12 Vebbestrup
.13 Visborg (including .04)
.14 Vive
.15 Øls

12.05 *Hornum District*

12.05 – Ansgar landsogn, now: .06
.01 Bislev
.02 Buderup
  – Budolfi landsogn, now: .06
.03 Ellidshøj
.04 Frejlev
.05 Gravlev
.06 Hasseris
.07 Nibe

.08 Nørholm
.09 Suldrup
.10 Svenstrup
.11 Sønderholm
.12 Sønderup
.13 Veggerby
.14 Vokslev
.15 Øster-Hornum
.16 Ålborg
.17 Årestrup

12.06 *Kær District*

12.06.01 Ajstrup
  – Aså-Melholt S
    (added to 10.02.03)
.02 Biersted
  – Egholm = .03
.03 Frue landsogn
.04 Hals
.05 Hammer
.06 Horsens
.07 Hvorup
.08 Lindholm
.09 Nørresundby
.10 Sulsted
.11 Ulsted
.12 Vadum
.13 Vester-Hassing
.14 Øster-Hassing
.15 Åby

12.07 *Slet District*

12.07.01 Farstrup
.02 Gundersted
.03 Kornum
.04 Lundby
.05 Løgsted
.06 Løgstør
.07 Malle
.08 Næsborg
.09 Oudrup
.10 Ranum
.11 Sebber
.12 Skarp-Salling
.13 Store-Ajstrup
.14 Vilsted
.15 Vindblæs

12.08 *Års District*

12.08 – Binderup N
    (added to 12.02.02)
.01 Blære

.02 Brorstrup
.03 Ejdrup
.04 Flejsborg
.05 Giver
  – Gundersted S
    (added to 12.07.02)
.06 Havbro
.07 Haverslev
.08 Hyllebjerg
.09 Overlade
.10 Ravnkilde
.11 Skivum
.12 Ulstrup
.13 Vester-Hornum
.14 Års

13. Viborg County

13.01 Fjends
13.02 Harre
13.03 Hids
13.04 Hindborg
13.05 Houlbjerg
13.06 Lysgård
13.07 Middelsom
13.08 Nørlyng
13.09 Rinds
13.10 Rødding
13.11 Salling Nørre
13.12 Sønderlyng

13.01 *Fjends District*

13.01.01 Daubjerg
.02 Dommerby
.03 Feldingbjerg
.04 Fly
  – Frederiks N
    (added to 13.06.03)
.05 Gammelstrup
.06 Højslev
.07 Kobberup
.08 Kvols
.09 Lundø
.10 Mønsted
.11 Nørre-Borris
.12 Resen
.13 Smollerup
.14 Tårup
.15 Vridsted
.16 Vroue
.17 Ørslevkloster
.18 Ørum

13.02 *Harre District*

13.02.01 Durup
  .02 Fur
  .03 Glyngøre
  .04 Harre
  .05 Hjerk
  .06 Nautrup
  .07 Roslev
  .08 Sæby
  .09 Tøndering
  .10 Vile
  .11 Åsted

13.03 *Hids District*

13.03.01 Balle
  .02 Engesvang
  .03 Funder
  .04 Gødvad
  .05 Kragelund
  .06 Lemming
  .07 Sejling
  .08 Serup
  .09 Sinding
  .10 Svostrup

13.04 *Hindborg District*

13.04.01 Brøndum
  .02 Dølby
  .03 Hem
  .04 Hindborg
  .05 Hvidbjerg
  .06 Oddense
  .07 Otting
  .08 Resen
  .09 Skive (including .10)
  .10 Skive landsogn (part of .09)
  .11 Volling

13.05 *Houlbjerg District*

13.05.01 Aidt
  – Bjerringbro S
    (added to 13.07.02)
  .02 Gerning
  .03 Granslev
  .04 Gullev
  .05 Haurum
  .06 Houlbjerg
  .07 Hvorslev
  .08 Sahl
  .09 Sall
  .10 Skjød
  .11 Thorsø

  .12 Vejerslev
  .13 Vellev

13.06 *Lysgård District*

13.06.01 Almind
  .02 Elsborg
  .03 Frederiks
  .04 Grønbæk
  .05 Hinge
  .06 Høbjerg
  .07 Hørup
  .08 Karup
  .09 Levring
  .10 Lysgård
  .11 Sjørslev
  .12 Torning
  .13 Vinderslev
  .14 Vium

13.07 *Middelsom District*

13.07.01 Bjerring (including .02)
  .02 Bjerringbro (part of .01)
  .03 Grensten
  .04 Helstrup
  .05 Hjermind
  .06 Hjorthede
  .07 Langå
  .08 Lee
  .09 Mammen
  .10 Skjern
  .11 Sønder-Rind
  .12 Sønder-Vinge
  .13 Torup
  – Vejrum S (added to 13.12.10)
  .14 Vester-Velling
  .15 Vindum
  .16 Vinkel
  – Viskum S (added to 13.12.11)
  .17 Øster-Velling

13.08 *Nørlyng District*

13.08.01 Asmild
  .02 Bigum
  .03 Dollerup
  .04 Finderup
  .05 Fiskbæk
  .06 Gråbrødre landsogn
    (part of .15)
  .07 Lindum
  .08 Løvel
  .09 Pederstrup
  .10 Ravnstrup

  .11 Romlund
  .12 Rødding
  .13 Tapdrup
  .14 Vammen
  .15 Viborg (including .06)
  .16 Vorde

13.09 *Rinds Herred*

13.09.01 Fjelsø
  .02 Gedsted
  .03 Hersom
  .04 Hvam
  .05 Hvilsom
  .06 Klejtrup
  .07 Lynderup
  .08 Låstrup
  .09 Roum
  .10 Simested
  .11 Skals
  .12 Testrup
  .13 Ulbjerg
  .14 Vester-Bjerregrav
  .15 Vester-Bølle
  .16 Vester-Tostrup
  .17 Øster-Bølle

13.10 *Rødding District*

13.10.01 Balling
  .02 Håsum
  .03 Krejbjerg
  .04 Lem
  .05 Lihme
  .06 Ramsing
  .07 Rødding
  .08 Vejby

13.11 *Salling Nørre District*

13.11.01 Grinderslev
  .02 Grønning
  .03 Jebjerg
  .04 Junget
  .05 Lyby
  – Roslev Ø (added to 13.02.07)
  .06 Rybjerg
  .07 Selde
  .08 Thise
  .09 Torum

13.12 *Sønderlyng District*

13.12.01 Hammershøj
  .02 Hornbæk
  .03 Kvorning

.04 Læsten
.05 Nørbæk
.06 Nørre-Vinge
.07 Sønderbæk
.08 Tjele
.09 Tånum
.10 Vejrum
.11 Viskum
.12 Vorning
.13 Ørum
.14 Øster-Bjerregrav
.15 Ålum

14. Randers County

14.01 Djurs Nørre
14.02 Djurs Sønder
14.03 Galten
14.04 Gjerlev
14.05 Mols
14.06 Nørhald
14.07 Onsild
14.08 Rougsø
14.09 Støvring
14.10 Sønderhald
14.11 Øster Lisbjerg

14.01 *Djurs Nørre District*

14.01.01 Anholt
.02 Enslev
.03 Fjellerup
.04 Gammelsogn (part of .08)
.05 Ginnerup
.06 Gjerrild
.07 Glesborg
.08 Grenå (including .04)
.09 Hammelev
.10 Hemmed
.11 Karlby
.12 Kastbjerg
.13 Nimtofte
.14 Rimsø
.15 Tøstrup
.16 Veggerslev
.17 Villersø
.18 Voldby
.19 Ørum

14.02 *Djurs Sønder District*

14.02.01 Albøge
.02 Ebdrup
.03 Feldballe

.04 Fuglslev
.05 Hoed
.06 Homå
.07 Hyllested
.08 Kolind
.09 Lyngby
.10 Nødager
.11 Rosmus
.12 Tirstrup
.13 Vejlby
.14 Ålsø

14.03 *Galten District*

14.03.01 Galten
.02 Hadbjerg
.03 Halling
.04 Haslund
.05 Laurbjerg
.06 Lerbjerg
.07 Rud
.08 Vissing
.09 Voldum
.10 Vorup
.11 Værum
.12 Ødum
.13 Ølst
.14 Ørum

14.04 *Gjerlev District*

14.04.01 Dalbyneder
.02 Dalbyover
.03 Enslev
.04 Gjerlev
.05 Kastbjerg
.06 Kærby
.07 Råby
.08 Sødring
.09 Udbyneder
.10 Vindblæs
.11 Øster-Tørslev

14.05 *Mols District*

14.05.01 Agri
.02 Dråby
.03 Ebeltoft (including .04)
.04 Ebeltoft landsogn (part of .03)
.05 Egens
.06 Helgenæs
.07 Knebel
.08 Rolsø
.09 Tved
.10 Vistoft

14.06 *Nørhald District*

14.06.01 Asferg
.02 Fårup
.03 Gassum
.04 Glenstrup
.05 Hald
.06 Kousted
.07 Linde
.08 Spentrup
.09 Tvede
.10 Vester-Tørslev

14.07 *Onsild District*

14.07.01 Falslev
.02 Hem
.03 Hobro
.04 Hvornum
.05 Mariager (including .06)
.06 Mariager landsogn
    (part of .05)
.07 Nørre-Onsild
.08 Sem
.09 Skjellerup
.10 Snæbum
.11 Svenstrup
.12 Sønder-Onsild

14.08 *Rougsø District*

14.08.01 Estruplund
.02 Holbæk
.03 Udby
.04 Voer
.05 Ørsted

14.09 *Støvring District*

14.09.01 Albæk
.02 Borup
.03 Dronningborg
.04 Gimming
.05 Harridslev
.06 Lem
.07 Mellerup
.08 Randers
.09 Råsted
.10 Støvring

14.10 *Sønderhald District*

14.10.01 Auning
.02 Essenbæk
.03 Fausing
.04 Gjesing
.05 Hvilsager

.06 Hørning
.07 Koed
.08 Kristrup
.09 Krogsbæk
.10 Lime
.11 Marie Magdalene
.12 Mygind
.13 Nørager
.14 Skader
.15 Skørring
.16 Søby
.17 Vejlby
.18 Vester-Alling
.19 Virring
.20 Vivild
– Ørsted NØ
(added to 14.08.05)
.21 Øster-Alling
.22 Årslev

14.11 *Øster-Lisbjerg District*

14.11.01 Bregnet
.02 Egå
.03 Hjortshøj
.04 Hornslet
.05 Mejlby
.06 Mørke
.07 Skarresø
.08 Skødstrup
.09 Thorsager
.10 Todbjerg

15. Århus County

15.01 Framlev
15.02 Hads
15.03 Hasle
15.04 Ning
15.05 Sabro
15.06 Vester-Lisbjerg

15.01 *Framlev District*

15.01.01 Borum
.02 Framlev
.03 Harlev
.04 Sjelle
.05 Skivholme
.06 Skovby
.07 Skørring
.08 Stjær
.09 Storring
.10 Sønder-Galten

15.02 *Hads District*

15.02.01 Alrø
.02 Bjerager
.03 Falling
.04 Gosmer
.05 Gylling
.06 Halling
.07 Hundslund
.08 Hvilsted
.09 Nølev
.10 Odder
.11 Randlev
.12 Saksild
.13 Torrild
.14 Ørting

15.03 *Hasle District*

15.03.01 Brabrand
.02 Hasle
.03 Kasted
.04 Lyngby
.05 Risskov (part of .09)
.06 Skejby
.07 Sønder-Årslev
.08 Tilst
.09 Vejlby (including .05)
.10 Åby
.11 Århus

15.04 *Ning District*

15.04.01 Astrup
.02 Beder
.03 Holme
.04 Kolt
.05 Malling
.06 Mårslet
.07 Ormslev
.08 Skåde
.09 Tiset
.10 Tranbjerg
.11 Tulstrup
.12 Tunø
.13 Viby
– Århus S (added to 15.03.11)

15.05 *Sabro District*

15.05.01 Folby
.02 Fårup
.03 Hadsten
.04 Haldum
.05 Lading
.06 Lyngå

.10 Veng
.07 Sabro
.08 Vitten

15.06 *Vester-Lisbjerg District*

15.06.01 Elev
.02 Elsted
.03 Grundfør
.04 Lisbjerg
.05 Spørring
.06 Søften
.07 Trige
.08 Ølsted

16. Skanderborg County

16.01 Gjern
16.02 Hjelmslev
16.03 Nim
16.04 Tyrsting
16.05 Voer
16.06 Vrads

16.01 *Gjern District*

16.01.01 Alling
.02 Dallerup
.03 Gjern
.04 Hammel
.05 Linå
.06 Låsby
.07 Røgen
.08 Silkeborg
.09 Skannerup
.10 Skorup
.11 Sporup
.12 Søby
.13 Tulstrup
.14 Tvilum (including .15)
.15 Voel (part of .14)
.16 Voldby

16.02 *Hjelmslev District*

16.02.01 Adslev
.02 Blegind
.03 Dover
.04 Fruering
.05 Hørning
.06 Mesing
.07 Skanderborg
.08 Skanderup
.09 Stilling

.11 Vitved

16.03 *Nim District*

16.03.01 Endelave
.02 Hornborg
.03 Horsens
.04 Hvirring
.05 Nim
.06 Tamdrup
.07 Underup

16.04 *Tyrsting District*

16.04.01 Bryrup
.02 Føvling
.03 Grædstrup
.04 Ring
.05 Rye
.06 Sønder-Vissing
.07 Træden
.08 Tyrsting
.09 Tønning
.10 Vinding
.11 Voerladegård

16.05 *Voer District*

16.05.01 Gangsted
.02 Hansted
.03 Hylke
.04 Kattrup
.05 Lundum
.06 Nebel
.07 Ovsted
.08 Søvind
.09 Tolstrup
.10 Tåning
.11 Vedslet
.12 Vær
.13 Yding
.14 Ørridslev
.15 Østbirk

16.06 *Vrads District*

16.06.01 Ejstrup
.02 Hammer
.03 Klovborg
.04 Linnerup
.05 Nørre-Snede
.06 Them
.07 Tørring
.08 Vrads
.09 Åle

17. Vejle County

17.01 Bjerre
17.02 Brusk
17.03 Elbo
17.04 Hatting
17.05 Holmans
17.06 Jerlev
17.07 Nørre-Tyrstrup
17.08 Nørvang
17.09 Tørrild

17.01 *Bjerre District*

17.01.01 As
.02 Barrit
.03 Bjerre
.04 Glud
.05 Hjarnø
.06 Hornum
.07 Klakring
.08 Nebsager
.09 Rårup
.10 Skjold
.11 Stouby
.12 Uth
.13 Vrigsted
.14 Ørum

17.02 *Brusk District*

17.02.01 Almind
.02 Eltang
.03 Harte
.04 Herslev
.05 Kolding
.06 Nørre-Bjert
.07 Nørre-Bramdrup
 – Smidstrup S
 (added to 17.05.06)
.08 Sønder-Vilstrup
.09 Vester-Nebel
.10 Viuf
.11 Øster-Starup

17.03 *Elbo District*

17.03.01 Bredstrup
.02 Erritsø
.03 Fredericia
.04 Taulov
.05 Trinitatis landsogn
 – Ullerup = .05
.06 Vejlby

17.04 *Hatting District*

17.04.01 Daugård
.02 Engum
.03 Hatting
.04 Hedensted
.05 Korning
.06 Løsning
.07 Stenderup
.08 Store-Dalby
.09 Torsted
.10 Tyrsted
.11 Urlev
.12 Ølsted

17.05 *Holmans District*

17.05.01 Gauerslund
.02 Gårslev
.03 Mølholm (part of .07)
.04 Pjedsted
.05 Skærup
.06 Smidstrup
.07 Vinding (including .03)

17.06 *Jerlev District*

17.06.01 Egtved
.02 Højen
.03 Jerlev
.04 Ødsted

17.07 *Nørre-Tyrstrup District*

17.07.01 Dalby
.02 Hejls
.03 Sønder-Bjert
.04 Sønder-Stenderup
.05 Taps
.06· Vejstrup
.07 Vonsild
.08 Ødis

17.08 *Nørvang District*

17.08.01 Blåhøj (part of .12)
.02 Brande
.03 Filskov (part of .12)
.04 Give
.05 Givskud
.06 Grejs
.07 Hornstrup
.08 Hvejsel
.09 Langskov
.10 Ringgive
.11 Sindbjerg

.12 Sønder-Omme
(including .01 and .03)
.13 Tyregod
.14 Uldum
.15 Vejle
.16 Vester
.17 Vindelev
.18 Øster-Nykirke
.19 Øster-Snede

17.09 *Tørrild District*

17.09.01 Bredsten
.02 Gadbjerg
.03 Hover
.04 Jelling
.05 Kollerup
.06 Lindeballe
.07 Nørup
.08 Randbøl
.09 Skibet

18. Ringkøbing County

18.01 Bølling
18.02 Ginding
18.03 Hammerum
18.04 Hind
18.05 Hjerm
18.06 Nørre-Horne
18.07 Skodborg
18.08 Ulfborg
18.09 Vandfuld

18.01 *Bølling District*

18.01.01 Bølling
.02 Dejbjerg
.03 Faster
.04 Fjelstervang (part of .13)
.05 Hanning
.06 Herborg (part of .13)
.07 Nørre-Vium
.08 Skjern
.09 Stavning
.10 Sædding
.11 Sønder-Borris
.12 Videbæk (part of .13)
.13 Vorgod
(including .04, .06 and .12)

18.02 *Ginding District*

18.02.01 Ejsing
.02 Estvad

.03 Grove
.04 Haderup
.05 Hodsager
.06 Ryde
.07 Rønbjerg
.08 Sahl
.09 Sevel

18.03 *Hammerum District*

18.03.01 Arnborg
.02 Assing
.03 Avlum
.04 Bording
.05 Gjellerup
.06 Herning
.07 Ikast
.08 Ilskov
.09 Nøvling
.10 Rind
.11 Simmelkær
.12 Sinding
.13 Skarrild
.14 Snejbjerg
.15 Studsgård-Havnstrup
.16 Sunds
.17 Sønder-Felding
.18 Tjørring
.19 Tvis
.20 Vildbjerg
– Vorgod Ø (added to 18.01.13)
.21 Ørre

18.04 *Hind District*

18.04.01 Brejning
.02 Gammelsogn
.03 Hee
.04 Holmsland Klit
.05 Hover
.06 No
.07 Nysogn
.08 Nørre-Omme
.09 Rindum
.10 Ringkøbing
.11 Stadil
.12 Sønder-Lem
.13 Tim
.14 Torsted
.15 Vedersø
.16 Velling
.17 Ølstrup

18.05 *Hjerm District*

18.05.01 Asp

.02 Borbjerg
.03 Bur
.04 Fovsing
.05 Gimsing
.06 Gørding
.07 Handbjerg
.08 Hjerm
.09 Holstebro
.10 Mejrup
.11 Måbjerg
.12 Navr
.13 Sir
.14 Struer
.15 Vejrum
.16 Vemb
.17 Ølby

18.06 *Nørre-Horne District*

18.06.01 Egvad
.02 Hemmet
.03 Hoven
.04 Lyne
.05 Lønborg
.06 Nørre-Bork
.07 Oddum
.08 Strellev
.09 Sønder-Bork
.10 Sønder-Vium

18.07 *Skodborg District*

18.07.01 Bøvling
.02 Fabjerg
.03 Flynder
.04 Gudum
.05 Heldum
.06 Humlum
.07 Lemvig
.08 Lomborg
.09 Møborg
.10 Nees
.11 Nørlem
.12 Nørre-Nissum
.13 Resen
.14 Rom
.15 Tørring
.16 Venø

18.08 *Ulfborg District*

18.08.01 Husby
.02 Idum
.03 Madum
.04 Nørre-Felding

.05 Råsted
.06 Staby
.07 Sønder-Nissum
.08 Timring
.09 Ulfborg
 – Vildbjerg V
  (added to 18.03.20)
.10 Vind
.11 Vinding

18.09 *Vandfuld District*

18.09.01 Dybe
.02 Engbjerg
.03 Ferring
.04 Fjaltring
.05 Harboør
.06 Hove
.07 Hygum
.08 Ramme
.09 Thyborøn
.10 Trans
.11 Vandborg

19. Ribe County

19.01 Anst
19.02 Gørding
19.03 Malt
19.04 Ribe
19.05 Skast
19.06 Slavs
19.07 Vester-Horne
19.08 Øster-Horne

19.01 *Anst District*

19.01.01 Anst
.02 Bække
.03 Gesten
.04 Hjarup
.05 Jordrup
.06 Lejrskov
.07 Seest
.08 Skanderup
.09 Vamdrup
.10 Verst

19.02 *Gørding District*

19.02.01 Bramminge
.02 Darum
.03 Gørding
.04 Hunderup
.05 Jernved
 – Sneum Ø (added to 19.05.11)

.06 Vejrup
.07 Vilslev
.08 Åstrup

19.03 *Malt District*

19.03.01 Brørup
.02 Folding
.03 Føvling
.04 Holsted
.05 Lindknud
.06 Læborg
.07 Malt
.08 Vejen

19.04 *Ribe District*

19.04.01 Farup
.02 Hjortlund
.03 Kalvslund
.04 Mandø
.05 Obbekær
.06 Ribe (divided into .08 and .09)
.07 Ribe Domkirke landsogn
.08 Ribe Domkirke
.09 Ribe Skt. Catharina
.10 Seem
.11 Vester-Vedsted

19.05 *Skast District*

19.05.01 Alslev
.02 Brøndum
.03 Esbjerg
.04 Fåborg
.05 Grimstrup
.06 Guldager
.07 Hostrup
 – Jerne, now .03
.08 Nordby
.09 Næsbjerg
.10 Nørre-Skast
.11 Sneum
.12 Sønderho
.13 Tjæreborg
 – Varde landsogn Ø
  (added to 19.07.13)
.14 Vester-Nebel
.15 Vester-Nykirke
.16 Vester-Starup
.17 Øse
.18 Årre

19.06 *Slavs District*

19.06.01 Grene

.02 Grindsted
.03 Hejnsvig
.04 Vorbasse

19.07 *Vester-Horne District*

19.07.01 Billum
.02 Henne
.03 Ho
.04 Janderup
.05 Kvong
.06 Lunde
.07 Lydum
.08 Lønne
.09 Nørre-Nebel
.10 Oksby
.11 Ovtrup
.12 Varde
.13 Varde landsogn
.14 Ål

19.08 *Øster-Horne District*

19.08.01 Ansager
.02 Hodde
.03 Horne
.04 Tistrup
.05 Torstrup
.06 Ølgod

20. Haderslev County

20.01 Frøs
20.02 Gram
20.03 Haderslev
20.04 Nørre-Rangstrup
20.05 Sønder-Tyrstrup

20.01 *Frøs District*

20.01.01 Fole
.02 Hjerting
.03 Lintrup
.04 Rødding
.05 Skodborg
.06 Skrave
.07 Sønder-Hygum
.08 Øster-Lindet

20.02 *Gram District*

20.02.01 Gram
.02 Hammelev
.03 Jegerup
.04 Jels
.05 Magstrup

.06 Nustrup
.07 Oksenvad
.08 Skrydstrup
.09 Sommersted
.10 Vedsted
.11 Vojens

20.03 *Haderslev District*

20.03.01 Frue landsogn (part of .04)
.02 Gammel Haderslev landsogn
(part of .04)
.03 Grarup
.04 Haderslev
(including .01 and .02)
.05 Halk
.06 Hoptrup
.07 Moltrup
.08 Sønder-Starup
.09 Vilstrup
.10 Vonsbæk
.11 Øsby
.12 Åstrup

20.04 *Nørre-Rangstrup District*

20.04.01 Agerskov
.02 Bevtoft
.03 Branderup
.04 Tislund
.05 Toftlund

20.05 *Sønder-Tyrstrup District*

20.05.01 Aller
.02 Bjerning
.03 Christiansfeld (part of .08)
.04 Fjelstrup
.05 Frørup
.06 Hjerndrup
.07 Stepping
.08 Tyrstrup (including .03)

21. Tønder County
21.01 Hviding
21.02 Højer
21.03 Lø
21.04 Slogs
21.05 Tønder

21.01 *Hviding District*

21.01.01 Arrild
.02 Brøns
.03 Hviding
.04 Højrup

.05 Rejsby
.06 Roager
.07 Skærbæk
.08 Spandet
.09 Vodder

21.02 *Højer District*

21.02.01 Daler
.02 Emmerlev
.03 Hjerpsted
.04 Højer
.05 Højer landsogn
.06 Sønder-Skast

21.03 *Lø District*

21.03.01 Ballum
.02 Brede
.03 Døstrup
.04 Løgumkloster (including .05)
.05 Løgumkloster landsogn
(part of .04)
.06 Mjolden
.07 Nørre-Løgum
.08 Randerup
.09 Rømø

21.04 *Slogs District*

21.04.01 Burkal
.02 Bylderup
.03 Hostrup
.04 Højst
.05 Ravsted
.06 Tinglev

21.05 *Tønder District*

21.05.01 Abild
.02 Møgeltønder
.03 Tønder
.04 Tønder landsogn
.05 Ubjerg
.06 Visby

22. Åbenrå County
22.01 Lundtoft
22.02 Rise
22.03 Sønder-Rangstrup

22.01 *Lundtoft District*

22.01.01 Adsbøl
.02 Bov
.03 Ensted
.04 Felsted

.05 Gråsten
.06 Holbøl
.07 Kliplev
.08 Kværs
.09 Rinkenæs
.10 Uge
.11 Varnæs

22.02 *Rise District*

22.02.01 Bjolderup
.02 Hjortkær
.03 Løjt
.04 Rise
.05 Åbenrå

22.03 *Sønder-Rangstrup District*

22.03.01 Bedsted
.02 Egvad
.03 Hellevad
.04 Øster-Løgum

23. Sønderborg County
23.01 Als Nørre
23.02 Als Sønder
23.03 Nybøl

23.01 *Als Nørre District*

23.01.01 Egen
.02 Havnbjerg
.03 Nordborg
.04 Oksbøl
.05 Svenstrup

23.02 *Als Sønder District*

23.02.01 Asserballe
.02 Augustenborg
.03 Hørup
.04 Kegnæs
.05 Ketting
.06 Lysabild
.07 Notmark
.08 Sønderborg
.09 Tandslet
.10 Ulkebøl

23.03 *Nybøl District*

23.03.01 Broager
.02 Dybbøl
.03 Nybøl
.04 Sottrup
.05 Ullerup

Appendix 2

Alphabetical Index for Place Name Register

PREFACE

The following lists have been compiled as a supplement to the *Stednummerfortegnelse* (: Place Name Register), National Museum Dept. I, published by the State Inspectorate of Local Museums in 1961. They include:

A list of Danish counties and districts arranged by place number, with an accompanying index map .... pp. 4-5
An alphabetical list of Danish districts with place numbers .... pp. 7-9
An alphabetical list of Danish parishes with place numbers .... pp. 10-37

There are also some corrections to the *Stednummerfortegnelse* of 1961; they include a few printing errors as well as revisions in accordance with the register of place names in Ringkøbing County published in 1962.

The lists are based on the names of parishes and districts in the *Stednummerfortegnelse*, which – like the post office directory – complies with the register of place names approved by the Government. No such registers have yet been issued, however, for the counties of Hjørring, Thisted and Ribe.

When the spelling and nomenclature of parishes differ from those given in the *Stednummerfortegnelse*, we have, as far as possible, included them in the lists with reference to the approved name, e.g. 1.03.06 Hjørlunde = Jørlunde, or 8.02.03 Brandsø = Bågø.

The National Museum, January 1963.

Olfert Voss   Mogens Ørsnes

---

1. Frederiksborg County
1.01 Holbo
1.02 Horns
1.03 Lynge-Frederiksborg
1.04 Lynge-Kronborg
1.05 Strø
1.06 Ølstykke

2. Københavns County
2.01 Ramsø
2.02 Smørum
2.03 Sokkelund
2.04 Sømme
2.05 Tune
2.06 Volborg

3. Holbæk County
3.01 Ars
3.02 Løve

3.03 Merløse
3.04 Ods
3.05 Samsø
3.06 Skippinge
3.07 Tuse

4. Sorø County
4.01 Alsted
4.02 Ringsted
4.03 Slagelse
4.04 V.-Flakkebjerg
4.05 Ø.-Flakkebjerg

5. Præstø County
5.01 Bjæverskov
5.02 Bårse
5.03 Fakse
5.04 Hammer
5.05 Mønbo

5.06 Stevns
5.07 Tybjerg

6. Bornholms County
6.01 Bornh.s. Nørre
6.02 Bornh.s Sønder
6.03 Bornh.s Vester
6.04 Bornh.s Øster

7. Maribo County
7.01 Falsters Nørre
7.02 Falsters Sønder
7.03 Fuglse
7.04 Lollands Nørre
7.05 Lollands Sdr.
7.06 Musse

8. Odense County
8.01 Bjerge
8.02 Båg
8.03 Lunde
8.04 Odense
8.05 Skam
8.06 Skovby
8.07 Vends
8.08 Åsum

9. Svendborg County
9.01 Gudme
9.02 Langelands Nr.
9.03 Langelands Sdr.
9.04 Sallinge
9.05 Sunds
9.06 Vindinge
9.07 Ærø

10. Hjørring County
10.01 Børglum
10.02 Dronninglund
10.03 Horns
10.04 Hvetbo
10.05 Læsø
10.06 Vennebjerg
10.07 Øster-Han

11. Thisted County
11.01 Hassing
11.02 Hillerslev
11.03 Hundborg
11.04 Morsø Nørre
11.05 Morsø Sønder
11.06 Refs
11.07 Vester-Han

12. Ålborg County
12.01 Fleskum
12.02 Gislum
12.03 Hellum
12.04 Hindsted
12.05 Hornum
12.06 Kær
12.07 Slet
12.08 Års

13. Viborg County
13.01 Fjends
13.02 Harre
13.03 Hids
13.04 Hindborg
13.05 Houlbjerg
13.06 Lysgård
13.07 Middelsom
13.08 Nørlyng
13.09 Rinds
13.10 Rødding
13.11 Salling Nørre
13.12 Sønderlyng

14. Randers County
14.01 Djurs Nørre
14.02 Djurs Sønder
14.03 Galten
14.04 Gjerlev
14.05 Mols
14.06 Nørhald
14.07 Onsild
14.08 Rougsø
14.09 Støvring
14.10 Sønderhald
14.11 Øster-Lisbjerg

15. Århus County
15.01 Framlev
15.02 Hads
15.03 Hasle
15.04 Ning
15.05 Sabro
15.06 V.-Lisbjerg

16. Skanderborg County
16.01 Gjern
16.02 Hjelmslev
16.03 Nim
16.04 Tyrsting
16.05 Voer
16.06 Vrads

17. Vejle County
17.01 Bjerre
17.02 Brusk
17.03 Elbo
17.04 Hatting
17.05 Holmans
17.06 Jerlev
17.07 N.-Tyrstrup
17.08 Nørvang
17.09 Tørrild

18. Ringkøbing County
18.01 Bølling
18.02 Ginding
18.03 Hammerum
18.04 Hind
18.05 Hjerm
18.06 Nørre-Horne
18.07 Skodborg
18.08 Ulfborg
18.09 Vandfuld

19. Ribe County
19.01 Anst
19.02 Gørding
19.03 Malt
19.04 Ribe
19.05 Skast
19.06 Slavs
19.07 Vester-Horne
19.08 Øster-Horne

20. Haderslev County
20.01 Frøs
20.02 Gram
20.03 Haderslev
20.04 N.-Rangstrup
20.05 S.-Tyrstrup

21. Tønder County
21.01 Hviding
21.02 Højer
21.03 Lø
21.04 Slogs
21.05 Tønder

22. Åbenrå County
22.01 Lundtoft
22.02 Rise
22.03 S.-Rangstrup

23. Sønderborg Conty

23.01 Als Nørre
23.02 Als Sønder
23.03 Nybøl

DANISH DISTRICTS

23.01 Als Nørre
23.02 Als Sønder
4.01 Alsted
19.01 Anst
3.01 Ars
3.01 Arts = Ars
8.01 Bjerge
17.01 Bjerre
5.01 Bjæverskov
6.01 Bornholms Nørre
6.02 Bornholms Sønder
6.03 Bornholms Vester
6.04 Bornholms Øster
17.02 Brusk
18.01 Bølling
10.01 Børglum
8.02 Båg
5.02 Bårse
14.01 Djurs Nørre
14.02 Djurs Sønder
10.02 Dronninglund
14.01 Dyrs, N = Djurs Nørre
14.02 Dyrs, S = Djurs Sønder
17.03 Elbo
5.03 Fakse
7.01 Falsters Nørre
7.02 Falsters Sønder
13.01 Fjends
12.01 Fleskum
15.01 Framlev
20.01 Frøs
7.03 Fuglse
14.03 Galten
14.04 Gerlev = Gjerlev
16.01 Gern = Gjern
18.02 Ginding
12.02 Gislum
14.04 Gjerlev
16.01 Gjern
20.02 Gram
9.01 Gudme
19.02 Gørding
20.03 Haderslev
15.02 Hads
5.04 Hammer
18.03 Hammerum
11.07 Han, V = Vester-Han
10.07 Han, Ø = Øster-Han

13.02 Harre
15.03 Hasle
11.01 Hassing
17.04 Hatting
12.03 Hellum
13.03 Hids
11.02 Hillerslev
18.04 Hind
13.04 Hindborg
12.04 Hindsted
18.04 Hing = Hind
16.02 Hjelmslev
18.05 Hjerm
1.01 Holbo
17.05 Holmans
18.06 Horne, N = Nørre-Horne
19.07 Horne, V = Vester-Horne
19.08 Horne, Ø = Øster-Horne
1.02 Horns
10.03 Horns
12.05 Hornum
13.05 Houlbjerg
11.03 Hundborg
10.04 Hvetbo
21.01 Hvidding = Hviding
21.01 Hviding
21.02 Højer
17.06 Jerlev
12.06 Kær
9.02 Langelands Nørre
9.03 Langelands Sønder
15.06 Lisbjerg, V = Vester-Lisbjerg
14.11 Lisbjerg, Ø = Øster-Lisbjerg
7.04 Lollands Nørre
7.05 Lollands Sønder
8.03 Lunde
22.01 Lundtoft
22.01 Lundtoft-Vis = Lundtoft
1.03 Lynge-Frederiksborg
1.04 Lynge-Kronborg
13.06 Lysgård
10.05 Læsø
21.03 Lø
3.02 Løve
19.03 Malt
3.03 Merløse
13.07 Middelsom
14.05 Mols
11.04 Morsø Nørre
11.05 Morsø Sønder
7.06 Musse
5.05 Mønbo
16.03 Nim
15.04 Ning
23.03 Nybøl
14.06 Nørhald
13.08 Nørlyng
18.06 Nørre-Horne

20.04 Nørre-Rangstrup
17.07 Nørre-Tyrstrup
17.08 Nørvang
8.04 Odense
3.04 Ods
14.07 Onsild
2.01 Ramsø
14.01 Randers, N = Djurs Nørre
14.02 Randers, S = Djurs Sønder
20.04 Rangstrup, N = Nørre-Rangstrup
22.03 Rangstrup, S = Sønder-Rangstrup
11.06 Refs
19.04 Ribe
13.09 Rinds
4.02 Ringsted
22.02 Rise
14.08 Rougsø
13.10 Rødding
15.05 Sabro
9.04 Sallinge
13.11 Salling Nørre
3.05 Samsø
19.05 Skads = Skast
8.05 Skam
19.05 Skast
3.06 Skippinge
18.07 Skodborg
8.06 Skovby
4.03 Slagelse
19.06 Slaugs = Slavs
19.06 Slavs
12.07 Slet
21.04 Slogs
2.02 Smørum
2.03 Sokkelund
5.06 Stevns
1.05 Strø
14.09 Støvring
9.05 Sunds
2.04 Sømme
14.10 Sønderhald
13.12 Sønderlyng
22.03 Sønder-Rangstrup
20.05 Sønder-Tyrstrup
3.07 Tudse = Tuse
2.05 Tune
3.07 Tuse
5.07 Tybjerg
16.04 Tyrsting
17.07 Tyrstrup, N = Nørre-Tyrstrup
20.05 Tyrstrup, S = Sønder-Tyrstrup
21.05 Tønder
17.09 Tørrild
18.08 Ulfborg
18.09 Vandfuld
8.07 Vends

10.06 Vennebjerg
4.04 Vester-Flakkebjerg
11.07 Vester-Han
19.07 Vester-Horne
15.06 Vester-Lisbjerg
9.06 Vindinge
16.05 Voer
2.06 Volborg
16.06 Vrads
9.07 Ærø
1.06 Ølstykke
4.05 Øster-Flakkebjerg
10.07 Øster-Han
19.08 Øster-Horne
14.11 Øster-Lisbjerg
12.08 Års
8.08 Åsum

DANISH PARISHES

21.05.01 Abild
22.01.01 Adsbøl
16.02.01 Adslev
8.01.01 Agedrup
20.04.01 Agerskov
4.04.01 Agersø
11.06.01 Agger
10.07.01 Aggersborg
3.06.01 Agnsø = Avnsø
14.05.01 Agri
13.05.01 Aidt
12.06.01 Ajstrup
12.07.13 Ajstrup, Store = Store-Ajstrup
10.02.01 Albæk
14.09.01 Albæk
14.02.01 Albøge
20.05.01 Aller
2.06.01 Allerslev
5.02.01 Allerslev
8.08.01 Allerup
8.03.01 Allese
9.04.01 Allested
4.02.01 Allindemagle
16.01.01 Alling
14.10.18 Alling, V = Vester-Alling
14.10.21 Alling, Ø = Øster-Alling
6.01.01 Allinge-Sandvig
13.06.01 Almind
17.02.01 Almind
17.02.01 Alminde = Almind
15.02.01 Alrø
12.04.01 Als
5.03.01 Alslev
19.05.01 Alslev
7.01.07 Alslev, N = Nørre-Alslev
7.02.11 Alslev, S = Sønder-Alslev

4.01.01 Alsted
11.04.01 Alsted
10.04.01 Alstrup
12.02.01 Alstrup
1.05.01 Alsønderup
19.08.01 Andsager = Ansager
19.01.01 Andst = Anst
14.01.01 Anholt
1.01.01 Annisse
19.08.01 Ansager
12.05.06 Ansager landsogn = Hasseris
19.01.01 Anst
12.04.10 Arden, Store = Store-Arden
18.03.01 Arnborg
7.05.01 Arninge
21.01.01 Arrild
11.07.01 Arup
17.01.01 As
22.01.01 Asbøl = Adsbøl
10.06.01 Asdal
14.06.01 Asferg
7.03.01 Askø
13.08.01 Asmild
1.04.01 Asminderød
3.04.08 Asmindrup, N = Nørre-Asmindrup
3.03.11 Asmindrup, S = Sønder-Asmindrup
3.04.01 Asnæs
18.05.01 Asp
8.07.01 Asperup
11.05.15 Assels, V = Vester-Assels
11.05.17 Assels, Ø = Øster-Assels
8.02.01 Assens
23.02.01 Asserballe
18.03.02 Assing
10.06.02 Astrup
12.04.02 Astrup
15.04.01 Astrup
10.02.02 Aså-Melholt
23.02.02 Augustenborg
14.10.01 Auning
9.04.02 Avernakø
5.07.01 Aversi
18.03.03 Avlum
7.05.02 Avnede
14.10.01 Avning = Auning
9.06.01 Avnslev
3.06.01 Avnsø
3.02.01 Bakkendrup
13.03.01 Balle
2.02.01 Ballerup
13.10.01 Balling
21.03.01 Ballum
8.07.02 Balslev
7.03.02 Bandholm
8.02.02 Barløse
17.01.02 Barrit

5.07.02 Bavelse
15.04.02 Beder
8.05.01 Bederslev
8.05.01 Bedeslev = Bederslev
11.01.01 Bedsted = Bested
22.03.01 Bedsted
10.07.02 Bejstrup
5.02.02 Beldringe
8.04.01 Bellinge
4.02.02 Benløse
3.05.01 Besser
11.01.01 Bested
20.04.02 Bevtoft
12.06.02 Biersted
13.08.02 Bigum
19.07.01 Billum
12.02.02 Binderup
10.03.01 Bindslev
8.01.02 Birkende
1.04.02 Birkerød
7.04.01 Birket
12.06.02 Birsted = Biersted
12.05.01 Bislev
15.02.02 Bjerager
15.02.02 Bjergager = Bjerager
10.06.03 Bjergby
11.04.02 Bjergby
3.06.02 Bjergsted
4.01.02 Bjernede
20.05.02 Bjerning
17.01.03 Bjerre
9.05.01 Bjerreby
13.09.14 Bjerregrav, V = Vester-Bjerregrav
13.12.14 Bjerregrav, Ø = Øster-Bjerregrav
13.07.01 Bjerring
13.07.02 Bjerringbro
17.02.06 Bjert, N = Nørre-Bjert
17.07.03 Bjert, S = Sønder-Bjert
22.02.01 Bjolderup
9.05.01 Bjærgby = Bjerreby
4.01.08 Bjærgby, Munke = Munke-Bjergby
4.03.15 Bjærgby, Slots = Slots-Bjergby
3.07.11 Bjærgby, Stigs = Stigs-Bjergby
17.01.03 Bjærge = Bjerre
4.04.15 Bjærge, S = Sønder-Bjerge
17.02.06 Bjært, N = Nørre-Bjert
17.07.03 Bjært, S = Sønder-Bjert
5.01.01 Bjæverskov
Bjørnsholm =
12.08.09   Overlade and
12.07.10   Ranum
9.04.07 Bjørnø = Fåborg landsogn
16.02.02 Blegind

12.03.01 Blenstrup
11.05.01 Blidstrup
1.01.02 Blistrup
11.05.01 Blistrup = Blidstrup
1.04.03 Blovstrød
12.08.01 Blære
17.08.01 Blåhøj
11.06.02 Boddum
6.02.01 Bodilsker
11.06.02 Bodum = Boddum
4.03.01 Boeslunde
8.06.01 Bogense
5.05.01 Bogø
18.05.02 Borbjerg
18.03.04 Bording
18.06.06 Bork, N = Nørre-Bork
18.06.09 Bork, S = Sønder-Bork
5.05.02 Borre
18.03.04 Borring = Bording
13.01.11 Borris, N = Nørre-Borris
18.01.11 Borris, S = Sønder-Borris
15.01.01 Borum
2.01.01 Borup
14.09.02 Borup
22.01.02 Bov
9.06.02 Bovense
15.03.01 Brabrand
9.04.03 Brahetrolleborg
17.02.07 Bramdrup, N =
Nørre-Bramdrup
19.02.01 Bramminge
17.08.02 Brande
7.04.02 Branderslev
20.04.03 Branderup
8.02.03 Brandsø = Bågø
7.01.01 Brarup
21.03.02 Brede
17.09.01 Bredsten
17.03.01 Bredstrup
14.11.01 Bregnet
3.06.03 Bregninge
7.06.01 Bregninge
9.05.02 Bregninge
9.07.01 Bregninge
18.04.01 Brejning
8.04.03 Brendekilde = Brændekilde
8.07.03 Brenderup
4.02.03 Bringstrup
23.03.01 Broager
9.04.18 Broby, N = Nørre-Broby
8.04.06 Broby, Næsbyhoved =
Næsbyhoved-Broby
9.04.21 Broby, S = Sønder-Broby
4.01.13 Broby, V = Vester-Broby
4.01.03 Bromme
12.08.02 Brorstrup
10.07.03 Brovst
9.01.01 Brudager

8.04.02 Brylle
16.04.01 Bryrup
8.04.03 Brændekilde
8.07.03 Brænderup = Brenderup
2.02.03 Brøndbyvester
2.02.02 Brøndbyøster
10.01.01 Brønderslev
10.01.19 Brønderslev, Ø =
Øster-Brønderslev
13.04.01 Brøndum
19.05.02 Brøndum
12.03.12 Brøndum, Store =
Store-Brøndum
21.01.02 Brøns
19.03.01 Brørup
4.02.23 Braaby, Ø = Øster-Broby
12.05.02 Buderup
12.05.06 Budolfi landsogn = Hasseris
3.02.02 Buerup
18.05.03 Bur
21.04.01 Burkal
7.03.03 Bursø
3.03.01 Butterup
21.04.02 Bylderup
10.05.01 Byrum
19.01.02 Bække
12.03.02 Bælum
13.09.15 Bølle, V = Vester-Bølle
13.09.17 Bølle, Ø = Øster-Bølle
18.01.01 Bølling
10.01.02 Børglum
9.02.01 Bøstrup
18.07.01 Bøvling
8.02.03 Bågø
5.02.03 Bårse
20.05.03 Christiansfeld
6.04.01 Christiansø
12.01.01 Dal = Dall
8.01.03 Dalby
17.07.01 Dalby
2.01.08 Dalby, N = Nørre-Dalby
17.04.08 Dalby, Store = Store-Dalby
5.03.08 Dalby, S = Sønder-Dalby
14.04.01 Dalbyneder
14.04.02 Dalbyover
21.02.01 Daler
12.01.01 Dall
16.01.02 Dallerup
8.04.04 Dalum
5.05.03 Damsholte
7.05.03 Dannemare
19.02.02 Darum
13.01.01 Daubjerg
17.04.01 Daugård
8.08.02 Davinde
18.01.02 Dejbjerg
9.04.04 Diernæs
13.08.03 Dollerup

13.01.02 Dommerby
16.02.03 Dover
11.04.03 Dragstrup
2.03.01 Dragør
9.05.03 Drejø
8.02.04 Dreslette
8.01.04 Drigstrup
14.09.03 Dronningborg
10.02.03 Dronninglund
3.02.03 Drøsselbjerg
1.02.01 Dråby
14.05.02 Dråby
11.04.13 Draaby, S = Sønder-Dråby
12.02.03 Durup
13.02.01 Durup
23.03.02 Dybbøl
18.09.01 Dybe
13.04.02 Dølby
7.06.02 Døllefjelde
12.04.03 Døstrup
21.03.03 Døstrup
2.01.02 Dåstrup
14.02.02 Ebdrup
14.05.03 Ebeltoft
14.05.04 Ebeltoft landsogn
3.04.02 Egebjerg
1.04.04 Egebæksvang
5.07.13 Egede, V = Vester-Egede
5.03.12 Egede, Ø = Øster-Egede
23.01.01 Egen
14.05.05 Egens
9.05.04 Egense
5.04.12 Egesborg, V =
Vester-Egesborg
5.02.16 Egesborg, Ø =
Øster-Egesborg
4.04.02 Eggeslevmagle
12.06.03 Egholm = Frue landsogn
17.06.01 Egtved
18.06.01 Egvad
22.03.02 Egvad
14.11.02 Egå
2.01.03 Ejby
8.07.04 Ejby
12.08.03 Ejdrup
11.04.04 Ejerslev
8.06.02 Ejlby
18.02.01 Ejsing
16.06.01 Ejstrup
15.06.01 Elev
9.06.03 Ellested
12.05.03 Ellidshøj
10.03.02 Elling
9.06.04 Ellinge
5.05.04 Elmelunde
13.06.02 Elsborg
15.06.02 Elsted
11.05.02 Elsø

17.02.02 Eltang
10.01.03 Em
10.01.03 Emb = Em
21.02.02 Emmerlev
16.03.01 Endelave
5.01.02 Endeslev
18.09.02 Engbjerg
7.06.03 Engestofte
13.03.02 Engesvang
17.04.02 Engom = Engum
17.04.02 Engum
14.01.02 Enslev
14.04.03 Enslev
22.01.03 Ensted
7.03.04 Errindlev
17.03.02 Erritsø
11.04.05 Erslev
19.05.03 Esbjerg
1.01.03 Esbønderup
7.01.02 Eskilstrup
3.03.04 Eskilstrup, Kirke =
 Kirke-Eskilstrup
9.04.05 Espe
14.10.02 Essenbæk
14.08.01 Estruplund
18.02.02 Estvad
5.02.04 Everdrup
18.07.02 Fabjerg
5.03.02 Fakse
7.02.01 Falkerslev
15.02.03 Falling
14.07.01 Falslev
5.05.05 Fanefjord
8.04.05 Fangel
4.02.04 Farendløse
12.07.01 Farstrup
12.02.04 Farsø
1.06.01 Farum
19.04.01 Farup
18.01.03 Faster
14.10.03 Fausing
14.10.03 Favsing = Fausing
18.05.04 Favsing = Fovsing
7.03.05 Fejø
14.02.03 Feldballe
18.08.04 Felding, N = Nørre-Felding
18.03.17 Felding, S = Sønder-Felding
13.01.03 Feldingbjerg
22.01.04 Felsted
7.03.06 Femø
5.07.03 Fensmark
18.09.03 Ferring
1.02.02 Ferslev
12.01.02 Ferslev
17.08.03 Filskov
3.02.04 Finderup
13.08.04 Finderup
13.08.05 Fiskbæk

18.09.04 Fjaltring
7.06.04 Fjelde
14.01.03 Fjellerup
8.07.05 Fjelsted
18.01.04 Fjelstervang
20.05.04 Fjelstrup
13.09.01 Fjelsø
4.01.04 Fjenneslev
7.06.04 Fjælde = Fjelde
10.03.03 Flade
11.04.06 Flade
4.04.03 Flakkebjerg
12.08.04 Flejsborg
8.02.05 Flemløse
4.01.06 Flinterup, Kirke =
 Kirke-Flinterup
13.01.04 Fly
18.07.03 Flynder
9.06.05 Flødstrup
2.04.01 Fløng
4.05.01 Fodby
9.03.01 Fodslette
15.05.01 Folby
19.03.02 Folding
20.01.01 Fole
18.05.04 Fousing = Fovsing
12.02.05 Fovlum
18.05.04 Fovsing
15.01.02 Framlev
8.08.03 Fraugde
17.03.03 Fredericia
13.06.03 Frederiks
1.03.01 Frederiksborg Slotssogn
10.03.04 Frederikshavn
1.03.02 Frederikssund
1.05.02 Frederiksværk
4.02.05 Freerslev
12.05.04 Frejlev
12.06.03 Frue landsogn
20.03.01 Frue landsogn
2.04.14 Frue, Roskilde Vor =
 Vor Frue
16.02.04 Fruering
3.07.01 Frydendal
12.03.03 Fræer
9.06.06 Frørup
20.05.05 Frørup
5.06.01 Frøslev
11.05.03 Frøslev
4.05.02 Fuglebjærg
3.01.02 Fuglede, Lille = Lille-Fuglede
3.01.06 Fuglede, Store =
 Store Fuglede
9.03.02 Fuglsbølle
7.03.07 Fuglse
14.02.04 Fuglslev
4.05.03 Fuirendal = Fyrendal
13.03.03 Funder

13.02.02 Fur
10.01.04 Furreby
4.05.03 Fyrendal
7.03.06 Fæmø = Femø
8.07.14 Fænø = Middelfart landsogn
3.06.04 Føllenslev
8.07.06 Føns
4.05.04 Førslev
4.02.21 Førslev, Øde = Øde-Førslev
16.04.02 Føvling
19.03.03 Føvling
9.04.06 Fåborg
19.05.04 Fåborg
9.04.07 Fåborg landsogn
4.04.04 Fårdrup
3.04.03 Fårvejle
14.06.02 Fårup
15.05.02 Fårup
17.09.02 Gadbjerg
2.01.04 Gadstrup
14.03.01 Galten
15.01.10 Galten
11.04.07 Galtrup
8.07.07 Gamborg
20.03.02 Gammel-Haderslev landsogn
14.01.04 Gammelsogn
18.04.02 Gammelsogn
13.01.05 Gammelstrup
8.02.06 Gamtofte
16.05.01 Gangsted
1.06.02 Ganløse
14.06.03 Gassum
17.05.01 Gauerslund
17.05.01 Gaverslund = Gauerslund
7.02.02 Gedesby
7.02.02 Gedeby = Gedesby
13.09.02 Gedsted
3.02.05 Geeslev = Gierslev
18.03.05 Gellerup = Gjellerup
8.07.08 Gelsted
18.05.05 Gemsing = Gimsing
2.03.02 Gentofte
12.03.04 Gerding
1.02.03 Gerlev
4.03.02 Gerlev
14.04.04 Gerlev = Gjerlev
16.01.03 Gern = Gjern
13.05.02 Gerning
14.01.06 Gerrild = Gjerrild
2.06.02 Gershøj
10.03.05 Gerum = Gærum
14.10.04 Gesing = Gjesing
8.04.08 Gestelev
19.01.03 Gesten
11.06.03 Gettrup
2.06.03 Gevninge
3.02.05 Gierslev
2.05.06 Gildebrønde = Kildebrønde

1.01.04 Gilleleje
4.04.05 Gimlinge
14.09.04 Gimming
18.05.05 Gimsing
14.01.05 Ginnerup
9.01.02 Gislev
3.07.02 Gislinge
12.02.06 Gislum
17.08.04 Give
12.08.05 Giver
17.08.05 Givskud
18.03.05 Gjellerup
12.03.04 Gjerding = Gerding
13.05.02 Gjerning = Gerning
14.04.04 Gjerlev
16.01.03 Gjern
14.01.06 Gjerrild
10.03.05 Gjerum = Gærum
14.10.04 Gjesing
19.02.03 Gjørding = Gørding
2.03.03 Gladsakse
14.06.04 Glenstrup
14.01.07 Glesborg
2.04.02 Glim
7.05.04 Gloslunde
2.02.04 Glostrup
17.01.04 Glud
5.07.04 Glumsø
13.02.03 Glyngøre
14.01.07 Glæsborg = Glesborg
7.06.05 Godsted
15.02.04 Gosmer
20.02.01 Gram
3.03.02 Grandløse
13.05.03 Granslev
20.03.03 Grarup
12.05.05 Gravlev
17.08.06 Grejs
19.06.01 Grene
13.07.03 Grensten
14.01.08 Grenå
14.01.04 Grenå Gammelsogn = Gammelsogn
2.05.01 Greve
3.04.04 Grevinge
19.05.05 Grimstrup
13.11.01 Grinderslev
8.05.02 Grindløse
18.02.03 Grove
19.06.02 Grindsted
15.06.03 Grundfør
11.01.02 Grurup
12.02.07 Grynderup
16.04.03 Grædstrup
1.03.03 Græse
7.05.05 Græshave
1.01.05 Græsted
3.04.04 Grævinge = Grevinge

13.06.04 Grønbæk
1.04.05 Grønholt
13.11.02 Grønning
13.08.06 Gråbrødre landsogn
22.01.05 Gråsten
9.01.03 Gudbjerg
6.04.02 Gudhjem
9.01.04 Gudme
4.03.03 Gudum
12.01.03 Gudum
18.07.04 Gudum
19.05.06 Guldager
8.06.03 Guldbjerg
13.05.04 Gullev
4.05.05 Gunderslev
12.07.02 Gundersted
12.01.04 Gunderup
7.01.03 Gundslev
2.04.03 Gundsømagle
7.05.06 Gurreby
15.02.05 Gylling
4.01.05 Gyrstinge
10.03.05 Gærum
13.03.04 Gødvad
10.04.02 Gøl
18.05.06 Gørding
19.02.03 Gørding
3.02.06 Gørlev
1.03.04 Gørløse
5.01.03 Gørslev
11.07.02 Gøttrup
17.05.02 Gårslev
14.03.02 Hadbjerg
20.03.04 Haderslev
20.03.02 Haderslev, Gammel = Gammel Haderslev landsogn
18.02.04 Haderup
15.05.03 Hadsten
12.04.04 Hadsund
23.01.02 Hagenbjerg = Havnbjerg
3.07.03 Hagested
14.06.05 Hald
4.05.06 Haldagerlille
15.05.04 Haldum
20.03.05 Halk
3.02.07 Hallenslev
14.03.03 Halling
15.02.06 Halling
10.02.04 Hallund
10.05.02 Hals
12.06.04 Hals
7.04.03 Halsted
16.01.04 Hammel
14.01.09 Hammelev
20.02.02 Hammelev
5.04.01 Hammer
12.06.05 Hammer
16.06.02 Hammer

13.12.01 Hammershøj
18.05.07 Hanbjerg = Handbjerg
18.05.07 Handbjerg
18.01.05 Hanning
10.06.11 Hans, Skt. = Skt. Hans
11.02.01 Hansted
16.05.02 Hansted
4.02.06 Haraldsted
18.09.05 Harboør
15.01.03 Harlev
8.07.09 Harndrup
13.02.04 Harre
10.06.04 Harreslev
10.06.04 Harridslev = Harreslev
14.09.05 Harridslev
11.01.03 Harring
17.02.03 Harte
6.01.02 Hasle
15.03.02 Hasle
6.01.03 Hasle landdistrikt
4.02.07 Haslev
14.03.04 Haslund
12.05.06 Hasseris
11.01.04 Hassing
12.06.13 Hassing, V = Vester-Hassing
12.06.14 Hassing, Ø = Øster-Hassing
17.04.03 Hatting
13.05.05 Haurum
12.08.06 Havbro
2.05.02 Havdrup
10.07.04 Haverslev
12.08.07 Haverslev
23.01.02 Havnbjerg
5.06.02 Havnelev
18.03.15 Havnstrup, Studsgård = Studsgård-Havnstrup
3.02.08 Havrebjerg
13.05.05 Havrum = Haurum
5.06.06 Heddinge, Lille = Lille-Heddinge
5.06.10 Heddinge, Store = Store-Heddinge
9.04.09 Heden
17.04.04 Hedensted
18.04.03 Hee
17.07.02 Hejls
4.03.04 Hejninge
19.06.03 Hejnsvig
18.07.05 Heldum
14.05.06 Helgenæs
1.04.06 Hellebæk
2.03.02 Hellerup = Gentofte
9.06.07 Hellerup
5.06.03 Hellested
10.02.05 Hellevad
22.03.03 Hellevad
5.07.05 Hellevmagle = Herlufmagle
11.06.04 Helligsø

10.02.06 Hellum
8.02.07 Helnæs
1.01.06 Helsinge
3.02.09 Helsinge, Kirke =
         Kirke-Helsinge
1.04.07 Helsingør
13.07.04 Helstrup
11.06.05 Heltborg
13.04.03 Hem
14.07.02 Hem
14.01.10 Hemmed
4.03.05 Hemmeshøj
18.06.02 Hemmet
19.07.02 Henne
18.01.06 Herborg
5.01.04 Herfølge
2.03.04 Herlev
1.03.09 Herlev, N = Nørre-Herlev
5.07.05 Herlufmagle
4.05.07 Herlufsholm
18.03.06 Herning
7.04.04 Herredskirke
9.06.08 Herrested
9.04.10 Herringe
7.06.06 Herritslev
2.04.04 Herslev
17.02.04 Herslev
13.09.03 Hersom
2.02.05 Herstedvester
2.02.06 Herstedøster
9.01.05 Hesselager
9.04.11 Hillerslev
11.02.02 Hillerslev
1.03.05 Hillerød
7.03.08 Hillested
14.02.07 Hillested = Hyllested
5.01.05 Himlingøje
2.04.05 Himmelev
13.04.04 Hindborg
13.06.05 Hinge
10.03.06 Hirsholmene
10.03.06 Hirtsholmene = Hirsholmene
8.03.02 Hjadstrup
11.02.03 Hjardemaal = Hjaremål
11.02.03 Hjaremål
17.01.05 Hjarnø
19.01.04 Hjarup
3.07.04 Hjembæk
13.02.05 Hjerk
18.05.08 Hjerm
10.04.08 Hjermeslev, V =
         Vester-Hjermeslev
13.07.05 Hjermind
20.05.06 Hjerndrup
21.02.03 Hjerpsted
20.01.02 Hjerting
22.02.02 Hjordkær = Hjortkær
11.07.03 Hjortdal

13.07.06 Hjorthede
14.11.03 Hjorthøj = Hjortshøj
22.02.02 Hjortkær
19.04.02 Hjortlund
14.11.03 Hjortshøj
9.06.11 Hjulby = Nyborg landsogn
1.03.06 Hjørlunde = Jørlunde
10.06.05 Hjørring
19.05.12 Ho, Sønder = Sønderho
19.07.03 Ho
14.07.03 Hobro
19.08.02 Hodde
18.02.05 Hodsager
14.02.05 Hoed
3.03.03 Holbæk
14.08.02 Holbæk
22.01.06 Holbøl
7.03.09 Holeby
8.02.08 Holevad
15.04.03 Holme
5.04.02 Holme-Olstrup
18.04.04 Holmsland Klit
3.06.05 Holmstrup
18.05.09 Holstebro
19.03.04 Holsted
4.04.06 Holsteinborg
5.06.04 Holtug
14.02.06 Homå
20.03.06 Hoptrup
7.02.03 Horbelev
16.03.02 Hornborg
1.04.08 Hornbæk
13.12.02 Hornbæk
9.04.12 Horne
10.06.06 Horne
19.08.03 Horne
14.11.04 Hornslet
17.08.07 Hornstrup
17.01.06 Hornum
14.07.04 Hornum, S = Hvornum
12.08.13 Hornum, V = Vester-Hornum
12.05.15 Hornum, Ø = Øster-Hornum
7.02.04 Horreby
12.06.06 Horsens
16.03.03 Horsens
13.05.07 Horslev = Hvorslev
7.04.05 Horslunde
9.04.14 Hostrup = Håstrup
19.05.07 Hostrup
21.04.03 Hostrup
13.05.06 Houlbjerg
9.02.02 Hov
18.09.06 Hove
18.06.03 Hoven
17.09.03 Hover
18.04.05 Hover
9.03.03 Humble
1.04.09 Humlebæk

18.07.06 Humlum
11.03.01 Hundborg
19.02.04 Hunderup
15.02.07 Hundslund
9.04.13 Hundstrup
10.04.03 Hune
7.06.07 Hunseby
11.02.04 Hunstrup
11.06.06 Hurup
8.07.10 Husby
18.08.01 Husby
2.06.04 Hvalsø, Kirke = Kirke-Hvalsø
13.09.04 Hvam
2.04.06 Hvedstrup
17.08.08 Hvejsel
11.01.05 Hvidbjerg
11.05.04 Hvidbjerg
11.06.07 Hvidbjerg
13.04.05 Hvidbjerg
21.01.03 Hviding
2.03.05 Hvidovre
14.10.05 Hvilsager
13.09.05 Hvilsom
15.02.08 Hvilsted
16.03.04 Hvirring
14.07.04 Hvornum
13.05.07 Hvorslev
12.06.07 Hvorup
18.09.07 Hygum
16.05.03 Hylke
12.08.08 Hyllebjerg
5.03.03 Hylleholt
4.04.07 Hyllested
14.02.07 Hyllested
4.05.08 Hyllinge
2.06.05 Hyllinge, Kirke =
         Kirke-Hyllinge
9.04.25 Hæsinge, V = Vester-Hæsinge
9.04.28 Hæsinge, Ø = Øster-Hæsinge
10.01.05 Hæstrup
13.06.06 Høbjerg
13.06.06 Højbjærg = Høbjerg
3.04.05 Højby
8.08.04 Højby
2.01.05 Højelse
17.06.02 Højen
21.02.04 Højer
21.02.05 Højer landsogn
5.06.05 Højerup
2.02.07 Høje Tåstrup
21.01.04 Højrup
8.05.05 Højrup, N = Nørre-Højrup
9.06.15 Højrup, S = Sønder-Højrup
13.01.06 Højslev
21.04.04 Højst
4.02.08 Høm
3.07.05 Hørby
10.02.07 Hørby

1.02.05 Kyndby
14.04.06 Kærby
8.02.11 Kærum
7.04.06 Købelev
2.03.06 København including
    Frederiksberg
2.01.07 Køge
2.01.07 Køge landdistrikt = Køge
8.01.06 Kølstrup
5.04.04 Køng
8.02.12 Køng
11.02.05 Kåstrup
15.05.05 Lading
7.05.08 Landet
9.05.07 Landet
17.08.09 Langskov
9.01.06 Langå
13.07.07 Langå
6.04.05 Larsker, Ø = Øster-Larsker
14.03.05 Laurbjerg
13.07.08 Le = Lee
2.02.09 Ledøje
13.07.08 Lee
2.06.01 Lejre = Allerslev
19.01.06 Lejrskov
5.01.07 Lellinge
13.10.04 Lem
14.09.06 Lem
18.07.11 Lem, N = Nørlem
18.04.12 Lem, S = Sønder-Lem
13.03.06 Lemming
18.07.07 Lemvig
10.03.08 Lendum
14.03.06 Lerbjerg
10.07.05 Lerup
13.06.09 Levring
5.01.08 Lidemark
13.10.05 Lihme
14.10.10 Lihme = Lime
11.07.07 Lild
7.01.05 Lillebrænde
3.01.02 Lille-Fuglede
5.06.06 Lille-Heddinge
1.05.04 Lille-Lyngby
1.03.07 Lillerød
12.01.06 Lillevorde
13.10.05 Lime = Lihme
14.10.10 Lime
14.06.07 Linde
17.09.06 Lindeballe
9.03.04 Lindelse
20.01.08 Lindet, Ø = Øster-Lindet
12.06.08 Lindholm
19.03.05 Lindknud
13.08.07 Lindum
16.06.04 Linnerup
20.01.03 Lintrup
16.01.05 Linå

15.06.04 Lisbjerg
11.05.07 Ljørslev = Lørslev
11.01.08 Lodbjerg
18.07.08 Lomborg
9.03.05 Longelse
12.02.09 Lovns
8.03.03 Lumby
5.04.05 Lundby
12.07.04 Lundby
8.03.04 Lunde
9.05.08 Lunde
19.07.06 Lunde
4.03.09 Lundforlund
2.03.07 Lundtofte = Lyngby-Tårbæk
16.05.05 Lundum
13.01.09 Lundø
13.11.05 Lyby
5.06.07 Lyderslev
19.07.07 Lydom = Lydum
19.07.07 Lydum
18.06.04 Lyhne = Lyne
2.06.09 Lyndby
8.08.05 Lyndelse, N = Nørre-Lyndelse
9.04.19 Lyndelse, Sandholts =
    Sandholts-Lyndelse
13.09.07 Lynderup
18.06.04 Lyne
10.01.07 Lyngby
12.03.06 Lyngby
14.02.09 Lyngby
15.03.04 Lyngby
2.03.07 Lyngby, Kgs. =
    Lyngby-Tårbæk
1.05.04 Lyngby, Lille = Lille-Lyngby
2.03.07 Lyngby-Tårbæk
1.03.08 Lynge
4.01.07 Lynge
11.06.09 Lyngs
15.05.06 Lyngå
23.02.06 Lysabild
13.06.10 Lysgård
9.04.17 Lyø
19.03.06 Læborg
13.12.04 Læsten
11.05.06 Lødderup
12.07.05 Løgsted
12.07.06 Løgstør
21.03.07 Løgum, N = Nørre-Løgum
22.03.04 Løgum, Ø = Øster-Løgum
21.03.04 Løgumkloster
21.03.05 Løgumkloster landsogn
22.02.03 Løjt
7.04.07 Løjtofte
18.06.05 Lønborg
19.07.08 Lønne
11.05.07 Lørslev
17.04.06 Løsning
13.08.08 Løvel

16.01.06 Låsby
13.09.08 Låstrup
18.08.03 Madum
7.01.06 Maglebrænde
4.04.11 Magleby
5.05.07 Magleby
9.03.06 Magleby
5.06.08 Magleby-Stevns
2.03.09 Magleby, Store =
    Store-Magleby
20.02.05 Magstrup
7.06.09 Majbølle
12.07.07 Malle
15.04.05 Malling
19.03.07 Malt
13.07.09 Mammen
19.04.04 Mandø
19.04.04 Manø = Mandø
14.07.05 Mariager
14.07.06 Mariager landsogn
7.06.10 Maribo
7.06.11 Maribo landsogn
14.10.11 Marie-Magdalene
6.03.05 Marie, V = Vester-Marie
6.04.06 Marie, Ø = Øster-Marie
8.01.07 Marslev
9.07.02 Marstal
9.07.03 Marstal landsogn
4.05.12 Marvede
14.11.05 Mejlby
18.05.10 Mejrup
1.05.05 Melby
8.06.05 Melby
10.02.02 Melholt, Aså = Aså-Melholt
14.09.07 Mellerup
3.03.03 Merløse, Tveje = Holbæk
5.02.07 Mern
16.02.06 Mesing
8.01.08 Mesinge
8.07.13 Middelfart
8.07.14 Middelfart landsogn
4.03.12 Mikkels landsogn, Skt. =
    Skt. Mikkels landsogn
21.03.06 Mjolden
5.04.06 Mogenstrup
11.05.08 Mollerup
20.03.07 Moltrup
5.07.07 Mortens, Skt. = Næstved
14.09.08 Mortens, Skt. = Randers
10.03.09 Mosbjerg
12.01.07 Mou
4.01.08 Munke-Bjergby
8.01.09 Munkebo
7.06.12 Musse
10.06.08 Mygdal
14.10.12 Mygind
18.07.09 Møborg
21.05.02 Møgeltønder

17.05.03 Mølholm	8.04.06 Næsbyhoved-Broby	8.04.07 Odense
13.01.10 Mønsted	5.04.07 Næstelsø	19.07.10 Oksby
14.11.06 Mørke	5.07.07 Næstved	23.01.04 Oksbøl
3.07.08 Mørkøv	14.02.10 Nødager	20.02.07 Oksenvad
18.05.11 Måbjerg	1.01.08 Nødebo	10.06.12 Olai, Skt. = Skt. Olai
2.02.10 Måløv	15.02.09 Nølev	9.05.09 Ollerup
15.04.06 Mårslet	14.10.13 Nørager	6.01.05 Olsker
1.01.07 Mårum	13.12.05 Nørbæk	7.03.12 Olstrup
10.06.09 Mårup	12.05.08 Nørholm	5.04.02 Olstrup, Holme =
7.04.08 Nakskov	11.03.04 Nørhå	Holme-Olstrup
13.02.06 Nautrup	18.07.11 Nørlem	18.04.08 Omme, N = Nørre-Omme
18.05.12 Navr	7.01.07 Nørre-Alslev	17.08.12 Omme, S = Sønder-Omme
7.03.11 Nebbelunde	3.04.08 Nørre-Asmindrup	4.04.12 Omø
16.05.06 Nebel	17.02.06 Nørre-Bjert	3.03.18 Ondløse = Undløse
19.07.09 Nebel, N = Nørre-Nebel	18.06.06 Nørre-Bork	3.05.04 Onsbjerg
17.02.09 Nebel, V = Vester-Nebel	13.01.11 Nørre-Borris	14.07.07 Onsild, N = Nørre-Onsild
19.05.14 Nebel, V = Vester-Nebel	17.02.07 Nørre-Bramdrup	14.07.12 Onsild, S = Sønder-Onsild
17.01.08 Nebsager	9.04.18 Nørre-Broby	1.03.10 Oppe-Sundby
18.07.10 Nees	2.01.08 Nørre-Dalby	2.03.02 Ordrup = Gentofte
6.02.02 Neksø	18.08.04 Nørre-Felding	8.06.07 Ore
18.07.10 Nes = Nees	14.03.01 Nørre-Galten = Galten	15.04.07 Ormslev
5.04.07 Nestelsø = Næstelsø	1.03.09 Nørre-Herlev	19.05.18 Orre = Årre
12.05.07 Nibe	8.05.05 Nørre-Højrup	8.02.13 Orte
3.03.06 Niløse	14.10.06 Nørre-Hørning = Hørning	3.07.09 Orø
16.03.05 Nim	3.03.07 Nørre-Jernløse	2.06.10 Osted
14.01.13 Nimtofte	7.01.08 Nørre-Kirkeby	8.03.06 Otterup
18.07.12 Nissum, N = Nørre-Nissum	12.03.07 Nørre-Kongerslev	4.03.11 Ottestrup
18.08.07 Nissum, S = Sønder-Nissum	18.07.11 Nørre-Lem = Nørlem	13.04.07 Otting
18.04.06 No	8.08.05 Nørre-Lyndelse	12.07.09 Oudrup
23.01.03 Nordborg	10.01.07 Nørre-Lyngby = Lyngby	9.01.07 Oure
3.05.03 Nordby	21.03.07 Nørre-Løgum	12.04.06 Ove
19.05.08 Nordby	19.07.09 Nørre-Nebel	12.08.09 Overlade
7.04.09 Nordlunde	18.07.12 Nørre-Nissum	16.05.07 Ovsted
4.03.10 Nordrupvester	8.05.06 Nørre-Nærå	11.05.10 Ovtrup
4.02.11 Nordrupøster	18.04.08 Nørre-Omme	19.07.11 Ovtrup
11.02.06 Nors	14.07.07 Nørre-Onsild	4.01.09 Pedersborg
8.03.05 Norup	8.06.06 Nørre-Sandager	4.03.13 Peders landsogn, Skt. =
23.02.07 Notmark	19.05.10 Nørre-Skast	Skt. Peders landsogn
20.02.06 Nustrup	16.06.05 Nørre-Snede	6.02.03 Pedersker
9.06.10 Nyborg	17.04.07 Nørre-Stenderup = Stenderup	13.08.09 Pederstrup
9.06.11 Nyborg landsogn	12.06.09 Nørresundby	17.05.04 Pjedsted
23.03.03 Nybøl	8.08.06 Nørre-Søby	6.02.04 Povlsker
6.03.02 Nyker	12.01.08 Nørre-Tranders	5.02.08 Præstø
19.05.15 Nykirke, V = Vester-Nykirke	7.01.09 Nørre-Vedby	5.02.09 Præstø landsogn
17.08.18 Nykirke, Ø = Øster-Nykirke	13.12.06 Nørre-Vinge	8.04.08 Pårup
7.02.07 Nykøbing F	18.01.07 Nørre-Vium	21.04.05 Rabsted = Ravsted
11.05.09 Nykøbing M	7.02.08 Nørre-Ørslev	7.06.15 Radsted
3.04.07 Nykøbing S	8.07.15 Nørre-Åby	10.01.08 Rakkeby
6.03.03 Nylarsker	14.10.22 Nørre-Aarslev = Årslev	11.05.11 Rakkeby
5.05.08 Nyord	17.09.07 Nørup	3.01.03 Raklev
18.04.07 Nysogn	12.01.09 Nøvling	1.01.09 Ramløse
7.06.13 Nysted	18.03.09 Nøvling	18.09.08 Ramme
7.06.14 Nysted landsogn	19.04.05 Obbekær	13.10.06 Ramsing
8.05.06 Nærå, N = Nørre-Nærå	11.06.10 Odby	17.09.08 Randbøl
8.08.10 Nærå, S = Sønder-Nærå	3.04.09 Odden	14.09.08 Randers
19.05.09 Næsbjerg	13.04.06 Oddense	21.03.08 Randerup
12.07.08 Næsborg	15.02.10 Odder	15.02.11 Randlev
5.07.06 Næsby	18.06.07 Oddum	12.07.10 Ranum

8.03.07 Skeby	15.01.07 Skørring	8.04.10 Stenløse
15.03.06 Skejby	7.03.15 Skørringe	1.06.05 Stenløse
5.07.10 Skelby	15.04.08 Skåde	4.01.12 Stenmagle
7.02.09 Skelby	9.05.10 Skårup	9.05.11 Stenstrup
3.02.12 Skellebjerg	4.03.14 Slagelse	10.01.11 Stenum
9.06.13 Skellerup	4.01.10 Slaglille	20.05.07 Stepping
14.07.09 Skellerup = Skjellerup	1.06.03 Slagslunde	3.07.11 Stigs-Bjergby
4.04.13 Skelskør = Skælskør	1.03.12 Slangerup	16.02.09 Stilling
12.04.09 Skelum = Skelund	7.06.18 Slemminge	4.03.07 Stillinge, Kirke =
12.04.09 Skelund	4.03.15 Slots-Bjergby	Kirke-Stillinge
2.05.07 Skensved, Kirke =	4.03.16 Sludstrup	15.01.08 Stjær
Kirke-Skensved	5.06.09 Smerup	9.02.07 Stoense
13.07.10 Skern = Skjern	17.05.06 Smidstrup	7.05.11 Stokkemarke
18.01.08 Skern = Skjern	13.01.13 Smollerup	12.07.13 Store-Ajstrup
9.04.26 Skerninge, V =	2.02.12 Smørum	12.04.10 Store-Arden
Vester-Skerninge	16.06.05 Snede, N = Nørre-Snede	12.03.12 Store-Brøndum
9.05.16 Skerninge, Ø =	17.08.19 Snede, Ø = Øster-Snede	17.04.08 Store-Dalby
Øster-Skerninge	11.01.10 Snedsted	3.01.06 Store-Fuglede
1.02.07 Skibby	18.03.14 Snejbjerg	5.06.10 Store-Heddinge
17.09.09 Skibet	5.02.11 Snesere	5.06.11 Store-Heddinge landsogn
5.02.10 Skibinge	4.02.15 Sneslev	2.03.09 Store-Magleby
12.03.09 Skibsted	19.05.11 Sneum	15.01.09 Store-Ring = Storring
11.03.06 Skinnerup	2.05.09 Snoldelev	3.03.10 Store-Tåstrup
13.04.09 Skive	1.06.04 Snostrup	15.01.09 Storring
13.04.10 Skive landsogn	14.07.10 Snæbum	12.01.12 Storvorde
15.01.05 Skiveholme = Skivholme	9.02.06 Snøde	17.01.11 Stouby
15.01.05 Skivholme	3.03.08 Soderup	12.02.12 Strandby
12.08.11 Skivum	3.02.13 Solbjerg	18.06.08 Strellev
14.07.09 Skjellerup	11.04.11 Solbjerg	8.07.18 Strib-Røjleskov
13.07.10 Skjern	12.03.11 Solbjerg	18.05.14 Struer
18.01.08 Skjern	2.05.10 Solrød	9.05.12 Strynø
17.01.10 Skjold	20.02.09 Sommersted	1.05.07 Strø
11.03.07 Skjoldborg	2.06.06 Sonnerup, Kirke =	5.06.12 Strøby
13.05.10 Skjød	Kirke-Sonnerup	7.01.11 Stubbekøbing
20.01.05 Skodborg	4.03.17 Sorterup	8.01.12 Stubberup
16.01.10 Skorup	4.01.11 Sorø	18.03.15 Studsgård-Havnstrup
8.06.08 Skovby	23.03.04 Sottrup	14.09.10 Støvring
15.01.06 Skovby	21.01.08 Spandet	12.05.09 Suldrup
7.05.10 Skovlænge	14.06.08 Spentrup	12.06.10 Sulsted
2.03.02 Skovshoved = Gentofte	5.03.07 Spjellerup	11.04.12 Sundby
20.01.06 Skrave	16.01.11 Sporup	12.06.09 Sundby, N = Nørresundby
20.02.08 Skrydstrup	15.06.05 Spørring	18.03.16 Sunds
10.07.06 Skræm	18.08.06 Staby	3.01.07 Svallerup
9.02.05 Skrøbelev	7.01.10 Stadager	6.04.04 Svaneke
1.02.08 Skuldelev	18.04.11 Stadil	9.04.20 Svanninge
8.02.15 Skydebjerg	11.01.11 Stagstrup	9.05.13 Svendborg
11.01.09 Skyum	20.03.08 Starup = Sønder-Starup	12.05.10 Svenstrup
4.04.13 Skælskør	19.05.16 Starup, V = Vester-Starup	14.07.11 Svenstrup
21.01.07 Skærbæk	17.02.11 Starup, Ø = Øster-Starup	23.01.05 Svenstrup
10.03.13 Skærum	18.01.09 Stavning	10.07.10 Svenstrup, Ø =
17.05.05 Skærup	5.05.09 Stege	Øster-Svenstrup
10.02.09 Skæve	5.05.10 Stege landdistrikt	9.01.10 Svindinge
1.05.06 Skævinge	5.05.11 Stege landsogn	3.07.12 Svinninge
13.05.10 Skød = Skjød	17.04.07 Stenderup	2.04.13 Svogerslev
14.11.08 Skødstrup	17.07.04 Stenderup, S =	13.03.10 Svostrup
12.03.10 Skørping	Sønder-Stenderup	5.04.09 Sværdborg
4.04.14 Skørpinge	12.02.11 Stenild	7.02.10 Systofte
14.10.15 Skørring	3.03.09 Stenlille	2.01.10 Syv

11.02.09 Tved	3.03.17 Uggerløse = Ugerløse	12.05.13 Veggerby
14.05.09 Tved	8.05.08 Uggerslev	7.02.13 Veggerløse = Væggerløse
14.06.09 Tvede	10.06.17 Ugilt	14.01.16 Veggerslev
3.03.03 Tveje-Merløse = Holbæk	13.09.13 Ulbjerg	1.01.13 Vejby
10.03.15 Tversted = Tværsted	9.04.22 Ulbølle	10.01.15 Vejby
16.01.14 Tvilum	17.08.14 Uldum	13.10.08 Vejby
18.03.19 Tvis	18.08.09 Ulfborg	19.03.08 Vejen
11.03.12 Tvorup	23.02.10 Ulkebøl	11.05.14 Vejerslev
10.03.15 Tværsted	9.06.16 Ullerslev	13.05.12 Vejerslev
5.07.11 Tybjerg	17.03.05 Ullerup = Trinitatis landsogn	12.01.14 Vejgård
17.08.13 Tyregod = Thyregod	23.03.05 Ullerup	8.07.20 Vejlby
17.04.10 Tyrsted	12.02.13 Ullits	14.02.13 Vejlby
16.04.08 Tyrsting	5.03.10 Ulse	14.10.17 Vejlby
20.05.08 Tyrstrup	7.06.21 Ulslev, V = Vester-Ulslev	15.03.09 Vejlby
4.05.13 Tystrup	7.06.24 Ulslev, Ø = Øster-Ulslev	17.03.06 Vejlby
5.07.12 Tyvelse	12.06.11 Ulsted	9.04.24 Vejle
11.05.13 Tæbring	12.08.12 Ulstrup	17.08.15 Vejle
11.04.14 Tødsø	10.02.12 Understed	7.03.20 Vejleby
3.03.16 Tølløse	16.03.07 Underup	9.04.24 Vejlev = Vejle
11.07.08 Tømmerby	3.03.18 Undløse	5.04.11 Vejlø
3.01.08 Tømmerup	17.04.11 Urlev	13.12.10 Vejrum
21.05.03 Tønder	17.01.12 Uth	18.05.15 Vejrum
21.05.04 Tønder landsogn	7.04.11 Utterslev	19.02.06 Vejrup
13.02.09 Tøndering	1.03.14 Uvelse	9.01.11 Vejstrup
16.04.09 Tønning	12.06.12 Vadum	17.07.06 Vejstrup
16.06.07 Tørring	1.01.12 Valby	1.06.06 Veksø
18.07.15 Tørring	3.04.11 Vallekilde	1.02.09 Vellerup
14.06.10 Tørslev, V = Vester-Tørslev	2.02.15 Vallensbæk	13.05.13 Vellev
14.04.11 Tørslev, Ø = Øster-Tørslev	4.05.14 Vallensved	18.04.16 Velling
14.01.15 Tøstrup	5.01.11 Valløby	13.07.14 Velling, V = Vester-Velling
7.03.19 Tågerup	12.04.11 Valsgård	13.07.17 Velling, Ø = Øster-Velling
16.05.10 Tåning	2.06.04 Valsø, Kirke = Kirke-Hvalsø	18.05.16 Vemb
13.12.09 Tånum	4.02.18 Valsølille	4.03.20 Vemmelev
4.03.19 Tårnborg	19.01.09 Vamdrup	5.03.11 Vemmetofte
2.03.11 Tårnby	13.08.14 Vammen	16.02.10 Veng
5.01.10 Tårnby	18.09.11 Vandborg	16.02.10 Venge = Veng
2.03.07 Tårbæk = Lyngby-Tårbæk	11.02.10 Vandet, V = Vester-Vandet	10.06.18 Vennebjerg
7.06.20 Tårs	11.02.13 Vandet, Ø = Øster-Vandet	4.04.19 Venslev
10.01.14 Tårs	11.03.13 Vang	18.07.16 Venø
13.01.14 Tårup	11.02.10 Vanned, V = Vester-Vandet	8.04.14 Verninge
2.02.07 Taastrup, Høje = Høje-Tåstrup	11.02.13 Vanned, Ø = Øster-Vandet	19.01.10 Verst
2.02.14 Tåstrup Nykirke	9.04.23 Vantinge	11.07.09 Vesløs = Vestløs
3.03.10 Taastrup, St. = Store-Tåstrup	19.07.12 Varde	7.05.14 Vestenskov
8.04.13 Ubberud	19.07.13 Varde landsogn	17.08.16 Vester
3.01.09 Ubby	22.01.11 Varnæs	14.10.18 Vester-Alling
21.05.05 Ubjerg	5.06.13 Varpelev	11.05.15 Vester-Assels
3.01.09 Udby = Ubby	12.04.12 Vebbestrup	13.09.14 Vester-Bjerregrav
3.07.14 Udby	7.01.09 Vedby, N = Nørre-Vedby	7.04.12 Vesterborg
5.02.12 Udby	3.02.11 Vedby, Ruds = Ruds-Vedby	4.01.13 Vester-Broby
8.07.19 Udby	2.03.10 Vedbæk = Søllerød	10.01.01 Vester-Brønderslev = Brønderslev
14.08.03 Udby	18.04.15 Vedersø	
14.04.09 Udbyneder	16.05.11 Vedslet	13.09.15 Vester-Bølle
1.03.02 Ude-Sundby = Frederikssund	10.04.07 Vedsted	5.07.13 Vester-Egede
22.01.10 Uge	19.04.11 Vedsted = Vester-Vedsted	5.04.12 Vester-Egesborg
3.03.17 Ugerløse	20.02.10 Vedsted	12.06.13 Vester-Hassing
1.03.13 Uggeløse	8.02.21 Vedtofte	10.04.08 Vester-Hjermeslev
10.06.16 Uggerby	19.01.10 Veerst = Verst	12.08.13 Vester-Hornum
	8.06.11 Veflinge	9.04.25 Vester-Hæsinge

15.06.04 Vester-Lisbjerg = Lisbjerg
6.03.05 Vester-Marie
17.02.09 Vester-Nebel
19.05.14 Vester-Nebel
19.05.15 Vester-Nykirke
9.04.26 Vester-Skerninge
23.03.04 Vester-Sottrup = Sottrup
19.05.16 Vester-Starup
11.07.10 Vester-Torup
13.09.16 Vester-Tostrup
14.06.10 Vester-Tørslev
7.06.21 Vester-Ulslev
11.02.10 Vester-Vandet
19.04.11 Vester-Vedsted
13.07.14 Vester-Velling
11.06.12 Vestervig
10.05.03 Vesterø
9.04.27 Vester-Åby
11.07.09 Vestløs
4.02.19 Vetterslev
13.08.15 Viborg
13.08.06 Viborg, Graabdr. =
　　　　　Gråbrødre landsogn
8.01.13 Viby
15.04.13 Viby
18.01.12 Videbæk
10.06.19 Vidstrup
3.04.12 Vig
8.06.12 Vigerslev
4.02.20 Vigersted
8.06.12 Vigslev = Vigerslev
7.06.22 Vigsnæs
11.02.11 Vigsø
1.06.06 Viksø = Veksø
18.03.20 Vildbjerg
13.02.10 Vile
11.01.13 Villerslev
14.01.17 Villersø
19.02.07 Vilslev
12.07.14 Vilsted
20.03.09 Vilstrup
17.02.08 Vilstrup, S = Sønder-Vilstrup
18.08.10 Vind
12.07.15 Vindblæs
14.04.10 Vindblæs
7.04.13 Vindeby
17.08.17 Vindelev
13.06.13 Vinderslev
1.05.10 Vinderød
16.04.10 Vinding
17.05.07 Vinding
18.08.11 Vinding
2.05.12 Vindinge
9.06.17 Vindinge
13.07.15 Vindum
13.12.06 Vinge, N = Nørre-Vinge
13.07.12 Vinge, S = Sønder-Vinge
13.07.16 Vinkel

14.10.19 Virring
2.03.07 Virum = Lyngby-Tårbæk
12.04.13 Visborg
11.01.14 Visby
21.05.06 Visby
3.06.09 Viskinge
13.12.11 Viskum
8.04.15 Vissenbjerg
14.03.08 Vissing
16.04.06 Vissing, S = Sønder-Vissing
14.05.10 Vistoft
15.05.08 Vitten
16.02.11 Vitved
17.02.10 Viuf
13.06.14 Vium
18.01.07 Vium, N = Nørre-Vium
18.06.10 Vium, S = Sønder-Vium
17.02.10 Viv = Viuf
12.04.14 Vive
14.10.20 Vivild
21.01.09 Vodder
16.01.15 Voel
10.02.13 Voer
14.08.04 Voer
16.04.11 Voerladegård
12.02.14 Vognsild
20.02.11 Vojens
12.05.14 Vokslev
14.01.18 Voldby
16.01.16 Voldby
14.03.09 Voldum
5.01.12 Vollerslev
13.04.11 Volling
12.01.15 Volsted
10.02.14 Volstrup
20.03.10 Vonsbæk
12.02.14 Vonsild = Vognsild
17.07.07 Vonsild
10.02.13 Vor = Voer
14.08.04 Vor = Voer
19.06.04 Vorbasse
13.08.16 Vorde
12.01.06 Vorde, Lille = Lillevorde
12.01.12 Vorde, Store = Storvorde
5.02.13 Vordingborg
5.02.14 Vordingborg landsogn
2.04.14 Vor Frue
18.01.13 Vorgod
16.04.11 Vorladegaard = Voerladegård
13.12.12 Vorning
14.03.10 Vorup
16.06.08 Vrads
5.07.14 Vrangstrup
10.01.16 Vrejlev
10.01.17 Vrensted
13.01.15 Vridsted
17.01.13 Vrigsted
13.01.16 Vrove = Vroue

13.01.16 Vroue
10.01.18 Vrå
5.01.13 Vråby
11.07.11 Vust
7.02.13 Væggerløse
16.05.12 Vær
2.02.16 Værløse
3.06.10 Værslev
14.03.11 Værum
8.06.11 Vævlinge = Veflinge
7.06.23 Våbensted
7.01.14 Vålse
11.06.13 Ydby
16.05.13 Yding
14.05.03 Æbeltoft = Ebeltoft
14.05.04 Æbeltoft landsogn =
　　　　　Ebeltoft landsogn
9.07.07 Ærøskøbing
4.02.21 Øde-Førslev
17.07.08 Ødis
17.06.04 Ødsted
14.03.12 Ødum
9.01.12 Øksendrup
10.07.09 Øland
18.05.17 Ølby
19.08.06 Ølgod
12.04.15 Øls
2.01.11 Ølsemagle
14.03.13 Ølst
1.05.11 Ølsted
15.06.08 Ølsted
17.04.12 Ølsted
18.04.17 Ølstrup
1.06.07 Ølstykke
7.01.15 Ønslev
9.06.18 Ørbæk
11.05.16 Ørding
18.03.21 Ørre
16.05.14 Ørridslev
3.02.15 Ørslev
4.02.22 Ørslev
4.04.20 Ørslev
5.02.15 Ørslev
8.07.21 Ørslev
7.02.08 Ørslev, N = Nørre-Ørslev
13.01.17 Ørslevkloster
2.01.12 Ørsted
8.02.22 Ørsted
14.08.05 Ørsted
15.02.14 Ørting
10.02.15 Ørum
11.01.15 Ørum
13.01.18 Ørum
13.12.13 Ørum
14.01.19 Ørum
14.03.14 Ørum
17.01.14 Ørum
20.03.11 Øsby

19.05.17 Øse
11.07.12 Øsløs = Østløs
19.05.17 Øsse = Øse
16.05.15 Østbirk
14.10.21 Øster-Alling
11.05.17 Øster-Assels
13.12.14 Øster-Bjerregrav
4.02.23 Øster-Broby
10.01.19 Øster-Brønderslev
13.09.17 Øster-Bølle
5.03.12 Øster-Egede
5.02.16 Øster-Egesborg
12.06.14 Øster-Hassing
12.05.15 Øster-Hornum
21.04.04 Øster-Højst = Højst
9.04.28 Øster-Hæsinge
11.02.12 Østerild
11.04.15 Øster-Jølby
6.04.05 Øster-Larsker
20.01.08 Øster-Lindet
22.03.04 Øster-Løgum
6.04.06 Øster-Marie
17.08.18 Øster-Nykirke

9.05.16 Øster-Skerninge
17.08.19 Øster-Snede
17.02.11 Øster-Starup
10.07.10 Øster-Svenstrup
14.04.11 Øster-Tørslev
7.06.24 Øster-Ulslev
11.02.13 Øster-Vandet
20.02.10 Øster-Vedsted = Vedsted
13.07.17 Øster-Velling
11.07.12 Østløs
7.03.21 Østofte
8.03.08 Østrup
22.02.05 Åbenrå
12.06.15 Åby
15.03.10 Åby
8.07.15 Aaby, N = Nørre-Åby
9.04.27 Aaby, V = Vester-Åby
18.06.07 Ådum = Oddum
2.04.15 Ågerup
3.03.19 Ågerup
6.02.05 Åker
6.02.06 Åkirkeby
19.07.14 Ål

12.05.16 Ålborg
12.06.03 Aalborg, Frue lds. =
          Frue landsogn
16.06.09 Åle
14.02.14 Ålsø
13.12.15 Ålum
3.01.10 Årby
12.05.17 Årestrup
15.03.11 Århus
19.05.18 Årre
12.08.14 Års
9.06.19 Årslev
14.10.22 Årslev
15.03.07 Aarslev, S = Sønder-Årslev
10.03.16 Åsted
13.02.11 Åsted
7.02.14 Åstrup
9.04.29 Åstrup
19.02.08 Åstrup
20.03.12 Åstrup
8.08.11 Åsum

Introduction to appendix 3-4

In 1873 the National Museum received an appropriation from the Danish government which enabled it to initiate a national survey of all archaeological monuments and sites in the landscape. The survey was carried out parish by parish and was therefore called the Parish Survey. It lasted from 1873 to approx. 1930 (Southern Jutland was not surveyed until after 1920, when it came back under Danish sovereignty). Today the Parish Survey is the backbone of both research and administration. It is a central register in the National Museum where all information of new recorded monuments, finds, excavations etc. must be registered. At present it is being computerized (Hansen 1982; Nielsen 1981). Today the Parish Survey comprises approx. 120,000 localities and has a yearly accession of approx. 1,000. The function as a central register of all archaeological finds and monuments, however, is more recent. Originally, the Parish Survey was a central record of all visible monuments in the landscape, supplemented with drawings and later photographs. The latter also constitute an important documentation of cultural landscapes which today have often vanished.

From a source-critical point of view it is important to know when the individual parishes were surveyed and by whom. This information is offered in appendix 3. A thorough analysis and evaluation of the Parish Survey has recently been carried out (Ebbesen 1984).

When archaeological monuments were generally protected by law in 1937, the National Museum was given responsibility to decide which monuments should be comprised by protection. A conservation survey, based on the Parish Survey, was therefore carried out between 1937 and 1957. The conservation survey was also carried out parish by parish, and the surveyors are listed in appendix 4. Approx. 26,000 monuments were scheduled during the survey, and this register of protected monuments is today the backbone of the administration in the National Agency for the Protection of Nature, Monuments and Sites in the Ministry of the Environment. Today it comprises approx. 28,000 scheduled monuments, and the yearly accession is approx. 100-200 monuments. Since 1980 a new updated registration of all protected monuments is carried out as a basis for future inspection, information and vegetational care (Fischer 1982).

REFERENCES

EBBESEN, KLAUS, 1984: *Fortidsminderegistreringen i Danmark*. Fredningsstyrelsen.

FISCHER, ANDERS, 1982: Fredningsstyrelsens besigtigelse og registrering af de fredede fortidsminder. *Antikvariske Studier 5*, Fredningsstyrelsen.

HANSEN, BERIT PAULI, 1982: EDB og arkæologi (EDP and Archaeology). *Antikvariske Studier 5*. Fredningsstyrelsen.

NIELSEN, POUL OTTO, 1981: Hundredtusind fortidsminder. Om den arkæologiske kortlægning af Danmark siden 1807. *Nationalmuseets Arbejdsmark*.

Appendix 3

The Parish Survey 1873-1930

	Surveyed by:	time	drawings	photos
1. Frederiksborg County				
1.01 Holbo	V. Boye, E. Löffler (C)	1885-86	x	
1.02 Horns	H. Petersen, E. Löffler	1873-74	x	
1.03 Lynge-Frederiksborg	V. Boye	1890	x	
1.04 Lynge-Kronborg	V. Boye, M. Petersen (C)	1884	x	
1.05 Strø	V. Boye	1887-88	x	
	E. Löffler (C)	1891	x	
1.06 Ølstykke	S. Müller, E. Schiödte	1875	x	
2. København County				
2.01 Ramsø	A. P. Madsen	1901	x	x
2.02 Smørum	C. Nergaard	1889-90		
2.03 Sokkelund	A. P. Madsen	1899		x
2.04 Sømme	V. Boye	1889	x	
2.05 Tune	J. Kornerup	1876	x	
2.06 Voldborg	Kr. Bahnson, E. Rondahl	1883	x	x
3. Holbæk County				
3.01 Ars	H. Petersen, E. Löffler (C)	1881	x	x
3.02 Løve	C. Fredstrup .01,.02,.05,.06,.07,.08,.11,.13,.14	1892	x	
	C. Nergaard – remaining parishes	1892	x	
3.03 Merløse	E. Petersen .07,.13,.14,.17,.18	1893		
	Chr. Blinkenberg .01,.05	1894		
	Chr. Blinkenberg, H. A. Kjær – remaining parishes	1896	x	x
3.04 Ods	H. Petersen, E. Löffler (C)	1874	x	
3.05 Samsø	C. Engelhardt, S. Müller, M. Petersen (C)	1874	x	
3.06 Skippinge	C. Nergaard	1891-92	x	x
3.07 Tuse	V. Boye	1891	x	
4. Sorø County				
4.01 Alsted	S. Müller, E. Schiödte (the estate of Sorø Academy only)	1877	x	
	H. Petersen, E. Löffler (C)	1882-83	x	
4.02 Ringsted	H. Petersen, E. Löffler (C)	1883-84	x	
4.03 Slagelse	Chr. Blinkenberg	1892-93	x	
4.04 V.-Flakkebjerg	E. Löffler (C)	1884, 1886	x	
	A. P. Madsen	1896	x	
4.05 Ø.-Flakkebjerg	A. P. Madsen	1904	x	

5. Præstø County

5.01 Bjæverskov	S. Müller, E. Schiödte	1875	x	
5.02 Bårse	S. Müller	1876-77	x	
5.03 Fakse	Chr. Blinkenberg	1894-95	x	x
5.04 Hammer	A. P. Madsen	1905	x	
5.05 Mønbo	H. Petersen	1880	x	x
5.06 Stevns	Chr. Blinkenberg .01,.03	1895		
	.02,.05,.06,.07,.09,.10,.11	1900		
	.04,.08	1901		
	.04,.12,.13	1902		
5.07 Tybjerg	Th. Thomsen .09,.12,.14	1910		x
	Th. Thomsen – remaining parishes	1914		x

6. Bornholms County

6.01 Bornh.s Nørre	S. Petersen .07	1877		
	J. A. Jørgensen .02,.03,.04,.06	1882		
	E. Löffler (C)	1882	x	
	S. Petersen .05,.01	1884		
	J. A. Jørgensen .07	1884		
6.02 Bornh.s Sønder	J. A. Jørgensen .01	1875	x	
	J. A. Jørgensen .02	1876		
	J. A. Jørgensen .03	1878	x	
	J. A. Jørgensen .05,.06	1879	x	
	J. A. Jørgensen .04	1880		
	E. Löffler (C)	1883	x	
6.03 Bornh.s Vester	J. A. Jørgensen	1878	x	
	E. Löffler (C)	1882	x	
6.04 Bornh.s Øster	J. A. Jørgensen	1880	x	
	E. Löffler (C)	1882		

7. Maribo County

7.01 Falster Nørre	K. Friis Johansen	1914		x
7.02 Falster Sønder	S. Müller	1880	x	x
7.03 Fuglse	C. Engelhardt, M. Petersen (C)	1878	x	x
7.04 Lollands Nørre	C. Engelhardt, M. Petersen (C)	1876	x	x
7.05 Lollands Sdr.	C. Engelhardt, M. Petersen (C)	1877	x	x
7.06 Musse	C. Engelhardt, M. Petersen (C)	1879-80	x	x

8. Odense County

8.01 Bjerge	J. E. Boesen, S. Müller (C), E. Schiödte (C)	1884	x	
8.02 Båg	A. P. Madsen	1897-98	x	
8.03 Lunde	H. Petersen, E. Löffler (C)	1882	x	
8.04 Odense	K. Klem .11,.15	1927		
8.05 Skam	J. E. Boesen	1891	x	
8.06 Skovby	J. E. Boesen	1892		
8.07 Vends	K. Friis Johansen	1915-16		
8.08 Åsum	J. E. Boesen	1890	x	

9. Svendborg County

9.01 Gudme	K. Friis Johansen	1916-17		
9.02 Langelands Nr.	H. Petersen, E. Löffler (C)	1875-76	x	
9.03 Langelands Sdr.	H. Petersen, E. Löffler (C)	1875-76	x	
9.04 Sallinge	H. Petersen .17,.02	1884		
	J. E. Boesen – remaining parishes	1885-86	x	
	E. Löffler (C)	1886	x	
9.05 Sunds	H. Petersen, E. Löffler (C) .01,.02	1876	x	
	Th. Thomsen – remaining parishes	1921	x	
9.06 Vindinge	C. A. Nordman	1916,17		x
9.07 Ærø	H. Petersen	1884	x	
	J. Jessen .02,.04,.06	1936		

10. Hjørring County

10.01 Børglum	Kr. Bahnson, E. Rondahl .01,.02,.03,.04,.06,.07,.08, .10,.11,.12,.13,.14,.16,.17,.18,.19	1884	x	
	H. A. Kjær, Th. Thomsen .01,.02,.03,.04,.06,.07,.08, .09,.10,.11,.12,.13,.14,.15,.16,.17,.18,.19	1907-09		x
10.02 Dronninglund	Kr. Bahnson, E. Schiödte	1881	x	
	H. A. Kjær, Th. Thomsen	1905-08	x	x
10.03 Horns	Kr. Bahnson	1882	x	
	Th. Thomsen .03,.05,.08,.13,.16	1906	x	x
	J. Brøndsted .01,.02,.03,.04,.06,.07, .09,.10,.11,.12,.13,.14,.15,.16	1923-24	x	x
10.04 Hvetbo	S. Müller, E. Schiödte	1882	x	
	J. Brøndsted	1928		
10.05 Læsø	J. Brøndsted	1926		
10.06 Vennebjerg	C. Engelhardt, M. Petersen (C)	1881	x	
	Th. Thomsen .12,.17	1908		
	H. A. Kjær .04,.07,.10,.11	1909		
	S. Schultz .09,.14,.15,.18,.19	1924		
	J. Brøndsted .02,.03,.08,.13,.16	1925		
	J. Brøndsted .01,.06,.12	1926		
	J. Brøndsted .04,.05,.07,.10,.11,.12,.17	1927		
10.07 Øster-Han	H. Petersen, E. Löffler (C)	1878	x	x

11. Thisted County

11.01 Hassing	C. Engelhardt	1877	x	
	Aa. Brusendorff .01,.02,.03,.04,.05,.06,.07,.08,.09, .11,.12,.13,.14,.15	1912		x
	H. A. Kjær .10	1913		
11.02 Hillerslev	C. Engelhardt, M. Petersen (C)	1875	x	x
	K. Friis Johansen .02,.03,.04,.05,.06,.08,.09,.11,.12	1912		
	H. A. Kjær – remaining parishes	1913		
11.03 Hundborg	C. Engelhardt, M. Petersen (C)	1875	x	
	H. A. Kjær	1912-14		x
11.04 Morsø Nørre	C. Engelhardt, M. Petersen (C)	1873	x	
	G. Hatt	1921, 1924-26		

11.05 Morsø Sønder	C. Engelhardt, M. Petersen (C)	1873	x	
	G. Hatt .01,.02,.03,.04,.06,.07,.08, .12,.14,.16	1921, 1924, 1926		x
11.06 Refs	C. Engelhardt, M. Petersen, E. Löffler	1877-78	x	
	H. A. Kjær	1914-16		x
11.07 Vester Han	C. Engelhardt, M. Petersen (C)	1880	x	
	Th. Thomsen .01,.09,.11,.12	1913		
	Th. Thomsen, S. Schultz	1914	x	x

12. Ålborg County

12.01 Fleskum	Kr. Bahnson, E. Rondahl	1887	x	
12.02 Gislum	D. Bruun	1892		
12.03 Hellum	Kr. Bahnson, E. Rondahl	1886	x	
12.04 Hindsted	Kr. Bahnson, E. Rondahl	1887-88	x	
12.05 Hornum	Kr. Bahnson, E. Rondahl	1887,1889	x	x
12.06 Kær	E. Petersen, E. Löffler (C)	1889	x	
	H. A. Kjær .01,.10	1909		
12.07 Slet	Kr. Bahnson, E. Rondahl	1885	x	x
12.08 Års	Kr. Bahnson, E. Rondahl	1885,1888	x	

13. Viborg County

13.01 Fjends	S. Müller	1886	x	
	Kr. Grüner .16	1899		
	G. V. Blom .01,.13	1899		
	Th. Thomsen – remaining parishes	1899-1900, 1903		x
13.02 Harre	Aa. Brusendorff	1909		
	F. Uldall (C)	?	x	
13.03 Hids	S. Müller, E. Schiödte	1885	x	
13.04 Hindborg	F. Uldall (C)	1873	x	
	Th. Thomsen .10	1901		
	G. Sarauw .06,.07,.11	1910		
	Aa. Brusendorff – remaining parishes	1911		
13.05 Houlbjerg	J. V. Nissen	1891-92		
	J. Brøndsted	1929-32		
13.06 Lysgård	S. Müller, E. Schiödte	1879-80	x	
13.07 Middelsom	H. A. Kjær	1899		x
13.08 Nørlyng	D. Bruun	1886, 1888-90		
13.09 Rinds	D. Bruun	1892		
13.10 Rødding	F. Uldall (C)	1875	x	
	H. A. Kjær	1910-11		x
13.11 Salling Nørre	F. Uldall (C)	1874	x	
	G. Sarauw .04,.07,.09	1910		
	Aa. Brusendorff – remaining parishes	1910-11		
13.12 Sønderlyng	D. Bruun	1892-93		

14. Randers County

14.01 Djurs Nørre	J. V. Nissen	?	x	x
	M. Petersen (C)	1886	x	
14.02 Djurs Sønder	J. V. Nissen	?	x	
	E. Löffler (C)	1880	x	

14.03 Galten	F. Uldall	1874-75		
14.04 Gjerlev	F. Uldall .04,.11	1875-76		
	D. Bruun	1891-92		
14.05 Mols	S. Müller, E. Schiödte	1877-78	x	
14.06 Nørhald	J. V. Nissen	1890		
14.07 Onsild	S. Müller (eastern part)	1882	x	
	Kr. Bahnson (western part)	1882	x	
14.08 Rougsø	J. V. Nissen	1891		
14.09 Støvring	F. Uldall .02,.04,.09	1874	x	
	A. P. Madsen – remaining parishes	1901		
14.10 Sønderhald	J. V. Nissen	1891-93		
14.11 Øster-Lisbjerg	F. Uldall .05,.10	1874-75		
	J. V. Nissen	1894		

15. Århus County

15.01 Framlev	S. Schultz	1918-19	x	x
15.02 Hads	H. A. Kjær	1903-04		x
15.03 Hasle	J. Brøndsted	1918-19		
15.04 Ning	C. I. W. Smith, A. Reeh .03,.04,.07,.10,.13	1893-94		
	H. A. Kjær – remaining parishes	1905-06		
15.05 Sabro	J. V. Nissen	1898		
15.06 V. Lisbjerg	J. Brøndsted	1918		

16. Skanderborg County

16.01 Gjern	Kr. Bahnson, Th. Thomsen .01,.02,.03,.05,.06,.10, .13,.14,.15	1894	x	
	G. V. Blom – remaining parishes	1896		
16.02 Hjelmslev	H. A. Kjær .03,.04,.07,.08	1897		x
	C. Fredstrup – remaining parishes	1897		x
16.03 Nim	M. Kristensen	1894-98		
16.04 Tyrsting	E. Löffler (C)	1877	x	x
	H. Petersen .08	1877		
	H. A. Kjær – remaining parishes	1902-03		
16.05 Voer	M. Kristensen	1894-95	x	
	R. P. Randløv .10	1933		
16.06 Vrads	H. Petersen, E. Löffler (C)	1877	x	

17. Vejle County

17.01 Bjerre	H. Petersen, Kr. Bahnson, E. Löffler (C)	1878-80	x	
17.02 Brusk	G. Sarauw	1908-09		
17.03 Elbo	J. Brøndsted	1919		
17.04 Hatting	G. Sarauw	1904-06		
17.05 Holmans	S. Müller, E. Schiödte	1878	x	
	G. Sarauw .06	1909		
17.06 Jerlev	G. Sarauw	1906-08		
17.07 N.-Tyrstrup	J. Helms (C)	1874		
	S. Müller, E. Schiödte	1886	x	
	H. C. Broholm	1931-32, 1935		
17.08 Nørvang	G. Sarauw	1896-97		
	G. Sarauw	1899		
	G. Sarauw	1902-04		
17.09 Tørrild	A. P. Madsen	1895		
	G. Sarauw .08	1908		

18. Ringkøbing County

18.01 Bølling	S. Müller, E. Schiödte	1883	x	
18.02 Ginding	H. C. Strandgaard .01,.02,.06,.07,.08,.09	1880		
	H. A. Kjær	1900-01		x
18.03 Hammerum	C. Nergaard .01,.13	1894		
	G. V. Blom .02,.03,.06,.09,.10,.12,.18,.19,.20	1894-95		
	G. Sarauw .04,.05,.07,.14,.16,.17,.21	1895		
18.04 Hind	E. Petersen	1892		
18.05 Hjerm	H. C. Strandgaard	1877		
	E. Löffler (C)	1880	x	
	K. Friis Johansen, H. C. Broholm	1918-19	x	x
18.06 Nørre-Horne	Th. Thomsen .03	1903		
	Sv. Müller .04,.08,.10	1904		
	Th. Thomsen – remaining parishes	1904		x
18.07 Skodborg	H. C. Strandgaard	1878		
	E. Löffler (C)	1879	x	
	H. A. Kjær .05,.08,.15	1919		
18.08 Ulfborg	G. V. Blom .01,.03,.05,.06,.07,.09	1901		
	Th. Thomsen – remaining parishes	1901-03		
18.09 Vandfuld	H. C. Strandgaard	1879	x	
	E. Löffler (C)	1880	x	
	H. A. Kjær	1917		

19. Ribe County

19.01 Anst	J. Helms (C)	1874	x	
	C. Fredstrup .01,.03,.04,.08,.09	1898		
	G. V. Blom – remaining parishes	1898		
19.02 Gørding	J. Helms (C)	1875	x	
	Sv. Müller	1906-07		
19.03 Malt	J. Helms (C)	?	x	
	Kr. Grüner .06	1897		
	G. V. Blom .03,.08	1897-98		
	C. Fredstrup .01,.02,.04,.07	1898	x	x
	H. A. Kjær .05	1898	x	x
19.04 Ribe	Aa. Brusendorff	1913		
19.05 Skast	J. Helms (C)	1873		
	A. P. Madsen .01,.02,.03,.04,.05,.06,.07,.09,.14, .15,.16,.17,.18	1891-92		
	A. P. Madsen .10,.11,.13	1900-01		
	Sv. Müller .08,.12	1905-06		
	S. Schultz .01,.02,.03,.04,.05,.06,.07,.09,.10,.11, .13,.14,.15,.16,.17,.18	1916		
19.06 Slavs	J. Helms (C)	1874		
	G. V. Blom	1896	x	x
19.07 Vester Horne	J. Helms (C)	?	x	
	A. P. Madsen .06	1902	x	
	Sv. Müller .05,.08,.09	1904		
	H. A. Kjær .04,.12,.13	1904		
	Sv. Müller .02,.07,.11	1905		
	H. A. Kjær .01,.03,.10,.14	1905		
	H. C. Broholm .13	1922		
19.08 Øster Horne	J. Helms (C)	?	x	
	A. P. Madsen	1893		
	Th. Thomsen	1915-16		

20. Haderslev County

20.01 Frøs	K. Friis Johansen .02,.04,.05,.06,.08	1925-26	
	H. C. Broholm – remaining parishes	1930	
20.02 Gram	H. C. Broholm	1924-25	x
	H. C. Broholm	1927-28	
20.03 Haderslev	H. C. Broholm	1929	
20.04 N.-Rangstrup	Th. Thomsen	1927-28	
20.05 S.-Tyrstrup	H. C. Broholm	1928	

21. Tønder County

21.01 Hviding	Th. Thomsen	1925	
21.02 Højer	Th. Thomsen	1925	
21.03 Lø	Th. Thomsen	1925	
21.04 Slogs	H. C. Broholm .05,.06	?	
	Th. Thomsen – remaining parishes	1925	
21.05 Tønder	Th. Thomsen	1925	

22. Åbenrå County

22.01 Lundtoft	J. Brøndsted .01,.04,.09,.11	1921	
	H. C. Broholm .02,.03,.06,.07,.08,.10	1921,1923-24	x
22.02 Rise	H. C. Broholm .01,.02,.04	1920-21	
	H. A. Kjær .03,.05	1921, 1923	
22.03 S.-Rangstrup	H. C. Broholm .02	1920	
	H. A. Kjær .04	1920	
	H. C. Broholm .01,.03	1922	

23. Sønderborg County

23.01 Als Nørre	K. Friis Johansen	1920-22	x
23.02 Als Sønder	K. Friis Johansen .01,.02,.05,.07	1920	x
	K. Friis Johansen .03,.04,.06,.09	1922-23	
	K. Friis Johansen .10	1925	
23.03 Nybøl	J. Brøndsted	1920-21	

Parish surveyors

Bahnson, Kr., museumsassistent, cand. mag.
Blinkenberg, Chr., museumsassistent, dr.
Blom, G. V., figurmaler, cand. polyt., docent.
Boesen, J. E., adjunkt, cand. mag. – Sorø
Boye, Vilhelm, museumsassistent
Broholm, H. C., museumsinspektør
Brusendorff, Aa., stud. mag.
Bruun, Daniel, premierløjtnant – Hobro
Brøndsted, Johs., museumsinspektør
Engelhardt, Conrad, professor
Fredstrup, Carl, museumsassistent, cand. mag.
Grüner, Kr., cand. phil.
Hatt, Gudmund, dr. phil., professor
Helms, J., pastor
Jessen, Jørgen, cand. mag.
Johansen, K. Friis, assistent, dr.
Jørgensen, J. A., lærer
Kjær, Hans A., stud. mag.
Klem, K.
Kornerup, Jacob, professor

Kristensen, Martin, lærer, seminarieforstander – Gjedved
Löffler, E., arkitekt
Madsen, A. P., kaptajn
Müller, Sophus, museumsassistent, cand. phil., dr. phil., museumsinspektør
Müller, Sven, cand. phil.
Nergaard, Carl, cand. phil., museumsassistent
Nissen, Jacob, V., lærer – Ramten
Nordman, C. A., underinspektør
Petersen, Egil, museumsassistent, cand. mag.
Petersen, Henry, cand. mag., museumsassistent, dr. phil.
Petersen, Magnus, professor
Petersen, S., lærer
Randløv, R. P., lærer
Reeh, A., overretssagfører
Rondahl, E., figurmaler, kunstmaler
Sarauw, Georg, museumsassistent
Schiödte, E., arkitket
Schultz, S., stud. mag.
Smith, C. I. W., kaptajn
Strandgaard, H. C., lærer
Thomsen, Thomas, stud. mag., assistent, inspektør
Uldall, F., arkitekt

Appendix 4

The Conservation Survey 1937-1957

	Surveyed by:	time
1. Frederiksborg County		
1.01 Holbo	H. Norling-Christensen .02,.13	1937
	H. Norling-Christensen – remaining parishes	1942
1.02 Horns	C. J. Becker	1942
1.03 Lynge-Frederiksborg	Th. Mathiassen	1942
1.04 Lynge-Kronborg	C. L. Vebæk	1942
1.05 Strø	C. J. Becker .03,.05,.09	1942
	H. Norling-Christensen – remaining parishes	1942
1.06 Ølstykke	Th. Mathiassen	1942
2. Københavns County		
2.01 Ramsø	M. B. Mackeprang	1941-42
2.02 Smørum	Th. Mathiassen	1938
2.03 Sokkelund	Th. Mathiassen	1938
2.04 Sømme	Th. Mathiassen .01,.03,.05,.06,.07,.08,.15	1942
	M. B. Mackeprang – remaining parishes	1942
2.05 Tune	M. B. Mackeprang	1942
2.06 Volborg	Th. Mathiassen .02,.04,.05,.06,.07,.09,.11,.12	1941
	M. B. Mackeprang – remaining parishes	1942
3. Holbæk County		
3.01 Ars	Th. Mathiassen .06,.07	1940
	P. V. Glob	1941
3.02 Løve	Th. Mathiassen	1940
3.03 Merløse	H. Norling-Christensen .04,.09,.10	1940
	Th. Mathiassen – remaining parishes	1940-41
3.04 Ods	C. J. Becker .01,.03,.06,.11	1941
	H. Norling-Christensen – remaining parishes	1941
3.05 Samsø	Th. Mathiassen	1941
3.06 Skippinge	Th. Mathiassen .01	1938
	Th. Mathiassen .06	1940
	Th. Mathiassen .05	1941
	C. J. Becker – remaining parishes	1941
3.07 Tuse	Th. Mathiassen	1941

4. Sorø County

4.01 Alsted	H. Norling-Christensen	1940
4.02 Ringsted	E. Albrectsen .05,.07,.16,.17,.21,.23	1939
	H. Norling-Christensen – remaining parishes	1940
4.03 Slagelse	Th. Mathiassen .07,.10,.12	1940
	C. J. Becker – remaining parishes	1940
4.04 V.-Flakkebjerg	Th. Mathiassen .06,.19	1937
	C. J. Becker	1940
4.05 Ø.-Flakkebjerg	P. V. Glob	1940

5. Præstø County

5.01 Bjæverskov	M. B. Mackeprang	1941
5.02 Bårse	P. V. Glob .13,.14	1940
	Th. Mathiassen – remaining parishes	1945
5.03 Fakse	E. Albrectsen .10	1939
	Th. Mathiassen – remaining parishes	1945
5.04 Hammer	P. V. Glob	1940
5.05 Mønbo	P. V. Glob .02,.04,.06,.07	1945
	M. B. Mackeprang – remaining parishes	1945
5.06 Stevns	M. B. Mackeprang	1941
5.07 Tybjerg	E. Albrectsen .13	1939
	M. B. Mackeprang – remaining parishes	1940

6. Bornholms County

6.01 Bornh.s. Nørre	C. J. Becker	1943
6.02 Bornh.s. Sønder	E. Albrectsen	1943
6.03 Bornh.s. Vester	C. J. Becker	1943
6.04 Bornh.s. Øster	E. Albrectsen	1943

7. Maribo County

7.01 Falsters Nørre	G. Kunwald	1954
7.02 Falsters Sønder	K. Thorvildsen	1954
7.03 Fuglse	Th. Mathiassen .02,.21	1949
	Th. Mathiassen .03,.04,.07,.09,.10,.14	1953
7.04 Lollands Nørre	Th. Mathiassen	1953
7.05 Lollands Sdr.	Th. Mathiassen .02,.03,.07,.11,.13,.14	1953
7.06 Musse	K. Thorvildsen .10,.11,.23 and a part of .08	1944
	Th. Mathiassen .07	1949
	Th. Mathiassen – remaining parishes	1954

8. Odense County

8.01 Bjerge	E. Albrectsen	1953
8.02 Båg	E. Albrectsen	1954
8.03 Lunde	E. Albrectsen	1953
8.04 Odense	E. Albrectsen	1953
8.05 Skam	E. Albrectsen	1953
8.06 Skovby	E. Albrectsen	1954
8.07 Vends	E. Albrectsen	1954
8.08 Åsum	E. Albrectsen .05,.06,.07,.10	1947
	E. Albrectsen – remaining parishes	1953

9. Svendborg County

9.01 Gudme	Th. Mathiassen	1947
9.02 Langelands Nr.	P. V. Glob	1947
9.03 Langelands Sdr.	Th. Mathiassen	1947
9.04 Sallinge	C. L. Vebæk	1947
9.05 Sunds	H. Norling-Christensen .01,.02,.03,.04,.05,.06, .07,.08,.09,.10,.11,.12,.13,.16	1947
	Th. Mathiassen	1947
9.06 Vindinge	P. V. Glob	1947
9.07 Ærø		

10. Hjørring County

10.01 Børglum	Th. Mathiassen .02,.04,.07,.12,.17	1939
	M. B. Mackeprang .01,.03,.05,.08,.09,.11,.15,.19	1939
	H. Norling-Christensen – remaining parishes	1939
10.02 Dronninglund	H. Norling-Christensen .06	1939
	M. B. Mackeprang .04,.05,.09,.15	1939
	K. Thorvildsen .01,.02,.03,.13	1939
	P. V. Glob – remaining parishes	1939
10.03 Horns	Th. Mathiassen .01,.03,.07,.09,.13,.14,.16	1938
	P. V. Glob – remaining parishes	1939
10.04 Hvetbo	Th. Mathiassen .03,.04,.05,.06	1939
	Th. Mathiassen – remaining parishes	1953
10.05 Læsø	not inspected	
10.06 Vennebjerg	Th. Mathiassen	1938
10.07 Øster-Han	Th. Mathiassen	1939

11. Thisted County

11.01 Hassing	G. Kunwald	1943
11.02 Hillerslev	A. Bæksted	1943
11.03 Hundborg	K. Thorvildsen	1943
11.04 Morsø Nørre	C. J. Becker .02,.05,.06,.07,.08,.09,.10,.11,.12, .14,.15	1949
	H. Norling-Christensen .02,.06,.07,.09,.12	1953
11.05 Morsø Sønder	C. J. Becker .01,.02,.03,.04,.05,.06,.07,.08,.10, .11,.12,.13,.14,.16,.17	1949
	H. Norling-Christensen .01,.06,.07,.08,.10,.11, .12,.14	1953
11.06 Refs	H. Norling-Christensen	1943
11.07 Vester-Han	P. Riismøller	1943

12. Ålborg County

12.01 Fleskum	P. Riismøller .15	1953
	P. Riismøller .03,.04,.05,.06,.07,.08,.10,.11, .12,.13,.14	1954
	Th. Ramskou – remaining parishes	1954
12.02 Gislum	H. Larsen .11	1938
	P. Riismøller .10	1945
	H. Norling-Christensen .01,.02,.03,.04,.05,.06, .07,.08,.09,.12,.13,.14	1953
	Th. Mathiassen .10	1954

12.03 Hellum	P. Riismøller .11	1948
	P. Riismøller .03,.10,.14	1950
	Th. Mathiassen .01,.02,.05,.07,.09,.13	1953
	P. Riismøller – remaining parishes	1953
12.04 Hindsted	H. Larsen .05,.15	1938
	P. Riismøller .06,.11	1942
	P. Riismøller .03,.08,.12	1945
	P. Riismøller .13,.14	1946
	P. Riismøller .01,.02,.04,.09	1947
	P. Riismøller .07,.10	1948
	P. Riismøller .10	1950
12.05 Hornum	E. Albrectsen .15	1939
	G. Kunwald .01,.09,.12,.13,.14	1953
	Th. Ramskou – remaining parishes	1953
12.06 Kær	P. Riismøller	1939
12.07 Slet	E. Thorvildsen .02,.09	1953
	Th. Mathiassen – remaining parishes	1953
12.08 Års	O. Klindt-Jensen .01,.02,.03,.05,.07,.11,.14	1953
	G. Kunwald .10	1953
	E. Thorvildsen – remaining parishes	1953

13. Viborg County

13.01 Fjends	H. Larsen .01,.10	1938
	H. Norling-Christensen .03,.05,.06,.07,.08,.09, .11,.12,.13,.14,.17,.18	1938
	Th. Mathiassen – remaining parishes	1950
13.02 Harre	Th. Mathiassen .01,.02,.03,.04,.05,.06,.07,.08, .10,.11	1949
13.03 Hids	Th. Mathiassen .02,.05	1937
	K. Thorvildsen – remaining parishes	1950
13.04 Hindborg	H. Norling Christensen .04,.06,.07	1941
	H. Norling Christensen – remaining parishes	1949
13.05 Houlbjerg	K. Thorvildsen .02,.04,.07,.08	1938
	Th. Ramskou – remaining parishes	1948
13.06 Lysgård	E. Albrectsen .01,.03,.10,.11,.14	1938
	E. Albrectsen .02,.05,.06,.07,.08,.09,.12,.13	1942
	K. Thorvildsen .04	1950
13.07 Middelsom	K. Thorvildsen .01,.02,.05,.06,.08,.09,.10,.11, .12,.14,.15,.16	1938
	Th. Ramskou – remaining parishes	1948
13.08 Nørlyng	E. Albrectsen .08,.09	1938
	M. B. Mackeprang .02,.07,.12,.14	1938
	H. C. Broholm – remaining parishes	1938
13.09 Rinds	P. V. Glob .01,.03,.04,.05,.06,.07,.08,.09,.11,.13, .14,.16	1938
	K. Thorvildsen – remaining parishes	1953
13.10 Rødding	H. Norling-Christensen	1949
13.11 Salling Nørre	Th. Mathiassen	1949
13.12 Sønderlyng	M. B. Mackeprang .01,.03,.06,.08,.10,.11,.12,.13	1938
	Th. Ramskou – remaining parishes	1948

14. Randers County

14.01 Djurs Nørre	P. Simonsen .03,.07,.13,.15,.19	1946
	Th. Ramskou – remaining parishes	1946
14.02 Djurs Sønder	O. Klindt-Jensen	1946
14.03 Galten	C. J. Becker	1948
14.04 Gjerlev	Th. Mathiassen .01,.02,.03,.04,.05,.06,.07,.09, .10,.11	1948
14.05 Mols	C. L. Vebæk	1946
14.06 Nørhald	H. Andersen	1948
14.07 Onsild	H. Larsen .03,.04,.07,.10,.12	1938
	H. Norling-Christensen – remaining parishes	1948
14.08 Rougsø	C. J. Becker	1948
14.09 Støvring	C. J. Becker	1948
14.10 Sønderhald	P. Simonsen .01,.04,.07,.11,.13,.17,.20	1945
	Th. Ramskou .10	1947
	C. J. Becker .02,.03,.06,.08,.09,.15,.16,.18,.19, .21,.22	1948
14.11 Øster-Lisbjerg	P. Simonsen .07	1945
	P. Simonsen .01,.06,.09	1946
	Th. Ramskou .04,.08	1947
	Th. Mathiassen .02,.03,.10	1948

15. Århus County

15.01 Framlev	Th. Mathiassen	1948
15.02 Hads	Th. Mathiassen	1952
15.03 Hasle	Th. Mathiassen	1948
15.04 Ning	Th. Mathiassen .03,.04,.06,.07,.09,.10,.13	1948
	Th. Mathiassen .01,.02,.05,.11	1952
15.05 Sabro	Th. Mathiassen	1948
15.06 V.-Lisbjerg	Th. Mathiassen	1948

16. Skanderborg County

16.01 Gjern	O. Klindt-Jensen	1948
16.02 Hjelmslev	K. Thorvildsen .01,.02,.03,.05,.06,.10	1948
	C. L. Vebæk – remaining parishes	1953
16.03 Nim	Th. Mathiassen	1951
16.04 Tyrsting	Th. Mathiassen	1951
16.05 Voer	Th. Mathiassen .05,.13,.15	1951
	C. L. Vebæk – remaining parishes	1953
16.06 Vrads	H. Norling-Christensen .01,.06,.08	1951
	K. Thorvildsen	1951

17. Vejle County

17.01 Bjerre	C. L. Vebæk .01,.02,.05,.06,.07,.09,.10,.11,.12,.14	1947
17.02 Brusk	O. Klindt-Jensen	1954
17.03 Elbo	O. Klindt-Jensen	1954
17.04 Hatting	Th. Mathiassen .03,.05,.06	1951
	C. L. Vebæk .01,.02,.04,.07,.08,.09,.10	1953
17.05 Holmans	O. Klindt-Jensen	1954
17.06 Jerlev	M. Ørsnes	1954
17.07 N. Tyrstrup	C. L. Vebæk	1955

17.08 Nørvang	H. Norling-Christensen .02	1951
	Th. Mathiassen .09,.11	1951
	C. J. Becker .04,.05,.08,.10,.13,.16,.18	1951
	K. Thorvildsen .01,.03,.12	1952
	H. Norling-Christensen .06,.07	1954
17.09 Tørrild	Th. Mathiassen .06,.08	1952
	H. Norling-Christensen – remaining parishes	1954

18. Ringkøbing County

18.01 Bølling	P. Simonsen .04,.05,.06,.07,.12,.13	1950
	O. Klindt-Jensen .01,.02,.03,.08,.10,.11	1951
18.02 Ginding	P. Simonsen .05,.06	1944
	O. Voss .09	1945
	O. Klindt-Jensen .08	1945
	E. Busch .01	1945
	M. Ørsnæs .09	1947
	Th. Mathiassen .02,.07	1949
	Th. Mathiassen – remaining parishes	1950
18.03 Hammerum	E. Busch .19	1943
	P. Simonsen .02,.17	1950
	C. J. Becker .03,.04,.05,.06,.07,.08,.09,.12,.16,.20,.21	1950
	H. Norling-Christensen .10,.14,.15,.18	1950
	O. Klindt-Jensen .02,.13,.17	1951
	K. Thorvildsen .01,.11	1952
18.04 Hind	P. Simonsen .02,.03,.04,.06,.07,.09,.11,.13,.15,.16	1943
	H. Andersen .05,.08,.14	1950
	P. Simonsen .01,.17	1950
	H. Norling-Christensen .12	1950
18.05 Hjerm	P. Simonsen .04,.07	1942
	E. Busch .05,.17	1942
	G. Kunwald .08,.15	1942
	H. Andersen .01,.12	1942
	C. L. Vebæk .02	1942
	E. Busch .09	1942
	B. Fabricius .11,.10,.13	1942
	H. Andersen .03,.06,.16	1943
18.06 Nørre-Horne	P. Simonsen .02,.05,.06,.09,.10	1943
	Th. Ramskou – remaining parishes	1950
18.07 Skodborg	P. V. Glob .06,.13,.16	1942
	C. L. Vebæk .01,.02,.03,.05,.08,.09,.10,.11,.12,.14,.15	1943
	C. L. Vebæk .04	1945
18.08 Ulfborg	E. Thorvildsen .02	1942
	H. Andersen .05	1943
	P. Simonsen .01	1943
	E. Busch .04	1943
	H. Andersen .03,.05,.06,.07,.08,.09,.10,.11	1950
18.09 Vandfuld	C. L. Vebæk .01,.02,.03,.07,.08,.10	1943
	H. Andersen, O. Klindt-Jensen .04,.05,.06,.11	1944

19. Ribe County

19.01 Anst	Th. Mathiassen .02,.03	1952
	C. L. Vebæk – remaining parishes	1954
19.02 Gørding	Th. Mathiassen .06,.08	1952
	M. Ørsnes – remaining parishes	1955
19.03 Malt	Th. Mathiassen .01,.04,.05,.06	1952
	C. L. Vebæk – remaining parishes	1955
19.04 Ribe	G. Kunwald	1955
19.05 Skast	W. Schuldt .01,.02,.03,.06,.07,.10,.11,.13,.14	1943
	G. Kunwald – remaining parishes	1952
19.06 Slavs	C. L. Vebæk	1952
19.07 Vester-Horne	E. Thorvildsen	1943
19.08 Øster-Horne	H. Norling-Christensen	1952

20. Haderslev County

20.01 Frøs	O. Klindt-Jensen	1956
20.02 Gram	H. C. Broholm .08,.10	1937
	Th. Mathiassen .02,.05,.09,.11	1955
	C. L. Vebæk .03,.04,.06,.07	1956
	O. Klindt-Jensen .01	1956
20.03 Haderslev	Th. Mathiassen	1955
20.04 N.-Rangstrup	H. Norling-Christensen	1956
20.05 S.-Tyrstrup	Th. Mathiassen	1955

21. Tønder County

21.01 Hviding	M. Ørsnes	1956
21.02 Højer	Th. Mathiassen	1956
21.03 Lø	Th. Mathiassen	1956
21.04 Slogs	Th. Mathiassen	1956
21.05 Tønder	Th. Mathiassen	1956

22. Åbenrå County

22.01 Lundtoft	K. Thorvildsen	1956
22.02 Rise	G. Kunwald	1956
22.03 S.-Rangstrup	E. Thorvildsen	1956

23. Sønderborg County

23.01 Als Nørre	H. Norling-Christensen	1955
23.02 Als Sønder	O. Klindt-Jensen	1955
23.03 Nybøl	K. Thorvildsen	1955

Conservation – Surveyors

Albrectsen, Erling, museumsinspektør
Andersen, Harald, stud. mag.
Becker, C. J., mag. art., dr. phil.
Broholm, H. C., museumsinspektør
Busch, Ebba, stud. mag.
Bæksted, A., cand. mag.
Fabricius, Bjørn, stud. mag.
Glob. P. V., mag. art.
Klindt-Jensen, Ole, dr. phil.
Kunwald, G., stud. mag.

Larsen, Helge, museumsinspektør
Mackeprang, M. B., museumsinspektør
Mathiassen, Therkel, dr., museumsinspektør
Norling-Christensen, H., mag. art.
Ramskou, Th., stud. mag.
Riismøller, Peter, cand. mag., museumsinspektør
Schuldt, Walter, stud. mag.
Simonsen, Poul, stud. mag.
Thorvildsen, Elise, stud. mag.
Thorvildsen, Knud, cand. mag., konservator
Vebæk, C. L., cand. mag., museumsinspektør
Voss, Olfert, stud. mag.
Ørsnes, Mogens, stud. mag.